# SATELLITE IMAGE OF CENTRAL SCOTLAND

This false-colour composite image was recorded in June. Glasgow and Edinburgh and other settlements in the Forth–Clyde Valley are clearly visible in blue. The bright red areas are fields of healthy crops. Imagery such as this is used to police EU agricultural subsidies. *(EROS)*

# PHILIP'S
# MODERN SCHOOL ATLAS

## 94TH EDITION

IN ASSOCIATION WITH
**THE ROYAL GEOGRAPHICAL SOCIETY**
WITH THE INSTITUTE OF BRITISH GEOGRAPHERS

# CONTENTS

| | |
|---|---|
| SUBJECT LIST AND MAP SYMBOLS | 3 |
| SCALE, LATITUDE AND LONGITUDE | 4 |
| MAP PROJECTIONS | 5 |

### REMOTE SENSING — 6–16

| | |
|---|---|
| SATELLITE IMAGERY AND REMOTE SENSING *INTRODUCTION* | 6–7 |
| COLOUR COMPOSITES | 8 |
| VEGETATION AND LANDFORMS | 9 |
| GLOBAL MONITORING | 10–11 |
| ENVIRONMENTAL MONITORING | 12 |
| URBAN MONITORING | 13 |
| GEOLOGICAL INTERPRETATION | 14 |
| SYNTHETIC APERTURE RADAR | 15 |
| DIGITAL ELEVATION MODELS AND LAND USE | 16 |

### BRITISH ISLES — 17–48

| | |
|---|---|
| NORTHERN SCOTLAND | 18–19 |
| SOUTHERN SCOTLAND | 20–21 |
| NORTHERN ENGLAND | 22–23 |
| SOUTH AND SOUTH-EAST ENGLAND | 24–25 |
| WALES AND SOUTH-WEST ENGLAND | 26–27 |
| IRELAND – NORTH | 28–29 |
| IRELAND – SOUTH | 30–31 |
| BRITISH ISLES *GEOLOGY* | 32 |
| BRITISH ISLES *RELIEF OF LAND* | 33 |
| BRITISH ISLES *CLIMATE* | 34–35 |
| BRITISH ISLES *WATER RESOURCES* | 36 |
| BRITISH ISLES *ENVIRONMENT, CONSERVATION AND POLLUTION* | 37 |
| BRITISH ISLES *AGRICULTURE AND FISHING* | 38–39 |
| BRITISH ISLES *INDUSTRY AND EMPLOYMENT* | 40 |
| BRITISH ISLES *ENERGY* | 41 |
| BRITISH ISLES *TRANSPORT* | 42 |
| BRITISH ISLES *TRADE AND TOURISM* | 43 |
| BRITISH ISLES *COUNTIES AND REGIONS* | 44–45 |
| BRITISH ISLES *POPULATION TRENDS* | 46–47 |
| BRITISH ISLES *STANDARDS OF LIVING* | 48 |

### THE WORLD — 49–122

| | |
|---|---|
| THE WORLD *RELIEF OF LAND* | 50–51 |
| THE WORLD *COUNTRIES* | 52–53 |
| ARCTIC OCEAN AND ANTARCTICA | 54–55 |
| EUROPE *RELIEF OF LAND* | 56 |
| EUROPE *COUNTRIES* | 57 |
| EUROPE *POPULATION* | 58 |
| EUROPE *ECONOMIC* | 59 |
| EUROPEAN UNION | 60–61 |
| EUROPE *CLIMATE AND NATURAL VEGETATION* | 62 |
| SCANDINAVIA AND THE BALTIC LANDS | 63 |
| BRITISH ISLES | 64 |
| BENELUX AND THE RUHR | 65 |
| CENTRAL EUROPE | 66–67 |
| FRANCE | 68 |
| SPAIN AND PORTUGAL | 69 |
| ITALY AND THE BALKAN STATES | 70–71 |
| EASTERN EUROPE AND TURKEY | 72–73 |
| ASIA *RELIEF OF LAND* | 74 |
| ASIA *COUNTRIES* | 75 |

| | |
|---|---|
| ASIA *POPULATION AND WEALTH* | 76 |
| ASIA *ECONOMIC* | 77 |
| ASIA *CLIMATE AND NATURAL VEGETATION* | 78 |
| RUSSIA AND CENTRAL ASIA | 79 |
| CHINA AND THE FAR EAST | 80–81 |
| JAPAN | 82 |
| SOUTH-EAST ASIA | 83 |
| SOUTH ASIA | 84–85 |
| THE MIDDLE EAST | 86–87 |
| ARABIA AND THE HORN OF AFRICA | 88 |
| AFRICA *CLIMATE AND NATURAL VEGETATION* | 89 |
| AFRICA *RELIEF OF LAND* | 90 |
| AFRICA *COUNTRIES* | 91 |
| AFRICA *POPULATION AND WEALTH* | 92 |
| AFRICA *ECONOMIC* | 93 |
| NORTHERN AFRICA | 94–95 |
| CENTRAL AND SOUTHERN AFRICA | 96–97 |
| AUSTRALIA AND OCEANIA | 98–99 |
| OCEANIA *CLIMATE AND NATURAL VEGETATION* | 100 |
| OCEANIA *POPULATION AND ECONOMIC* | 101 |
| PACIFIC OCEAN | 102–103 |
| NORTH AMERICA *RELIEF OF LAND AND CLIMATE* | 104 |
| NORTH AMERICA *COUNTRIES, CLIMATE AND NATURAL VEGETATION* | 105 |
| NORTH AMERICA *POPULATION AND WEALTH* | 106 |
| NORTH AMERICA *ECONOMIC* | 107 |
| CANADA | 108–109 |
| UNITED STATES | 110–111 |
| NORTH-EAST UNITED STATES AND THE ST LAWRENCE | 112–113 |
| MEXICO, CENTRAL AMERICA AND THE CARIBBEAN | 114–115 |
| SOUTH AMERICA *RELIEF OF LAND* | 116 |
| SOUTH AMERICA *CLIMATE AND NATURAL VEGETATION* | 117 |
| SOUTH AMERICA *POPULATION AND WEALTH* | 118 |
| SOUTH AMERICA *ECONOMIC* | 119 |
| SOUTH AMERICA | 120–121 |
| SOUTH-EASTERN BRAZIL | 122 |

### WORLD THEMES — 123–160

| | |
|---|---|
| THE WORLD *GEOLOGY, VOLCANOES AND EARTHQUAKES* | 124–125 |
| THE WORLD *TEMPERATURE AND OCEAN CURRENTS* | 126 |
| THE WORLD *PRESSURE, WINDS AND PRECIPITATION* | 127 |
| THE WORLD *CLIMATE* | 128–129 |
| THE WORLD *CLIMATE STATISTICS* | 130–131 |
| THE WORLD *NATURAL VEGETATION* | 132–133 |
| THE WORLD *ENVIRONMENTAL CONCERNS* | 134–135 |
| THE WORLD *AGRICULTURE* | 136–137 |
| THE WORLD *ENERGY AND MINERALS* | 138–139 |
| THE WORLD *INDUSTRY AND TRADE* | 140–141 |
| THE WORLD *TRAVEL AND TOURISM* | 142–143 |
| THE WORLD *STANDARDS OF LIVING* | 144–145 |
| THE WORLD *POPULATION DISTRIBUTION* | 146–147 |
| THE WORLD *POPULATION TRENDS* | 148–149 |
| THE WORLD *LANGUAGES AND RELIGIONS* | 150 |
| THE WORLD *INTERNATIONAL ORGANIZATIONS* | 151 |
| THE WORLD *HUMAN CONCERNS* | 152–153 |
| THE WORLD *SOCIAL AND ECONOMIC STATISTICS* | 154–159 |
| THE WORLD *PHYSICAL DIMENSIONS* | 160 |

### INDEX — 161–184

Published in Great Britain in 2003 by Philip's,
a division of Octopus Publishing Group Limited,
2–4 Heron Quays, London E14 4JP

Cartography by Philip's

Ninety-fourth edition
Copyright © 2003 Philip's
Reprinted 2004

ISBN 0-540-08088-8 Paperback edition
ISBN 0-540-08087-X Hardback edition

Printed in Hong Kong

Philip's World Atlases are published in association with The Royal Geographical
Society (with The Institute of British Geographers).

The Society was founded in 1830 and given a Royal Charter in 1859 for
'the advancement of geographical science'. Today it is a leading world centre
for geographical learning – supporting education, teaching, research and
expeditions, and promoting public understanding of the subject.

Further information about the Society and how to join may be found on its
website at: **www.rgs.org**

PHOTOGRAPHIC ACKNOWLEDGEMENTS
All satellite images in the atlas are courtesy of NPA Group Ltd, Edenbridge, Kent,
with the exception of the following: p. 17 M-SAT Ltd/Science Photo Library;
p. 49 PLI/Science Photo Library; p. 134 NASA/GSFC.

## SUBJECT LIST

| Acid rain | 37, 135 |
| Agriculture | 38–9, 136–7, 140 |
| Aid (international) | 92, 152 |
| AIDS and HIV | 153 |
| Air travel | 42, 61, 142 |
| Alternative energy | 139 |
| Assisted areas | 40 |
| Carbon dioxide emissions | 37, 134 |
| Child mortality | 149 |
| Climate regions | 128 |
| Climate statistics | 35, 130–1 |
| Coal/oil/gas | 138 |
| Conservation | 37, 134–5 |
| Continental drift | 124 |
| Conflicts | 153 |
| Debt | 92, 152 |
| Deforestation | 135 |
| Desertification | 135 |
| Drugs | 153 |
| Earthquakes | 125 |
| Education | 48, 61, 145 |
| Electricity | 41, 139 |
| El Niño | 129 |
| Employment | 39, 40, 140 |
| Energy | 41, 138 |
| Ethnic groups | 47 |
| European Union | 60–1 |
| Exports | 141 |
| Family size | 149 |
| Famine | 135 |
| Fishing | 39, 136–7 |
| Flood risk | 36 |
| Food production | 38, 136–7 |
| Foot-and-mouth disease | 38 |
| Forestry | 37, 39, 137 |
| Fuel | 41, 138 |
| Gender development index (GDI) | 145 |
| Geology | 32, 124 |
| Global warming | 134 |
| Greenhouse effect | 37, 134 |
| Gross domestic product (GDP) | 144 |
| Health care | 48, 61, 145 |
| Human development index (HDI) | 144 |
| Hydroelectricity | 139 |
| Illiteracy | 145 |
| Industry | 40, 61, 140 |
| Internet | 141 |
| Languages | 58, 150 |
| Latitude and longitude | 4 |
| Life expectancy | 149 |
| Literacy | 145 |
| Manufacturing | 40, 140–1 |
| Map projections | 5 |
| Migration | 47, 152 |
| Monsoon | 128 |
| Multinational corporations | 141 |
| National parks | 37 |
| Natural vegetation | 37, 132–3 |
| North Sea fishing | 137 |
| Nuclear power | 139 |
| Ocean currents | 126 |
| Oil spills | 135 |
| Ozone layer | 37, 134 |
| Plate tectonics | 124–5 |
| Population change | 47, 146, 148 |
| Population density | 46, 146–8 |
| Population pyramids | 47, 146 |
| Precipitation | 34, 127 |
| Rainfall | 35, 130–1 |
| Refugees | 152 |
| Religions | 150 |
| Remote sensing | 6–16 |
| Renewable energy | 41, 139 |
| Research and development | 140 |
| Satellite imagery | 6–16 |
| Scale | 4 |
| Services | 40, 140 |
| Soils | 132–3 |
| Standards of living | 48, 144 |
| Telecommunications | 141 |
| Temperature | 35, 126 |
| Time zones | 142 |
| Tourism | 43, 113, 143 |
| Trade | 43, 60, 141 |
| Transport | 42, 61 |
| Travel | 42–3, 142 |
| Unemployment | 40, 61 |
| United Nations | 151 |
| Urban population | 47, 148 |
| Volcanoes | 125 |
| Water pollution | 36, 135 |
| Water supply | 36, 144 |
| Wealth | 48, 61, 144 |
| Wind power | 139 |
| Wind-chill effect | 129 |
| World Heritage Sites | 37, 143 |

## MAP SYMBOLS

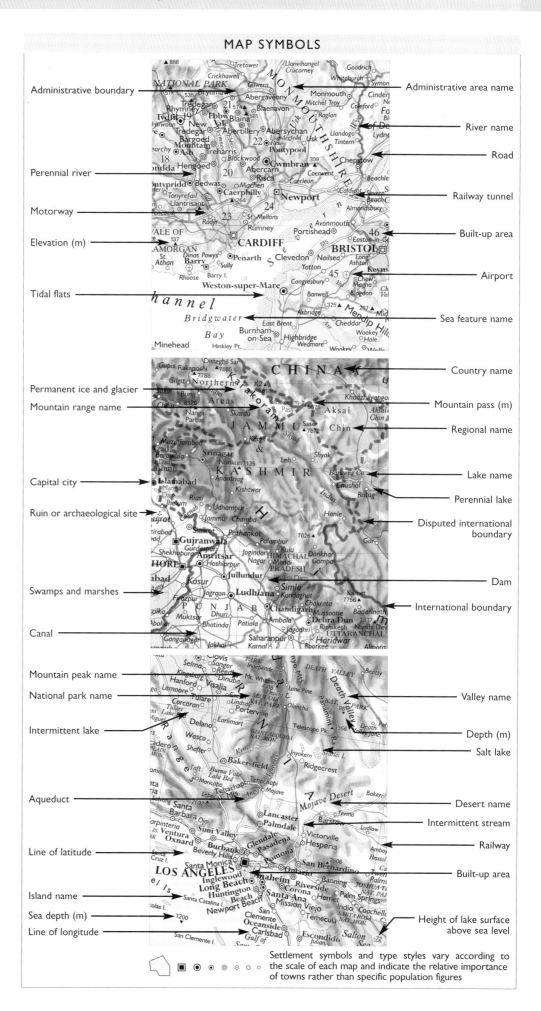

Administrative boundary
Administrative area name
River name
Perennial river
Road
Railway tunnel
Motorway
Built-up area
Elevation (m)
Airport
Tidal flats
Sea feature name

Permanent ice and glacier
Country name
Mountain range name
Mountain pass (m)
Regional name
Capital city
Lake name
Perennial lake
Ruin or archaeological site
Disputed international boundary
Dam
Swamps and marshes
International boundary
Canal

Mountain peak name
National park name
Valley name
Intermittent lake
Depth (m)
Salt lake
Aqueduct
Desert name
Intermittent stream
Railway
Line of latitude
Built-up area
Island name
Sea depth (m)
Line of longitude
Height of lake surface above sea level

Settlement symbols and type styles vary according to the scale of each map and indicate the relative importance of towns rather than specific population figures

## SCALE

The scale of a map is the relationship of the distance between two points shown on the map and the distance between the same two points on the Earth's surface. For instance, 1 inch on the map represents 1 mile on the ground, or 10 kilometres on the ground is represented by 1 centimetre on the map.

Instead of saying 1 centimetre represents 10 kilometres, we could say that 1 centimetre represents 1 000 000 centimetres on the map. If the scale is stated so that the same unit of measurement is used on both the map and the ground, then the proportion will hold for any unit of measurement. Therefore, the scale is usually written 1:1 000 000. This is called a 'representative fraction' and usually appears at the top of the map page, above the scale bar.

Calculations can easily be made in centimetres and kilometres by dividing the second figure in the representative fraction by 100 000 (i.e. by deleting the last five zeros). Thus at a scale of 1:5 000 000, 1 cm on the map represents 50 km on the ground. This is called a 'scale statement'. The calculation for inches and miles is more laborious, but 1 000 000 divided by 63 360 (the number of inches in a mile) shows that 1:1 000 000 can be stated as 1 inch on the map represents approximately 16 miles on the ground.

Many of the maps in this atlas feature a scale bar. This is a bar divided into the units of the map – miles and kilometres – so that a map distance can be measured with a ruler, dividers or a piece of paper, then placed along the scale bar, and the distance read off. To the left of the zero on the scale bar there are usually more divisions. By placing the ruler or dividers on the nearest rounded figure to the right of the zero, the smaller units can be counted off to the left.

The map extracts to the right show Los Angeles and its surrounding area at six different scales. The representative fraction, scale statement and scale bar are positioned above each map. Map 1 is at 1:27 000 and is the largest scale extract shown. Many of the individual buildings are identified and most of the streets are named, but at this scale only part of central Los Angeles can be shown within the given area. Map 2 is much smaller in scale at 1:250 000. Only a few important buildings and streets can be named, but the whole of central Los Angeles is shown. Maps 3, 4 and 5 show how greater areas can be depicted as the map scale decreases, down to Map 6 at 1:35 000 000. At this small scale, the entire Los Angeles conurbation is depicted by a single town symbol and a large part of the south-western USA and part of Mexico is shown.

The scales of maps must be used with care since large distances on small-scale maps can be represented by one or two centimetres. On certain projections scale is only correct along certain lines, parallels or meridians. As a general rule, the larger the map scale, the more accurate and reliable will be the distance measured.

## LATITUDE AND LONGITUDE

Accurate positioning of individual points on the Earth's surface is made possible by reference to the geometric system of latitude and longitude.

Latitude is the distance of a point north or south of the Equator measured at an angle with the centre of the Earth, whereby the Equator is latitude 0 degrees,

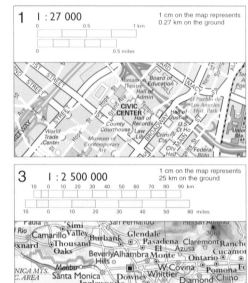

**1  1 : 27 000**  — 1 cm on the map represents 0.27 km on the ground

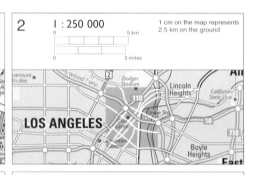

**2  1 : 250 000**  — 1 cm on the map represents 2.5 km on the ground

**3  1 : 2 500 000**  — 1 cm on the map represents 25 km on the ground

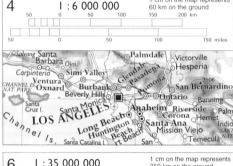

**4  1 : 6 000 000**  — 1 cm on the map represents 60 km on the ground

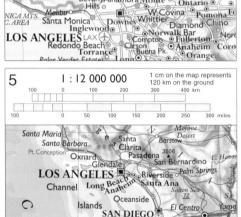

**5  1 : 12 000 000**  — 1 cm on the map represents 120 km on the ground

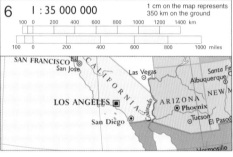

**6  1 : 35 000 000**  — 1 cm on the map represents 350 km on the ground

the North Pole is 90 degrees north and the South Pole 90 degrees south. Latitude parallels are drawn west–east around the Earth, parallel to the Equator, decreasing in diameter from the Equator until they become a point at the poles. On the maps in this atlas the lines of latitude are represented by blue lines running across the map in smooth curves, with the degree figures in blue at the sides of the maps. The degree interval depends on the scale of the map.

Lines of longitude are meridians drawn north–south, cutting the lines of latitude at right angles on the Earth's surface and intersecting with one another at the poles. Longitude is measured by an angle at the centre of the Earth from the prime meridian (0 degrees), which passes through Greenwich in London. It is given as a measurement east or west of the Greenwich Meridian from 0 to 180 degrees. The meridians are normally drawn north–south vertically down the map, with the degree figures

in blue in the top and bottom margins of the map.

In the index each place name is followed by its map page number, its letter-figure grid reference, and then its latitude and longitude. The unit of measurement is the degree, which is subdivided into 60 minutes. An index entry states the position of a place in degrees and minutes. The latitude is followed by N(orth) or S(outh) and the longitude E(ast) or W(est).

For example:
Helston, U.K.                    27 G3    50 7N    5 17W
Helston is on map page 27, in grid square G3, and is 50 degrees 7 minutes north of the Equator and 5 degrees 17 minutes west of Greenwich.

McKinley, Mt., U.S.A.        108 B4    63 4N    151 0W
Mount McKinley is on map page 108, in grid square B4, and is 63 degrees 4 minutes north of the Equator and 151 degrees west of Greenwich.

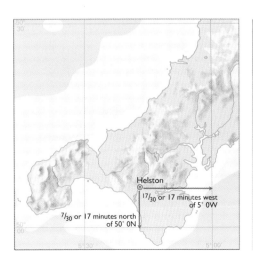

### How to locate a place or feature

The two diagrams (*left*) show how to estimate the required distance from the nearest line of latitude or longitude on the map page, in order to locate a place or feature listed in the index (such as Helston in the UK and Mount McKinley in the USA, as detailed in the above example).

In the left-hand diagram there are 30 minutes between the lines and so to find the position of Helston an estimate has to be made: 7 parts of the 30 degrees north of the 50 0N latitude line, and 17 parts of the 30 degrees west of the 5 0W longitude line.

In the right-hand diagram it is more difficult to estimate because there is an interval of 10 degrees between the lines. In the example of Mount McKinley, the reader has to estimate 3 degrees 4 minutes north of 60 0N and 1 degree west of 150 0W.

## MAP PROJECTIONS

A map projection is the systematic depiction of the imaginary grid of lines of latitude and longitude from a globe on to a flat surface. The grid of lines is called the 'graticule' and it can be constructed either by graphical means or by mathematical formulae to form the basis of a map. As a globe is three dimensional, it is not possible to depict its surface on a flat map without some form of distortion. Preservation of one of the basic properties listed below can only be secured at the expense of the others and thus the choice of projection is often a compromise solution.

### Correct area
In these projections the areas from the globe are to scale on the map. This is particularly useful in the mapping of densities and distributions. Projections with this property are termed 'equal area', 'equivalent' or 'homolographic'.

### Correct distance
In these projections the scale is correct along the meridians, or, in the case of the 'azimuthal equidistant', scale is true along any line drawn from the centre of the projection. They are called 'equidistant'.

### Correct shape
This property can only be true within small areas as it is achieved only by having a uniform scale distortion along both the 'x' and 'y' axes of the projection. The projections are called 'conformal' or 'orthomorphic'.

Map projections can be divided into three broad categories – **'azimuthal'**, **'conic'** and **'cylindrical'**. Cartographers use different projections from these categories depending on the map scale, the size of the area to be mapped, and what they want the map to show.

### AZIMUTHAL OR ZENITHAL PROJECTIONS

These are constructed by the projection of part of the graticule from the globe on to a plane tangential to any single point on it. This plane may be tangential to the equator (equatorial case), the poles (polar case) or any other point (oblique case). Any straight line drawn from the point at which the plane touches the globe is the shortest distance from that point and is known as a 'great circle'. In its 'gnomonic' construction any straight line on the map is a great circle, but there is great exaggeration towards the edges and this reduces its general uses. There are five different ways of transferring the graticule on to the plane and these are shown below. The diagrams below also show how the graticules vary, using the polar case as the example.

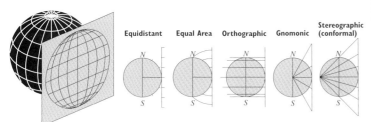

Equidistant  Equal Area  Orthographic  Gnomonic  Stereographic (conformal)

### Polar case
The polar case is the simplest to construct and the diagram on the right shows the differing effects of all five methods of construction, comparing their coverage, distortion, etc., using North America as the example.

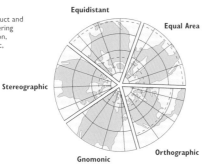

Equidistant
Equal Area
Stereographic
Gnomonic
Orthographic

### Oblique case
The plane touches the globe at any point between the Equator and poles. The oblique orthographic uses the distortion in azimuthal projections away from the centre to give a graphic depiction of the Earth as seen from any desired point in space.

### Equatorial case
The example shown here is Lambert's Equivalent Azimuthal. It is the only projection which is both equal area and where bearing is true from the centre.

### CONICAL PROJECTIONS

These use the projection of the graticule from the globe on to a cone which is tangential to a line of latitude (termed the 'standard parallel'). This line is always an arc and scale is always true along it. Because of its method of construction, it is used mainly for depicting the temperate latitudes around the standard parallel, i.e. where there is least distortion. To reduce the distortion and include a larger range of latitudes, the projection may be constructed with the cone bisecting the surface of the globe so that there are two standard parallels, each of which is true to scale. The distortion is thus spread more evenly between the two chosen parallels.

**Simple Conical with one standard parallel**

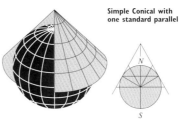

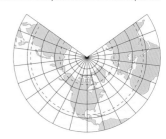

### Bonne
This is a modification of the simple conic, whereby the true scale along the meridians is sacrificed to enable the accurate representation of areas. However, scale is true along each parallel but shapes are distorted at the edges.

### Albers Conical Equal Area
This projection uses two standard parallels. The selection of these relative to the land area to be mapped is very important. It is equal area and is especially useful for large land masses oriented east–west, such as the USA.

### CYLINDRICAL AND OTHER WORLD PROJECTIONS

This group of projections are those which permit the whole of the Earth's surface to be depicted on one map. They are a very large group of projections and the following are only a few of them. Cylindrical projections are constructed by the projection of the graticule from the globe on to a cylinder tangential to the globe. Although cylindrical projections can depict all the main land masses, there is considerable distortion of shape and area towards the poles. One cylindrical projection, Mercator, overcomes this shortcoming by possessing the unique navigational property that any straight line drawn on it is a line of constant bearing ('loxodrome'). It is used for maps and charts between 15° either side of the Equator. Beyond this, enlargement of area is a serious drawback, although it is used for navigational charts at all latitudes.

**Simple Cylindrical**

**Cylindrical with two standard parallels**

**Mercator**

**Eckert IV**
(pseudo-cylindrical equal area)

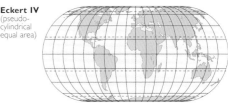

**Hammer**
(polyconic equal area)

The first satellite to monitor our environment systematically was launched as long ago as April 1961. It was called TIROS-1 and was designed specifically to record atmospheric change. The first of the generation of Earth resources satellites was Landsat-1, launched in July 1972.

The succeeding decades have seen a revolution in our ability to survey and map our global environment. Digital sensors mounted on satellites now scan vast areas of the Earth's surface day and night. They collect and relay back to Earth huge volumes of geographical data which is processed and stored by computers.

### Satellite imagery and remote sensing

Continuous development and refinement, and freedom from national access restrictions, have meant that sensors on these satellite platforms are increasingly replacing surface and airborne data-gathering techniques. Twenty-four hours a day, satellites are scanning and measuring the Earth's surface and atmosphere, adding to an ever-expanding range of geographic and geophysical data available to help us identify and manage the problems of our human and physical environments. Remote sensing is the science of extracting information from such images.

### Satellite orbits

Most Earth-observation satellites (such as the Landsat, SPOT and IRS series) are in a near-polar, Sun-synchronous orbit (*see diagram opposite*). At altitudes of around 700–900 km the satellites revolve around the Earth approximately every 100 minutes and on each orbit cross a particular line of latitude at the same local (solar) time. This ensures that the satellite can obtain coverage of most of the globe, replicating the coverage typically within 2–3 weeks. In more recent satellites, sensors can be pointed sideways from the orbital path, and 'revisit' times with high-resolution frames can thus be reduced to a few days.

Exceptions to these Sun-synchronous orbits include the geo-stationary meteorological satellites, such as Meteosat. These have a 36,000 km high orbit and rotate around the Earth every 24 hours, thus remaining above the same point on the Equator.

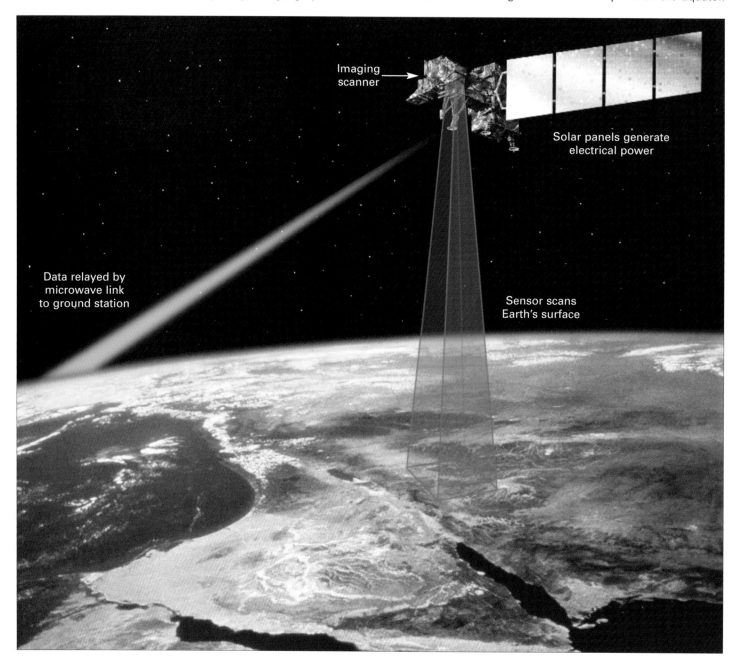

Imaging scanner

Solar panels generate electrical power

Data relayed by microwave link to ground station

Sensor scans Earth's surface

**Landsat-7**
*This is the latest addition to the Landsat Earth-observation satellite programme, orbiting at 705 km above the Earth. With onboard recorders, the satellite can store data until it passes within range of a ground station. Basic geometric and radiometric corrections are then applied before distribution of the imagery to users.*

These satellites acquire frequent images showing cloud and atmospheric moisture movements for almost a full hemisphere.

In addition, there is the Global Positioning System (GPS) satellite 'constellation', which orbits at a height of 20,200 km, consisting of 24 satellites. These circle the Earth in six different orbital planes, enabling us to fix our position on the Earth's surface to an accuracy of a few centimetres. Although developed for military use, this system is now available to individuals through hand-held receivers and in-car navigation systems. The other principal commercial uses are for surveying and air and sea navigation.

### Digital sensors

Early satellite designs involved images being exposed to photographic film and returned to Earth by capsule for processing, a technique still sometimes used today. However, even the first commercial satellite imagery, from Landsat-1, used digital imaging sensors and transmitted the data back to ground stations (*see diagram opposite*).

Passive, or optical, sensors record the radiation reflected from the Earth for specific wavebands. Active sensors transmit their own microwave radiation, which is reflected from the Earth's surface back to the satellite and recorded. The SAR (Synthetic Aperture Radar) Radarsat images on page 15 are examples of the latter.

Whichever scanning method is used, each satellite records image data of constant width but potentially several thousand kilometres in length. Once the data has been received on Earth, it is usually split into approximately square sections or 'scenes' for distribution.

### Spectral resolution, wavebands and false-colour composites

Satellites can record data from many sections of the electromagnetic spectrum (wavebands) simultaneously. Since we can only see images made from the three primary colours (red, green and blue), a selection of any three wavebands needs to be made in order to form a picture that will enable visual interpretation of the scene to be made. When any combination other than the visible bands are used, such as near or middle infrared, the resulting image is termed a 'false-colour composite'. An example of this is shown on page 8.

The selection of these wavebands depends on the purpose of the final image – geology, hydrology, agronomy and environmental requirements each have their own optimum waveband combinations.

## GEOGRAPHIC INFORMATION SYSTEMS

A Geographic Information System (GIS) enables any available geospatial data to be compiled, presented and analysed using specialized computer software.

Many aspects of our lives now benefit from the use of GIS – from the management and maintenance of the networks of pipelines and cables that supply our homes, to the exploitation or protection of the natural resources that we use. Much of this is at a regional or national scale and the data collected from satellites form an important part of our interpretation and understanding of the world around us.

GIS systems are used for many aspects of central planning and modern life, such as defence, land use, reclamation, telecommunications and the deployment of emergency services. Commercial companies can use demographic and infrastructure data within a GIS to plan marketing strategies, identifying where their services would be most needed, and thus decide where best to locate their businesses. Insurance companies use GIS to determine premiums based on population distribution, crime figures and the likelihood of natural disasters, such as flooding or subsidence.

Whatever the application, all the geographically related information that is available can be input and prepared in a GIS, so that a user can display the specific information of interest, or combine data to produce further information which might answer or help resolve a specific problem. From analysis of the data that has been acquired, it is often possible to use a GIS to generate a 'model' of possible future situations and to see what impact might result from decisions and actions taken. A GIS can also monitor change over time, to aid the observation and interpretation of long-term change.

A GIS can utilize a satellite image to extract useful information and map large areas, which would otherwise take many man-years of labour to achieve on the ground. For industrial applications, including hydrocarbon and mineral exploration, forestry, agriculture, environmental monitoring and urban development, such dramatic and beneficial increases in efficiency have made it possible to evaluate and undertake projects and studies in parts of the world that were previously considered inaccessible, and on a scale that would not have been possible before.

| SELECTED REMOTE SENSING SATELLITES | | | |
|---|---|---|---|
| **Year Launched** | **Satellite** | **Country** | **Pixel Size (Resolution)** |
| *Passive Sensors (Optical)* | | | |
| 1972 | Landsat-1 MSS | USA | 80 m |
| 1975 | Landsat-2 MSS | USA | 80 m |
| 1978 | Landsat-3 MSS | USA | 80 m |
| 1978 | NOAA AVHRR | USA | 1.1 km |
| 1981 | Cosmos TK-350 | Russia | 10 m |
| 1982 | Landsat-4 TM | USA | 30 m |
| 1984 | Landsat-5 TM | USA | 30 m |
| 1986 | SPOT-1 | France | 10 / 20 m |
| 1988 | IRS-1A | India | 36 / 72 m |
| 1988 | SPOT-2 | France | 10 / 20 m |
| 1989 | Cosmos KVR-1000 | Russia | 2 m |
| 1991 | IRS-1B | India | 36 / 72 m |
| 1992 | SPOT-3 | France | 10 / 20 m |
| 1995 | IRS-1C | India | 5.8 / 23.5 m |
| 1997 | IRS-1D | India | 5.8 / 23.5 m |
| 1998 | SPOT-4 | France | 10 / 20 m |
| 1999 | Landsat-7 ETM | USA | 15 / 30 m |
| 1999 | UoSAT-12 | UK | 10 / 32 m |
| 1999 | IKONOS-2 | USA | 1.0 / 4 m |
| 1999 | ASTER | USA | 15 m |
| 2000 | Hyperion | USA | 30 m |
| 2000 | EROS-A1 | International | 1.8 m |
| 2001 | Quickbird | USA | 0.61 / 2.4 m |
| 2002 | SPOT-5 | France | 2.5 / 5 / 10 m |
| *Active Sensors (Synthetic Aperture Radar)* | | | |
| 1991 | ERS-1 | Europe | 25 m |
| 1992 | JERS-1 | Japan | 18 m |
| 1995 | ERS-2 | Europe | 25 m |
| 1995 | Radarsat | Canada | 8–100 m |
| 2002 | ENVISAT | Europe | 25 m |

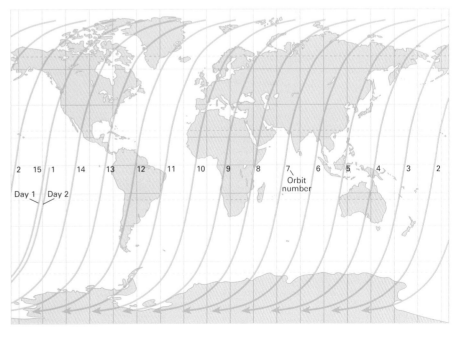

**Satellite orbits**
*Landsat-7 makes over 14 orbits per day in its Sun-synchronous orbit. During the full 16 days of a repeat cycle, coverage of the areas between those shown is achieved.*

**Natural-colour and false-colour composites**
These images show the salt ponds at the southern end of San Francisco Bay, which now form the San Francisco Bay National Wildlife Refuge. They demonstrate the difference between 'natural colour' (*top*) and 'false colour' (*bottom*) composites.

The top image is made from visible red, green and blue wavelengths. The colours correspond closely to those one would observe from an aircraft. The salt ponds appear green or orange-red due to the colour of the sediments they contain. The urban areas appear grey and vegetation is either dark green (trees) or light brown (dry grass).

The bottom image is made up of near-infrared, visible red and visible green wavelengths. These wavebands are represented here in red, green and blue, respectively. Since chlorophyll in healthy vegetation strongly reflects near-infrared light, this is clearly visible as red in the image.

False-colour composite imagery is therefore very sensitive to the presence of healthy vegetation. The bottom image thus shows better discrimination between the 'leafy' residential urban areas, such as Palo Alto (south-west of the Bay) from other urban areas by the 'redness' of the trees. The high chlorophyll content of watered urban grass areas shows as bright red, contrasting with the dark red of trees and the brown of natural, dry grass. *(EROS)*

**Western Grand Canyon, Arizona, USA**
This false-colour image shows in bright red the sparse vegetation on the limestone plateau, including sage, mesquite and grasses. Imagery such as this is used to monitor this and similar fragile environments. The sediment-laden river, shown as blue-green, can be seen dispersing into Lake Mead to the north-west. Side canyons cross the main canyon in straight lines, showing where erosion along weakened fault lines has occurred. *(EROS)*

**Ayers Rock and Mt Olga, Northern Territory, Australia**
These two huge outliers are the remnants of Precambrian mountain ranges created some 500 million years ago and then eroded away. Ayers Rock (*seen at right*) rises 345 m above the surrounding land and has been a part of Aboriginal life for over 10,000 years. Their dramatic coloration, caused by oxidized iron in the sandstone, attracts visitors from around the world. *(EROS)*

**Mount St Helens, Washington, USA**
A massive volcanic eruption on 18 May 1980 killed 60 people and devastated around 400 sq km of forest within minutes. The blast reduced the mountain peak by 400 m to its current height of 2,550 m, and volcanic ash rose some 25 km into the atmosphere. The image shows Mount St Helens eight years after the eruption in 1988. The characteristic volcanic cone has collapsed in the north, resulting in the devastating 'liquid' flow of mud and rock. *(EROS)*

**Niger Delta, West Africa**
The River Niger is the third longest river in Africa after the Nile and Congo. Deltas are by nature constantly evolving sedimentary features and often contain many ecosystems within them. In the case of the Niger Delta, there are also vast hydro-carbon reserves beneath it with associated wells and pipelines. Satellite imagery helps to plan activity and monitor this fragile and changing environment. *(EROS)*

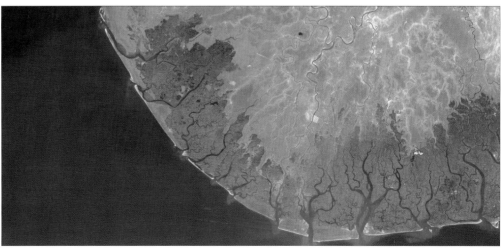

**Europe at night**
This image was derived as part of the Defense Meteorological Satellite Program. The sensor recorded all the emissions of near-infrared radiation at night, mainly the lights from cities, towns and villages. Note also the 'lights' in the North Sea from the flares of the oil production platforms. This project was the first systematic attempt to record human settlement on a global scale using remote sensing. *(NOAA)*

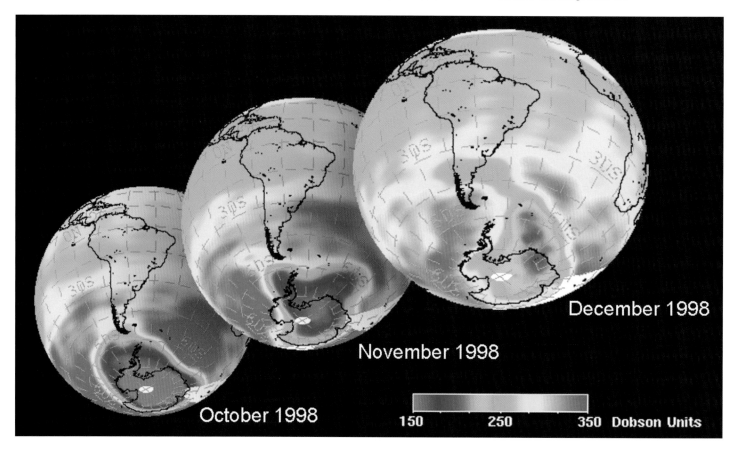

December 1998

November 1998

October 1998

150    250    350  **Dobson Units**

**Ozone distribution**
The Global Ozone Monitoring Experiment (GOME) sensor was launched in April 1995. This instrument can measure a range of atmospheric trace constituents, in particular global ozone distributions. Environmental and public health authorities need this up-to-date information to alert people to health risks. Low ozone levels result in increased UV-B radiation, which is harmful and can cause cancers, cataracts and impact the human immune system. 'Dobson Units' indicate the level of ozone depletion (normal levels are around 280DU). *(DLR)*

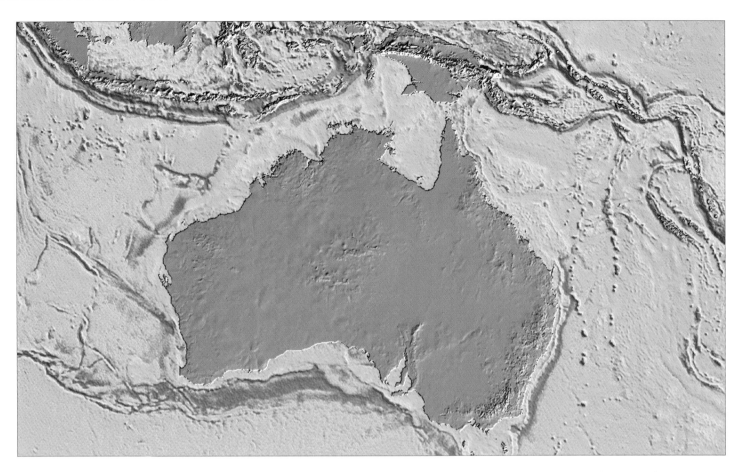

### Gravitational fields

The strength of the Earth's gravitational field at its surface varies according to the ocean depth and the density of local rocks. This causes local variations in the sea level. Satellites orbiting in precisely determined orbits are able to measure the sea level to an accuracy of a few centimetres. These variations give us a better understanding of the geological structure of the sea floor. Information from these sensors can also be used to determine ocean wave heights, which relate to surface wind speed, and are therefore useful in meteorological forecasting. *(NPA)*

### Weather monitoring

Geostationary and polar orbiting satellites monitor the Earth's cloud and atmospheric moisture movements, giving us an insight into the global workings of the atmosphere and permitting us to predict weather change. *(J-2)*

### Hurricane Andrew

Although Hurricane Andrew, which hit Florida on 23 August 1992, was the most expensive natural disaster ever to strike the USA, its effects would have been even worse had its path not been tracked by images such as this from the AVHRR sensor. *(NOAA)*

**Kuwait City, Kuwait**
This image (*right*) shows Kuwait after the 1991 war with
Iraq. During this conflict, more than 600 oil wells were set
on fire and over 300 oil lakes were formed (visible as dark
areas to the south). Satellite imagery helped reduce the
costs of mapping these oil spills and enabled the level
of damage to be determined prior to clean-up operations.
*(Space Imaging)*

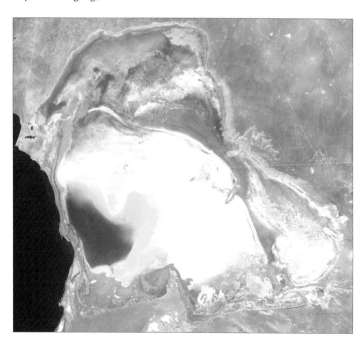

**Kara-Bogaz-Gol, Turkmenistan**
The Kara-Bogaz-Gol (*above and below*) is a large, shallow
lagoon joined by a narrow, steep-sided strait to the Caspian Sea.
Evaporation makes it one of the most saline bodies of water
in the world. Believing the Caspian sea level was falling, the
straight was dammed by the USSR in 1980 with the intention
of conserving the water to sustain the salt industry. However, by
1983 it had dried up completely (*above*), leading to widespread
wind-blown salt, soil poisoning and health problems downwind
to the east. In 1992 the Turkmenistan government began to
demolish the dam to re-establish the flow of water from the
Caspian Sea (*below*). Satellite imagery has helped to monitor
and map the Kara-Bogaz-Gol as it has fluctuated in size. *(EROS)*

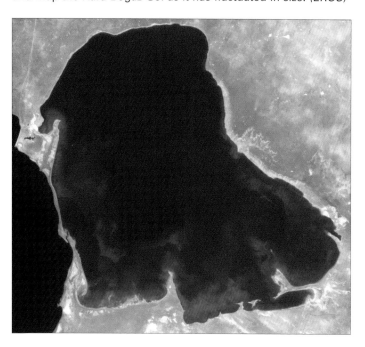

**Lake Amadeus, Northern Territory, Australia**
This saline lake system (*below*) is an important wetland environment at the heart of one of the most arid areas in Australia. It
supports a wide range of complex habitats and exists due to
seepage from the central groundwater system. Changes in its
extent in an otherwise remote site can be monitored using
satellite imagery such as this Landsat ETM scene. *(EROS)*

### Gulf of Izmit, north-west Turkey

An earthquake measuring 7.4 on the Richter scale caused extensive damage and loss of life around Izmit on 17 August 1999. The image above is a composite of two black-and-white images, one recorded on 7 August 1999 and the other on 24 September 1999. The colours indicate change: orange highlights damaged buildings and areas where debris has been deposited during the rescue operation; blue indicates areas submerged beneath sea level as a result of the Earth's movement during the earthquake and fire-damaged oil tanks in the north-west. *(NPA)*

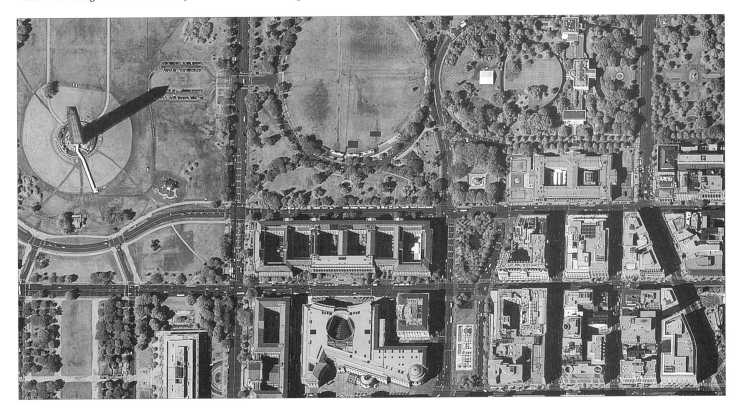

### Washington, DC, USA

This image, with the White House seen at top right and the Washington Monument to the left, was recorded on 30 September 1999 by Space Imaging's IKONOS-2 satellite. It was the first satellite image to be commercially available with a ground-sampling interval (pixel size) of 1 m. With a directional sensor, image acquisition attempts can be made in as little as 1–3 days (cloud cover permitting). This level of resolution enables satellite imagery to be used as a data source for many applications that otherwise require expensive aerial surveys to be flown. In addition, data can be readily acquired for projects in remote regions of the world or areas where access is restricted. *(Space Imaging)*

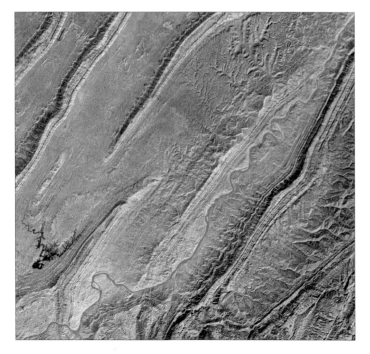

**Sichuan Basin, China**
The north-east/south-west trending ridges in this image are anticlinal folds developed in the Earth's crust as a result of plate collision and compression. Geologists map these folds and the lowlands between them formed by synclinal folds, as they are often the areas where oil or gas are found in commercial quantities. The river shown in this image is the Yangtze, near Chongqing. *(China RSGS)*

**North Anatolian Fault, Turkey**
The east–west trending valley running through the centre of this image is formed by the North Anatolian wrench fault. It is the result of Arabia colliding with southern Eurasia, forcing most of Turkey westwards towards Greece. The valley was created by the Kelkit river removing the loosened rock formed by the two tectonic plates grinding together. This active fault has also caused considerable damage further east in the Gulf of Izmit *(see page 13)*. *(EROS)*

**Wadi Hadhramaut, Yemen**
Yemen is extremely arid – however, in the past it was more humid and wet, enabling large river systems to carve out the deep and spectacular gorges and dried-out river beds (*wadis*) seen in this image. The erosion has revealed many contrasting rock types. The image has been processed to exaggerate this effect, producing many shades of red, pink and purple, which make geological mapping easier and more cost-effective. *(EROS)*

**Zagros Mountains, Iran**
These mountains were formed as Arabia collided with Southern Eurasia. The upper half of this colour-enhanced image shows an anticline that runs east–west. The dark grey features are called *diapirs*, which are bodies of viscous rock salt that are very buoyant and sometimes rise to the surface, spilling and spreading out like a glacier. The presence of salt in the region is important as it stops oil escaping to the surface. *(EROS)*

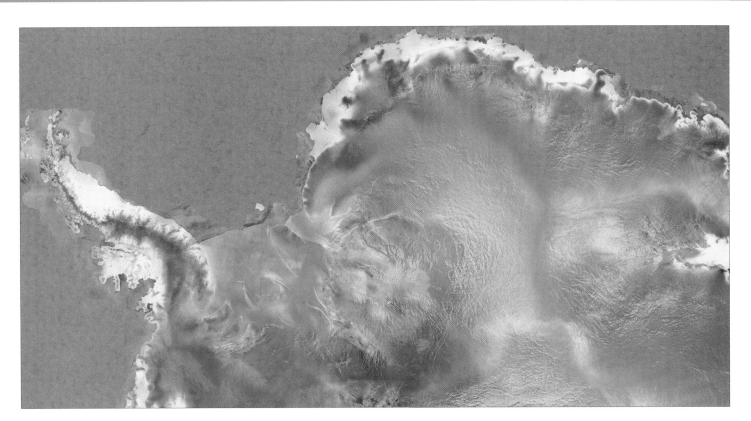

**Antarctic Peninsula**
Synthetic Aperture Radar (SAR) image brightness is dependent on surface texture. This image of part of Antarctica clearly shows the ice tongues projecting from the Wilkins and George VI Ice Shelves at the south-west end of the peninsula, as well as other coastal ice features. Images can be received, even during the winter 'night', and over a period of time form a valuable resource in our ability to monitor the recession of the ice. *(Radarsat)*

**Montserrat, Caribbean Sea**
SAR sensors send out a microwave signal and create an image from the radiation reflected back. The signal penetrates cloud cover and does not need any solar illumination. This image of Montserrat shows how the island can still be seen, despite clouds and the continuing eruption of the Soufrière volcano in the south. The delta visible in the sea to the east is being formed by lava flows pouring down the Tar River Valley. *(Radarsat)*

**Las Vegas, Nevada, USA**
Two satellite images viewing the same area of ground from different orbits can be used to compile a Digital Elevation Model (DEM) of the Earth's surface. A computer compares the images and calculates the ground surface elevation to a vertical precision of 8–15 m, preparing this for thousands of square kilometres in just a few minutes. Overlaying a colour satellite image on to a DEM produced the picture of Las Vegas shown here. *(NPA)*

Urban (tall)
Urban dense
Urban
Industrial
Paved
Urban / Tree mix
Trees (coniferous)
Trees (deciduous)
Forest clearing
Grass or crops
Open
Water

**Seattle, Washington, USA**
Image-processing software can use the differing spectral properties of land cover to 'classify' a multispectral satellite image. This classification of the area around Seattle was used together with elevation data to model the transmission of mobile phone signals before installation of the network. Microwave signals are affected by the absorption, reflection and scattering of the signal from vegetation and urban structures as well as the topography. *(NPA)*

BRITISH ISLES

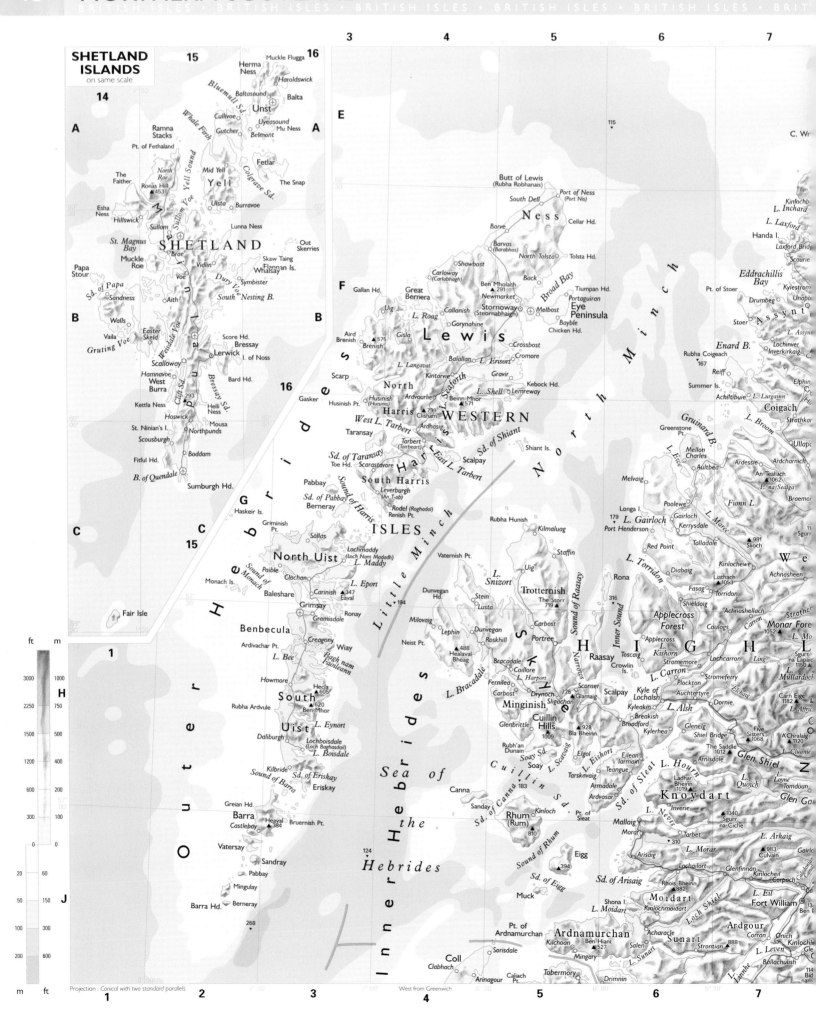

**SHETLAND ISLANDS**
on same scale

15  14  16

Muckle Flugga
Herma Ness
Haroldswick
Bluemull Sd.
Baltasound
Balta
Cullivoe  Unst
Whale Firth  Gutcher  Uyeasound  Mu Ness
Belmont

**A**
Ramna Stacks
Pt. of Fethaland
Fetlar
The Snap
The Faither
North Roe  Mid Yell
Ronas Hill ▲453  Yell  Colgrave Sd.
Esha Ness  The Snap
Hillswick  Ulsta  Burravoe
Sullom  Lunna Ness

**B**
St. Magnus Bay
Papa Stour  Muckle Roe  SHETLAND  Out Skerries
Sandness  "Brae"  Skaw Taing
Vidlin  Flannan Is.
Walls  Aith  Whalsay
Vaila  Voe  Symbister
Gruting Voe  South Nesting B.
Easter Skeld  Score Hd.
Bressay  Dury Voe
Scalloway  Lerwick  I. of Noss
Hamnavoe  Bard Hd.
West Burra  Cliff Sd.  Bressay Sd.
Kettla Ness  293  Helli Ness
Hoswick  Mousa
St. Ninian's I.  Northpunds
Scousburgh  Boddam
Fitful Hd.
B. of Quendale  Sumburgh Hd.

15

Fair Isle

---

**Scale (left margin)**

ft / m
3000 / 1000
2250 / 750
1500 / 500
1200 / 400
600 / 200
300 / 100
0 / 0
20 / 60
50 / 150
100 / 300
200 / 600

m / ft

Projection : Conical with two standard parallels

---

**E**
115
C. Wr

Butt of Lewis
(Rubha Robhanais)
Port of Ness
(Port Nis)
South Dell
**Ness**
Cellar Hd.
Borve
Barvas  North Tolsta
(Barabhas)  Tolsta Hd.
Shawbost  Back
Carloway  Ben Mholach  Broad Bay
(Carlabhagh)  ▲291  Tiumpan Hd.
Gallan Hd.  Newmarket  Portaguiran
Great Bernera  Stornoway  Eye Peninsula
Uig  (Steornabhaigh)  Melbost
L. Roag  Callanish  Bayble
Aird  Gorynahine  Chicken Hd.
Brenish  **Lewis**
▲575  Balallan  L. Erisort
Brenish  Crossbost
Gisla  L. Langavat  Cromore
Scarp  Kintarvie  L. Seaforth  Gravir
Husinish  L. Shell  Kebock Hd.
(Huisinis)  Ardvourlie  Lemreway
Gasker  Husinish Pt.  Beinn Mhor
**Harris**  Clisham ▲571
West L. Tarbert  ▲799
Taransay  Ardhasig
Sd. of Taransay  Tarbert
Toe Hd.  Scarastavore  (Tairbeart)  East L. Tarbert
**WESTERN**  Sd. of Shiant
Shiant Is.
Pabbay  South Harris  Scalpay
Sd. of Pabbay  Leverburgh
Berneray  (An T-ob)
Haskeir Is.  Rodel (Roghadal)
Renish Pt.  **ISLES**
Griminish Pt.  Rubha Hunish
Sollas  Kilmaluag
North Uist  Staffin
Lochmaddy  Vaternish Pt.
Paible  (Loch Nam Madadh)
Monach Is.  L. Maddy  Uig
Clachan  Dunvegan Hd.
Baleshare  Carinish  L. Eport  L. Snizort
Grimsay  ▲347 Eaval  Stein  **Trotternish**
Benbecula  Ronay  194  Lusta  The Storr ▲719
Ardivachar Pt.  Gramsdale  Milovaig  Carbost
Creagory  Dunvegan  Portree
L. Bee  Wiay  Lephin  Roskhill
Howmore  Bagh nam  Neist Pt.  Bracadale
Faoileann  Healaval  Coillore
South  Hecla  Bheag ▲488  L. Harport
Uist  ▲605  Carbost
Rubha Ardvule  Ben Mhor  Ferniea
▲620  L. Bracadale  Carbost
L. Eynort  Glenbrittle  Drynoch
Daliburgh  Lochboisdale  Minginish  Sligachan
(Loch Baghasdail)  Cuillin  Bla Bheinn
Kilbride  L. Boisdale  Hills  ▲928
Sd. of Eriskay  Rubh'an  ▲1009
Eriskay  Dunain  Soay Sd.  Elgol
Sea of  Soay  L. Scavaig
Greian Hd.  the  Canna
Barra  Hebrides  Sanday
Castlebay  Heaval ▲384  Kinloch
Vatersay  Bruernish Pt.  Rhum
Sandray  (Rum)
Pabbay  124  810  Eigg
Mingulay  ▲394
Berneray  Sd. of Eigg
Barra Hd.  Muck

268

**Inner Hebrides**

Coll
Clabhach
Pt. of Ardnamurchan
Sorisdale
Arinagour  Caliach Pt.
Kilchoan

---

**Right side (mainland)**

Kinlochbervie  L. Inchard
L. Laxford
Handa I.
Laxford Bridge
Scourie
**Eddrachillis Bay**  Kylestrome
Pt. of Stoer  Unapool
Drumbeg  **Assynt**
Stoer  L. Assynt
**Enard B.**  Lochinver
Inverkirkaig
Rubha Coigeach  Achiltibuie  L. Lurgainn
167  Elphin
Reiff  Summer Is.  **Coigach**
Strathkanaird
L. Broom  Ullapool
Greenstone Pt.  Gruinard B.  Mellon Charles
Mellon  Ardessie  Ardcharnich
Poolewe  Charles  An Teallach ▲1062
L. Ewe  Fionn L.  L. na Sealga  Braemore
Melvaig  Aultbea
Longa I.  Gairloch
Port Henderson  179 L. Gairloch  Kerrysdale
Red Point  981 Slioch
Talladale  Kinlochewe  We
Diabaig  L. Maree  11 Sgurr
Rona  Achnasheen
L. Torridon  Liathach ▲1053  Achnashellach
Fasag  Torridon  Strother
Shieldaig  Sound of Raasay  Carron  Strome
Applecross Forest  316  Coulags  Monar Fore
Applecross  Caulags  ▲1052  L. Mo
Toscaig  L. Kishorn  **HIGH** Carn Eige
Raasay  Stromemore  Lochcarron  Ling  ▲1182
Crowlin Is.  L. Carron  A'Chralaig
Sconser  Plockton  Stromeferry  ▲1120
Sligachan  775  Kyle of Lochalsh  Sgurr na Lapaich  L. Mullardoch
Scalpay  Glamaig  Dornie  ▲1150
Glenelg  Breakish  Kyleakin  Five Sisters
Broadford  Kylerhea  Shiel Bridge ▲1068  L. Cluanie
Eilean Iarmain  The Saddle ▲1012  A'Chralaig
Teangue  Arnisdale  Glen Shiel
Armadale  Ladhar Bheinn ▲1019  L. Quoich  L. Loyne
Tarskavaig  Ardvasar  **Knoydart**  Tomdoun  Glen Ga
Pt. of Sleat  Inverie  Glen Ga
Sd. of Sleat  L. Hourn  L. Neevis
Mallaig  ▲1040 Sgurr na Ciche
Morar  Tarbet  L. Arkaig
310  L. Morar  ▲983 Culvain
Arisaig  Glenfinnan  Kinlocheil
Sd. of Arisaig  Lochailort  Corpach
Rhois Bheinn  L. Eil
Shona I.  ▲882  Fort William
Kinlochmoidart  **Moidart**  Loch Shiel  **Ardgour**
L. Moidart  Kinlochleven
**Ardnamurchan**  Acharacle  Corran
Ben Hiant ▲527  L. Sunart  Onich
Mingary  Salen  **Sunart**  Strontian ▲888  L. Leven
Tobermory  Drimnin  L. Linnhe  Ballachulish

West from Greenwich

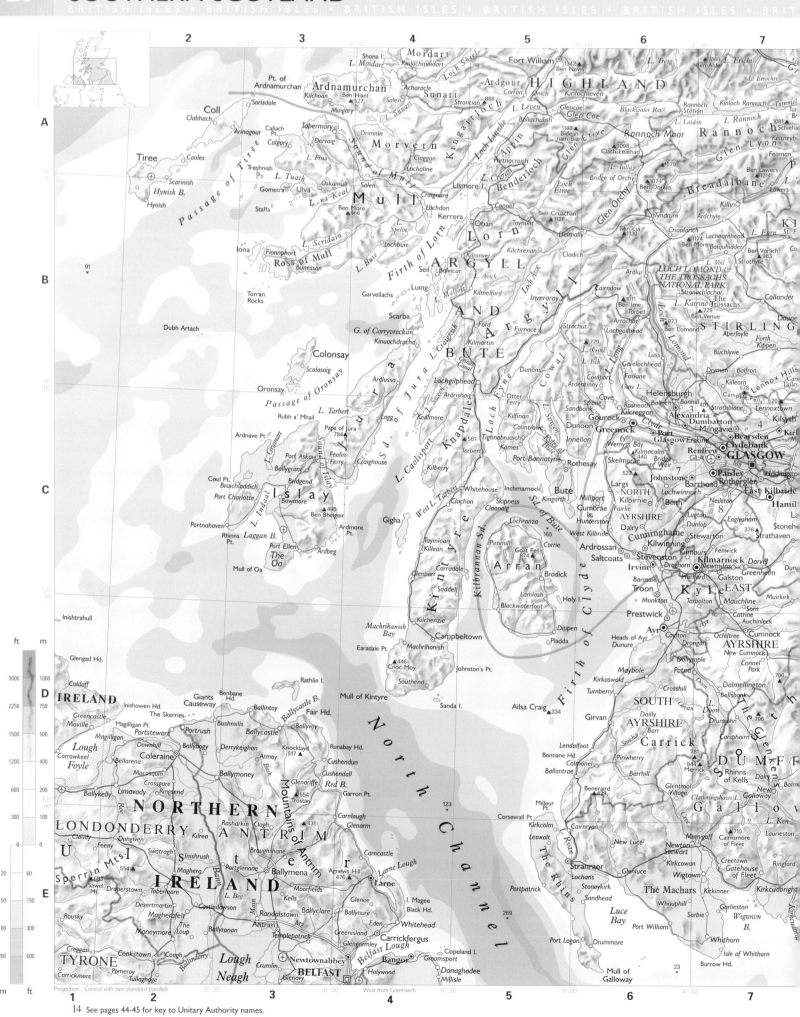

Projection : Conical with two standard parallels

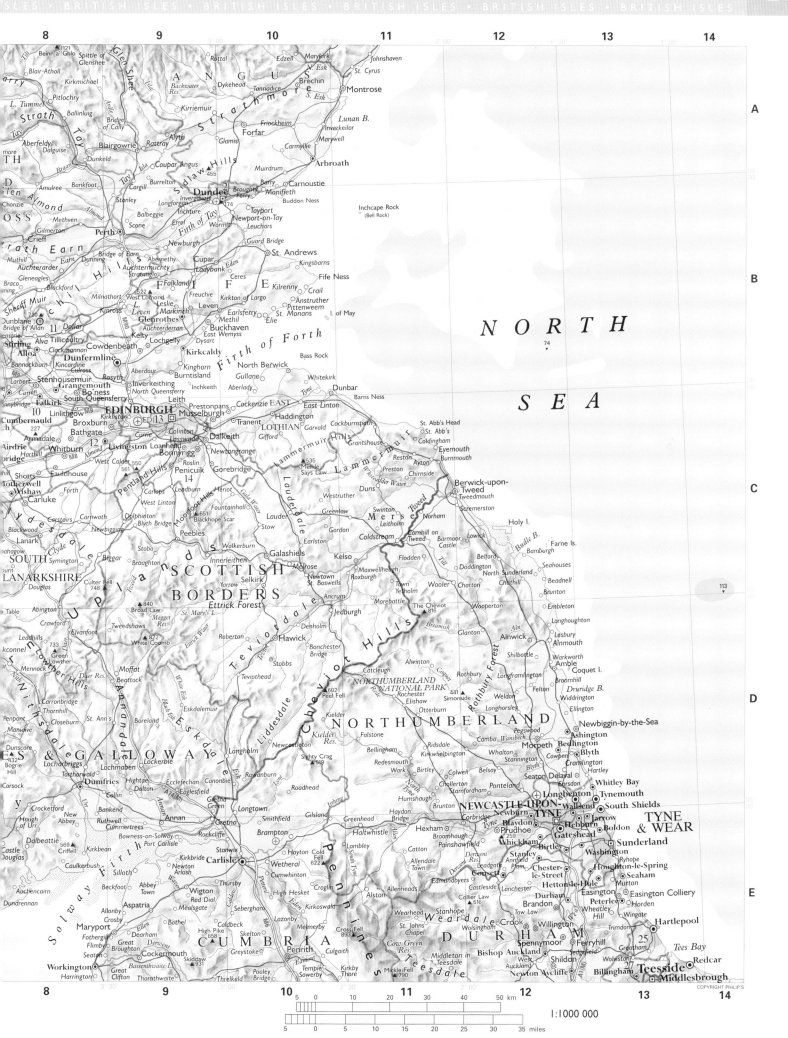

**NORTH**

**SEA**

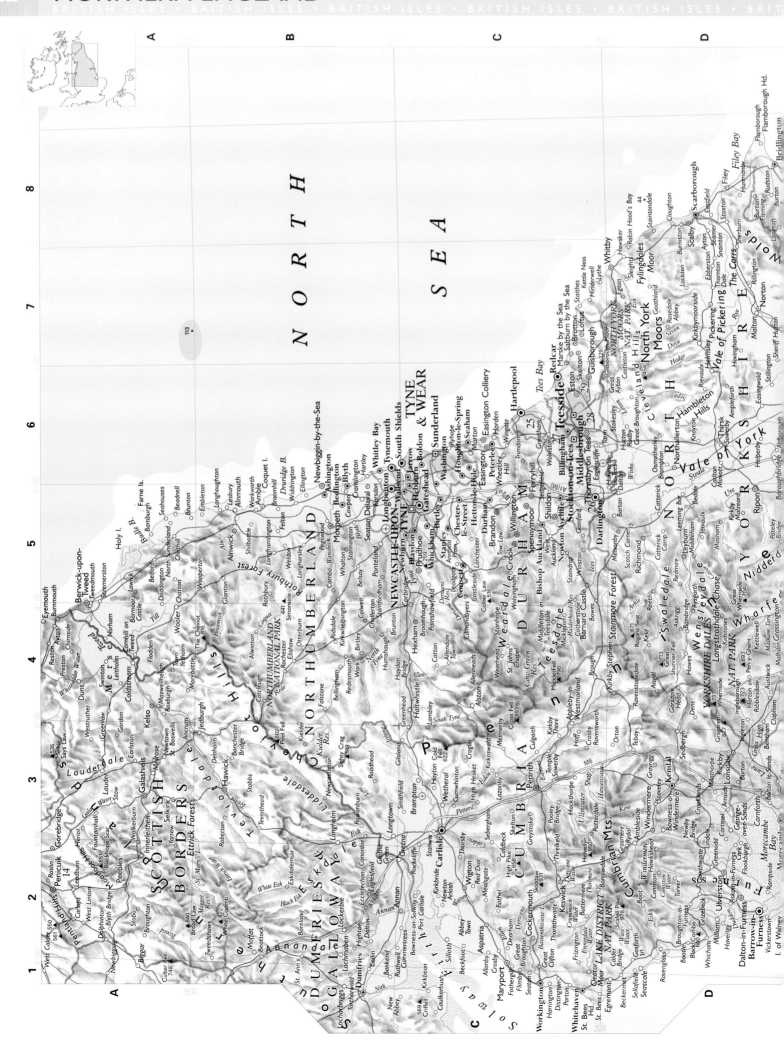

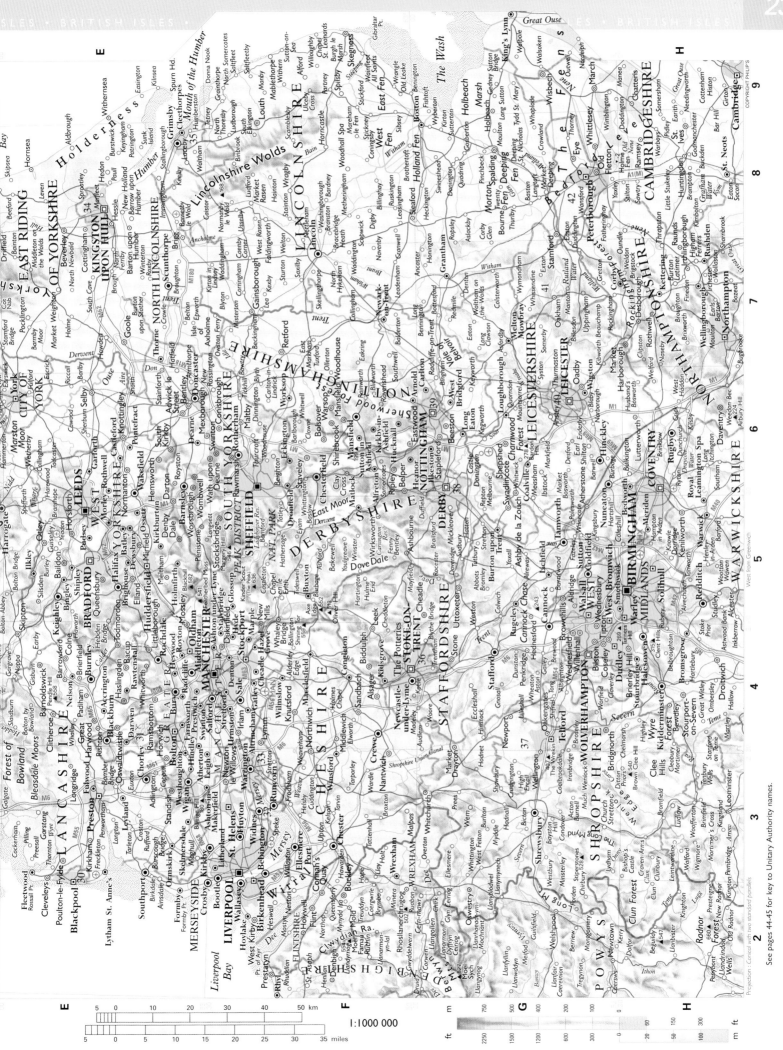

Great Ouse

King's Lynn

The Wash

COPYRIGHT PHILIP'S

9

**E**

Skipsea
Hornsea

Withernsea

Aldbrough
Burstwick
Keyingham
Patrington
Sunk Island

Spurn Hd.

Withernsea

**H** o l d e r n e s s

Leven
Beeford

Skeffling

Cleethorpes

Grimsby

Mouth of the Humber

35

Spurn Hd.

Cot Ness
Donna Nook
North Somercotes
Saltfleet

Mablethorpe
Sutton-on-
Sea

Chapel
St. Leonards

Skegness

Wolferton
Walpole
Walsoken
Outwell

8

B r e c k l a n d

Wisbech

March

CAMBRIDGESHIRE

St. Ives

Cambridge

**H**

See pages 44–45 for key to Unitary Authority names.

West from Greenwich

Projection : Conical with two standard parallels

**E**        5   0    10     20     30     40     50 km      **F**        **G**        **H**

5   0    5     10    15    20    25    30    35 miles

1:1 000 000

# SOUTH AND SOUTH-EAST ENGLAND

Major areas and regions labelled on the map:

POWYS · CARMARTHENSHIRE · SHROPSHIRE · STAFFORDSHIRE · HEREFORDSHIRE · WORCESTERSHIRE · WARWICKSHIRE · WEST MIDLANDS · BIRMINGHAM · WOLVERHAMPTON · COVENTRY · LEICESTER · NOTTINGHAM · DERBY

MONMOUTHSHIRE · GLOUCESTERSHIRE · OXFORDSHIRE · GLAMORGAN · CARDIFF · SWANSEA · Port Talbot · Newport

WILTSHIRE · WEST BERKSHIRE · SOMERSET · DORSET · DEVON · HAMPSHIRE · SOUTHAMPTON · ISLE OF WIGHT

Black Mountains · Brecon Beacons National Park · Mynydd Du (Black Mt.) / Fforest Fawr · Cambrian Mountains · Mynydd Epynt

Cotswold Hills · Mendip Hills · Salisbury Plain · Marlborough Downs · Berkshire Downs · Vale of White Horse · Vale of Pewsey · Cranborne Chase · Blackmoor Vale · North Dorset Downs · South Dorset Downs · Blackdown Hills · Quantock Hills · Brendon Hills · Polden Hills · New Forest

EXMOOR · EXMOOR NATIONAL PARK

Bristol Channel · Bridgwater Bay · Swansea Bay · Lyme Bay · Poole Harbour · Chesil Beach · The Solent · Spithead

Selected towns and cities: Shrewsbury · Telford · Stafford · Cannock · Lichfield · Tamworth · Nuneaton · Rugby · Leamington Spa · Warwick · Redditch · Bromsgrove · Kidderminster · Worcester · Great Malvern · Hereford · Leominster · Ludlow · Ross-on-Wye · Monmouth · Abergavenny · Merthyr Tydfil · Aberdare · Pontypridd · Caerphilly · Cardiff · Newport · Chepstow · Gloucester · Cheltenham · Cirencester · Stroud · Oxford · Witney · Banbury · Swindon · Chippenham · Calne · Marlborough · Devizes · Trowbridge · Bath · Bristol · Kingswood · Keynsham · Weston-super-Mare · Bridgwater · Taunton · Wellington · Tiverton · Exeter · Yeovil · Sherborne · Shaftesbury · Blandford Forum · Dorchester · Weymouth · Poole · Bournemouth · Christchurch · Wimborne Minster · Ringwood · Salisbury · Warminster · Frome · Shepton Mallet · Wells · Glastonbury · Street · Winchester · Eastleigh · Southampton · Romsey · Andover · Newbury

20 See pages 44-45 for key to Unitary Authority names.
Projection : Conical with two standard parallels · West from Greenwich
1  2  3  4  5  6

Scale bar (elevation):
ft / m
2250 / 750
1500 / 500
1200 / 400
600 / 200
300 / 100
0 / 0

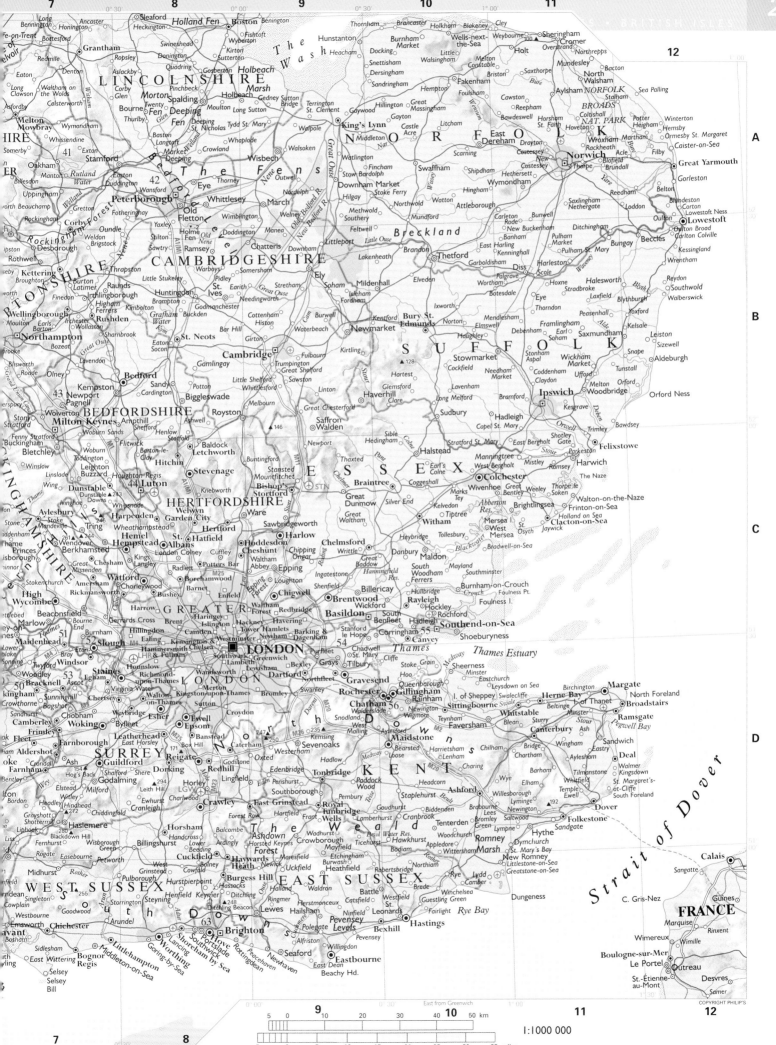

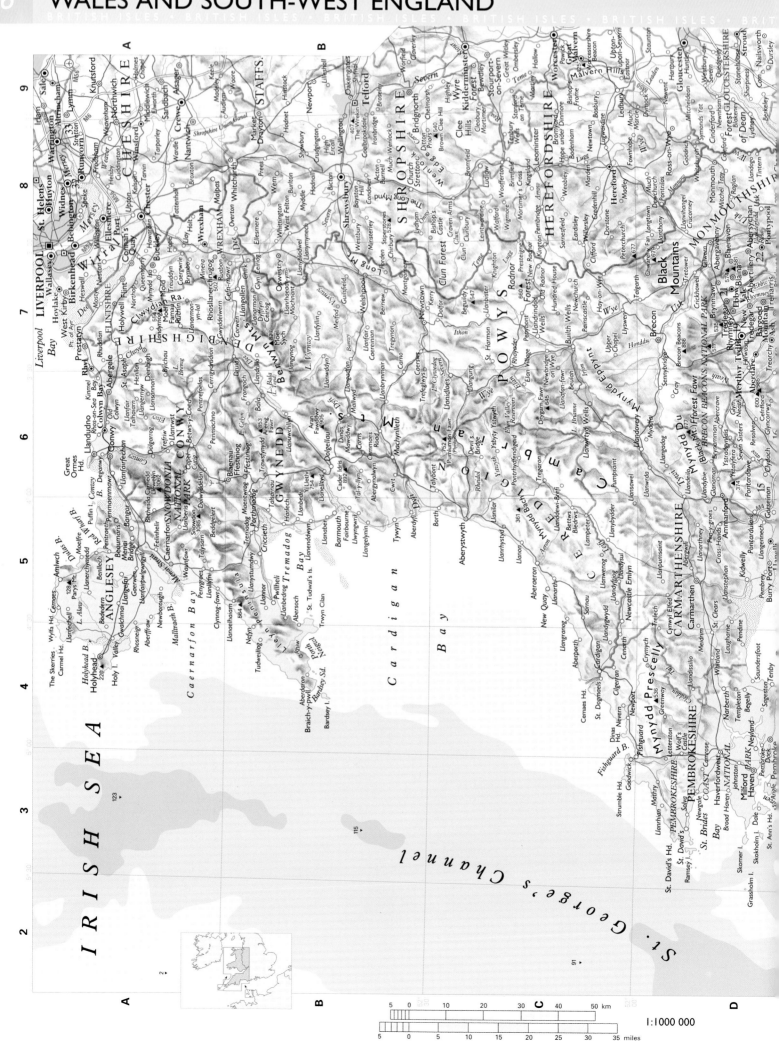

1:1 000 000

**IS. OF SCILLY**
on same scale

Isles of Scilly

**CHANNEL ISLANDS**
on same scale

FRANCE

Guernsey

Jersey

CHANNEL ISLANDS

Bristol Channel

Lundy

SOMERSET

DEVON

CORNWALL

DORSET

Dartmoor National Park

Exmoor National Park

COPYRIGHT PHILIPS

Projection: Conical with two standard parallels

57 See pages 44-45 for key to Unitary Authority names.

West from Greenwich

1:1000 000

5  0    10    20    30    40    50 km

5    0    5    10    15    20    25    30    35 miles

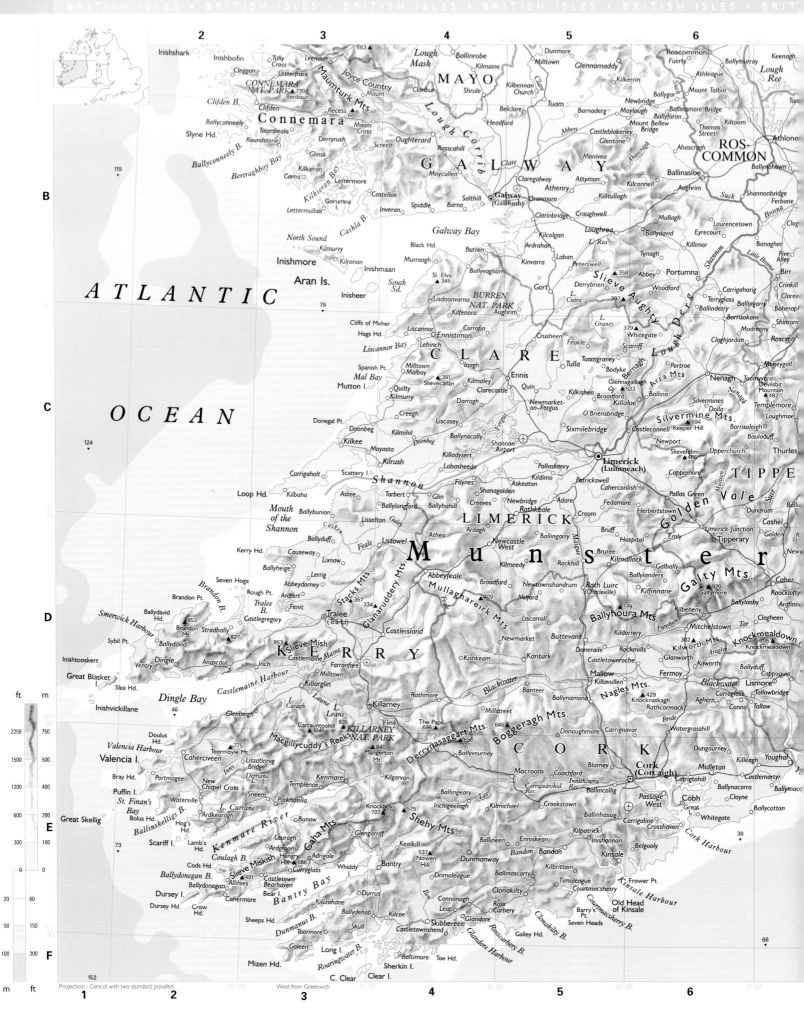

ATLANTIC

OCEAN

MAYO

GALWAY

CONNEMARA

ROS-COMMON

CLARE

LIMERICK

Munster

KERRY

Munster

CORK

TIPPE

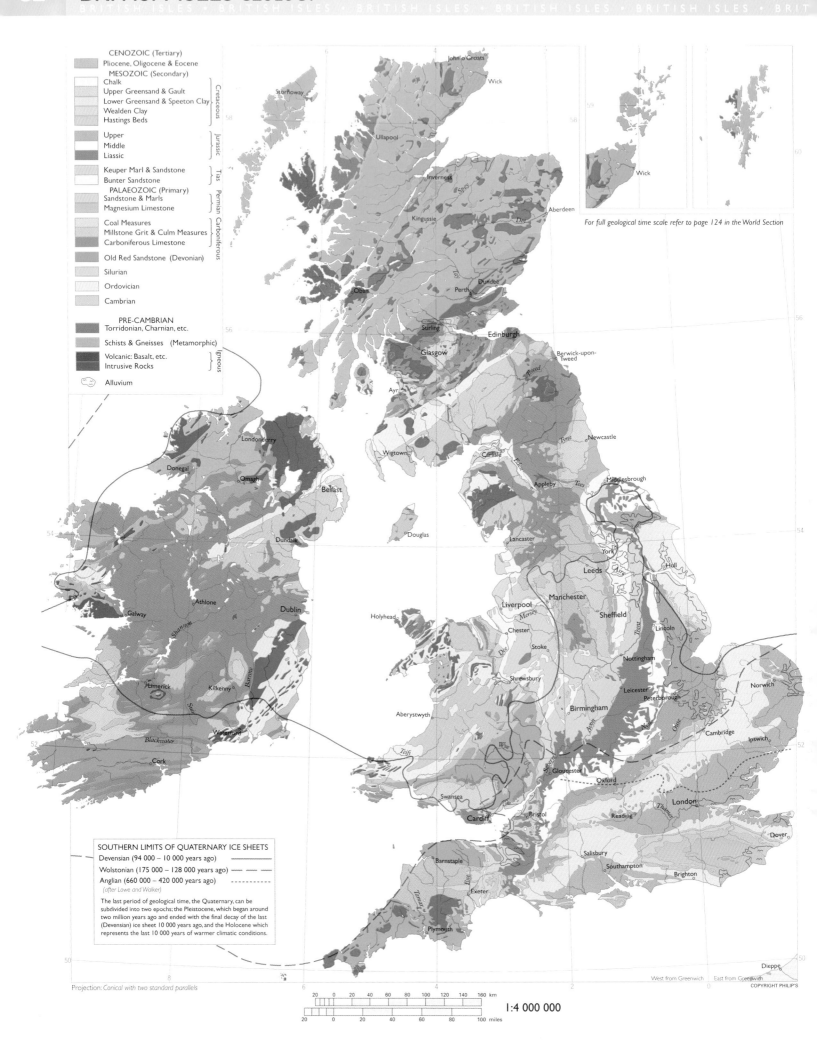

CENOZOIC (Tertiary)
Pliocene, Oligocene & Eocene
MESOZOIC (Secondary)
Chalk
Upper Greensand & Gault
Lower Greensand & Speeton Clay  | Cretaceous
Wealden Clay
Hastings Beds

Upper
Middle  | Jurassic
Liassic

Keuper Marl & Sandstone  | Trias
Bunter Sandstone
PALAEOZOIC (Primary)
Sandstone & Marls  | Permian
Magnesium Limestone

Coal Measures
Millstone Grit & Culm Measures  | Carboniferous
Carboniferous Limestone

Old Red Sandstone (Devonian)

Silurian

Ordovician

Cambrian

PRE-CAMBRIAN
Torridonian, Charnian, etc.

Schists & Gneisses  (Metamorphic)

Volcanic: Basalt, etc.  | Igneous
Intrusive Rocks

Alluvium

For full geological time scale refer to page 124 in the World Section

SOUTHERN LIMITS OF QUATERNARY ICE SHEETS
Devensian (94 000 – 10 000 years ago)  ————
Wolstonian (175 000 – 128 000 years ago)  — — —
Anglian (660 000 – 420 000 years ago)  ··········
(after Lowe and Walker)

The last period of geological time, the Quaternary, can be
subdivided into two epochs; the Pleistocene, which began around
two million years ago and ended with the final decay of the last
(Devensian) ice sheet 10 000 years ago, and the Holocene which
represents the last 10 000 years of warmer climatic conditions.

Projection: Conical with two standard parallels

West from Greenwich   East from Greenwich
COPYRIGHT PHILIP'S

20  0  20  40  60  80  100  120  140  160 km
20  0  20  40  60  80  100 miles
1:4 000 000

Projection: *Conical with two standard parallels*

West from Greenwich   East from Greenwich

1:4 000 000

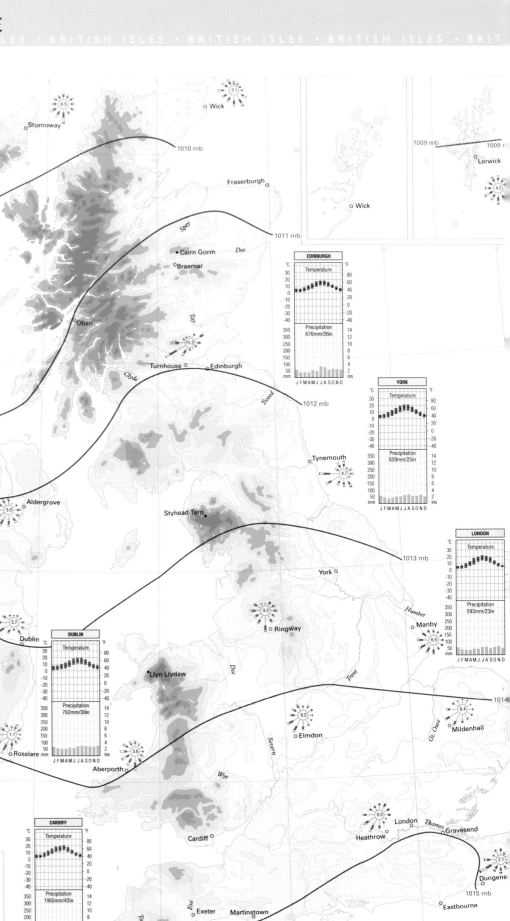

## ANNUAL PRECIPITATION

mm
2,500
2,000
1,500
1,250
1,000
750
625
500

—— Annual isobars
in millibars

## WIND

% calms in a year

Direction the wind
blows from

% frequency of
wind from a direction

Force of wind
(Beaufort scale)

| BEAUFORT FORCE | SPEED (km/h) | CATEGORY |
|---|---|---|
| 1 – 3 | 1 – 20 | Light breeze |
| 4 | 21 – 29 | Moderate breeze |
| 5 – 6 | 30 – 50 | Fresh to strong wind |
| 7 | 51 – 61 | Near gale |
| 8 – 12 | over 62 | Gale, storm or hurricane |

## UK WEATHER EXTREMES

**Air Temperature (1.25 m above the ground)**
Highest recorded: 38.1°C Gravesend, Kent on 10 August 2003
Lowest recorded: −27.2°C Braemar, Grampian on 11 February 1895 and
10 January 1982

**Rainfall**
Maximum recorded in 1 day: 279 mm Martinstown, Dorset on 18 July 1955
Highest monthly rainfall: 1,436 mm Llyn Llydaw, Snowdonia in October 1909
Wettest place: Styhead Tarn, Cumbria average annual rainfall is 4,391 mm

**Sunshine (duration in 1 month)**
Maximum recorded: 389.9 hours Eastbourne, E. Sussex in July 1911
Minimum recorded: 0.0 hours Westminster, Greater London in December 1890

**Winds (highest gusts)**
High level site: 150 knots (278 km/h) Cairn Gorm, Grampian on 20 March 1989
Low level site : 123 knots (229 km/h) Fraserburgh, Aberdeenshire on
13 February 1989

Projection: Conical with two standard parallels

Based partly on information supplied by the Meteorological Office
and on the Climatological Atlas of the British Isles

1 : 4 000 000

COPYRIGHT PHIL

# CLIMATE GRAPHS

Average monthly minimum temperature in degrees Celsius

Average monthly maximum temperature in degrees Celsius

Height of meteorological station above sea level in metres

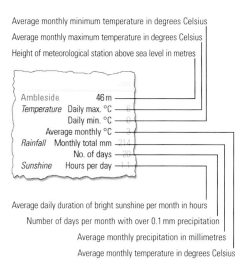

Ambleside — 46 m
*Temperature* Daily max. °C — 6
Daily min. °C — 0
Average monthly °C — 3
*Rainfall* Monthly total mm — 214
No. of days — 20
*Sunshine* Hours per day — 1.1

Average daily duration of bright sunshine per month in hours

Number of days per month with over 0.1 mm precipitation

Average monthly precipitation in millimetres

Average monthly temperature in degrees Celsius

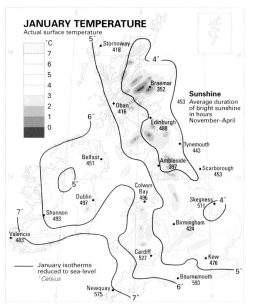

**JANUARY TEMPERATURE**
Actual surface temperature

°C
7
6
5
4
3
2
1
0

Stornoway 418
Braemar 352
Oban 416
Edinburgh 488
Tynemouth 443
Belfast 451
Ambleside 397
Scarborough 453
Colwyn Bay 496
Dublin 497
Skegness 511
Shannon 493
Birmingham 424
Valencia 483
Cardiff 527
Kew 476
Bournemouth 593
Newquay 575

**Sunshine**
453 Average duration of bright sunshine in hours November–April

January isotherms reduced to sea-level
° *Celsius*

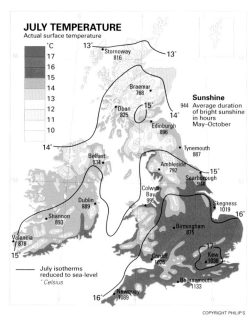

**JULY TEMPERATURE**
Actual surface temperature

°C
17
16
15
14
13
12
11
10

Stornoway 816
Braemar 768
Oban 825
Edinburgh 896
Tynemouth 887
Belfast 834
Ambleside 792
Scarborough 944
Colwyn Bay 995
Dublin 889
Skegness 1019
Shannon 893
Birmingham 875
Valencia 878
Cardiff 1026
Kew 1038
Bournemouth 1133
Newquay 1089

**Sunshine**
944 Average duration of bright sunshine in hours May–October

July isotherms reduced to sea-level
° *Celsius*

COPYRIGHT PHILIP'S

|  |  | Jan | Feb | Mar | Apr | May | June | July | Aug | Sept | Oct | Nov | Dec | Year |
|---|---|---|---|---|---|---|---|---|---|---|---|---|---|---|
| **Ambleside** | **46 m** |  |  |  |  |  |  |  |  |  |  |  |  |  |
| *Temperature* | Daily max. °C | 6 | 7 | 9 | 12 | 16 | 19 | 20 | 19 | 17 | 13 | 9 | 7 | 13 |
|  | Daily min. °C | 0 | 0 | 2 | 4 | 6 | 9 | 11 | 11 | 9 | 6 | 3 | 1 | 5 |
|  | Average monthly °C | 3 | 4 | 6 | 8 | 11 | 14 | 15 | 15 | 13 | 10 | 6 | 4 | 9 |
| *Rainfall* | Monthly total mm | 214 | 146 | 112 | 101 | 90 | 111 | 134 | 139 | 184 | 196 | 209 | 215 | 1,851 |
|  | No. of days | 20 | 17 | 15 | 15 | 14 | 15 | 18 | 17 | 18 | 19 | 19 | 21 | 208 |
| *Sunshine* | Hours per day | 1.1 | 2 | 3.2 | 4.5 | 6 | 5.7 | 4.5 | 4.2 | 3.3 | 2.2 | 1.4 | 1 | 3.3 |
| **Belfast** | **4 m** |  |  |  |  |  |  |  |  |  |  |  |  |  |
| *Temperature* | Daily max. °C | 6 | 7 | 9 | 12 | 15 | 18 | 18 | 18 | 16 | 13 | 9 | 7 | 12 |
|  | Daily min. °C | 2 | 2 | 3 | 4 | 6 | 9 | 11 | 11 | 9 | 7 | 4 | 3 | 6 |
|  | Average monthly °C | 4 | 4 | 6 | 8 | 11 | 13 | 15 | 15 | 13 | 10 | 7 | 5 | 9 |
| *Rainfall* | Monthly total mm | 80 | 52 | 50 | 48 | 52 | 68 | 94 | 77 | 80 | 83 | 72 | 90 | 845 |
|  | No. of days | 20 | 17 | 16 | 16 | 15 | 16 | 19 | 17 | 18 | 19 | 19 | 21 | 213 |
| *Sunshine* | Hours per day | 1.5 | 2.3 | 3.4 | 5 | 6.3 | 6 | 4.4 | 4.4 | 3.6 | 2.6 | 1.8 | 1.1 | 3.5 |
| **Birkenhead** | **60 m** |  |  |  |  |  |  |  |  |  |  |  |  |  |
| *Temperature* | Daily max. °C | 6 | 6 | 9 | 11 | 15 | 17 | 19 | 19 | 16 | 13 | 9 | 7 | 12 |
|  | Daily min. °C | 2 | 2 | 3 | 5 | 8 | 11 | 13 | 13 | 11 | 8 | 5 | 3 | 7 |
|  | Average monthly °C | 4 | 4 | 6 | 8 | 11 | 14 | 16 | 16 | 14 | 10 | 7 | 5 | 10 |
| *Rainfall* | Monthly total mm | 64 | 46 | 40 | 41 | 55 | 55 | 67 | 80 | 66 | 71 | 76 | 65 | 726 |
|  | No. of days | 18 | 13 | 13 | 13 | 13 | 13 | 15 | 15 | 15 | 14 | 17 | 19 | 181 |
| *Sunshine* | Hours per day | 1.6 | 2.4 | 3.5 | 5.3 | 6.3 | 6.7 | 5.7 | 5.4 | 4.2 | 2.9 | 1.8 | 1.3 | 3.9 |
| **Birmingham** | **163 m** |  |  |  |  |  |  |  |  |  |  |  |  |  |
| *Temperature* | Daily max. °C | 5 | 6 | 9 | 12 | 16 | 19 | 20 | 20 | 17 | 13 | 9 | 6 | 13 |
|  | Daily min. °C | 2 | 2 | 3 | 5 | 7 | 10 | 12 | 12 | 10 | 7 | 5 | 3 | 7 |
|  | Average monthly °C | 3 | 4 | 6 | 8 | 11 | 15 | 16 | 16 | 14 | 10 | 7 | 5 | 10 |
| *Rainfall* | Monthly total mm | 74 | 54 | 50 | 53 | 64 | 50 | 69 | 69 | 61 | 69 | 84 | 67 | 764 |
|  | No. of days | 17 | 15 | 13 | 13 | 14 | 13 | 15 | 14 | 14 | 14 | 15 | 17 | 178 |
| *Sunshine* | Hours per day | 1.4 | 2.1 | 3.2 | 4.6 | 5.4 | 6 | 5.4 | 5.1 | 3.9 | 2.8 | 1.6 | 1.2 | 3.6 |
| **Cambridge** | **12 m** |  |  |  |  |  |  |  |  |  |  |  |  |  |
| *Temperature* | Daily max. °C | 6 | 7 | 11 | 14 | 17 | 21 | 22 | 22 | 19 | 15 | 10 | 7 | 14 |
|  | Daily min. °C | 1 | 1 | 2 | 4 | 7 | 10 | 12 | 12 | 10 | 6 | 4 | 2 | 6 |
|  | Average monthly °C | 3 | 4 | 6 | 9 | 12 | 15 | 17 | 17 | 14 | 10 | 7 | 5 | 10 |
| *Rainfall* | Monthly total mm | 49 | 35 | 36 | 37 | 45 | 45 | 58 | 55 | 51 | 51 | 54 | 41 | 558 |
|  | No. of days | 15 | 13 | 10 | 11 | 11 | 11 | 12 | 11 | 11 | 13 | 14 | 14 | 147 |
| *Sunshine* | Hours per day | 1.7 | 2.5 | 3.8 | 5.1 | 6.2 | 6.7 | 6 | 5.7 | 4.6 | 3.4 | 1.9 | 1.4 | 4.1 |
| **Craibstone** | **91 m** |  |  |  |  |  |  |  |  |  |  |  |  |  |
| *Temperature* | Daily max. °C | 5 | 6 | 8 | 10 | 13 | 16 | 18 | 17 | 15 | 12 | 8 | 6 | 11 |
|  | Daily min. °C | 0 | 0 | 2 | 3 | 5 | 8 | 10 | 10 | 8 | 6 | 3 | 1 | 5 |
|  | Average monthly °C | 3 | 3 | 5 | 7 | 9 | 12 | 14 | 13 | 12 | 9 | 6 | 4 | 8 |
| *Rainfall* | Monthly total mm | 78 | 55 | 53 | 51 | 63 | 54 | 95 | 75 | 67 | 92 | 93 | 80 | 856 |
|  | No. of days | 19 | 16 | 15 | 15 | 14 | 14 | 18 | 15 | 16 | 18 | 19 | 18 | 197 |
| *Sunshine* | Hours per day | 1.8 | 2.9 | 3.5 | 4.9 | 5.9 | 6.1 | 5.1 | 4.8 | 4.3 | 3..1 | 2 | 1.5 | 3.8 |
| **Durham** | **102 m** |  |  |  |  |  |  |  |  |  |  |  |  |  |
| *Temperature* | Daily max. °C | 6 | 6 | 9 | 12 | 15 | 18 | 20 | 19 | 17 | 13 | 9 | 7 | 13 |
|  | Daily min. °C | 0 | 0 | 1 | 3 | 6 | 9 | 11 | 10 | 9 | 6 | 3 | 2 | 5 |
|  | Average monthly °C | 3 | 3 | 5 | 7 | 10 | 13 | 15 | 15 | 13 | 9 | 6 | 4 | 9 |
| *Rainfall* | Monthly total mm | 59 | 51 | 38 | 38 | 51 | 49 | 61 | 67 | 60 | 63 | 66 | 55 | 658 |
|  | No. of days | 17 | 15 | 14 | 13 | 14 | 13 | 14 | 14 | 14 | 16 | 17 | 17 | 179 |
| *Sunshine* | Hours per day | 1.7 | 2.5 | 3.3 | 4.6 | 5.4 | 6 | 5.1 | 4.8 | 4.1 | 3 | 1.9 | 1.4 | 3.6 |

|  |  | Jan | Feb | Mar | Apr | May | June | July | Aug | Sept | Oct | Nov | Dec | Year |
|---|---|---|---|---|---|---|---|---|---|---|---|---|---|---|
| **Lerwick** | **82 m** |  |  |  |  |  |  |  |  |  |  |  |  |  |
| *Temperature* | Daily max. °C | 5 | 5 | 6 | 8 | 11 | 13 | 14 | 14 | 13 | 10 | 8 | 6 | 9 |
|  | Daily min. °C | 1 | 1 | 2 | 3 | 5 | 7 | 10 | 10 | 8 | 6 | 4 | 3 | 5 |
|  | Average monthly °C | 3 | 3 | 4 | 5 | 8 | 10 | 12 | 12 | 11 | 8 | 6 | 4 | 7 |
| *Rainfall* | Monthly total mm | 109 | 87 | 69 | 68 | 52 | 55 | 72 | 71 | 87 | 104 | 111 | 118 | 1,003 |
|  | No. of days | 25 | 22 | 20 | 21 | 15 | 15 | 17 | 17 | 19 | 23 | 24 | 25 | 243 |
| *Sunshine* | Hours per day | 0.8 | 1.8 | 2.9 | 4.4 | 5.3 | 5.3 | 4 | 3.8 | 3.5 | 2.2 | 2.2 | 0.5 | 3 |
| **Plymouth** | **27 m** |  |  |  |  |  |  |  |  |  |  |  |  |  |
| *Temperature* | Daily max. °C | 8 | 8 | 10 | 12 | 15 | 18 | 19 | 19 | 18 | 15 | 11 | 9 | 14 |
|  | Daily min. °C | 4 | 4 | 5 | 6 | 8 | 11 | 13 | 13 | 12 | 9 | 7 | 5 | 8 |
|  | Average monthly °C | 6 | 6 | 7 | 9 | 12 | 15 | 16 | 16 | 15 | 12 | 9 | 7 | 11 |
| *Rainfall* | Monthly total mm | 99 | 74 | 69 | 53 | 63 | 53 | 70 | 77 | 78 | 91 | 113 | 110 | 950 |
|  | No. of days | 19 | 15 | 14 | 12 | 12 | 12 | 14 | 14 | 15 | 16 | 17 | 18 | 178 |
| *Sunshine* | Hours per day | 1.9 | 2.9 | 4.3 | 6.1 | 7.1 | 7.4 | 6.4 | 6.4 | 5.1 | 3.7 | 2.2 | 1.7 | 4.6 |
| **Renfrew** | **6 m** |  |  |  |  |  |  |  |  |  |  |  |  |  |
| *Temperature* | Daily max. °C | 5 | 7 | 9 | 12 | 15 | 18 | 19 | 19 | 16 | 13 | 9 | 7 | 12 |
|  | Daily min. °C | 1 | 1 | 2 | 4 | 6 | 9 | 11 | 11 | 9 | 6 | 4 | 2 | 6 |
|  | Average monthly °C | 3 | 4 | 6 | 8 | 11 | 14 | 15 | 15 | 13 | 9 | 7 | 4 | 9 |
| *Rainfall* | Monthly total mm | 111 | 85 | 69 | 67 | 63 | 70 | 97 | 93 | 102 | 119 | 106 | 127 | 1,109 |
|  | No. of days | 19 | 16 | 15 | 14 | 15 | 15 | 17 | 17 | 17 | 18 | 18 | 20 | 201 |
| *Sunshine* | Hours per day | 1.1 | 2.1 | 2.9 | 4.7 | 6 | 6.1 | 5.1 | 4.4 | 3.7 | 2.3 | 1.4 | 0.8 | 3.4 |
| **St Mary's** | **50 m** |  |  |  |  |  |  |  |  |  |  |  |  |  |
| *Temperature* | Daily max. °C | 9 | 9 | 11 | 12 | 14 | 17 | 19 | 19 | 18 | 15 | 12 | 10 | 14 |
|  | Daily min. °C | 6 | 6 | 7 | 7 | 9 | 12 | 13 | 14 | 13 | 11 | 9 | 7 | 9 |
|  | Average monthly °C | 8 | 7 | 9 | 10 | 12 | 14 | 16 | 16 | 15 | 13 | 10 | 9 | 12 |
| *Rainfall* | Monthly total mm | 91 | 71 | 69 | 46 | 56 | 49 | 61 | 64 | 67 | 80 | 96 | 94 | 844 |
|  | No. of days | 22 | 17 | 16 | 13 | 14 | 11 | 16 | 15 | 16 | 17 | 19 | 21 | 200 |
| *Sunshine* | Hours per day | 2 | 2.9 | 4.2 | 6.4 | 7.6 | 7.6 | 6.7 | 6.7 | 5.2 | 3.9 | 2.5 | 1.8 | 4.8 |
| **Southampton** | **20 m** |  |  |  |  |  |  |  |  |  |  |  |  |  |
| *Temperature* | Daily max. °C | 7 | 8 | 11 | 14 | 17 | 20 | 22 | 22 | 19 | 15 | 10 | 8 | 15 |
|  | Daily min. °C | 2 | 2 | 3 | 5 | 8 | 11 | 13 | 13 | 11 | 7 | 5 | 3 | 7 |
|  | Average monthly °C | 5 | 5 | 7 | 10 | 13 | 16 | 17 | 17 | 15 | 11 | 8 | 6 | 11 |
| *Rainfall* | Monthly total mm | 83 | 56 | 52 | 45 | 56 | 49 | 60 | 69 | 70 | 86 | 94 | 84 | 804 |
|  | No. of days | 17 | 13 | 13 | 12 | 12 | 12 | 13 | 14 | 14 | 16 | 17 | 166 |  |
| *Sunshine* | Hours per day | 1.8 | 2.6 | 4 | 5.7 | 6.7 | 7.2 | 6.5 | 6.4 | 4.9 | 3.6 | 2.2 | 1.6 | 4.5 |
| **Tiree** | **9 m** |  |  |  |  |  |  |  |  |  |  |  |  |  |
| *Temperature* | Daily Max. °C | 7 | 7 | 9 | 10 | 13 | 15 | 16 | 16 | 15 | 12 | 10 | 8 | 12 |
|  | Daily Min. °C | 4 | 3 | 4 | 5 | 7 | 10 | 11 | 11 | 10 | 8 | 6 | 5 | 7 |
|  | Average Monthly °C | 5 | 5 | 6 | 8 | 10 | 12 | 14 | 14 | 13 | 10 | 8 | 6 | 9 |
| *Rainfall* | Monthly Total mm | 117 | 77 | 67 | 64 | 55 | 70 | 91 | 90 | 118 | 129 | 122 | 128 | 1,128 |
|  | No. of Days | 23 | 19 | 17 | 17 | 15 | 16 | 20 | 18 | 20 | 23 | 22 | 24 | 234 |
| *Sunshine* | Hours per Day | 1.3 | 2.6 | 3.7 | 5.7 | 7.5 | 6.8 | 5.2 | 5.3 | 4.2 | 2.6 | 1.6 | 0.9 | 4 |
| **Valencia** | **9 m** |  |  |  |  |  |  |  |  |  |  |  |  |  |
| *Temperature* | Daily max. °C | 9 | 9 | 11 | 13 | 15 | 17 | 18 | 18 | 17 | 14 | 12 | 10 | 14 |
|  | Daily min. °C | 5 | 4 | 5 | 6 | 8 | 11 | 12 | 13 | 11 | 9 | 7 | 6 | 8 |
|  | Average monthly °C | 7 | 7 | 8 | 9 | 11 | 14 | 15 | 15 | 14 | 12 | 9 | 8 | 11 |
| *Rainfall* | Monthly total mm | 165 | 107 | 103 | 75 | 86 | 81 | 107 | 95 | 122 | 140 | 151 | 168 | 1,400 |
|  | No. of days | 20 | 15 | 14 | 13 | 13 | 13 | 15 | 15 | 16 | 17 | 18 | 21 | 190 |
| *Sunshine* | Hours per day | 1.6 | 2.5 | 3.5 | 5.2 | 6.5 | 5.9 | 4.7 | 4.9 | 3.8 | 2.8 | 2 | 1.3 | 3.7 |

## WATER SUPPLY

Regions of reliably high rainfall (more than 1,250 mm in at least 70% of the years)

③ Major reservoirs (capacity over 20 million cubic metres, see list opposite for details)

→ Existing inter-regional transfers of water (by pipeline and river)

→ Proposed inter-regional transfers of water (by pipeline and river)

□ Proposed estuary storage site

▽ Proposed groundwater storage site

Principal sources of groundwater (porous and jointed aquifers)

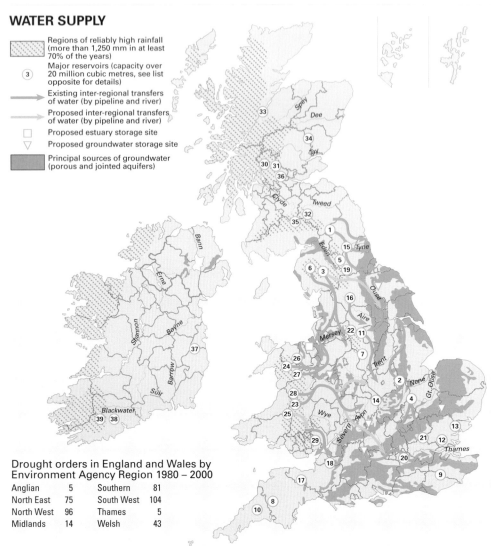

### Drought orders in England and Wales by Environment Agency Region 1980 – 2000

| | | | |
|---|---|---|---|
| Anglian | 5 | Southern | 81 |
| North East | 75 | South West | 104 |
| North West | 96 | Thames | 5 |
| Midlands | 14 | Welsh | 43 |

## MAJOR RESERVOIRS (with capacity in million n

### England
| | | |
|---|---|---|
| 1 | Kielder Res. | 198 |
| 2 | Rutland Water | 123 |
| 3 | Haweswater | 85 |
| 4 | Grafham Water | 59 |
| 5 | Cow Green Res. | 41 |
| 6 | Thirlmere | 41 |
| 7 | Carsington Res. | 36 |
| 8 | Roadford Res. | 35 |
| 9 | Bewl Water Res. | 31 |
| 10 | Colliford Lake | 29 |
| 11 | Ladybower Res. | 28 |
| 12 | Hanningfield Res. | 27 |
| 13 | Abberton Res. | 25 |
| 14 | Draycote Water | 23 |
| 15 | Derwent Res. | 22 |
| 16 | Grimwith Res. | 22 |
| 17 | Wimbleball Lake | 21 |
| 18 | Chew Valley Lake | 20 |
| 19 | Balderhead Res. | 20 |
| 20 | Thames Valley (linked reservoirs) | |
| 21 | Lea Valley (linked reservoirs) | |
| 22 | Longendale (linked reservoirs) | |

### Wales
| | | |
|---|---|---|
| 23 | Elan Valley | 99 |
| 24 | Llyn Celyn | 74 |
| 25 | Llyn Brianne | 62 |
| 26 | Llyn Brenig | 60 |
| 27 | Llyn Vyrnwy | 60 |
| 28 | Llyn Clywedog | 48 |
| 29 | Llandegfedd Res. | 22 |

### Scotland
| | | |
|---|---|---|
| 30 | Loch Lomond | 86 |
| 31 | Loch Katrine | 64 |
| 32 | Megget Res. | 64 |
| 33 | Loch Ness | 26 |
| 34 | Blackwater Res. | 25 |
| 35 | Daer Res. | 23 |
| 36 | Carron Valley Res. | 21 |

### Ireland
| | | |
|---|---|---|
| 37 | Poulaphouca Res. | 168 |
| 38 | Inishcarra Res. | 57 |
| 39 | Carrigadrohid Res. | 33 |

## WATER SUPPLY IN THE UK

The pie graph represents the 18,002 million litres a day that were supplied by the public water authority and services companies in the UK in 1999.

Total water abstraction in England and Wales in 1999 was approximately 37,000 million litres a day.

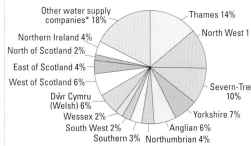

Other water supply companies* 18%
Northern Ireland 4%
North of Scotland 2%
East of Scotland 4%
West of Scotland 6%
Dŵr Cymru (Welsh) 6%
Wessex 2%
South West 2%
Southern 3%
Northumbrian 4%
Anglian 6%
Yorkshire 7%
Severn-Tre 10%
North West 1
Thames 14%

*This is a group of 17 privately-owned companies who are not connected with the other water authorities

## WATER ABSTRACTIONS

THAMES Environment Agency Region

1883 (16%) Water supply* in megalitres per day (with percentage of total abstraction from groundwater in brackets)

*Piped mains water, excluding water abstracted for agricultural and industrial use

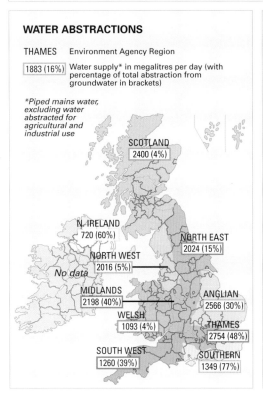

SCOTLAND 2400 (4%)

N. IRELAND 720 (60%)

NORTH EAST 2024 (15%)

NORTH WEST 2016 (5%)

No data

MIDLANDS 2198 (40%)

ANGLIAN 2566 (30%)

WELSH 1093 (4%)

THAMES 2754 (48%)

SOUTH WEST 1260 (39%)

SOUTHERN 1349 (77%)

## WATER QUALITY

The percentage of all rivers and canals of very good quality within each Environment Agency Region 2000

Under 15%
15% – 30%
30% – 60%
Over 60%

The percentage of bathing beaches complying with EC standards in 2001

100%
90% – 99%
80% – 89%

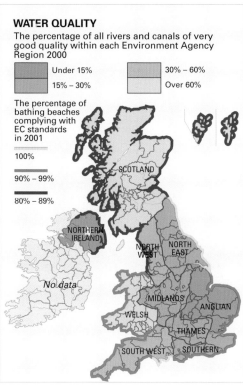

SCOTLAND

NORTHERN IRELAND

No data

NORTH WEST

NORTH EAST

MIDLANDS

ANGLIAN

WELSH

THAMES

SOUTH WEST

SOUTHERN

## FLOOD RISK IN ENGLAND AND WALES

Areas at greatest risk from flooding (as designated by the Environment Agency in 2002)

Settlements with over 100 properties flooded in 2001

Ponteland
Skinningrove
Malton and Norton
Stockbridge
York
Barlby
Gowdall
Catcliffe
Mold
Ruthin
Halton
Shrewsbury
Bewdley
Newport
Waltham Abbey
Weking
Wanstead
Portsmouth
Uckfield
Lewes

## EU AIR QUALITY Emissions in thousand tonnes

| | Sulphur dioxide | | | Nitrogen oxides | | |
|---|---|---|---|---|---|---|
| | 1975 | 1990 | 2000 | 1975 | 1990 | 2000 |
| Austria | – | 90 | 41 | – | 221 | 184 |
| Belgium/Lux. | – | 105 | 162 | – | 172 | 315 |
| Denmark | 418 | 183 | 27 | 182 | 270 | 206 |
| Finland | – | 260 | 76 | – | 290 | 236 |
| France | 3,329 | 1,200 | 715 | 1,608 | 1,487 | 1,508 |
| Germany | 3,325 | 5,633 | 795 | 2,532 | 3,033 | 1,600 |
| Greece | – | – | 483 | – | 338 | 321 |
| Ireland | 186 | 187 | 131 | 60 | 128 | 123 |
| Italy | 3,250 | 1,682 | 758 | 1,499 | 2,041 | 1,372 |
| Netherlands | 386 | 204 | 91 | 447 | 575 | 421 |
| Portugal | 178 | 286 | 339 | 104 | 216 | 394 |
| Spain | – | 2,205 | 1,495 | – | 1,247 | 1,405 |
| Sweden | – | 169 | 58 | – | 411 | 247 |
| United Kingdom | 5,310 | 3,754 | 1,166 | 2,365 | 2,731 | 1,520 |

## FORESTRY

The percentage of the total area covered by woodland and forest

- Over 20%
- 15% – 20%
- 10% – 15%
- 5% – 10%
- Under 5%
- △ Over 50% coniferous
- ◇ Over 50% broadleaves

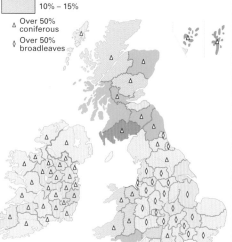

...tatistics are taken from ...e latest inventory for ...ch county

## NATURAL VEGETATION

The plant cover associated with a particular environment if it is unaffected by human activity

- Oak
- Beech and Oak
- Ash and Oak
- Birch and Oakwood
- Scots Pine
- Heath, moorland, water meadows, fen, bog and marsh

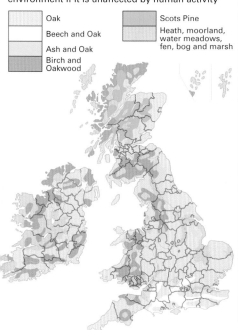

## ACID RAIN

Average acidity of precipitation in the UK (pH scale)

- 4.29 and under (most acidic)
- 4.30 – 4.39
- 4.40 – 4.49
- 4.50 – 4.59
- 4.60 – 4.69
- 4.70 – 4.79
- 4.80 and over (least acidic)

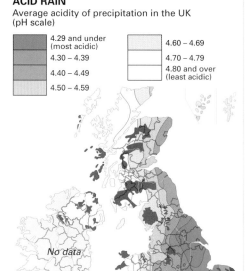

No data

**ESAs**
Environmentally Sensitive Areas in the UK

## GROUND LEVEL OZONE

The number of days each year with 8 hour periods with ozone levels exceeding 50 parts per billion

- More than 50
- 40 – 50
- 30 – 40
- 20 – 30
- Less than 20

**Greenhouse Gas Emissions**
- Carbon Dioxide
- Methane
- Nitrous Oxide

131 Total emissions in million tonnes of Carbon Equivalent

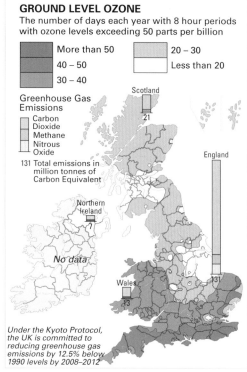

Scotland 21
Northern Ireland 7
England 131
Wales 43

No data

*Under the Kyoto Protocol, the UK is committed to reducing greenhouse gas emissions by 12.5% below 1990 levels by 2008–2012*

## CONSERVATION

- National Parks
- Areas of Outstanding Natural Beauty
- National Scenic Areas
- Forest Parks, Regional Parks in Scotland and Special Protected Areas
- Green Belts (and the urban areas they surround)
- Heritage Coast (England and Wales)/Coastal Conservation Zones (Scotland)

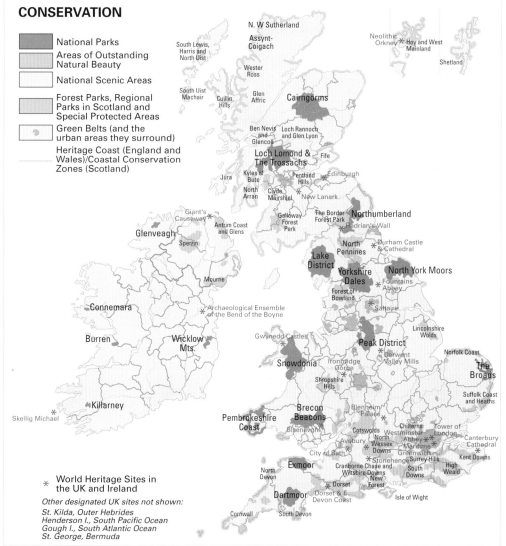

* World Heritage Sites in the UK and Ireland

*Other designated UK sites not shown:*
*St. Kilda, Outer Hebrides*
*Henderson I., South Pacific Ocean*
*Gough I., South Atlantic Ocean*
*St. George, Bermuda*

## TYPES OF FARM

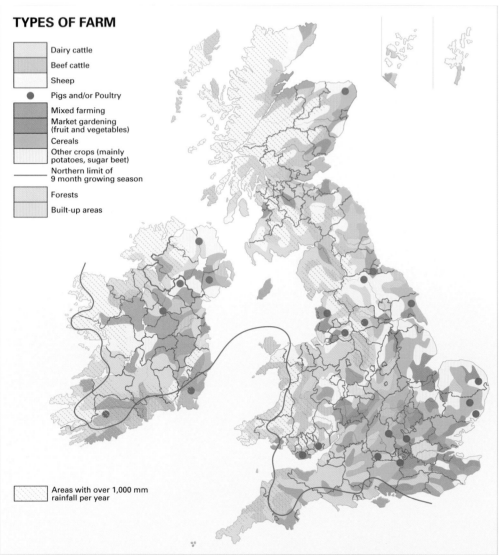

Dairy cattle
Beef cattle
Sheep
● Pigs and/or Poultry
Mixed farming
Market gardening (fruit and vegetables)
Cereals
Other crops (mainly potatoes, sugar beet)
Northern limit of 9 month growing season
Forests
Built-up areas

Areas with over 1,000 mm rainfall per year

## CEREAL FARMING

The percentage of the total farmland used for growing cereals in 2000 (Ireland 1999)

Over 40%
30 – 40%
20 – 30%
10 – 20%
0 – 10%
No data

*Cereal Production (2000)*
*UK 24 million tonnes*
*Ireland 2 million tonnes*

## AGRICULTURAL LAND USE IN THE UK

Other agricultural land 18.0%
Wheat 8.8%
Barley 6.7%
Oats 0.6%
Potatoes 0.9%
Sugar beet 1.0
Rapeseed 2.2%
Horticultural 1.8%
Rough grazing 23.9%
Pasture 36.6%

Total agricultural land area (2001) 18.5 million hectares

## DAIRY FARMING

The number of dairy cows per 100 hectares of farmland in 2000 (Ireland 1999)

Over 40
30 – 40
20 – 30
10 – 20
0 – 10
No data

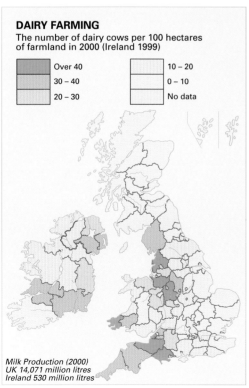

*Milk Production (2000)*
*UK 14,071 million litres*
*Ireland 530 million litres*

## LIVESTOCK FARMING

The number of cattle, sheep and pigs per 100 hectares of farmland in 2000 (Ireland 1999)

Over 400
300 – 400
200 – 300
100 – 200
0 – 100
No data

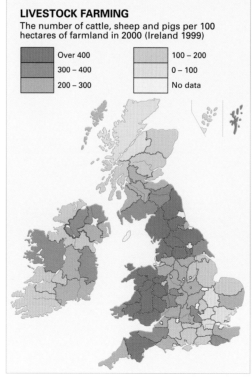

## FOOT-AND-MOUTH DISEASE

The number of confirmed cases of foot-and-mouth disease in 2001

Over 200
100 – 200
50 – 100
25 – 50
0 – 25
Unaffected areas

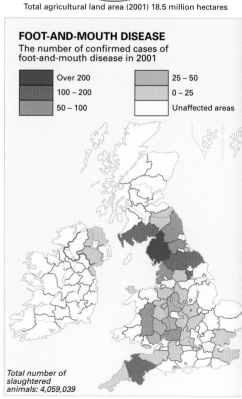

*Total number of slaughtered animals: 4,059,039*

## NUMBER AND SIZE OF AGRICULTURAL HOLDINGS IN THE UK

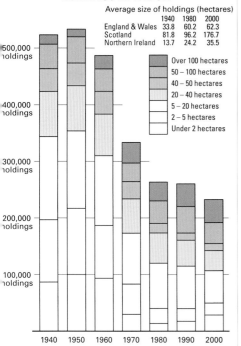

Average size of holdings (hectares)

| | 1940 | 1980 | 2000 |
|---|---|---|---|
| England & Wales | 33.8 | 60.2 | 62.3 |
| Scotland | 81.8 | 96.2 | 176.7 |
| Northern Ireland | 13.7 | 24.2 | 35.5 |

Over 100 hectares
50 – 100 hectares
40 – 50 hectares
20 – 40 hectares
5 – 20 hectares
2 – 5 hectares
Under 2 hectares

## LAND UNDER AGRICULTURE

The percentage of the total land area used for agriculture in 2000 (Ireland 1999)

Over 80%
60 – 80%
40 – 60%
20 – 40%
0 – 20%
No data

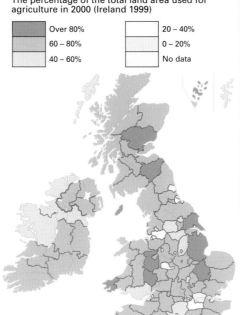

## EMPLOYMENT IN AGRICULTURE

The percentage of the total workforce employed in agriculture in 2000

Over 10%
2.5 – 10%
1 – 2.5%
0 – 1%

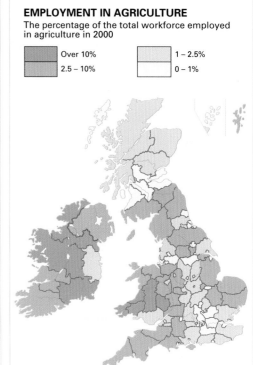

## FISHING

Quantities of fish landed at major ports in 2001 (Ireland 2000)

('000 tonnes)
100
50
25
10
5

Type of fish landed
Demersal (Deep Sea Fish)
Pelagic (Shallow Water Fish)
Shellfish

Fishing Regions
IV    North Sea
VIa    West Scotland
VIIa    Irish Sea
VIIb/h/j    W. Ireland & Sole Bank
VIId/e    English Channel
VIIf/g    Bristol Ch. & S.E. Ireland
— Region boundary

Fish landed according to region of capture (2001)
Demersal
Pelagic
Shellfish
One fish represents 10,000 tonnes caught

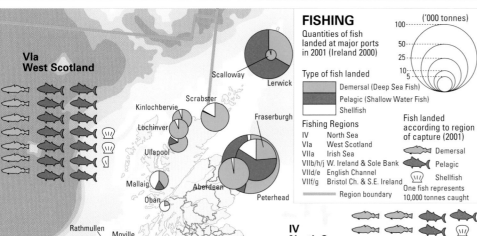

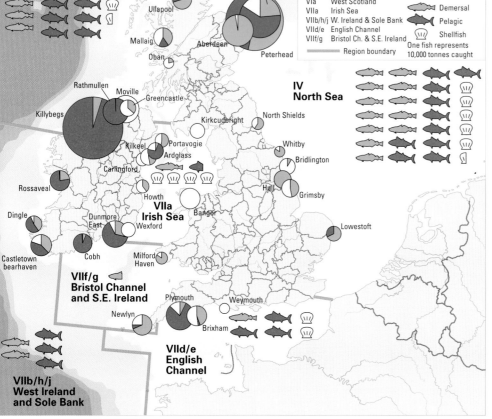

VIa West Scotland

Scalloway
Lerwick
Scrabster
Kinlochbervie
Fraserburgh
Lochinver
Ullapool
Mallaig
Aberdeen
Oban
Peterhead

IV North Sea

Rathmullen
Moville
Greencastle
Killybegs
Kilkeel
Portavogie
Ardglass
Carlingford
Rossaveal
Dingle
Dunmore East
Wexford
Castletown bearhaven
Cobh
Milford Haven

Kirkcudbright
North Shields
Whitby
Bridlington
Hull
Grimsby
Lowestoft

VIIa Irish Sea
Bangor
Howth

VIIf/g Bristol Channel and S.E. Ireland

Plymouth
Weymouth
Newlyn
Brixham

VIId/e English Channel

VIIb/h/j West Ireland and Sole Bank

1000  500  200  100  50  m

## CHANGES IN THE UK FISHING INDUSTRY

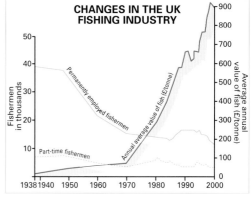

Permanently employed fishermen
Part-time fishermen
Annual average value of fish (£/tonne)

Fishermen in thousands
50
40
30
20
10

Average annual value of fish (£/tonne)
900
800
700
600
500
400
300
200
100
0

1938 1940  1950  1960  1970  1980  1990  2000

## FORESTRY – WOODLAND COVER

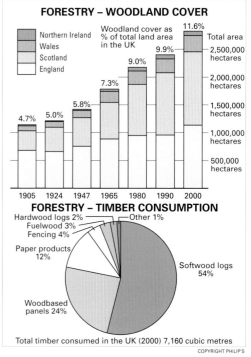

Northern Ireland
Wales
Scotland
England

Woodland cover as % of total land area in the UK

Total area
2,500,000 hectares
2,000,000 hectares
1,500,000 hectares
1,000,000 hectares
500,000 hectares

4.7%  5.0%  5.8%  7.3%  9.0%  9.9%  11.6%

1905  1924  1947  1965  1980  1990  2000

## FORESTRY – TIMBER CONSUMPTION

Hardwood logs 2%
Fuelwood 3%
Fencing 4%
Other 1%
Paper products 12%
Woodbased panels 24%
Softwood logs 54%

Total timber consumed in the UK (2000) 7,160 cubic metres

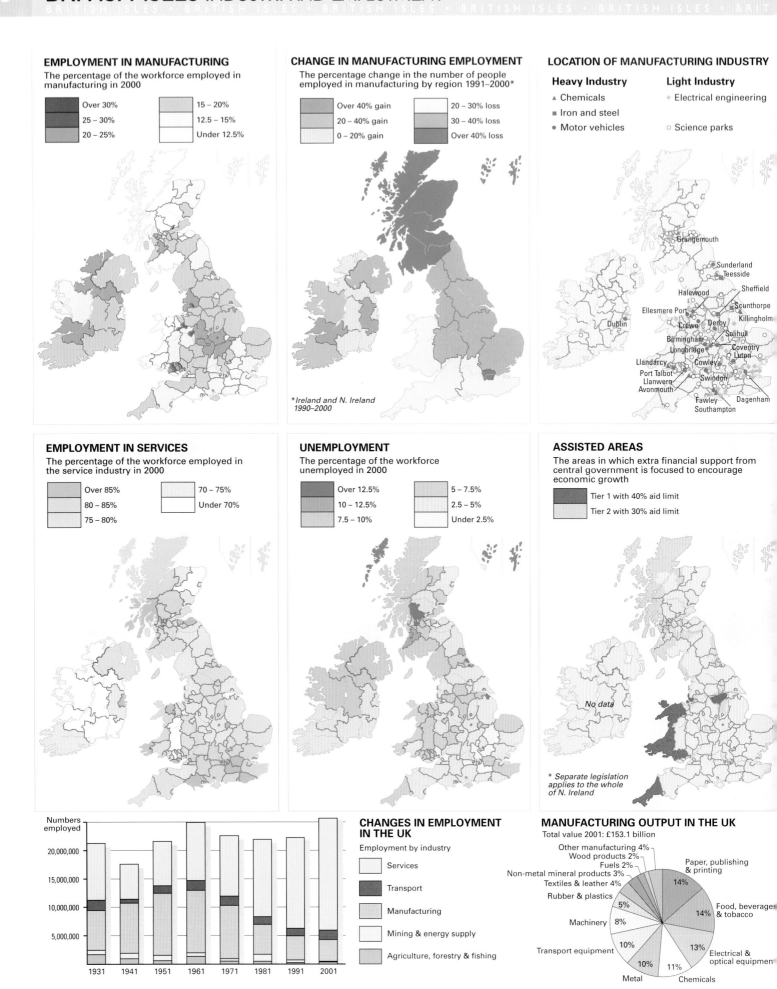

## EMPLOYMENT IN MANUFACTURING

The percentage of the workforce employed in manufacturing in 2000

- Over 30%
- 25 – 30%
- 20 – 25%
- 15 – 20%
- 12.5 – 15%
- Under 12.5%

## CHANGE IN MANUFACTURING EMPLOYMENT

The percentage change in the number of people employed in manufacturing by region 1991–2000*

- Over 40% gain
- 20 – 40% gain
- 0 – 20% gain
- 20 – 30% loss
- 30 – 40% loss
- Over 40% loss

*Ireland and N. Ireland 1990–2000*

## LOCATION OF MANUFACTURING INDUSTRY

**Heavy Industry**
- ▲ Chemicals
- ■ Iron and steel
- ● Motor vehicles

**Light Industry**
- ◆ Electrical engineering
- ○ Science parks

Grangemouth
Sunderland
Teesside
Halewood
Sheffield
Ellesmere Port
Scunthorpe
Killingholm
Dublin
Crewe
Derby
Solihull
Birmingham
Coventry
Longbridge
Luton
Llandarcy
Cowley
Port Talbot
Swindon
Llanwern
Avonmouth
Fawley
Dagenham
Southampton

## EMPLOYMENT IN SERVICES

The percentage of the workforce employed in the service industry in 2000

- Over 85%
- 80 – 85%
- 75 – 80%
- 70 – 75%
- Under 70%

## UNEMPLOYMENT

The percentage of the workforce unemployed in 2000

- Over 12.5%
- 10 – 12.5%
- 7.5 – 10%
- 5 – 7.5%
- 2.5 – 5%
- Under 2.5%

## ASSISTED AREAS

The areas in which extra financial support from central government is focused to encourage economic growth

- Tier 1 with 40% aid limit
- Tier 2 with 30% aid limit

No data

*Separate legislation applies to the whole of N. Ireland*

## CHANGES IN EMPLOYMENT IN THE UK

Numbers employed

20,000,000
15,000,000
10,000,000
5,000,000

1931 1941 1951 1961 1971 1981 1991 2001

Employment by industry
- Services
- Transport
- Manufacturing
- Mining & energy supply
- Agriculture, forestry & fishing

## MANUFACTURING OUTPUT IN THE UK

Total value 2001: £153.1 billion

- Other manufacturing 4%
- Wood products 2%
- Fuels 2%
- Non-metal mineral products 3%
- Textiles & leather 4%
- Rubber & plastics 5%
- Machinery 8%
- Transport equipment 10%
- Metal 10%
- Chemicals 11%
- Electrical & optical equipmen 13%
- Food, beverages & tobacco 14%
- Paper, publishing & printing 14%

### OSSIL FUELS

- Oilfield
- Gasfield
- Gas condensate field
- Oil pipeline
- Gas pipeline
- Tanker terminal
- Oil terminal
- Gas terminal
- Oil refinery
- International dividing line
- Coalfield

ATLANTIC OCEAN

NORWAY

Magnus
Snorre
Visund
Statfjord
Gullfaks
Mongstad
Thistle
Tern
Cormorant
Brent
Kvitebjørn
Huldra
Stura
Kollsnes
Bergen
Troll
Clair
Ninian
Dunbar
Alpha
Brage
Schiehallion
Foinaven
Shetland Islands
Sullom Voe
Oseberg
Frigg
Bruce
Heimdal
Beryl
Jotun
Haugesund
Orkney Islands
Harding
Balder
Grane
Kårstø
Flotta
Brae
Sleipner
Stavanger
Sola
Captain
Scapa
Piper
Scott
Beatrice
Britannia
Alba
NORWEGIAN SECTOR
Nigg
Forties
Everest
Inverness
St. Fergus
Nelson
Mungo
Cruden Bay
Heron
Pierce
Ula
Aberdeen
Elgin
Gyda
UNITED KINGDOM SECTOR
Bittern
Joanne
Tor
Ekofisk
Eldfisk
Valhal
Siri
Harald
DANISH SECTOR
Svend
Syd Arne
Valdemar
Tyra
Finnart
Gorm
Rolf
Halfdan
Grangemouth
Mossmorran
Edinburgh
Skjold
Dan
Glasgow
Bathgate
Dalmeny
North Sea
Outer Hebrides

Ballylumford
Belfast
Newcastle
Jarrow
South Shields
Sunderland
Teesside
Hanze
F3
UNITED KINGDOM
Barrow-in-Furness
Millom
Morecambe
Heysham
Tyne
Murdock
DUTCH SECTOR
L9
Trent
Ravenspurn
Boulton
Schooner
Markham
Immingham
West Sole
Leeds
Lennox
Hamilton
Amlwch
Liverpool
Hull
Easington
Barque
K4B-K5A
K6
L4-A
Point of Ayr
Killingholme
Pickerill
Audrey
Viking
Galleon
K7
K8
KN
L8
L11A
Manchester
Sheffield
Stanlow
Beckingham
Clipper
Vulcan
Sean
Kotter
Logger
L10
Ellesmere Port
Egmanton
Theddlethorpe
Indefatigable
Haven
Hoorn
Nottingham
Bacton
Hewitt
Leman
Helder
RELAND
Dublin
Irish Sea
Kingsbury
Tamworth
Kings Lynn
Norwich
Helm
IJmuiden
Horizon
Birmingham
Bedworth
Amsterdam
Rijn
The Hague
Bromford
Northampton
Wymondham
P15
P18
Milford Haven
Pembroke
Avonmouth
Buncefield
Ipswich
Felixstowe
Europoort
Rotterdam
Swansea
Cardiff
Westerleigh
Slough
Dalston
Coryton
Vlissingen
Llandarcy
Barry
Bristol
Theale
Heathrow
London
Grays
Canvey I.
Grain
Zeebrugge
Celtic Sea
Stockbridge
Southampton
Fawley
Hamble
Great Marsh
Brighton
Dunkerque
Gent
Brussels
BELGIUM
Feluy
Plymouth
Exeter
Poole
Cowes
Wytch Farm
English Channel
Lille
FRANCE
Valenciennes
Portland

### ELECTRICITY GENERATION
Power Stations (with capacity) 2002

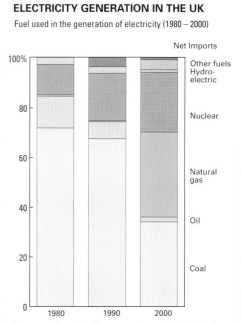

- Coal-fired (over 1,000 MW)
- Peat-fired (over 50 MW)
- Oil-fired (over 500 MW)
- Combined Cycle Gas Turbine (over 1,000 MW)
- Nuclear (over 1,000 MW)
- Pumped storage scheme
- Hydro-electric (over 40 MW)
- Coal & gas-fired (over 1,000 MW)

Fasnakyle
Foyers
Peterhead
Rannoch
Errochty
Cruachan
Clunie
Lochay
Clachan
Sloy
Cockenzie
Longannet
Torness
Hunterston
Ballylumford
Hartlepool
Teesside
Lanesboro
Heysham
Shannonbridge
Poolbeg
Ferrybridge
Saltend
Connahs Quay
Drax
Turlough Hill
Dinorwig
Fiddler's Ferry
Eggborough
West Burton
Tarbert
Ardnacrusha
Ffestiniog
Rugeley
Cottam
Ratcliffe
Rheidol
Sizewell
Aberthaw
Didcot
Barking
Tilbury
Hinkley Point
Littlebrook
Grain
Kingsnorth
Fawley
Dungeness

### ELECTRICITY GENERATION IN THE UK
Fuel used in the generation of electricity (1980 – 2000)

Net Imports
Other fuels
Hydro-electric
Nuclear
Natural gas
Oil
Coal

The use of coal in the generation of electricity has dropped over the 20-year period, while the use of nuclear power has increased by 58%.

### RENEWABLE ENERGY SOURCES

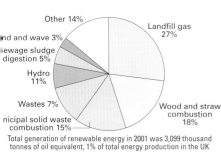

- Other 14%
- Landfill gas 27%
- nd and wave 3%
- ewage sludge digestion 5%
- Hydro 11%
- Wastes 7%
- nicipal solid waste combustion 15%
- Wood and straw combustion 18%

Total generation of renewable energy in 2001 was 3,099 thousand tonnes of oil equivalent, 1% of total energy production in the UK

### PRODUCTION OF PRIMARY FUELS IN THE UK

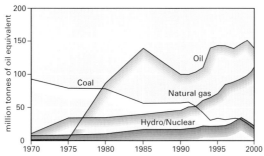

million tonnes of oil equivalent

Oil
Coal
Natural gas
Hydro/Nuclear

1970　1975　1980　1985　1990　1995　2000

### ENERGY CONSUMPTION BY FUEL IN THE UK

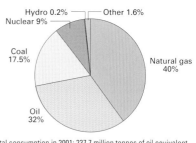

- Hydro 0.2%
- Other 1.6%
- Nuclear 9%
- Coal 17.5%
- Natural gas 40%
- Oil 32%

Total consumption in 2001: 237.7 million tonnes of oil equivalent

## ROADS AND FERRIES

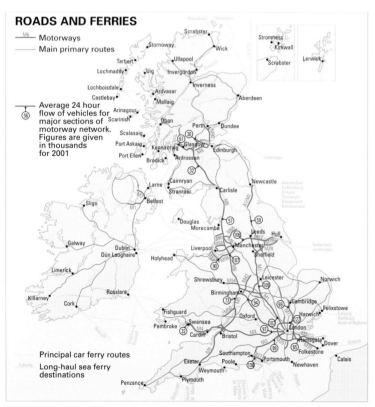

— M6 — Motorways

—— Main primary routes

56 — Average 24 hour flow of vehicles for major sections of motorway network. Figures are given in thousands for 2001

—— Principal car ferry routes

• Long-haul sea ferry destinations

## RAILWAYS

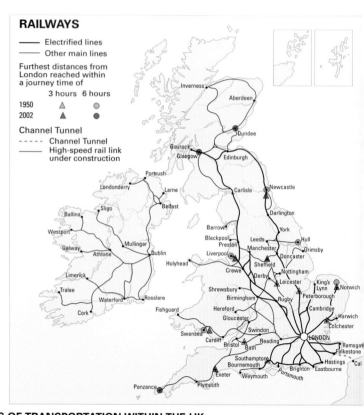

—— Electrified lines

—— Other main lines

Furthest distances from London reached within a journey time of

| | 3 hours | 6 hours |
| --- | --- | --- |
| 1950 | △ | ○ |
| 2002 | ▲ | ● |

Channel Tunnel

- - - - Channel Tunnel

—— High-speed rail link under construction

## CHANNEL TUNNEL & HIGH-SPEED LINKS IN EUROPE

Estimated journey times between London and other European cities

London – Berlin

London – Amsterdam

London – Paris

London – Brussels

5   10   15   20
Hours

1990 — Best time achievable using existing networks

2002 — Since opening of Channel Tunnel in 1994 and completion of high-speed links in Europe

2007 — Estimated journey times on completion of new link from London to Folkestone

## MEANS OF TRANSPORTATION WITHIN THE UK

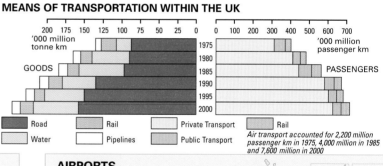

200 175 150 125 100 75 50 25 0    '000 million tonne km

GOODS

0 100 200 300 400 500 600 700   '000 million passenger km

PASSENGERS

1975
1980
1985
1990
1995
2000

Road  Rail  Private Transport  Rail
Water  Pipelines  Public Transport

*Air transport accounted for 2,200 million passenger km in 1975, 4,000 million in 1985 and 7,600 million in 2000*

## SEAPORTS

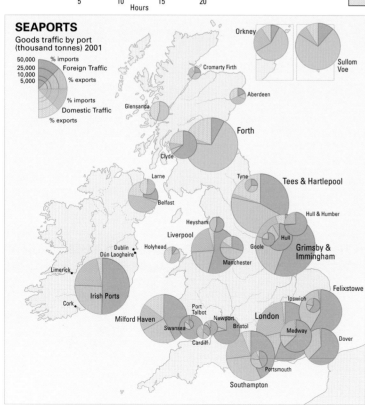

Goods traffic by port (thousand tonnes) 2001

50,000
25,000
10,000
5,000

% imports
Foreign Traffic
% exports

% imports
Domestic Traffic
% exports

## AIRPORTS

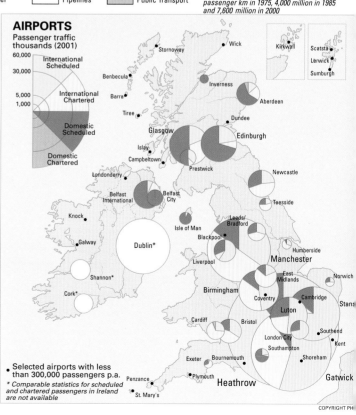

Passenger traffic thousands (2001)

60,000
International Scheduled

30,000
International Chartered

5,000
1,000

Domestic Scheduled

Domestic Chartered

• Selected airports with less than 300,000 passengers p.a.

*Comparable statistics for scheduled and chartered passengers in Ireland are not available*

COPYRIGHT PH

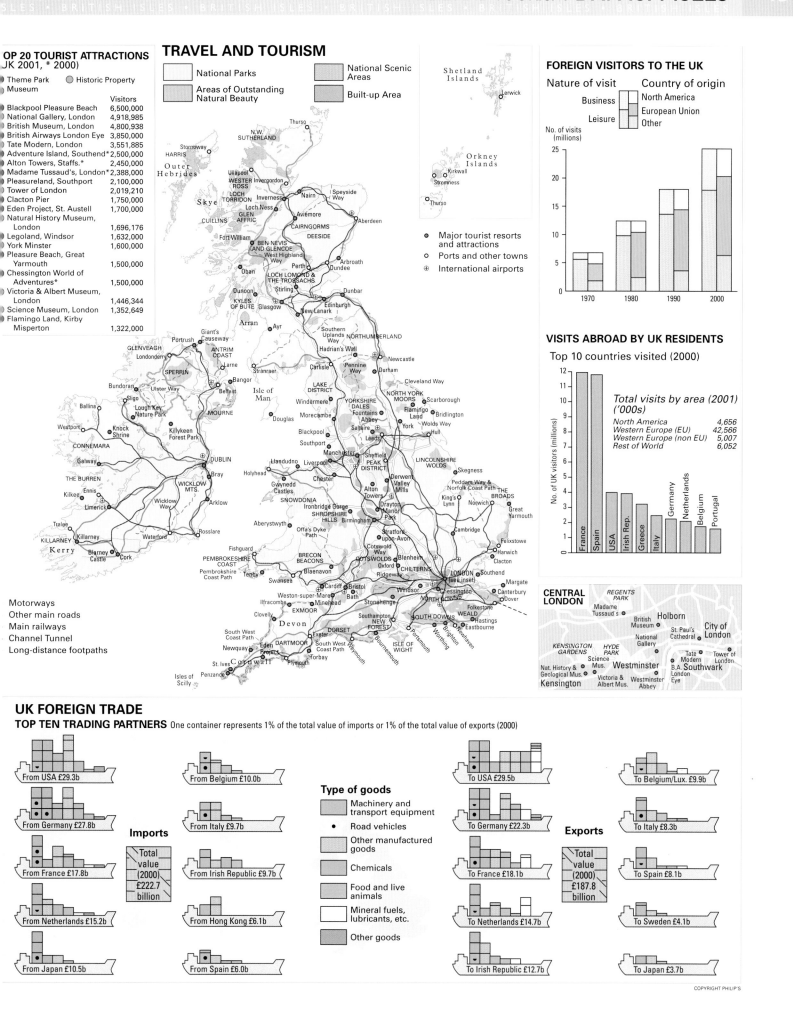

## TOP 20 TOURIST ATTRACTIONS
UK 2001, * 2000

- Theme Park
- Museum
- Historic Property

| | Visitors |
|---|---|
| Blackpool Pleasure Beach | 6,500,000 |
| National Gallery, London | 4,918,985 |
| British Museum, London | 4,800,938 |
| British Airways London Eye | 3,850,000 |
| Tate Modern, London | 3,551,885 |
| Adventure Island, Southend* | 2,500,000 |
| Alton Towers, Staffs.* | 2,450,000 |
| Madame Tussaud's, London* | 2,388,000 |
| Pleasureland, Southport | 2,100,000 |
| Tower of London | 2,019,210 |
| Clacton Pier | 1,750,000 |
| Eden Project, St. Austell | 1,700,000 |
| Natural History Museum, London | 1,696,176 |
| Legoland, Windsor | 1,632,000 |
| York Minster | 1,600,000 |
| Pleasure Beach, Great Yarmouth | 1,500,000 |
| Chessington World of Adventures* | 1,500,000 |
| Victoria & Albert Museum, London | 1,446,344 |
| Science Museum, London | 1,352,649 |
| Flamingo Land, Kirby Misperton | 1,322,000 |

## TRAVEL AND TOURISM

- National Parks
- Areas of Outstanding Natural Beauty
- National Scenic Areas
- Built-up Area

- Major tourist resorts and attractions
- Ports and other towns
- International airports

- Motorways
- Other main roads
- Main railways
- Channel Tunnel
- Long-distance footpaths

## FOREIGN VISITORS TO THE UK

Nature of visit
- Business
- Leisure

Country of origin
- North America
- European Union
- Other

No. of visits (millions): 1970, 1980, 1990, 2000

## VISITS ABROAD BY UK RESIDENTS
Top 10 countries visited (2000)

France, Spain, USA, Irish Rep., Greece, Italy, Germany, Netherlands, Belgium, Portugal

Total visits by area (2001) ('000s)

| | |
|---|---|
| North America | 4,656 |
| Western Europe (EU) | 42,566 |
| Western Europe (non EU) | 5,007 |
| Rest of World | 6,052 |

## CENTRAL LONDON

Regents Park, Madame Tussaud's, British Museum, Holborn, St. Paul's Cathedral, City of London, National Gallery, Kensington Gardens, Hyde Park, Science Mus., Nat. History & Geological Mus., Victoria & Albert Mus., Westminster, Westminster Abbey, London Eye, B.A. Southwark, Tate Modern, Tower of London, Kensington

## UK FOREIGN TRADE

### TOP TEN TRADING PARTNERS
One container represents 1% of the total value of imports or 1% of the total value of exports (2000)

**Imports**
- From USA £29.3b
- From Germany £27.8b
- From France £17.8b
- From Netherlands £15.2b
- From Japan £10.5b
- From Belgium £10.0b
- From Italy £9.7b
- From Irish Republic £9.7b
- From Hong Kong £6.1b
- From Spain £6.0b

Total value (2000) £222.7 billion

**Exports**
- To USA £29.5b
- To Germany £22.3b
- To France £18.1b
- To Netherlands £14.7b
- To Irish Republic £12.7b
- To Belgium/Lux. £9.9b
- To Italy £8.3b
- To Spain £8.1b
- To Sweden £4.1b
- To Japan £3.7b

Total value (2000) £187.8 billion

**Type of goods**
- Machinery and transport equipment
- Road vehicles
- Other manufactured goods
- Chemicals
- Food and live animals
- Mineral fuels, lubricants, etc.
- Other goods

COPYRIGHT PHILIP'S

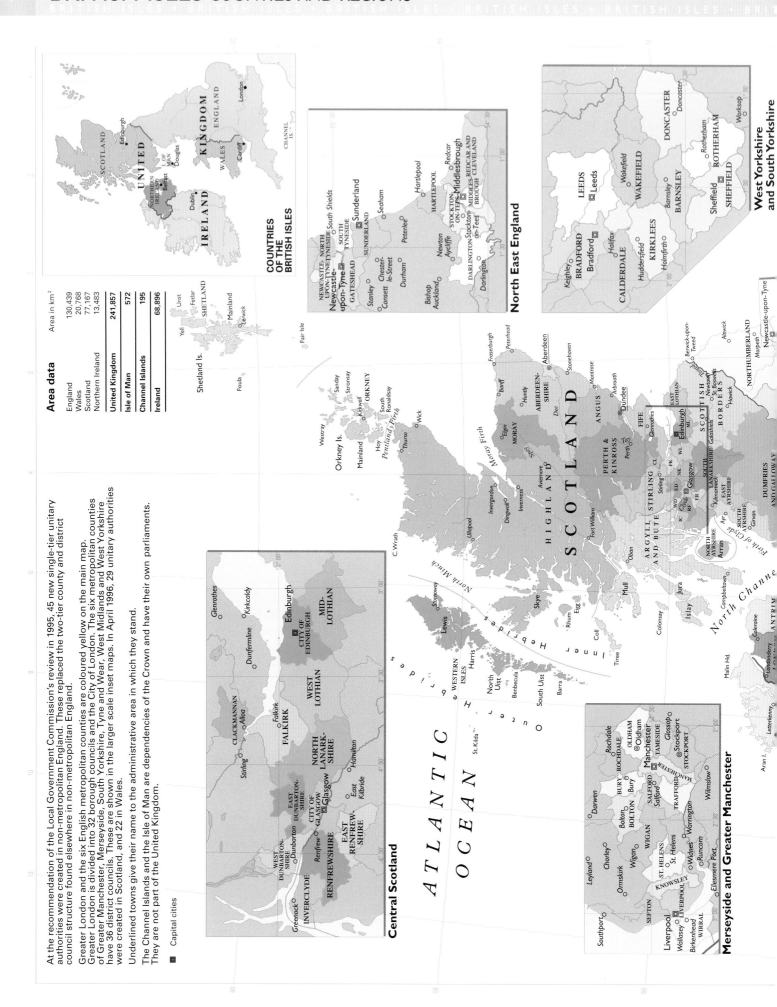

At the recommendation of the Local Government Commission's review in 1995, 45 new single-tier unitary authorities were created in non-metropolitan England. These replaced the two-tier county and district council structure found elsewhere in non-metropolitan England.

Greater London and the six English metropolitan counties are coloured yellow on the main map. Greater London is divided into 32 borough councils and the City of London. The six metropolitan counties of Greater Manchester, Merseyside, South Yorkshire, Tyne and Wear, West Midlands and West Yorkshire have 36 district councils. These are shown in the larger scale inset maps. In April 1996, 29 unitary authorities were created in Scotland, and 22 in Wales.

Underlined towns give their name to the administrative area in which they stand.

The Channel Islands and the Isle of Man are dependencies of the Crown and have their own parliaments. They are not part of the United Kingdom.

■ Capital cities

### Area data

| | Area in km² |
|---|---|
| England | 130,439 |
| Wales | 20,768 |
| Scotland | 77,167 |
| Northern Ireland | 13,483 |
| **United Kingdom** | **241,857** |
| Isle of Man | 572 |
| Channel Islands | 195 |
| Ireland | 68,896 |

**COUNTRIES OF THE BRITISH ISLES**

**North East England**

**West Yorkshire and South Yorkshire**

**Central Scotland**

**Merseyside and Greater Manchester**

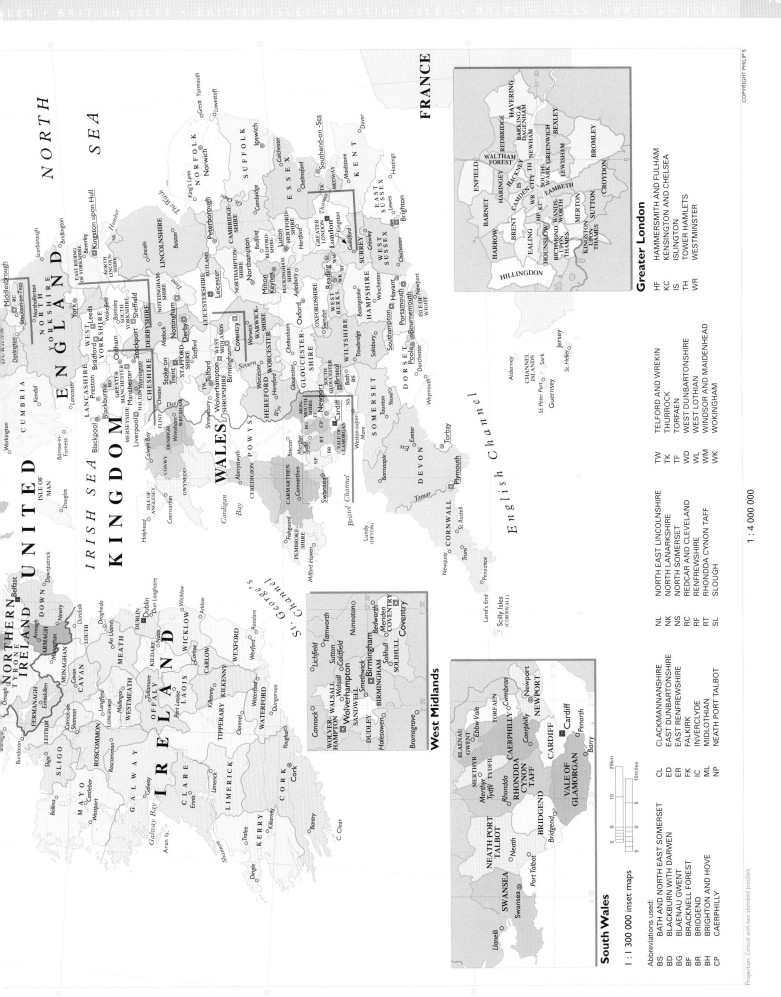

**FRANCE**

**NORTH**

**SEA**

*N O R T H*

*S E A*

**UNITED**

**KINGDOM**

**ENGLAND**

*N o r t h*

**NORTHERN**
**IRELAND**

*I R I S H   S E A*

**WALES**

*IRELAND*

*St. George's*
*Channel*

*E n g l i s h   C h a n n e l*

*Bristol Channel*

**Greater London**

| | |
|---|---|
| HF | HAMMERSMITH AND FULHAM |
| KC | KENSINGTON AND CHELSEA |
| IS | ISLINGTON |
| TH | TOWER HAMLETS |
| WR | WESTMINSTER |

ENFIELD
BARNET
HARROW
HILLINGDON
EALING
BRENT
HARINGEY
WALTHAM FOREST
REDBRIDGE
HAVERING
BARKING & DAGENHAM
NEWHAM
HACKNEY
CAMDEN
HOUNSLOW
RICHMOND UPON THAMES
KINGSTON UPON THAMES
MERTON
WANDSWORTH
LAMBETH
SOUTHWARK
GREENWICH
BEXLEY
LEWISHAM
SUTTON
CROYDON
BROMLEY

**West Midlands**
1 : 300 000

Cannock
Lichfield
Tamworth
WOLVERHAMPTON
WALSALL
Sutton Coldfield
Nuneaton
Bedworth
Meriden
SANDWELL
Smethwick
BIRMINGHAM
Solihull
SOLIHULL
COVENTRY
Coventry
DUDLEY
Halesowen
Bromsgrove

**South Wales**
1 : 1 300 000

BLAENAU GWENT
MERTHYR TYDFIL
Merthyr Tydfil
RHONDDA CYNON TAFF
Rhondda
Ebbw Vale
TORFAEN
CAERPHILLY
Cwmbran
Caerphilly
NEWPORT
Newport
NEATH PORT TALBOT
Neath
BRIDGEND
Bridgend
VALE OF GLAMORGAN
CARDIFF
Cardiff
Penarth
Barry
SWANSEA
Swansea
Llanelli
Port Talbot

Abbreviations used:

| | | | | | |
|---|---|---|---|---|---|
| BS | BATH AND NORTH EAST SOMERSET | CL | CLACKMANNANSHIRE | NL | NORTH EAST LINCOLNSHIRE | TW | TELFORD AND WREKIN |
| BD | BLACKBURN WITH DARWEN | ED | EAST DUNBARTONSHIRE | NK | NORTH LANARKSHIRE | TK | THURROCK |
| BG | BLAENAU GWENT | ER | EAST RENFREWSHIRE | NS | NORTH SOMERSET | TF | TORFAEN |
| BF | BRACKNELL FOREST | FK | FALKIRK | RC | REDCAR AND CLEVELAND | WD | WEST DUNBARTONSHIRE |
| BR | BRIDGEND | IC | INVERCLYDE | RF | RENFREWSHIRE | WL | WEST LOTHIAN |
| BH | BRIGHTON AND HOVE | ML | MIDLOTHIAN | RT | RHONDDA CYNON TAFF | WM | WINDSOR AND MAIDENHEAD |
| CP | CAERPHILLY | NP | NEATH PORT TALBOT | SL | SLOUGH | WK | WOKINGHAM |

COPYRIGHT PHILIP'S

1 : 4 000 000

Projection: Conical with two standard parallels

0   5   10   20km
0   5   10miles

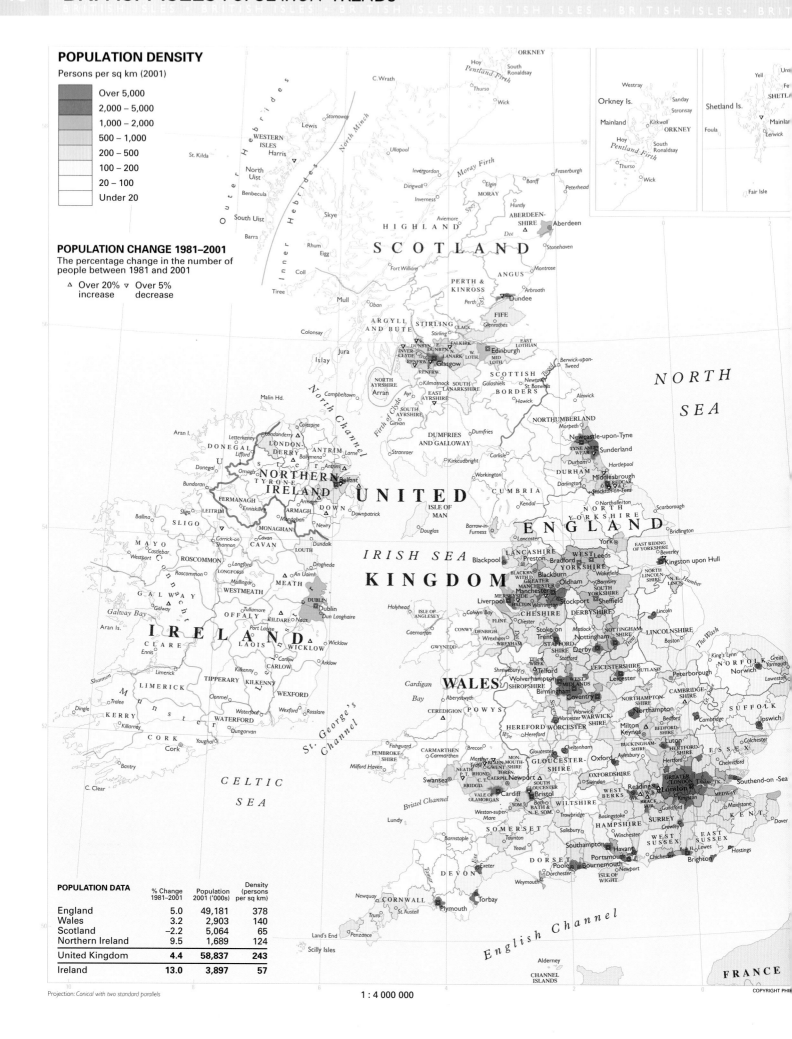

## POPULATION DENSITY

Persons per sq km (2001)

- Over 5,000
- 2,000 – 5,000
- 1,000 – 2,000
- 500 – 1,000
- 200 – 500
- 100 – 200
- 20 – 100
- Under 20

## POPULATION CHANGE 1981–2001

The percentage change in the number of
people between 1981 and 2001

△ Over 20%    ▽ Over 5%
increase          decrease

| POPULATION DATA | % Change 1981–2001 | Population 2001 ('000s) | Density (persons per sq km) |
|---|---|---|---|
| England | 5.0 | 49,181 | 378 |
| Wales | 3.2 | 2,903 | 140 |
| Scotland | –2.2 | 5,064 | 65 |
| Northern Ireland | 9.5 | 1,689 | 124 |
| United Kingdom | 4.4 | 58,837 | 243 |
| Ireland | 13.0 | 3,897 | 57 |

Projection: Conical with two standard parallels

1 : 4 000 000

COPYRIGHT PHI

## POPULATION DENSITY IN 1891

Persons per sq km

- Over 1,000
- 500 – 1,000
- 200 – 500
- 100 – 200
- 50 – 100
- 25 – 50
- Under 25

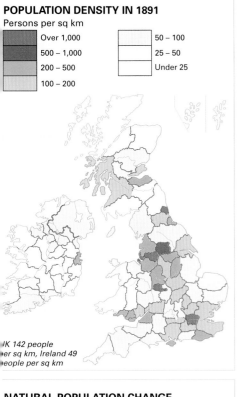

UK 142 people
per sq km, Ireland 49
people per sq km

## ETHNIC GROUPS

Ethnic minorities as a % of total population in 2000–1

- Over 6%
- 4 – 6%
- 2 – 4%
- 0 – 2%

Ethnic minority groups

- Indian/ Pakistani/ Bangladeshi
- W. Indian/ African
- Other

77 000  Total number of ethnic minority people in each region

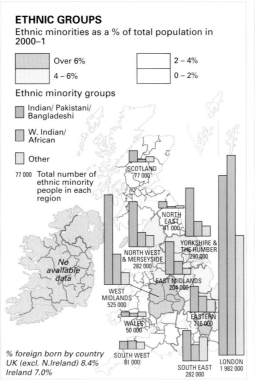

% foreign born by country
UK (excl. N.Ireland) 8.4%
Ireland 7.0%

## MIGRATION

The difference between the number moving in and the number moving away (per 1,000 inhabitants)*

- Over 10 moved in
- 5 – 10 moved in
- 0 – 5 moved in
- 0 – 5 moved away
- 5 – 10 moved away
- Over 10 moved away

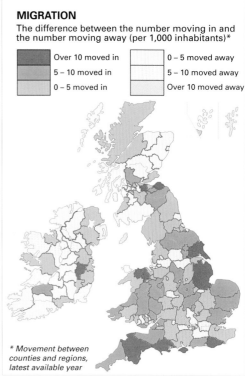

* Movement between counties and regions, latest available year

## NATURAL POPULATION CHANGE

The difference between the number of births and the number of deaths per thousand inhabitants in 2000

- Over 7.5 more births
- 5 – 7.5 more births
- 2.5 – 5 more births
- 0 – 2.5 more births
- 0 – 2.5 more deaths
- Over 2.5 more deaths

UK 1.2 more
births than deaths
Ireland 6.1 more
births than deaths

## YOUNG PEOPLE

The percentage of the population under 15 years old in 2000 (Ireland 2002)

- Over 22.5%
- 20 – 22.5%
- 19 – 20%
- 18 – 19%
- Under 18%

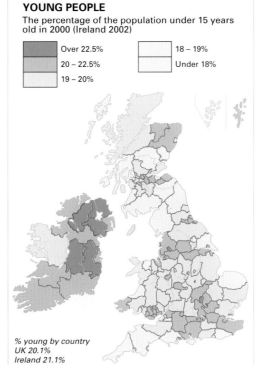

% young by country
UK 20.1%
Ireland 21.1%

## OLD PEOPLE

The percentage of the population over pensionable age* in 2000 (Ireland 2002)

- Over 25%
- 20 – 25%
- 17.5 – 20%
- 15 – 17.5%
- 12.5 – 15%
- Under 12.5%

*Pensionable age is 65 for males, 60 for females

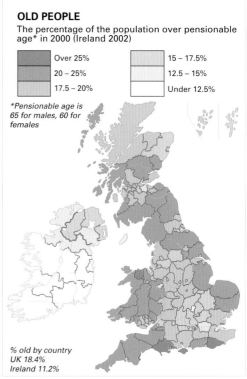

% old by country
UK 18.4%
Ireland 11.2%

## K VITAL STATISTICS (1900–2000)

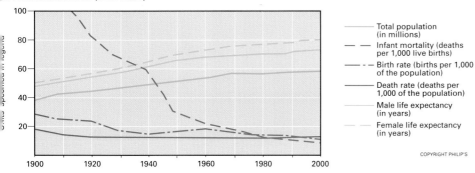

- Total population (in millions)
- Infant mortality (deaths per 1,000 live births)
- Birth rate (births per 1,000 of the population)
- Death rate (deaths per 1,000 of the population)
- Male life expectancy (in years)
- Female life expectancy (in years)

COPYRIGHT PHILIP'S

## AGE STRUCTURE OF THE UK

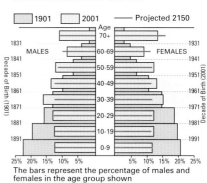

- 1901
- 2001
- Projected 2150

The bars represent the percentage of males and females in the age group shown

## HOME OWNERSHIP

The percentage of dwellings which are owner-occupied in 2000

| | |
|---|---|
| Over 75% | 60 – 65% |
| 70 – 75% | Under 60% |
| 65 – 70% | |

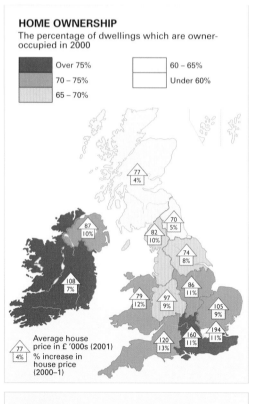

77 / 4% Average house price in £ '000s (2001)
% increase in house price (2000–1)

## CAR OWNERSHIP

The number of new cars per thousand people in 2001* (N. Ireland 2000*)

| | |
|---|---|
| Over 50 | 20 – 30 |
| 40 – 50 | 10 – 20 |
| 30 – 40 | |

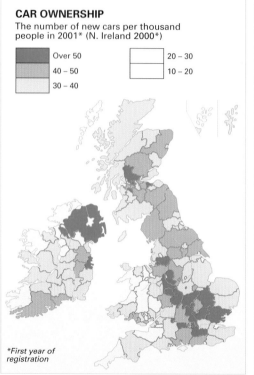

*First year of registration

## INCOME

The average gross weekly earnings of males and females in full employment in 2000 (Ireland 1999)

| | |
|---|---|
| Over £400 | £325 – £350 |
| £375 – £400 | £300 – £325 |
| £350 – £375 | Under £300 |

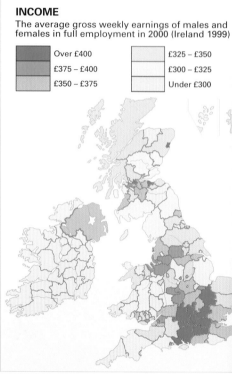

## HEALTH

The number of doctors per 100,000 people by region

| | |
|---|---|
| Over 65 | 50 – 55 |
| 60 – 65 | 45 – 50 |
| 55 – 60 | Under 45 |

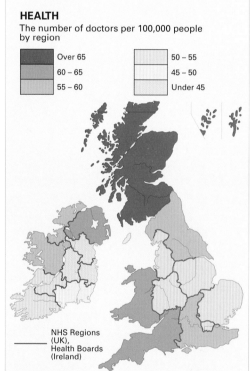

NHS Regions (UK), Health Boards (Ireland)

## EDUCATION

The percentage of pupils aged 16 staying on in education in 1999–2000

| | |
|---|---|
| Over 90% | 75 – 80% |
| 85 – 90% | 70 – 75% |
| 80 – 85% | Under 70% |

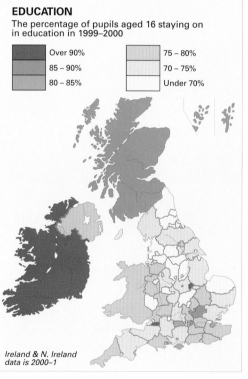

*Ireland & N. Ireland data is 2000–1*

## CRIME RATE

The number of recorded crimes per thousand people in 2001–2 (Ireland 2000)

| | |
|---|---|
| Over 100 | 25 – 50 |
| 75 – 100 | Under 25 |
| 50 – 75 | |

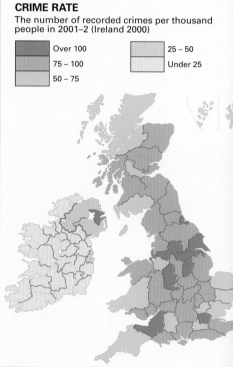

## COMPARISON OF HOUSEHOLD EXPENDITURE IN THE UK

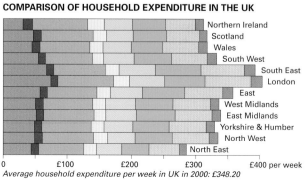

Northern Ireland
Scotland
Wales
South West
South East
London
East
West Midlands
East Midlands
Yorkshire & Humber
North West
North East

0   £100   £200   £300   £400 per week

*Average household expenditure per week in UK in 2000: £348.20*

| | |
|---|---|
| | Housing |
| | Fuel, light & power |
| | Food, beverages and tobacco |
| | Clothing and footwear |
| | Household goods & services |
| | Transport & communication |
| | Leisure goods & services |
| | Miscellaneous goods |

COPYRIGHT PHILIP'S

## CHANGES IN LIFESTYLE IN THE U

Percentage of househol owning goods listed belo

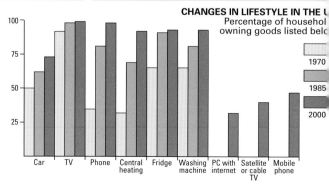

Car   TV   Phone   Central heating   Fridge   Washing machine   PC with internet   Satellite or cable TV   Mobile phone

1970
1985
2000

Equatorial Scale 1 : 89 000 000

Projection: *Hammer Equal Area*

Projection: *Hammer Equal Area*

Hanoi ◉ Capital Cities

Equatorial Scale 1:95 000 000

COPYRIGHT PHILIP'S

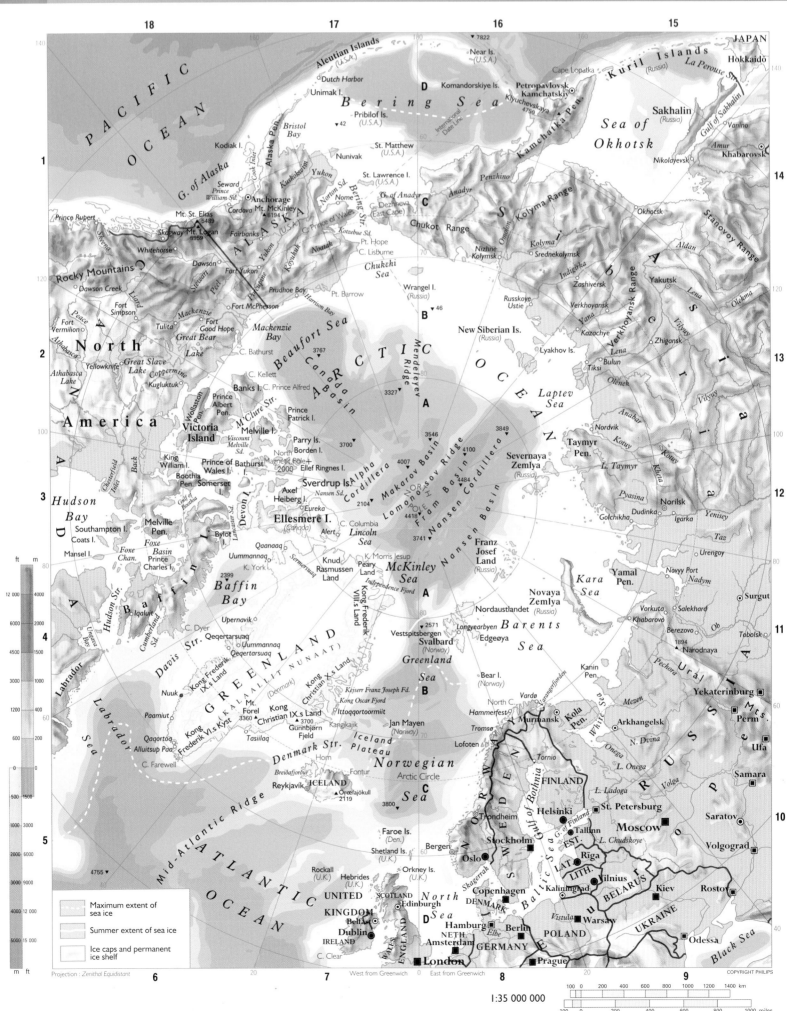

Projection : Zenithal Equidistant

1:35 000 000

Maximum extent of sea ice

Summer extent of sea ice

Ice caps and permanent ice shelf

COPYRIGHT PHILIPS

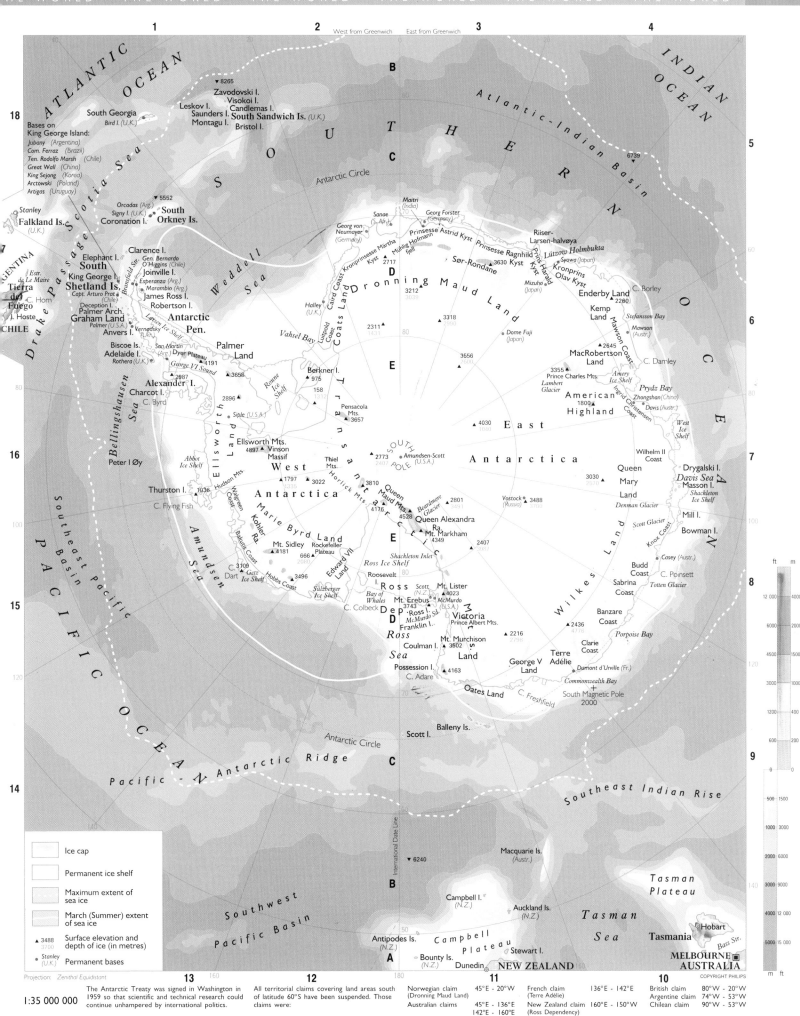

**Legend:**

- Ice cap
- Permanent ice shelf
- Maximum extent of sea ice
- March (Summer) extent of sea ice
- ▲ 3488 / 3700 — Surface elevation and depth of ice (in metres)
- ● Stanley (U.K.) — Permanent bases

Projection: Zenithal Equidistant

1:35 000 000

COPYRIGHT PHILIPS

The Antarctic Treaty was signed in Washington in 1959 so that scientific and technical research could continue unhampered by international politics.

All territorial claims covering land areas south of latitude 60°S have been suspended. Those claims were:

| | | | |
|---|---|---|---|
| Norwegian claim (Dronning Maud Land) | 45°E – 20°W | French claim (Terre Adélie) | 136°E – 142°E |
| Australian claims | 45°E – 136°E / 142°E – 160°E | New Zealand claim (Ross Dependency) | 160°E – 150°W |
| | | British claim | 80°W – 20°W |
| | | Argentine claim | 74°W – 53°W |
| | | Chilean claim | 90°W – 53°W |

**Elevation scale (ft / m):**
12 000 / 4000
6000 / 2000
4500 / 1500
3000 / 1000
1200 / 400
600 / 200
0 / 0
500 / 1500
1000 / 3000
2000 / 6000
3000 / 9000
4000 / 12 000
5000 / 15 000
m / ft

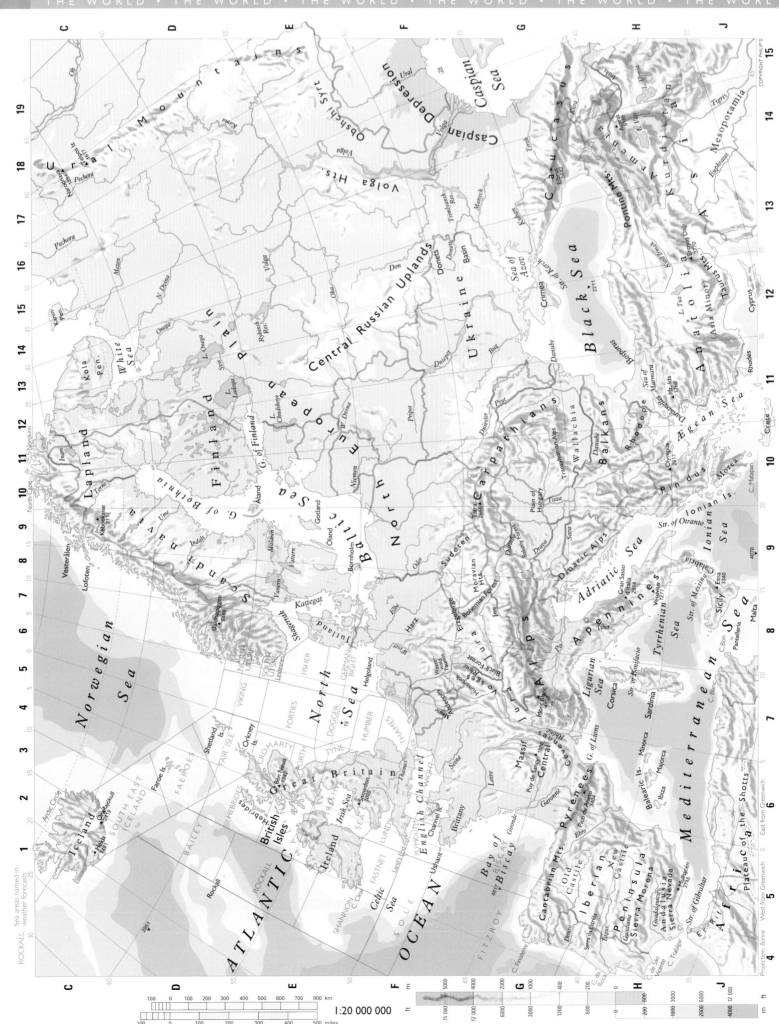

ROCKALL   Sea areas named in
weather forecasts

1:20 000 000

East from Greenwich   West from Greenwich

Projection: Bonne

1:20 000 000

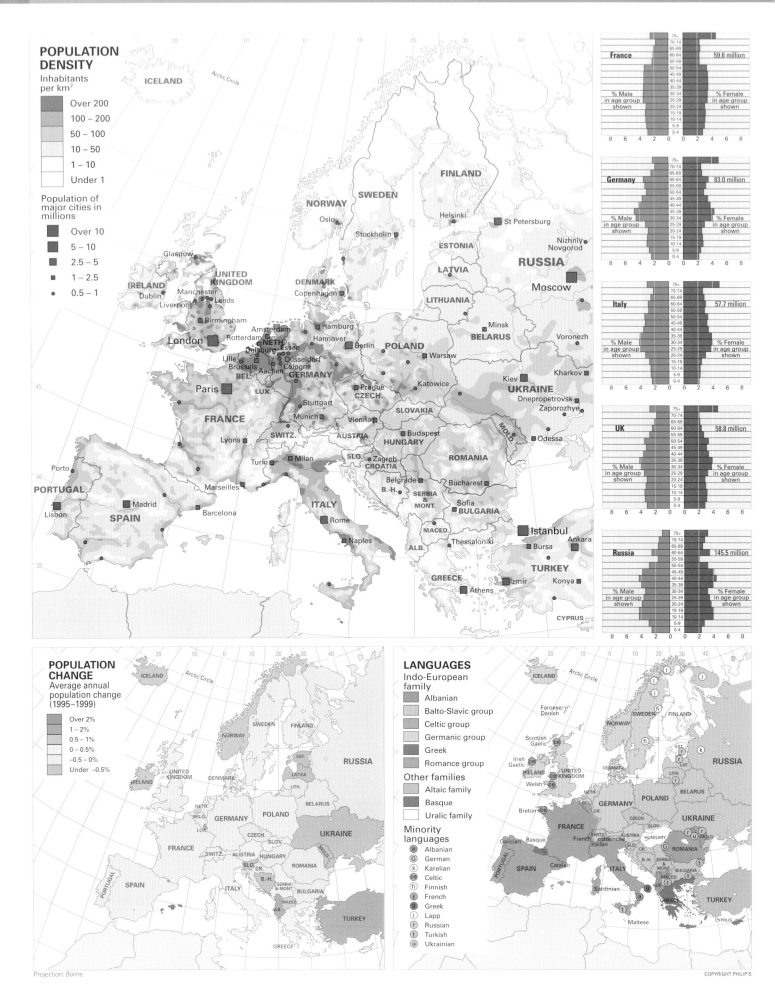

## POPULATION DENSITY

Inhabitants per km²

- Over 200
- 100 – 200
- 50 – 100
- 10 – 50
- 1 – 10
- Under 1

Population of major cities in millions

- Over 10
- 5 – 10
- 2.5 – 5
- 1 – 2.5
- 0.5 – 1

## POPULATION CHANGE

Average annual population change (1995–1999)

- Over 2%
- 1 – 2%
- 0.5 – 1%
- 0 – 0.5%
- -0.5 – 0%
- Under -0.5%

## LANGUAGES

Indo-European family

- Albanian
- Balto-Slavic group
- Celtic group
- Germanic group
- Greek
- Romance group

Other families

- Altaic family
- Basque
- Uralic family

Minority languages

- a  Albanian
- G  German
- k  Karelian
- ce Celtic
- fi Finnish
- f  French
- g  Greek
- l  Lapp
- r  Russian
- t  Turkish
- u  Ukrainian

France  59.6 million
Germany  83.0 million
Italy  57.7 million
UK  58.8 million
Russia  145.5 million

% Male in age group shown   % Female in age group shown

Projection: Bonne

COPYRIGHT PHILIP'S

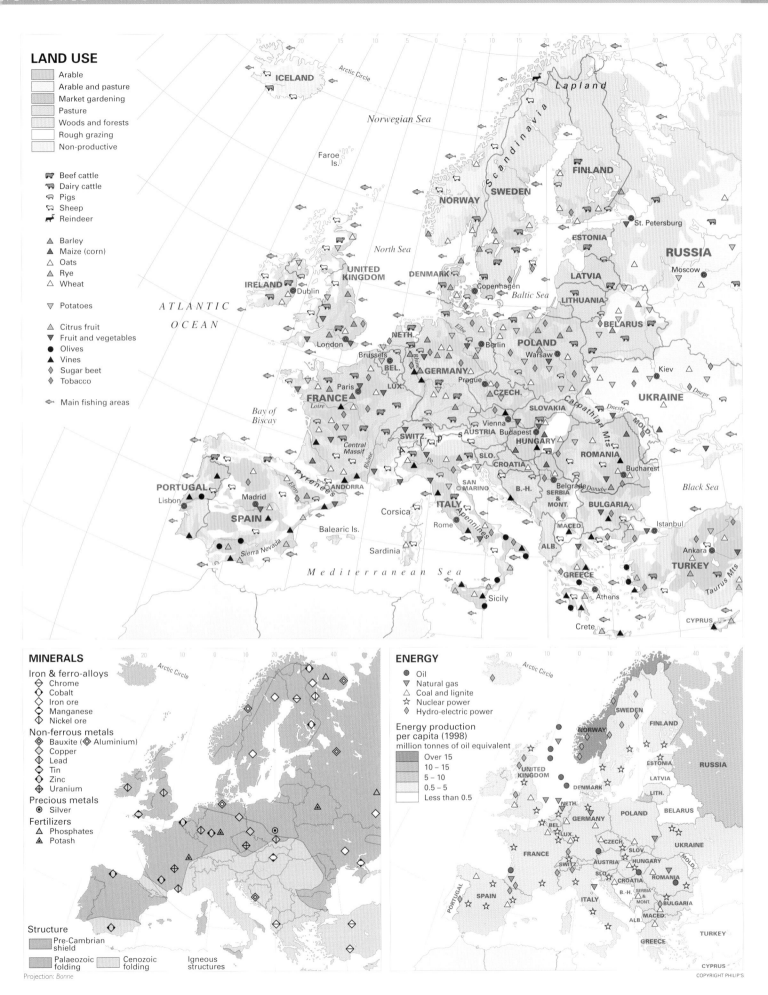

**LAND USE**

- Arable
- Arable and pasture
- Market gardening
- Pasture
- Woods and forests
- Rough grazing
- Non-productive

- Beef cattle
- Dairy cattle
- Pigs
- Sheep
- Reindeer

- Barley
- Maize (corn)
- Oats
- Rye
- Wheat

- Potatoes

- Citrus fruit
- Fruit and vegetables
- Olives
- Vines
- Sugar beet
- Tobacco

- Main fishing areas

**MINERALS**

Iron & ferro-alloys
- Chrome
- Cobalt
- Iron ore
- Manganese
- Nickel ore

Non-ferrous metals
- Bauxite (◈ Aluminium)
- Copper
- Lead
- Tin
- Zinc
- Uranium

Precious metals
- Silver

Fertilizers
- Phosphates
- Potash

Structure
- Pre-Cambrian shield
- Palaeozoic folding
- Cenozoic folding
- Igneous structures

Projection: *Bonne*

**ENERGY**

- Oil
- Natural gas
- Coal and lignite
- Nuclear power
- Hydro-electric power

Energy production per capita (1998)
million tonnes of oil equivalent
- Over 15
- 10 – 15
- 5 – 10
- 0.5 – 5
- Less than 0.5

COPYRIGHT PHILIP'S

## COUNTRIES OF THE EU

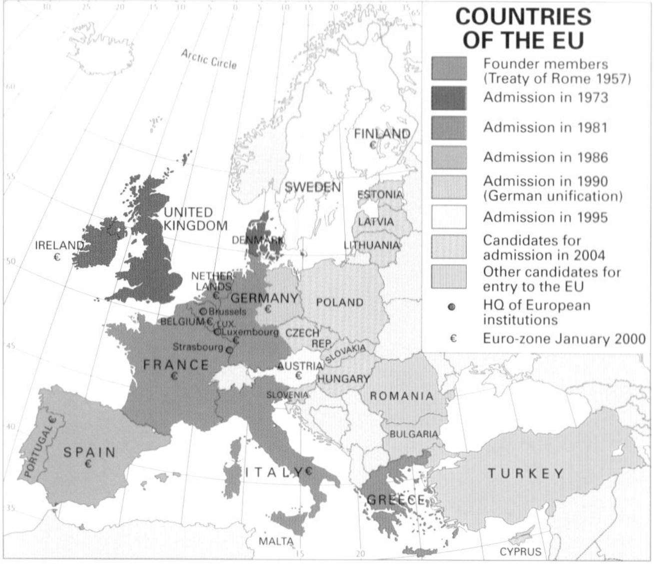
Founder members (Treaty of Rome 1957)
Admission in 1973
Admission in 1981
Admission in 1986
Admission in 1990 (German unification)
Admission in 1995
Candidates for admission in 2004
Other candidates for entry to the EU
HQ of European institutions
€ Euro-zone January 2000
Arctic Circle
FINLAND €
SWEDEN
ESTONIA
LATVIA
LITHUANIA
UNITED KINGDOM
IRELAND €
DENMARK
NETHERLANDS
GERMANY €
POLAND
Brussels
BELGIUM €
LUX.
Luxembourg
CZECH REP.
SLOVAKIA
Strasbourg
FRANCE €
AUSTRIA €
HUNGARY
SLOVENIA
ROMANIA
BULGARIA
PORTUGAL €
SPAIN €
ITALY €
TURKEY
GREECE
MALTA
CYPRUS

## EU BUDGET

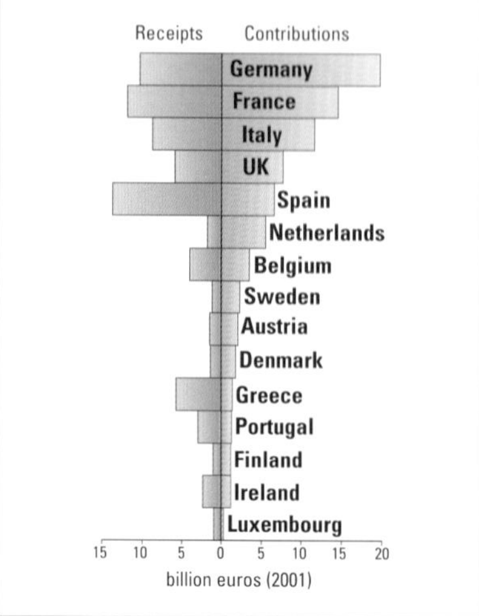
Receipts
Contributions
Germany
France
Italy
UK
Spain
Netherlands
Belgium
Sweden
Austria
Denmark
Greece
Portugal
Finland
Ireland
Luxembourg
15 10 5 0 5 10 15 20
billion euros (2001)

## EU TRADE

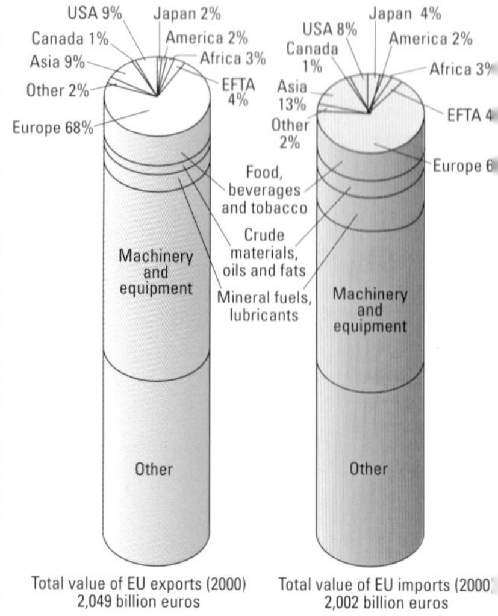
USA 9%
Japan 2%
Canada 1%
America 2%
Asia 9%
Africa 3%
EFTA 4%
Other 2%
Europe 68%
USA 8%
Japan 4%
Canada 1%
America 2%
Africa 3%
Asia 13%
Other 2%
EFTA 4
Europe 6
Food, beverages and tobacco
Crude materials, oils and fats
Mineral fuels, lubricants
Machinery and equipment
Machinery and equipment
Other
Other
Total value of EU exports (2000) 2,049 billion euros
Total value of EU imports (2000) 2,002 billion euros

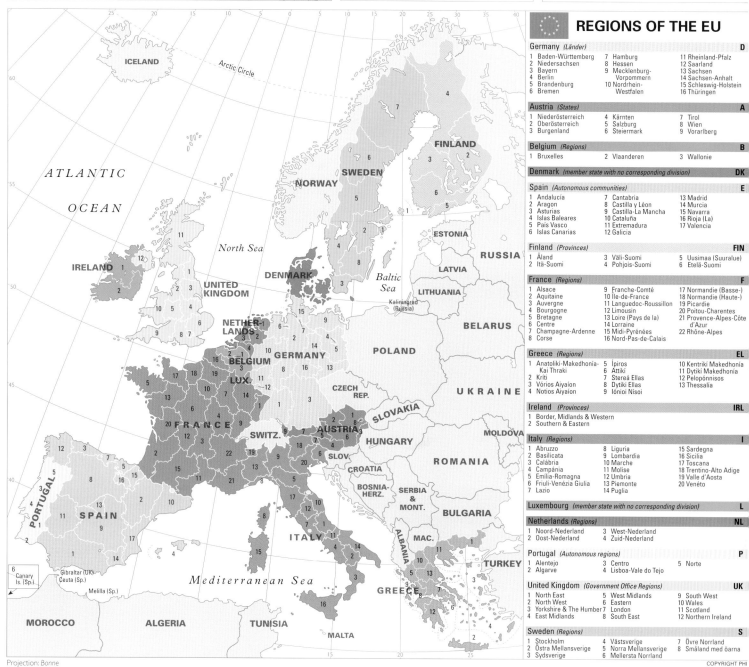

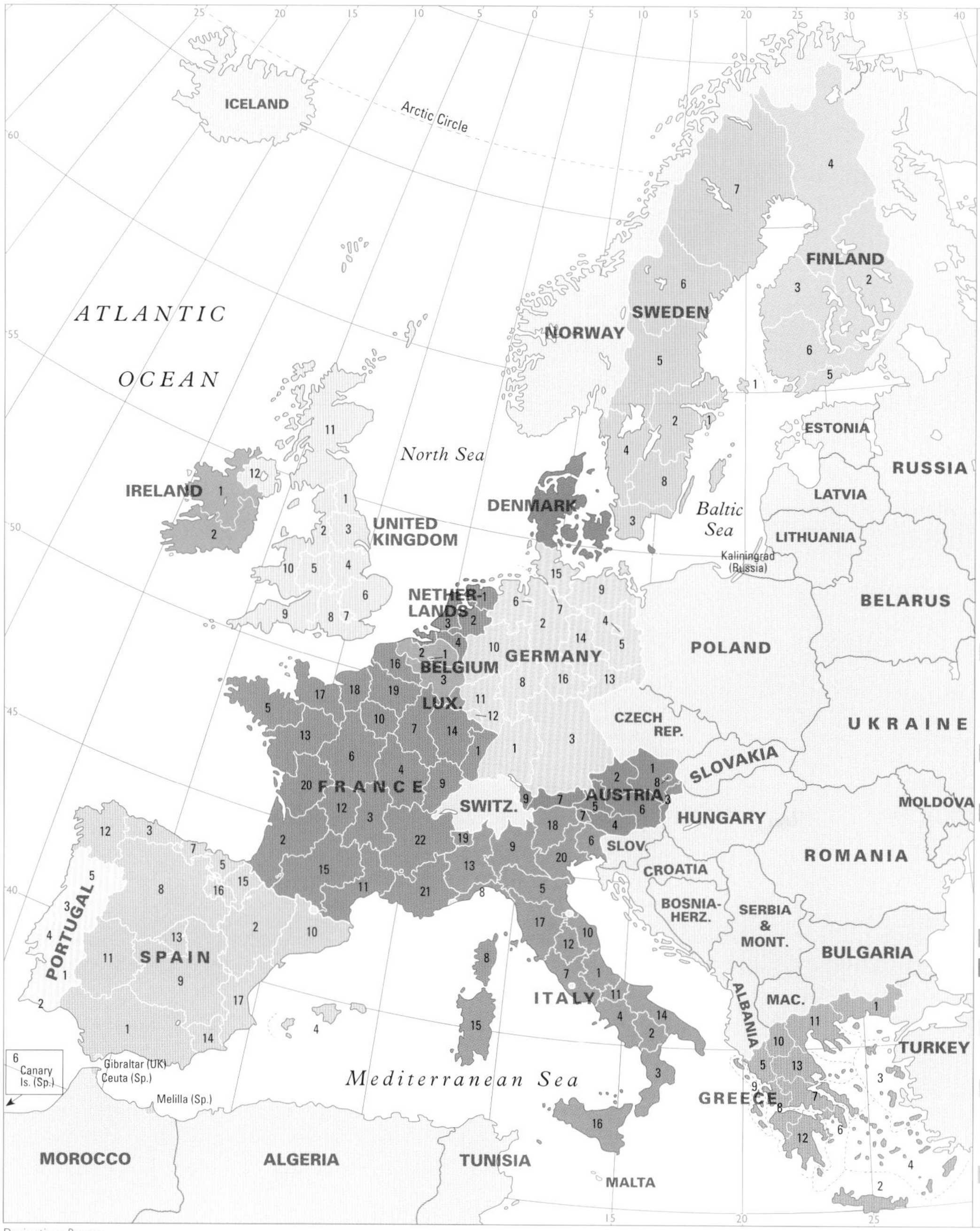
ICELAND
Arctic Circle
ATLANTIC OCEAN
NORWAY
SWEDEN
FINLAND
ESTONIA
RUSSIA
LATVIA
LITHUANIA
Kaliningrad (Russia)
BELARUS
North Sea
IRELAND
UNITED KINGDOM
DENMARK
Baltic Sea
NETHERLANDS
POLAND
BELGIUM
GERMANY
LUX.
CZECH REP.
UKRAINE
SLOVAKIA
MOLDOVA
FRANCE
SWITZ.
AUSTRIA
HUNGARY
SLOV.
CROATIA
ROMANIA
BOSNIA-HERZ.
SERBIA & MONT.
BULGARIA
PORTUGAL
SPAIN
ITALY
ALBANIA
MAC.
TURKEY
GREECE
Canary Is. (Sp.)
Gibraltar (UK)
Ceuta (Sp.)
Melilla (Sp.)
Mediterranean Sea
MOROCCO
ALGERIA
TUNISIA
MALTA

Projection: Bonne

## REGIONS OF THE EU

**Germany** *(Länder)* **D**
1 Baden-Württemberg
2 Niedersachsen
3 Bayern
4 Berlin
5 Brandenburg
6 Bremen
7 Hamburg
8 Hessen
9 Mecklenburg-Vorpommern
10 Nordrhein-Westfalen
11 Rheinland-Pfalz
12 Saarland
13 Sachsen
14 Sachsen-Anhalt
15 Schleswig-Holstein
16 Thüringen

**Austria** *(States)* **A**
1 Niederösterreich
2 Oberösterreich
3 Burgenland
4 Kärnten
5 Salzburg
6 Steiermark
7 Tirol
8 Wien
9 Vorarlberg

**Belgium** *(Regions)* **B**
1 Bruxelles
2 Vlaanderen
3 Wallonie

**Denmark** *(member state with no corresponding division)* **DK**

**Spain** *(Autonomous communities)* **E**
1 Andalucía
2 Aragon
3 Asturias
4 Islas Baleares
5 Pais Vasco
6 Islas Canarias
7 Cantabria
8 Castilla y Léon
9 Castilla-La Mancha
10 Cataluña
11 Extremadura
12 Galicia
13 Madrid
14 Murcia
15 Navarra
16 Rioja (La)
17 Valencia

**Finland** *(Provinces)* **FIN**
1 Åland
2 Itä-Suomi
3 Väli-Suomi
4 Pohjois-Suomi
5 Uusimaa (Suuralue)
6 Etelä-Suomi

**France** *(Regions)* **F**
1 Alsace
2 Aquitaine
3 Auvergne
4 Bourgogne
5 Bretagne
6 Centre
7 Champagne-Ardenne
8 Corse
9 Franche-Comté
10 Île-de-France
11 Languedoc-Roussillon
12 Limousin
13 Loire (Pays de la)
14 Lorraine
15 Midi-Pyrénées
16 Nord-Pas-de-Calais
17 Normandie (Basse-)
18 Normandie (Haute-)
19 Picardie
20 Poitou-Charentes
21 Provence-Alpes-Côte d'Azur
22 Rhône-Alpes

**Greece** *(Regions)* **EL**
1 Anatoliki-Makedhonia-Kai Thraki
2 Kríti
3 Vórios Aiyaíon
4 Notios Aiyaíon
5 Ípiros
6 Attikí
7 Stereá Ellas
8 Dytiki Ellas
9 Iónioi Nísoi
10 Kentriki Makedhonia
11 Dytiki Makedhonia
12 Pelopónnisos
13 Thessalia

**Ireland** *(Provinces)* **IRL**
1 Border, Midlands & Western
2 Southern & Eastern

**Italy** *(Regions)* **I**
1 Abruzzo
2 Basilicata
3 Calábria
4 Campània
5 Emília-Romagna
6 Friuli-Venézia Giulia
7 Lazio
8 Liguria
9 Lombardia
10 Marche
11 Molise
12 Umbria
13 Piemonte
14 Puglia
15 Sardegna
16 Sicilia
17 Toscana
18 Trentino-Alto Adige
19 Valle d'Aosta
20 Venéto

**Luxembourg** *(member state with no corresponding division)* **L**

**Netherlands** *(Regions)* **NL**
1 Noord-Nederland
2 Oost-Nederland
3 West-Nederland
4 Zuid-Nederland

**Portugal** *(Autonomous regions)* **P**
1 Alentejo
2 Algarve
3 Centro
4 Lisboa-Vale do Tejo
5 Norte

**United Kingdom** *(Government Office Regions)* **UK**
1 North East
2 North West
3 Yorkshire & The Humber
4 East Midlands
5 West Midlands
6 Eastern
7 London
8 South East
9 South West
10 Wales
11 Scotland
12 Northern Ireland

**Sweden** *(Regions)* **S**
1 Stockholm
2 Östra Mellansverige
3 Sydsverige
4 Västsverige
5 Norra Mellansverige
6 Mellersta Norrland
7 Övre Norrland
8 Småland med öarna

# WEALTH

Gross Domestic
Product expressed as
Purchasing Power
Parity in Euros per
capita (2000)

- Over 35,000
- 30,000 – 35,000
- 25,000 – 30,000
- 20,000 – 25,000
- 15,000 – 20,000
- Under 15,000

Government debt as
percentage of GDP
(2001)

| | |
|---|---|
| Italy | 109.8% |
| Belgium | 107.6% |
| Greece | 107.0% |
| Austria | 63.2% |
| Germany | 59.5% |
| UK | 39.0% |

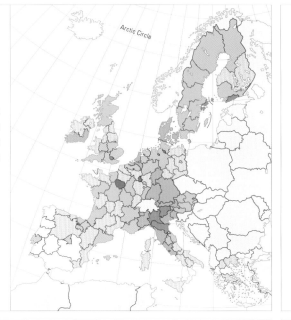

# HEALTH

Number of doctors
per thousand
inhabitants (2000)

- Over 7
- 6 – 7
- 5 – 6
- 4 – 5
- 3 – 4
- 2 – 3
- Under 2

Deaths by circulatory
causes, deaths per
100,000 by country
(1999)

- Over 500
- 400 – 500
- 300 – 400
- Under 300

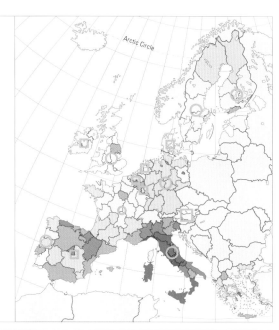

# OUT OF WORK

The percentage of
the workforce
unemployed (2001)

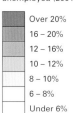

- Over 20%
- 16 – 20%
- 12 – 16%
- 10 – 12%
- 8 – 10%
- 6 – 8%
- Under 6%

Unemployment rate
for people under
25 years old (2001)

- Over 30%
- 20 – 30%
- Under 20%

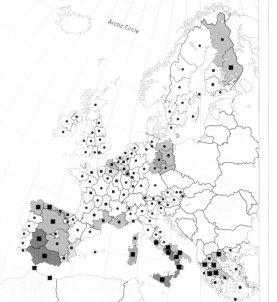

# EDUCATION

The percentage of
people aged 15 – 24
in education (2000)

- Over 70%
- 60 – 70%
- 50 – 60%
- 40 – 50%
- 30 – 40%
- Under 30%

Expenditure on
education as
percentage of GDP by
country (1995–97)

- Over 7%
- 5% – 7%
- Under 5%

# TRANSPORT

Airports with over
10 million passengers
a year (2000)

- 50 million
- 25 million
- 10 million

— European high-
speed rail
network built or
planned for 2010

Planned journey times
by rail from London

| | 1990 | 2010 |
|---|---|---|
| Amsterdam | 7 h 38 | 3 h 45 |
| Barcelona | 20 h 00 | 6 h 40 |
| Berlin | 16 h 35 | 8 h 25 |
| Brussels | 4 h 55 | 2 h 05 |
| Bordeaux | 9 h 48 | 4 h 45 |
| Frankfurt | 11 h 26 | 5 h 00 |
| Lyons | 9 h 04 | 4 h 00 |
| Madrid | 21 h 32 | 9 h 20 |
| Paris | 5 h 15 | 2 h 10 |
| Venice | 20 h 45 | 7 h 45 |

# INDUSTRY

The percentage
of the workforce
employed in
industry (2001)

- Over 40%
- 35 – 40%
- 30 – 35%
- 25 – 30%
- 20 – 25%
- Under 20%

**SERVICES**
Percentage of total
employment in
services by country
(2001)

- Over 75%
- 65 – 75%
- Under 65%

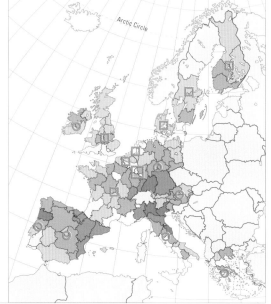

ction: Bonne        Data Source: Eurostat 2000–1        COPYRIGHT PHILIP'S

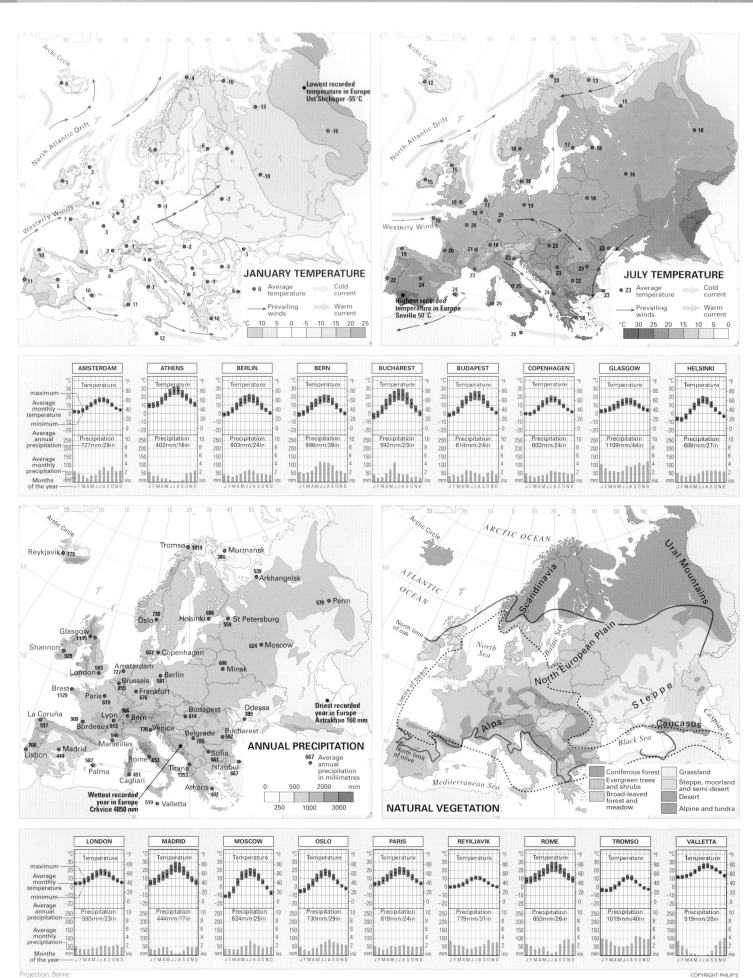

**JANUARY TEMPERATURE**

Lowest recorded temperature in Europe Ust'Shchugor -55°C

- 6 Average temperature
- Prevailing winds
- Cold current
- Warm current

°C 10 5 0 -5 -10 -15 -20 -25

**JULY TEMPERATURE**

Highest recorded temperature in Europe Seville 50°C

- 23 Average temperature
- Prevailing winds
- Cold current
- Warm current

°C 30 25 20 15 10 5 0

AMSTERDAM · ATHENS · BERLIN · BERN · BUCHAREST · BUDAPEST · COPENHAGEN · GLASGOW · HELSINKI

Temperature — maximum / Average monthly temperature / minimum
Precipitation — Average annual precipitation
Average monthly precipitation
Months of the year — J F M A M J J A S O N D

Precipitation 727mm/29in · 402mm/16in · 603mm/24in · 986mm/39in · 592mm/23in · 614mm/24in · 603mm/24in · 1109mm/44in · 688mm/27in

**ANNUAL PRECIPITATION**

Tromsø 1019 · Murmansk 386
Reykjavik 779
539 Arkhangelsk
570 Perm
730 Oslo · 688 Helsinki · St Petersburg 559
624 Moscow
Glasgow 1109
Shannon 929
603 Copenhagen
606 Minsk
593 Amsterdam 727
London
Brussels 855
Brest 1129 · Berlin 581 · Frankfurt 676
Paris 619
986 Bern
La Coruña 900 · Lyon 813
Bordeaux 937 · 770 Venice
546 Budapest 614
Marseilles · Belgrade 700 · Odessa 389
708 Madrid 444 · Bucharest 592
Lisbon · 587 Rome 653 · Sofia 661
Palma · 451 Cagliari · Tirana 1353 · Istanbul 667
Athens 402
519 Valletta

Driest recorded year in Europe Astrakhan 160 mm

Wettest recorded year in Europe Crkvice 4850 mm

667 Average annual precipitation in millimetres

0 · 250 · 500 · 1000 · 2000 · 3000 mm

**NATURAL VEGETATION**

ARCTIC OCEAN
ATLANTIC OCEAN
Scandinavia
Ural Mountains
North limit of oak
North Sea
Baltic Sea
North European Plain
Steppe
Limits of beech
Caucasus
Caspian Sea
Alps
Black Sea
North limit of olive
Mediterranean Sea

- Coniferous forest
- Evergreen trees and shrubs
- Broad-leaved forest and meadow
- Grassland
- Steppe, moorland and semi-desert
- Desert
- Alpine and tundra

LONDON · MADRID · MOSCOW · OSLO · PARIS · REYKJAVIK · ROME · TROMSO · VALLETTA

Temperature — maximum / Average monthly temperature / minimum
Precipitation — Average annual precipitation
Average monthly precipitation
Months of the year — J F M A M J J A S O N D

Precipitation 593mm/23in · 444mm/17in · 624mm/25in · 730mm/29in · 619mm/24in · 779mm/31in · 653mm/26in · 1019mm/40in · 519mm/20in

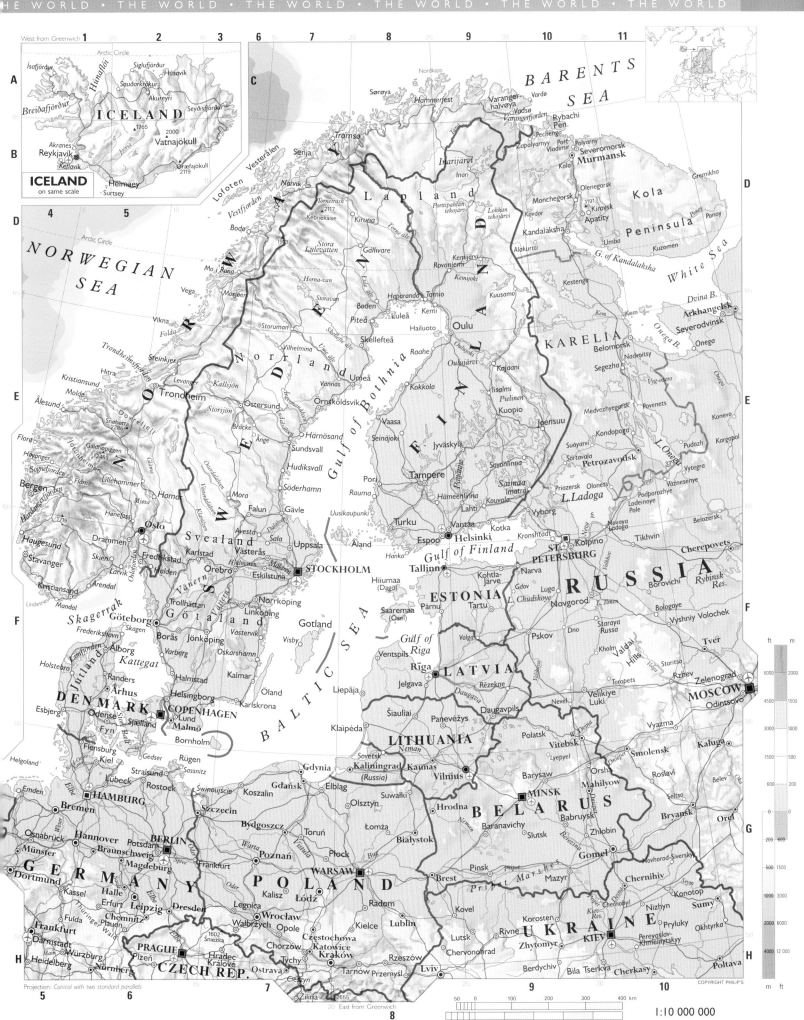

Projection: Conical with two standard parallels

1:5 000 000

East from Greenwich
COPYRIGHT PHILIP'S

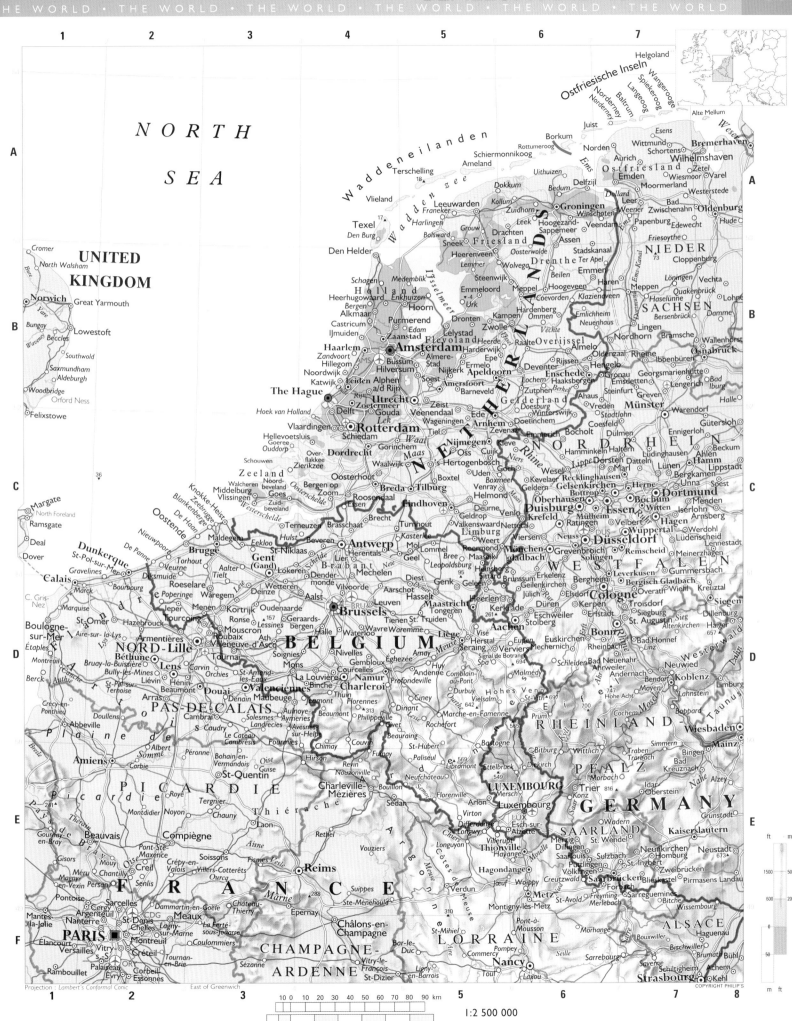

1:2 500 000

East from Greenwich

COPYRIGHT PHILIP'S

1:5 000 000

50  25  0  25  50  75  100  125  150  175 km
50  0  25  50  75  100  125 miles

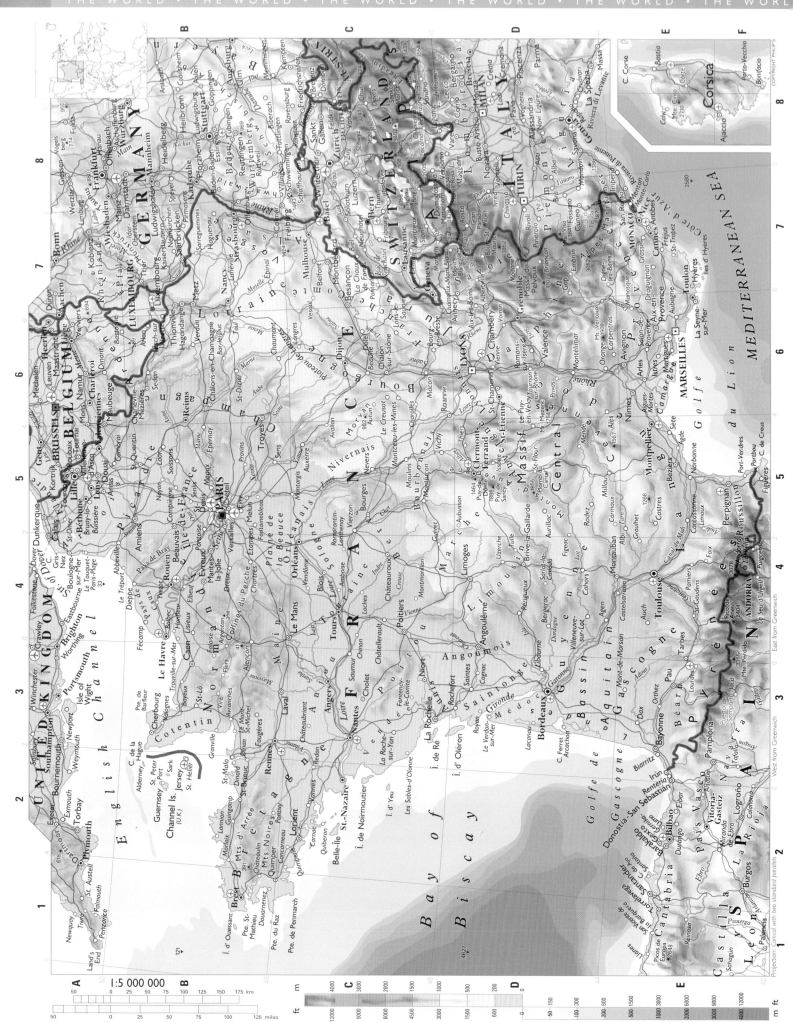

1:5 000 000

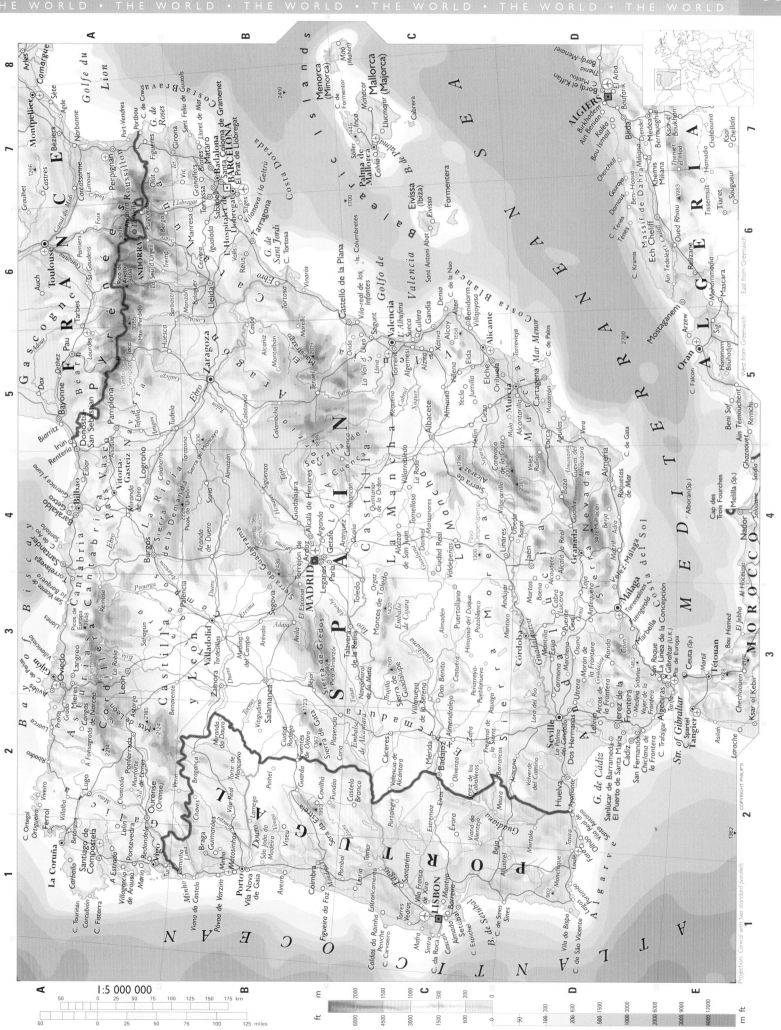

1:5 000 000

Projection: Conical with two standard parallels

East from Greenwich

1:5 000 000

1:10 000 000

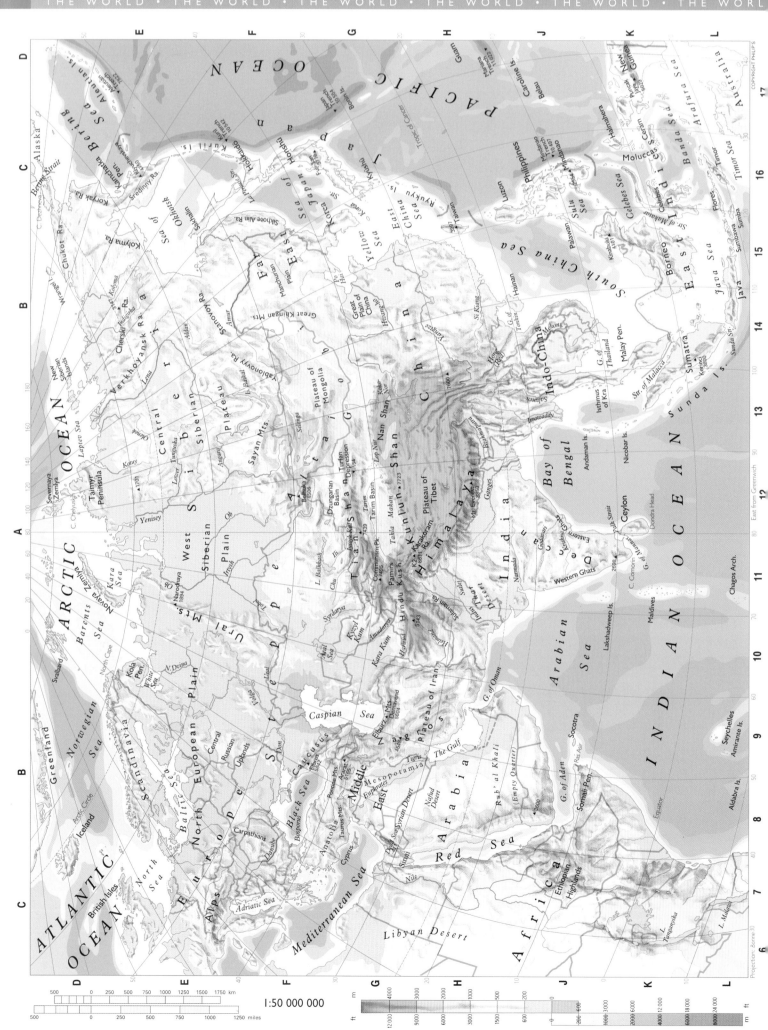

1:50 000 000

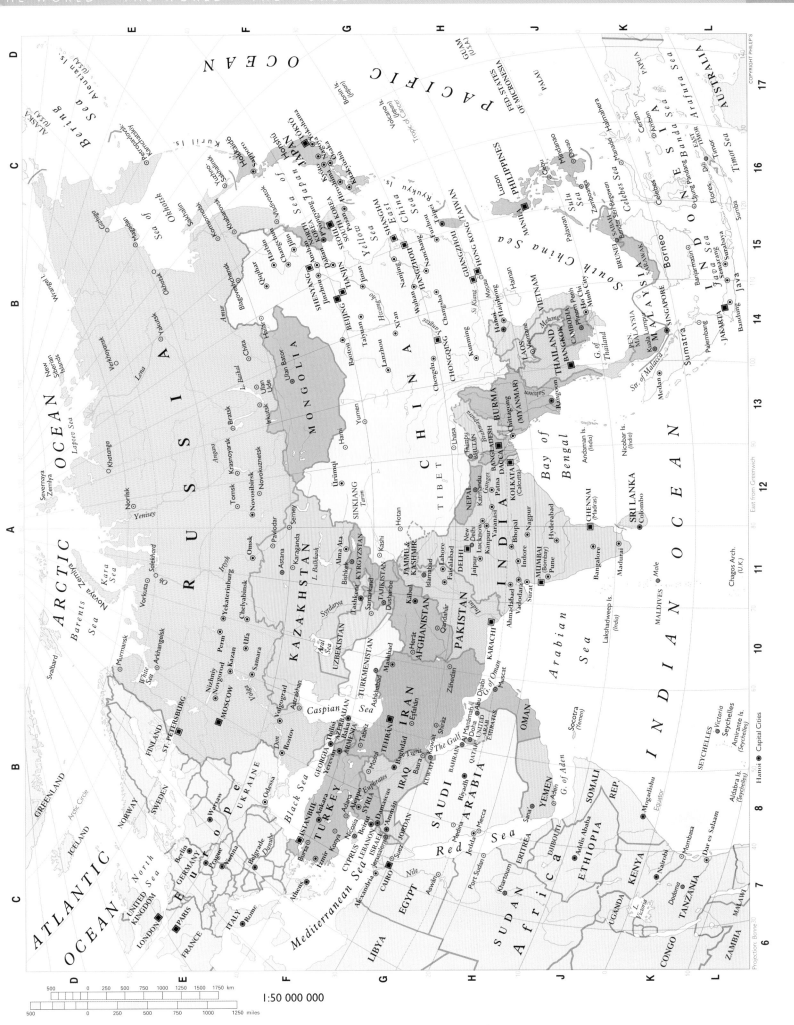

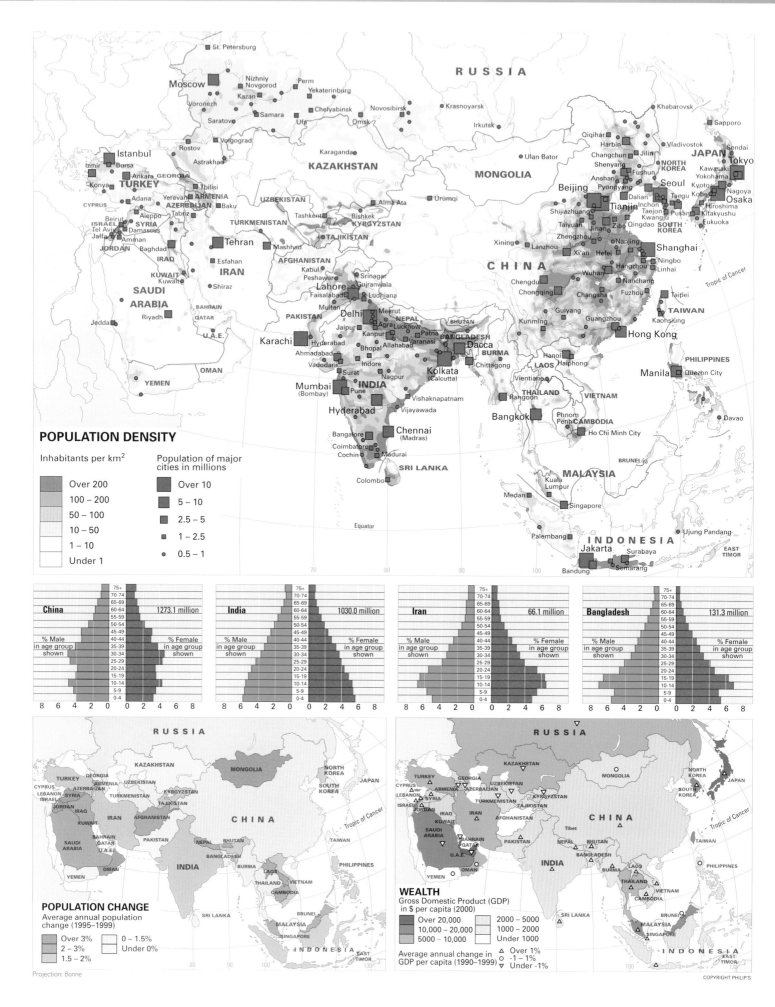

## POPULATION DENSITY

Inhabitants per km²

Over 200
100 – 200
50 – 100
10 – 50
1 – 10
Under 1

Population of major cities in millions

Over 10
5 – 10
2.5 – 5
1 – 2.5
0.5 – 1

**China** 1273.1 million
% Male in age group shown / % Female in age group shown

**India** 1030.0 million
% Male in age group shown / % Female in age group shown

**Iran** 66.1 million
% Male in age group shown / % Female in age group shown

**Bangladesh** 131.3 million
% Male in age group shown / % Female in age group shown

75+ / 70-74 / 65-69 / 60-64 / 55-59 / 50-54 / 45-49 / 40-44 / 35-39 / 30-34 / 25-29 / 20-24 / 15-19 / 10-14 / 5-9 / 0-4

8 6 4 2 0 2 4 6 8

## POPULATION CHANGE

Average annual population change (1995–1999)

Over 3%
2 – 3%
1.5 – 2%
0 – 1.5%
Under 0%

## WEALTH

Gross Domestic Product (GDP) in $ per capita (2000)

Over 20,000
10,000 – 20,000
5000 – 10,000
2000 – 5000
1000 – 2000
Under 1000

Average annual change in GDP per capita (1990–1999)

△ Over 1%
○ -1 – 1%
▽ Under -1%

Projection: Bonne

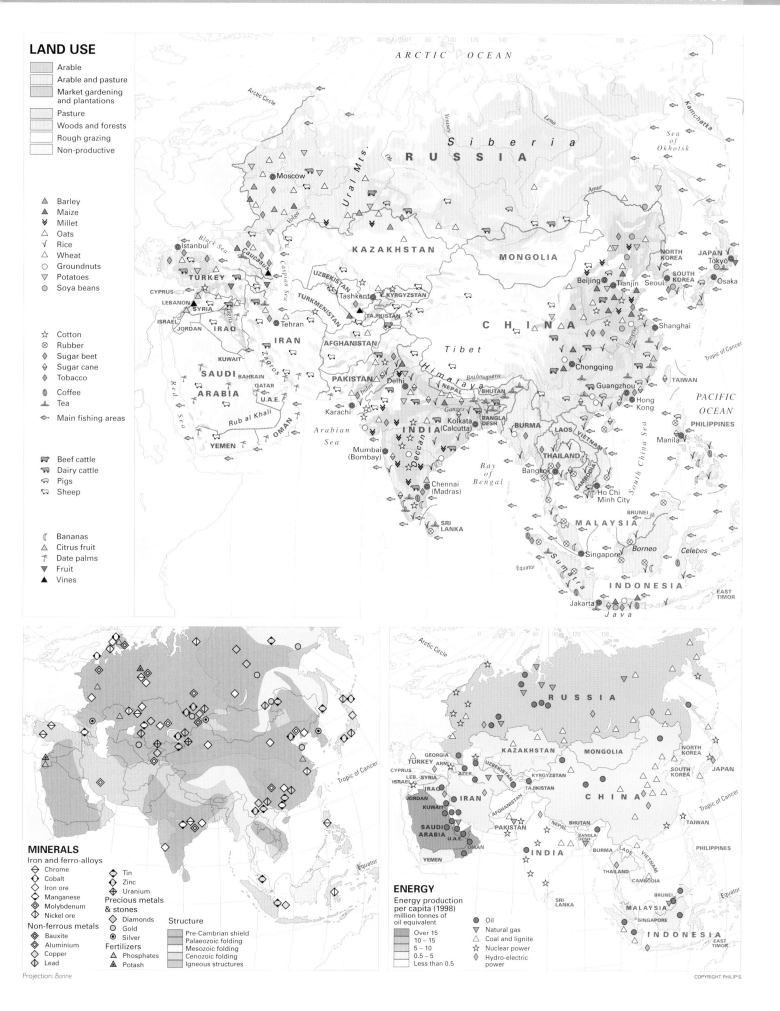

## LAND USE

- Arable
- Arable and pasture
- Market gardening and plantations
- Pasture
- Woods and forests
- Rough grazing
- Non-productive

- △ Barley
- ▲ Maize
- ⋎ Millet
- △ Oats
- √ Rice
- △ Wheat
- ○ Groundnuts
- ▽ Potatoes
- ⬤ Soya beans

- ☆ Cotton
- ⊗ Rubber
- ◇ Sugar beet
- ◇ Sugar cane
- ◇ Tobacco
- ● Coffee
- ⚘ Tea
- ⬱ Main fishing areas

- Beef cattle
- Dairy cattle
- Pigs
- Sheep

- ☾ Bananas
- △ Citrus fruit
- ⫟ Date palms
- ▽ Fruit
- ▲ Vines

### MINERALS
Iron and ferro-alloys
- ◇ Chrome
- ◇ Cobalt
- ◇ Iron ore
- ◇ Manganese
- ◈ Molybdenum
- ◇ Nickel ore

Non-ferrous metals
- ◈ Bauxite
- ◈ Aluminium
- ◇ Copper
- ◇ Lead
- ◇ Tin
- ◇ Zinc
- ⊕ Uranium

Precious metals & stones
- ◇ Diamonds
- ◯ Gold
- ⊙ Silver

Fertilizers
- △ Phosphates
- ▲ Potash

Structure
- Pre-Cambrian shield
- Palaeozoic folding
- Mesozoic folding
- Cenozoic folding
- Igneous structures

### ENERGY
Energy production per capita (1998)
million tonnes of oil equivalent

- Over 15
- 10 – 15
- 5 – 10
- 0.5 – 5
- Less than 0.5

- ● Oil
- ▽ Natural gas
- △ Coal and lignite
- ☆ Nuclear power
- ◇ Hydro-electric power

Projection: *Bonne*

COPYRIGHT PHILIP'S

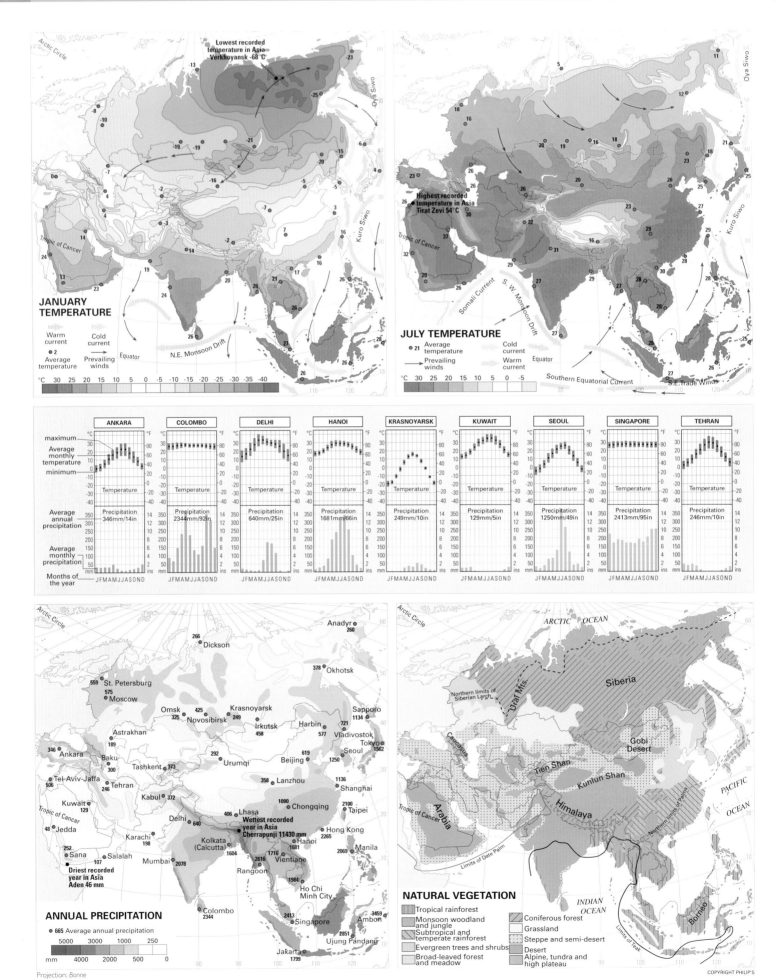

## JANUARY TEMPERATURE

Lowest recorded temperature in Asia Verkhoyansk -68°C

Warm current
Cold current
● 2 Average temperature
Prevailing winds
Equator
N.E. Monsoon Drift

°C 30 25 20 15 10 5 0 -5 -10 -15 -20 -25 -30 -35 -40

## JULY TEMPERATURE

Highest recorded temperature in Asia Tirat Zevi 54°C

● 21 Average temperature
Prevailing winds
Cold current
Warm current
Equator
Somali Current
S.W. Monsoon Drift
Southern Equatorial Current
S.E. Trade Winds

°C 30 25 20 15 10 5 0 -5

### Climate graphs

ANKARA — Temperature — Precipitation 346mm/14in
COLOMBO — Temperature — Precipitation 2344mm/92in
DELHI — Temperature — Precipitation 640mm/25in
HANOI — Temperature — Precipitation 1681mm/66in
KRASNOYARSK — Temperature — Precipitation 249mm/10in
KUWAIT — Temperature — Precipitation 129mm/5in
SEOUL — Temperature — Precipitation 1250mm/49in
SINGAPORE — Temperature — Precipitation 2413mm/95in
TEHRAN — Temperature — Precipitation 246mm/10in

maximum
Average monthly temperature
minimum
Average annual precipitation
Average monthly precipitation
Months of the year

JFMAMJJASOND

## ANNUAL PRECIPITATION

Anadyr 260
Dickson 266
Okhotsk 378
St. Petersburg 559
Moscow 575
Omsk 325
Novosibirsk 425
Krasnoyarsk 249
Irkutsk 458
Sapporo 1134
Harbin 577
Vladivostok 721
Tokyo 1562
Astrakhan 189
Ankara 346
Baku 300
Tashkent 373
Urumqi 292
Beijing 619
Seoul 1250
Tel-Aviv-Jaffa 506
Tehran 246
Kabul 372
Lanzhou 358
Shanghai 1136
Lhasa 406
Chongqing 1090
Taipei 2100
Kuwait 129
Delhi 640
Wettest recorded year in Asia Cherrapunji 11430 mm
Hong Kong 2265
Jedda 48
Karachi 198
Kolkata (Calcutta) 1604
Hanoi 1681
Manila 2069
Sana 252
Salalah 107
Mumbai 2078
Rangoon 2616
Vientiane 1716
Driest recorded year in Asia Aden 46 mm
Ho Chi Minh City 1984
Colombo 2344
Singapore 2413
Ambon 3459
Ujung Pandang 2851
Jakarta 1799

● 665 Average annual precipitation

mm 5000 4000 3000 2000 1000 500 250 0

## NATURAL VEGETATION

ARCTIC OCEAN
Siberia
Ural Mts.
Northern limits of Siberian Larch
Gobi Desert
Caucasus
Tien Shan
Kunlun Shan
Arabia
Tropic of Cancer
Himalaya
Northern limits of Palms
PACIFIC OCEAN
Limits of Date Palm
INDIAN OCEAN
Borneo
Limits of Teak

Tropical rainforest
Monsoon woodland and jungle
Subtropical and temperate rainforest
Evergreen trees and shrubs
Broad-leaved forest and meadow
Coniferous forest
Grassland
Steppe and semi-desert
Desert
Alpine, tundra and high plateau

Projection: Bonne

COPYRIGHT PHILIP'S

1:35 000 000

COPYRIGHT PHILIP'S

1:15 000 000

CHINA

RUSSIA

Linkou
Novokachalinsk
Kamen-Rybolov
L. Khanka
Spassk Dalniy
Suifenhe
Lipovcy
Manzovka
Ussuriysk
Arsenev
Kavalerovo
Lesozavodsk
Kirovskiy
Ariadnoye
Rakitnoye
Terney
Plastun
Dalnegorsk
1855
Trudovoye
Yakovleyka
Margaritovo
1498
Vladivostok
Slavyanka
Nakhodka
Preobrazheniye
Khasan
Najin
Chŏngjin

NORTH KOREA

SEA OF JAPAN

(EAST SEA)

JAPAN

Ullŭng-do (S. Korea)
Tok-do

SOUTH KOREA

Pohang

Korea Strait

Tsushima (Japan)
Iki
Karatsu
Imari
Goto-Retto
Fukue-Shima
Sasebo
Isahaya
Nagasaki
Yatsushiro
Amakusa-Shoto
Ushibuka
Koshikijima-Retto
Sata-Misaki

Wakkanai
Rebun-To
Rishiri-To
Teshio
Haboro
Rumoi
Embetsu
Otoineppu
Esashi
Ōmu
Mombetsu
Yūbetsu
Nayoro
Engaru
Abashiri-Wan
Abashiri
Rausu-Dake 1661
Nemuro
Kunashir
Nakashibetsu
Shibecha
Akkeshi
Kushiro
Hiroo
Samani
Erimo-misaki
Muroran
Tomakomai
SAPPORO
Otaru
Iwanai
Suttsu
Setana
Okushiri-To
Yakumo
Esashi
Matsumae
Hakodate
Esan-Misaki
Asahigawa 2290
Daisetsu-Zan 2077
Hokkaidō
Takikawa
Bibai
Iwamizawa
Ebetsu
Obihiro
Poroshiri-Dake 2052
Honbetsu
Kitami
Shari
Ishikari-Wan
Kamui-Misaki
Shikotu-Ko
Toya-Ko
Uchiura-Wan

Tsugaru Strait
Shiriya-Zaki
Matsumae
Shiragami-Misaki
Ohata
Mutsu
Mutsu-Wan
Kanagi
Goshogawara
Aomori
Henashi-Misaki
Towada-Ko
Towada
Hachinohe
Hirosaki
Odate
Kuji
Iwaizumi
Noshiro
Oga
Iwate-San 2041
Morioka
Miyako
Oga-Hantō
Akita
Omagari
1914
Kamaishi
Honjō
Hanamaki
Sakata
2230
Ichinoseki
Kesennuma
Tsuruoka
Minami-Gawa 1980
Furukawa
Ishinomaki
Yamagata
Sendai
Sendai-Wan
Sōma
Haranomachi
Niigata
Shibata
Fukushima
Aizuwakamatsu
Kōriyama
Higashiyama-San 2024
Honshū
Sado
Ryōtsu
Aikawa
Niitsu
Sanjo
Nagaoka
Sukagawa
Iwaki
Tokamachi
Tajima
2578
Tanakura
Kitaibaraki
Hitachi
Wajima
Suzu-Misaki
Suzu-Wan
Takada
Nagano
Maebashi
Kiryū
Utsunomiya
Mito
Nanao
Toyama-Wan
Himi
Toyama
Matsumoto
Takasaki
Kumagaya
Kawagoe
Tsuchiura
Takaoka
Hodaka-Dake 3190
Ina
3063
Kōfu
Fuji-San 3776
Odawara
YOKOHAMA
Yokosuka
Kanazawa
Komatsu
Takayama
2782
Takada
TŌKYŌ
KAWASAKI
Funabashi
Chiba
Ichihara
Fukui
3192
Numazu
Itō
Ō-Shima
Takefu
Tsuruga
Iida
Fuji
Shizuoka
Tateyama
Nojima-Zaki
Kyō-ga-Saki
Wakasa-Wan
Maizuru
Ōgaki
Gifu
Ichinomiya
Toyota
Okazaki
Toyohashi
Iwata
Hamamatsu
Suruga-Wan
Irō-Zaki
Izu-Shotō
Nii-Jima
Matsue
Yonago
Tottori
Toyooka
Fukuchiyama
Ayabe
NAGOYA
Yokkaichi
Izumo
Ōda
1712
Tsuyama
KYŌTO
Ōtsu
Matsusaka
Miyake-Jima
Hamada
Masuda
Fuchū
Himeji
Amagasaki
Higashiosaka
Ise-Wan
Chūgoku-Sanchi
Okayama
KOBE
ŌSAKA
Izumi-Sano
Owase
Daiō-Misaki
Aoga-Shima
HIROSHIMA
Fukuyama
Takamatsu
Naruto
Wakayama
Yamaguchi
Iwakuni
Kure
Marugame
Awaji-Shima
Tokushima
1915
Tanabe
Shimonoseki
Ube
Tokuyama
Imabari
Ikeda
Anan
Shingū
Hachijō-Jima
Hōfu
Matsuyama
1955
Mugi
Kushimoto
Kii Channel
Shio-no-Misaki
KITAKYŪSHŪ
Nōgata
Buzen
FUKUOKA
Kōchi
Muroto
Saga
Kurume
Beppu
Ōita
Yawatahama
Tosa-Wan
Muroto-Misaki
Ōmuta
1787
Saiki
Uwajima
Shikoku
Kumamoto
Nakamura
Sukumo
Ashizuri-Zaki
Minamata
Nobeoka
Hyūga
Miyazaki
Miyakonojō
Kagoshima
Nichinan
Kanoya
Ibusuki
Makurazaki
Sendai
Bungo Channel
Inland Sea
Kyūshū

PACIFIC OCEAN

Nampo-Shoto

8412
9076

ft     m
9000  3000
6000  2000
4500  1500
3000  1000
1200   400
600    200
0      0
600    200
6000   2000
12000  4000
18000  6000
24000  8000
ft     m

Projection: Conical with two standard parallels    East from Greenwich

50  0  25  50  75  100  125  150  175 km
50     0     25     50     75     100  125 miles

1:6 400 000

COPYRIGHT PHILIP'S

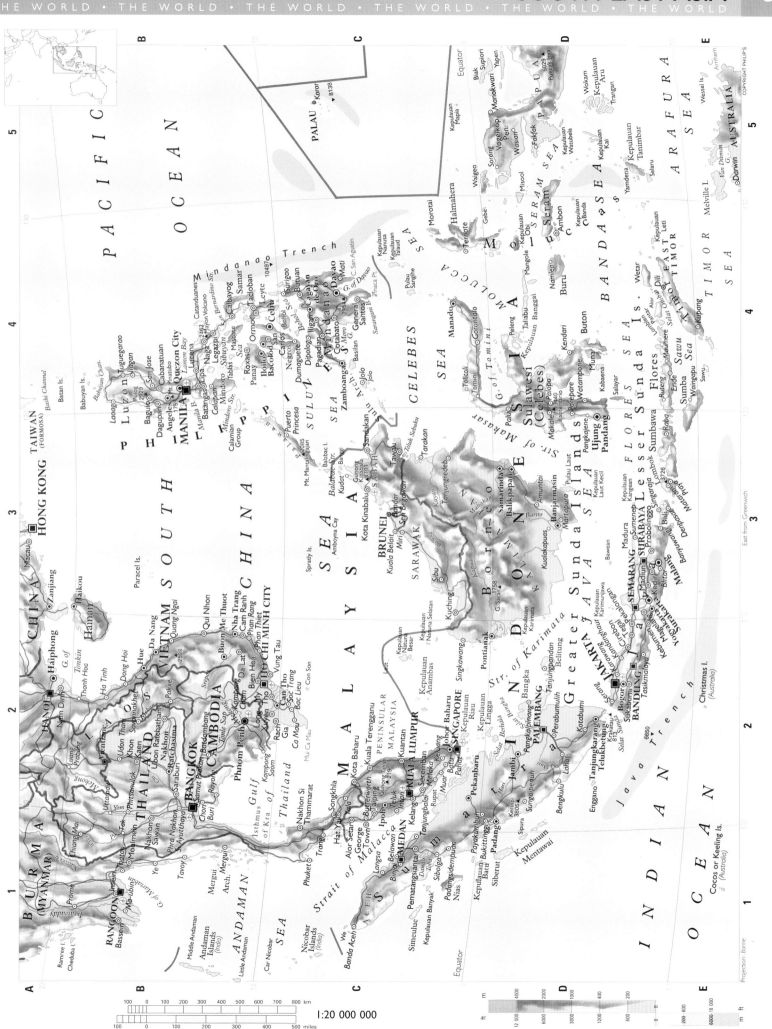

Projection: Bonne

1:20 000 000

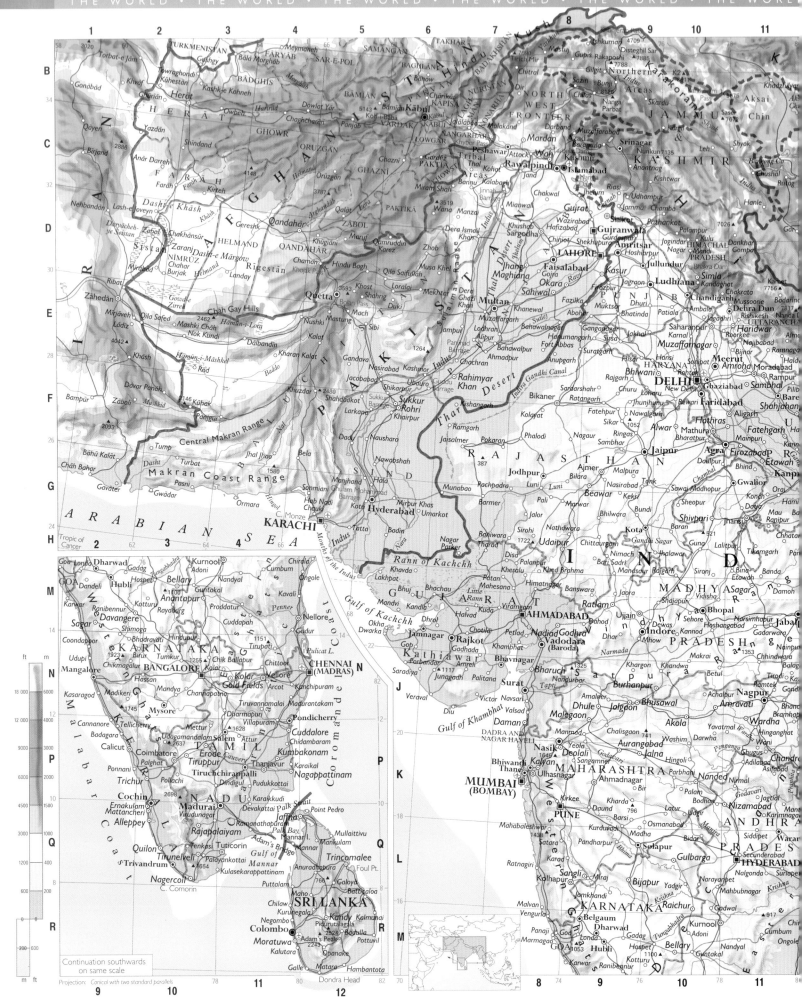

SINKIANG

Pulu

nlun Shan

Kun lun

Tibet

QINGHAI

Ngoring Hu

Hwang-ho

Dogai Coring

Gyaring Hu

6094

T I B E T

C H I (Dangla) Shan

N A

Yushu

Dainkog

Garzê

Tanggula

Tanggula Shankou

Nangqen

(X I Z A N G)

Bagên

Dêngqên

Qamdo

Baiyü

Xinlong

SICHUAN

Mapam Yumco

Ombu

Silling Co

Nagqu

Lhorong

Zhaxizê

Ningjing

Yidun

Litang

Yajiang

Coqên

Xainza

Nam Co

Gongbo'gyamda

Lhari

Zhongdian

Nyainqentanglha Shan

Lhasa

Tsangpo (Brahmaputra)

Namcha

Riga

Weixi

Lijiang

NEPAL

Mustang

Muktinath

Xigaze

Gyangze

Nang Xian

Cona

Kangto

ARUNACHAL PRADESH

Putao

Konglu

Jianchuan

Katmandu

Bhaktapur

SIKKIM

BHUTAN

Thimphu

Gangtok

Punakha

A S S A M

Guwahati

KACHIN

YUNNAN

Yunlong

Baoshan

Tengchong

Changning

Lucknow

Faizabad

Gorakhpur

Darbhanga

Biratnagar

Shiliguri

Jalpaiguri

Koch Bihar

Goalpara

Brahmapur

Shillong

NAGALAND

Kohima

Myitkyina

Mogaung

Bhamo

Longling

Patna

B I H A R

Gaya

Bhagalpur

Dinajpur

B A N G L A D E S H

Rangpur

Tura

MEGHALAYA

Cherrapunji

SYLHET

MANIPUR

Imphal

Shwegu

Katha

JHARKHAND

Ranchi

Jamshedpur

Asansol

Durgapur

WEST BENGAL

DHAKA

TRIPURA

Agartala

MIZORAM

Aizawl

CHIN

Mandalay

CHHATTISGARH

Raipur

ORISSA

KOLKATA (CALCUTTA)

Haora

BARISAL

Chittagong

B U R M A

(M Y A N M A R)

SHAN

Taunggyi

Brahmapur

Cuttack

Bhubaneswar

Puri

The Sundarbans

Mouths of the Ganges

Cox's Bazar

ARAKAN

Sittwe (Akyab)

MAGWE

PEGU

KAYAH

THAILAND

Chiang Mai

Vishakhapatnam

B A Y   O F   B E N G A L

Irrawaddy

RANGOON

MON

Moulmein

IRRAWADDY

Bassein

G. of Martaban

Amherst

I N D I A N   O C E A N

Preparis North Channel

Pariparit Kyun (Burma)

Mouths of the Irrawaddy

Ye

Sangkhla

Koko Kyunzu (Burma)

Tavoy

East from Greenwich

1:10 000 000

COPYRIGHT PHILIP'S

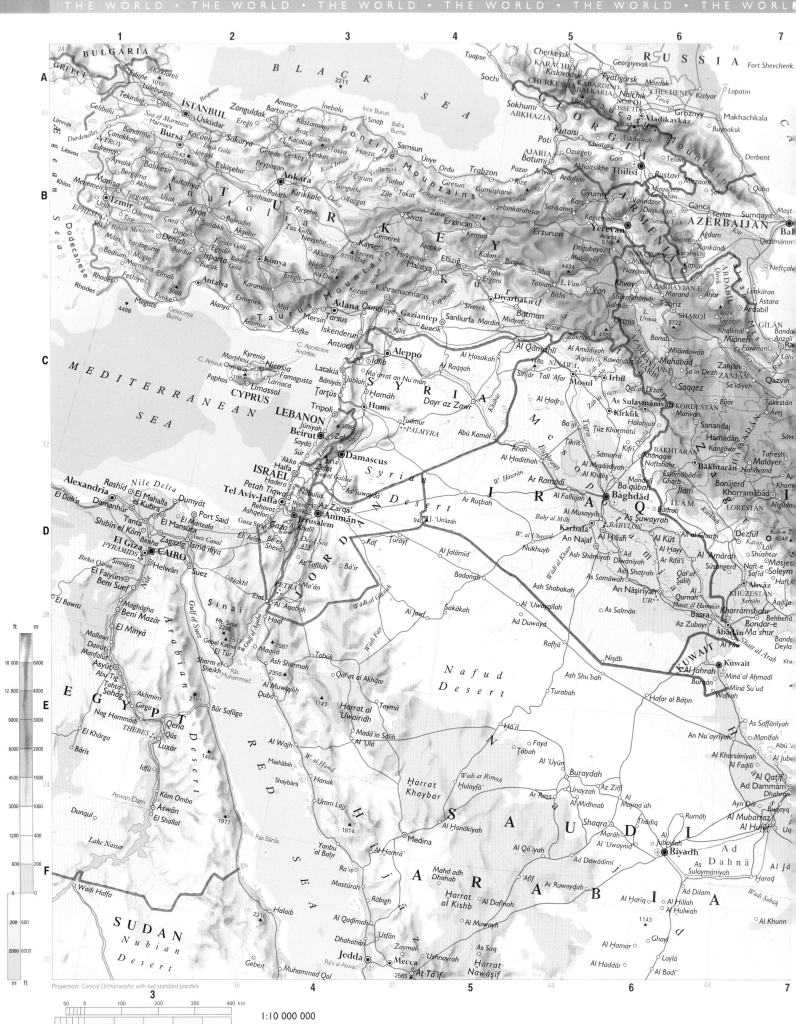

Projection: Conical Orthomorphic with two standard parallels

1:10 000 000

50   0   100   200   300   400 km

50   0   50   100   150   200   250 miles

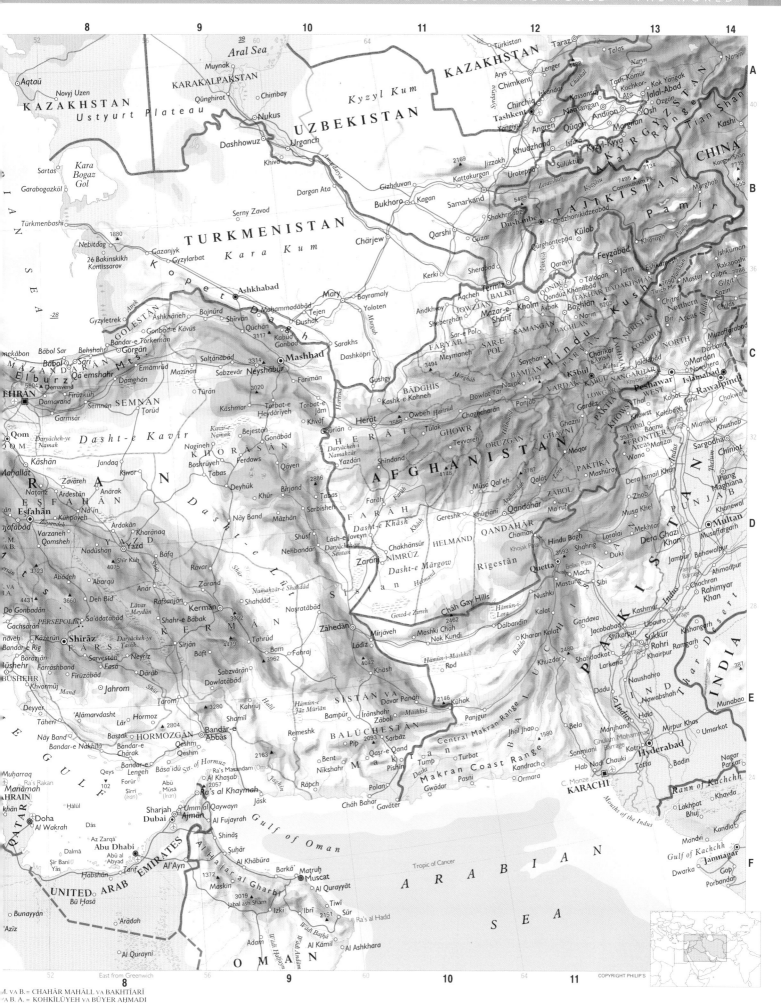

KAZAKHSTAN

KARAKALPAKSTAN

Aral Sea

KAZAKHSTAN

Türkistan          Taraz

Talas

Aqtaū          Novyj Uzen

Muynak

Chimbay

Kyzyl Kum

Chirchiq     Tashkent

CHINA

KYRGYZSTAN     Tian Shan

Ustyurt Plateau

Qünghirot          Nukus

UZBEKISTAN

Dashhowuz

Khiva          Urganch

Kara Bogaz Gol

Garabogazköl

Sartas

TURKMENISTAN

TAJIKISTAN     Pamir

Dushanbe

Türkmenbashi

Kara Kum

Ashkhabad

Mary

Bayramaly

Nebitdag

26 Bakinskikh Komissarov

Gyzylarbat

Kopet Dagh

TEHRAN

MAZANDARAN     Elburz Mts

Mashhad

Neyshābūr

AFGHANISTAN

Hindu Kush

Kabul

Peshawar

Islamabad
Rawalpindi

PAKISTAN

Herāt

HERĀT

GHOWR

Qom

Dasht-e Kavir

KHORĀSĀN

Eşfahān

ESFAHĀN

YAZD

Yazd

FARAH

Qandahār

QANDAHĀR

Quetta

PUNJAB

Multan

INDIA

Kermān

KERMĀN

Zāhedān

SISTĀN VA BALŪCHESTĀN

BALŪCHISTĀN

Shirāz

FĀRS

BUSHEHR

HORMOZGĀN

Bandar-e Abbas

Karachi

Hyderabad

Gulf of Oman

QATAR

Doha

Dubai

Abu Dhabi

UNITED ARAB EMIRATES

Muscat

OMAN

ARABIAN SEA

Tropic of Cancer

PERSIAN GULF

BAHRAIN

Manāmah

East from Greenwich

M. VA B. = CHAHĀR MAHĀLL VA BAKHTĪĀRĪ
VA B. A. = KOHKĪLŪYEH VA BŪYER AḤMADĪ

COPYRIGHT PHILIP'S

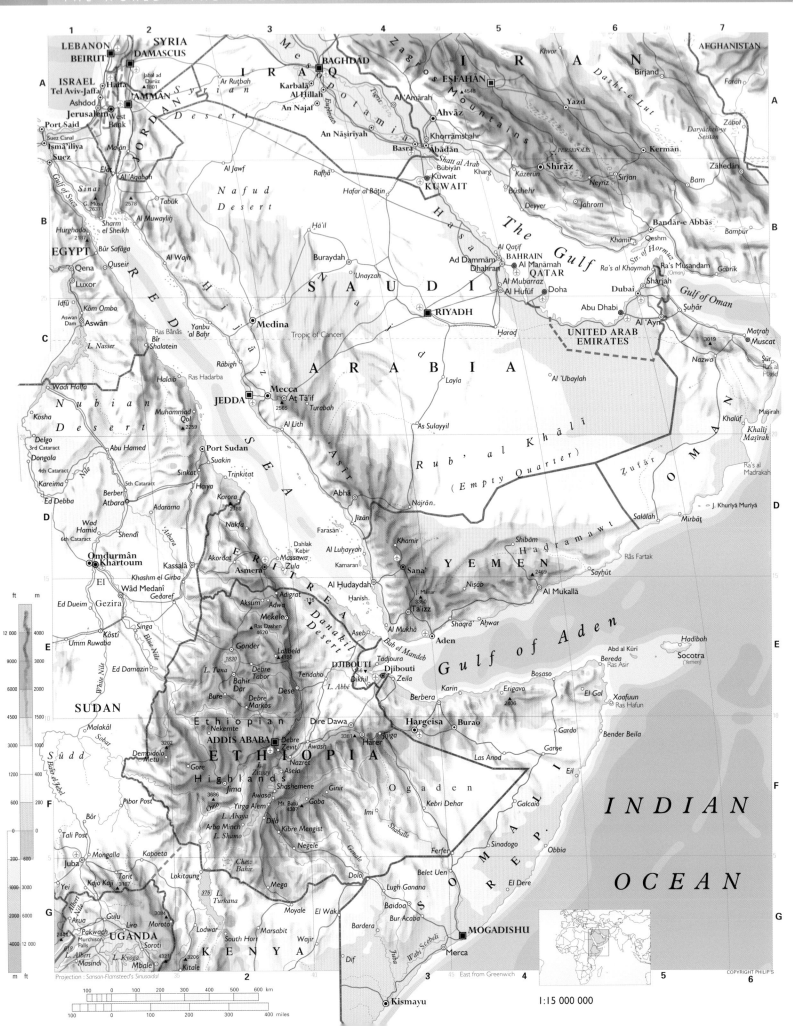

AFGHANISTAN

LEBANON
BEIRUT
SYRIA
DAMASCUS
ISRAEL
Tel Aviv-Jaffa
Haifa
Jabal ad
Druze
Ashdod
AMMAN
Jerusalem
West
Bank
JORDAN
Port Said
Isma'iliya
Suez
Suez Canal
Ma'ān
El'Aţ
Al 'Aqabah
Sinai
G. Mūsà
2637
EGYPT
Hurghada
2187
Bûr Safâga
Qena
Luxor
Quseir
Idfû
Kôm Ombo
Aswan
Aswan
Dam
Ras Bânâs
Bîr
Shalatein

BAGHDAD
Ar Ruţbah
IRAQ
Karbalā
Al Hillah
An Najaf
An Nāşirīyah
Al 'Amārah
Basra
Ābādān
Khorramshahr
ESFAHĀN
4548
Ahvāz
IRAN
Khvor
Birjand
Farāh
Yazd
Daryācheh-ye
Seistan
Kermān
Zābol
Zāhedān

Jabal ad
Druze
1801
Al Jawf
Syrian
Desert
Rafḥā
Hafar al Bāţin
KUWAIT
Shatt al Arab
Būbiyān
Kharg
Kāzerūn
Shīrāz
Būshehr
Deyyer
Neyrīz
Sirjān
Jahrom
Bam

Nafud
Desert
Ḥā'il
Ħāşa
Bandar-e Abbās
Khamīr
Qeshm
Bampūr
Ra's al Khaymah
Ra's Musandam
(Oman)
Gābrīk

Al Muwayliḥ
Tabūk
2578
Buraydah
Unayzah
Ad Dammām
BAHRAIN
Al Manāmah
QATAR
Sharjah
Gulf of Oman
Stwel
Dhahran
Al Mubarraz
Al Hufūf
Doha
Dubai
Abu Dhabi
Al 'Ayn
Suḥār
Maţraḥ
Muscat
Shūr
Ra's al
Ḥadd

SAUDI
RIYADH
Ħaraḍ
UNITED ARAB
EMIRATES
3019
OMAN
Nazwa

Al Wajh
Medina
Tropic of Cancer
Yanbu
al Baḥr
Rābigh
ARABIA

JEDDA
Mecca
Aţ Ţā'if
2565
Turabah
Layla
Al 'Ubaylah
Khalūf
Khalij
Maşīrah

Halaib
Ras Hadarba
Muhammad
Qol
2259
Al Līth
As Sulayyil
Masīrah

Nubian
Desert
Port Sudan
Suakin
Trinkitat
Sinkat
Haiya
Karora
2780
Nakfa

Rub' al Khālī
(Empty Quarter)
Zufār
Ra's al
Madrakah

Kosha
Delgo
3rd Cataract
Dongola
4th Cataract
Kareima
Ed Debba
Abu Hamed
Berber
Atbara
Adarama

ERITREA
Dahlak
Kebir
Massawa
Zula
Farasān
Jīzān
Abhā
Najrān
Khamir
Salālah
Mirbāţ
J. Khurīyā Murīyā

Wad
Hamid
6th Cataract
Shendî
Omdurmân
Khartoum
Kassalā
Akordat
Asmera
Al Luḥayyah
Kamaran
Shibām
2469
Ra's Fartak

SUDAN
El
Khashm el Girba
Wâd Medanî
Gedaref
Adigrat
Aksum
Adwa
-116
Al Ḥudaydah
Ħanīsh
Sana'
Nişāb
Hadramawt
Sayḥūt
Al Mukallā
YEMEN
J. Mānar
3350
Ta'izz

Gezira
Ed Dueim
Umm Ruwaba
Singa
Mekele
Ras Dashen
4620
Danakil
Desert
Al Mukhā
Shaqrā
Aḥwar
Gulf of Aden
Hadiboh
Socotra
(Yemen)

Gonder
1830
Lalibela
4198
Aseb
Bab el Mandeb
Aden
Abd al Kūri
Bereda
Ras Asir

Kôstî
Blue Nile
Ed Damazin
L. Tana
Debre
Tabor
DJIBOUTI
Tadjoura
Djibouti
Zeila
Bosaso
Xaafuun
Ras Hafun

SUDAN
Bahir
Dar
Bure
Debre
Markos
Dese
Tendaho
Dikhil
L. Abbē
Karin
Berbera
Erigavo
2406
El Gal

Malakâl
Sobat
Nekemte
ADDIS ABABA
Debre
Zeyit
Awash
Dire Dawa
Harer
3381
Jijiga
Hargeisa
Burao
Gardo
Bender Beila

Sûdd
Bahr el Zabol
3202
Dembidolo
Metu
Gore
ETHIOPIA
Highlands
Nazret
Asela
Ziway
Shashemene
Ginir
Kebri Dehar
Ogaden
Las Anod
Garoe
Eil

Pibor Post
Jima
3686
Omo
Yirga Alem
Awasa
Mt. Batu
4307
Goba
Imi
Galcaio

Bôr
Tali Post
L. Abaya
Arba Minch
L. Shamo
Dila
Kibre Mengist
Shabelle
Sinadogo
Obbia

INDIAN
OCEAN

Juba
Mongalla
Kapoeta
Chew
Bahr
Negele
Gestro
Ferfer
El Dere

Yei
Lokichokio
375
Mega
Dolo
Belet Uen
Baidoa

UGANDA
Kajo Kaji
3187
L. Turkana
Moyale
El Wak
Bur Acaba
Bardera

Arua
Gulu
Liria
Moroto
Lodwar
Marsabit
Wajir
Dif
Fiitha
Merca
MOGADISHU

L. Albert
2444
Murchison
Falls
Pakwach
Soroti
3084
Mbale
Kitale
KENYA
Baardheere
Kismayu

East from Greenwich

COPYRIGHT PHILIP'S

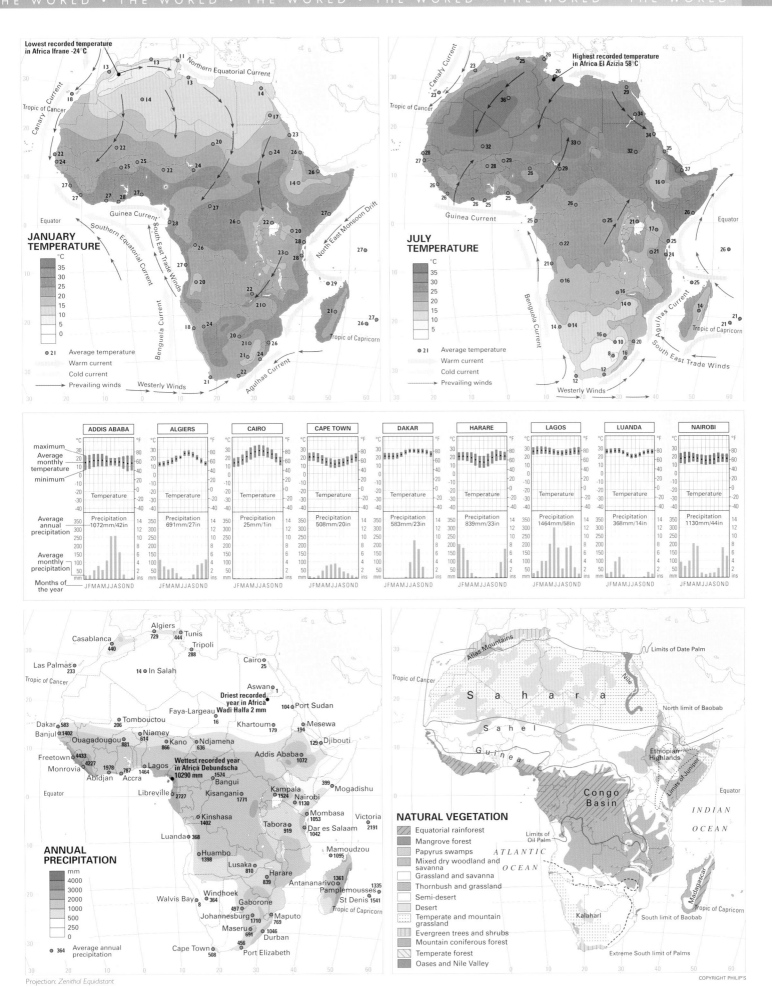

**JANUARY TEMPERATURE**

Lowest recorded temperature in Africa Ifrane -24°C

°C
35
30
25
20
15
10
5
0

⊙ 21  Average temperature
⊙   Warm current
⊙   Cold current
→   Prevailing winds

Northern Equatorial Current
Canary Current
Guinea Current
Southern Equatorial Current
South East Trade Winds
Benguela Current
North East Monsoon Drift
Agulhas Current
Westerly Winds
Equator
Tropic of Cancer
Tropic of Capricorn

**JULY TEMPERATURE**

Highest recorded temperature in Africa El Azizia 58°C

°C
35
30
25
20
15
10
5

⊙ 21  Average temperature
⊙   Warm current
⊙   Cold current
→   Prevailing winds

Canary Current
Guinea Current
Benguela Current
Agulhas Current
South East Trade Winds
Westerly Winds
Equator
Tropic of Cancer
Tropic of Capricorn

| | ADDIS ABABA | ALGIERS | CAIRO | CAPE TOWN | DAKAR | HARARE | LAGOS | LUANDA | NAIROBI |
|---|---|---|---|---|---|---|---|---|---|
| Average annual precipitation | 1072mm/42in | 691mm/27in | 25mm/1in | 508mm/20in | 583mm/23in | 839mm/33in | 1464mm/58in | 368mm/14in | 1130mm/44in |

maximum
Average monthly temperature
minimum
Temperature
Average monthly precipitation
Months of the year
JFMAMJJASOND

**ANNUAL PRECIPITATION**

Algiers 729
Tunis 444
Tripoli 288
Casablanca 440
Las Palmas 233
14 In Salah
Cairo 25
Aswan 1
Driest recorded year in Africa Wadi Halfa 2 mm
Faya-Largeau 16
104 Port Sudan
Tombouctou 206
Dakar 583
Banjul 1402
Khartoum 179
Mesewa 194
Niamey 614
Ouagadougou 881
Kano 866
Ndjamena 636
129 Djibouti
Freetown 4433
4227
Monrovia
1978
Abidjan
787
Accra
1464
Lagos
Addis Ababa 1072
Wettest recorded year in Africa Debundscha 10290 mm
1574
Bangui
399 Mogadishu
Libreville 2727
Kisangani 636
Kampala 1524
Nairobi 1771
Kinshasa 1402
Mombasa 1053
Tabora 919
Victoria 2191
Luanda 368
Dar es Salaam 1042
Mamoudzou 1095
Huambo 1398
Lusaka 810
Harare 839
Antananarivo 1361
1335
Pamplemousses
St Denis 1541
Walvis Bay 8
Windhoek 364
Gaborone 497
Johannesburg 1710
Maputo 769
Maseru 691
Durban 1046
Cape Town 508
Port Elizabeth 456

mm
4000
3000
2000
1000
500
250
0

⊙ 364  Average annual precipitation

Equator
Tropic of Cancer
Tropic of Capricorn

**NATURAL VEGETATION**

Atlas Mountains
Limits of Date Palm
Sahara
Sahel
Guinea
North limit of Baobab
Nile
Ethiopian Highlands
Limits of Juniper
Congo Basin
Limits of Oil Palm
ATLANTIC OCEAN
INDIAN OCEAN
Kalahari
South limit of Baobab
Madagascar
Extreme South limit of Palms
Equator
Tropic of Cancer
Tropic of Capricorn

Equatorial rainforest
Mangrove forest
Papyrus swamps
Mixed dry woodland and savanna
Grassland and savanna
Thornbush and grassland
Semi-desert
Desert
Temperate and mountain grassland
Evergreen trees and shrubs
Mountain coniferous forest
Temperate forest
Oases and Nile Valley

Projection: Zenithal Equidistant

COPYRIGHT PHILIP'S

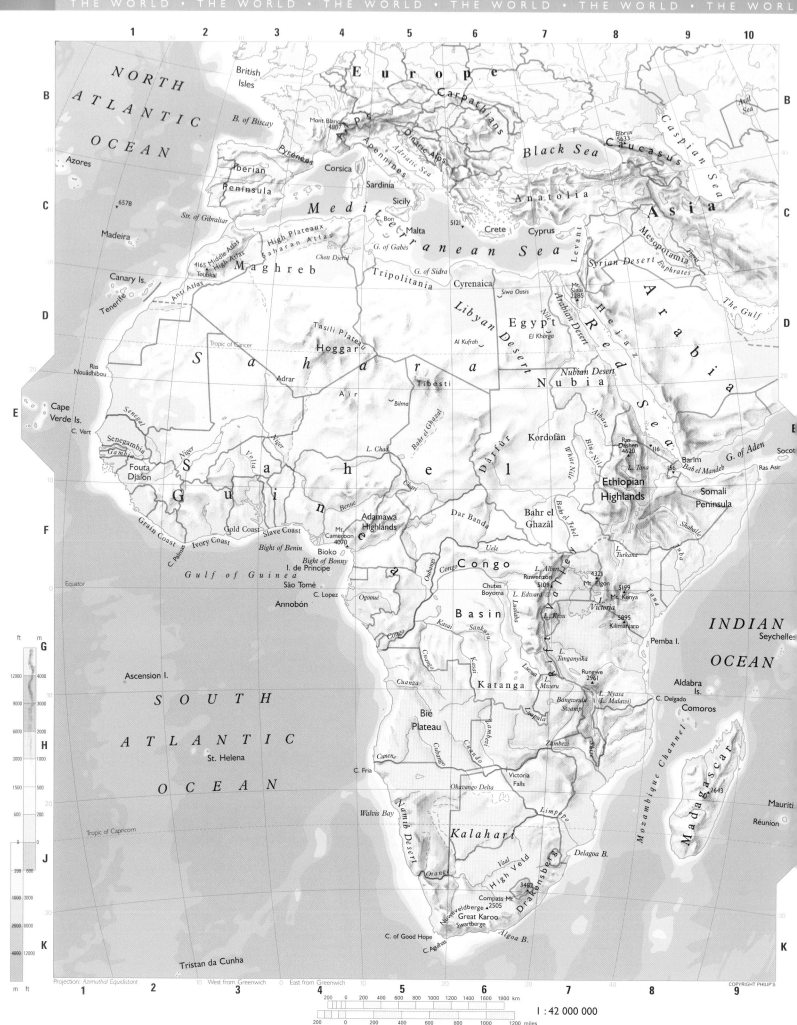

1 : 42 000 000

NORTH

ATLANTIC

OCEAN

Azores
(Port.)

Madeira
(Port.)

Canary Is.
(Sp.)

E VERDE IS.

St-Louis
C. Vert
Praia
Dakar

SOUTH

ATLANTIC

OCEAN

Ascension I.
(U.K.)

St. Helena
(U.K.)

Tristan da Cunha
(U.K.)

Projection: Azimuthal Equidistant

UNITED
KINGDOM
LONDON
NETH.
BELG.
PARIS
FRANCE
B. of Biscay
PORTUGAL
Lisbon
SPAIN
Madrid
Rabat
Casablanca
Tétouan
Fès
MOROCCO
Marrakesh
Algiers
Constantine
Annaba
Tunis
TUNISIA
Sfax
Chott Djerid

GERMANY POLAND
Prague
CZECH REP.
Vienna
SLOVAK REP.
SWITZ.
AUSTRIA
HUNGARY
CROATIA
BOS.-
HERZ.
SERBIA
& MONT.
ITALY
Rome
Sardinia
Corsica
Adriatic
Sea
ALB.
MAC.
BULGARIA
GREECE
Athens
Crete
Sicily
MALTA
Tripoli
Misrātah
Benghazi

Warsaw
Kiev
UKRAINE
ROMANIA
Odessa
Black Sea
GEORGIA
ARM.
AZER.
Ankara
TURKEY
CYPRUS
SYRIA
Aleppo
LEB.
Tel Aviv
Jaffa
Damascus
ISRAEL
Jerusalem
JORDAN
Alexandria
Port Said
Suez
CAIRO
El Faiyûm
El Jawf
EGYPT
Aswân

RUSSIA
Volgograd
KAZAKHSTAN
Aral
Sea
Caspian
Sea
Baku
TURKMEN.
Mosul
TEHRĀN
Eşfahān
Baghdād
IRAQ
Basra
KUWAIT
The Gulf
BAHRAIN
QATAR
Riyadh
SAUDI
ARABIA
Medina
Mecca
Jedda
YEMEN
IRAN

Mediterranean Sea

ALGERIA
In Salah
LIBYA
Marzūq

WESTERN SAHARA
El Aaiún
Dakhla
Ras
Nouâdhibou
Fdérik
Tropic of Cancer

S a h a r a

MAURITANIA
Nouakchott
Tombouctou
SENEGAL
Senegal
GAMBIA
Banjul
GUINEA
BISSAU
Bissau
Conakry
Freetown
SIERRA
LEONE
LIBERIA
Monrovia
MALI
Bamako
Niger
BURKINA
FASO
Ouagadougou
Bobo-
Dioulasso
IVORY
COAST
Yamoussoukro
Bouaké
GHANA
Kumasi
Abidjan
Sekondi-
Takoradi
TOGO
BENIN
Lomé
Accra
Porto
Novo
Bight of Benin

NIGER
Agadès
Niamey
Kano
NIGERIA
Maiduguri
Abuja
Ibadan
Lagos
Enugu
Benue
CAMEROON
Douala
Malabo
Yaoundé
EQUATORIAL
GUINEA
SÃO TOMÉ & PRÍNCIPE
Port
Harcourt

CHAD
L. Chad
Abéché
Ndjamena
Chari
CENTRAL
AFRICAN REP.
Bangui
Oubangui

Red Sea

SUDAN
El Fâsher
El Obeid
Khartoum
Omdurmân
Atbara
Wâd Medani
Malakâl
Wau
Bahr el Jebel
White Nile
Blue Nile
Wadi Halfa
Port Sudan

ERITREA
Mesewa
Asmera
DJIBOUTI
Djibouti
Harer
Berbera
Ras Asir
Socotra
(Yemen)
G. of Aden

ETHIOPIA
Addis Ababa
L. Tana
SOMALI REP.
Mogadishu

Gulf of Guinea
C. Lopez
Annobón
GABON
Libreville
CONGO
Brazzaville
Pointe-Noire
CABINDA
(Angola)
Matadi
Congo
Kasai
CONGO
(DEM. REP. OF THE)
Kinshasa
Mbandaka
Kisangani
L. Albert
L. Edward
UGANDA
Kampala
RWANDA
Kigali
L. Kivu
BURUNDI
Bujumbura
L. Tanganyika
Kananga
L. Victoria
Kisumu
KENYA
Nairobi
Mombasa
L. Turkana
Juba
Shabelle
Kismayu

Equator

TANZANIA
Dodoma
Dar es Salaam
Zanzibar
SEYCHELLES

INDIAN

OCEAN

Aldabra
Is.

ANGOLA
Luanda
Lobito
Huambo
Namibe
C. Fria
Cunene
Cubango
L. Mweru
Likasi
Lubumbashi
ZAMBIA
Ndola
Lusaka
Kafue
Zambezi
L. Malawi
MALAWI
Lilongwe
Blantyre
MOZAMBIQUE
C. Delgado
COMOROS
Moroni
Moçambique
Mozambique Channel
Mamoudzou
Mayotte
(Fr.)
Antsiranana
Mahajanga
Toamasina
MADAGASCAR
Antananarivo
Fianarantsoa
MAURITIUS
St-Denis
Réunion
(Fr.)
Port
Louis

ZIMBABWE
Livingstone
Harare
Bulawayo
Beira
Limpopo
BOTSWANA
Gaborone
NAMIBIA
Windhoek
Tropic of Capricorn

SOUTH AFRICA
Johannesburg
Pretoria
Mbabane
SWAZ.
Maputo
LESOTHO
Maseru
Kimberley
Vaal
Orange
Durban
Cape Town
C. of Good Hope
C. Agulhas
East
London
Port
Elizabeth

West from Greenwich    East from Greenwich

200  0  200  400  600  800  1000 1200 1400 1600 1800 km

1 : 42 000 000    ● Dakar  Capital Cities

200  0  200  400  600  800  1000  1200 miles

COPYRIGHT PHILIP'S

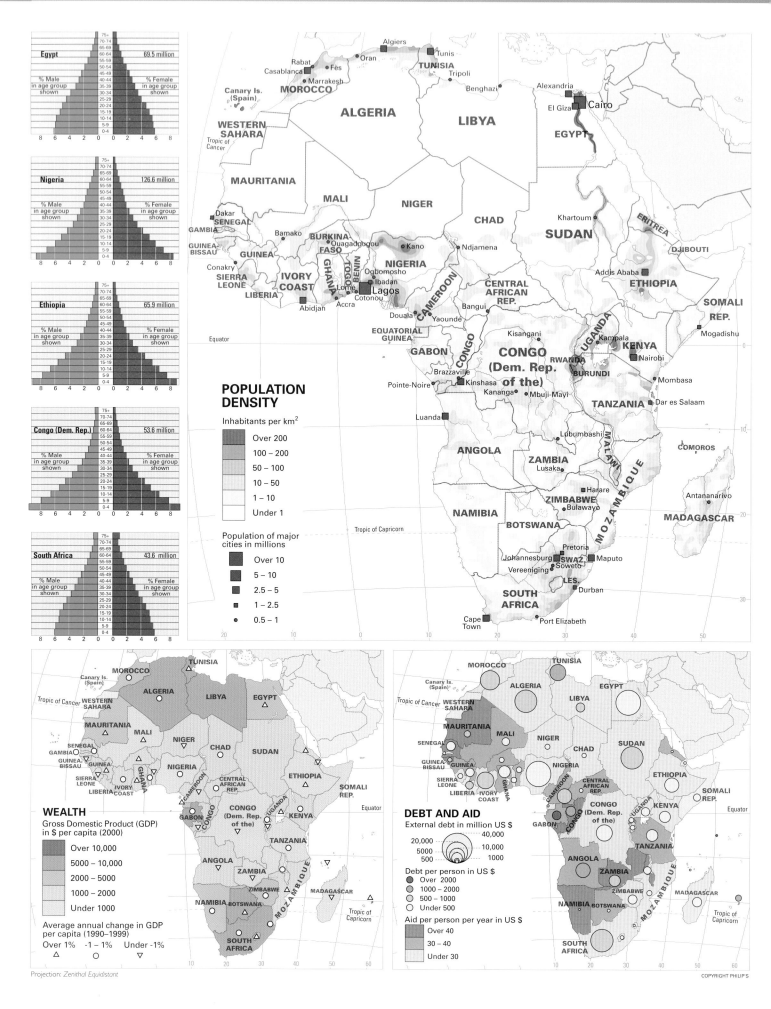

POPULATION PYRAMIDS

Egypt — 69.5 million
% Male in age group shown / % Female in age group shown

Nigeria — 126.6 million
% Male in age group shown / % Female in age group shown

Ethiopia — 65.9 million
% Male in age group shown / % Female in age group shown

Congo (Dem. Rep.) — 53.6 million
% Male in age group shown / % Female in age group shown

South Africa — 43.6 million
% Male in age group shown / % Female in age group shown

## POPULATION DENSITY

Inhabitants per km²

- Over 200
- 100 – 200
- 50 – 100
- 10 – 50
- 1 – 10
- Under 1

Population of major cities in millions

- Over 10
- 5 – 10
- 2.5 – 5
- 1 – 2.5
- 0.5 – 1

## WEALTH

Gross Domestic Product (GDP) in $ per capita (2000)

- Over 10,000
- 5000 – 10,000
- 2000 – 5000
- 1000 – 2000
- Under 1000

Average annual change in GDP per capita (1990–1999)

Over 1%  /  -1 – 1%  /  Under -1%
△  /  ○  /  ▽

Projection: *Zenithal Equidistant*

## DEBT AND AID

External debt in million US $

- 40,000
- 20,000
- 10,000
- 5000
- 1000
- 500

Debt per person in US $

- Over 2000
- 1000 – 2000
- 500 – 1000
- Under 500

Aid per person per year in US $

- Over 40
- 30 – 40
- Under 30

COPYRIGHT PHILIP'S

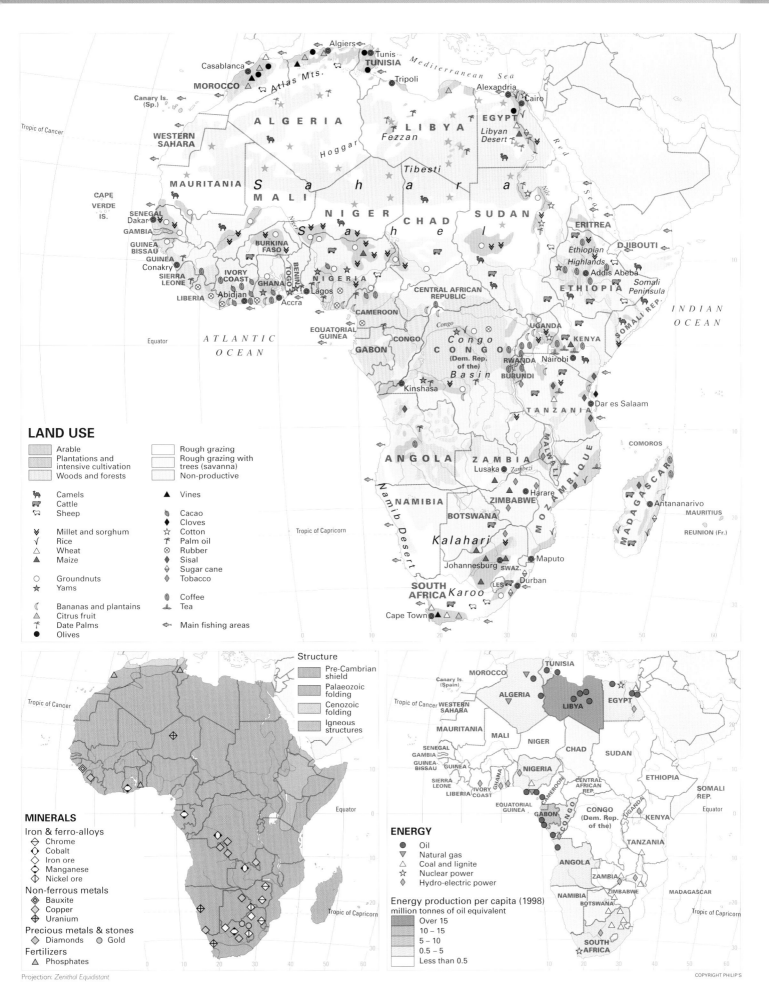

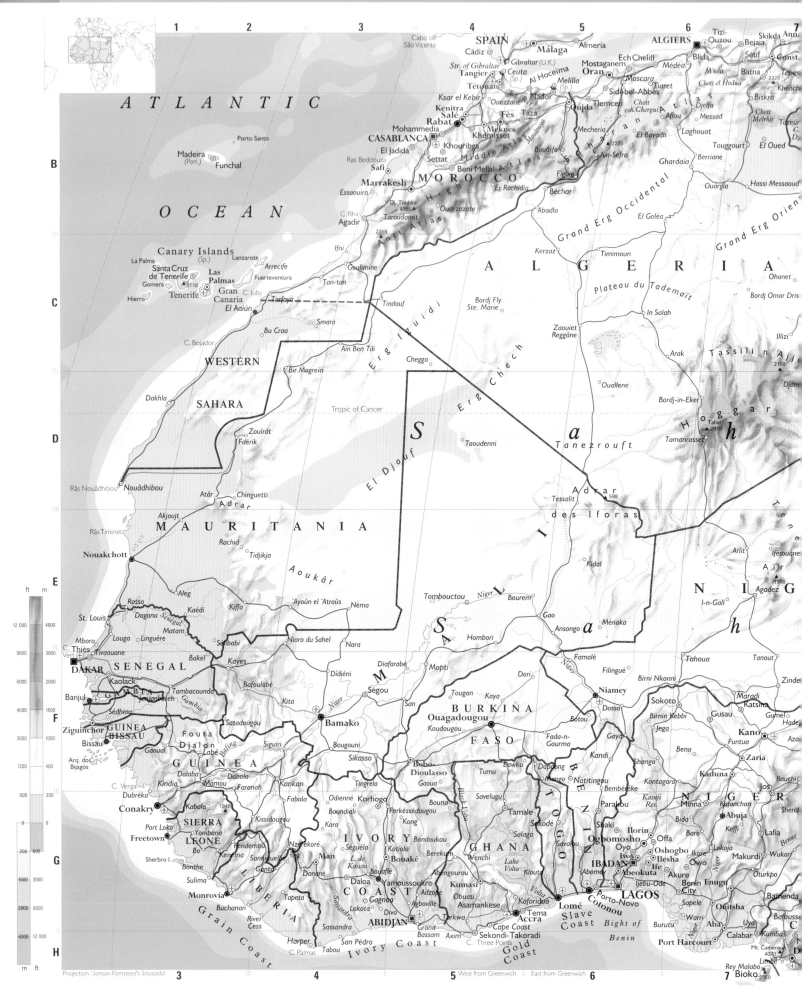

Bizerte
Ariana
CARTHAGE
Beja
TUNIS
Nabeul
Sousse
Mahdia
Sfax
G. of Gabès
Ile de Djerba
Zarzis
Médenine
Tataouine
Dehibat

Sicily

MALTA
Valletta

M E D I T E R R A N E A N   S E A

GREECE

Iráklion
Crete

Rhodes

TURKEY
Antalya
Antakya
CYPRUS
Nicosia
Latakia

ADANA
ALEPPO
Euphrates

SYRIA

Homs
Tripoli
LEBANON
BEIRUT
Tel Aviv-Jaffa
ISRAEL
Ashdod

Hama
Jabal ad Drūz
1801

DAMASCUS
AMMAN

IRAQ
Ar Ruṭbah

Syrian Desert

Zuwārah
Tripoli
Al Khums
Az Zāwiyah
Gharyān
968
Misrātah

Surt

G. of Sidra

Benghazi
Al Marj
Darnah
Tubruq
Suluq
Ajdābiya
Bardīyah
Salūm
ALEXANDRIA
Marsā Matrūh
El Alamein
Damanhūr
El Mahalla el Kubra
Tanta
Zagazig
Port Said
Ismā'īliya
Dumyāt
El Mansûra
Jerusalem
West Bank
Mo'ān
Elat
Al 'Aqabah

JORDAN
Al Jawf

SAUDI

Tripolitania

Daraj
Ghadāmis

Mizdah

Hūn

Zillah

Ajdābiya

Awjilah

C y r e n a i c a

Al Jaghbūb

Siwa
-133
Qattâra Depression

EL GÎZA
Helwân
El Faiyûm
Beni Suef
Maghâgha
El Minyâ
Mallawi
Manfalût
Asyût

Suez
Gulf of Suez
Sinai
G. Mûsa
2637
2578
Tabūk

Arabian Desert

Hurghada
2187
Bûr Safâga

ARABIA

I d e h a n   A w b ā r i

Brach

Sabhah

▲1200

L I B Y A

Qasr Farâfra

Tahta
Sohâg
Girga
Mût
Qena
KARNAK
THEBES
Luxor

Quseir
Al Wajh

RED

Awbārī

Marzūq

Wāw al Kabīr

L i b y a n

D e s e r t

El Wâhât el-Dakhla

El Wâhât el-Khârga

Idfû
Kom Ombo

Bir Shalatein

Ras Bânâs

F e z z a n

Ghat

Al Qaṭrūn

R e b i a n a   D e s e r t

Al Jawf

Al Kufrah

Aswan Dam
Aswân

L. Nasser

Yanbu 'al Bahr

Râbigh

Halaib
Ras Hadarba

S E A

S a h a r a

Toummo
Madama

Chirfa

Bardai
Pic Toussidé
3265
Zouar
T i b e s t i
Emi Koussi
3415

Aozou
Tarso Emissi
3150

Aozou Strip

Ma'tan as Sarra

▲1082

J. Uweinat
1893

Wadi Halfa

El Wâhât el Selîma

ABU SIMBEL

N u b i a n

Kosha
Delgo
3rd Cataract
Dongola

Muhammad Qol
2259▲

Port Sudan
Suakin
Trinkitat

Bilma

Fachi

Grand Erg du Bilma

B o r k o u

Faya-Largeau

Ounianga Sérir

Dépression du Mourdi

Fada
▲1310
E n n e d i

Z a g a o u a

Oum Chalouba

Bir 'Atrun

Abu Hamed

D e s e r t

Kareima
4th Cataract
Berber
Atbara
5th Cataract

Ed Debba
Adarama
Haiya

Karora

Nakfa

ERITREA
Akordat

N I G E R

Erg du Djourab

C H A D

Zigey
Mao
L. Chad

Bahr el Ghazal

Biltine

Kutum
1954

Malha
Sodiri

Wad Hamid
6th Cataract
Shendi

S U D A N

El Wuz

Khashm el Girba
Kassalâ

Maiduguri
Nguigmi
Bosso
Gashua
Geidam

Moussoro
Ati
Massakory

Abéché

Al Junaynah

El Fâsher
Djebel Marra
3088
Nyâlâ

Umm Keddada

En Nahud

El Odaiya

Abu Zabad

Umm Ruwaba

El Obeid

Ed Dueim

Er Rahad

Omdurmân
Khartoum

El Gezira
Wâd Medanî
Gedaref

Singa
Kôstî

1830

Gonder
L. Tana

Potiskum
Bama
Bajoga
Biu
Mubi
Numan
Yola

Maroua
Guider

Ndjamena
Kousseri
Massenya
Bokoro
Mongo
Goz Beïda

D a r f u r

Birao

Songo

Sa'id Bundas

Malakâl
Sobat

Singa
Ed Damazin
1325

Kâdugli

K o r d o f â n

W h i t e   N i l e

B l u e   N i l e

Bahir Dar
Bure
Debre Markos
Nekemté

3202
ETHIOPIA

Garoua
Moundou
Doba

Chari
Logone

Pala
Laï
Koumra
Sarh

Ndélé

1226

Raga

Wâw

B a h r   e l

Bahr el Arab

S û d d

Gogriâl

Tonj

Bahr el Ghazal
Jur

Bôr

3686
Jima

L. Abaya
Dembidolo

Metu
Gore

CAMEROON

Yaoundé

Bétaré Oya
Bouar
Bossangoa

Ngaoundéré
Banyo

Baïbokoum

C E N T R A L   A F R I C A N
R E P U B L I C

Kaga Bandoro

Bozoum

Sibut

Bambari

Yalinga

Bakouma

G h a z â l

Rumbêk

Toinya

Amadi

Tali Post

Pibor Post

El Istwa'îya

Mongalla

3686

Gore

Jima

375

Nanga-Eboko
Abong-Mbang
Yoko

Bertoua
Batouri

Bossembélé
Carnot
Berbérati

Bangui
Mbaïki

Ippy

Bozoum

Zongo
Libenge

Mobaye
Mobayi
Bosobolo
Bondo

Obo

Bomu

Uele
Dungu
Faradje

Yambio
Yei

Juba
Kajo Kaji
3187

Kapoeta

Torit
Lokitaung

L. Turkana

Chew Bahir

L. Shamo
Arba Minch
Abaya

8    9    10    11    12    13

100  0  100  200  300  400  500  600 km
100  0  100  200  300  400 miles

1:15 000 000

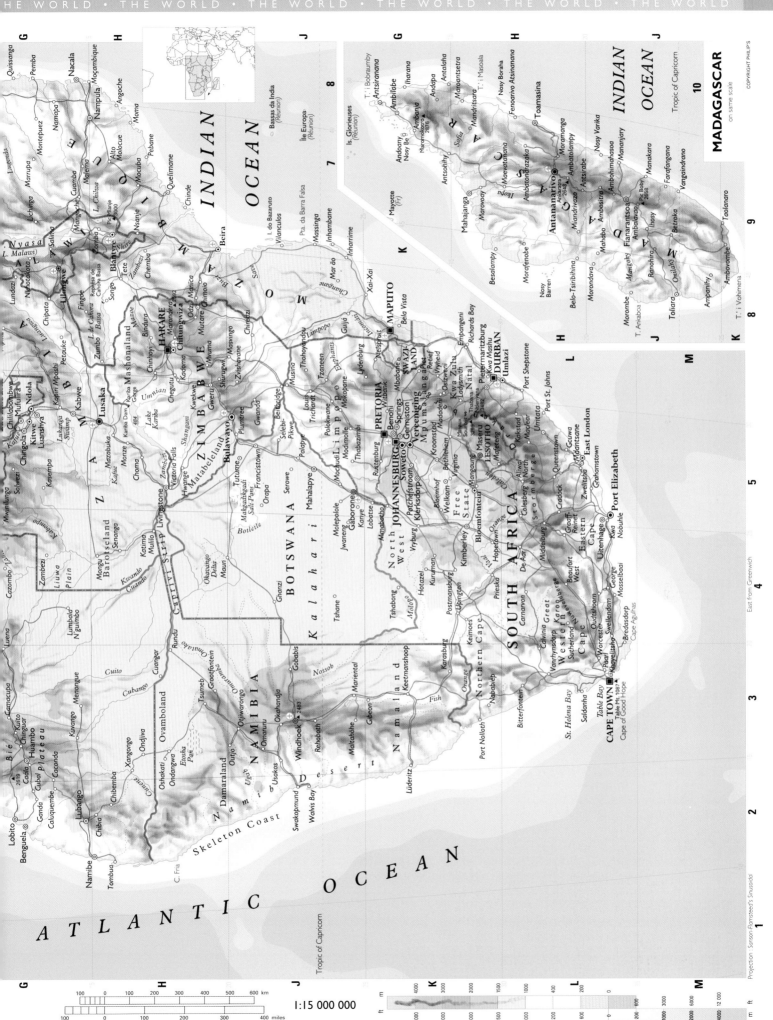

**MADAGASCAR**
on same scale

INDIAN

OCEAN

Tropic of Capricorn

INDIAN

OCEAN

ATLANTIC OCEAN

Tropic of Capricorn

Skeleton Coast

**SOUTH AFRICA**

NAMIBIA

BOTSWANA

ZIMBABWE

ZAMBIA

Kalahari

East from Greenwich

Projection : Sanson-Flamsteed's Sinusoidal

1:15 000 000

100    0    100   200   300   400   500   600 km

100    0    100    200    300    400 miles

ft m    4000    3000    2000    1500    1000    400    200    0

12 000    9000    6000    4500    3000    1500    600    200    0    200 600

Projection: Lambert's Equivalent Azimuthal

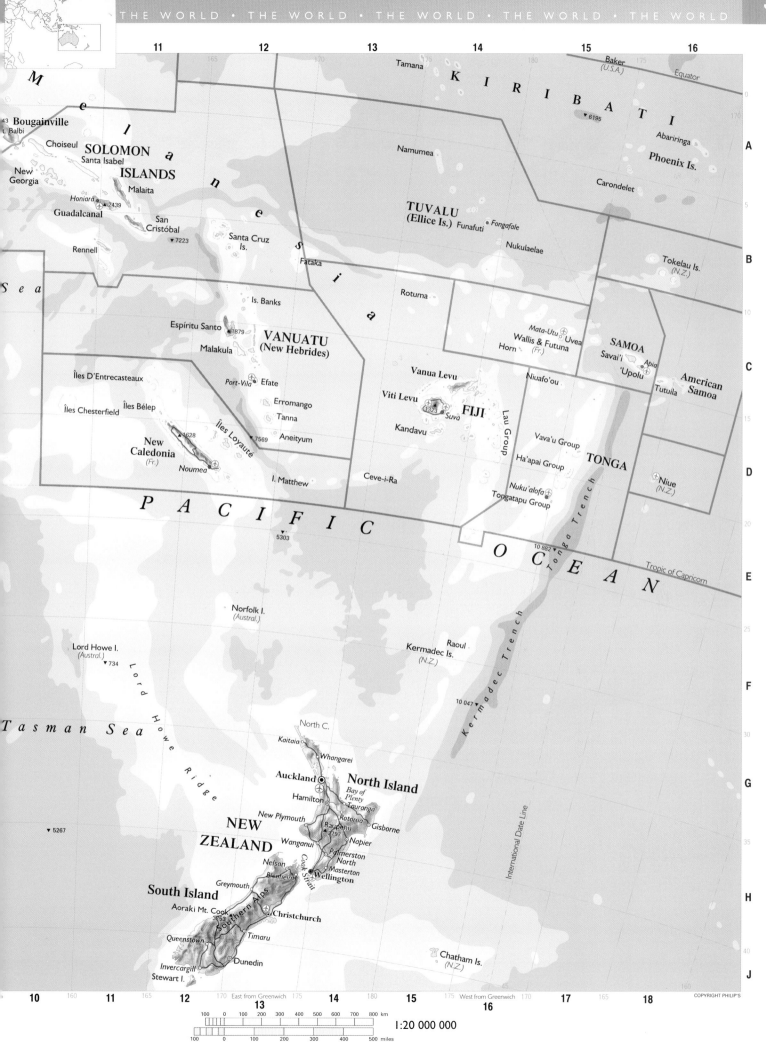

M e l a n e s i a

43 Bougainville
t. Balbi

SOLOMON
ISLANDS
Choiseul
Santa Isabel
New
Georgia
Malaita
Honiara ▲ 2439
Guadalcanal
San
Cristóbal
Rennell
▽ 7223

Sea

Santa Cruz
Is.

Fataka

Is. Banks

Espíritu Santo ▼ 1879
VANUATU
(New Hebrides)
Malakula

Îles D'Entrecasteaux
Port-Vila ⊕ Efate
Erromango
Îles Chesterfield
Îles Bélep
Tanna
Îles Loyauté
▲ 1628
New
Caledonia
(Fr.)
Noumea ⊕
I. Matthew
Aneityum
▼ 7569

Tamana

K I R I B A T I

Namumea

TUVALU
(Ellice Is.) Funafuti ⊙ Fongafale
Nukulaelae

Rotuma

Mata-Utu ⊕ Uvea
Wallis & Futuna
Horn (Fr.)

Vanua Levu
Viti Levu
▲ 1323
Suva
FIJI
Kandavu

Niuafo'ou

Lau Group

Vava'u Group
Ha'apai Group
TONGA

Nuku'alofa ⊕
Tongatapu Group

Ceve-i-Ra

Baker
(U.S.A.)
Equator

▼ 6195

Abariringa

Phoenix Is.

Carondelet

Tokelau Is.
(N.Z.)

SAMOA
Savai'i ○ Apia
'Upolu ⊕
Tutuila
American
Samoa

Niue
(N.Z.)

P A C I F I C

▼ 5303

O C E A N

Tonga Trench

10 882 ▼

Tropic of Capricorn

Norfolk I.
(Austral.)

Lord Howe I.
(Austral.)
▼ 734

Raoul
Kermadec Is.
(N.Z.)

Kermadec Trench

10 047 ▼

International Date Line

T a s m a n   S e a

Lord Howe Ridge

North C.
Kaitaia
Whangarei
Auckland ⊙
Hamilton
North Island
Bay of
Plenty
Tauranga
New Plymouth
Rotorua
Gisborne
Raupehu
▲ 2797
NEW
ZEALAND
Wanganui
Napier
Palmerston
North
Nelson
Masterton
Blenheim
Cook Strait
Wellington ⊙
South Island
Greymouth
Aoraki Mt. Cook
3753 ▲
Southern Alps
Christchurch
Queenstown
Timaru
Invercargill
Dunedin
Stewart I.

▼ 5267

Chatham Is.
(N.Z.)

1:20 000 000

100   0   100   200   300   400   500   600   700   800 km
100   0   100   200   300   400   500 miles

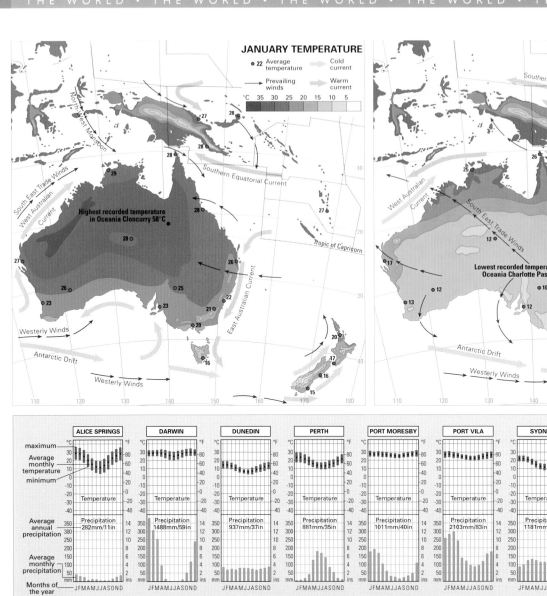

## JANUARY TEMPERATURE

- 22 Average temperature
- → Prevailing winds
- ⇒ Cold current
- ⇒ Warm current

°C 35 30 25 20 15 10 5

Highest recorded temperature in Oceania Cloncurry 58°C

North West Monsoon
South East Trade Winds
West Australian Current
Southern Equatorial Current
East Australian Current
Westerly Winds
Antarctic Drift
Westerly Winds

## JULY TEMPERATURE

- 18 Average temperature
- → Prevailing winds
- ⇒ Cold current
- ⇒ Warm current

°C 25 20 15 10 5 0

Southern Equatorial Current
West Australian Current
South East Trade Winds
Lowest recorded temperature in Oceania Charlotte Pass -22°C
East Australian Current
Antarctic Drift
Westerly Winds

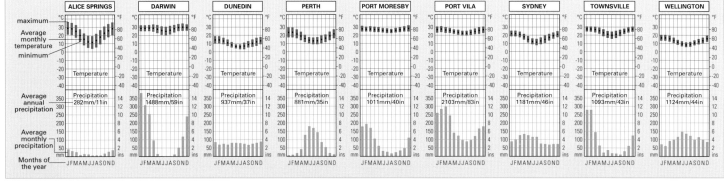

Climate graphs: ALICE SPRINGS, DARWIN, DUNEDIN, PERTH, PORT MORESBY, PORT VILA, SYDNEY, TOWNSVILLE, WELLINGTON

maximum
Average monthly temperature
minimum
Average annual precipitation
Average monthly precipitation
Months of the year

- ALICE SPRINGS — Precipitation 282mm/11in
- DARWIN — Precipitation 1488mm/59in
- DUNEDIN — Precipitation 937mm/37in
- PERTH — Precipitation 881mm/35in
- PORT MORESBY — Precipitation 1011mm/40in
- PORT VILA — Precipitation 2103mm/83in
- SYDNEY — Precipitation 1181mm/46in
- TOWNSVILLE — Precipitation 1093mm/43in
- WELLINGTON — Precipitation 1124mm/44in

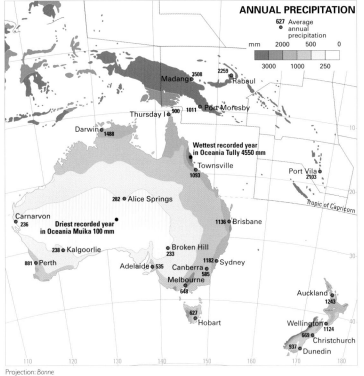

## ANNUAL PRECIPITATION

- 627 Average annual precipitation

mm 2000 500 0
3000 1000 250

Madang 3508
Rabaul 2259
Port Moresby 1011
Thursday I 900
Darwin 1488
Townsville 1093
Wettest recorded year in Oceania Tully 4550 mm
Port Vila 2103
Alice Springs 282
Carnarvon 236
Driest recorded year in Oceania Muika 100 mm
Brisbane 1136
Broken Hill 233
Kalgoorlie 238
Perth 881
Adelaide 535
Canberra 585
Sydney 1182
Melbourne 648
Auckland 1243
Hobart 627
Wellington 1124
Christchurch 669
Dunedin 937

Projection: Bonne

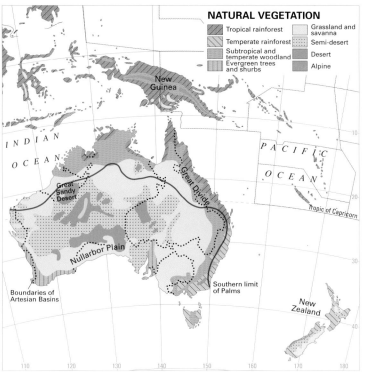

## NATURAL VEGETATION

- Tropical rainforest
- Temperate rainforest
- Subtropical and temperate woodland
- Evergreen trees and shrubs
- Grassland and savanna
- Semi-desert
- Desert
- Alpine

New Guinea
INDIAN OCEAN
PACIFIC OCEAN
Great Sandy Desert
Great Divide
Nullarbor Plain
Tropic of Capricorn
Boundaries of Artesian Basins
Southern limit of Palms
New Zealand

COPYRIGHT PHILIP'S

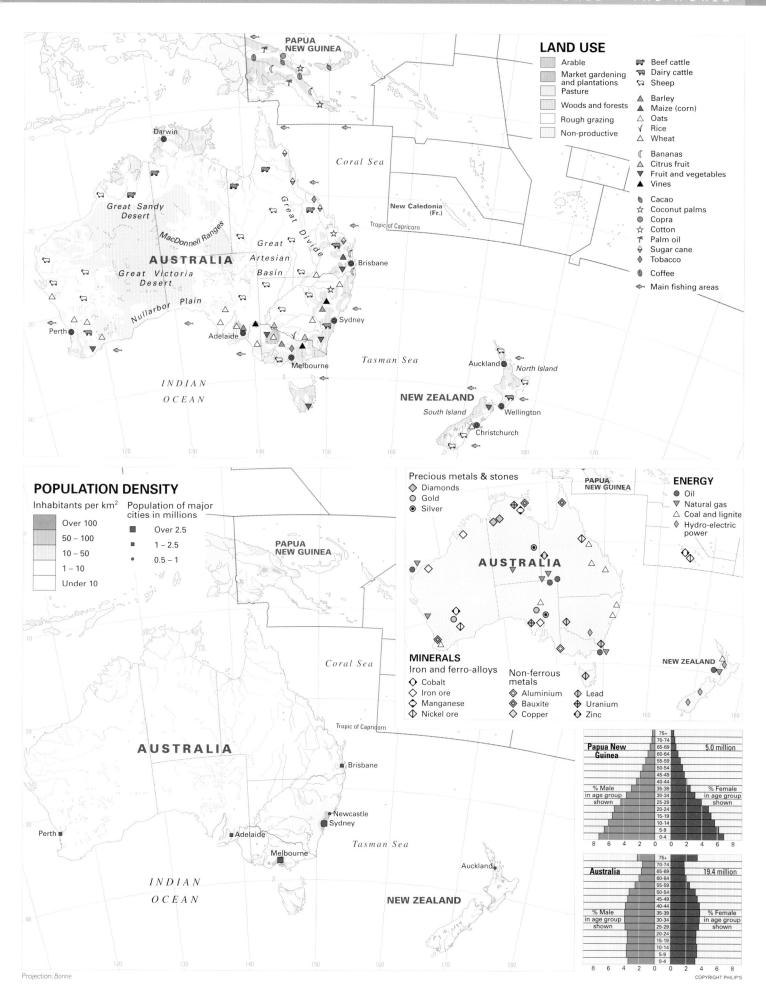

## LAND USE

| | |
|---|---|
| Arable | |
| Market gardening and plantations | |
| Pasture | |
| Woods and forests | |
| Rough grazing | |
| Non-productive | |

- Beef cattle
- Dairy cattle
- Sheep

- Barley
- Maize (corn)
- Oats
- Rice
- Wheat

- Bananas
- Citrus fruit
- Fruit and vegetables
- Vines

- Cacao
- Coconut palms
- Copra
- Cotton
- Palm oil
- Sugar cane
- Tobacco

- Coffee

- Main fishing areas

PAPUA NEW GUINEA

Darwin

Coral Sea

New Caledonia (Fr.)

Tropic of Capricorn

Great Sandy Desert

MacDonnell Ranges

AUSTRALIA

Great Victoria Desert

Great Artesian Basin

Great Divide

Brisbane

Nullarbor Plain

Perth

Adelaide

Sydney

Melbourne

Tasman Sea

INDIAN OCEAN

Auckland
North Island

NEW ZEALAND

South Island    Wellington

Christchurch

## POPULATION DENSITY

Inhabitants per km²

| | |
|---|---|
| Over 100 | |
| 50 – 100 | |
| 10 – 50 | |
| 1 – 10 | |
| Under 10 | |

Population of major cities in millions

- Over 2.5
- 1 – 2.5
- 0.5 – 1

PAPUA NEW GUINEA

Coral Sea

Tropic of Capricorn

AUSTRALIA

Brisbane

Newcastle
Sydney

Perth

Adelaide

Tasman Sea

Melbourne

INDIAN OCEAN

Auckland

NEW ZEALAND

Projection: Bonne

## Precious metals & stones

- Diamonds
- Gold
- Silver

PAPUA NEW GUINEA

AUSTRALIA

## MINERALS

### Iron and ferro-alloys

- Cobalt
- Iron ore
- Manganese
- Nickel ore

### Non-ferrous metals

- Aluminium
- Bauxite
- Copper
- Lead
- Uranium
- Zinc

## ENERGY

- Oil
- Natural gas
- Coal and lignite
- Hydro-electric power

NEW ZEALAND

| Papua New Guinea | | 5.0 million |
|---|---|---|
| 75+ | | |
| 70-74 | | |
| 65-69 | | |
| 60-64 | | |
| 55-59 | | |
| 50-54 | | |
| 45-49 | | |
| 40-44 | | |
| % Male in age group shown | 35-39 | % Female in age group shown |
| | 30-34 | |
| | 25-29 | |
| | 20-24 | |
| | 15-19 | |
| | 10-14 | |
| | 5-9 | |
| | 0-4 | |

8  6  4  2  0  0  2  4  6  8

| Australia | | 19.4 million |
|---|---|---|
| 75+ | | |
| 70-74 | | |
| 65-69 | | |
| 60-64 | | |
| 55-59 | | |
| 50-54 | | |
| 45-49 | | |
| 40-44 | | |
| % Male in age group shown | 35-39 | % Female in age group shown |
| | 30-34 | |
| | 25-29 | |
| | 20-24 | |
| | 15-19 | |
| | 10-14 | |
| | 5-9 | |
| | 0-4 | |

8  6  4  2  0  0  2  4  6  8

MOSCOW
Yekaterinburg
Tomsk
Ob
Okhotsk
Sea of Okhotsk
Beri
Sea
Komandorskiye Islands (Russia)
Near Is. (U.S.A.)
Andreanof (U.S.A.)
Novosibirsk
Irkutsk
L. Baikal
Chita
Amur
Khabarovsk
Petropavlovsk-Kamchatskiy
Kamchatka Pen.
Aleutian Trench
Astana
Semey
RUSSIA
Lena
KAZAKHSTAN
Aral Sea
L. Balkhash
Altai
MONGOLIA
Ulan Bator
Blagoveshchensk
Sakhalin
7822
Aleutia
Alma Ata
Ürümqi
Harbin
Vladivostok
La Pérouse Str.
Kuril Is.
10,542
Kuril Trench
Emperor Seamount Chain
Tashkent
KYRGYZSTAN
SHENYANG
Changchun
Sapporo
Hakodate
TAJIKISTAN
BEIJING
TIANJIN
Taiyuan
Dalian
SOUL
Sea of Japan
Sendai
AFGHANISTAN
CHINA
Hwang-Ho
NORTH KOREA
SOUTH KOREA
Nagoya
Fuji-San 3776
TOKYO
Yokohama
Kabul
Srinagar
Lanzhou
Xi'an
Qingdao
Kyoto
Osaka
JAPAN
PAKISTAN
Kunlun Shan
TIBET
Nanjing
Kitakyūshū
Shikoku
Midway Is. (U.S.A.)
DELHI
Lhasa
8850 Mt. Everest
Himalaya
Wuhan
CHONGQING
SHANGHAI
Kyūshū
Japan Trench
Lahore
NEPAL
Ganges
Brahmaputra
HANGZHOU
East China Sea
Ogasawara Gunto (Japan)
Lisianski I. (U.S.A.)
Kanpur
Changsha
South Honshu Ridge
Minami-Tori-Shima (Japan)
Hyderabad
KOLKATA (Calcutta)
DHAKA
BANGLADESH
Mandalay
Kunming
Fuzhou
Taipei
Ryukyu Is. (Japan)
Kazan-Rettō (Japan)
Marcus
Necker Ridge
Wake I. (U.S.A.)
INDIA
BURMA
GUANGZHOU
HONG KONG
TAIWAN
NORTHERN MARIANAS (U.S.A.)
P
A
Irrawaddy
LAOS
Hanoi
Hainan
Saipan
MARSHALL IS.
Salween
Bay of Bengal
Rangoon
THAILAND
Mekong
C. Engano
Luzon
Paracel Is.
MANILA
PHILIPPINES
GUAM (U.S.A.) 11,022
Mariana Trench
Micronesia
CHENNAI (Madras)
Andaman Is. (India)
BANGKOK
CAMBODIA
VIETNAM
South China
Mindoro
Samar
10,497
Yap
Caroline Is.
Truk
Enewetak Atoll
Bikini Atoll
Phnom Penh
Palawan
Koror
Pohnpei
Palikir
Jaluit I.
Dalap-Uliga-Darrit
SRI LANKA
Nicobar Is. (India)
Ho Chi Minh City
Sulu Sea
Mindanao
Mindanao Trench
PALAU
FEDERATED STATES OF MICRONESIA
Butaritari
Colombo
MALAYSIA
Celebes Sea
4101
BRUNEI
SABAH
Tarawa
Gilbert Is.
Howland I. (U.)
Baker I. (U.)
Kuala Lumpur
PEN. MALAYSIA
SARAWAK
Celebes Sea
Halmahera
Melanesia
NAURU
Banaba
Phoenix Is.
Abariringa
Enderbury
Sumatra
SINGAPORE
Borneo
Sulawesi
Seram
PAPUA NEW GUINEA
Admiralty Is.
New Ireland
KI
Palembang
Ujung Pandang
Buru
Moluccas
Banda Sea
PAPUA
5029 Puncak Jaya
New Guinea
Bismarck Arch.
New Britain
Rabaul
Bougainville
SOLOMON IS.
Fongafale
TUVALU
Tokelau (N.Z.)
JAKARTA
Jawa
Java Sea
Surabaya
Flores Sea
Bali
Sumbawa
Flores
7440
EAST TIMOR
Arafura Sea
Torres Strait
Lae
Port Moresby
Honiara
Guadalcanal
Santa Cruz Is. 9165
Rotuma
Is. Wallis & Futuna (Fr.)
SAMO
Apia
INDIAN
Java Trench
Cocos Is. (Austral.)
Christmas I. (Austral.)
Sumba
Timor
C. Arnhem
Darwin
Gulf of Carpentaria
C. York
Louisiade Arch.
Coral Sea
Espíritu Santo
VANUATU
Vanua Levu
OCEAN
North West C.
Broome
Cairns
Townsville
Is. Chesterfield
Port Vila
Viti Levu
Suva
Nuku'alofa
TONG
Mount Isa
NEW CALEDONIA (Fr.)
7670
Nouméa
Is. Loyauté
FIJI
10,822
Tonga Trench
AUSTRALIA
Alice Springs
Rockhampton
Great Dividing Ra.
Brisbane
Norfolk I. (Austral.)
Kermadec Is. (N.Z.)
Geraldton
L. Eyre
Darling
Lord Howe I. (Austral.)
Kermadec Trench 10,047
Perth
Great Australian Bight
Sydney
Canberra
Mt. Kosciuszko 2230
NEW ZEALAND
Albany
Murray
Adelaide
Tasman Sea
Auckland
Cook Strait
Nouvelle Amsterdam (Fr.)
I. St. Paul (Fr.)
Melbourne
Bass Str.
Aoraki Mt. Cook 3753
Christchurch
Chatham I. (N.Z.)
Mid-Indian Ridge
Tasmania
Hobart
Dunedin
Bounty Is. (N.Z.)
Is. Crozet (Fr.)
Invercargill
Antipodes Is. (N.Z.)
Kerguelen (Fr.)
Auckland Is. (N.Z.)
Campbell I. (N.Z.)
Heard I. (Austral.)
Macquarie Is. (Austral.)

ft m
12 000 4000
9000 3000
6000 2000
3000 1000
1500 500
600 200
0 0
200 600
1000 3000
2000 6000
4000 12 000
6000 18 000
8000 24 000
m ft

16  17  18  19  20

ALASKA
(U.S.A.)
Anchorage

5959

Juneau

B

Bristol Bay

Gulf of Alaska

R  O  C  K  Y

C  A  N  A  D  A

Prince of Wales I.
(U.S.A.)  Prince Rupert

Is. (U.S.A.)

Queen Charlotte Is.
(Canada)

Edmonton

L. Winnipeg

Newfoundland

Vancouver
Vancouver I.
Victoria
Seattle

Calgary

Regina

Winnipeg

L. Superior

St. Lawrence

Québec

St. John's

NORTH

C

Portland

Boise

Minneapolis

L. Huron
L. Michigan

Montréal
Ottawa

Boston

Salt Lake
City

Missouri

Toronto
Detroit
L. Erie
Buffalo
Pittsburgh

Denver

Kansas City

CHICAGO
Cincinnati

NEW YORK CITY
PHILADELPHIA
Baltimore
Washington D.C.

Sacramento

SAN FRANCISCO

4418

Colorado

St. Louis

UNITED STATES

Appalachian Mts.

ATLANTIC

D

6741

Oklahoma City  Memphis

Atlanta

C. Hatteras

C. Mendocino

LOS ANGELES
San Diego

Phoenix

Dallas

Houston

San Antonio

New
Orleans

Jacksonville

Bermuda
(U.K.)

Ciudad
Juárez

Baja California

M

Gulf of Mexico  Miami

Sargasso Sea

OCEAN

E

Tropic of Cancer

Honolulu

Oahu
4205
HAWAIIAN IS.
(U.S.A.)

Hawaii

an Ridge

Johnston I.
(U.S.A.)

Guadalupe
(Mex.)

C. San Lucas

Is. Revilla Gigedo
(Mex.)

Guadalajara

E  X  I  C  O

Monterrey

Mérida

Canal de Yucatán

Havana

Florida Str.

CUBA

BAHAMAS

West Indies

PACIFIC

North West Christmas I. Ridge

Palmyra Is.
(U.S.A.)

Teraina

Tabuaeran
Kiritimati

Acapulco

MEXICO
Puebla

5610

BELIZE

7680

JAMAICA

9200

HAITI

DOMINICAN REP.

Kingston

PUERTO
RICO
(U.S.A.)

Leeward
Is.

F

GUATEMALA
Guatemala
San Salvador
EL SALVADOR

HONDURAS

Caribbean Sea

BARBADOS

Windward Is.

Managua
NICARAGUA

I. Clipperton
(Fr.)

Barranquilla

Maracaibo

P  O  L  Y

Jarvis I.
(U.S.A.)

Line Is.

Equator

COSTA
RICA
Colón
PANAMA

San José
Panamá

I. del Coco
(Costa Rica)

Medellín

Caracas

Orinoco

VENEZUELA

G

N  E  S  I  A

KIRIBATI

Malden I.

Starbuck I.

Galápagos
(Ecuador)

I. de Malpelo
(Colombia)

Cali

Bogotá

COLOMBIA

OCEAN

Quito
ECUADOR

Guayaquil

C. Paliñas

Iquitos

Amazonas

BRAZIL

H

Tongareva

Is. Marquises

Trujillo

Pukapuka

Manihiki

Vostok I.

Caroline I.
(Millennium I.)

Flint I.

East Pacific Ridge

6369

PERU

MER.
MOA
U.S.A.)

Suwarrow Is.

Is. de la
Société
Papeete Tahiti

Is. Tuamotu

LIMA

Cuzco

L. Titicaca

Nevada Ancohuma
6550

Niue
(N.Z.)

Australi Seamount Chain

FRENCH POLYNESIA

Tuamotu Ridge

Arequipa

6866

Peru-

La Paz

BOLIVIA

J

Cook Is.
(N.Z.)

Rarotonga

Is. Tubuai

Mururoa

Arica

Iquique

Tropic of Capricorn

Antofagasta

Chile

PARAGUAY

Asunción

Ducie I.

Pitcairn I.
(U.K.)

Rapa

Sala-y-Gómez
(Chile)

I. de Pascua
(Chile)

San Felix
(Chile)

San Ambrosio
(Chile)

8050
Trench

San Miguel
de Tucumán

K

Porto
Alegre

Arch. de
Juan Fernández
(Chile)

Córdoba
Aconcagua
6962

Valparaíso
SANTIAGO

Rosario

Concepción

BUENOS
AIRES

URUGUAY
Montevideo

Río de la Plata

L

Chile Rise

ARGENTINA

ANTILLES

Patagonia

SOUTH

ATLANTIC

M

Pacific-Antarctic Ridge

6212

OCEAN

Punta Arenas

Est. de Magallanes
Tierra del Fuego

Falkland Is.
(U.K.)

South Georgia
(U.K.)

N

C. de Hornos

11  12  13  14  15  16  17  18  19  20

West from Greenwich

COPYRIGHT PHILIP'S

1:54 000 000

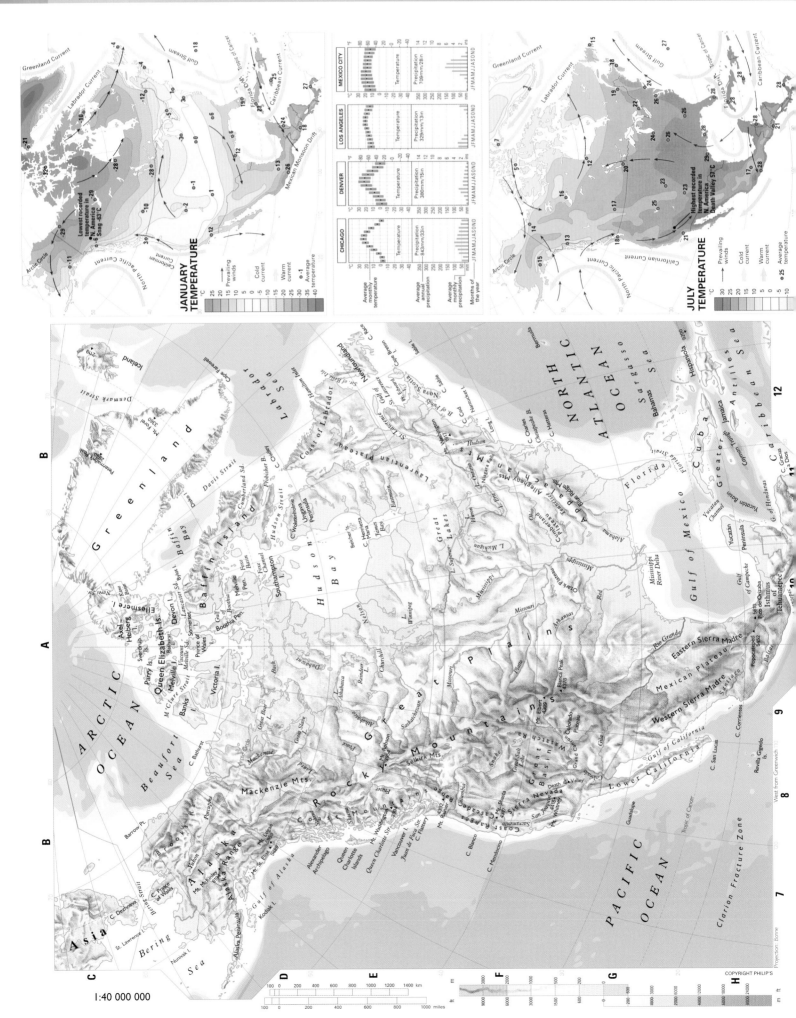

**JANUARY TEMPERATURE**

Lowest recorded temperature in N. America –63°C Snag –63°C

| | Prevailing winds |
| | Cold current |
| | Warm current |
| ●25 | Average temperature |

°C 25 20 15 10 5 0 –5 –10 –15 –20 –25 –30 –35 –40

**JULY TEMPERATURE**

Highest recorded temperature in N. America Death Valley 57°C

| | Prevailing winds |
| | Cold current |
| | Warm current |
| ●25 | Average temperature |

°C 30 25 20 15 10 5 –5 –10

MEXICO CITY — Temperature — Precipitation 705mm/28in
LOS ANGELES — Temperature — Precipitation 329mm/13in
DENVER — Temperature — Precipitation 380mm/15in
CHICAGO — Temperature — Precipitation 843mm/33in

Average monthly temperature
Average annual precipitation
Average monthly precipitation
Months of the year

1:40 000 000

COPYRIGHT PHILIP'S

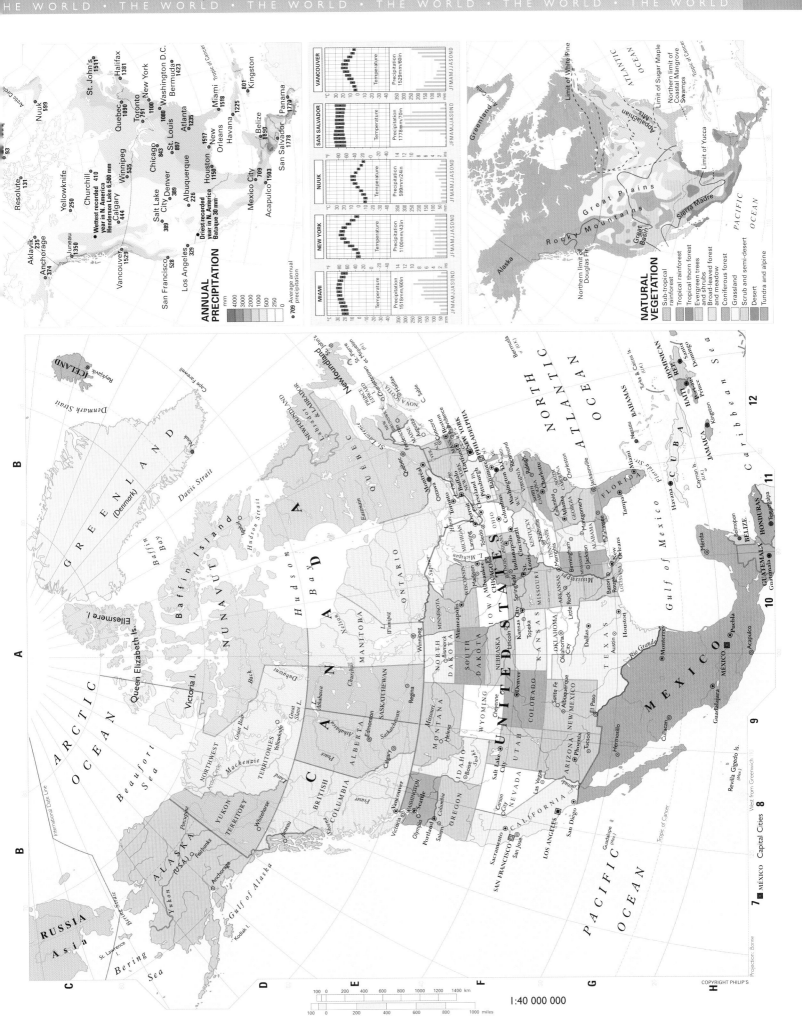

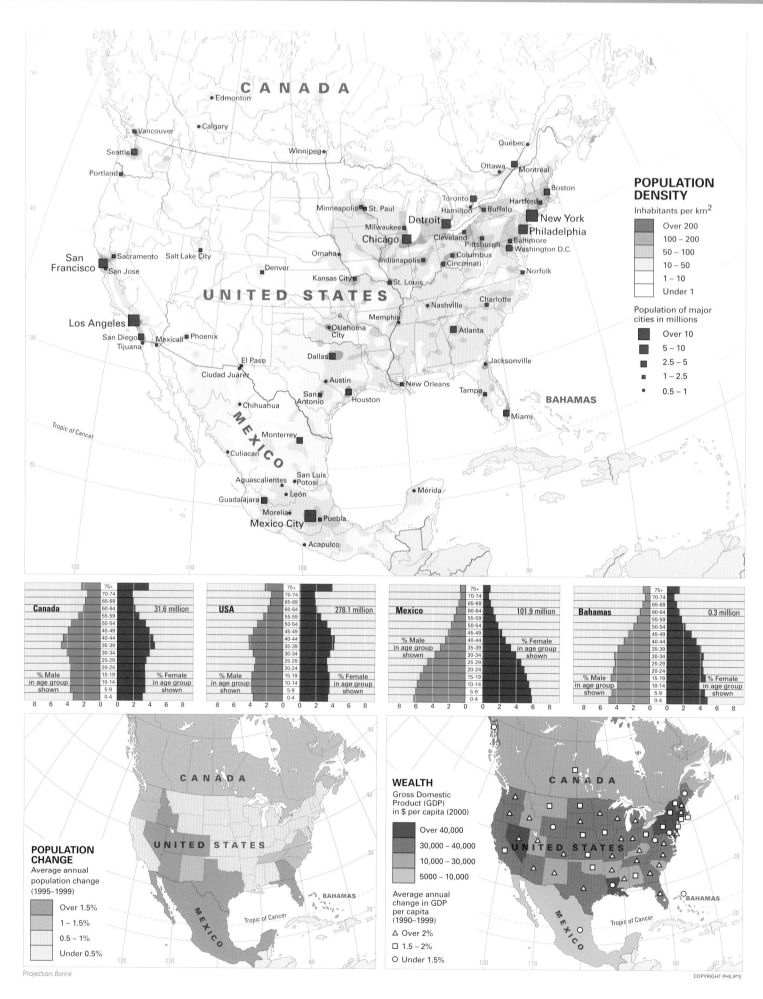

**POPULATION DENSITY**

Inhabitants per km²

- Over 200
- 100 – 200
- 50 – 100
- 10 – 50
- 1 – 10
- Under 1

Population of major cities in millions

- Over 10
- 5 – 10
- 2.5 – 5
- 1 – 2.5
- 0.5 – 1

**Canada** 31.6 million

**USA** 278.1 million

**Mexico** 101.9 million

**Bahamas** 0.3 million

% Male in age group shown — % Female in age group shown

**POPULATION CHANGE**

Average annual population change (1995–1999)

- Over 1.5%
- 1 – 1.5%
- 0.5 – 1%
- Under 0.5%

**WEALTH**

Gross Domestic Product (GDP) in $ per capita (2000)

- Over 40,000
- 30,000 – 40,000
- 10,000 – 30,000
- 5000 – 10,000

Average annual change in GDP per capita (1990–1999)

- △ Over 2%
- ☐ 1.5 – 2%
- ○ Under 1.5%

Projection: *Bonne*

COPYRIGHT PHILIP'S

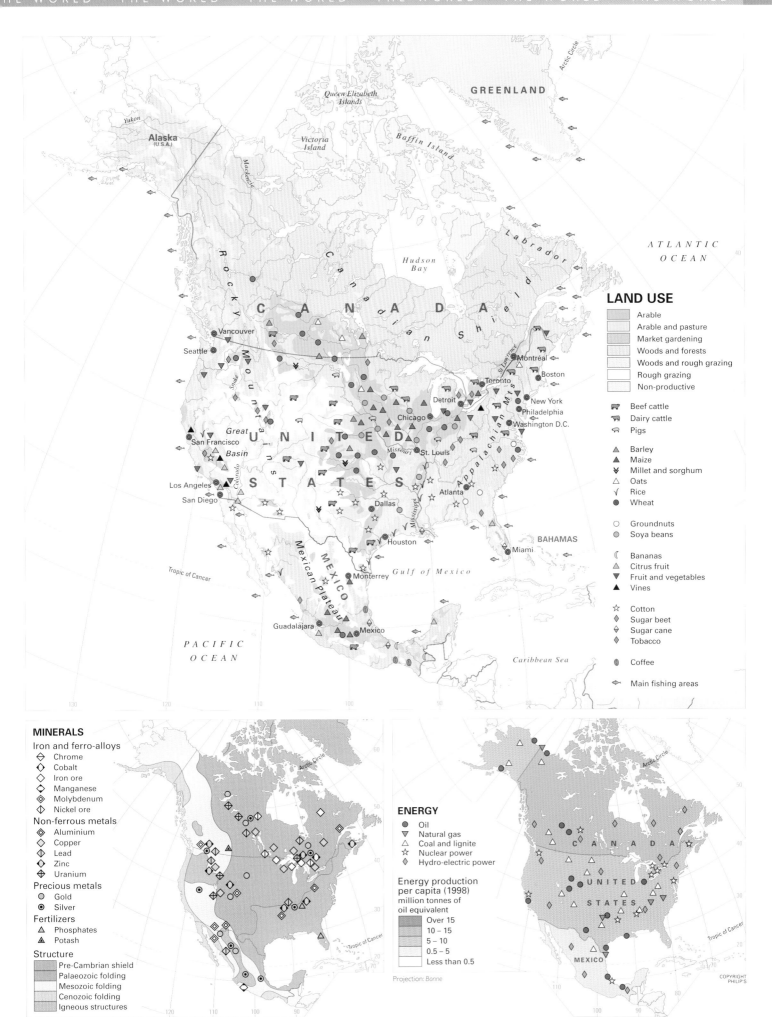

GREENLAND

*Queen Elizabeth Islands*

*Yukon*

**Alaska** (U.S.A.)

*Victoria Island*

*Baffin Island*

*Mackenzie*

*ATLANTIC OCEAN*

C A N A D A

*Canadian Shield*

*Hudson Bay*

*Labrador*

Vancouver

Seattle

*Rocky Mountains*

*Snake*

Montréal

Boston

Toronto

U N I T E D

*Great Basin*

San Francisco

*Colorado*

Los Angeles

San Diego

S T A T E S

Detroit

Chicago

*Missouri*

St. Louis

New York

Philadelphia

Washington D.C.

*Appalachian Mts.*

Atlanta

Dallas

*Mississippi*

BAHAMAS

Houston

Miami

M E X I C O

*Mexican Plateau*

Monterrey

*Gulf of Mexico*

*Tropic of Cancer*

Guadalajara

Mexico

*PACIFIC OCEAN*

*Caribbean Sea*

## LAND USE

- Arable
- Arable and pasture
- Market gardening
- Woods and forests
- Woods and rough grazing
- Rough grazing
- Non-productive

- Beef cattle
- Dairy cattle
- Pigs

- △ Barley
- ▲ Maize
- ⋎ Millet and sorghum
- △ Oats
- √ Rice
- ● Wheat

- ○ Groundnuts
- ● Soya beans

- ☾ Bananas
- △ Citrus fruit
- ▽ Fruit and vegetables
- ▲ Vines

- ☆ Cotton
- ◇ Sugar beet
- ◆ Sugar cane
- ◇ Tobacco

- ● Coffee

- ⬄ Main fishing areas

## MINERALS

### Iron and ferro-alloys
- ◈ Chrome
- ◇ Cobalt
- ◇ Iron ore
- ◇ Manganese
- ◈ Molybdenum
- ◈ Nickel ore

### Non-ferrous metals
- ◈ Aluminium
- ◇ Copper
- ◇ Lead
- ◇ Zinc
- ✦ Uranium

### Precious metals
- ◎ Gold
- ◉ Silver

### Fertilizers
- △ Phosphates
- ▲ Potash

### Structure
- Pre-Cambrian shield
- Palaeozoic folding
- Mesozoic folding
- Cenozoic folding
- Igneous structures

## ENERGY

- ● Oil
- ▽ Natural gas
- △ Coal and lignite
- ☆ Nuclear power
- ◇ Hydro-electric power

### Energy production per capita (1998)
million tonnes of oil equivalent

- Over 15
- 10 – 15
- 5 – 10
- 0.5 – 5
- Less than 0.5

C A N A D A

U N I T E D

S T A T E S

MEXICO

Projection: Bonne

COPYRIGHT PHILIP'S

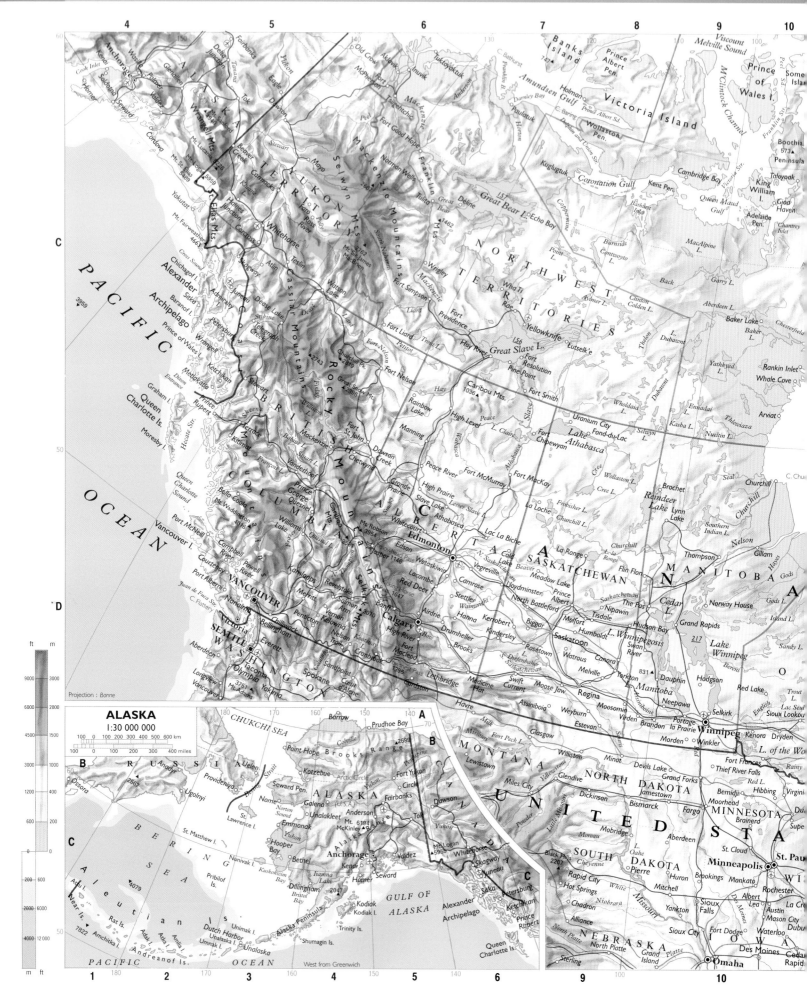

PACIFIC OCEAN

ALASKA
1:30 000 000

CHUKCHI SEA

RUSSIA

BERING SEA

ALASKA (U.S.A.)

GULF OF ALASKA

PACIFIC OCEAN

West from Greenwich

Projection : Bonne

100   0   100   200   300   400   500   600 km

100   0   100   200   300   400 miles

1:15 000 000

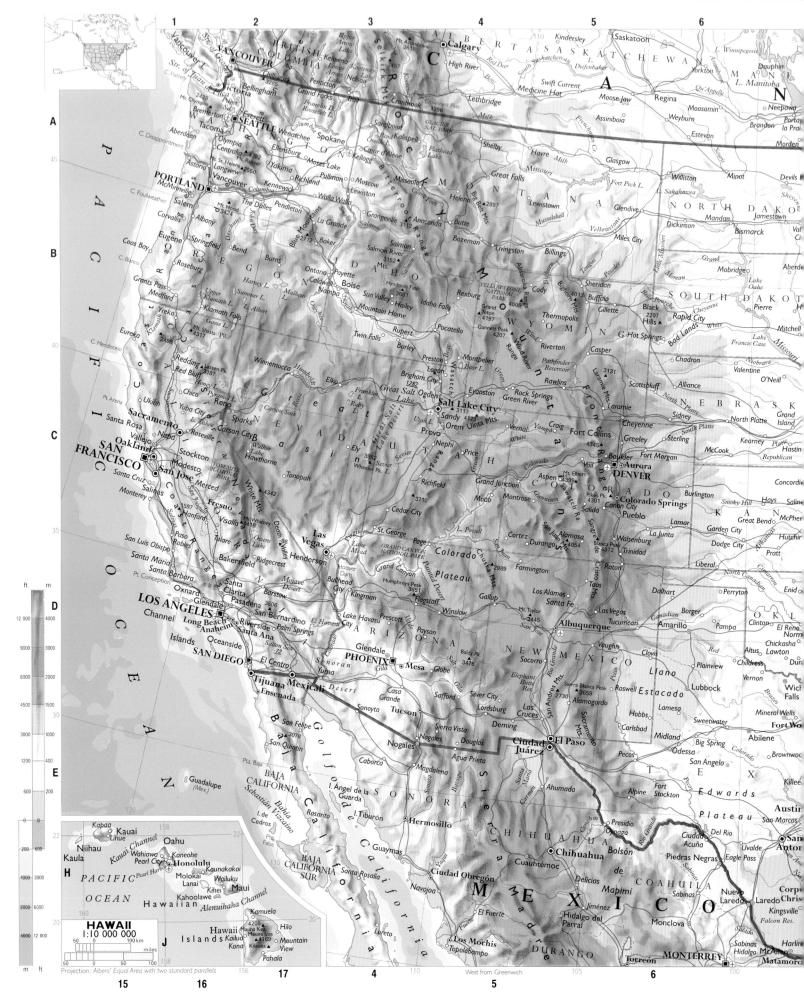

Projection: Albers' Equal Area with two standard parallels

## HAWAII 1:10 000 000

1:12 000 000

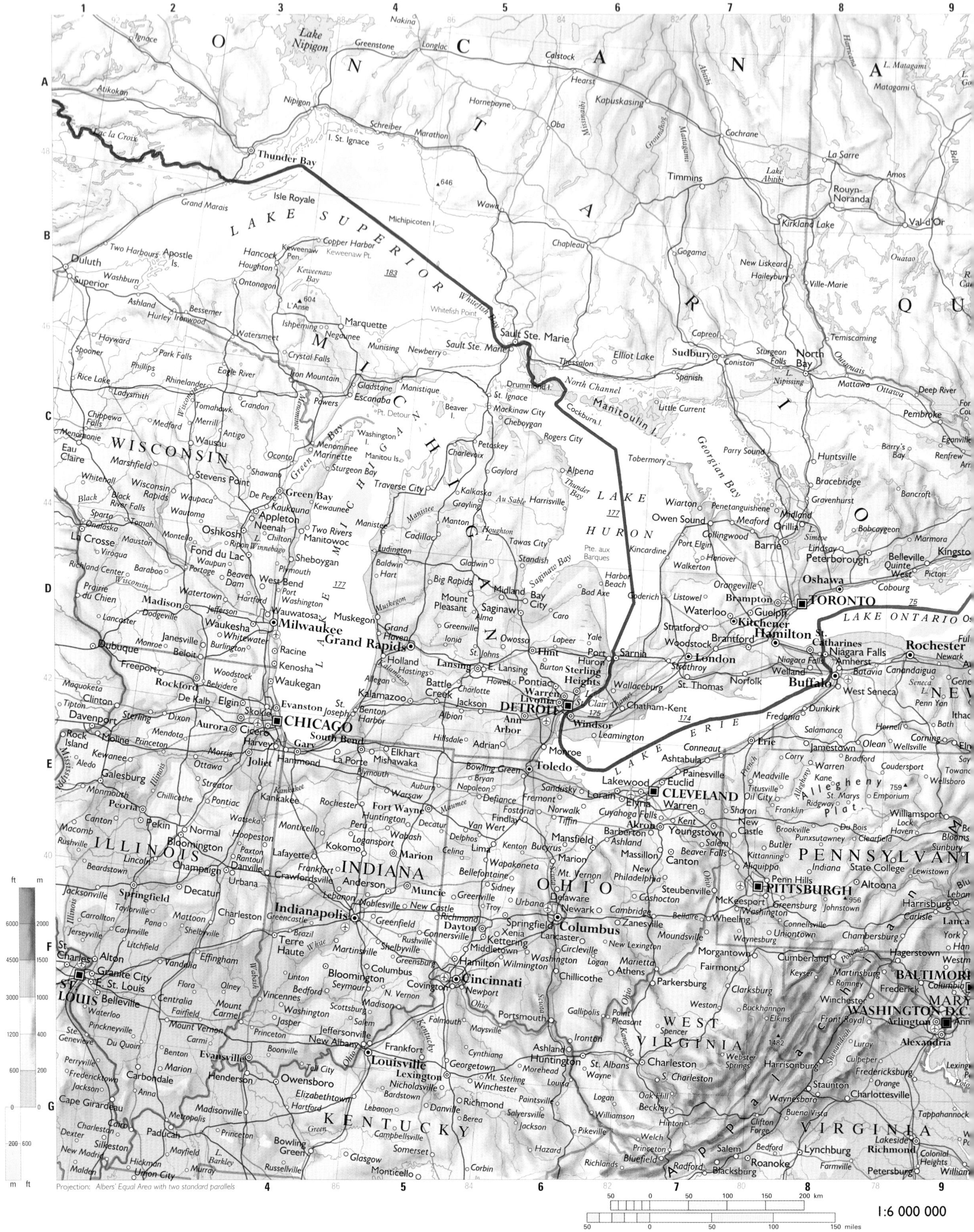

CANADA

**Lake Superior**
**Lake Huron**
**Lake Michigan**
**Lake Erie**
**Lake Ontario**
Lake Nipigon
Georgian Bay

QUÉBEC
ONTARIO
WISCONSIN
MICHIGAN
ILLINOIS
INDIANA
OHIO
KENTUCKY
WEST VIRGINIA
VIRGINIA
PENNSYLVANIA
NEW YORK
MARYLAND

Duluth, Superior, Washburn, Ashland, Thunder Bay, Isle Royale, Grand Marais, Two Harbours, Apostle Is., Hancock, Houghton, Keweenaw Pen., Copper Harbor, Keweenaw Pt., Ontonagon, L'Anse, Keweenaw Bay, Ishpeming, Negaunee, Marquette, Munising, Newberry, Sault Ste. Marie, Sudbury, North Bay, Coniston, Sturgeon Falls, Timmins, Kapuskasing, Cochrane, Hearst, Calstock, Longlac, Greenstone, Nakina

CHICAGO, Milwaukee, Madison, Green Bay, Appleton, Oshkosh, Fond du Lac, Racine, Kenosha, Waukegan, Rockford, Aurora, Joliet, Gary, Hammond, South Bend, Elkhart, Fort Wayne, Lansing, E. Lansing, Flint, Saginaw, Bay City, Midland, Grand Rapids, Muskegon, Holland, Kalamazoo, Battle Creek, Jackson, Ann Arbor, DETROIT, Livonia, Warren, Sterling Heights, Pontiac, Windsor, Toledo, Monroe, Sandusky, Lorain, Elyria, CLEVELAND, Euclid, Lakewood, Akron, Canton, Youngstown

Indianapolis, Anderson, Muncie, Kokomo, Lafayette, Terre Haute, Bloomington, Columbus, Cincinnati, Dayton, Springfield, Columbus, Newark, Zanesville, Marion, Mansfield, Lima

Louisville, Lexington, Frankfort, Owensboro, Evansville, Henderson, Bowling Green

PITTSBURGH, Penn Hills, McKeesport, Altoona, Johnstown, State College, Williamsport, Erie, Buffalo, Niagara Falls, Rochester, Hamilton, Toronto, Oshawa, Kitchener, Guelph, Brampton, London, Sarnia, Barrie, Peterborough, Kingston

WASHINGTON D.C., BALTIMORE, Arlington, Alexandria, Frederick, Hagerstown, Cumberland, Harrisburg, Charleston, Huntington, Roanoke, Lynchburg, Richmond

ft m
6000 2000
4500 1500
3000 1000
1200 400
600 200
0 0
200 600
m ft

Projection: Albers' Equal Area with two standard parallels

50 0 50 100 150 200 km
50 0 50 100 150 miles

1:6 000 000

## TOURISM IN THE USA

Olympic N.P.
North Cascades N.P.
Seattle
Mt. Rainier N.P.
Glacier N.P.
Voyageurs N.P.
Isle Royale N.P.
Acadia N.P.
Boston
Redwood N.P.
Crater Lake N.P.
Theodore Roosevelt N.P.
Niagara Falls
New York
San Francisco
Lassen Volcanic N.P.
Yellowstone N.P.
Badlands N.P.
Minneapolis
Detroit
Philadelphia
Atlantic City
Grand Teton N.P.
Wind Cave N.P.
Yosemite N.P.
Capitol Reef N.P.
Rocky Mt. N.P.
Chicago
Shenandoah N.P.
Washington
Kings Canyon N.P.
Bryce Canyon N.P.
Arches N.P.
Denver
Kansas City
St. Louis
Great Smoky Mountains N.P.
Sequoia N.P.
Death Valley N.P.
Zion N.P.
Mesa Verde N.P.
Mammoth Cave N.P.
Channel Islands N.P.
Las Vegas
Grand Canyon N.P.
Petrified Forest N.P.
Hot Springs N.P.
Atlanta
Los Angeles
Phoenix
Saguaro N.P.
Carlsbad Caverns N.P.
Dallas
San Diego
Guadalupe Mountains N.P.
Big Bend N.P.
Houston
Orlando
Tampa
New Orleans
Dry Tortugas N.P.
Miami
Everglades N.P.

Major tourist centres

Major concentration of hotels

Major National Parks

COPYRIGHT PHILIP'S

**JAMAICA**
1:3 000 000

CARIBBEAN SEA

JAMAICA

**GUADELOUPE**
(Fr.)

**MARTINIQUE**
(Fr.)

**GUADELOUPE AND MARTINIQUE**
1:2 000 000

Projection : Bonne

Projection: *Lambert's Azimuthal Equal Area*

1:28 000 000

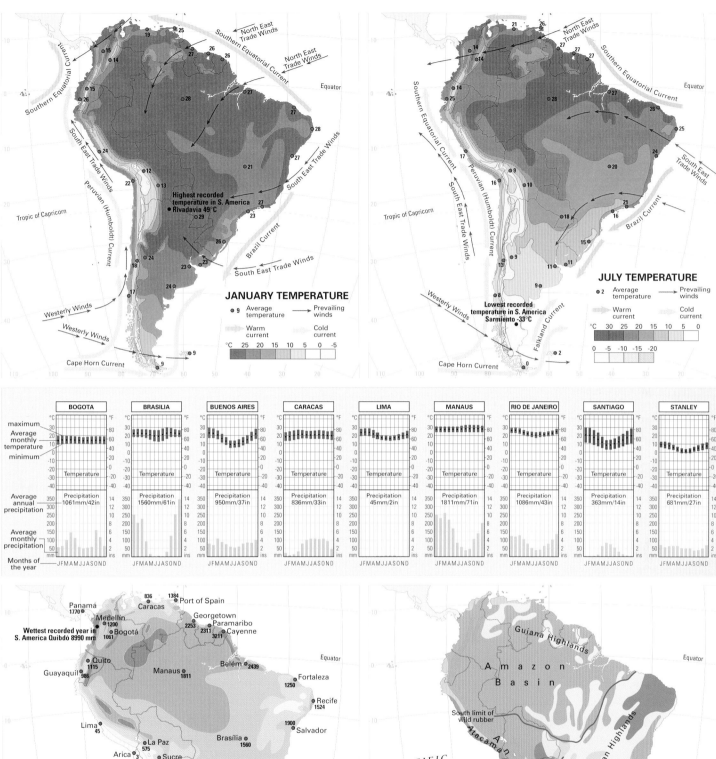

### JANUARY TEMPERATURE

North East Trade Winds
Southern Equatorial Current
North East Trade Winds
Southern Equatorial Current
Equator
South East Trade Winds
Peruvian (Humboldt) Current
Tropic of Capricorn
Brazil Current
South East Trade Winds
South East Trade Winds
**Highest recorded temperature in S. America Rivadavia 49°C**
Westerly Winds
Westerly Winds
Cape Horn Current

● 9 Average temperature
→ Prevailing winds
Warm current
Cold current
°C 25 20 15 10 5 0 -5

### JULY TEMPERATURE

North East Trade Winds
North East Trade Winds
Southern Equatorial Current
Equator
Southern Equatorial Current
Peruvian (Humboldt) Current
South East Trade Winds
Tropic of Capricorn
South East Trade Winds
Brazil Current
South East Trade Winds
Westerly Winds
**Lowest recorded temperature in S. America Sarmiento -33°C**
Falkland Current
Cape Horn Current

● 2 Average temperature
→ Prevailing winds
Warm current
Cold current
°C 30 25 20 15 10 5 0
0 -5 -10 -15 -20

### Climate Graphs

| BOGOTA | BRASILIA | BUENOS AIRES | CARACAS | LIMA | MANAUS | RIO DE JANEIRO | SANTIAGO | STANLEY |
|---|---|---|---|---|---|---|---|---|

maximum
Average monthly temperature
minimum
Temperature

Average annual precipitation
Average monthly precipitation
Precipitation

- BOGOTA — Precipitation 1061mm/42in
- BRASILIA — Precipitation 1560mm/61in
- BUENOS AIRES — Precipitation 950mm/37in
- CARACAS — Precipitation 836mm/33in
- LIMA — Precipitation 45mm/2in
- MANAUS — Precipitation 1811mm/71in
- RIO DE JANEIRO — Precipitation 1086mm/43in
- SANTIAGO — Precipitation 363mm/14in
- STANLEY — Precipitation 681mm/27in

Months of the year: JFMAMJJASOND

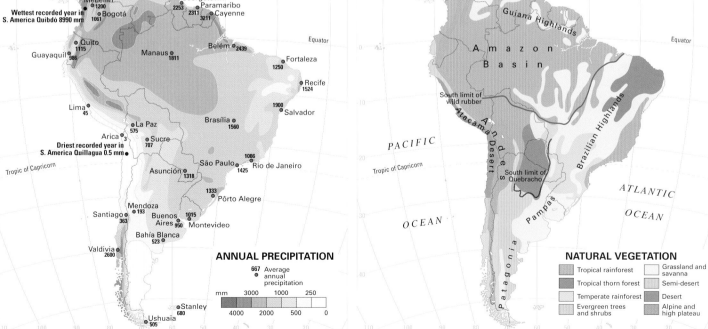

### ANNUAL PRECIPITATION

- Panamá 1770
- Caracas 836
- Port of Spain 1384
- Medellín 1200
- **Wettest recorded year in S. America Quibdó 8990 mm**
- Bogotá 1061
- Georgetown 2253
- Paramaribo 2311
- Cayenne 3211
- Quito 1115
- Guayaquil 986
- Manaus 1811
- Belém 2439
- Equator
- Fortaleza 1250
- Recife 1524
- Lima 45
- La Paz 575
- Arica 3
- Sucre 707
- **Driest recorded year in S. America Quillagua 0.5 mm**
- Brasília 1560
- Salvador 1900
- São Paulo 1086
- Rio de Janeiro 1425
- Asunción 1318
- Pôrto Alegre 1333
- Tropic of Capricorn
- Mendoza 193
- Santiago 363
- Buenos Aires 950
- Montevideo 1015
- Bahía Blanca 523
- Valdivia 2600
- Stanley 680
- Ushuaïa 505

● 667 Average annual precipitation
mm 4000 3000 2000 1000 500 250 0

### NATURAL VEGETATION

Guiana Highlands
Amazon Basin
Equator
South limit of wild rubber
Andes
Atacama Desert
Brazilian Highlands
PACIFIC OCEAN
Tropic of Capricorn
South limit of Quebracho
Pampas
ATLANTIC OCEAN
Patagonia

- Tropical rainforest
- Tropical thorn forest
- Temperate rainforest
- Evergreen trees and shrubs
- Grassland and savanna
- Semi-desert
- Desert
- Alpine and high plateau

Projection: Lambert's Equivalent Azimuthal

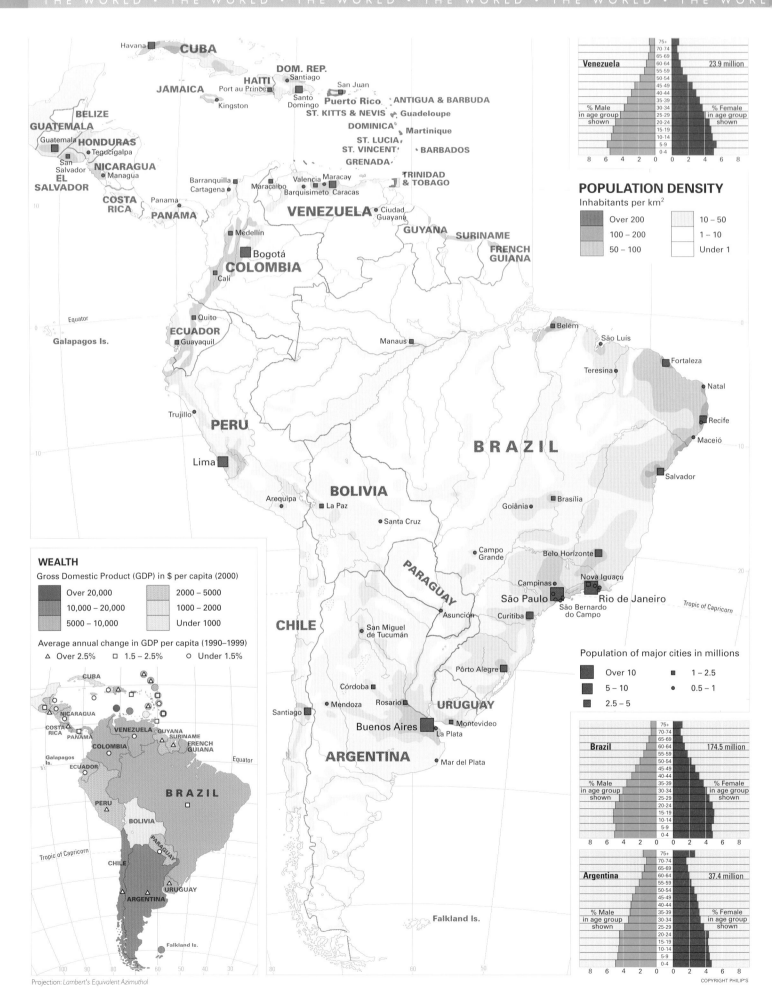

Venezuela 23.9 million
% Male in age group shown
% Female in age group shown
75+
70-74
65-69
60-64
55-59
50-54
45-49
40-44
35-39
30-34
25-29
20-24
15-19
10-14
5-9
0-4
8 6 4 2 0 0 2 4 6 8

## POPULATION DENSITY
Inhabitants per km²

| | |
|---|---|
| Over 200 | 10 – 50 |
| 100 – 200 | 1 – 10 |
| 50 – 100 | Under 1 |

### WEALTH
Gross Domestic Product (GDP) in $ per capita (2000)

| | |
|---|---|
| Over 20,000 | 2000 – 5000 |
| 10,000 – 20,000 | 1000 – 2000 |
| 5000 – 10,000 | Under 1000 |

Average annual change in GDP per capita (1990–1999)
△ Over 2.5%   □ 1.5 – 2.5%   ○ Under 1.5%

Population of major cities in millions

| | |
|---|---|
| Over 10 | 1 – 2.5 |
| 5 – 10 | 0.5 – 1 |
| 2.5 – 5 | |

Brazil 174.5 million
% Male in age group shown
% Female in age group shown
75+
70-74
65-69
60-64
55-59
50-54
45-49
40-44
35-39
30-34
25-29
20-24
15-19
10-14
5-9
0-4
8 6 4 2 0 0 2 4 6 8

Argentina 37.4 million
% Male in age group shown
% Female in age group shown
75+
70-74
65-69
60-64
55-59
50-54
45-49
40-44
35-39
30-34
25-29
20-24
15-19
10-14
5-9
0-4
8 6 4 2 0 0 2 4 6 8

Projection: Lambert's Equivalent Azimuthal

COPYRIGHT PHILIP'S

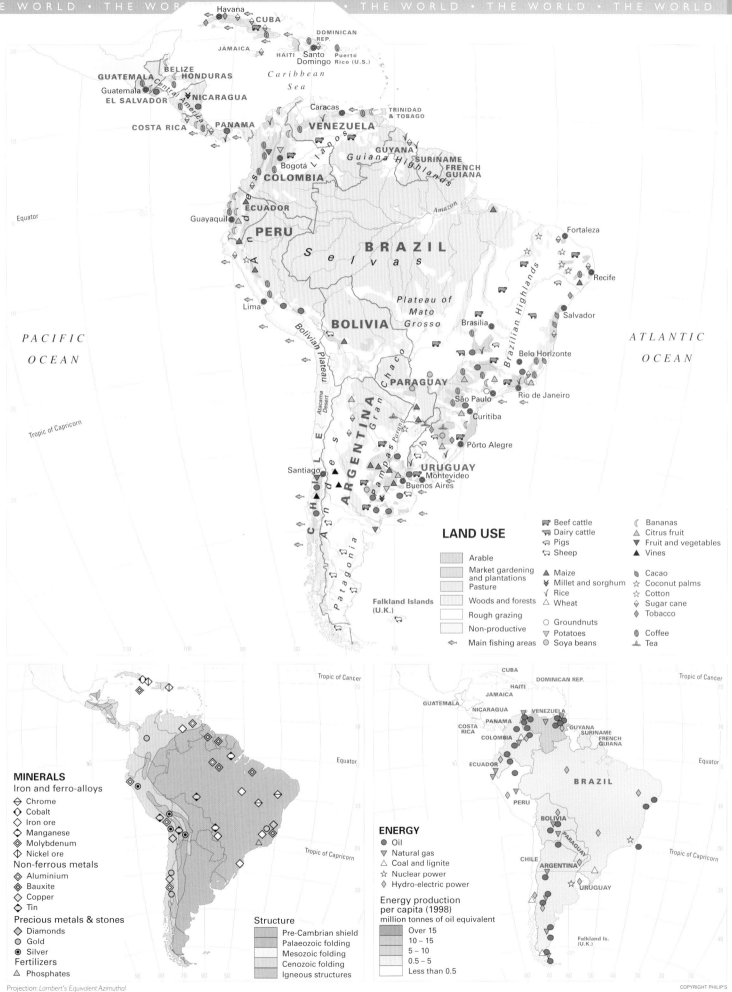 

Havana
CUBA
DOMINICAN REP.
JAMAICA
HAITI   Santo   Puerto Rico (U.S.)
Domingo
Caribbean Sea
GUATEMALA   BELIZE
HONDURAS
Guatemala
EL SALVADOR   NICARAGUA
COSTA RICA   PANAMA
Caracas
TRINIDAD & TOBAGO
VENEZUELA
GUYANA
Bogotá   Guiana Highlands   SURINAME   FRENCH GUIANA
COLOMBIA
Equator
ECUADOR
Guayaquil   Amazon
PERU   BRAZIL   Fortaleza
Selvas   Recife
Lima   Plateau of Mato Grosso   Salvador
BOLIVIA   Brasília
Belo Horizonte
PACIFIC OCEAN   Brazilian Highlands   ATLANTIC OCEAN
PARAGUAY   Rio de Janeiro
São Paulo
Curitiba
Tropic of Capricorn   Pôrto Alegre
Santiago   ARGENTINA   URUGUAY
Buenos Aires   Montevideo

Patagonia

## LAND USE

Falkland Islands (U.K.)

| | |
|---|---|
| | Arable |
| | Market gardening and plantations |
| | Pasture |
| | Woods and forests |
| | Rough grazing |
| | Non-productive |
| ⤆ | Main fishing areas |

Beef cattle      Bananas
Dairy cattle     Citrus fruit
Pigs             Fruit and vegetables
Sheep            Vines

Maize            Cacao
Millet and sorghum   Coconut palms
Rice             Cotton
Wheat            Sugar cane
                 Tobacco
Groundnuts       Coffee
Potatoes         Tea
Soya beans

## MINERALS

### Iron and ferro-alloys

◇ Chrome
◇ Cobalt
◇ Iron ore
◇ Manganese
◈ Molybdenum
◇ Nickel ore

### Non-ferrous metals

◆ Aluminium
◆ Bauxite
◇ Copper
◇ Tin

### Precious metals & stones

◇ Diamonds
○ Gold
◉ Silver

### Fertilizers

△ Phosphates

Tropic of Cancer
CUBA
DOMINICAN REP.
HAITI
JAMAICA
GUATEMALA
NICARAGUA
PANAMA   VENEZUELA
COSTA RICA   GUYANA
COLOMBIA   SURINAME   FRENCH GUIANA
Equator
ECUADOR
PERU   BRAZIL
BOLIVIA
Tropic of Capricorn
PARAGUAY
CHILE
ARGENTINA
URUGUAY
Falkland Is. (U.K.)

### Structure

| | |
|---|---|
| | Pre-Cambrian shield |
| | Palaeozoic folding |
| | Mesozoic folding |
| | Cenozoic folding |
| | Igneous structures |

## ENERGY

● Oil
▼ Natural gas
△ Coal and lignite
☆ Nuclear power
◇ Hydro-electric power

### Energy production per capita (1998)
million tonnes of oil equivalent

| | |
|---|---|
| | Over 15 |
| | 10 – 15 |
| | 5 – 10 |
| | 0.5 – 5 |
| | Less than 0.5 |

Projection: *Lambert's Equivalent Azimuthal*

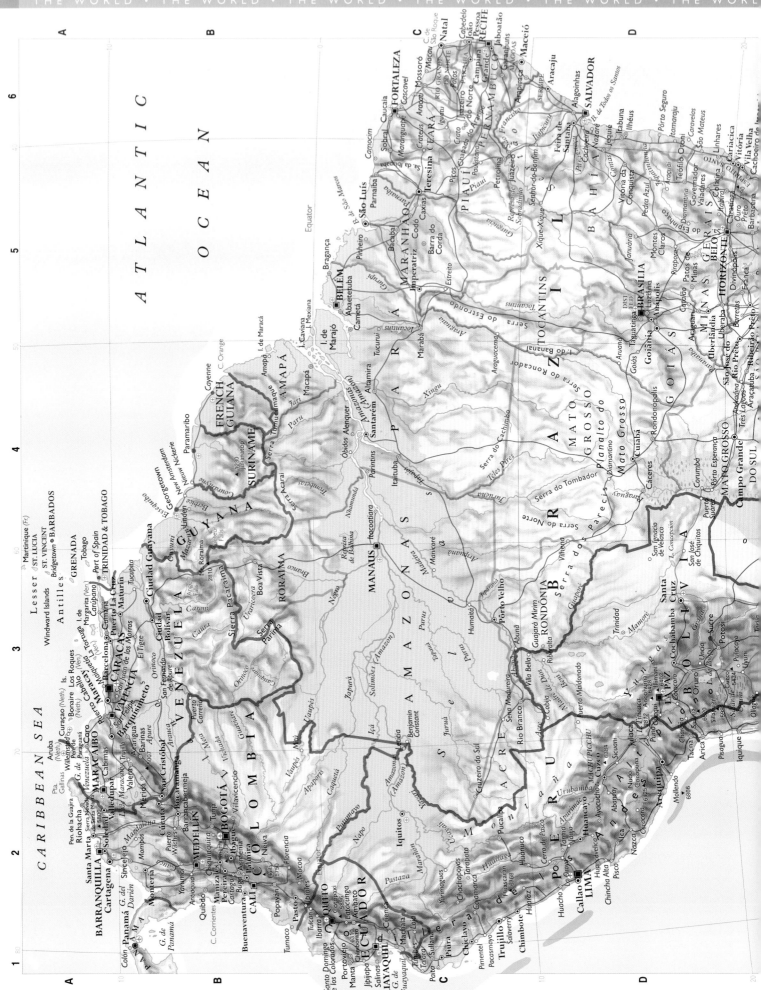

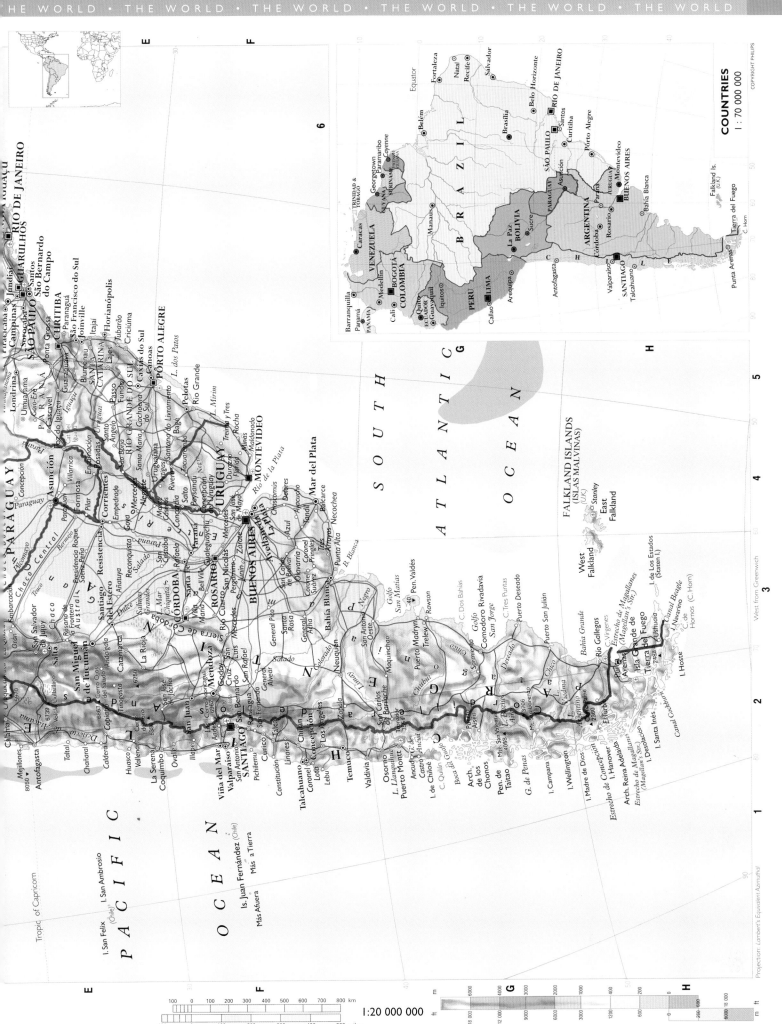

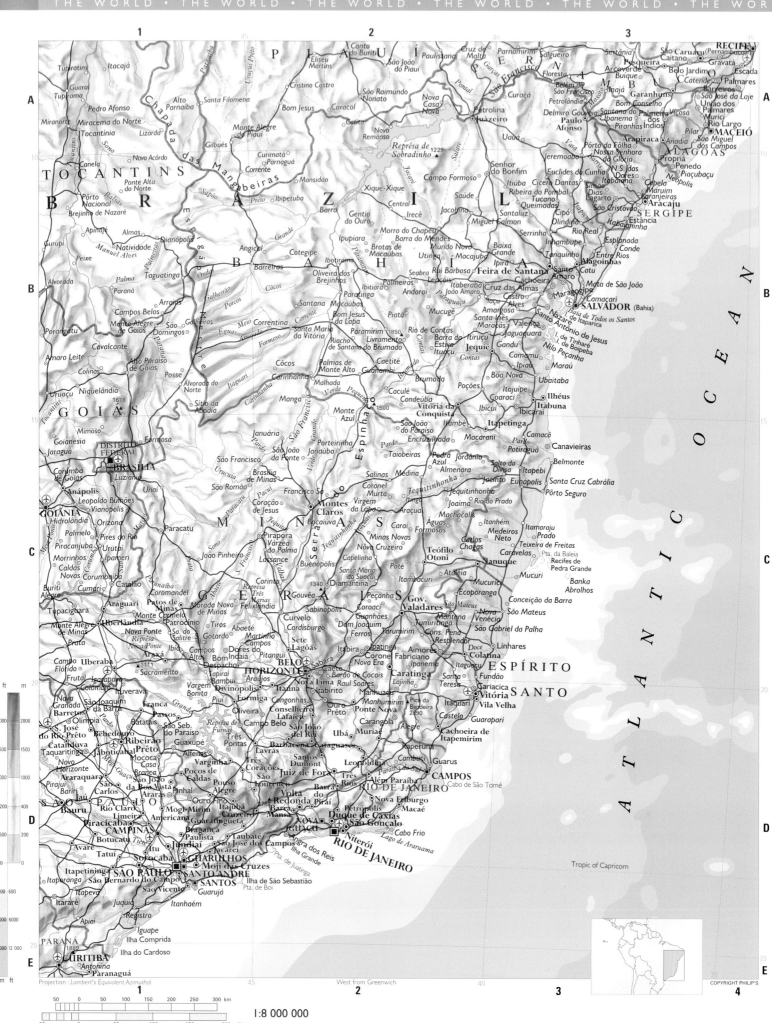

Projection : Lambert's *Equivalent* Azimuthal

West from Greenwich

COPYRIGHT PHILIP'S

1:8 000 000

50    0    50    100    150    200    250    300 km

50    0    50    100    150    200 miles

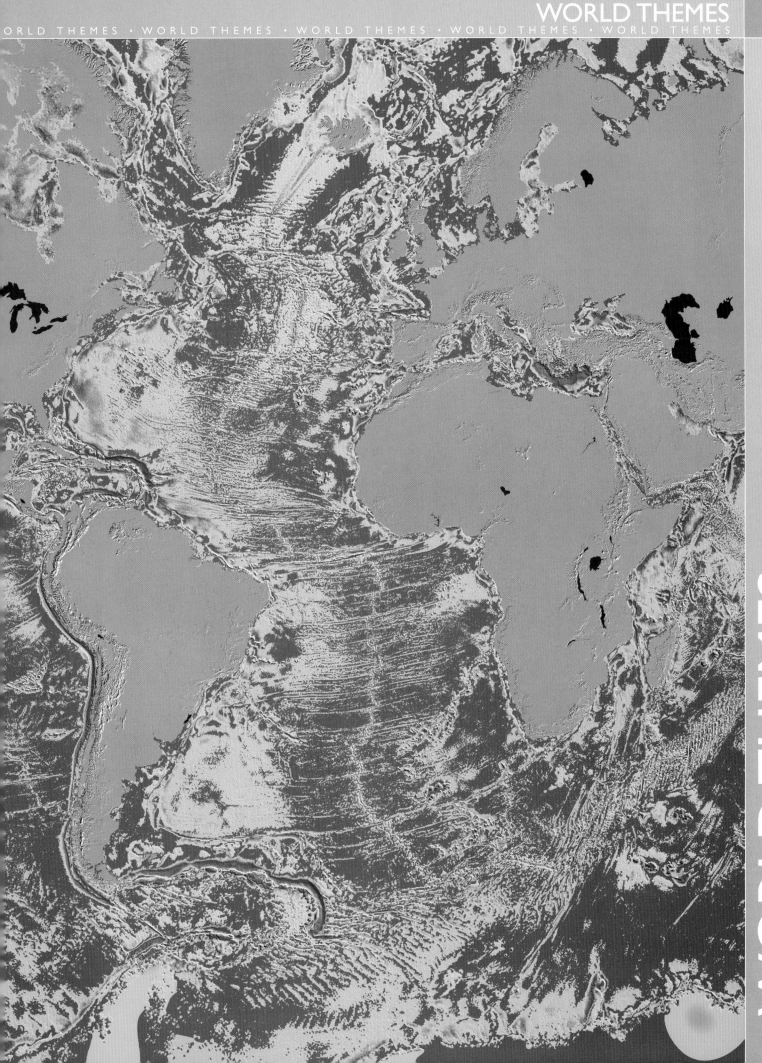

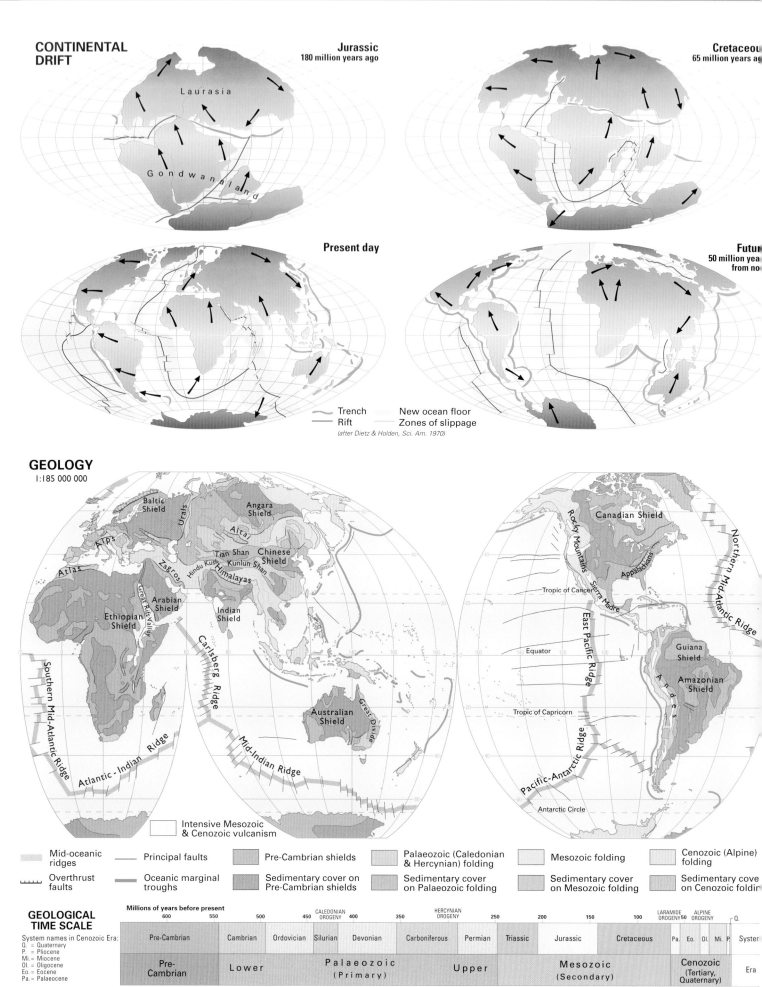

## CONTINENTAL DRIFT

**Jurassic**
180 million years ago

Laurasia

Gondwanaland

**Cretaceou**
65 million years ag

**Present day**

**Futur**
50 million yea
from no

Trench — New ocean floor
Rift — Zones of slippage

*(after Dietz & Holden, Sci. Am. 1970)*

## GEOLOGY
1:185 000 000

Baltic Shield
Urals
Angara Shield
Altai
Alps
Atlas
Tian Shan  Chinese Shield
Zagros
Hindu Kush  Kunlun Shan
Himalayas
Great Rift Valley
Arabian Shield
Ethiopian Shield
Indian Shield
Carlsberg Ridge
Australian Shield
Great Divide
Southern Mid-Atlantic Ridge
Atlantic - Indian Ridge
Mid-Indian Ridge

Rocky Mountains
Canadian Shield
Appalachians
Sierra Madre
Tropic of Cancer
Equator
East Pacific Ridge
Northern Mid-Atlantic Ridge
Guiana Shield
Amazonian Shield
Andes
Tropic of Capricorn
Pacific-Antarctic Ridge
Antarctic Circle

☐ Intensive Mesozoic & Cenozoic vulcanism

| Mid-oceanic ridges | Principal faults | Pre-Cambrian shields | Palaeozoic (Caledonian & Hercynian) folding | Mesozoic folding | Cenozoic (Alpine) folding |
| Overthrust faults | Oceanic marginal troughs | Sedimentary cover on Pre-Cambrian shields | Sedimentary cover on Palaeozoic folding | Sedimentary cover on Mesozoic folding | Sedimentary cove on Cenozoic foldin |

## GEOLOGICAL TIME SCALE

System names in Cenozoic Era:
Q. = Quaternary
P. = Pliocene
Mi. = Miocene
Ol. = Oligocene
Eo. = Eocene
Pa. = Palaeocene

Millions of years before present

| | 600 | 550 | 500 | 450 | CALEDONIAN OROGENY | 400 | 350 | HERCYNIAN OROGENY | 250 | 200 | 150 | 100 | LARAMIDE OROGENY 50 | ALPINE OROGENY | Q. | |
|---|---|---|---|---|---|---|---|---|---|---|---|---|---|---|---|---|
| | Pre-Cambrian | | Cambrian | Ordovician | Silurian | Devonian | | Carboniferous | Permian | Triassic | Jurassic | Cretaceous | Pa. | Eo. | Ol. | Mi. P. | System |
| | Pre-Cambrian | | Lower | | Palaeozoic (Primary) | | | Upper | | | Mesozoic (Secondary) | | | Cenozoic (Tertiary, Quaternary) | | Era |

# VOLCANOES AND PLATE TECTONICS

1:185 000 000

'Ring of Fire'
Constructive boundary (plates moving apart)
Destructive boundary (plates colliding)
Conservative boundary (plates sliding past each other)
7.2 ← Direction of movement along plate boundaries (cm/year)

○ Submarine volcanoes
✦ Geysers
△ Land volcanoes active since 1700

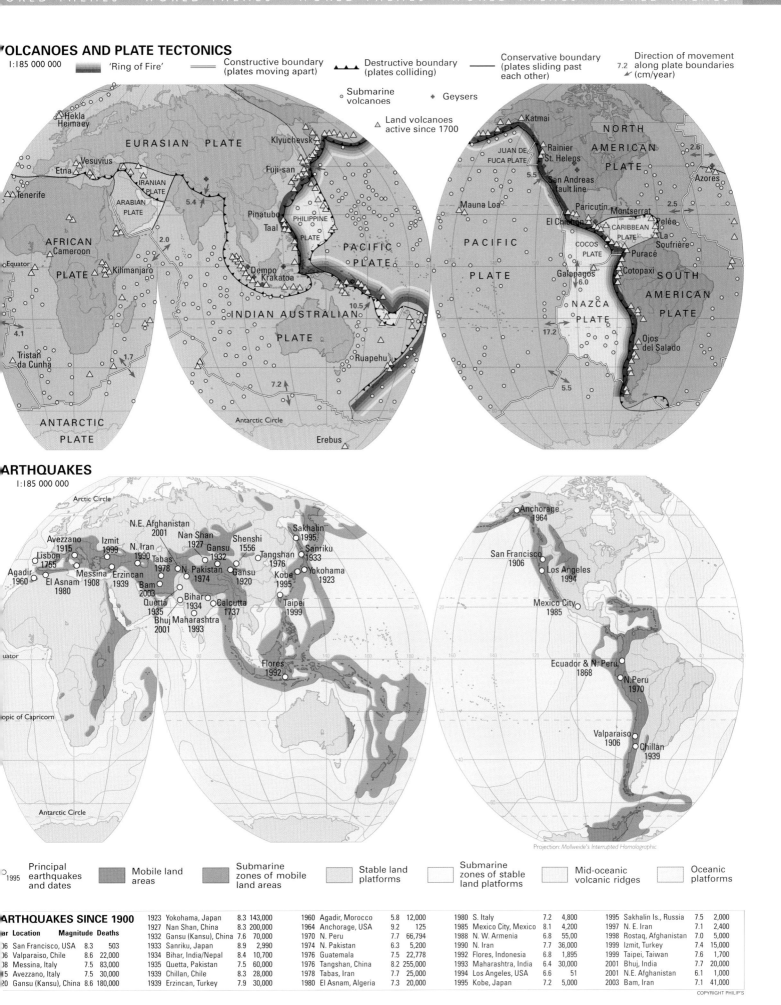

EURASIAN PLATE

Hekla
Heimaey
Vesuvius
Etna
Tenerife
ARABIAN PLATE
IRANIAN PLATE
AFRICAN PLATE
Cameroon
Equator
Kilimanjaro
Tristan da Cunha
ANTARCTIC PLATE

Klyuchevsk
Fuji-san
Pinatubo
Taal
PHILIPPINE PLATE
Dempo
Krakatoa
INDIAN AUSTRALIAN PLATE
Ruapehu
Erebus
Antarctic Circle

PACIFIC PLATE

5.4
2.0
4.1
1.7
7.2
10.5

Katmai
NORTH AMERICAN PLATE
JUAN DE FUCA PLATE
Rainier
St. Helens
San Andreas Fault line
Mauna Loa
Paricutín
Montserrat
El Chichón
CARIBBEAN PLATE
Pelée
La Soufrière
COCOS PLATE
Purace
Galapagos
Cotopaxi
NAZCA PLATE
SOUTH AMERICAN PLATE
Ojos del Salado
Azores

PACIFIC PLATE

2.6
5.5
2.5
6.0
17.2
5.5

# EARTHQUAKES

1:185 000 000

Arctic Circle
Equator
Tropic of Capricorn
Antarctic Circle

Avezzano 1915
Lisbon 1755
Agadir 1960
El Asnam 1980
Messina 1908
Izmit 1999
N. Iran 1990
Tabas 1978
Erzincan 1939
Bam 2003
Quetta 1935
Bihar 1934
Bhuj 2001
Maharashtra 1993
N.E. Afghanistan 2001
Nan Shan 1927
Gansu 1932
N. Pakistan 1974
Calcutta 1737
Shenshi 1556
Tangshan 1976
Gansu 1920
Sakhalin 1995
Sanriku 1933
Kobe 1995
Yokohama 1923
Taipei 1999
Flores 1992

Anchorage 1964
San Francisco 1906
Los Angeles 1994
Mexico City 1985
Ecuador & N. Peru 1868
N. Peru 1970
Valparaiso 1906
Chillan 1939

Projection: Mollweide's Interrupted Homolographic

○ 1995 Principal earthquakes and dates
Mobile land areas
Submarine zones of mobile land areas
Stable land platforms
Submarine zones of stable land platforms
Mid-oceanic volcanic ridges
Oceanic platforms

## EARTHQUAKES SINCE 1900

| Year | Location | Magnitude | Deaths |
|------|----------|-----------|--------|
| 1906 | San Francisco, USA | 8.3 | 503 |
| 1906 | Valparaiso, Chile | 8.6 | 22,000 |
| 1908 | Messina, Italy | 7.5 | 83,000 |
| 1915 | Avezzano, Italy | 7.5 | 30,000 |
| 1920 | Gansu (Kansu), China | 8.6 | 180,000 |
| 1923 | Yokohama, Japan | 8.3 | 143,000 |
| 1927 | Nan Shan, China | 8.3 | 200,000 |
| 1932 | Gansu (Kansu), China | 7.6 | 70,000 |
| 1933 | Sanriku, Japan | 8.9 | 2,990 |
| 1934 | Bihar, India/Nepal | 8.4 | 10,700 |
| 1935 | Quetta, Pakistan | 7.5 | 60,000 |
| 1939 | Chillan, Chile | 8.3 | 28,000 |
| 1939 | Erzincan, Turkey | 7.9 | 30,000 |
| 1960 | Agadir, Morocco | 5.8 | 12,000 |
| 1964 | Anchorage, USA | 9.2 | 125 |
| 1970 | N. Peru | 7.7 | 66,794 |
| 1974 | N. Pakistan | 6.3 | 5,200 |
| 1976 | Guatemala | 7.5 | 22,778 |
| 1976 | Tangshan, China | 8.2 | 255,000 |
| 1978 | Tabas, Iran | 7.7 | 25,000 |
| 1980 | El Asnam, Algeria | 7.3 | 20,000 |
| 1980 | S. Italy | 7.2 | 4,800 |
| 1985 | Mexico City, Mexico | 8.1 | 4,200 |
| 1988 | N. W. Armenia | 6.8 | 55,00 |
| 1990 | N. Iran | 7.7 | 36,000 |
| 1992 | Flores, Indonesia | 6.8 | 1,895 |
| 1993 | Maharashtra, India | 6.4 | 30,000 |
| 1994 | Los Angeles, USA | 6.6 | 51 |
| 1995 | Kobe, Japan | 7.2 | 5,000 |
| 1995 | Sakhalin Is., Russia | 7.5 | 2,000 |
| 1997 | N. E. Iran | 7.1 | 2,400 |
| 1998 | Rostaq, Afghanistan | 7.0 | 5,000 |
| 1999 | Izmit, Turkey | 7.4 | 15,000 |
| 1999 | Taipei, Taiwan | 7.6 | 1,700 |
| 2001 | Bhuj, India | 7.7 | 20,000 |
| 2001 | N.E. Afghanistan | 6.1 | 1,000 |
| 2003 | Bam, Iran | 7.1 | 41,000 |

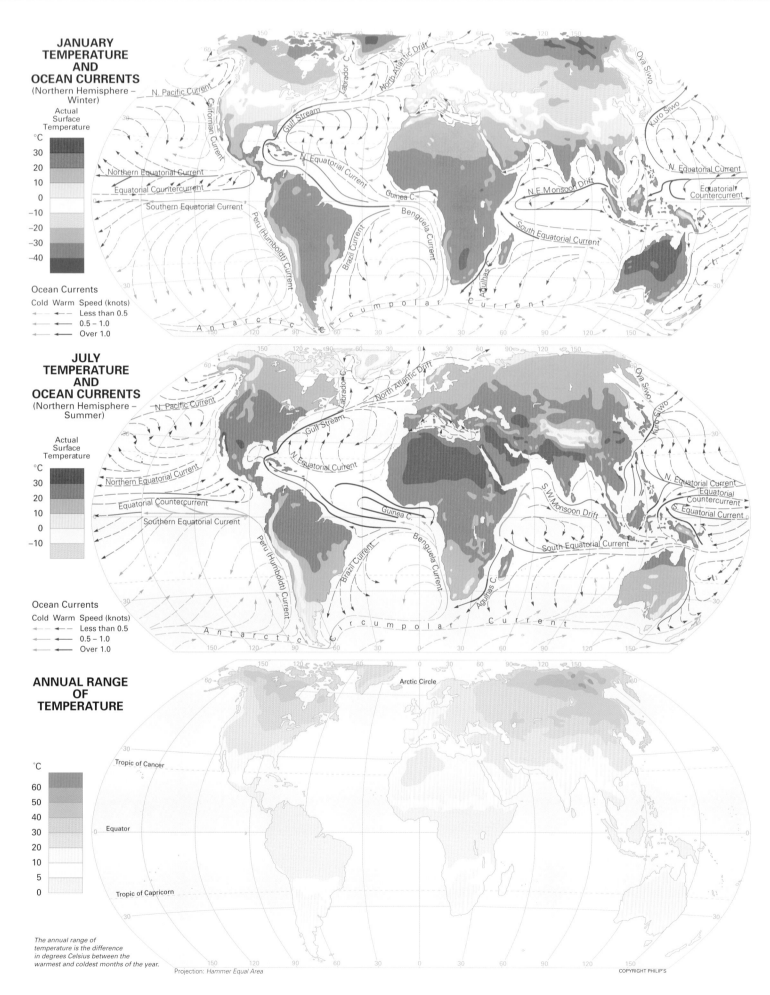

## JANUARY TEMPERATURE AND OCEAN CURRENTS
(Northern Hemisphere – Winter)

Actual Surface Temperature

°C
30
20
10
0
-10
-20
-30
-40

Ocean Currents

Cold Warm Speed (knots)
Less than 0.5
0.5 – 1.0
Over 1.0

## JULY TEMPERATURE AND OCEAN CURRENTS
(Northern Hemisphere – Summer)

Actual Surface Temperature

°C
30
20
10
0
-10

Ocean Currents

Cold Warm Speed (knots)
Less than 0.5
0.5 – 1.0
Over 1.0

## ANNUAL RANGE OF TEMPERATURE

°C
60
50
40
30
20
10
5
0

*The annual range of temperature is the difference in degrees Celsius between the warmest and coldest months of the year.*

Projection: *Hammer Equal Area*

COPYRIGHT PHILIP'S

1 : 190 000 000

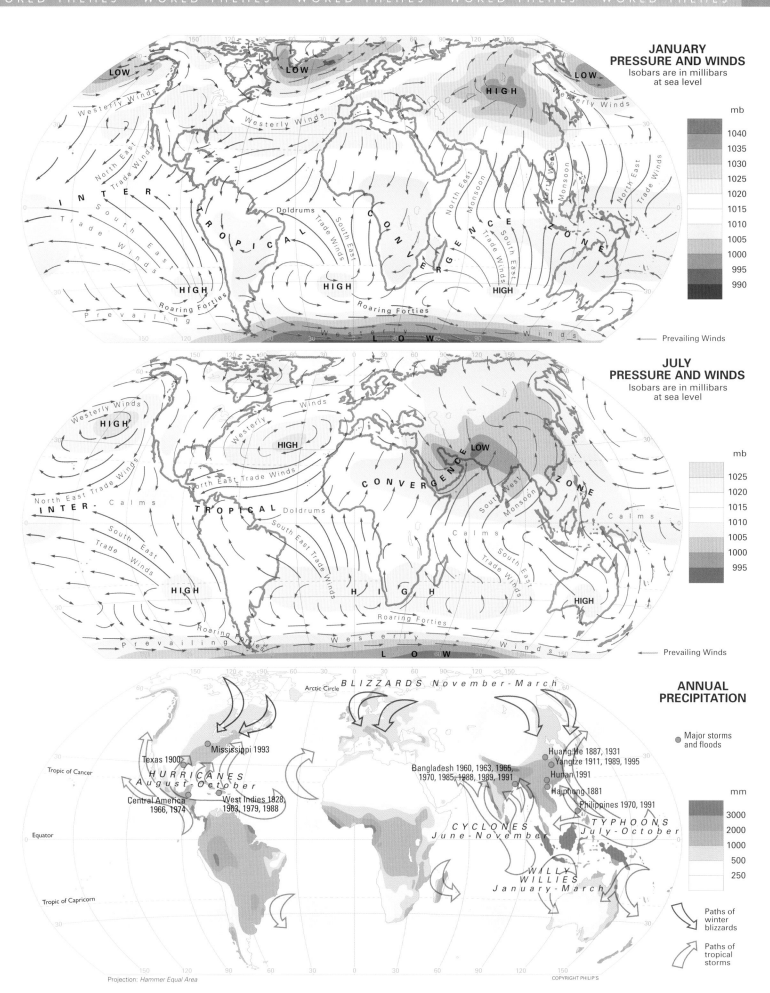

**JANUARY PRESSURE AND WINDS**

Isobars are in millibars at sea level

mb
1040
1035
1030
1025
1020
1015
1010
1005
1000
995
990

← Prevailing Winds

**JULY PRESSURE AND WINDS**

Isobars are in millibars at sea level

mb
1025
1020
1015
1010
1005
1000
995

← Prevailing Winds

**ANNUAL PRECIPITATION**

● Major storms and floods

mm
3000
2000
1000
500
250

Paths of winter blizzards

Paths of tropical storms

Projection: *Hammer Equal Area*

COPYRIGHT PHILIP'S

## CLIMATE REGIONS (after Köppen)

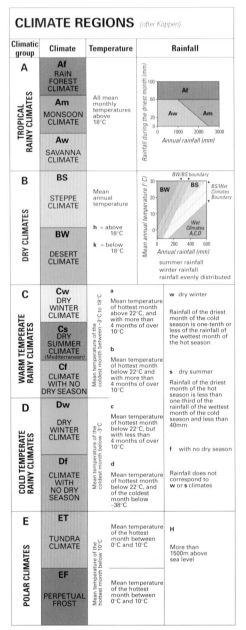

| Climatic group | Climate | Temperature | Rainfall |
|---|---|---|---|
| **A** TROPICAL RAINY CLIMATES | **Af** RAIN FOREST CLIMATE / **Am** MONSOON CLIMATE / **Aw** SAVANNA CLIMATE | All mean monthly temperatures above 18°C | *(graph: Rainfall during the driest month (mm) vs Annual rainfall (mm); regions Af, Aw, Am)* |
| **B** DRY CLIMATES | **BS** STEPPE CLIMATE / **BW** DESERT CLIMATE | Mean annual temperature; **h** = above 18°C; **k** = below 18°C | *(graph: Mean annual temperature (°C) vs Annual rainfall (mm); BW, BS, Wet Climates A,C,D; summer rainfall / winter rainfall / rainfall evenly distributed)* |
| **C** WARM TEMPERATE RAINY CLIMATES | **Cw** DRY WINTER CLIMATE / **Cs** DRY SUMMER CLIMATE (Mediterranean) / **Cf** CLIMATE WITH NO DRY SEASON | Mean temperature of the coldest month between −3°C to 18°C | **a** Mean temperature of hottest month above 22°C, and with more than 4 months of over 10°C / **b** Mean temperature of hottest month below 22°C and with more than 4 months of over 10°C / **w** dry winter — Rainfall of the driest month of the cold season is one-tenth or less of the rainfall of the wettest month of the hot season / **s** dry summer — Rainfall of the driest month of the hot season is less than one-third of the rainfall of the wettest month of the cold season and less than 40mm |
| **D** COLD TEMPERATE RAINY CLIMATES | **Dw** DRY WINTER CLIMATE / **Df** CLIMATE WITH NO DRY SEASON | Mean temperature of the coldest month below −3°C | **c** Mean temperature of hottest month below 22°C, but with less than 4 months of over 10°C / **d** Mean temperature of hottest month below 22°C, and of the coldest month below −38°C / **f** with no dry season — Rainfall does not correspond to **w** or **s** climates |
| **E** POLAR CLIMATES | **ET** TUNDRA CLIMATE / **EF** PERPETUAL FROST | Mean temperature of the hottest month between 0°C and 10°C / Mean temperature of the hottest month between 0°C and 10°C | **H** More than 1500m above sea level |

## CLIMATE RECORDS

**Highest recorded temperature:** Al Aziziyah, Libya, 58°C, 13 September 1922.

**Lowest recorded temperature (outside poles):** Verkhoyansk, Siberia, −68°C, 6 February 1933. Verkhoyansk also registered the greatest annual range of temperature: −70°C to 37°C.

**Highest barometric pressure:** Agata, Siberia, 1,083.8 mb at altitude 262 m, 31 December 1968.

**Lowest barometric pressure:** Typhoon Tip, 480 km west of Guam, Pacific Ocean, 870 mb, 12 October 1979.

**Driest place:** Quillagua, N. Chile, 0.5 mm, 1964–2001.

**Wettest place (12 months):** Cherrapunji, Meghalaya, N.E. India, August 1860 to August 1861. Cherrapunji also holds the record for rainfall in one month: 2930 mm, July 1861.

**Highest recorded wind speed:** Mt Washington, New Hampshire, USA, 371 km/h, 12 April 1934. This is three times as strong as hurricane force on the Beaufort Scale.

**Windiest place:** Commonwealth Bay, George V Coast, Antarctica, where gales frequently reach over 320 km/h.

Projection: Interrupted Mollweide's Homolographic

## THE MONSOON

In early March, which normally marks the end of the subcontinent's cool season and the start of the hot season, winds blow outwards from the mainland. But as the overhead sun and the ITCZ move northwards, the land is intensely heated, and a low-pressure system develops. The south-east trade winds, which are drawn across the Equator, change direction and are sucked into the interior to become south-westerly winds, bringing heavy rain. By November, the overhead sun and the ITCZ have again moved southwards and the wind directions are again reversed. Cool winds blow from the Asian interior to the sea, losing any moisture on the Himalayas before descending to the coast.

Monthly rainfall

| mm | |
|---|---|
| 400 | → wind direction |
| 200 | |
| 100 | ▬ ITCZ (intertropic convergen zone) |
| 50 | |
| 25 | |

**March** – Start of the hot, dry season, the ITCZ is over the southern Indian Ocean.

**July** – The rainy season, the ITCZ has migrated northwards; winds blow onshore.

**November** – The ITCZ has returned so the offshore winds are cool and dry.

## EL NIÑO

In a normal year, south-easterly trade winds drive surface waters westwards off the coast of South America, drawing cold, nutrient-rich water up from below. In an El Niño year (which occurs every 2–7 years), warm water from the west Pacific suppresses up-welling in the east, depriving the region of nutrients. The water is warmed by as much as 7°C, disturbing the tropical atmospheric circulation. During an intense El Niño, the south-east trade winds change direction and become equatorial westerlies, resulting in climatic extremes in many regions of the world, such as drought in parts of Australia and India, and heavy rainfall in south-eastern USA. An intense El Niño occurred in 1997–8, with resultant freak weather conditions across the entire Pacific region.

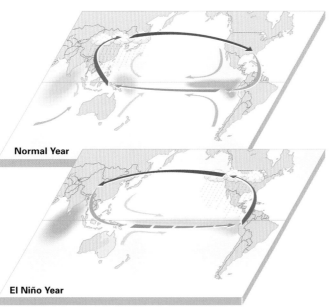

**Normal Year**

**El Niño Year**

## WINDCHILL FACTOR

In sub-zero weather, even moderate winds significantly reduce effective temperatures. The chart below shows the windchill effect across a range of speeds.

| | Wind speed (km/h) | | | | |
| | 16 | 32 | 48 | 64 | 80 |
|---|---|---|---|---|---|
| 0°C | −8 | −14 | −17 | −19 | −20 |
| −5°C | −14 | −21 | −25 | −27 | −28 |
| −10°C | −20 | −28 | −33 | −35 | −36 |
| −15°C | −26 | −36 | −40 | −43 | −44 |
| −20°C | −32 | −42 | −48 | −51 | −52 |
| −25°C | −38 | −49 | −56 | −59 | −60 |
| −30°C | −44 | −57 | −63 | −66 | −68 |
| −35°C | −51 | −64 | −72 | −74 | −76 |
| −40°C | −57 | −71 | −78 | −82 | −84 |
| −45°C | −63 | −78 | −86 | −90 | −92 |
| −50°C | −69 | −85 | −94 | −98 | −100 |

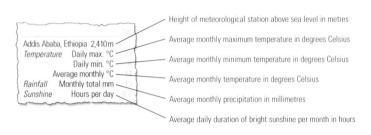

Addis Ababa, Ethiopia 2,410 m — Height of meteorological station above sea level in metres
*Temperature* Daily max. °C — Average monthly maximum temperature in degrees Celsius
Daily min. °C — Average monthly minimum temperature in degrees Celsius
Average monthly °C — Average monthly temperature in degrees Celsius
*Rainfall* Monthly total mm — Average monthly precipitation in millimetres
*Sunshine* Hours per day — Average daily duration of bright sunshine per month in hours

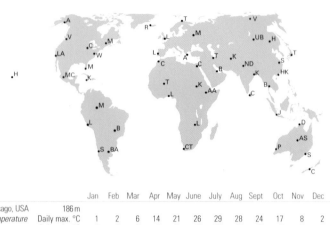

| Addis Ababa, Ethiopia 2,410 m | Jan | Feb | Mar | Apr | May | June | July | Aug | Sept | Oct | Nov | Dec | Year |
|---|---|---|---|---|---|---|---|---|---|---|---|---|---|
| *Temperature* Daily max. °C | 23 | 24 | 25 | 24 | 25 | 23 | 20 | 20 | 21 | 22 | 23 | 22 | 23 |
| Daily min. °C | 6 | 7 | 9 | 10 | 9 | 10 | 11 | 11 | 10 | 7 | 5 | 5 | 8 |
| Average monthly °C | 14 | 15 | 17 | 17 | 17 | 16 | 16 | 15 | 15 | 15 | 14 | 14 | 15 |
| *Rainfall* Monthly total mm | 13 | 35 | 67 | 91 | 81 | 117 | 247 | 255 | 167 | 29 | 8 | 5 | 1,115 |
| *Sunshine* Hours per day | 8.7 | 8.2 | 7.6 | 8.1 | 6.5 | 4.8 | 2.8 | 3.2 | 5.2 | 7.6 | 6.7 | 7 | 6.4 |

| Alice Springs, Australia 580 m | Jan | Feb | Mar | Apr | May | June | July | Aug | Sept | Oct | Nov | Dec | Year |
|---|---|---|---|---|---|---|---|---|---|---|---|---|---|
| *Temperature* Daily max. °C | 35 | 35 | 32 | 27 | 23 | 19 | 19 | 23 | 27 | 31 | 33 | 35 | 28 |
| Daily min. °C | 21 | 20 | 17 | 12 | 8 | 5 | 4 | 6 | 10 | 15 | 18 | 20 | 13 |
| Average monthly °C | 28 | 27 | 25 | 20 | 15 | 12 | 12 | 14 | 18 | 23 | 25 | 27 | 21 |
| *Rainfall* Monthly total mm | 44 | 33 | 27 | 10 | 15 | 13 | 7 | 8 | 7 | 18 | 29 | 38 | 249 |
| *Sunshine* Hours per day | 10.3 | 10.4 | 9.3 | 9.2 | 8 | 8 | 8.9 | 9.8 | 10 | 9.7 | 10.1 | 10 | 9.5 |

| Anchorage, USA 183 m | Jan | Feb | Mar | Apr | May | June | July | Aug | Sept | Oct | Nov | Dec | Year |
|---|---|---|---|---|---|---|---|---|---|---|---|---|---|
| *Temperature* Daily max. °C | –7 | –3 | 0 | 7 | 13 | 18 | 19 | 17 | 13 | 6 | –2 | –6 | –6 |
| Daily min. °C | –15 | –12 | –9 | –2 | 4 | 8 | 10 | 9 | 5 | –2 | –9 | –14 | –2 |
| Average monthly °C | –11 | –7 | –4 | 3 | 9 | 13 | 15 | 13 | 9 | 2 | –5 | –10 | –4 |
| *Rainfall* Monthly total mm | 20 | 18 | 13 | 11 | 13 | 25 | 47 | 64 | 64 | 47 | 28 | 24 | 374 |
| *Sunshine* Hours per day | 2.4 | 4.1 | 6.6 | 8.3 | 8.3 | 9.2 | 8.5 | 6 | 4.4 | 3.1 | 2.6 | 1.6 | 5.4 |

| Athens, Greece 107 m | Jan | Feb | Mar | Apr | May | June | July | Aug | Sept | Oct | Nov | Dec | Year |
|---|---|---|---|---|---|---|---|---|---|---|---|---|---|
| *Temperature* Daily max. °C | 13 | 14 | 16 | 20 | 25 | 30 | 33 | 33 | 29 | 24 | 19 | 15 | 23 |
| Daily min. °C | 6 | 7 | 8 | 11 | 16 | 20 | 23 | 23 | 19 | 15 | 12 | 8 | 14 |
| Average monthly °C | 10 | 10 | 12 | 16 | 20 | 25 | 28 | 28 | 24 | 20 | 15 | 11 | 18 |
| *Rainfall* Monthly total mm | 62 | 37 | 37 | 23 | 23 | 14 | 6 | 7 | 15 | 51 | 56 | 71 | 402 |
| *Sunshine* Hours per day | 3.9 | 5.2 | 5.8 | 7.7 | 8.9 | 10.7 | 11.9 | 11.5 | 9.4 | 6.8 | 4.8 | 3.8 | 7.3 |

| Bahrain City, Bahrain 2 m | Jan | Feb | Mar | Apr | May | June | July | Aug | Sept | Oct | Nov | Dec | Year |
|---|---|---|---|---|---|---|---|---|---|---|---|---|---|
| *Temperature* Daily max. °C | 20 | 21 | 25 | 29 | 33 | 36 | 37 | 38 | 36 | 32 | 27 | 22 | 30 |
| Daily min. °C | 14 | 15 | 18 | 22 | 25 | 29 | 31 | 32 | 29 | 25 | 22 | 16 | 23 |
| Average monthly °C | 17 | 18 | 21 | 25 | 29 | 32 | 34 | 35 | 32 | 29 | 25 | 19 | 26 |
| *Rainfall* Monthly total mm | 18 | 12 | 10 | 9 | 2 | 0 | 0 | 0 | 0 | 0.4 | 3 | 16 | 70 |
| *Sunshine* Hours per day | 5.9 | 6.9 | 7.9 | 8.8 | 10.6 | 13.2 | 12.1 | 12 | 12 | 10.3 | 7.7 | 6.4 | 9.5 |

| Bangkok, Thailand 10 m | Jan | Feb | Mar | Apr | May | June | July | Aug | Sept | Oct | Nov | Dec | Year |
|---|---|---|---|---|---|---|---|---|---|---|---|---|---|
| *Temperature* Daily max. °C | 32 | 33 | 34 | 35 | 34 | 33 | 32 | 32 | 32 | 31 | 31 | 31 | 33 |
| Daily min. °C | 20 | 23 | 24 | 26 | 25 | 25 | 25 | 24 | 24 | 24 | 23 | 20 | 24 |
| Average monthly °C | 26 | 28 | 29 | 30 | 30 | 29 | 28 | 28 | 28 | 28 | 27 | 26 | 28 |
| *Rainfall* Monthly total mm | 9 | 30 | 36 | 82 | 165 | 153 | 168 | 183 | 310 | 239 | 55 | 8 | 1,438 |
| *Sunshine* Hours per day | 8.2 | 8 | 8 | 10 | 7.5 | 6.1 | 4.7 | 5.2 | 5.2 | 6.1 | 7.3 | 7.8 | 7 |

| Brasilia, Brazil 910 m | Jan | Feb | Mar | Apr | May | June | July | Aug | Sept | Oct | Nov | Dec | Year |
|---|---|---|---|---|---|---|---|---|---|---|---|---|---|
| *Temperature* Daily max. °C | 28 | 28 | 28 | 28 | 27 | 27 | 27 | 29 | 30 | 29 | 28 | 27 | 28 |
| Daily min. °C | 18 | 18 | 18 | 17 | 15 | 13 | 13 | 14 | 16 | 18 | 18 | 18 | 16 |
| Average monthly °C | 23 | 23 | 23 | 22 | 21 | 20 | 20 | 21 | 23 | 24 | 23 | 22 | 22 |
| *Rainfall* Monthly total mm | 252 | 204 | 227 | 93 | 17 | 3 | 6 | 3 | 30 | 127 | 255 | 343 | 1,560 |
| *Sunshine* Hours per day | 5.8 | 5.7 | 6 | 7.4 | 8.7 | 9.3 | 9.6 | 9.8 | 7.9 | 6.5 | 4.8 | 4.4 | 7.2 |

| Buenos Aires, Argentina 25 m | Jan | Feb | Mar | Apr | May | June | July | Aug | Sept | Oct | Nov | Dec | Year |
|---|---|---|---|---|---|---|---|---|---|---|---|---|---|
| *Temperature* Daily max. °C | 30 | 29 | 26 | 22 | 18 | 14 | 14 | 16 | 18 | 21 | 25 | 28 | 22 |
| Daily min. °C | 17 | 17 | 16 | 12 | 9 | 5 | 6 | 6 | 8 | 10 | 14 | 16 | 11 |
| Average monthly °C | 23 | 23 | 21 | 17 | 13 | 10 | 10 | 11 | 13 | 15 | 19 | 22 | 16 |
| *Rainfall* Monthly total mm | 79 | 71 | 109 | 89 | 76 | 61 | 56 | 61 | 79 | 86 | 84 | 99 | 950 |
| *Sunshine* Hours per day | 9.2 | 8.5 | 7.5 | 6.8 | 4.9 | 3.5 | 3.8 | 5.2 | 6 | 6.8 | 8.1 | 8.5 | 6.6 |

| Cairo, Egypt 75 m | Jan | Feb | Mar | Apr | May | June | July | Aug | Sept | Oct | Nov | Dec | Year |
|---|---|---|---|---|---|---|---|---|---|---|---|---|---|
| *Temperature* Daily max. °C | 19 | 21 | 24 | 28 | 32 | 35 | 35 | 35 | 33 | 30 | 26 | 21 | 28 |
| Daily min. °C | 9 | 9 | 12 | 14 | 18 | 20 | 22 | 22 | 20 | 18 | 14 | 10 | 16 |
| Average monthly °C | 14 | 15 | 18 | 21 | 25 | 28 | 29 | 28 | 26 | 24 | 20 | 16 | 22 |
| *Rainfall* Monthly total mm | 4 | 4 | 3 | 1 | 2 | 1 | 0 | 0 | 1 | 1 | 3 | 7 | 27 |
| *Sunshine* Hours per day | 6.9 | 8.4 | 8.7 | 9.7 | 10.5 | 11.9 | 11.7 | 11.3 | 10.4 | 9.4 | 8.3 | 6.4 | 9.5 |

| Cape Town, South Africa 44 m | Jan | Feb | Mar | Apr | May | June | July | Aug | Sept | Oct | Nov | Dec | Year |
|---|---|---|---|---|---|---|---|---|---|---|---|---|---|
| *Temperature* Daily max. °C | 26 | 26 | 25 | 23 | 20 | 18 | 17 | 18 | 19 | 21 | 24 | 25 | 22 |
| Daily min. °C | 15 | 15 | 14 | 11 | 9 | 7 | 7 | 7 | 8 | 10 | 13 | 15 | 11 |
| Average monthly °C | 21 | 20 | 20 | 17 | 14 | 13 | 12 | 12 | 14 | 16 | 18 | 20 | 16 |
| *Rainfall* Monthly total mm | 12 | 19 | 17 | 42 | 67 | 98 | 68 | 76 | 36 | 45 | 12 | 13 | 505 |
| *Sunshine* Hours per day | 11.4 | 10.2 | 9.4 | 7.7 | 6.1 | 5.7 | 6.4 | 6.6 | 7.6 | 8.6 | 10.2 | 10.9 | 8.4 |

| Casablanca, Morocco 59 m | Jan | Feb | Mar | Apr | May | June | July | Aug | Sept | Oct | Nov | Dec | Year |
|---|---|---|---|---|---|---|---|---|---|---|---|---|---|
| *Temperature* Daily max. °C | 17 | 18 | 20 | 21 | 22 | 24 | 26 | 26 | 26 | 24 | 21 | 18 | 22 |
| Daily min. °C | 8 | 9 | 11 | 12 | 15 | 18 | 19 | 20 | 18 | 15 | 12 | 10 | 14 |
| Average monthly °C | 13 | 13 | 15 | 16 | 18 | 21 | 23 | 23 | 22 | 20 | 17 | 14 | 18 |
| *Rainfall* Monthly total mm | 78 | 61 | 54 | 37 | 20 | 3 | 0 | 1 | 6 | 28 | 58 | 94 | 440 |
| *Sunshine* Hours per day | 5.2 | 6.3 | 7.3 | 9 | 9.4 | 9.7 | 10.2 | 9.7 | 9.1 | 7.4 | 5.9 | 5.3 | 7.9 |

| Chicago, USA 186 m | Jan | Feb | Mar | Apr | May | June | July | Aug | Sept | Oct | Nov | Dec | Year |
|---|---|---|---|---|---|---|---|---|---|---|---|---|---|
| *Temperature* Daily max. °C | 1 | 2 | 6 | 14 | 21 | 26 | 29 | 28 | 24 | 17 | 8 | 2 | 15 |
| Daily min. °C | –7 | –6 | –2 | 5 | 11 | 16 | 20 | 19 | 14 | 8 | 0 | –5 | –6 |
| Average monthly °C | –3 | –2 | 2 | 9 | 16 | 21 | 24 | 23 | 19 | 13 | 4 | –2 | 4 |
| *Rainfall* Monthly total mm | 47 | 41 | 70 | 77 | 96 | 103 | 86 | 80 | 69 | 71 | 56 | 48 | 844 |
| *Sunshine* Hours per day | 4 | 5 | 6.6 | 6.9 | 8.9 | 10.2 | 10 | 9.2 | 8.2 | 6.9 | 4.5 | 3.7 | 7 |

| Christchurch, New Zealand 5 m | Jan | Feb | Mar | Apr | May | June | July | Aug | Sept | Oct | Nov | Dec | Year |
|---|---|---|---|---|---|---|---|---|---|---|---|---|---|
| *Temperature* Daily max. °C | 21 | 21 | 19 | 17 | 13 | 11 | 10 | 11 | 14 | 17 | 19 | 21 | 16 |
| Daily min. °C | 12 | 12 | 10 | 7 | 4 | 2 | 1 | 3 | 5 | 7 | 8 | 11 | 7 |
| Average monthly °C | 16 | 16 | 15 | 12 | 9 | 6 | 6 | 7 | 9 | 12 | 13 | 16 | 11 |
| *Rainfall* Monthly total mm | 56 | 46 | 43 | 46 | 76 | 69 | 61 | 58 | 51 | 51 | 51 | 61 | 669 |
| *Sunshine* Hours per day | 7 | 6.5 | 5.6 | 4.7 | 4.3 | 3.9 | 4.1 | 4.7 | 5.6 | 6.1 | 6.9 | 6.3 | 5.5 |

| Colombo, Sri Lanka 10 m | Jan | Feb | Mar | Apr | May | June | July | Aug | Sept | Oct | Nov | Dec | Year |
|---|---|---|---|---|---|---|---|---|---|---|---|---|---|
| *Temperature* Daily max. °C | 30 | 31 | 31 | 31 | 30 | 30 | 29 | 29 | 30 | 29 | 29 | 30 | 30 |
| Daily min. °C | 22 | 22 | 23 | 24 | 25 | 25 | 25 | 25 | 25 | 24 | 23 | 22 | 24 |
| Average monthly °C | 26 | 26 | 27 | 28 | 28 | 27 | 27 | 27 | 27 | 27 | 26 | 26 | 27 |
| *Rainfall* Monthly total mm | 101 | 66 | 118 | 230 | 394 | 220 | 140 | 102 | 174 | 348 | 333 | 142 | 2,368 |
| *Sunshine* Hours per day | 7.9 | 9 | 8.1 | 7.2 | 6.4 | 5.4 | 6.1 | 6.3 | 6.2 | 6.5 | 6.4 | 7.8 | 6.9 |

| Darwin, Australia 30 m | Jan | Feb | Mar | Apr | May | June | July | Aug | Sept | Oct | Nov | Dec | Year |
|---|---|---|---|---|---|---|---|---|---|---|---|---|---|
| *Temperature* Daily max. °C | 32 | 32 | 33 | 33 | 33 | 31 | 31 | 32 | 33 | 34 | 34 | 33 | 33 |
| Daily min. °C | 25 | 25 | 25 | 24 | 23 | 21 | 19 | 21 | 23 | 25 | 26 | 26 | 24 |
| Average monthly °C | 29 | 29 | 29 | 29 | 28 | 26 | 25 | 26 | 28 | 29 | 30 | 29 | 28 |
| *Rainfall* Monthly total mm | 405 | 309 | 279 | 77 | 8 | 2 | 0 | 1 | 15 | 48 | 108 | 214 | 1,466 |
| Sunshine Hours per day | 5.8 | 5.8 | 6.6 | 9.8 | 9.3 | 10 | 9.9 | 10.4 | 10.1 | 9.4 | 9.6 | 6.8 | 8.6 |

| Harbin, China 175 m | Jan | Feb | Mar | Apr | May | June | July | Aug | Sept | Oct | Nov | Dec | Year |
|---|---|---|---|---|---|---|---|---|---|---|---|---|---|
| *Temperature* Daily max. °C | –14 | –9 | 0 | 12 | 21 | 26 | 29 | 27 | 20 | 12 | –1 | –11 | 9 |
| Daily min. °C | –26 | –23 | –12 | –1 | 7 | 14 | 18 | 16 | 8 | 0 | –12 | –22 | –3 |
| Average monthly °C | –20 | –16 | –6 | 6 | 14 | 20 | 23 | 22 | 14 | 6 | –7 | –17 | 3 |
| *Rainfall* Monthly total mm | 4 | 6 | 17 | 23 | 44 | 92 | 167 | 119 | 52 | 36 | 12 | 5 | 577 |
| *Sunshine* Hours per day | 6.4 | 7.8 | 8 | 7.8 | 8.3 | 8.6 | 8.6 | 8.2 | 7.2 | 6.9 | 6.1 | 5.7 | 7.5 |

| Hong Kong, China 35 m | Jan | Feb | Mar | Apr | May | June | July | Aug | Sept | Oct | Nov | Dec | Year |
|---|---|---|---|---|---|---|---|---|---|---|---|---|---|
| *Temperature* Daily max. °C | 18 | 18 | 20 | 24 | 28 | 30 | 31 | 31 | 30 | 27 | 24 | 20 | 25 |
| Daily min. °C | 13 | 13 | 16 | 19 | 23 | 26 | 26 | 26 | 25 | 23 | 19 | 15 | 20 |
| Average monthly °C | 16 | 15 | 18 | 22 | 25 | 28 | 28 | 28 | 27 | 25 | 21 | 17 | 23 |
| *Rainfall* Monthly total mm | 30 | 60 | 70 | 133 | 332 | 479 | 286 | 415 | 364 | 33 | 46 | 17 | 2,265 |
| *Sunshine* Hours per day | 4.7 | 3.5 | 3.1 | 3.8 | 5 | 5.4 | 6.8 | 6.5 | 6.6 | 7 | 6.2 | 5.5 | 5.3 |

| Honolulu, Hawaii 5 m | Jan | Feb | Mar | Apr | May | June | July | Aug | Sept | Oct | Nov | Dec | Year |
|---|---|---|---|---|---|---|---|---|---|---|---|---|---|
| *Temperature* Daily max. °C | 26 | 26 | 26 | 27 | 28 | 29 | 29 | 29 | 30 | 29 | 28 | 26 | 28 |
| Daily min. °C | 19 | 19 | 19 | 20 | 21 | 22 | 23 | 23 | 23 | 22 | 21 | 20 | 21 |
| Average monthly °C | 23 | 22 | 23 | 23 | 24 | 26 | 26 | 26 | 26 | 26 | 24 | 23 | 24 |
| *Rainfall* Monthly total mm | 96 | 84 | 73 | 33 | 25 | 8 | 11 | 23 | 25 | 47 | 55 | 76 | 556 |
| *Sunshine* Hours per day | 7.3 | 7.7 | 8.3 | 8.6 | 8.8 | 9.1 | 9.4 | 9.3 | 9.2 | 8.3 | 7.5 | 6.2 | 8.3 |

| Jakarta, Indonesia 10 m | Jan | Feb | Mar | Apr | May | June | July | Aug | Sept | Oct | Nov | Dec | Year |
|---|---|---|---|---|---|---|---|---|---|---|---|---|---|
| *Temperature* Daily max. °C | 29 | 29 | 30 | 31 | 31 | 31 | 31 | 31 | 31 | 31 | 30 | 29 | 30 |
| Daily min. °C | 23 | 23 | 23 | 24 | 24 | 23 | 23 | 23 | 23 | 23 | 23 | 23 | 23 |
| Average monthly °C | 26 | 26 | 27 | 27 | 27 | 27 | 27 | 27 | 27 | 27 | 27 | 26 | 27 |
| *Rainfall* Monthly total mm | 300 | 300 | 211 | 147 | 114 | 97 | 64 | 43 | 66 | 112 | 142 | 203 | 1,799 |
| *Sunshine* Hours per day | 6.1 | 6.5 | 7.7 | 8.5 | 8.4 | 8.5 | 9.1 | 9.5 | 9.6 | 9 | 7.7 | 7.1 | 8.1 |

| Kabul, Afghanistan 1,791 m | Jan | Feb | Mar | Apr | May | June | July | Aug | Sept | Oct | Nov | Dec | Year |
|---|---|---|---|---|---|---|---|---|---|---|---|---|---|
| *Temperature* Daily max. °C | 2 | 4 | 12 | 19 | 26 | 31 | 33 | 33 | 30 | 22 | 17 | 8 | 20 |
| Daily min. °C | –8 | –6 | 1 | 6 | 11 | 13 | 16 | 15 | 11 | 6 | 1 | –3 | 5 |
| Average monthly °C | –3 | –1 | 6 | 13 | 18 | 22 | 25 | 24 | 20 | 14 | 9 | 3 | 12 |
| *Rainfall* Monthly total mm | 28 | 61 | 72 | 117 | 33 | 1 | 7 | 1 | 0 | 1 | 37 | 14 | 372 |
| *Sunshine* Hours per day | 5.9 | 6 | 5.7 | 6.8 | 10.1 | 11.5 | 11.4 | 11.2 | 9.8 | 9.4 | 7.8 | 6.1 | 8.5 |

| Khartoum, Sudan 380 m | Jan | Feb | Mar | Apr | May | June | July | Aug | Sept | Oct | Nov | Dec | Year |
|---|---|---|---|---|---|---|---|---|---|---|---|---|---|
| *Temperature* Daily max. °C | 32 | 33 | 37 | 40 | 42 | 41 | 38 | 36 | 38 | 39 | 35 | 32 | 37 |
| Daily min. °C | 16 | 17 | 20 | 23 | 26 | 27 | 26 | 25 | 25 | 25 | 21 | 17 | 22 |
| Average monthly °C | 24 | 25 | 28 | 32 | 34 | 34 | 32 | 30 | 32 | 32 | 28 | 25 | 30 |
| *Rainfall* Monthly total mm | 0 | 0 | 0 | 1 | 7 | 5 | 56 | 80 | 28 | 2 | 0 | 0 | 179 |
| *Sunshine* Hours per day | 10.6 | 11.2 | 10.4 | 10.8 | 10.4 | 10.1 | 8.6 | 8.6 | 9.6 | 10.3 | 10.8 | 10.6 | 10.2 |

| Kingston, Jamaica 35 m | Jan | Feb | Mar | Apr | May | June | July | Aug | Sept | Oct | Nov | Dec | Year |
|---|---|---|---|---|---|---|---|---|---|---|---|---|---|
| *Temperature* Daily max. °C | 30 | 30 | 30 | 31 | 31 | 32 | 32 | 32 | 32 | 31 | 31 | 31 | 31 |
| Daily min. °C | 20 | 20 | 20 | 21 | 22 | 24 | 23 | 23 | 23 | 23 | 22 | 21 | 22 |
| Average monthly °C | 25 | 25 | 25 | 26 | 26 | 28 | 28 | 28 | 27 | 27 | 26 | 26 | 26 |
| *Rainfall* Monthly total mm | 23 | 15 | 23 | 31 | 102 | 89 | 38 | 91 | 99 | 180 | 74 | 36 | 801 |
| *Sunshine* Hours per day | 8.3 | 8.8 | 8.7 | 8.7 | 8.3 | 7.8 | 8.5 | 8.5 | 7.6 | 7.3 | 8.3 | 7.7 | 8.2 |

### Kolkata (Calcutta), India  5m

| | Jan | Feb | Mar | Apr | May | June | July | Aug | Sept | Oct | Nov | Dec | Year |
|---|---|---|---|---|---|---|---|---|---|---|---|---|---|
| Temperature Daily max. °C | 27 | 29 | 34 | 36 | 35 | 34 | 32 | 32 | 32 | 32 | 29 | 26 | 31 |
| Daily min. °C | 13 | 15 | 21 | 24 | 25 | 26 | 26 | 26 | 26 | 23 | 18 | 13 | 21 |
| Average monthly °C | 20 | 22 | 27 | 30 | 30 | 30 | 29 | 29 | 29 | 28 | 23 | 20 | 26 |
| Rainfall Monthly total mm | 10 | 30 | 34 | 44 | 140 | 297 | 325 | 332 | 253 | 114 | 20 | 5 | 1,604 |
| Sunshine Hours per day | 8.6 | 8.7 | 8.9 | 9 | 8.7 | 5.4 | 4.1 | 4.1 | 5.1 | 6.5 | 8.3 | 8.4 | 7.1 |

### Lagos, Nigeria  40m

| | Jan | Feb | Mar | Apr | May | June | July | Aug | Sept | Oct | Nov | Dec | Year |
|---|---|---|---|---|---|---|---|---|---|---|---|---|---|
| Temperature Daily max. °C | 32 | 33 | 33 | 32 | 31 | 29 | 28 | 28 | 29 | 30 | 31 | 32 | 31 |
| Daily min. °C | 22 | 23 | 23 | 23 | 23 | 22 | 22 | 21 | 22 | 22 | 23 | 22 | 22 |
| Average monthly °C | 27 | 28 | 28 | 28 | 27 | 26 | 25 | 24 | 25 | 26 | 27 | 27 | 26 |
| Rainfall Monthly total mm | 28 | 41 | 99 | 99 | 203 | 300 | 180 | 56 | 180 | 190 | 63 | 25 | 1,464 |
| Sunshine Hours per day | 5.9 | 6.8 | 6.3 | 6.1 | 5.6 | 3.8 | 2.8 | 3.3 | 3 | 5.1 | 6.6 | 6.5 | 5.2 |

### Lima, Peru  120m

| | Jan | Feb | Mar | Apr | May | June | July | Aug | Sept | Oct | Nov | Dec | Year |
|---|---|---|---|---|---|---|---|---|---|---|---|---|---|
| Temperature Daily max. °C | 28 | 29 | 29 | 27 | 24 | 20 | 20 | 19 | 20 | 22 | 24 | 26 | 24 |
| Daily min. °C | 19 | 20 | 19 | 17 | 16 | 15 | 14 | 14 | 14 | 15 | 16 | 17 | 16 |
| Average monthly °C | 24 | 24 | 24 | 22 | 20 | 17 | 17 | 16 | 17 | 18 | 20 | 21 | 20 |
| Rainfall Monthly total mm | 1 | 1 | 1 | 1 | 5 | 5 | 8 | 8 | 8 | 3 | 3 | 1 | 45 |
| Sunshine Hours per day | 6.3 | 6.8 | 6.9 | 6.7 | 4 | 1.4 | 1.1 | 1 | 1.1 | 2.5 | 4.1 | 5 | 3.9 |

### Lisbon, Portugal  77m

| | Jan | Feb | Mar | Apr | May | June | July | Aug | Sept | Oct | Nov | Dec | Year |
|---|---|---|---|---|---|---|---|---|---|---|---|---|---|
| Temperature Daily max. °C | 14 | 15 | 17 | 20 | 21 | 25 | 27 | 28 | 26 | 22 | 17 | 15 | 21 |
| Daily min. °C | 8 | 8 | 10 | 12 | 13 | 15 | 17 | 17 | 17 | 14 | 11 | 9 | 13 |
| Average monthly °C | 11 | 12 | 14 | 16 | 17 | 20 | 22 | 23 | 21 | 18 | 14 | 12 | 17 |
| Rainfall Monthly total mm | 111 | 76 | 109 | 54 | 44 | 16 | 3 | 4 | 33 | 62 | 93 | 103 | 708 |
| Sunshine Hours per day | 4.7 | 5.9 | 6 | 8.3 | 9.1 | 10.6 | 11.4 | 10.7 | 8.4 | 6.7 | 5.2 | 4.6 | 7.7 |

### London (Kew), UK  5m

| | Jan | Feb | Mar | Apr | May | June | July | Aug | Sept | Oct | Nov | Dec | Year |
|---|---|---|---|---|---|---|---|---|---|---|---|---|---|
| Temperature Daily max. °C | 6 | 7 | 10 | 13 | 17 | 20 | 22 | 21 | 19 | 14 | 10 | 7 | 14 |
| Daily min. °C | 2 | 2 | 3 | 6 | 8 | 12 | 14 | 13 | 11 | 8 | 5 | 4 | 7 |
| Average monthly °C | 4 | 5 | 7 | 9 | 12 | 16 | 18 | 17 | 15 | 11 | 8 | 5 | 11 |
| Rainfall Monthly total mm | 54 | 40 | 37 | 37 | 46 | 45 | 57 | 59 | 49 | 57 | 64 | 48 | 593 |
| Sunshine Hours per day | 1.7 | 2.3 | 3.5 | 5.7 | 6.7 | 7 | 6.6 | 6 | 5 | 3.3 | 1.9 | 1.4 | 4.3 |

### Los Angeles, USA  30m

| | Jan | Feb | Mar | Apr | May | June | July | Aug | Sept | Oct | Nov | Dec | Year |
|---|---|---|---|---|---|---|---|---|---|---|---|---|---|
| Temperature Daily max. °C | 18 | 18 | 18 | 19 | 20 | 22 | 24 | 24 | 24 | 23 | 22 | 19 | 21 |
| Daily min. °C | 7 | 8 | 9 | 11 | 13 | 15 | 17 | 17 | 16 | 14 | 11 | 9 | 12 |
| Average monthly °C | 12 | 13 | 14 | 15 | 17 | 18 | 21 | 21 | 20 | 18 | 16 | 14 | 17 |
| Rainfall Monthly total mm | 69 | 74 | 46 | 28 | 3 | 3 | 0 | 0 | 5 | 10 | 28 | 61 | 327 |
| Sunshine Hours per day | 6.9 | 8.2 | 8.9 | 8.8 | 9.5 | 10.3 | 11.7 | 11 | 10.1 | 8.6 | 8.2 | 7.6 | 9.2 |

### Lusaka, Zambia  1,154m

| | Jan | Feb | Mar | Apr | May | June | July | Aug | Sept | Oct | Nov | Dec | Year |
|---|---|---|---|---|---|---|---|---|---|---|---|---|---|
| Temperature Daily max. °C | 26 | 26 | 26 | 27 | 25 | 23 | 23 | 26 | 29 | 31 | 29 | 27 | 27 |
| Daily min. °C | 17 | 17 | 16 | 15 | 12 | 10 | 9 | 11 | 15 | 18 | 18 | 17 | 15 |
| Average monthly °C | 22 | 22 | 21 | 21 | 18 | 17 | 16 | 19 | 22 | 25 | 23 | 22 | 21 |
| Rainfall Monthly total mm | 224 | 173 | 90 | 19 | 3 | 1 | 0 | 1 | 1 | 17 | 85 | 196 | 810 |
| Sunshine Hours per day | 5.1 | 5.4 | 6.9 | 8.9 | 9 | 9 | 9.1 | 9.6 | 9.5 | 9 | 7 | 5.5 | 7.8 |

### Manaus, Brazil  45m

| | Jan | Feb | Mar | Apr | May | June | July | Aug | Sept | Oct | Nov | Dec | Year |
|---|---|---|---|---|---|---|---|---|---|---|---|---|---|
| Temperature Daily max. °C | 31 | 31 | 31 | 31 | 31 | 31 | 32 | 33 | 34 | 34 | 33 | 32 | 32 |
| Daily min. °C | 24 | 24 | 24 | 24 | 24 | 24 | 24 | 24 | 24 | 25 | 25 | 24 | 24 |
| Average monthly °C | 28 | 28 | 28 | 27 | 28 | 28 | 28 | 29 | 29 | 29 | 29 | 28 | 28 |
| Rainfall Monthly total mm | 278 | 278 | 300 | 287 | 193 | 99 | 61 | 41 | 62 | 112 | 165 | 220 | 2,096 |
| Sunshine Hours per day | 3.9 | 4 | 3.6 | 3.9 | 5.4 | 6.9 | 7.9 | 8.2 | 7.5 | 6.6 | 5.9 | 4.9 | 5.7 |

### Mexico City, Mexico  2,309m

| | Jan | Feb | Mar | Apr | May | June | July | Aug | Sept | Oct | Nov | Dec | Year |
|---|---|---|---|---|---|---|---|---|---|---|---|---|---|
| Temperature Daily max. °C | 21 | 23 | 26 | 27 | 26 | 25 | 23 | 24 | 23 | 22 | 21 | 21 | 24 |
| Daily min. °C | 5 | 6 | 7 | 9 | 10 | 11 | 11 | 11 | 11 | 9 | 6 | 5 | 8 |
| Average monthly °C | 13 | 15 | 16 | 18 | 18 | 18 | 17 | 17 | 17 | 16 | 14 | 13 | 16 |
| Rainfall Monthly total mm | 8 | 4 | 9 | 23 | 57 | 111 | 160 | 149 | 119 | 46 | 16 | 7 | 709 |
| Sunshine Hours per day | 7.3 | 8.1 | 8.5 | 8.1 | 7.8 | 7 | 6.2 | 6.4 | 5.6 | 6.3 | 7 | 7.3 | 7.1 |

### Miami, USA  2m

| | Jan | Feb | Mar | Apr | May | June | July | Aug | Sept | Oct | Nov | Dec | Year |
|---|---|---|---|---|---|---|---|---|---|---|---|---|---|
| Temperature Daily max. °C | 24 | 25 | 27 | 28 | 30 | 31 | 32 | 32 | 31 | 29 | 27 | 25 | 28 |
| Daily min. °C | 14 | 15 | 16 | 19 | 21 | 23 | 24 | 24 | 24 | 22 | 18 | 15 | 20 |
| Average monthly °C | 19 | 20 | 21 | 23 | 25 | 27 | 28 | 28 | 27 | 25 | 22 | 20 | 24 |
| Rainfall Monthly total mm | 51 | 48 | 58 | 99 | 163 | 188 | 170 | 178 | 241 | 208 | 71 | 43 | 1,518 |
| Sunshine Hours per day | 7.7 | 8.3 | 8.7 | 9.4 | 8.9 | 8.5 | 8.7 | 8.4 | 7.1 | 6.5 | 7.5 | 7.1 | 8.1 |

### Montreal, Canada  57m

| | Jan | Feb | Mar | Apr | May | June | July | Aug | Sept | Oct | Nov | Dec | Year |
|---|---|---|---|---|---|---|---|---|---|---|---|---|---|
| Temperature Daily max. °C | −6 | −4 | 2 | 11 | 18 | 23 | 26 | 25 | 20 | 14 | 5 | −3 | 11 |
| Daily min. °C | −13 | −11 | −5 | 2 | 9 | 14 | 17 | 16 | 11 | 6 | 0 | −9 | 3 |
| Average monthly °C | −9 | −8 | −2 | 6 | 13 | 19 | 22 | 20 | 16 | 10 | 3 | −6 | 7 |
| Rainfall Monthly total mm | 87 | 76 | 86 | 83 | 81 | 91 | 98 | 87 | 96 | 84 | 89 | 89 | 1,047 |
| Sunshine Hours per day | 2.8 | 3.4 | 4.5 | 5.2 | 6.7 | 7.7 | 8.2 | 7.7 | 5.6 | 4.3 | 2.4 | 2.2 | 5.1 |

### Moscow, Russia  156m

| | Jan | Feb | Mar | Apr | May | June | July | Aug | Sept | Oct | Nov | Dec | Year |
|---|---|---|---|---|---|---|---|---|---|---|---|---|---|
| Temperature Daily max. °C | −6 | −4 | 1 | 9 | 18 | 22 | 24 | 22 | 17 | 10 | 1 | −5 | 9 |
| Daily min. °C | −14 | −16 | −11 | −1 | 5 | 9 | 12 | 9 | 4 | −2 | −6 | −12 | −2 |
| Average monthly °C | −10 | −10 | −5 | 4 | 12 | 15 | 18 | 16 | 10 | 4 | −2 | −8 | 4 |
| Rainfall Monthly total mm | 31 | 28 | 33 | 35 | 52 | 67 | 74 | 74 | 58 | 51 | 36 | 36 | 575 |
| Sunshine Hours per day | 1 | 1.9 | 3.7 | 5.2 | 7.8 | 8.3 | 8.4 | 7.1 | 4.4 | 2.4 | 1 | 0.6 | 4.4 |

### New Delhi, India  220m

| | Jan | Feb | Mar | Apr | May | June | July | Aug | Sept | Oct | Nov | Dec | Year |
|---|---|---|---|---|---|---|---|---|---|---|---|---|---|
| Temperature Daily max. °C | 21 | 24 | 29 | 36 | 41 | 39 | 35 | 34 | 34 | 34 | 28 | 23 | 32 |
| Daily min. °C | 6 | 10 | 14 | 20 | 26 | 28 | 27 | 26 | 24 | 17 | 11 | 7 | 18 |
| Average monthly °C | 14 | 17 | 22 | 28 | 33 | 34 | 31 | 30 | 29 | 26 | 20 | 15 | 25 |
| Rainfall Monthly total mm | 25 | 21 | 13 | 8 | 13 | 77 | 178 | 184 | 123 | 10 | 2 | 11 | 665 |
| Sunshine Hours per day | 7.7 | 8.2 | 8.2 | 8.7 | 9.2 | 7.9 | 6 | 6.3 | 6.9 | 9.4 | 8.7 | 8.3 | 8 |

### Perth, Australia  60m

| | Jan | Feb | Mar | Apr | May | June | July | Aug | Sept | Oct | Nov | Dec | Year |
|---|---|---|---|---|---|---|---|---|---|---|---|---|---|
| Temperature Daily max. °C | 29 | 30 | 27 | 25 | 21 | 18 | 17 | 18 | 19 | 21 | 25 | 27 | 23 |
| Daily min. °C | 17 | 18 | 16 | 14 | 12 | 10 | 9 | 9 | 10 | 11 | 14 | 16 | 13 |
| Average monthly °C | 23 | 24 | 22 | 19 | 16 | 14 | 13 | 13 | 15 | 16 | 19 | 22 | 18 |
| Rainfall Monthly total mm | 8 | 13 | 22 | 44 | 128 | 189 | 177 | 145 | 84 | 58 | 19 | 13 | 900 |
| Sunshine Hours per day | 10.4 | 9.8 | 8.8 | 7.5 | 5.7 | 4.8 | 5.4 | 6 | 7.2 | 8.1 | 9.6 | 10.4 | 7.8 |

### Reykjavik, Iceland  18m

| | Jan | Feb | Mar | Apr | May | June | July | Aug | Sept | Oct | Nov | Dec | Year |
|---|---|---|---|---|---|---|---|---|---|---|---|---|---|
| Temperature Daily max. °C | 2 | 3 | 5 | 6 | 10 | 13 | 15 | 14 | 12 | 8 | 5 | 4 | 8 |
| Daily min. °C | −3 | −3 | −1 | 1 | 4 | 7 | 9 | 8 | 6 | 3 | 0 | −2 | 3 |
| Average monthly °C | 0 | 0 | 2 | 4 | 7 | 10 | 12 | 11 | 9 | 5 | 3 | 1 | 5 |
| Rainfall Monthly total mm | 89 | 64 | 62 | 56 | 42 | 42 | 50 | 56 | 67 | 94 | 78 | 79 | 779 |
| Sunshine Hours per day | 0.8 | 2 | 3.6 | 4.5 | 5.9 | 6.1 | 5.8 | 5.4 | 3.5 | 2.3 | 1.1 | 0.3 | 3.7 |

### Santiago, Chile  520m

| | Jan | Feb | Mar | Apr | May | June | July | Aug | Sept | Oct | Nov | Dec | Year |
|---|---|---|---|---|---|---|---|---|---|---|---|---|---|
| Temperature Daily max. °C | 30 | 29 | 27 | 24 | 19 | 15 | 15 | 17 | 19 | 22 | 26 | 29 | 23 |
| Daily min. °C | 12 | 11 | 10 | 7 | 5 | 3 | 3 | 4 | 6 | 7 | 9 | 11 | 7 |
| Average monthly °C | 21 | 20 | 18 | 15 | 12 | 9 | 9 | 10 | 12 | 15 | 17 | 20 | 15 |
| Rainfall Monthly total mm | 3 | 3 | 5 | 13 | 64 | 84 | 76 | 56 | 31 | 15 | 8 | 5 | 363 |
| Sunshine Hours per day | 10.8 | 8.9 | 8.5 | 5.5 | 3.6 | 3.3 | 3.3 | 3.6 | 4.8 | 6.1 | 8.7 | 10.1 | 6.4 |

### Shanghai, China  5m

| | Jan | Feb | Mar | Apr | May | June | July | Aug | Sept | Oct | Nov | Dec | Year |
|---|---|---|---|---|---|---|---|---|---|---|---|---|---|
| Temperature Daily max. °C | 8 | 8 | 13 | 19 | 24 | 28 | 32 | 32 | 27 | 23 | 17 | 10 | 20 |
| Daily min. °C | −1 | 0 | 4 | 9 | 14 | 19 | 23 | 23 | 19 | 13 | 7 | 2 | 11 |
| Average monthly °C | 3 | 4 | 8 | 14 | 19 | 23 | 27 | 27 | 23 | 18 | 12 | 6 | 15 |
| Rainfall Monthly total mm | 48 | 59 | 84 | 94 | 94 | 180 | 147 | 142 | 130 | 71 | 51 | 36 | 1,136 |
| Sunshine Hours per day | 4 | 3.7 | 4.4 | 4.8 | 5.4 | 4.7 | 6.9 | 7.5 | 5.3 | 5.6 | 4.7 | 4.5 | 5.1 |

### Sydney, Australia  40m

| | Jan | Feb | Mar | Apr | May | June | July | Aug | Sept | Oct | Nov | Dec | Year |
|---|---|---|---|---|---|---|---|---|---|---|---|---|---|
| Temperature Daily max. °C | 26 | 26 | 25 | 22 | 19 | 17 | 17 | 18 | 20 | 22 | 24 | 25 | 22 |
| Daily min. °C | 18 | 19 | 17 | 14 | 11 | 9 | 8 | 9 | 11 | 13 | 16 | 17 | 14 |
| Average monthly °C | 22 | 22 | 21 | 18 | 15 | 13 | 12 | 13 | 16 | 18 | 20 | 21 | 18 |
| Rainfall Monthly total mm | 89 | 101 | 127 | 135 | 127 | 117 | 117 | 76 | 74 | 71 | 74 | 74 | 1,182 |
| Sunshine Hours per day | 7.5 | 7 | 6.4 | 6.1 | 5.7 | 5.3 | 6.1 | 7 | 7.3 | 7.5 | 7.5 | 7.5 | 6.8 |

### Tehran, Iran  1,191m

| | Jan | Feb | Mar | Apr | May | June | July | Aug | Sept | Oct | Nov | Dec | Year |
|---|---|---|---|---|---|---|---|---|---|---|---|---|---|
| Temperature Daily max. °C | 9 | 11 | 16 | 21 | 29 | 30 | 37 | 36 | 29 | 24 | 16 | 11 | 22 |
| Daily min. °C | −1 | 1 | 4 | 10 | 16 | 20 | 23 | 23 | 18 | 12 | 6 | 1 | 11 |
| Average monthly °C | 4 | 6 | 10 | 15 | 22 | 25 | 30 | 29 | 23 | 18 | 11 | 6 | 17 |
| Rainfall Monthly total mm | 37 | 23 | 36 | 31 | 14 | 2 | 1 | 1 | 1 | 5 | 29 | 27 | 207 |
| Sunshine Hours per day | 5.9 | 6.7 | 7.5 | 7.4 | 8.6 | 11.6 | 11.2 | 11 | 10.1 | 7.6 | 6.9 | 6.3 | 8.4 |

### Timbuktu, Mali  269m

| | Jan | Feb | Mar | Apr | May | June | July | Aug | Sept | Oct | Nov | Dec | Year |
|---|---|---|---|---|---|---|---|---|---|---|---|---|---|
| Temperature Daily max. °C | 31 | 35 | 38 | 41 | 43 | 42 | 38 | 35 | 38 | 40 | 37 | 31 | 37 |
| Daily min. °C | 13 | 16 | 18 | 22 | 26 | 27 | 25 | 24 | 24 | 23 | 18 | 14 | 21 |
| Average monthly °C | 22 | 25 | 28 | 31 | 34 | 34 | 32 | 30 | 31 | 31 | 28 | 23 | 29 |
| Rainfall Monthly total mm | 0 | 0 | 0 | 1 | 4 | 20 | 54 | 93 | 31 | 3 | 0 | 0 | 206 |
| Sunshine Hours per day | 9.1 | 9.6 | 9.6 | 9.7 | 9.8 | 9.4 | 9.6 | 9 | 9.3 | 9.5 | 9.5 | 8.9 | 9.4 |

### Tokyo, Japan  5m

| | Jan | Feb | Mar | Apr | May | June | July | Aug | Sept | Oct | Nov | Dec | Year |
|---|---|---|---|---|---|---|---|---|---|---|---|---|---|
| Temperature Daily max. °C | 9 | 9 | 12 | 18 | 22 | 25 | 29 | 30 | 27 | 20 | 16 | 11 | 19 |
| Daily min. °C | −1 | −1 | 3 | 4 | 13 | 17 | 22 | 23 | 19 | 13 | 7 | 1 | 10 |
| Average monthly °C | 4 | 4 | 8 | 11 | 18 | 21 | 25 | 26 | 23 | 17 | 11 | 6 | 14 |
| Rainfall Monthly total mm | 48 | 73 | 101 | 135 | 131 | 182 | 146 | 147 | 217 | 220 | 101 | 61 | 1,562 |
| Sunshine Hours per day | 6 | 5.9 | 5.7 | 6 | 6.2 | 5 | 5.8 | 6.6 | 4.5 | 4.4 | 4.8 | 5.4 | 5.5 |

### Tromsø, Norway  100m

| | Jan | Feb | Mar | Apr | May | June | July | Aug | Sept | Oct | Nov | Dec | Year |
|---|---|---|---|---|---|---|---|---|---|---|---|---|---|
| Temperature Daily max. °C | −2 | −2 | 0 | 3 | 7 | 12 | 16 | 14 | 10 | 5 | 2 | 0 | 5 |
| Daily min. °C | −6 | −6 | −5 | −2 | 1 | 6 | 9 | 8 | 5 | 1 | −2 | −4 | 0 |
| Average monthly °C | −4 | −4 | −3 | 0 | 4 | 9 | 13 | 11 | 7 | 3 | 0 | −2 | 3 |
| Rainfall Monthly total mm | 96 | 79 | 91 | 65 | 61 | 59 | 56 | 80 | 109 | 115 | 88 | 95 | 994 |
| Sunshine Hours per day | 0.1 | 1.6 | 2.9 | 6.1 | 5.7 | 6.9 | 7.9 | 4.8 | 3.5 | 1.7 | 0.3 | 0 | 3.5 |

### Ulan Bator, Mongolia  1,305m

| | Jan | Feb | Mar | Apr | May | June | July | Aug | Sept | Oct | Nov | Dec | Year |
|---|---|---|---|---|---|---|---|---|---|---|---|---|---|
| Temperature Daily max. °C | −19 | −13 | −4 | 7 | 13 | 21 | 22 | 21 | 14 | 6 | −6 | −16 | 4 |
| Daily min. °C | −32 | −29 | −22 | −8 | −2 | 7 | 11 | 8 | 2 | −8 | −20 | −28 | −11 |
| Average monthly °C | −26 | −21 | −13 | −1 | 6 | 14 | 16 | 14 | 8 | −1 | −13 | −22 | −4 |
| Rainfall Monthly total mm | 1 | 1 | 2 | 5 | 10 | 28 | 76 | 51 | 23 | 5 | 5 | 2 | 209 |
| Sunshine Hours per day | 6.4 | 7.8 | 8 | 7.8 | 8.3 | 8.6 | 8.6 | 8.2 | 7.2 | 6.9 | 6.1 | 5.7 | 7.5 |

### Vancouver, Canada  5m

| | Jan | Feb | Mar | Apr | May | June | July | Aug | Sept | Oct | Nov | Dec | Year |
|---|---|---|---|---|---|---|---|---|---|---|---|---|---|
| Temperature Daily max. °C | 6 | 7 | 10 | 14 | 17 | 20 | 23 | 22 | 19 | 14 | 9 | 7 | 14 |
| Daily min. °C | 0 | 1 | 3 | 5 | 8 | 11 | 13 | 12 | 10 | 7 | 3 | 2 | 6 |
| Average monthly °C | 3 | 4 | 6 | 9 | 13 | 16 | 18 | 17 | 14 | 10 | 6 | 4 | 10 |
| Rainfall Monthly total mm | 214 | 161 | 151 | 90 | 69 | 65 | 39 | 44 | 83 | 172 | 198 | 243 | 1,529 |
| Sunshine Hours per day | 1.6 | 3 | 3.8 | 5.9 | 7.5 | 7.4 | 9.5 | 8.2 | 6 | 3.7 | 2 | 1.4 | 5 |

### Verkhoyansk, Russia  137m

| | Jan | Feb | Mar | Apr | May | June | July | Aug | Sept | Oct | Nov | Dec | Year |
|---|---|---|---|---|---|---|---|---|---|---|---|---|---|
| Temperature Daily max. °C | −47 | −40 | −20 | −1 | 11 | 21 | 24 | 21 | 12 | −8 | −33 | −42 | −8 |
| Daily min. °C | −51 | −48 | −40 | −25 | −7 | 4 | 6 | 1 | −6 | −20 | −39 | −50 | −23 |
| Average monthly °C | −49 | −44 | −30 | −13 | 2 | 12 | 15 | 11 | 3 | −14 | −36 | −46 | −16 |
| Rainfall Monthly total mm | 7 | 5 | 5 | 4 | 5 | 25 | 33 | 30 | 13 | 11 | 10 | 7 | 155 |
| Sunshine Hours per day | 0 | 2.6 | 6.9 | 9.6 | 9.7 | 10 | 9.7 | 7.5 | 4.1 | 2.4 | 0.6 | 0 | 5.4 |

### Washington, USA  22m

| | Jan | Feb | Mar | Apr | May | June | July | Aug | Sept | Oct | Nov | Dec | Year |
|---|---|---|---|---|---|---|---|---|---|---|---|---|---|
| Temperature Daily max. °C | 7 | 8 | 12 | 19 | 25 | 29 | 31 | 30 | 26 | 20 | 14 | 8 | 19 |
| Daily min. °C | −1 | −1 | 2 | 8 | 13 | 18 | 21 | 20 | 16 | 10 | 4 | −1 | 9 |
| Average monthly °C | 3 | 3 | 7 | 13 | 19 | 24 | 26 | 25 | 21 | 15 | 9 | 4 | 14 |
| Rainfall Monthly total mm | 84 | 68 | 96 | 85 | 103 | 88 | 108 | 120 | 100 | 78 | 75 | 75 | 1,080 |
| Sunshine Hours per day | 4.4 | 5.7 | 6.7 | 7.4 | 8.2 | 8.8 | 8.6 | 8.2 | 7.5 | 6.5 | 5.3 | 4.5 | 6.8 |

## Tropical Rain Forest

Tall broadleaved evergreen forest, trees 30–50m high with climbers and epiphytes forming continuous canopies. Associated with wet climate 2–3000mm precipitation per year and high temperatures 24–28°C. High diversity of species, typically 100 per ha including lianas, bamboo, palms, rubber, mahogany. Mangrove swamps form in coastal areas.

Diagram shows the highly stratified nature of the tropical rain forest. Crowns of trees form numerous layers at different heights and the dense shade limits undergrowth.

## Temperate Deciduous and Coniferous Forest

A transition zone between broadleaves and conifers. Broadleaves are better suited to the warmer, damper and flatter locations.

## Northern Coniferous Forest (Taiga)

Forming a large continuous belt across Northern America and Eurasia with a uniformity in tree species. Characteristically trees are tall, conical with short branches and wax-covered needle-shaped leaves to retain moisture. Cold climate with prolonged harsh winters and cool summers where average temperatures for more than six months of the year are under 0°C. Undergrowth is sparse with mosses and lichens. Tree species include pine, fir, spruce, larch, tamarisk.

## Mountainous Forest, mainly Coniferous

Mild winters, high humidity and high levels of rainfall throughout the year provide habitat for dense needle-leaf evergreen forests and the largest trees in the world, up to 100m, including the Douglas fir, redwood and giant sequoia.

## High Plateau Steppe and Tundra

Similar to arctic tundra with frozen ground for the majority of the year. Very sparse ground coverage of low, shallow-rooted herbs, small shrubs, mosses, lichens and heather interspersed with bare soil.

## Arctic Tundra

Average temperatures are 0°C, precipitation is mainly snowfall and the ground remains frozen for 10 months of the year. Vegetation flourishes when the shallow surface layer melts in the long summer days. Underlying permafrost remains frozen and surface water cannot drain away, making conditions marshy. Consisting of sedges, snow lichen, arctic meadow grass, cotton grasses and dwarf willow.

## Polar and Mountainous Ice Desert

Areas of bare rock and ice with patches of rock-strewn lithosols, low in organic matter and low water content. In sheltered patches only a few mosses, lichens and low shrubs can grow, including woolly moss and purple saxifrage.

## Subtropical and Temperate Rain Forest

Precipitation which is less than in the Tropical Rain Forest falls in the long wet season interspersed with a season of reduced rainfall and lower temperatures. As a result there are fewer species, a thinner canopy, fewer lianas and denser ground level foliage. Vegetation consists of evergreen oak, laurel, bamboo, magnolia and tree ferns.

## Monsoon Woodland and Open Jungle

Mostly deciduous trees because of the long dry season and lower temperatur. Trees can reach 30m but are sparser than in the rain forests; there is le competition for light and thick jungle vegetation grows at lower levels. H species diversity including lianas, bamboo, teak, sandalwood, sal and bany

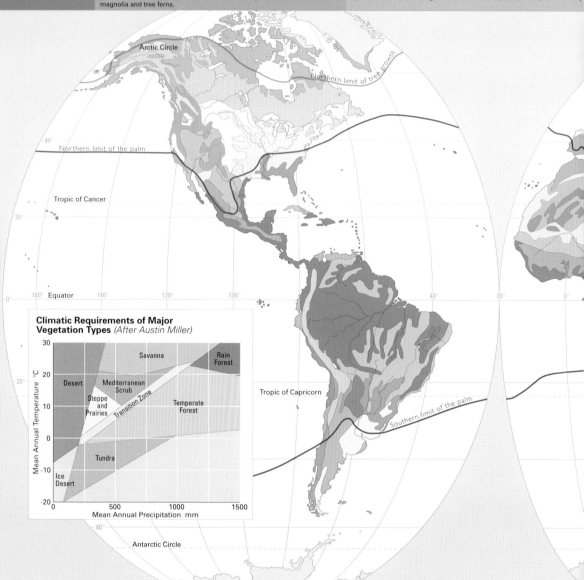

**Climatic Requirements of Major Vegetation Types** *(After Austin Miller)*

Projection: Interrupted Mollweide's Homolographic

## SOIL REGIONS

1:220 000 000

- Tundra soil
- Podzols
- Brown forest soil
- Lightly leached dry forest soil
- Red and yellow subtropical forest soil
- Reddish savanna soil and tropical red earths
- Laterites
- Chernozem
- Degraded chernozem
- Black savanna soil
- Chestnut steppe soil
- Desertic (arid) soil
- Alluvium
- Mountain and high plateau soils
- Oases soil
- Tropical and mangrove swamp

*(after Glinka, Stremme, Marbut, and others)*

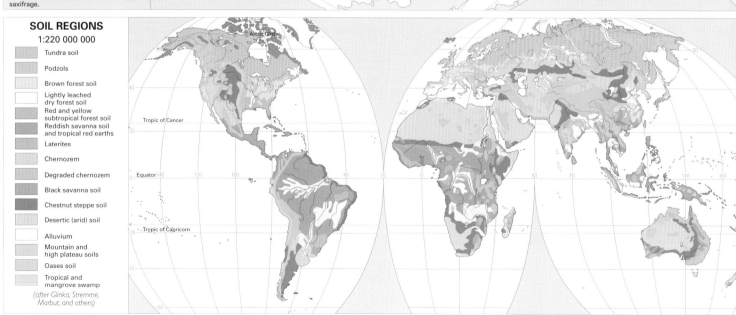

## btropical and Temperate Woodland, Scrub and Bush

st clearings with woody shrubs and tall grasses. Trees are fire-resistant and
er deciduous or xerophytic because of long dry periods. Species include
calyptus, acacia, mimosa and euphorbia.

## Tropical Savanna with Low Trees and Bush

Tall, coarse grass with enough precipitation to support a scattering of short
deciduous trees and thorn scrub. Vegetation consisting of elephant grass,
acacia, palms and baobob is limited by aridity, grazing animals and periodic
fires; trees have developed thick, woody bark, small leaves or thorns.

## Tropical Savanna and Grassland

Areas with a hot climate and long dry season. Extensive areas of tall grasses
often reaching 3.5m with scattered fire and drought resistant bushes, low trees
and thickets of elephant grass. Shrubs include acacia, baobab and palms.

# NATURAL VEGETATION
### (after Austin Miller)

### 1:116 000 000

### Dry Semi-desert with Shrub and Grass
Xerophytic shrubs with thin grass cover and
few trees, limited by a long dry season and
short, hot, rainy period. Sagebrush, bunch
grass and acacia shrubs are common.

### Desert Shrub
Scattered xerophytic plants able to withstand
daytime extremes in temperature and long
periods of drought. There is a large diversity
of desert flora such as cacti, yucca, tamarisk,
hard grass and artemisia.

### Desert
Precipitation less than 250mm per year;
vegetation is very sparse, mainly bare rock,
sand dunes and salt flats. Vegetation
comprises a few xerophytic shrubs and
ephemeral flowers.

### Dry Steppe and Shrub
Semi-arid with cold, dry winters and hot
summers. Bare soil with sparsely
distributed short grasses and scattered
shrubs and short trees. Species include acacia,
artemisia, saksaul and tamarisk.

### Temperate Grasslands, Prairie and Steppe
Continuous, tall, dense and deep-rooted
swards of ancient grasslands, considered to
be natural climax vegetation as determined
by soil and climate. Average precipitation
250–750mm with a long dry season, limiting
growth of trees and shrubs. Includes Stipa
grass, buffalo grass, blue stems and loco
weed.

### Mediterranean Hardwood Forest and Scrub
Areas with hot and arid summers. Sparse
evergreen trees are short and twisted
with thick bark, interspersed with areas of
scrub land. Trees have waxy leaves or thorns
and deep root systems to resist drought.
Many of the hardwood forests have been
cleared by man, resulting in extensive scrub
formation – maquis and chaparral. Species
found are evergreen oak, stone pine, cork,
olive and myrtle.

### Temperate Deciduous Forest and Meadow
Areas of relatively high, well-distributed
rainfall and temperatures favourable for forest
growth. The tall broadleaved trees form a
canopy in the summer, but shed their leaves
in the winter. The undergrowth is sparse and
poorly developed, but in the spring, herbs
and flowers develop quickly. Diverse species
with up to 20 per ha, including oak, beech,
birch, maple, ash, elm, chestnut and
hornbeam. Many of these forests have been
cleared for urbanization and farming.

# OIL DEGRADATION
### 1:220 000 000

### reas of Concern
- Areas of serious concern
- Areas of some concern
- Stable terrain
- Non-vegetated land

### auses of soil egradation by region)
- Grazing practices
- Other agricultural practices
- Industrialization
- Deforestation
- Fuelwood collection

*(after Wageningen 1990)*

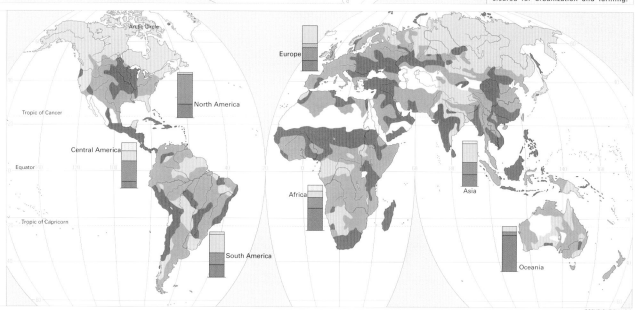

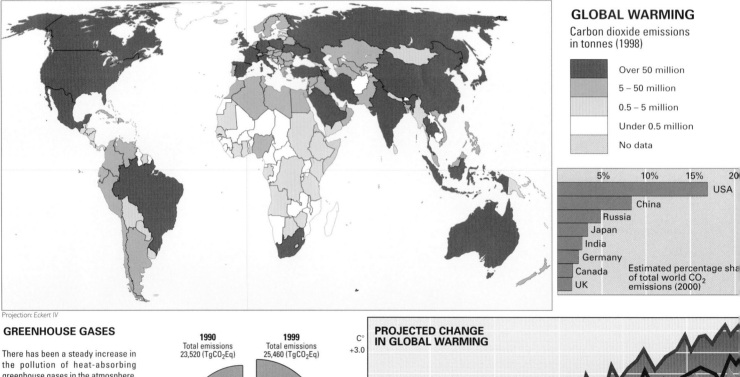

## GLOBAL WARMING
Carbon dioxide emissions in tonnes (1998)

- Over 50 million
- 5 – 50 million
- 0.5 – 5 million
- Under 0.5 million
- No data

Estimated percentage share of total world $CO_2$ emissions (2000)

5% 10% 15% 20

USA
China
Russia
Japan
India
Germany
Canada
UK

Projection: *Eckert IV*

### GREENHOUSE GASES

There has been a steady increase in the pollution of heat-absorbing greenhouse gases in the atmosphere. With the dangers of ozone depletion caused by CFCs in particular (see below), many countries have banned them and the pie charts show a dramatic drop in emissions.
The global warming potential of each gas is measured in equivalent units of $CO_2$ warming potential, or teragrams of $CO_2$ ($TgCO_2Eq$).

**1990** Total emissions 23,520 ($TgCO_2Eq$)
- Carbon Dioxide 70%
- Methane & $NO_2$ 9%
- CFCs & HCFCs 21%

**1999** Total emissions 25,460 ($TgCO_2Eq$)
- Carbon Dioxide 82%
- Methane & $NO_2$ 9%
- CFCs & HCFCs 9%

### PROJECTED CHANGE IN GLOBAL WARMING

Rise in average temperatures assuming present trends in $CO_2$ emissions continue
Assuming some cuts are made in emissions
Assuming drastic cuts are made in emissions

1950 1970 1990 2010 2030 2050

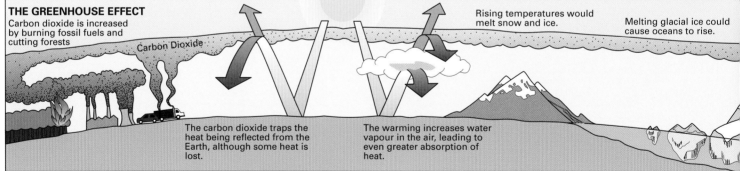

### THE GREENHOUSE EFFECT
Carbon dioxide is increased by burning fossil fuels and cutting forests

Carbon Dioxide

Rising temperatures would melt snow and ice.

Melting glacial ice could cause oceans to rise.

The carbon dioxide traps the heat being reflected from the Earth, although some heat is lost.

The warming increases water vapour in the air, leading to even greater absorption of heat.

**Northern Hemisphere**    **Southern Hemisphere**

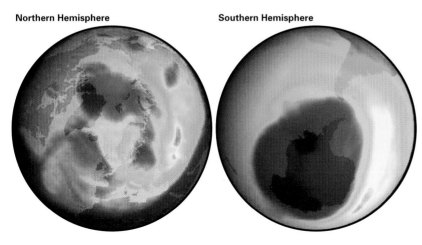

### THINNING OZONE LAYER
Total atmospheric ozone concentration in the southern and northern hemispheres (Dobson Units, 2000)

In 1985, scientists working in Antarctica discovered a thinning of the ozone layer, comm known as an 'ozone hole'. This caused immediate alarm because the ozone layer abs most of the Sun's dangerous ultraviolet radiation, which is believed to cause an increa skin cancer, cataracts and damage to the immune system. Since 1985, ozone depletion increased and, by 1996, the ozone hole over the South Pole was estimated to be as larg North America. The false colour images, left, show the total atmospheric ozone concentr in the southern hemisphere (in September 2000) and the northern hemisphere (in March 2 with the ozone hole clearly identifiable at the centre. The data is from the Tiros Ozone Ve Sounder, an instrument on the American TIROS weather satellite. The colours represen ozone concentration in Dobson Units (DU). Scientists agree that ozone depletion is cause CFCs, a group of manufactured chemicals used in air conditioning systems and refrigera In a 1987 treaty most industrial nations agreed to phase out CFCs and a complete ban on CFCs was agreed after the end of 1995. However, scientists believe that the chemicals remain in the atmosphere for 50 to 100 years. As a result, ozone depletion will continu many years.

## WATER POLLUTION

Severely polluted sea areas and lakes

Less polluted sea areas and lakes

Areas of frequent oil pollution by shipping

Major oil tanker spills ⑨ ○

Major oil rig blow-outs ▲

Offshore dumpsites for industrial and municipal waste ▼

Severely polluted rivers and estuaries ——

| Tanker Name | Tonnes Spilt | Year |
|---|---|---|
| ① Atlantic Empress | 287,000 | 1979 |
| ② ABT Summer | 260,000 | 1991 |
| ③ Castillo de Bellver | 252,000 | 1983 |
| ④ Amoco Cadiz | 223,000 | 1978 |
| ⑤ Haven | 144,000 | 1991 |
| ⑥ Odyssey | 132,000 | 1988 |
| ⑦ Torrey Canyon | 119,000 | 1967 |
| ⑧ Urquiola | 100,000 | 1976 |
| ⑨ Hawaiian Patriot | 95,000 | 1977 |
| ⑩ Independenta | 95,000 | 1979 |

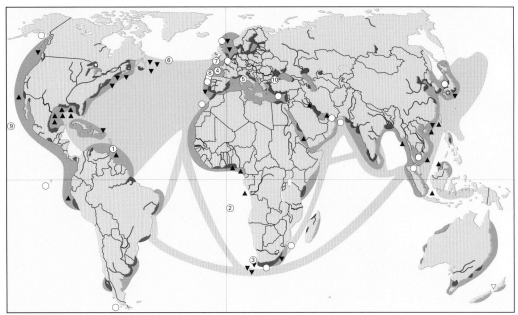

## ACID RAIN

Acid rain is caused by high levels of sulphur and nitrogen in the atmosphere. They combine with water vapour and oxygen to form acids ($H_2SO_4$ and $HNO_3$) which fall as precipitation.

Main areas of sulphur and nitrogen emissions (from the burning of fossil fuels)

● Major cities with levels of air pollution exceeding World Health Organization guidelines

**Areas of acid deposition**

(pH numbers measure acidity: normal rain is pH 5.6)

pH less than 4.0 (most acidic)

pH 4.0 – 4.5

pH 4.5 – 5.0

Potential problem areas

## DESERTIFICATION AND DEFORESTATION

Existing deserts

Areas with a high risk of desertification

Areas with a moderate risk of desertification

Former areas of rainforest

Existing rainforest

■ Major famines since 1900 (with dates)

### Deforestation 1990–2000

| | Annual Deforestation (thous. hectares) | Annual Deforestation Rate (%) |
|---|---|---|
| Brazil | 2,309 | 0.4 |
| Indonesia | 1,312 | 1.2 |
| Mexico | 631 | 1.1 |
| Congo (Dem. Rep.) | 532 | 0.4 |
| Burma (Myanmar) | 517 | 1.4 |
| Nigeria | 398 | 2.6 |
| Peru | 269 | 1.4 |

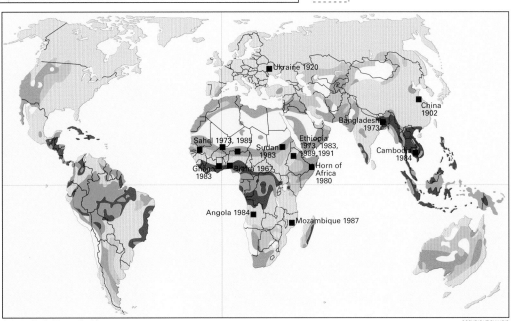

Ukraine 1920
China 1902
Bangladesh 1973
Sahel 1973, 1985
Sudan 1983
Ethiopia 1973, 1983, 1989, 1991
Cambodia 1984
Ghana 1983
Biafra 1967
Horn of Africa 1980
Angola 1984
Mozambique 1987

Projection: Modified Hammer Equal Area

COPYRIGHT PHILIP'S

# AGRICULTURAL PRODUCTION

## Staple Crops

### Wheat

China 16.0%
India 11.7%
USA 9.1%
Russia 8.0%
France 5.4%

World total (2001): 582,692,000 tonnes

### Rice

China 30.6%
India 22.2%
Indonesia 8.5%
Bangladesh 6.6%
Vietnam 5.4%

World total (2001): 592,831,000 tonnes

### Millet

India 32.5%
Nigeria 20.9%
China 8.4%
Niger 8.3%
Russia 4.5%

World total (2001): 29,207,000 tonnes

### Rye

Russia 26.4%
Germany 22.7%
Poland 21.7%
Belarus 6.6%
Ukraine 6.6%

World total (2001): 22,718,000 tonnes

### Maize

USA 39.6%
China 19.0%
Brazil 6.8%
Mexico 3.1%

World total (2001): 609,182,000 tonnes

### Potatoes

China 20.8%
Russia 11.2%
India 8.1%
Poland 6.6%
USA 6.5%

World total (2001): 308,195,000 tonnes

### Soybeans

USA 44.5%
Brazil 21.3%
Argentina 15.1%
China 8.7%

World total (2001): 176,639,000 tonnes

### Cassava

Nigeria 18.9%
Brazil 13.5%
Thailand 10.2%
Indonesia 9.0%
Dem. Rep. Congo 8.3%

World total (2001): 178,868,000 tonnes

## Animal Products

### Milk

India 14.4%
USA 12.8%
Russia 5.5%
Germany 4.8%
Pakistan 4.5%

World total (2001): 584,651,000 tonnes

### Butter and Ghee

India 30.0%
USA 7.7%
Pakistan 6.2%
France 5.9%
Germany 5.6%
New Zealand 4.7%

World total (2001): 7,503,000 tonnes

### Lamb and Mutton

China 19.1%
Australia 8.8%
N. Zealand 7.3%
Turkey 3.2%
Iran 3.7%

World total (2001): 7,532,000 tonnes

### Beef and Veal

USA 21.1%
Brazil 11.8%
China 9.1%
Argentina 4.7%

World total (2001): 56,647,000 tonnes

### Pigmeat

China 46.8%
USA 9.5%
Germany 4.5%

World total (2001): 91,188,000 tonnes

## Sugars

### Sugar Cane

Brazil 27.0%
India 22.8%
China 8.4%
Mexico 3.9%

World total (2001): 1,254,857,000 tonnes

### Sugar Beet

France 11.4%
Germany 10.4%
USA 8.6%
Ukraine 6.6%
Russia 6.2%
Turkey 6.2%
Poland 5.5%

World total (2001): 234,245,000 tonnes

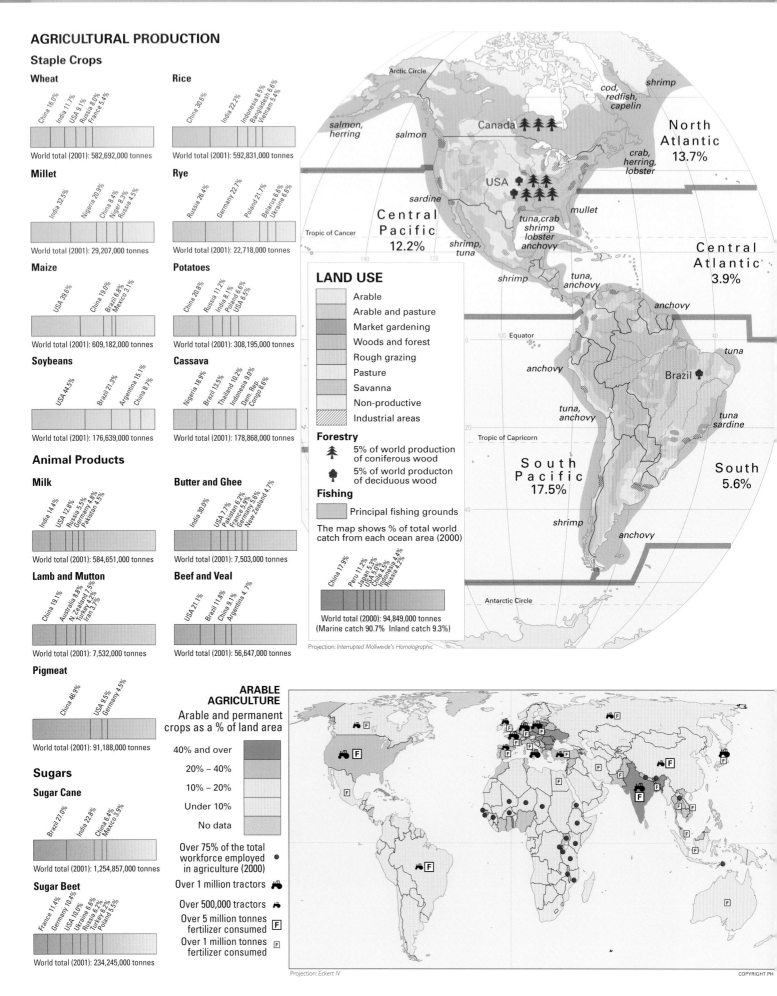

## LAND USE

- Arable
- Arable and pasture
- Market gardening
- Woods and forest
- Rough grazing
- Pasture
- Savanna
- Non-productive
- Industrial areas

### Forestry

🌲 5% of world production of coniferous wood

🌳 5% of world producton of deciduous wood

### Fishing

Principal fishing grounds

The map shows % of total world catch from each ocean area (2000)

China 17.9%
Peru 11.2%
Japan 5.3%
USA 5.0%
Chile 4.5%
Indonesia 4.4%
Russia 4.2%

World total (2000): 94,849,000 tonnes
(Marine catch 90.7% Inland catch 9.3%)

Projection: Interrupted Mollweide's Homolographic

North Atlantic 13.7%
Central Pacific 12.2%
Central Atlantic 3.9%
South Pacific 17.5%
South 5.6%

## ARABLE AGRICULTURE

Arable and permanent crops as a % of land area

- 40% and over
- 20% – 40%
- 10% – 20%
- Under 10%
- No data

● Over 75% of the total workforce employed in agriculture (2000)

🚜 Over 1 million tractors

🚜 Over 500,000 tractors

F Over 5 million tonnes fertilizer consumed

F Over 1 million tonnes fertilizer consumed

Projection: Eckert IV

COPYRIGHT PH

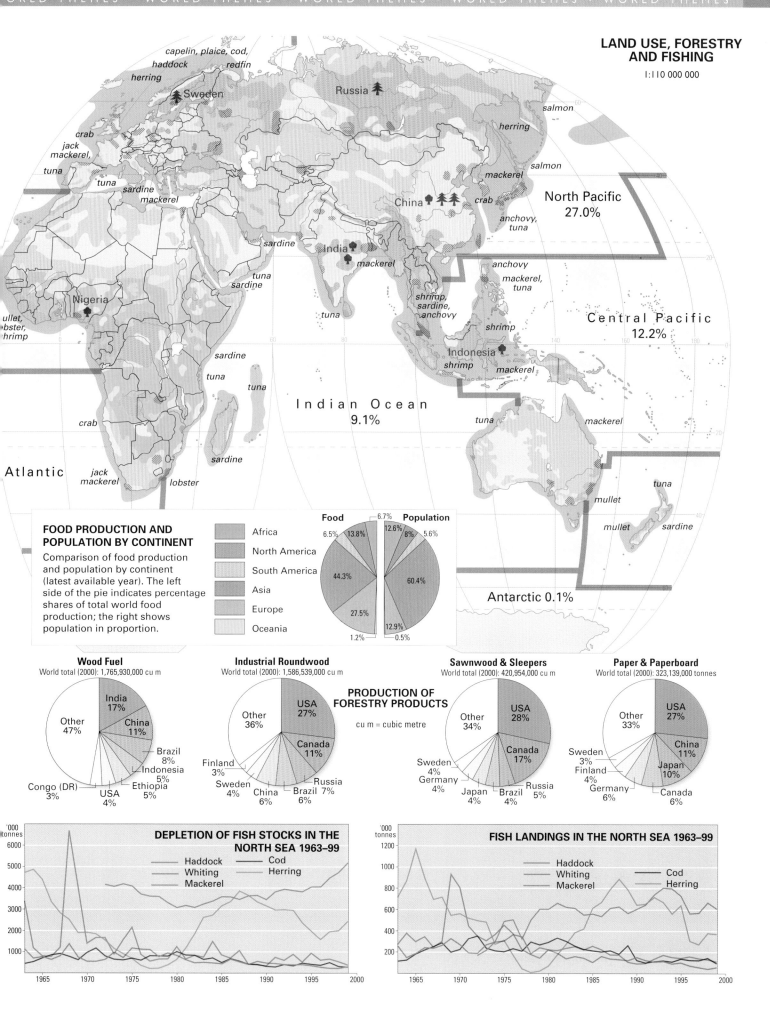

**LAND USE, FORESTRY AND FISHING**

1:110 000 000

*capelin, plaice, cod, haddock, redfin*
*herring*
Sweden

Russia

*salmon*

*herring*

*crab*
*jack mackerel,*
*tuna*

*tuna*

*salmon*

*sardine*
*mackerel*

China

*mackerel*

*crab*

North Pacific
**27.0%**

*anchovy, tuna*

*sardine*

India

*mackerel*

*anchovy*

*mackerel, tuna*

*tuna*
*sardine*

*shrimp, sardine, anchovy*

*shrimp*

Central Pacific
**12.2%**

Nigeria

*ullet, bster, hrimp*

*tuna*

*sardine*
*tuna*

*tuna*

Indonesia
*shrimp*

*mackerel*

Indian Ocean
**9.1%**

*tuna*

*mackerel*

*crab*

*sardine*

Atlantic

*jack mackerel*
*lobster*

*sardine*

*tuna*

*mullet*

*mullet*

*sardine*

Antarctic **0.1%**

**FOOD PRODUCTION AND POPULATION BY CONTINENT**

Comparison of food production and population by continent (latest available year). The left side of the pie indicates percentage shares of total world food production; the right shows population in proportion.

- Africa
- North America
- South America
- Asia
- Europe
- Oceania

**Food** | **Population**
6.7%
6.5% 13.8% | 12.6% 8% 5.6%
44.3% | 60.4%
27.5%
1.2% 0.5% | 12.9%

**PRODUCTION OF FORESTRY PRODUCTS**

cu m = cubic metre

**Wood Fuel**
World total (2000): 1,765,930,000 cu m

Other 47%
India 17%
China 11%
Brazil 8%
Indonesia 5%
Ethiopia 5%
USA 4%
Congo (DR) 3%

**Industrial Roundwood**
World total (2000): 1,586,539,000 cu m

Other 36%
USA 27%
Canada 11%
Russia
Brazil 7%
China 6%
Sweden 4%
Finland 3%

**Sawnwood & Sleepers**
World total (2000): 420,954,000 cu m

Other 34%
USA 28%
Canada 17%
Russia 5%
Brazil 4%
Japan 4%
Germany 4%
Sweden 4%

**Paper & Paperboard**
World total (2000): 323,139,000 tonnes

Other 33%
USA 27%
China 11%
Japan 10%
Canada 6%
Germany 6%
Finland 4%
Sweden 3%

**DEPLETION OF FISH STOCKS IN THE NORTH SEA 1963–99**

'000 tonnes

— Haddock
— Whiting
— Mackerel
— Cod
— Herring

**FISH LANDINGS IN THE NORTH SEA 1963–99**

'000 tonnes

— Haddock
— Whiting
— Mackerel
— Cod
— Herring

## ENERGY PRODUCTION BY REGION

Each square represents 1% of world energy production (2000)

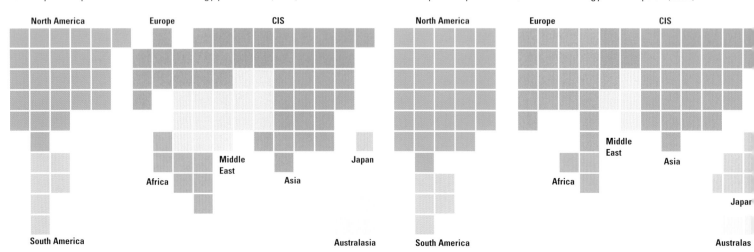

North America • Europe • CIS • Middle East • Africa • Asia • Japan • South America • Australasia

## ENERGY CONSUMPTION BY REGION

Each square represents 1% of world energy consumption (2000)

North America • Europe • CIS • Middle East • Africa • Asia • Japan • South America • Australasia

## ENERGY BALANCE

Difference between energy production and consumption in millions of tonnes of oil equivalent (MtOe) 2000

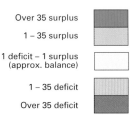

↑ Energy surplus in MtOe

- Over 35 surplus
- 1 – 35 surplus
- 1 deficit – 1 surplus (approx. balance)
- 1 – 35 deficit
- Over 35 deficit

↓ Energy deficit in MtOe

### Fossil fuel production

| | Principal | Secondary |
|---|---|---|
| Oilfields | ● | ● |
| Gasfields | ▽ | ▽ |
| Coalfields | ▲ | ▲ |

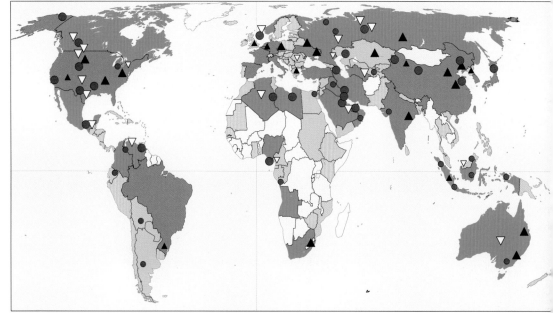

Projection: Eck

## OIL RESERVES

World oil reserves by region and country, thousand million tonnes (2001)

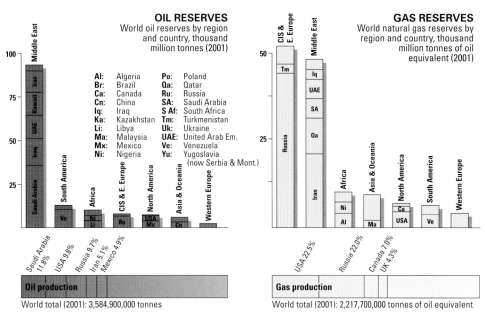

| Al: | Algeria | Po: | Poland |
|---|---|---|---|
| Br: | Brazil | Qa: | Qatar |
| Ca: | Canada | Ru: | Russia |
| Cn: | China | SA: | Saudi Arabia |
| Iq: | Iraq | S Af: | South Africa |
| Ka: | Kazakhstan | Tm: | Turkmenistan |
| Li: | Libya | Uk: | Ukraine |
| Ma: | Malaysia | UAE: | United Arab Em. |
| Mx: | Mexico | Ve: | Venezuela |
| Ni: | Nigeria | Yu: | Yugoslavia |
| | | | (now Serbia & Mont.) |

Middle East — Iran, Kuwait, UAE, Iraq, Saudi Arabia
South America — Ve
Africa — Ni, Li
CIS & E. Europe — Ru
North America — USA, Mx
Asia & Oceania — Cn
Western Europe

Saudi Arabia 11.8%
USA 9.8%
Russia 9.7%
Iran 5.1%
Mexico 4.9%

**Oil production**

World total (2001): 3,584,900,000 tonnes

## GAS RESERVES

World natural gas reserves by region and country, thousand million tonnes of oil equivalent (2001)

CIS & E. Europe — Tm, Russia
Middle East — Iq, UAE, SA, Qa, Iran
Africa — Ni, Al
Asia & Oceania — Ma
North America — Ca, USA
South America — Ve
Western Europe

USA 22.5%
Russia 22.0%
Canada 7.0%
UK 4.3%

**Gas production**

World total (2001): 2,217,700,000 tonnes of oil equivalent

## COAL RESERVES

World coal reserves by region and country, thousand million tonnes (2001, including lignite)

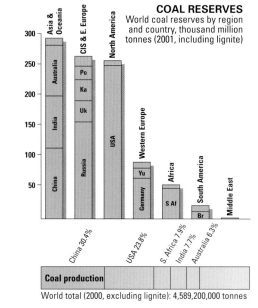

Asia & Oceania — Australia, India, China
CIS & E. Europe — Po, Ka, Uk, Russia
North America — USA
Western Europe — Germany, Yu
Africa — S Af
South America — Br
Middle East

China 30.4%
USA 23.8%
S. Africa 7.9%
India 7.7%
Australia 6.3%

**Coal production**

World total (2000, excluding lignite): 4,589,200,000 tonnes

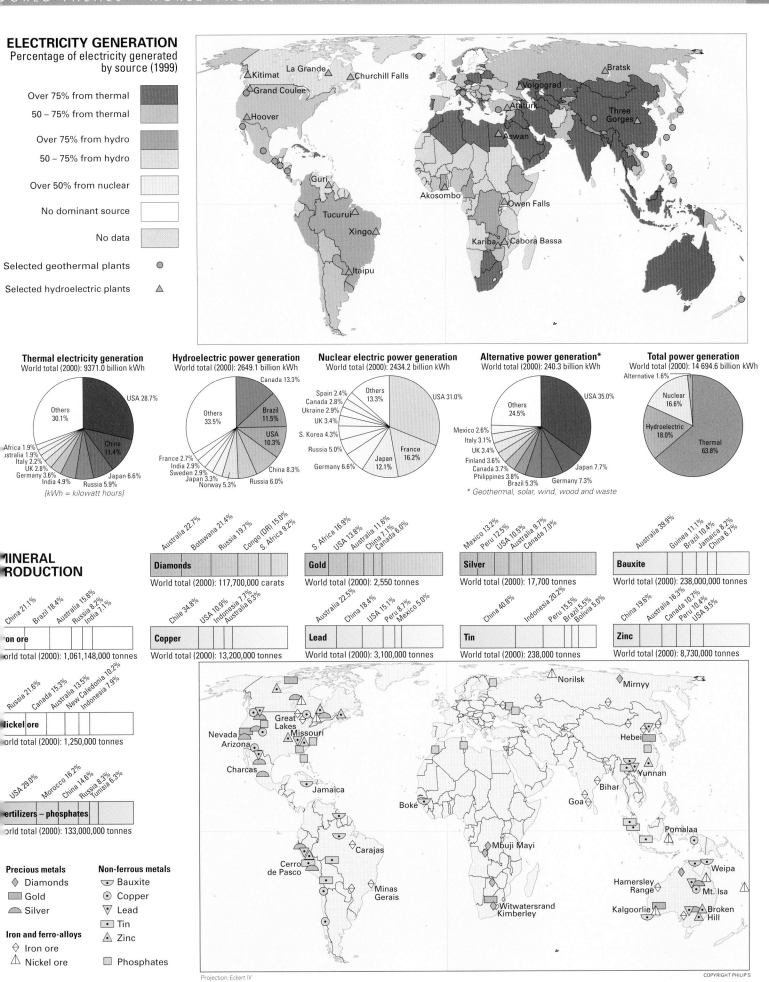

# ELECTRICITY GENERATION
Percentage of electricity generated by source (1999)

- Over 75% from thermal
- 50 – 75% from thermal
- Over 75% from hydro
- 50 – 75% from hydro
- Over 50% from nuclear
- No dominant source
- No data
- ⬤ Selected geothermal plants
- △ Selected hydroelectric plants

Map labels: Kitimat, La Grande, Grand Coulee, Churchill Falls, Bratsk, Volgograd, Ataturk, Three Gorges, Hoover, Aswan, Guri, Akosombo, Owen Falls, Tucurui, Xingo, Kariba, Cabora Bassa, Itaipu

## Thermal electricity generation
World total (2000): 9371.0 billion kWh

- USA 28.7%
- Others 30.1%
- China 11.4%
- Japan 6.6%
- Russia 5.9%
- India 4.9%
- Germany 3.6%
- UK 2.8%
- Italy 2.2%
- Australia 1.9%
- Africa 1.9%

[kWh = kilowatt hours]

## Hydroelectric power generation
World total (2000): 2649.1 billion kWh

- Canada 13.3%
- Brazil 11.5%
- USA 10.3%
- Others 33.5%
- China 8.3%
- Russia 6.0%
- Norway 5.3%
- Japan 3.3%
- Sweden 2.9%
- India 2.9%
- France 2.7%

## Nuclear electric power generation
World total (2000): 2434.2 billion kWh

- USA 31.0%
- Others 13.3%
- Spain 2.4%
- Canada 2.8%
- Ukraine 2.9%
- UK 3.4%
- S. Korea 4.3%
- Russia 5.0%
- Germany 6.6%
- Japan 12.1%
- France 16.2%

## Alternative power generation*
World total (2000): 240.3 billion kWh

- USA 35.0%
- Others 24.5%
- Mexico 2.6%
- Italy 3.1%
- UK 3.4%
- Finland 3.6%
- Canada 3.7%
- Philippines 3.8%
- Brazil 5.3%
- Germany 7.3%
- Japan 7.7%

*Geothermal, solar, wind, wood and waste

## Total power generation
World total (2000): 14 694.6 billion kWh

- Alternative 1.6%
- Nuclear 16.6%
- Hydroelectric 18.0%
- Thermal 63.8%

# MINERAL PRODUCTION

**Diamonds** — World total (2000): 117,700,000 carats
- Australia 22.7%
- Botswana 21.4%
- Russia 19.7%
- Congo (DR) 15.0%
- S. Africa 9.2%

**Gold** — World total (2000): 2,550 tonnes
- S. Africa 16.9%
- USA 13.8%
- Australia 11.6%
- China 7.1%
- Canada 6.0%

**Silver** — World total (2000): 17,700 tonnes
- Mexico 13.2%
- Peru 12.5%
- USA 10.5%
- Australia 9.7%
- Canada 7.0%

**Bauxite** — World total (2000): 238,000,000 tonnes
- Australia 39.9%
- Guinea 11.1%
- Brazil 10.4%
- Jamaica 8.2%
- China 6.7%

**Copper** — World total (2000): 13,200,000 tonnes
- Chile 34.8%
- USA 10.9%
- Indonesia 7.7%
- Australia 6.3%

**Lead** — World total (2000): 3,100,000 tonnes
- Australia 22.5%
- China 18.4%
- USA 15.1%
- Peru 8.7%
- Mexico 5.0%

**Tin** — World total (2000): 238,000 tonnes
- China 40.8%
- Indonesia 20.2%
- Peru 15.5%
- Brazil 5.5%
- Bolivia 5.0%

**Zinc** — World total (2000): 8,730,000 tonnes
- China 19.6%
- Australia 16.3%
- Canada 10.7%
- Peru 10.4%
- USA 9.5%

**Iron ore** — World total (2000): 1,061,148,000 tonnes
- China 21.1%
- Brazil 18.4%
- Australia 15.8%
- Russia 8.2%
- India 7.1%

**Nickel ore** — World total (2000): 1,250,000 tonnes
- Russia 21.6%
- Canada 15.3%
- Australia 13.5%
- New Caledonia 10.2%
- Indonesia 7.9%

**Fertilizers – phosphates** — World total (2000): 133,000,000 tonnes
- USA 29.0%
- Morocco 16.2%
- China 14.6%
- Russia 8.3%
- Tunisia 6.3%

### Precious metals
- ◇ Diamonds
- ▢ Gold
- ◖ Silver

### Iron and ferro-alloys
- ◇ Iron ore
- △ Nickel ore

### Non-ferrous metals
- ▽ Bauxite
- ⊙ Copper
- ▽ Lead
- ▪ Tin
- △ Zinc
- ▢ Phosphates

Map labels: Norilsk, Mirnyy, Great Lakes, Missouri, Hebei, Nevada, Arizona, Yunnan, Charcas, Bihar, Goa, Jamaica, Boke, Pomalaa, Mbuji Mayi, Weipa, Carajas, Cerro de Pasco, Hamersley Range, Mt. Isa, Minas Gerais, Witwatersrand, Kimberley, Kalgoorlie, Broken Hill

Projection: Eckert IV

COPYRIGHT PHILIP'S

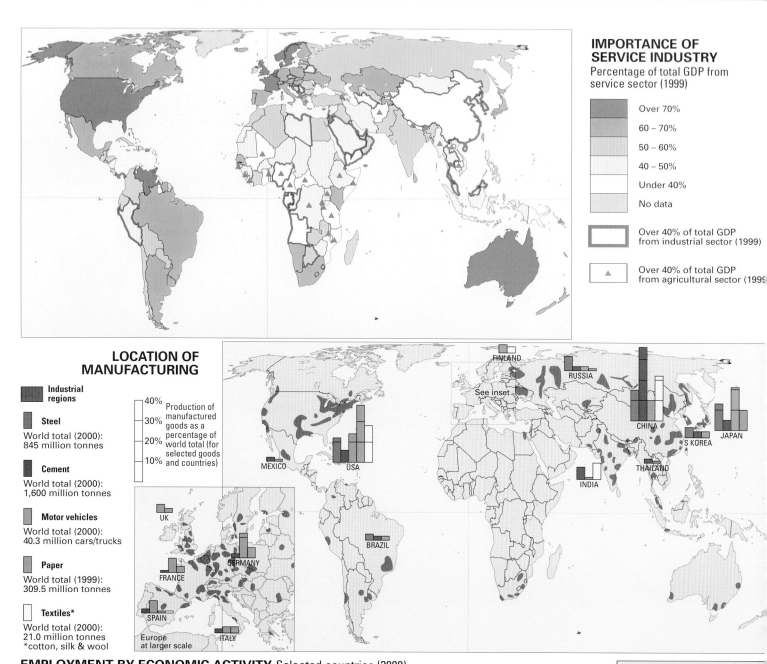

## IMPORTANCE OF SERVICE INDUSTRY
Percentage of total GDP from service sector (1999)

- Over 70%
- 60 – 70%
- 50 – 60%
- 40 – 50%
- Under 40%
- No data

Over 40% of total GDP from industrial sector (1999)

▲ Over 40% of total GDP from agricultural sector (1999)

## LOCATION OF MANUFACTURING

- **Industrial regions**

- **Steel**
World total (2000):
845 million tonnes

- **Cement**
World total (2000):
1,600 million tonnes

- **Motor vehicles**
World total (2000):
40.3 million cars/trucks

- **Paper**
World total (1999):
309.5 million tonnes

- **Textiles***
World total (2000):
21.0 million tonnes
*cotton, silk & wool

40%
30%
20%
10%
Production of manufactured goods as a percentage of world total (for selected goods and countries)

FINLAND
RUSSIA
See inset
CHINA
S KOREA
JAPAN
MEXICO
USA
THAILAND
INDIA
BRAZIL

UK
GERMANY
FRANCE
SPAIN
ITALY
Europe at larger scale

## EMPLOYMENT BY ECONOMIC ACTIVITY Selected countries (2000)

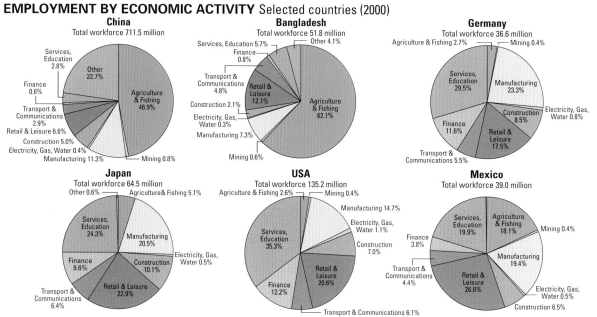

### China
Total workforce 711.5 million
- Services, Education 2.8%
- Other 22.7%
- Finance 0.6%
- Transport & Communications 2.9%
- Retail & Leisure 6.6%
- Construction 5.0%
- Electricity, Gas, Water 0.4%
- Manufacturing 11.3%
- Mining 0.8%
- Agriculture & Fishing 46.9%

### Bangladesh
Total workforce 51.8 million
- Services, Education 5.7%
- Other 4.1%
- Finance 0.8%
- Transport & Communications 4.8%
- Retail & Leisure 12.1%
- Construction 2.1%
- Electricity, Gas, Water 0.3%
- Manufacturing 7.3%
- Mining 0.6%
- Agriculture & Fishing 62.1%

### Germany
Total workforce 36.6 million
- Agriculture & Fishing 2.7%
- Mining 0.4%
- Services, Education 29.5%
- Manufacturing 23.3%
- Construction 8.5%
- Electricity, Gas, Water 0.8%
- Retail & Leisure 17.5%
- Finance 11.6%
- Transport & Communications 5.5%

### Japan
Total workforce 64.5 million
- Other 0.6%
- Agriculture & Fishing 5.1%
- Services, Education 24.3%
- Manufacturing 20.5%
- Electricity, Gas, Water 0.5%
- Finance 9.6%
- Construction 10.1%
- Transport & Communications 6.4%
- Retail & Leisure 22.9%

### USA
Total workforce 135.2 million
- Agriculture & Fishing 2.6%
- Mining 0.4%
- Manufacturing 14.7%
- Electricity, Gas, Water 1.1%
- Construction 7.0%
- Services, Education 35.3%
- Retail & Leisure 20.6%
- Finance 12.2%
- Transport & Communications 6.1%

### Mexico
Total workforce 39.0 million
- Services, Education 19.9%
- Agriculture & Fishing 18.1%
- Mining 0.4%
- Finance 3.8%
- Manufacturing 19.4%
- Transport & Communications 4.4%
- Retail & Leisure 26.6%
- Electricity, Gas, Water 0.5%
- Construction 6.5%

## RESEARCH & DEVELOPMENT
Scientists and engineers in R&D (per million people) 1990–2000

| Country | Total |
| --- | --- |
| Iceland | 5,686 |
| Japan | 4,960 |
| Sweden | 4,507 |
| USA | 4,103 |
| Norway | 4,095 |
| Russia | 3,397 |
| Australia | 3,320 |
| Denmark | 3,240 |
| Switzerland | 3,058 |
| Canada | 3,009 |
| Germany | 2,873 |
| Azerbaijan | 2,735 |
| France | 2,686 |
| UK | 2,678 |
| Netherlands | 2,490 |
| Belgium | 2,307 |
| Belarus | 2,296 |
| New Zealand | 2,197 |
| Singapore | 2,182 |
| Estonia | 2,164 |

## WORLD TRADE

Percentage share of total
world exports by value (2000)

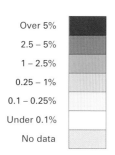

Over 5%

2.5 – 5%

1 – 2.5%

0.25 – 1%

0.1 – 0.25%

Under 0.1%

No data

The members of 'G8', the inner circle
of OECD, account for more than half
the total. The majority of nations
contribute less than one quarter of 1%
to the worldwide total of exports;
EU countries account for 35%; the
Pacific Rim nations over 50%

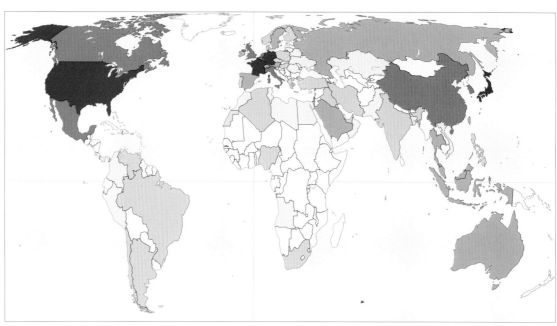

## MAJOR EXPORTS Leading manufactured items and their exporters

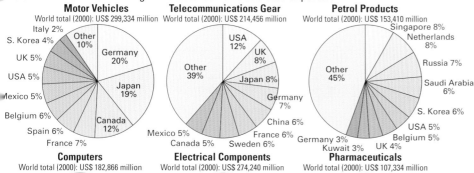

### Motor Vehicles
World total (2000): US$ 299,334 million

Italy 2%
S. Korea 4%
UK 5%
USA 5%
Mexico 5%
Belgium 6%
Spain 6%
France 7%
Other 10%
Germany 20%
Japan 19%
Canada 12%

### Telecommunications Gear
World total (2000): US$ 214,456 million

USA 12%
UK 8%
Other 39%
Japan 8%
Germany 7%
China 6%
France 6%
Mexico 5%
Canada 5%
Sweden 6%

### Petrol Products
World total (2000): US$ 153,410 million

Singapore 8%
Netherlands 8%
Russia 7%
Saudi Arabia 6%
S. Korea 6%
USA 5%
Belgium 5%
UK 4%
Kuwait 3%
Germany 3%
Other 45%

### Computers
World total (2000): US$ 182,866 million

USA 17%
Other 33%
Singapore 11%
Neth. 8%
Mexico 5%
S. Korea 5%
China 6%
UK 8%
Japan 8%

### Electrical Components
World total (2000): US$ 274,240 million

Thailand 17%
Other 23%
Hungary 16%
Germ. 6%
China 6%
Kuwait 6%
Portugal 13%
Ireland 9%
Japan 6%

### Pharmaceuticals
World total (2000): US$ 107,334 million

USA 12%
Germany 12%
Other 34%
UK 10%
Switzerland 10%
France 10%
Belgium 6%
Italy 6%

## MULTINATIONAL CORPORATIONS (MNCs)

Country of origin of world's top 200 MNCs
(top 200 are ranked by revenue, 2002)

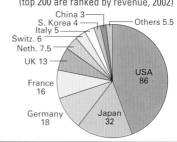

China 3
S. Korea 4
Italy 5
Others 5.5
Switz. 6
Neth. 7.5
UK 13
USA 86
France 16
Germany 18
Japan 32

### Top ten MNCs by revenue (million US$), 2002

| | | | |
|---|---|---|---|
| Wal-Mart | Supermarket chain | 219,812 | USA |
| Exxon Mobil | Petroleum | 191,581 | USA |
| General Motors | Motor vehicles | 177,260 | USA |
| BP | Petroleum | 174,218 | UK |
| Ford Motor | Motor vehicles | 162,412 | USA |
| Enron* | Energy | 138,718 | USA |
| DaimlerChrysler | Motor vehicles | 136,897 | Germany |
| Royal Dutch/Shell | Petroleum | 135,211 | Neth/UK |
| General Electric | Energy and finance | 125,913 | USA |
| Toyota Motor | Motor vehicles | 120,814 | Japan |

*Enron ceased trading in 2002

## INTERNET AND TELECOMMUNICATIONS

Percentage of total population
using the Internet (2000)

World total 513.4 million Internet users

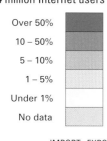

Over 50%

10 – 50%

5 – 10%

1 – 5%

Under 1%

No data

IMPORT  EXPORT

### Telecommunications

Trade in office machines and
telecom equipment,
percentage of world total
(2001)

40%
30%
20%
10%

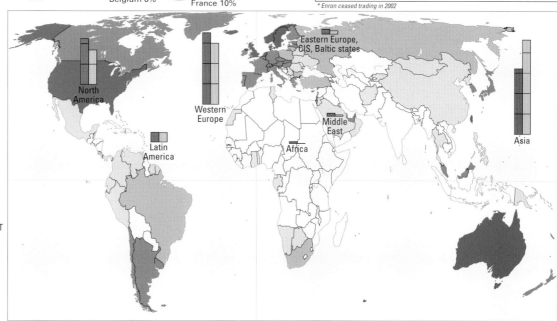

Eastern Europe,
CIS, Baltic states

North America

Western Europe

Middle East

Latin America

Africa

Asia

Projection: Eckert IV

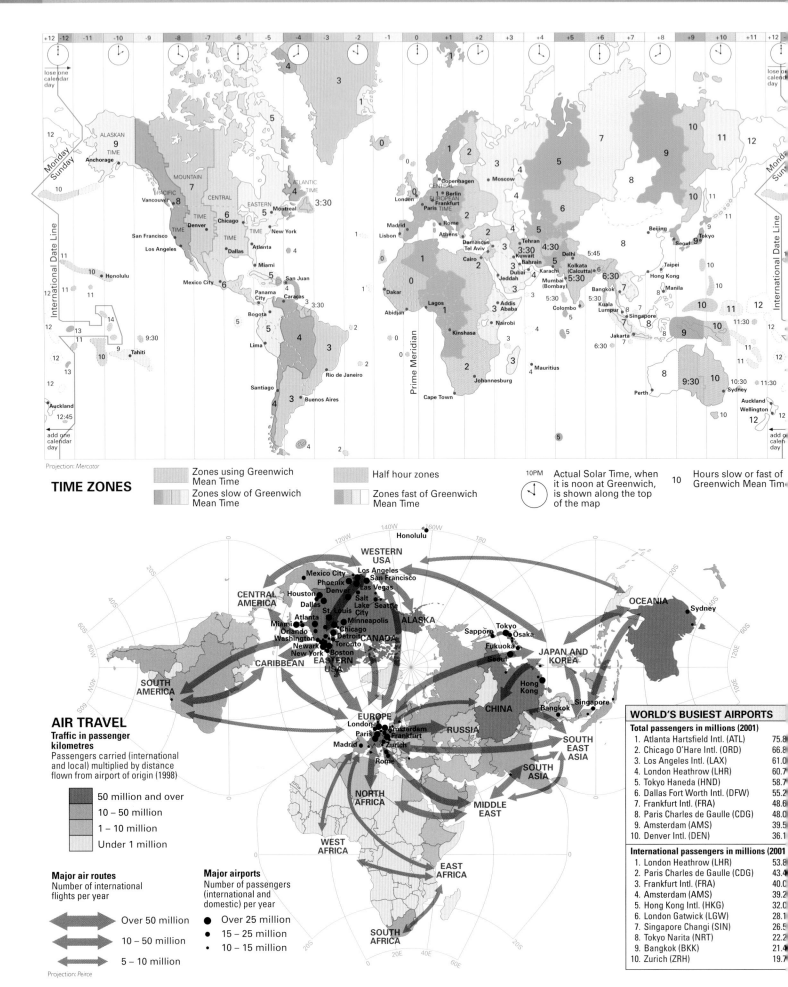

## TIME ZONES

Projection: *Mercator*

Zones using Greenwich Mean Time

Zones slow of Greenwich Mean Time

Half hour zones

Zones fast of Greenwich Mean Time

10PM Actual Solar Time, when it is noon at Greenwich, is shown along the top of the map

10 Hours slow or fast of Greenwich Mean Tim

## AIR TRAVEL

**Traffic in passenger kilometres**

Passengers carried (international and local) multiplied by distance flown from airport of origin (1998)

50 million and over
10 – 50 million
1 – 10 million
Under 1 million

**Major air routes**
Number of international flights per year

Over 50 million
10 – 50 million
5 – 10 million

**Major airports**
Number of passengers (international and domestic) per year

● Over 25 million
● 15 – 25 million
○ 10 – 15 million

Projection: *Peirce*

### WORLD'S BUSIEST AIRPORTS

**Total passengers in millions (2001)**
1. Atlanta Hartsfield Intl. (ATL)    75.8
2. Chicago O'Hare Intl. (ORD)    66.8
3. Los Angeles Intl. (LAX)    61.0
4. London Heathrow (LHR)    60.7
5. Tokyo Haneda (HND)    58.7
6. Dallas Fort Worth Intl. (DFW)    55.2
7. Frankfurt Intl. (FRA)    48.6
8. Paris Charles de Gaulle (CDG)    48.0
9. Amsterdam (AMS)    39.5
10. Denver Intl. (DEN)    36.1

**International passengers in millions (2001**
1. London Heathrow (LHR)    53.8
2. Paris Charles de Gaulle (CDG)    43.4
3. Frankfurt Intl. (FRA)    40.0
4. Amsterdam (AMS)    39.2
5. Hong Kong Intl. (HKG)    32.0
6. London Gatwick (LGW)    28.1
7. Singapore Changi (SIN)    26.5
8. Tokyo Narita (NRT)    22.2
9. Bangkok (BKK)    21.4
10. Zurich (ZRH)    19.7

## UNESCO WORLD HERITAGE SITES 2002

Total sites = 730 (563 cultural, 144 natural and 23 mixed)

| Region | Natural sites | Cultural sites |
|---|---|---|
| Europe | 21 | 285 |
| Middle East and Turkey | 1 | 31 |
| Asia and Russia | 29 | 106 |
| Canada and USA | 18 | 13 |
| Mexico and Central America | 11 | 35 |
| South America | 19 | 36 |
| Africa | 32 | 57 |
| Oceania | 13 | 0 |

**Destinations**

- ■ Cultural & historical centres
- □ Coastal resorts
- □ Ski resorts
- Centres of entertainment
- Places of pilgrimage
- Places of great natural beauty

Other tourist destinations

## TOURIST DESTINATIONS

Projection: Peirce

## TOURIST EARNINGS

Countries receiving the most from overseas tourism, US$ million (2000)

**Movement of tourists**

More than 10 million

5 – 10 million

3 – 5 million

Less than 3 million

## TOURIST SPENDING

Countries spending the most on overseas tourism, US$ million (2000)

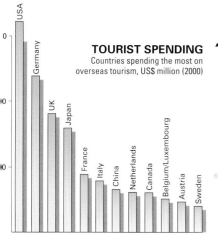

## IMPORTANCE OF TOURISM

Tourism receipts as a percentage of Gross National Income (1999)

- 10% and over
- 5 – 10%
- 2.5 – 5%
- 1 – 2.5%
- Under 1%
- No data

Arrivals from abroad in millions (2001)

| | |
|---|---|
| France | 75.6 |
| Spain | 49.5 |
| USA | 45.5 |
| Italy | 39.0 |
| China | 33.2 |

(UK = 23.4 million)

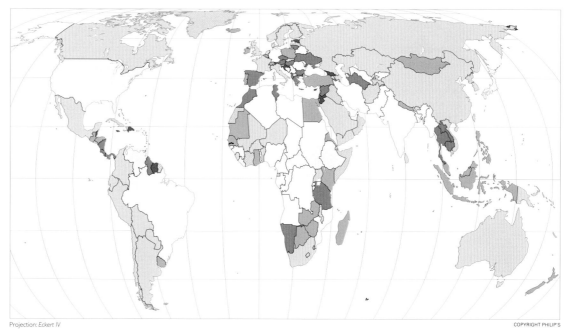

Projection: Eckert IV

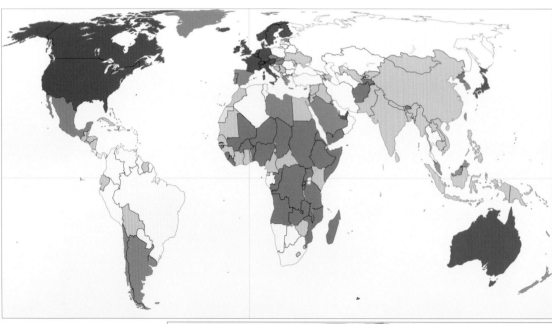

## WEALTH

### Gross Domestic Product per capita PPP (2000)

Annual value of goods and services divided by the population, using purchasing power parity (PPP) which gives real prices instead of variable exchange rates

 250% and over world average

100 – 250% world average

**World average: 8,527 US$**

50 – 100% world average

15 – 50% world average

Under 15% world average

No data

| Highest GDP (US$) | | Lowest GDP (US$) | |
|---|---|---|---|
| Lux'bourg | 36,400 | Sierra Leone | 510 |
| USA | 36,200 | Congo (D.Rep.) | 600 |
| San Marino | 32,000 | Ethiopia | 600 |
| Switzerland | 28,600 | Somalia | 600 |
| Norway | 27,700 | Eritrea | 710 |

(UK = 22,800 US$)

## WATER SUPPLY

Percentage of total population with access to safe drinking water (2000)

| | |
|---|---|
| 90% and over | |
| 75 – 90% | |
| 60 – 75% | |
| 45 – 60% | |
| 30 – 45% | |
| Under 30% | |

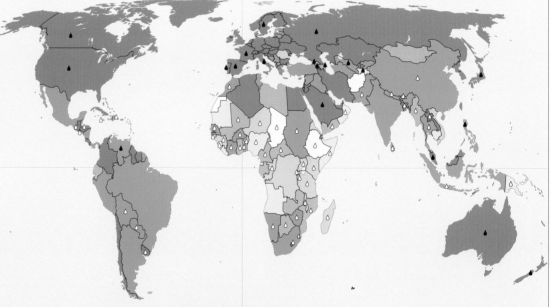

### Least amount of safe drinking water

| | | | |
|---|---|---|---|
| Afghanistan | 13% | Cambodia | 30% |
| Ethiopia | 24% | Mauritania | 37% |
| Chad | 27% | Angola | 38% |
| Sierra Leone | 28% | Oman | 39% |

Daily consumption per capita

△ Under 80 litres   ◆ Over 320 litres

*80 litres a day is considered necessary for a reasonable quality of life*

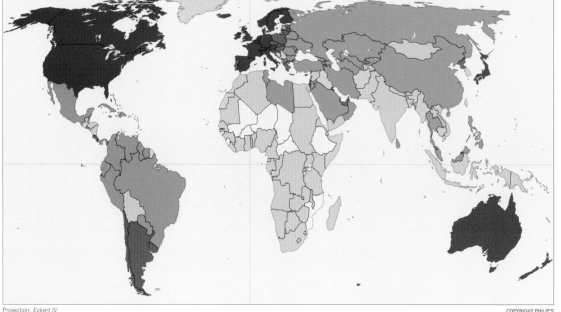

## HUMAN DEVELOPMENT INDEX (HDI)

HDI (calculated by the UNDP) gives a value to countries using indicators of life expectancy, education and standards of living in 2000. Higher values show more developed countries

| | |
|---|---|
| 0.9 and over | |
| 0.8 – 0.9 | |
| 0.7 – 0.8 | |
| 0.4 – 0.7 | |
| Under 0.4 | |
| No data | |

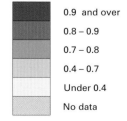

| Highest values | | Lowest values | |
|---|---|---|---|
| Norway | 0.942 | Sierra Leone | 0.275 |
| Sweden | 0.941 | Niger | 0.277 |
| Canada | 0.940 | Burundi | 0.313 |
| USA | 0.939 | Mozambique | 0.322 |
| Belgium | 0.939 | Burkina Faso | 0.325 |

(UK = 0.928)

## HEALTH CARE

### Number of people per qualified doctor (1999)

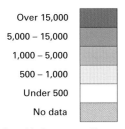

| | |
|---|---|
| Over 15,000 | |
| 5,000 – 15,000 | |
| 1,000 – 5,000 | |
| 500 – 1,000 | |
| Under 500 | |
| No data | |

Countries with the most and least people per doctor

| Most people | | Least people | |
|---|---|---|---|
| Eritrea | 33,333 | Italy | 181 |
| Chad | 30,303 | Belarus | 226 |
| Burkina Faso | 29,412 | Georgia | 229 |
| Niger | 28,517 | Spain | 236 |
| Tanzania | 24,390 | Russia | 238 |

(UK = 610 people)

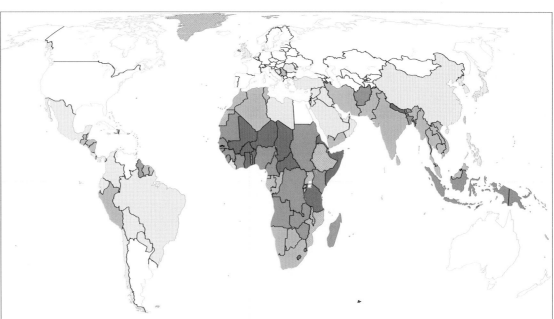

## ILLITERACY AND EDUCATION

### Percentage of adult population unable to read or write (2000)

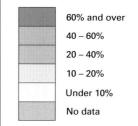

| | |
|---|---|
| 60% and over | |
| 40 – 60% | |
| 20 – 40% | |
| 10 – 20% | |
| Under 10% | |
| No data | |

Countries with the highest and lowest illiteracy rates

| Highest (%) | | Lowest (%) | |
|---|---|---|---|
| Niger | 84 | Australia | 0 |
| Burkina Faso | 76 | Denmark | 0 |
| Gambia | 63 | Estonia | 0 |
| Afghanistan | 63 | Finland | 0 |
| Senegal | 63 | Luxembourg | 0 |

(UK = 1%)

## GENDER DEVELOPMENT INDEX (GDI)

GDI shows economic and social differences between men and women by using various UNDP indicators (2002). Countries with higher values of GDI have more equality between men and women

| | |
|---|---|
| 0.8 and over | |
| 0.6 – 0.8 | |
| 0.4 – 0.6 | |
| Under 0.4 | |
| No data | |

| Highest values | | Lowest values | |
|---|---|---|---|
| Norway | 0.941 | Niger | 0.263 |
| Australia | 0.938 | Burundi | 0.306 |
| Canada | 0.938 | Mozambique | 0.307 |
| USA | 0.937 | Burkina Faso | 0.312 |
| Sweden | 0.936 | Ethiopia | 0.313 |

(UK = 0.925)

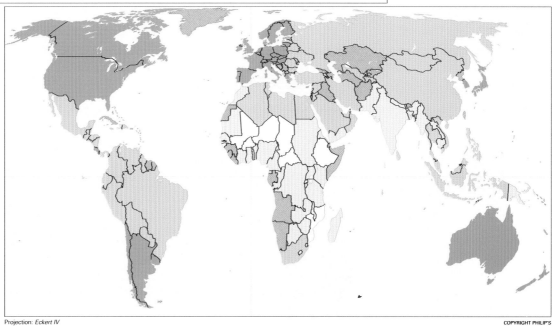

Projection: *Eckert IV*

## AGE DISTRIBUTION PYRAMIDS (2000)

The bars represent the percentage of the total population (males plus females) in each age group. Developed countries such as New Zealand have populations spread evenly across age groups and usually a growing percentage of elderly people. Developing countries such as Kenya have the great majority of their people in the younger age groups, about to enter their most fertile years.

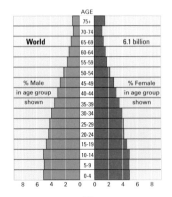

World — 6.1 billion

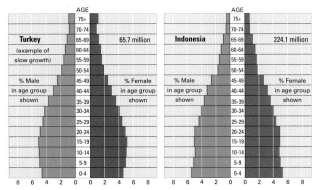

New Zealand — 3.8 million

Spain (example of negative growth) — 40.0 million

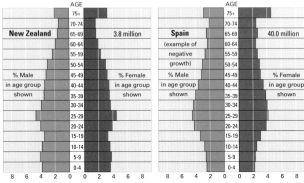

Turkey (example of slow growth) — 65.7 million

Indonesia — 224.1 million

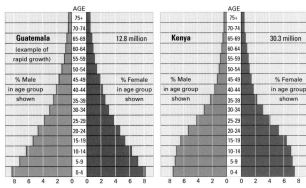

Guatemala (example of rapid growth) — 12.8 million

Kenya — 30.3 million

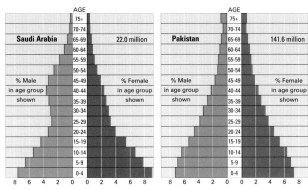

Saudi Arabia — 22.0 million

Pakistan — 141.6 million

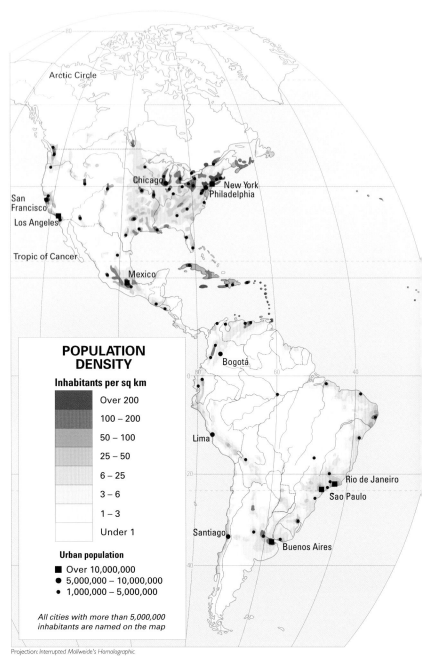

## POPULATION DENSITY

### Inhabitants per sq km

- Over 200
- 100 – 200
- 50 – 100
- 25 – 50
- 6 – 25
- 3 – 6
- 1 – 3
- Under 1

### Urban population

- ■ Over 10,000,000
- ● 5,000,000 – 10,000,000
- • 1,000,000 – 5,000,000

*All cities with more than 5,000,000 inhabitants are named on the map*

Projection: Interrupted Mollweide's Homolographic

## POPULATION CHANGE 1930–2020     Population totals are in millions

*Figures in italics represent the percentage average annual increase for the period show*

|  | 1930 | 1930–1960 | 1960 | 1960–1990 | 1990 | 1990–2020 | 2020 |
|---|---|---|---|---|---|---|---|
| World | 2,013 | *1.4%* | 3,019 | *1.9%* | 5,292 | *1.4%* | 8,062 |
| Africa | 155 | *2.0%* | 281 | *2.85* | 648 | *2.7%* | 1,441 |
| North America | 135 | *1.3%* | 199 | *1.1%* | 276 | *0.6%* | 327 |
| Latin America* | 129 | *1.8%* | 218 | *2.4%* | 448 | *1.6%* | 719 |
| Asia | 1,073 | *1.5%* | 1,669 | *2.1%* | 3,108 | *1.4%* | 4,680 |
| Europe | 355 | *0.6%* | 425 | *0.55* | 498 | *0.1%* | 514 |
| Oceania | 10 | *1.4%* | 16 | *1.75* | 27 | *1.1%* | 37 |
| CIS† | 176 | *0.7%* | 214 | *1.0%* | 288 | *0.6%* | 343 |

*\* South America plus Central America, Mexico and the West Indies*
*† Commonwealth of Independent States, formerly the USSR*

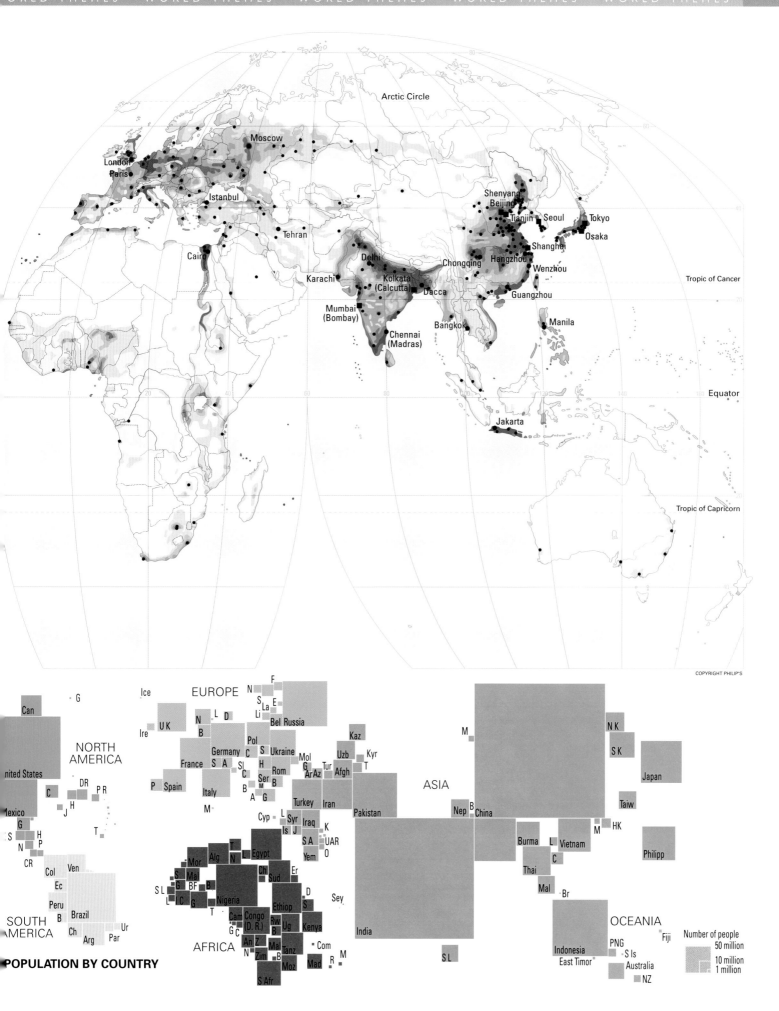

Arctic Circle

Moscow

London
Paris

Istanbul

Tehran

Cairo

Shenyang
Beijing
Tianjin    Seoul    Tokyo
Osaka
Shanghai
Delhi    Chongqing    Hangzhou
Karachi    Wenzhou
Kolkata
(Calcutta)    Dacca    Tropic of Cancer
Mumbai    Guangzhou
(Bombay)
Chennai    Bangkok    Manila
(Madras)

Equator

Jakarta

Tropic of Capricorn

COPYRIGHT PHILIP'S

**POPULATION BY COUNTRY**

EUROPE

G

Ice

Can

NORTH
AMERICA

F
N
S E
La
Li
Bel Russia

L D
N
UK
B

Ire

nited States

C
DR P R
J H

Germany
France
S A
C
Sl
P Spain
Italy
A G
M

Pol
S
H
Ser
B

Kaz

Uzb
Kyr
T

ASIA

M

N K

S K

Japan

Mexico

G
S
N
H
P
CR

Col    Ven
Ec
Peru
B    Brazil
Ch    Ur
Arg    Par

SOUTH
AMERICA

Mol
ArAz
Tur Afgh

Turkey
Iran

Cyp
Syr
L
Is J
Iraq
K
S A
UAR
Yem
O

Pakistan

Nep B
China

Taiw
M HK

Burma L
Vietnam
Thai    C
Mal    Br

Philipp

T
Mor
Alg
S
Mal
G BF B
S L
L
C
G
T N
Ch Sud Er
N Egypt

Nigeria

D
S
Ethiop
Cam Congo Rw Ug Kenya
G C (D. R.) B
An Z
N Zim Tanz Com
B
Moz Mad R M

S Afr

Sey

India

S L

AFRICA

OCEANIA

PNG    Fiji
Indonesia    S Is
East Timor    Australia

NZ

Number of people
50 million

10 million
1 million

## POPULATION DENSITY

Density of people per
square kilometre (2001)

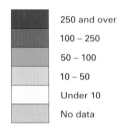

250 and over

100 – 250

50 – 100

10 – 50

Under 10

No data

### Most and least densely populated countries

| Most | | Least | |
|---|---|---|---|
| Singapore | 7,049.2 | W. Sahara | 0.9 |
| Malta | 1,234.4 | Mongolia | 1.7 |
| Maldives | 1,036.7 | Namibia | 2.0 |
| Bangladesh | 1,008.5 | Australia | 2.5 |
| Bahrain | 934.8 | Mauritania | 2.7 |

(UK = 247.6 people)

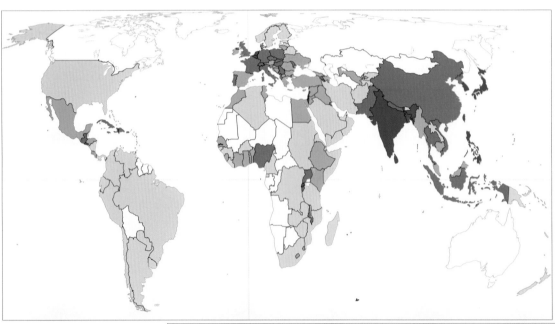

## POPULATION CHANGE

Change in total population
(1990 – 2000)

Over 40% gain

20 – 40% gain

10 – 20% gain

0 – 10% gain

Loss or no change

No data

### Greatest population gains and losses

| Greatest gains (%) | | Greatest losses (%) | |
|---|---|---|---|
| Kuwait | 75.9 | Germany | – 3.2 |
| Namibia | 69.4 | Tonga | – 3.2 |
| Afghanistan | 60.1 | Grenada | – 2.4 |
| Mali | 55.5 | Hungary | – 0.2 |
| Tanzania | 54.6 | Belgium | – 0.1 |

(UK = 2% gain)

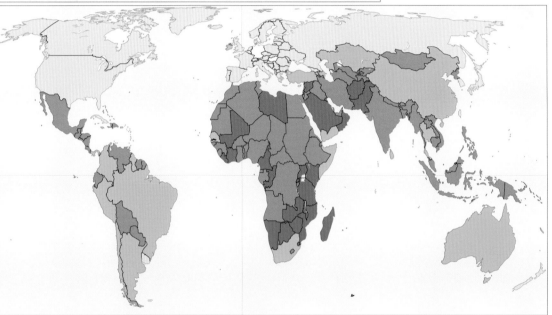

## URBAN POPULATION

People living in urban areas
as a percentage of
total population (2000)

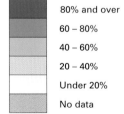

80% and over

60 – 80%

40 – 60%

20 – 40%

Under 20%

No data

### Countries that are the most and least urbanized (%)

| Most urbanized | | Least urbanized | |
|---|---|---|---|
| Singapore | 100 | Rwanda | 6.4 |
| Nauru | 100 | Bhutan | 7.3 |
| Monaco | 100 | East Timor | 7.4 |
| Vatican City | 100 | Burundi | 9.2 |
| Belgium | 97.3 | Nepal | 10.8 |

(UK = 89.3%)

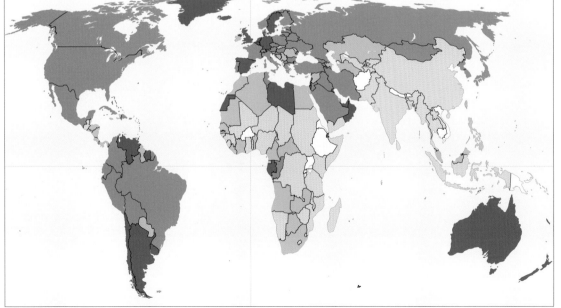

## CHILD MORTALITY

Deaths of children under 1 year
old per 1000 live births (2001)

| | |
|---|---|
| 100 and over | |
| 50 – 100 | |
| 25 – 50 | |
| 10 – 25 | |
| Under 10 | |
| No data | |

Countries with the highest and
lowest child mortality

| Highest | | Lowest | |
|---|---|---|---|
| Angola | 194 | Sweden | 3 |
| Afghanistan | 147 | Iceland | 4 |
| Sierra Leone | 147 | Singapore | 4 |
| Mozambique | 139 | Finland | 4 |
| Liberia | 132 | Japan | 4 |

(UK = 6 deaths)

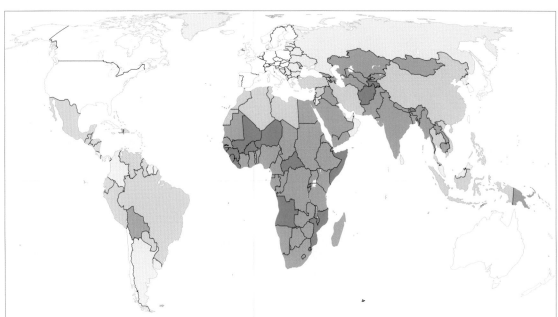
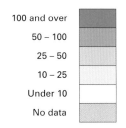

## LIFE EXPECTANCY

Life expectancy at birth in years
(2001)

| | |
|---|---|
| 75 and over | |
| 65 – 75 | |
| 55 – 65 | |
| 45 – 55 | |
| Under 45 | |
| No data | |

Countries with the longest and shortest
life expectancy at birth in years

| Longest | | Shortest | |
|---|---|---|---|
| Andorra | 83.5 | Mozambique | 36.5 |
| San Marino | 81.2 | Botswana | 37.1 |
| Japan | 80.8 | Zimbabwe | 37.1 |
| Singapore | 80.2 | Zambia | 37.3 |
| Australia | 79.9 | Angola | 38.6 |

(UK = 77.8 years)

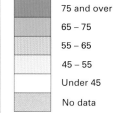

## FAMILY SIZE

Children born per woman (2001)

| | |
|---|---|
| More than 5 | |
| 4 – 5 | |
| 3 – 4 | |
| 2 – 3 | |
| 1 – 2 | |
| No data | |

Countries with the largest and
smallest family size

| Largest | | Smallest | |
|---|---|---|---|
| Somalia | 7.1 | Bulgaria | 1.1 |
| Niger | 7.1 | Latvia | 1.2 |
| Ethiopia | 7.0 | Spain | 1.2 |
| Yemen | 7.0 | Czech Rep. | 1.2 |
| Uganda | 7.0 | Italy | 1.2 |

(UK = 1.7 children)

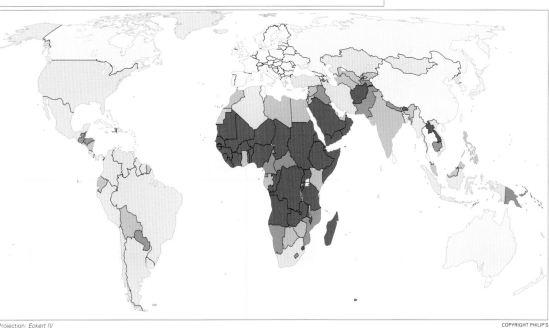
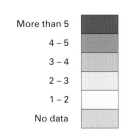

Projection: *Eckert IV*

COPYRIGHT PHILIP'S

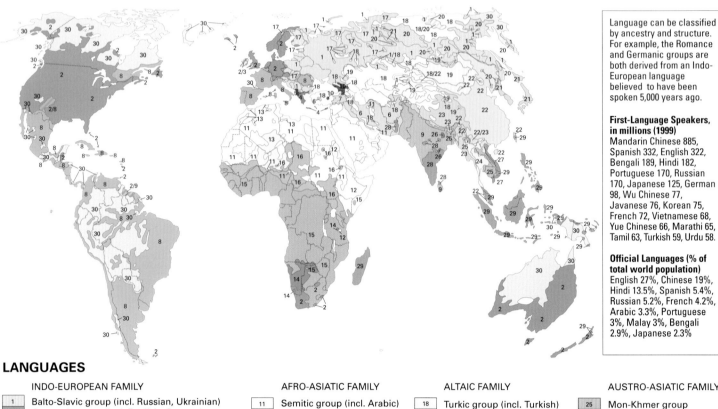

Language can be classified by ancestry and structure. For example, the Romance and Germanic groups are both derived from an Indo-European language believed to have been spoken 5,000 years ago.

**First-Language Speakers, in millions (1999)**
Mandarin Chinese 885, Spanish 332, English 322, Bengali 189, Hindi 182, Portuguese 170, Russian 170, Japanese 125, German 98, Wu Chinese 77, Javanese 76, Korean 75, French 72, Vietnamese 68, Yue Chinese 66, Marathi 65, Tamil 63, Turkish 59, Urdu 58.

**Official Languages (% of total world population)**
English 27%, Chinese 19%, Hindi 13.5%, Spanish 5.4%, Russian 5.2%, French 4.2%, Arabic 3.3%, Portuguese 3%, Malay 3%, Bengali 2.9%, Japanese 2.3%

## LANGUAGES

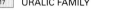

**INDO-EUROPEAN FAMILY**

| | |
|---|---|
| 1 | Balto-Slavic group (incl. Russian, Ukrainian) |
| 2 | Germanic group (incl. English, German) |
| 3 | Celtic group |
| 4 | Greek |
| 5 | Albanian |
| 6 | Iranian group |
| 7 | Armenian |
| 8 | Romance group (incl. Spanish, Portuguese, French, Italian) |
| 9 | Indo-Aryan group (incl. Hindi, Bengali, Urdu, Punjabi, Marathi) |
| 10 | CAUCASIAN FAMILY |

**AFRO-ASIATIC FAMILY**

| | |
|---|---|
| 11 | Semitic group (incl. Arabic) |
| 12 | Kushitic group |
| 13 | Berber group |
| 14 | KHOISAN FAMILY |
| 15 | NIGER-CONGO FAMILY |
| 16 | NILO-SAHARAN FAMILY |
| 17 | URALIC FAMILY |

**ALTAIC FAMILY**

| | |
|---|---|
| 18 | Turkic group (incl. Turkish) |
| 19 | Mongolian group |
| 20 | Tungus-Manchu group |
| 21 | Japanese and Korean |

**SINO-TIBETAN FAMILY**

| | |
|---|---|
| 22 | Sinitic (Chinese) languages (incl. Mandarin, Wu, Yue) |
| 23 | Tibetic-Burmic languages |
| 24 | TAI FAMILY |

**AUSTRO-ASIATIC FAMILY**

| | |
|---|---|
| 25 | Mon-Khmer group |
| 26 | Munda group |
| 27 | Vietnamese |
| 28 | DRAVIDIAN FAMILY (incl. Telugu, Tamil) |
| 29 | AUSTRONESIAN FAMILY (incl. Malay-Indonesian, Javanese) |
| 30 | OTHER LANGUAGES |

## RELIGIONS

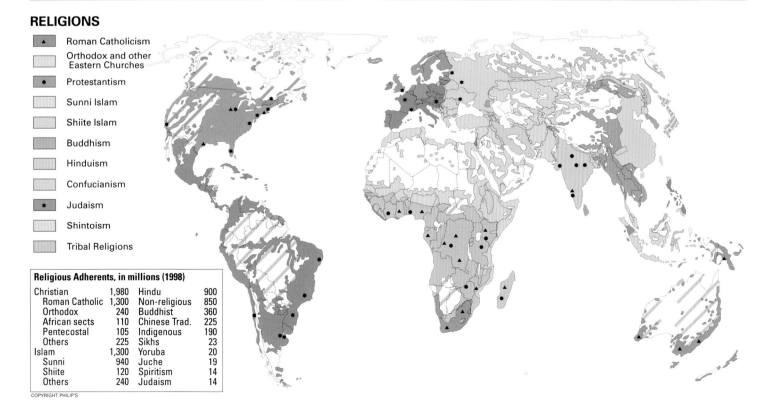

- ▲ Roman Catholicism
- Orthodox and other Eastern Churches
- • Protestantism
- Sunni Islam
- Shiite Islam
- Buddhism
- Hinduism
- Confucianism
- ✶ Judaism
- Shintoism
- Tribal Religions

**Religious Adherents, in millions (1998)**

| | | | |
|---|---|---|---|
| Christian | 1,980 | Hindu | 900 |
|   Roman Catholic | 1,300 | Non-religious | 850 |
|   Orthodox | 240 | Buddhist | 360 |
|   African sects | 110 | Chinese Trad. | 225 |
|   Pentecostal | 105 | Indigenous | 190 |
|   Others | 225 | Sikhs | 23 |
| Islam | 1,300 | Yoruba | 20 |
|   Sunni | 940 | Juche | 19 |
|   Shiite | 120 | Spiritism | 14 |
|   Others | 240 | Judaism | 14 |

## UNITED NATIONS

Created in 1945 to promote peace and co-operation and based in New York, the United Nations is the world's largest international organization, with 191 members and an annual budget of US$1.3 billion (2002). Each member of the General Assembly has one vote, while the five permanent members of the 15-nation Security Council – China, France, Russia, UK and USA – hold a veto. The Secretariat is the UN's principal administrative arm. The 54 members of the Economic and Social Council are responsible for economic, social, cultural, educational, health and related matters. The UN has 16 specialized agencies – based in Canada, France, Switzerland and Italy, as well as the USA – which help members in fields such as education (UNESCO), agriculture (FAO), medicine (WHO) and finance (IFC). By the end of 1994, all the original 11 trust territories of the Trusteeship Council had become independent.

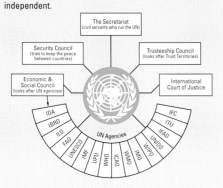

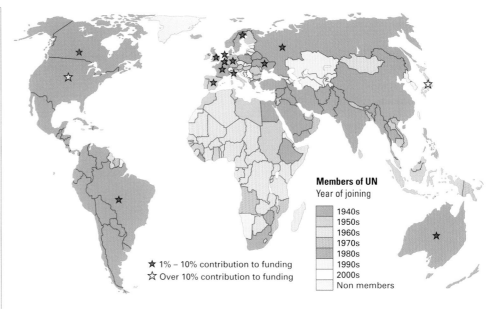

**Members of UN**
Year of joining

- 1940s
- 1950s
- 1960s
- 1970s
- 1980s
- 1990s
- 2000s
- Non members

★ 1% – 10% contribution to funding
☆ Over 10% contribution to funding

**MEMBERSHIP OF THE UN** In 1945 there were 51 members; by the end of 2002 membership had increased to 191 following the admission of East Timor and Switzerland. There are 2 independent states which are not members of the UN – Taiwan and the Vatican City. All the successor states of the former USSR had joined by the end of 1992. The official languages of the UN are Chinese, English, French, Russian, Spanish and Arabic.

**FUNDING** The UN regular budget for 2002 was US$1.3 billion. Contributions are assessed by the members' ability to pay, with the maximum 22% of the total (USA's share), the minimum 0.01%. The 15-country European Union pays over 37% of the budget.

**PEACEKEEPING** The UN has been involved in 54 peacekeeping operations worldwide since 1948.

## INTERNATIONAL ORGANIZATIONS

**ACP** African-Caribbean-Pacific (formed in 1963). Members have economic ties with the EU.

**ARAB LEAGUE** (formed in 1945). The League's aim is to promote economic, social, political and military co-operation. There are 22 member nations.

**ASEAN** Association of South-east Asian Nations (formed in 1967). Cambodia joined in 1999.

**AU** The African Union replaced the Organization of African Unity (formed in 1963) in 2002. Its 53 members represent over 94% of Africa's population. Arabic, French, Portuguese and English are recognized as working languages.

**CIS** The Commonwealth of Independent States (formed in 1991) comprises the countries of the former Soviet Union except for Estonia, Latvia and Lithuania.

**COLOMBO PLAN** (formed in 1951). Its 25 members aim to promote economic and social development in Asia and the Pacific.

**COMMONWEALTH** The Commonwealth of Nations evolved from the British Empire. Pakistan was suspended in 1999, and Zimbabwe in 2002. In response to its continued suspension, Zimbabwe left the Commonwealth in December 2003. It now comprises 16 Queen's realms, 31 republics and 6 indigenous monarchies, giving a total of 53 member states.

**EFTA** European Free Trade Association (formed in 1960). Portugal left the original 'Seven' in 1989 to join what was then the EC, followed by Austria, Finland and Sweden in 1995. Only 4 members remain: Norway, Iceland, Switzerland and Liechtenstein.

**EU** European Union (evolved from the European Community in 1993). The 15 members – Austria, Belgium, Denmark, Finland, France, Germany, Greece, Ireland, Italy, Luxembourg, Netherlands, Portugal, Spain, Sweden and the UK – aim to integrate economies, co-ordinate social developments and bring about political union. Cyprus, the Czech Republic, Estonia, Hungary, Latvia, Lithuania, Malta, Poland, the Slovak Republic and Slovenia are joining the EU in 2004. Bulgaria and Romania are expected to join in 2007.

**LAIA** Latin American Integration Association (1980). Its aim is to promote freer regional trade.

**NATO** North Atlantic Treaty Organization (formed in 1949). It continues after 1991 despite the winding up of the Warsaw Pact. The Czech Republic, Hungary and Poland were the latest members to join in 1999.

**OAS** Organization of American States (formed in 1948). It aims to promote social and economic co-operation between developed countries of North America and developing nations of Latin America.

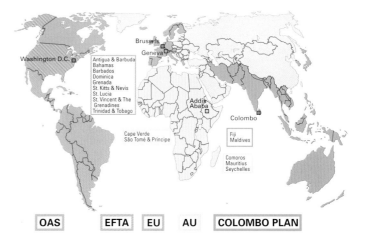

| OAS | EFTA | EU | AU | COLOMBO PLAN |

**OECD** Organization for Economic Co-operation and Development (formed in 1961). It comprises 30 major free-market economies. Poland, Hungary and South Korea joined in 1996, and the Slovak Republic in 2000. 'G8' is its 'inner group' of leading industrial nations, comprising Canada, France, Germany, Italy, Japan, Russia, UK and USA.

**OPEC** Organization of Petroleum Exporting Countries (formed in 1960). It controls about three-quarters of the world's oil supply. Gabon left the organization in 1996.

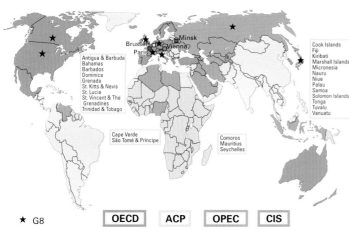

★ G8 | OECD | ACP | OPEC | CIS |

| NATO | LAIA | ARAB LEAGUE | COMMONWEALTH | ASEAN |

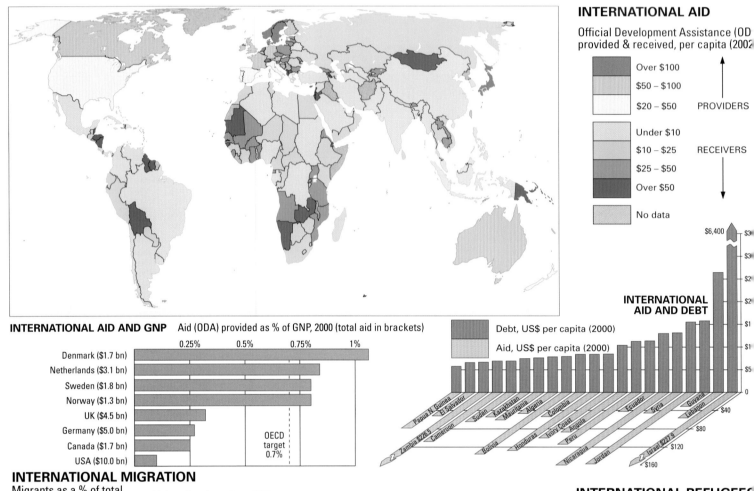

## INTERNATIONAL AID

Official Development Assistance (OD
provided & received, per capita (2002

| | |
|---|---|
| Over $100 | |
| $50 – $100 | PROVIDERS |
| $20 – $50 | |
| Under $10 | |
| $10 – $25 | RECEIVERS |
| $25 – $50 | |
| Over $50 | |
| No data | |

## INTERNATIONAL AID AND GNP

Aid (ODA) provided as % of GNP, 2000 (total aid in brackets)

| | 0.25% | 0.5% | 0.75% | 1% |
|---|---|---|---|---|
| Denmark ($1.7 bn) | | | | |
| Netherlands ($3.1 bn) | | | | |
| Sweden ($1.8 bn) | | | | |
| Norway ($1.3 bn) | | | | |
| UK ($4.5 bn) | | | | |
| Germany ($5.0 bn) | | OECD target 0.7% | | |
| Canada ($1.7 bn) | | | | |
| USA ($10.0 bn) | | | | |

## INTERNATIONAL AID AND DEBT

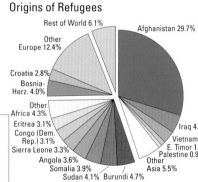

Debt, US$ per capita (2000)
Aid, US$ per capita (2000)

$6,400

Zambia $26.5, Papua N. Guinea, Cameroon, El Salvador, Sudan, Bolivia, Kazakhstan, Honduras, Mauritania, Ivory Coast, Algeria, Peru, Colombia, Angola, Ecuador, Nicaragua, Syria, Jordan, Guyana, Israel $27.9, Lebanon

$40, $80, $120, $160

## INTERNATIONAL MIGRATION

Migrants as a % of total population (foreign born and refugees, 2000)

| | |
|---|---|
| Over 20% | |
| 10 – 20% | |
| 5 – 10% | |
| 2 – 5% | |
| Under 2% | |

**Major migrations since 1945**

1. 18m E. Europeans to Germany 1945 –
2. 4m Europeans to N. America 1945 –
3. 2.4m Jews to Israel 1945 –
4. 2m Irish & Commonwealth to UK 1945 –
5. 2m Europeans to Australia 1945 –
6. 2m N. Africans & S. Europeans to France 1946 –
7. 5m Chinese to Japan & Korea 1947 –
8. 2.9m Palestinian refugees 1947
9. 25m Indian & Pakistani refugees 1947–
10. 9m Mexicans to N. America 1950 –
11. 5m Korean refugees 1950–54
12. 4.7m C. Americans & W. Indians to N. America 1960–
13. 1.5m workers to S. Africa 1960 –
14. 2.4m S. Asian workers to the Gulf 1970 –
15. 3m workers to Nigeria & Ivory Coast 1970 –
16. 2m Bangladeshi & Pakistani refugees 1972 –
17. 1.5m Vietnamese & Cambodian refugees 1975 –
18. 6.1m Afghan refugees 1979 –
19. 2.9m Egyptian workers to Libya & the Gulf 1980 –
20. 2m workers to Argentina 1980 –
21. 1.7m Mozambique refugees 1985 –
22. 1.7m Yugoslav refugees 1992 –
23. 2.6m Rwanda & Burundi refugees 1994 –

## INTERNATIONAL REFUGEES

World Total (2000): 12.1 million

### Origins of Refugees

Afghanistan 29.7%
Rest of World 6.1%
Other Europe 12.4%
Croatia 2.8%
Bosnia-Herz. 4.0%
Other Africa 4.3%
Eritrea 3.1%
Congo (Dem. Rep.) 3.1%
Sierra Leone 3.3%
Angola 3.6%
Somalia 3.9%
Sudan 4.1%
Burundi 4.7%
Iraq 4.4
Vietnam
E. Timor 1.0
Palestine 0.9
Other Asia 5.5%

### Refugee Destinations

2,000,000

Pakista
Iran
Germany
Gaza Strip (1996)
Tanzania
USA
Yugo-slavia

1,000,000

500,000

Refugees in host country

Refugees as a proportion of host country's population

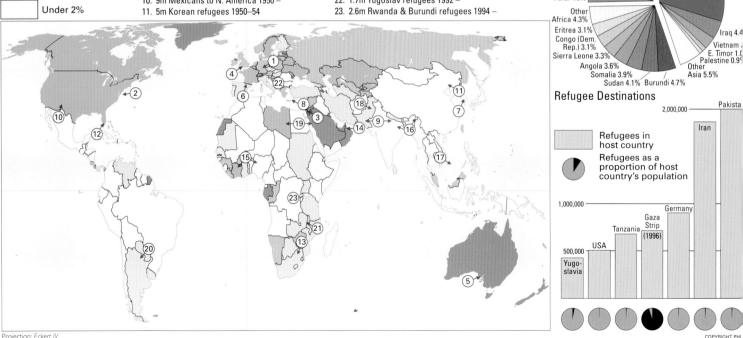

Projection: *Eckert IV*

COPYRIGHT PHI

## CONFLICTS

Conflicts during and since the 1990s

| | Past | Current |
|---|---|---|
| Major international war | | |
| Minor international war | | |
| Major civil war | | |
| Minor civil war | | |
| Long-running terrorist campaign | | |

### MAJOR WARS SINCE 1900

| War | Military deaths |
|---|---|
| Second World War (1939–45) | 20,000,000 |
| First World War (1914–18) | 8,500,000 |
| Korean War (1950–53) | 1,200,000 |
| Chinese Civil War (1945–49) | 1,200,000 |
| Vietnam War (1965–73) | 1,200,000 |

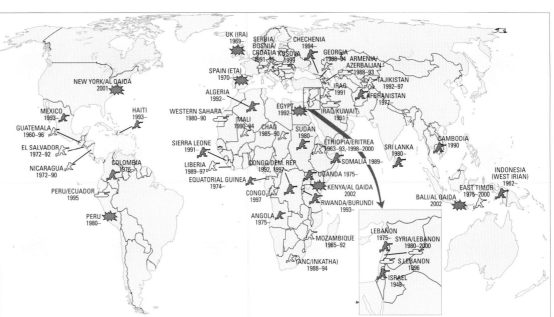

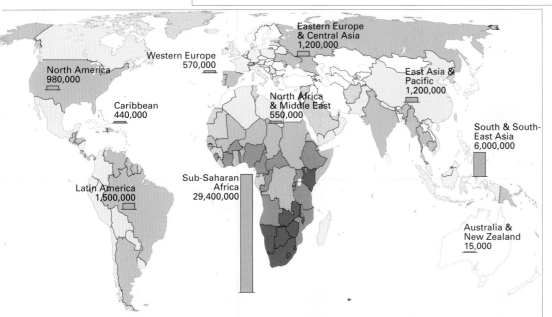

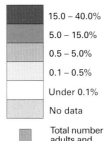

## HIV/AIDS

Percentage of adults (15 – 49 years) living with HIV/AIDS (2001)

- 15.0 – 40.0%
- 5.0 – 15.0%
- 0.5 – 5.0%
- 0.1 – 0.5%
- Under 0.1%
- No data

Total number of adults and children living with HIV/AIDS by region (2002)

Human Immunodeficiency Virus (HIV) is passed from one person to another and attacks the body's defence against illness. It develops into the Acquired Immunodeficiency Syndrome (AIDS) when a particularly severe illness, such as cancer, takes hold. The pandemic started just over 20 years ago and, by 2002, 42 millon people were living with HIV or AIDS.

## DRUGS

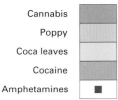

Countries producing illegal drugs

- Cannabis
- Poppy
- Coca leaves
- Cocaine
- Amphetamines ■

Major routes of drug trafficking

- Opium
- Coca leaves
- Cocaine
- Heroin
- Hashish and marijuana
- Amphetamines (usually used within producing countries)
- Conflicts relating to drug trafficking ✸

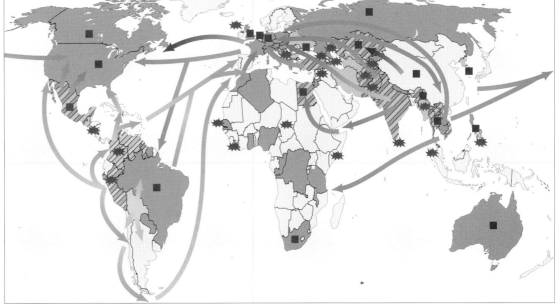

Projection: Eckert IV

COPYRIGHT PHILIP'S

| COUNTRY | POPULATION | | | | | | | | LAND AND AGRICULTURE | | | | | ENERGY AND TRADE | | | |
|---|---|---|---|---|---|---|---|---|---|---|---|---|---|---|---|---|---|
| | Population total (millions) | Population density (persons per km²) | Life expectancy (years) | Average annual population change (%) | Birth rate (births per thousand) | Death rate (deaths per thousand) | Fertility rate (children born per woman) | Urban population (% of total) | Land area (thousand km²) | Arable & permanent crops (% of land area) | Permanent pasture (% of land area) | Forest (% of land area) | Agricultural workforce (% of total workforce) | Energy produced (tonnes of oil equiv. per capita) | Energy consumed (tonnes of oil equiv. per capita) | Imports (US$ per capita) | Export (US$ per capita) |
| | 2001 | 2001 | 2001 | 2002 est. | 2001 | 2001 | 2001 | 2001 | 1999 | 1999 | 2000 | 2000 | 2000 | 2000 | 2000 | 2000 | 2000 |
| Afghanistan | 26.8 | 41 | 46 | 3.4 | 41 | 18 | 5.8 | 22 | 625 | 12 | 46 | 2 | 67 | 0.01 | 0.02 | 6 | 3 |
| Albania | 3.5 | 128 | 72 | 1.1 | 19 | 7 | 2.3 | 42 | 27 | 26 | 16 | 36 | 48 | 0.47 | 0.56 | 285 | 88 |
| Algeria | 31.7 | 13 | 70 | 1.7 | 23 | 5 | 2.7 | 57 | 2,382 | 3 | 14 | 1 | 24 | 4.93 | 0.98 | 290 | 618 |
| Angola | 10.4 | 8 | 39 | 2.2 | 47 | 25 | 6.5 | 34 | 1,247 | 3 | 43 | 56 | 72 | 3.93 | 0.22 | 241 | 752 |
| Argentina | 37.4 | 14 | 75 | 1.1 | 18 | 8 | 2.4 | 88 | 2,737 | 10 | 52 | 13 | 10 | 2.39 | 1.83 | 674 | 709 |
| Armenia | 3.3 | 118 | 66 | −0.2 | 11 | 10 | 1.5 | 67 | 28 | 20 | 30 | 12 | 13 | 0.31 | 0.74 | 274 | 85 |
| Australia | 19.4 | 3 | 80 | 1.0 | 13 | 7 | 1.8 | 91 | 7,682 | 6 | 53 | 21 | 5 | 12.53 | 6.35 | 3,978 | 3,564 |
| Austria | 8.2 | 99 | 78 | 0.2 | 10 | 10 | 1.4 | 67 | 83 | 18 | 23 | 47 | 5 | 1.76 | 4.32 | 8,048 | 7,754 |
| Azerbaijan | 7.8 | 90 | 63 | 0.4 | 18 | 10 | 2.2 | 52 | 87 | 23 | 29 | 13 | 27 | 2.70 | 1.72 | 180 | 244 |
| Bahamas | 0.3 | 30 | 70 | 0.9 | 19 | 7 | 2.3 | 88 | 10 | 1 | 0 | 84 | 4 | – | 4.71 | 5,805 | 1,264 |
| Bahrain | 0.6 | 935 | 73 | 1.7 | 20 | 4 | 2.8 | 92 | 1 | 9 | 6 | – | 1 | 17.20 | 15.61 | 6,512 | 8,992 |
| Bangladesh | 131.3 | 1,009 | 61 | 1.6 | 25 | 9 | 2.8 | 25 | 130 | 65 | 5 | 10 | 56 | 0.07 | 0.10 | 62 | 45 |
| Barbados | 0.3 | 688 | 73 | 0.5 | 13 | 9 | 1.6 | 50 | 1 | 40 | 5 | 5 | 4 | 0.27 | 1.67 | 2,910 | 945 |
| Belarus | 10.4 | 50 | 68 | −0.1 | 10 | 14 | 1.3 | 69 | 207 | 30 | 14 | 45 | 13 | 0.21 | 2.62 | 802 | 715 |
| Belgium | 10.3 | 311 | 78 | 0.2 | 11 | 10 | 1.6 | 97 | 30 | 25 | 21 | 22 | 2 | 1.22 | 6.73 | 16,181 | 17,682 |
| Belize | 0.3 | 11 | 71 | 2.7 | 32 | 5 | 4.1 | 48 | 23 | 4 | 2 | 59 | 30 | – | 0.33 | 1,613 | 92 |
| Benin | 6.6 | 60 | 50 | 2.9 | 44 | 15 | 6.2 | 42 | 111 | 17 | 5 | 24 | 54 | 0.02 | 0.05 | 86 | 60 |
| Bhutan | 2.0 | 44 | 53 | 2.2 | 36 | 14 | 5.1 | 7 | 47 | 3 | 6 | 64 | 94 | 0.25 | 0.10 | 131 | 75 |
| Bolivia | 8.3 | 8 | 64 | 1.7 | 27 | 8 | 3.5 | 62 | 1,084 | 2 | 31 | 49 | 44 | 0.66 | 0.46 | 224 | 152 |
| Bosnia-Herzegovina | 3.9 | 77 | 72 | 0.8 | 13 | 8 | 1.7 | 43 | 51 | 13 | 24 | 45 | 5 | 0.20 | 0.57 | 625 | 242 |
| Botswana | 1.6 | 3 | 37 | 0.2 | 29 | 24 | 3.7 | 49 | 567 | 1 | 45 | 22 | 45 | 0.39 | 0.83 | 1,387 | 1,639 |
| Brazil | 174.5 | 21 | 63 | 0.9 | 18 | 9 | 2.1 | 81 | 8,457 | 8 | 22 | 63 | 17 | 0.94 | 1.31 | 320 | 316 |
| Brunei | 0.3 | 65 | 74 | 2.1 | 20 | 3 | 2.4 | 72 | 5 | 1 | 1 | 84 | 1 | 71.70 | 6.33 | 3,779 | 7,413 |
| Bulgaria | 7.7 | 70 | 71 | −1.1 | 8 | 15 | 1.1 | 67 | 111 | 41 | 15 | 33 | 7 | 1.54 | 3.06 | 766 | 623 |
| Burkina Faso | 12.3 | 45 | 46 | 2.6 | 45 | 17 | 6.4 | 17 | 274 | 13 | 22 | 26 | 92 | 0.01 | 0.02 | 50 | 18 |
| Burma (Myanmar) | 42.0 | 64 | 55 | 0.6 | 20 | 12 | 2.3 | 28 | 658 | 15 | 1 | 52 | 70 | 0.09 | 0.09 | 60 | 31 |
| Burundi | 6.2 | 242 | 46 | 2.4 | 40 | 16 | 6.2 | 9 | 26 | 43 | 43 | 4 | 90 | 0.01 | 0.03 | 18 | 5 |
| Cambodia | 12.5 | 71 | 57 | 2.2 | 33 | 11 | 4.7 | 17 | 177 | 22 | 8 | 53 | 70 | 0.01 | 0.02 | 104 | 75 |
| Cameroon | 15.8 | 34 | 55 | 2.4 | 36 | 12 | 4.8 | 49 | 465 | 15 | 4 | 51 | 59 | 0.35 | 0.13 | 101 | 133 |
| Canada | 31.6 | 4 | 80 | 1.0 | 11 | 7 | 1.6 | 79 | 9,221 | 5 | 3 | 27 | 2 | 14.51 | 10.42 | 7,540 | 8,619 |
| Cape Verde Is. | 0.4 | 10 | 69 | 0.9 | 29 | 7 | 4.1 | 62 | 40 | 10 | 6 | 21 | 23 | – | 0.13 | 617 | 99 |
| Central African Rep. | 3.6 | 6 | 44 | 1.8 | 37 | 19 | 4.9 | 41 | 623 | 3 | 5 | 37 | 73 | 0.01 | 0.03 | 43 | 46 |
| Chad | 8.7 | 7 | 51 | 3.3 | 48 | 15 | 6.6 | 24 | 1,259 | 3 | 36 | 10 | 75 | – | 0.01 | 26 | 20 |
| Chile | 15.3 | 21 | 76 | 1.1 | 17 | 6 | 2.2 | 86 | 749 | 3 | 17 | 21 | 16 | 0.46 | 1.70 | 1,109 | 1,174 |
| China | 1,273.1 | 137 | 72 | 0.9 | 16 | 7 | 1.8 | 36 | 9,327 | 15 | 43 | 18 | 67 | 0.69 | 0.73 | 155 | 182 |
| Colombia | 40.3 | 39 | 71 | 1.6 | 22 | 6 | 2.7 | 75 | 1,039 | 4 | 40 | 48 | 20 | 1.93 | 0.74 | 307 | 359 |
| Comoros | 0.6 | 267 | 60 | 3.0 | 40 | 10 | 5.3 | 33 | 2 | 53 | 7 | 4 | 74 | 0.01 | 0.05 | 92 | 13 |
| Congo | 2.9 | 9 | 48 | 2.2 | 38 | 16 | 5.0 | 65 | 342 | 1 | 29 | 65 | 41 | 4.88 | 0.13 | 301 | 898 |
| Congo (Dem. Rep.) | 53.6 | 24 | 49 | 2.8 | 46 | 15 | 6.8 | 30 | 2,267 | 3 | 7 | 60 | 63 | 0.05 | 0.05 | 12 | 18 |
| Costa Rica | 3.8 | 74 | 76 | 1.6 | 20 | 4 | 2.5 | 59 | 51 | 10 | 46 | 39 | 20 | 0.55 | 0.97 | 1,564 | 1,590 |
| Croatia | 4.3 | 78 | 74 | 1.1 | 13 | 11 | 1.9 | 58 | 56 | 28 | 28 | 32 | 8 | 1.06 | 2.38 | 1,800 | 992 |
| Cuba | 11.2 | 102 | 76 | 0.4 | 12 | 7 | 1.6 | 75 | 110 | 41 | 20 | 21 | 14 | 0.29 | 0.87 | 304 | 161 |
| Cyprus | 0.8 | 83 | 77 | 0.6 | 13 | 8 | 1.9 | 70 | 9 | 15 | 0 | 13 | 9 | – | 3.40 | 5,245 | 1,378 |
| Czech Republic | 10.3 | 133 | 75 | −0.1 | 9 | 11 | 1.2 | 75 | 77 | 43 | 12 | 34 | 8 | 2.55 | 3.55 | 3,059 | 2,757 |
| Denmark | 5.4 | 126 | 77 | 0.3 | 12 | 11 | 1.7 | 85 | 42 | 54 | 8 | 11 | 4 | 5.31 | 4.13 | 8,145 | 9,490 |
| Djibouti | 0.5 | 20 | 51 | 2.6 | 41 | 15 | 5.7 | 84 | 23 | – | 56 | 0 | – | – | 1.22 | 954 | 564 |
| Dominican Republic | 8.6 | 177 | 73 | 1.6 | 25 | 5 | 3.0 | 65 | 48 | 32 | 43 | 28 | 17 | 0.04 | 0.60 | 1,119 | 670 |
| East Timor | 0.7 | 50 | – | 7.3 | – | – | – | 7 | 15 | 5 | 10 | – | 82 | – | – | – | – |
| Ecuador | 13.2 | 48 | 72 | 2.0 | 26 | 5 | 3.1 | 63 | 277 | 11 | 18 | 38 | 26 | 1.83 | 0.67 | 258 | 425 |
| Egypt | 69.5 | 70 | 64 | 1.7 | 25 | 8 | 3.1 | 43 | 995 | 3 | – | 0 | 33 | 0.96 | 0.74 | 244 | 105 |
| El Salvador | 6.2 | 301 | 70 | 1.8 | 29 | 6 | 3.3 | 60 | 21 | 39 | 38 | 6 | 29 | 0.12 | 0.46 | 737 | 449 |
| Equatorial Guinea | 0.5 | 17 | 54 | 2.5 | 38 | 13 | 4.9 | 48 | 28 | 8 | 4 | 62 | 70 | 16.92 | 0.14 | 617 | 1,770 |
| Eritrea | 4.3 | 43 | 56 | 3.8 | 43 | 12 | 5.9 | 19 | 121 | 5 | 69 | 16 | 78 | – | 0.11 | 130 | 6 |
| Estonia | 1.4 | 34 | 70 | −0.5 | 9 | 13 | 1.2 | 69 | 42 | 27 | 7 | 49 | 11 | 0.01 | 1.62 | 2,811 | 2,178 |
| Ethiopia | 65.9 | 66 | 45 | 2.6 | 45 | 18 | 7.0 | 16 | 1,120 | 11 | 20 | 5 | 82 | 0.01 | 0.02 | 19 | 7 |
| Fiji | 0.8 | 46 | 68 | 1.4 | 23 | 6 | 2.9 | 49 | 18 | 16 | 10 | 45 | 40 | 0.14 | 0.55 | 774 | 636 |
| Finland | 5.2 | 17 | 78 | 0.1 | 11 | 10 | 1.7 | 59 | 305 | 7 | 0 | 72 | 5 | 2.23 | 6.30 | 6,318 | 8,578 |
| France | 59.6 | 108 | 79 | 0.4 | 12 | 9 | 1.8 | 75 | 550 | 35 | 19 | 28 | 3 | 2.14 | 4.40 | 5,374 | 5,458 |
| Gabon | 1.2 | 5 | 50 | 1.0 | 27 | 17 | 3.7 | 81 | 258 | 2 | 18 | 85 | 38 | 14.92 | 1.06 | 819 | 2,785 |
| Gambia, The | 1.4 | 141 | 54 | 3.1 | 42 | 13 | 5.7 | 31 | 10 | 20 | 46 | 48 | 79 | – | 0.05 | 144 | 89 |
| Gaza Strip (OPT)* | 1.2 | 3,100 | 71 | 4.0 | 42 | 4 | 6.4 | – | 1 | 66 | – | – | – | – | – | 765 | 209 |
| Georgia | 5.0 | 72 | 65 | −0.6 | 11 | 15 | 1.5 | 56 | 70 | 15 | 28 | 43 | 20 | 0.34 | 0.86 | 180 | 75 |
| Germany | 83.0 | 233 | 78 | 0.3 | 9 | 11 | 1.4 | 88 | 357 | 34 | 14 | 31 | 3 | 1.58 | 4.24 | 6,082 | 6,961 |
| Ghana | 19.9 | 87 | 57 | 1.7 | 29 | 10 | 3.8 | 36 | 228 | 23 | 37 | 28 | 57 | 0.07 | 0.14 | 111 | 80 |
| Greece | 10.6 | 82 | 79 | 0.2 | 10 | 10 | 1.3 | 60 | 129 | 30 | 40 | 28 | 17 | 0.97 | 3.17 | 3,191 | 1,487 |

| WEALTH | | | | | | | SOCIAL INDICATORS | | | | | | | | | COUNTRY |
|---|---|---|---|---|---|---|---|---|---|---|---|---|---|---|---|---|
| GNI million US$ | GNI per capita (PPP US$) | GDP per capita (PPP US$) | Average annual growth GDP per capita (%) | Agriculture (% of GDP) | Industry (% of GDP) | Services (% of GDP) | HDI, Human Develop. Index (value) | Food supply (calories per capita per day) | Population per doctor | Adults living with HIV/AIDS (% 15–49 year olds) | GDI, Gender Develop. Index (value) | Female illiteracy (% female adults) | Male illiteracy (% male adults) | Aid donated (−)/received (US$ per capita) | Military spending (US$ per capita) | |
| 1999 | 1999 | 2000 | 1990–99 | 1999 | 1999 | 1999 | 2000 | 2000 | 1999 | 1999 | 2000 | 1999 | 1999 | 2000 | 1999 | |
| – | – | 800 | – | 52 | 29 | 19 | – | 1,539 | 9,091 | – | – | 79 | 49 | – | – | Afghanistan |
| 3,146 | 3,240 | 3,000 | 2.8 | 55 | 24 | 21 | 0.733 | 2,864 | 775 | 0.1 | 0.729 | 23 | 9 | 91 | 14 | Albania |
| 46,548 | 4,840 | 5,500 | –0.5 | 11 | 37 | 52 | 0.697 | 2,944 | 1,182 | 0.1 | 0.679 | 44 | 23 | 5 | 63 | Algeria |
| 3,276 | 1,100 | 1,000 | –2.8 | 7 | 60 | 33 | 0.403 | 1,903 | 12,987 | 3.0 | – | 72 | 44 | 30 | 94 | Angola |
| 76,097 | 11,940 | 12,900 | 3.6 | 6 | 32 | 62 | 0.844 | 3,181 | 373 | 0.7 | 0.836 | 3 | 3 | 2 | 118 | Argentina |
| 1,878 | 2,360 | 3,000 | –3.9 | 40 | 25 | 35 | 0.754 | 1,944 | 316 | 0.1 | 0.751 | 3 | 1 | 65 | 20 | Armenia |
| 97,345 | 23,850 | 23,200 | 2.9 | 3 | 26 | 71 | 0.939 | 3,176 | 417 | 0.2 | 0.938 | 1 | 1 | –51 | 365 | Australia |
| 05,743 | 24,600 | 25,000 | 1.4 | 2 | 30 | 68 | 0.926 | 3,757 | 331 | 0.2 | 0.921 | 1 | 1 | –52 | 210 | Austria |
| 3,705 | 2,450 | 3,000 | –10.7 | 22 | 33 | 45 | 0.741 | 2,468 | 278 | 0.1 | – | – | – | 18 | 15 | Azerbaijan |
| 4,526 | 15,500 | 15,000 | –0.1 | 3 | 7 | 90 | 0.826 | 2,443 | 659 | 4.1 | 0.825 | 4 | 5 | 18 | 67 | Bahamas |
| 4,909 | 12,060 | 15,900 | 0.8 | 1 | 46 | 53 | 0.831 | – | 1,000 | 0.2 | 0.822 | 18 | 10 | 76 | 530 | Bahrain |
| 47,071 | 1,530 | 1,570 | 3.1 | 30 | 18 | 52 | 0.478 | 2,103 | 5,000 | 0.1 | 0.468 | 71 | 48 | 9 | 4 | Bangladesh |
| 2,294 | 14,010 | 14,500 | 1.5 | 4 | 16 | 80 | 0.871 | 3,022 | 797 | 1.2 | – | – | – | 1 | – | Barbados |
| 26,299 | 6,880 | 7,500 | –2.9 | 13 | 46 | 41 | 0.788 | 2,902 | 226 | 0.3 | 0.786 | 1 | 1 | 4 | 15 | Belarus |
| 52,051 | 25,710 | 25,300 | 1.4 | 1 | 26 | 73 | 0.939 | 3,701 | 253 | 0.2 | 0.933 | 1 | 1 | –80 | 245 | Belgium |
| 673 | 4,750 | 3,200 | 0.7 | 18 | 24 | 58 | 0.784 | 2,888 | 1,825 | 2.0 | 0.764 | 7 | 7 | 57 | 85 | Belize |
| 2,320 | 920 | 1,030 | 1.8 | 38 | 14 | 48 | 0.420 | 2,558 | 17,544 | 2.5 | 0.404 | 76 | 45 | 36 | 4 | Benin |
| 399 | 1,260 | 1,100 | 3.4 | 38 | 37 | 25 | 0.494 | – | 6,250 | 0.1 | – | – | – | 26 | – | Bhutan |
| 8,092 | 2,300 | 2,600 | 1.8 | 16 | 31 | 53 | 0.653 | 2,218 | 770 | 0.1 | 0.645 | 21 | 8 | 57 | 18 | Bolivia |
| 4,706 | 1,210 | 1,700 | 32.7 | 19 | 23 | 58 | – | 2,661 | 699 | 0.1 | – | – | – | – | – | Bosnia-Herzegovina |
| 5,139 | 6,540 | 6,600 | 1.8 | 4 | 46 | 50 | 0.572 | 2,255 | 4,202 | 35.8 | 0.566 | 21 | 26 | 19 | 41 | Botswana |
| 30,424 | 6,840 | 6,500 | 1.5 | 9 | 29 | 62 | 0.757 | 2,985 | 786 | 0.6 | 0.751 | 15 | 15 | 2 | 80 | Brazil |
| 7,753 | 24,620 | 17,600 | –0.5 | 5 | 46 | 49 | 0.856 | 2,832 | 1,179 | 0.2 | 0.851 | 13 | 6 | 2 | 1143 | Brunei |
| 11,572 | 5,070 | 6,200 | –2.1 | 15 | 29 | 56 | 0.779 | 2,467 | 290 | 0.1 | 0.778 | 2 | 1 | 40 | 43 | Bulgaria |
| 2,602 | 960 | 1,000 | 1.4 | 26 | 27 | 47 | 0.325 | 2,293 | 29,412 | 6.4 | 0.312 | 87 | 67 | 27 | 6 | Burkina Faso |
| – | – | 1,500 | 5.1 | 42 | 17 | 41 | 0.552 | 2,842 | 3,367 | 2.0 | 0.548 | 20 | 11 | 3 | 1 | Burma (Myanmar) |
| 823 | 570 | 720 | –5.0 | 50 | 18 | 32 | 0.313 | 1,605 | – | 11.3 | 0.306 | 61 | 44 | 15 | 9 | Burundi |
| 3,023 | 1,350 | 1,300 | 1.9 | 50 | 15 | 35 | 0.543 | 2,070 | 3,367 | 4.0 | 0.537 | – | 20 | 32 | 9 | Cambodia |
| 8,798 | 1,490 | 1,700 | –1.5 | 43 | 20 | 37 | 0.512 | 2,255 | 13,514 | 7.7 | 0.500 | 31 | 19 | 24 | 8 | Cameroon |
| 14,003 | 25,440 | 24,800 | 1.7 | 3 | 31 | 66 | 0.940 | 3,174 | 436 | 0.3 | 0.938 | 1 | 1 | –55 | 246 | Canada |
| 569 | 4,450 | 1,700 | 3.2 | 13 | 19 | 68 | 0.715 | 3,278 | 5,848 | – | 0.704 | 35 | 16 | 232 | 10 | Cape Verde Is. |
| 1,035 | 1,150 | 1,700 | –0.3 | 53 | 20 | 27 | 0.375 | 1,946 | 28,571 | 13.8 | 0.364 | 67 | 41 | 21 | 8 | Central African Rep. |
| 1,555 | 840 | 1,000 | –0.9 | 40 | 14 | 46 | 0.365 | 2,046 | 30,303 | 2.7 | 0.353 | 68 | 50 | 15 | 5 | Chad |
| 69,602 | 8,410 | 10,100 | 5.6 | 8 | 38 | 54 | 0.831 | 2,882 | 907 | 0.2 | 0.824 | 5 | 4 | 3 | 167 | Chile |
| 79,894 | 3,550 | 3,600 | 9.5 | 15 | 50 | 35 | 0.726 | 3,029 | 618 | 0.1 | 0.724 | 25 | 9 | 1 | 10 | China |
| 90,007 | 5,580 | 6,200 | 1.4 | 19 | 26 | 55 | 0.772 | 2,597 | 862 | 0.3 | 0.767 | 9 | 9 | 5 | 73 | Colombia |
| 189 | 1,430 | 720 | –3.1 | 40 | 4 | 56 | 0.511 | 1,753 | 13,514 | 0.1 | 0.505 | 48 | 34 | 31 | – | Comoros |
| 1,571 | 540 | 1,100 | –3.3 | 10 | 48 | 42 | 0.512 | 2,223 | 3,984 | 6.4 | 0.506 | 27 | 13 | 11 | 38 | Congo |
| 4,985 | 710 | 600 | –8.1 | 58 | 17 | 25 | 0.431 | 1,514 | 14,493 | 5.1 | 0.420 | 51 | 28 | 3 | 5 | Congo (Dem. Rep.) |
| 12,828 | 7,880 | 6,700 | 3.0 | 13 | 31 | 56 | 0.820 | 2,783 | 709 | 0.5 | 0.814 | 5 | 5 | 3 | 18 | Costa Rica |
| 20,222 | 7,260 | 5,800 | 1.0 | 10 | 19 | 71 | 0.809 | 2,483 | 437 | 0.1 | 0.806 | 3 | 1 | 15 | 122 | Croatia |
| – | – | 1,700 | – | 7 | 37 | 56 | 0.795 | 2,564 | 189 | 0.1 | – | – | – | 4 | – | Cuba |
| 9,086 | 19,080 | 13,800 | 2.8 | 7 | 22 | 71 | 0.883 | 3,259 | 392 | 0.1 | 0.879 | 5 | 1 | 71 | 463 | Cyprus |
| 51,623 | 12,840 | 12,900 | 0.9 | 4 | 42 | 54 | 0.849 | 3,104 | 330 | 0.1 | 0.846 | 1 | 1 | 43 | 117 | Czech Republic |
| 70,685 | 25,600 | 25,500 | 2.0 | 3 | 25 | 72 | 0.926 | 3,396 | 345 | 0.2 | 0.924 | 1 | 1 | –311 | 466 | Denmark |
| 511 | 2,120 | 1,300 | –5.1 | 3 | 22 | 75 | 0.445 | 2,050 | 7,143 | 11.8 | – | 47 | 25 | 155 | 38 | Djibouti |
| 16,130 | 5,210 | 5,700 | 3.9 | 11 | 32 | 57 | 0.727 | 2,325 | 464 | 2.8 | 0.718 | 17 | 17 | 7 | 22 | Dominican Republic |
| – | – | – | – | – | – | – | – | – | – | – | – | – | – | – | – | East Timor |
| 16,841 | 2,820 | 2,900 | 0.0 | 14 | 36 | 50 | 0.732 | 2,693 | 590 | 0.3 | 0.718 | 11 | 7 | 11 | 52 | Ecuador |
| 86,544 | 3,460 | 3,600 | 2.4 | 17 | 32 | 51 | 0.642 | 3,346 | 495 | 0.1 | 0.628 | 57 | 34 | 19 | 61 | Egypt |
| 11,806 | 4,260 | 4,000 | 2.8 | 12 | 28 | 60 | 0.706 | 2,503 | 934 | 0.6 | 0.696 | 24 | 19 | 29 | 18 | El Salvador |
| 516 | 3,910 | 2,000 | 16.3 | 20 | 60 | 20 | 0.679 | – | 4,065 | 0.5 | 0.669 | 27 | 8 | 44 | 8 | Equatorial Guinea |
| 779 | 1,040 | 710 | 2.2 | 16 | 27 | 57 | 0.421 | 1,665 | 33,333 | 2.9 | 0.410 | 61 | 34 | 41 | 46 | Eritrea |
| 4,906 | 8,190 | 10,000 | –0.3 | 4 | 31 | 65 | 0.826 | 3,376 | 337 | 0.1 | – | 1 | 1 | 45 | 50 | Estonia |
| 6,524 | 620 | 600 | 2.4 | 45 | 12 | 43 | 0.327 | 2,023 | – | 10.6 | 0.313 | 68 | 57 | 11 | 2 | Ethiopia |
| 1,848 | 4,780 | 7,300 | 1.2 | 16 | 30 | 54 | 0.758 | 2,861 | 2,101 | 0.1 | 0.746 | 10 | 5 | 34 | 30 | Fiji |
| 27,764 | 22,600 | 22,900 | 2.0 | 4 | 28 | 68 | 0.930 | 3,227 | 334 | 0.1 | 0.928 | 1 | 1 | –72 | 346 | Finland |
| 53,211 | 23,020 | 24,400 | 1.1 | 3 | 26 | 71 | 0.928 | 3,591 | 330 | 0.4 | 0.926 | 1 | 1 | –69 | 675 | France |
| 3,987 | 5,280 | 6,300 | 0.6 | 10 | 60 | 30 | 0.637 | 2,564 | – | 4.2 | – | – | – | 10 | 76 | Gabon |
| 415 | 1,550 | 1,100 | –0.6 | 21 | 12 | 67 | 0.405 | 2,474 | 28,571 | 2.0 | 0.397 | 72 | 57 | 35 | 2 | Gambia, The |
| 5,063 | 1,780 | 1,000 | –0.2 | 9 | 28 | 63 | – | – | – | – | – | – | – | – | – | Gaza Strip (OPT)* |
| 3,362 | 2,540 | 4,600 | – | 32 | 23 | 45 | 0.748 | 2,412 | 229 | 0.1 | – | – | – | 34 | 4 | Georgia |
| 03,804 | 23,510 | 23,400 | 1.0 | 1 | 31 | 68 | 0.925 | 3,451 | 286 | 0.1 | 0.920 | 1 | 1 | –61 | 400 | Germany |
| 7,451 | 1,850 | 1,900 | 1.6 | 36 | 25 | 39 | 0.548 | 2,699 | 16,129 | 3.6 | 0.544 | 39 | 21 | 31 | 3 | Ghana |
| 27,648 | 15,800 | 17,200 | 1.8 | 8 | 28 | 64 | 0.885 | 3,705 | 255 | 0.2 | 0.879 | 4 | 2 | –21 | 577 | Greece |

| COUNTRY | POPULATION | | | | | | | | LAND AND AGRICULTURE | | | | | ENERGY AND TRADE | | | |
|---|---|---|---|---|---|---|---|---|---|---|---|---|---|---|---|---|---|
| | Population total (millions) | Population density (persons per km²) | Life expectancy (years) | Average annual population change (%) | Birth rate (births per thousand) | Death rate (deaths per thousand) | Fertility rate (children born per woman) | Urban population (% of total) | Land area (thousand km²) | Arable & permanent crops (% of land area) | Permanent pasture (% of land area) | Forest (% of land area) | Agricultural workforce (% of total workforce) | Energy produced (tonnes of oil equiv. per capita) | Energy consumed (tonnes of oil equiv. per capita) | Imports (US$ per capita) | Export (US$ per capita) |
| | 2001 | 2001 | 2001 | 2002 est. | 2001 | 2001 | 2001 | 2001 | 1999 | 1999 | 2000 | 2000 | 2000 | 2000 | 2000 | 2000 | 2000 |
| Guatemala | 13.0 | 120 | 67 | 2.3 | 35 | 7 | 4.6 | 40 | 108 | 18 | 24 | 26 | 46 | 0.15 | 0.30 | 339 | 224 |
| Guinea | 7.6 | 31 | 46 | 2.2 | 40 | 18 | 5.4 | 28 | 246 | 6 | 44 | 28 | 84 | 0.01 | 0.07 | 83 | 108 |
| Guinea-Bissau | 1.3 | 47 | 50 | 2.2 | 39 | 15 | 5.2 | 32 | 28 | 12 | 38 | 78 | 83 | – | 0.08 | 42 | 6 |
| Guyana | 0.7 | 4 | 63 | 0.2 | 18 | 9 | 2.1 | 36 | 197 | 3 | 6 | 86 | 18 | 0.01 | 0.77 | 947 | 818 |
| Haiti | 7.0 | 253 | 49 | 1.4 | 32 | 15 | 4.4 | 36 | 28 | 33 | 18 | 3 | 62 | 0.01 | 0.08 | 172 | 27 |
| Honduras | 6.4 | 58 | 69 | 2.3 | 32 | 6 | 4.2 | 53 | 112 | 16 | 13 | 48 | 32 | 0.09 | 0.38 | 437 | 312 |
| Hungary | 10.1 | 109 | 72 | –0.3 | 9 | 13 | 1.3 | 65 | 92 | 55 | 12 | 20 | 11 | 1.13 | 2.63 | 2,731 | 2,494 |
| Iceland | 0.3 | 3 | 80 | 0.5 | 15 | 7 | 2.0 | 92 | 100 | 0 | 23 | 0 | 8 | 7.71 | 11.33 | 7,914 | 7,194 |
| India | 1,030.0 | 346 | 63 | 1.5 | 24 | 9 | 3.0 | 28 | 2,973 | 57 | 4 | 22 | 60 | 0.23 | 0.31 | 59 | 42 |
| Indonesia | 227.7 | 126 | 68 | 1.5 | 22 | 6 | 2.6 | 41 | 1,812 | 17 | 6 | 58 | 48 | 0.85 | 0.43 | 177 | 284 |
| Iran | 66.1 | 41 | 70 | 0.8 | 17 | 5 | 2.0 | 64 | 1,636 | 12 | 27 | 5 | 26 | 3.98 | 1.80 | 227 | 378 |
| Iraq | 23.3 | 53 | 67 | 2.8 | 35 | 6 | 4.8 | 68 | 437 | 13 | 9 | 2 | 10 | 6.08 | 1.18 | 591 | 934 |
| Ireland | 3.9 | 57 | 77 | 1.1 | 15 | 8 | 1.9 | 59 | 69 | 16 | 48 | 10 | 10 | 0.36 | 3.93 | 11,898 | 19,136 |
| Israel | 5.9 | 288 | 79 | 1.5 | 19 | 6 | 2.6 | 92 | 21 | 21 | 7 | 6 | 3 | 0.01 | 3.35 | 5,911 | 5,305 |
| Italy | 57.7 | 196 | 79 | 0.1 | 9 | 10 | 1.2 | 67 | 294 | 39 | 16 | 34 | 5 | 0.60 | 3.47 | 4,012 | 4,180 |
| Ivory Coast | 16.4 | 52 | 45 | 2.5 | 40 | 17 | 5.7 | 44 | 318 | 23 | 41 | – | 49 | 0.13 | 0.17 | 153 | 232 |
| Jamaica | 2.7 | 246 | 75 | 0.6 | 18 | 5 | 2.1 | 56 | 11 | 25 | 21 | 30 | 21 | 0.07 | 1.49 | 1,125 | 638 |
| Japan | 126.8 | 348 | 81 | 0.2 | 10 | 8 | 1.4 | 79 | 375 | 13 | 1 | 64 | 4 | 0.86 | 4.33 | 2,800 | 3,550 |
| Jordan | 5.2 | 58 | 78 | 2.9 | 25 | 3 | 3.3 | 79 | 89 | 4 | 9 | 1 | 11 | 0.05 | 1.08 | 776 | 388 |
| Kazakhstan | 16.7 | 6 | 63 | 0.1 | 17 | 11 | 2.1 | 56 | 2,670 | 11 | 68 | 5 | 18 | 4.44 | 2.70 | 412 | 526 |
| Kenya | 30.8 | 54 | 47 | 1.2 | 29 | 14 | 3.5 | 33 | 569 | 8 | 37 | 30 | 75 | 0.03 | 0.13 | 98 | 55 |
| Korea, North | 22.0 | 182 | 71 | 1.1 | 19 | 7 | 2.3 | 60 | 120 | 17 | 0 | 68 | 30 | 2.97 | 3.22 | 44 | 24 |
| Korea, South | 47.9 | 485 | 75 | 0.9 | 15 | 6 | 1.7 | 82 | 99 | 19 | 1 | 63 | 10 | 0.61 | 4.14 | 3,350 | 3,603 |
| Kuwait | 2.0 | 115 | 76 | 3.3 | 22 | 2 | 3.2 | 96 | 18 | 0 | 8 | 0 | 1 | 64.76 | 12.52 | 3,722 | 113,614 |
| Kyrgyzstan | 4.8 | 25 | 63 | 1.5 | 26 | 9 | 3.2 | 34 | 192 | 7 | 48 | 5 | 26 | 0.82 | 1.16 | 122 | 101 |
| Laos | 5.6 | 24 | 53 | 2.5 | 38 | 13 | 5.1 | 19 | 231 | 4 | 4 | 54 | 76 | 0.05 | 0.05 | 96 | 57 |
| Latvia | 2.4 | 38 | 69 | –0.8 | 8 | 15 | 1.2 | 60 | 62 | 30 | 10 | 47 | 12 | 0.24 | 1.64 | 1,342 | 88 |
| Lebanon | 3.6 | 355 | 72 | 1.4 | 20 | 6 | 2.1 | 90 | 10 | 30 | 2 | 4 | 4 | 0.02 | 1.69 | 1,709 | 193 |
| Lesotho | 2.1 | 72 | 49 | 1.3 | 31 | 16 | 4.1 | 28 | 30 | 11 | 66 | 0 | 38 | – | 0.04 | 322 | 80 |
| Liberia | 3.2 | 34 | 51 | 1.9 | 47 | 16 | 6.4 | 45 | 96 | 3 | 21 | 36 | 68 | – | 0.05 | 53 | 17 |
| Libya | 5.2 | 3 | 76 | 2.4 | 28 | 4 | 3.6 | 88 | 1,760 | 1 | 8 | 0 | 6 | 15.98 | 2.79 | 1,450 | 2,652 |
| Lithuania | 3.6 | 56 | 69 | –0.3 | 10 | 13 | 1.4 | 69 | 65 | 46 | 8 | 31 | 12 | 0.74 | 1.87 | 1,357 | 1,025 |
| Luxembourg | 0.4 | 174 | 77 | 1.3 | 12 | 9 | 1.7 | 92 | 3 | – | – | – | 2 | 0.13 | 12.17 | 22,573 | 17,156 |
| Macedonia (FYROM) | 2.0 | 81 | 74 | 0.4 | 14 | 8 | 1.8 | 59 | 25 | 25 | 26 | 36 | 13 | 0.96 | 1.58 | 978 | 684 |
| Madagascar | 16.0 | 28 | 55 | 3.0 | 43 | 12 | 5.8 | 29 | 582 | 5 | 41 | 20 | 74 | 0.01 | 0.04 | 43 | 43 |
| Malawi | 10.5 | 112 | 37 | 1.4 | 38 | 23 | 5.2 | 15 | 94 | 21 | 20 | 28 | 83 | 0.02 | 0.05 | 41 | 39 |
| Malaysia | 22.2 | 68 | 71 | 1.9 | 25 | 5 | 3.2 | 57 | 329 | 23 | 1 | 59 | 19 | 3.64 | 2.11 | 3,716 | 4,404 |
| Mali | 11.0 | 9 | 47 | 3.0 | 49 | 19 | 6.8 | 30 | 1,220 | 4 | 25 | 11 | 81 | 0.01 | 0.02 | 52 | 44 |
| Malta | 0.4 | 1,234 | 78 | 0.7 | 13 | 8 | 1.9 | 91 | 1 | 28 | – | – | 1 | – | 3.24 | 6,582 | 5,063 |
| Mauritania | 2.7 | 3 | 51 | 3.0 | 43 | 14 | 6.2 | 58 | 1,025 | 1 | 38 | 0 | 53 | 0.01 | 0.45 | 111 | 121 |
| Mauritius | 1.2 | 586 | 71 | 0.9 | 17 | 7 | 2.0 | 41 | 2 | 52 | 3 | 8 | 12 | 0.03 | 0.75 | 1,933 | 1,345 |
| Mexico | 101.9 | 53 | 72 | 1.5 | 23 | 5 | 2.6 | 74 | 1,909 | 14 | 42 | 29 | 21 | 2.31 | 1.53 | 1,728 | 1,649 |
| Micronesia, Fed. States | 0.1 | 193 | – | – | – | – | – | 28 | 1 | 51 | 14 | – | – | – | – | 1,244 | 54 |
| Moldova | 4.4 | 135 | 65 | 0.1 | 13 | 13 | 1.7 | 42 | 33 | 66 | 11 | 10 | 23 | 0.02 | 0.64 | 172 | 113 |
| Mongolia | 2.7 | 2 | 64 | 1.5 | 22 | 7 | 2.4 | 57 | 1,567 | 1 | 75 | 7 | 24 | 0.43 | 0.62 | 192 | 171 |
| Morocco | 30.6 | 69 | 69 | 1.7 | 24 | 6 | 3.1 | 55 | 446 | 21 | 47 | 7 | 36 | 0.01 | 0.35 | 398 | 248 |
| Mozambique | 19.4 | 25 | 36 | 1.1 | 37 | 24 | 4.8 | 32 | 784 | 4 | 56 | 39 | 81 | 0.09 | 0.04 | 72 | 20 |
| Namibia | 1.8 | 2 | 41 | 1.2 | 35 | 21 | 4.8 | 31 | 823 | 1 | 46 | 10 | 41 | – | 0.36 | 890 | 779 |
| Nepal | 25.3 | 177 | 58 | 2.3 | 33 | 10 | 4.6 | 12 | 143 | 21 | 12 | 27 | 93 | 0.01 | 0.06 | 47 | 19 |
| Netherlands | 16.0 | 472 | 78 | 0.5 | 12 | 9 | 1.7 | 89 | 34 | 28 | 30 | 11 | 3 | 3.93 | 6.16 | 12,590 | 13,159 |
| New Zealand | 3.9 | 14 | 78 | 1.1 | 14 | 8 | 1.8 | 86 | 268 | 12 | 50 | 30 | 9 | 4.25 | 5.36 | 3,701 | 3,778 |
| Nicaragua | 4.9 | 41 | 69 | 2.1 | 28 | 5 | 3.2 | 56 | 121 | 23 | 40 | 27 | 20 | 0.03 | 0.30 | 325 | 128 |
| Niger | 10.4 | 8 | 42 | 2.7 | 51 | 23 | 7.1 | 21 | 1,267 | 4 | 9 | 1 | 88 | 0.01 | 0.04 | 31 | 37 |
| Nigeria | 126.6 | 139 | 51 | 2.5 | 40 | 14 | 5.6 | 44 | 911 | 34 | 43 | 15 | 33 | 1.02 | 0.17 | 84 | 175 |
| Norway | 4.5 | 15 | 79 | 0.5 | 13 | 10 | 1.8 | 75 | 307 | 3 | 1 | 29 | 5 | 57.10 | 10.05 | 7,817 | 13,147 |
| Oman | 2.6 | 12 | 72 | 3.4 | 38 | 4 | 6.0 | 76 | 212 | 0 | 5 | 0 | 36 | 22.91 | 3.33 | 1,716 | 4,233 |
| Pakistan | 144.6 | 188 | 61 | 2.1 | 31 | 9 | 4.4 | 33 | 771 | 28 | 6 | 3 | 47 | 0.21 | 0.33 | 66 | 59 |
| Panama | 2.8 | 38 | 76 | 1.3 | 19 | 5 | 2.3 | 56 | 74 | 9 | 20 | 39 | 20 | 0.32 | 1.40 | 2,424 | 2,003 |
| Papua New Guinea | 5.0 | 11 | 63 | 2.4 | 32 | 8 | 4.3 | 17 | 453 | 1 | 0 | 68 | 74 | 0.78 | 0.23 | 198 | 416 |
| Paraguay | 5.7 | 14 | 74 | 2.6 | 31 | 5 | 4.1 | 56 | 397 | 6 | 55 | 59 | 34 | 2.44 | 0.52 | 576 | 610 |
| Peru | 27.5 | 22 | 70 | 1.7 | 24 | 6 | 3.0 | 73 | 1,280 | 3 | 21 | 51 | 30 | 0.36 | 0.51 | 269 | 255 |
| Philippines | 82.8 | 278 | 68 | 2.0 | 27 | 6 | 3.4 | 59 | 298 | 34 | 4 | 19 | 40 | 0.09 | 0.37 | 422 | 459 |
| Poland | 38.6 | 127 | 73 | –0.1 | 10 | 10 | 1.4 | 62 | 304 | 47 | 13 | 31 | 22 | 1.99 | 2.40 | 1,105 | 735 |
| Portugal | 9.4 | 103 | 76 | 0.2 | 12 | 10 | 1.5 | 64 | 92 | 30 | 16 | 40 | 13 | 0.36 | 2.89 | 4,341 | 2,764 |
| Qatar | 0.7 | 70 | 73 | 3.0 | 16 | 4 | 3.2 | 93 | 11 | 2 | 5 | 0 | 1 | 101.49 | 23.74 | 4,941 | 12,744 |

| WEALTH | | | | | | | SOCIAL INDICATORS | | | | | | | | | COUNTRY |
|---|---|---|---|---|---|---|---|---|---|---|---|---|---|---|---|---|
| GNI million US$ | GNI per capita (PPP US$) | GDP per capita (PPP US$) | Average annual growth GDP per capita (%) | Agriculture (% of GDP) | Industry (% of GDP) | Services (% of GDP) | HDI, Human Develop. Index (value) | Food supply (calories per capita per day) | Population per doctor | Adults living with HIV/AIDS (% 15–49 year olds) | GDI, Gender Develop. Index (value) | Female illiteracy (% female adults) | Male illiteracy (% male adults) | Aid donated (–)/received (US$ per capita) | Military spending (US$ per capita) | |
| 1999 | 1999 | 2000 | 1990–99 | 1999 | 1999 | 1999 | 2000 | 2000 | 1999 | 1999 | 2000 | 1999 | 1999 | 2000 | 1999 | |
| 18,625 | 3,630 | 3,700 | 1.5 | 23 | 20 | 57 | 0.631 | 2,171 | 2,020 | 1.4 | 0.617 | 40 | 24 | 20 | 11 | Guatemala |
| 3,556 | 1,870 | 1,300 | 1.5 | 22 | 35 | 43 | 0.414 | 2,353 | 7,692 | 1.5 | – | – | – | 20 | 7 | Guinea |
| 194 | 630 | 850 | –1.9 | 54 | 15 | 31 | 0.349 | 2,333 | 6,024 | 2.5 | 0.325 | 82 | 42 | 61 | 7 | Guinea-Bissau |
| 651 | 3,330 | 4,800 | 5.2 | 35 | 32 | 33 | 0.708 | 2,582 | 5,525 | 3.0 | 0.698 | 2 | 1 | 155 | 9 | Guyana |
| 3,584 | 1,470 | 1,800 | –3.4 | 32 | 20 | 48 | 0.471 | 2,056 | 11,905 | 5.2 | 0.467 | 53 | 49 | 30 | – | Haiti |
| 4,829 | 2,270 | 2,700 | 0.3 | 16 | 32 | 52 | 0.638 | 2,395 | 1,202 | 1.9 | 0.628 | 26 | 26 | 70 | 6 | Honduras |
| 46,751 | 11,050 | 11,200 | 1.4 | 5 | 35 | 60 | 0.835 | 3,458 | 280 | 0.1 | 0.833 | 1 | 1 | 25 | 82 | Hungary |
| 8,197 | 27,210 | 24,800 | 1.8 | 15 | 21 | 64 | 0.936 | 3,342 | 307 | 0.1 | 0.934 | 1 | 1 | – | – | Iceland |
| 41,834 | 2,230 | 2,200 | 4.1 | 25 | 24 | 51 | 0.577 | 2,428 | 2,083 | 0.7 | 0.560 | 56 | 32 | 1 | 13 | India |
| 25,043 | 2,660 | 2,900 | 3.0 | 21 | 35 | 44 | 0.684 | 2,902 | 6,250 | 0.1 | 0.678 | 19 | 9 | 8 | 5 | Indonesia |
| 13,729 | 5,520 | 6,300 | 1.9 | 24 | 28 | 48 | 0.721 | 2,913 | 1,176 | 0.1 | 0.703 | 31 | 17 | 2 | 84 | Iran |
| – | – | 2,500 | – | 6 | 13 | 81 | – | 2,197 | 1,818 | 0.1 | – | – | – | – | – | Iraq |
| 80,559 | 22,460 | 21,600 | 6.1 | 4 | 38 | 58 | 0.925 | 3,613 | 457 | 0.1 | 0.917 | 1 | 1 | –61 | 194 | Ireland |
| 99,574 | 18,070 | 18,900 | 2.3 | 4 | 37 | 59 | 0.896 | 3,562 | 260 | 0.1 | 0.891 | 6 | 2 | 135 | 1,475 | Israel |
| 62,910 | 22,000 | 22,100 | 1.2 | 3 | 30 | 67 | 0.913 | 3,661 | 181 | 0.4 | 0.907 | 2 | 1 | –24 | 360 | Italy |
| 10,387 | 1,540 | 1,600 | 0.6 | 32 | 18 | 50 | 0.428 | 2,590 | 11,111 | 10.8 | 0.411 | 63 | 46 | 21 | 6 | Ivory Coast |
| 6,311 | 3,390 | 3,700 | –6.0 | 7 | 35 | 58 | 0.742 | 2,693 | 714 | 0.7 | 0.739 | 10 | 18 | 4 | 12 | Jamaica |
| 4,054,545 | 25,170 | 24,900 | 1.1 | 2 | 35 | 63 | 0.933 | 2,762 | 518 | 0.1 | 0.927 | 1 | 1 | –107 | 339 | Japan |
| 7,717 | 3,880 | 3,500 | 1.1 | 3 | 25 | 72 | 0.717 | 2,749 | 602 | 0.1 | 0.701 | 17 | 6 | 107 | 127 | Jordan |
| 18,732 | 4,790 | 5,000 | –4.9 | 10 | 30 | 60 | 0.750 | 2,991 | 283 | 0.1 | – | 2 | 1 | 11 | 20 | Kazakhstan |
| 10,696 | 1,010 | 1,500 | –0.3 | 25 | 13 | 62 | 0.513 | 1,965 | 7,576 | 14.0 | 0.511 | 25 | 12 | 17 | 7 | Kenya |
| – | – | 1,000 | – | 30 | 42 | 28 | 0.882 | 2,185 | 337 | – | – | – | – | – | 196 | Korea, North |
| 397,910 | 15,530 | 16,100 | 4.7 | 6 | 41 | 53 | – | 3,093 | 735 | 0.1 | 0.875 | 4 | 1 | 4 | 259 | Korea, South |
| – | – | 15,000 | – | 0 | 55 | 45 | 0.813 | 3,132 | 529 | 0.1 | 0.804 | 21 | 16 | 1 | 1,056 | Kuwait |
| 1,465 | 2,420 | 2,700 | –6.4 | 39 | 22 | 39 | 0.712 | 2,871 | 332 | 0.1 | – | – | – | 45 | 3 | Kyrgyzstan |
| 1,476 | 1,430 | 1,700 | 3.8 | 51 | 22 | 27 | 0.485 | 2,266 | 4,115 | 0.1 | 0.472 | 68 | 37 | 50 | 11 | Laos |
| 5,913 | 6,220 | 7,200 | –3.7 | 5 | 33 | 62 | 0.800 | 2,855 | 355 | 0.1 | 0.798 | 1 | 1 | 38 | 25 | Latvia |
| 15,796 | 4,410 | 5,000 | 5.7 | 12 | 27 | 61 | 0.755 | 3,155 | 476 | 0.1 | 0.739 | 20 | 8 | 54 | 101 | Lebanon |
| 1,158 | 2,350 | 2,400 | 2.1 | 18 | 38 | 44 | 0.535 | 2,300 | 18,519 | 23.6 | 0.521 | 7 | 28 | 19 | 17 | Lesotho |
| – | – | 1,100 | – | 60 | 10 | 30 | – | 2,076 | 43,478 | – | – | 33 | 10 | – | – | Liberia |
| – | – | 8,900 | – | 7 | 47 | 46 | 0.773 | 3,305 | 781 | 0.1 | 0.753 | – | – | 3 | 250 | Libya |
| 9751 | 6,490 | 7,300 | –3.9 | 10 | 33 | 57 | 0.808 | 3,040 | 253 | 0.1 | 0.806 | – | – | 27 | 49 | Lithuania |
| 18,545 | 41,230 | 36,400 | 3.8 | 1 | 30 | 69 | 0.925 | 3,701 | 368 | 0.2 | 0.914 | 1 | 1 | –287 | 328 | Luxembourg |
| 3,348 | 4,590 | 4,400 | –1.5 | 12 | 25 | 63 | 0.772 | 3,006 | 490 | 0.1 | – | – | – | 123 | 38 | Macedonia (FYROM) |
| 3,712 | 790 | 800 | –1.2 | 30 | 14 | 56 | 0.469 | 2,007 | 9,346 | 0.2 | 0.463 | 41 | 27 | 20 | 2 | Madagascar |
| 1,961 | 570 | 900 | 0.9 | 37 | 29 | 34 | 0.400 | 2,181 | – | 16.0 | 0.389 | 55 | 26 | 42 | 1 | Malawi |
| 76,944 | 7,640 | 10,300 | 4.7 | 14 | 44 | 42 | 0.782 | 2,919 | 1,520 | 0.4 | 0.776 | 17 | 9 | 2 | 78 | Malaysia |
| 2,577 | 740 | 850 | 1.1 | 46 | 21 | 33 | 0.386 | 2403 | 21277 | 2.0 | 0.739 | 67 | 53 | 33 | 5 | Mali |
| 3,492 | 14,930 | 14,300 | 4.2 | 3 | 26 | 71 | 0.875 | 3543 | 383 | 0.1 | 0.378 | 8 | 9 | 54 | 150 | Malta |
| 1,001 | 1,550 | 2,000 | 1.3 | 25 | 31 | 44 | 0.438 | 2638 | 7,246 | 0.5 | 0.860 | 69 | 48 | 77 | 16 | Mauritania |
| 4,157 | 8,950 | 10,400 | 3.9 | 10 | 29 | 61 | 0.772 | 2985 | 1,176 | 0.1 | 0.429 | 19 | 12 | 17 | 9 | Mauritius |
| 28,877 | 8,070 | 9,100 | 1.0 | 5 | 27 | 68 | 0.796 | 3165 | 536 | 0.3 | 0.762 | 11 | 7 | 1 | 41 | Mexico |
| 212 | 1,830 | 2,000 | –1.8 | 19 | 4 | 77 | – | – | 1,745 | – | 0.789 | – | – | – | – | Micronesia, Fed. States |
| 1,481 | 2,100 | 2,500 | –10.8 | 31 | 35 | 34 | 0.701 | 3764 | 286 | 0.2 | 0.698 | 2 | 1 | 28 | 1 | Moldova |
| 927 | 1,610 | 1,780 | –0.6 | 36 | 22 | 42 | 0.655 | 1981 | 411 | 0.1 | 0.653 | 48 | 27 | 82 | 10 | Mongolia |
| 33,715 | 3,320 | 3,500 | 0.4 | 15 | 33 | 52 | 0.602 | 2964 | 2,174 | 0.1 | 0.585 | 65 | 39 | 14 | 48 | Morocco |
| 3,804 | 810 | 1,000 | 3.8 | 44 | 19 | 37 | 0.322 | 1927 | – | 13.2 | 0.307 | 72 | 41 | 45 | 2 | Mozambique |
| 3,211 | 5,580 | 4,300 | 0.8 | 12 | 25 | 63 | 0.610 | 2649 | 3,390 | 19.5 | 0.604 | 20 | 18 | 84 | 61 | Namibia |
| 5,173 | 1,280 | 1,360 | 2.3 | 41 | 22 | 37 | 0.490 | 2436 | 25,000 | 0.3 | 0.470 | 77 | 42 | 15 | 2 | Nepal |
| 397,384 | 24,410 | 24,400 | 2.1 | 3 | 27 | 70 | 0.935 | 3,294 | 398 | 0.2 | 0.930 | 1 | 1 | –196 | 411 | Netherlands |
| 53,299 | 17,630 | 17,700 | 1.8 | 8 | 23 | 69 | 0.917 | 3,252 | 460 | 0.1 | 0.914 | 1 | 1 | –29 | 239 | New Zealand |
| 2,012 | 2,060 | 2,700 | 0.4 | 31 | 23 | 46 | 0.635 | 2,227 | 1,168 | 0.1 | 0.629 | 30 | 33 | 114 | 5 | Nicaragua |
| 1,974 | 740 | 1,000 | –1.0 | 40 | 18 | 42 | 0.277 | 2,089 | 28,571 | 1.4 | 0.263 | 92 | 77 | 20 | 2 | Niger |
| 31,600 | 770 | 950 | –0.5 | 40 | 40 | 20 | 0.462 | 2,850 | 5,405 | 5.1 | 0.449 | 46 | 29 | 1 | 3 | Nigeria |
| 149,280 | 28,140 | 27,700 | 3.2 | 2 | 25 | 73 | 0.942 | 3,414 | 242 | 0.1 | 0.941 | 1 | 1 | –281 | 708 | Norway |
| – | – | 7,700 | 0.3 | 3 | 40 | 57 | 0.751 | – | 752 | 0.1 | 0.722 | 40 | 21 | 17 | 960 | Oman |
| 62,915 | 1,860 | 2,000 | 1.3 | 25 | 25 | 50 | 0.499 | 2,452 | 1,754 | 0.1 | 0.468 | 70 | 41 | 5 | 18 | Pakistan |
| 8,657 | 5,450 | 6,000 | 2.4 | 7 | 17 | 76 | 0.787 | 2,488 | 600 | 1.5 | 0.784 | 9 | 8 | 6 | 46 | Panama |
| 3,834 | 2,260 | 2,500 | 2.3 | 30 | 35 | 35 | 0.535 | 2,175 | 13,699 | 0.2 | 0.530 | 44 | 29 | 55 | 9 | Papua New Guinea |
| 8,374 | 4,380 | 4,750 | –0.2 | 28 | 21 | 51 | 0.740 | 2,533 | 911 | 0.1 | 0.727 | 8 | 6 | 14 | 23 | Paraguay |
| 53,705 | 4,480 | 4,550 | 3.2 | 15 | 42 | 43 | 0.747 | 2,624 | 107 | 0.4 | 0.729 | 15 | 6 | 15 | 40 | Peru |
| 77,967 | 3,990 | 3,800 | 0.9 | 20 | 32 | 48 | 0.754 | 2,379 | 813 | 0.1 | 0.751 | 5 | 5 | 7 | 13 | Philippines |
| 157,429 | 8,390 | 8,500 | 4.4 | 4 | 36 | 60 | 0.833 | 3,376 | 424 | 0.1 | 0.831 | 1 | 1 | 36 | 82 | Poland |
| 110,175 | 15,860 | 15,800 | 2.3 | 4 | 36 | 60 | 0.880 | 3,716 | 321 | 0.7 | 0.876 | 11 | 6 | –29 | 246 | Portugal |
| – | – | 20,300 | – | 1 | 49 | 50 | 0.803 | – | 794 | 0.1 | 0.794 | 17 | 20 | 1 | 1,205 | Qatar |

| COUNTRY | POPULATION | | | | | | | | LAND AND AGRICULTURE | | | | | ENERGY AND TRADE | | | |
|---|---|---|---|---|---|---|---|---|---|---|---|---|---|---|---|---|---|
| | Population total (millions) | Population density (persons per km²) | Life expectancy (years) | Average annual population change (%) | Birth rate (births per thousand) | Death rate (deaths per thousand) | Fertility rate (children born per woman) | Urban population (% of total) | Land area (thousand km²) | Arable & permanent crops (% of land area) | Permanent pasture (% of land area) | Forest (% of land area) | Agricultural workforce (% of total workforce) | Energy produced (tonnes of oil equiv. per capita) | Energy consumed (tonnes of oil equiv. per capita) | Imports (US$ per capita) | Export (US$ p capita) |
| | 2001 | 2001 | 2001 | 2002 est. | 2001 | 2001 | 2001 | 2001 | 1999 | 1999 | 1999 | 2000 | 2000 | 2000 | 2000 | 2000 | 2000 |
| Romania | 22.4 | 97 | 70 | −0.2 | 11 | 12 | 1.4 | 55 | 230 | 43 | 21 | 28 | 15 | 1.42 | 1.79 | 532 | 50 |
| Russia | 145.5 | 9 | 67 | −0.3 | 9 | 14 | 1.3 | 73 | 16,996 | 8 | 5 | 50 | 10 | 7.50 | 4.86 | 304 | 722 |
| Rwanda | 7.3 | 296 | 39 | 1.2 | 34 | 21 | 4.9 | 6 | 25 | 45 | 22 | 12 | 90 | 0.01 | 0.04 | 34 | 9 |
| St Lucia | 0.2 | 259 | 73 | 1.2 | 22 | 5 | 2.4 | 38 | 1 | 28 | 3 | 15 | – | – | 0.35 | 1,958 | 432 |
| Saudi Arabia | 22.8 | 11 | 68 | 3.3 | 37 | 6 | 6.3 | 86 | 2,150 | 2 | 79 | 1 | 10 | 23.34 | 5.05 | 1,323 | 3,568 |
| Senegal | 10.3 | 53 | 63 | 2.9 | 37 | 8 | 5.1 | 47 | 193 | 12 | 29 | 32 | 74 | 0.01 | 0.16 | 126 | 93 |
| Serbia & Montenegro | 10.7 | 105 | 74 | −0.1 | 13 | 11 | 1.8 | 52 | 102 | 37 | 17 | 3 | 20 | 1.18 | 1.40 | 309 | 140 |
| Sierra Leone | 5.4 | 76 | 46 | 3.2 | 45 | 19 | 6.0 | 37 | 72 | 16 | – | 67 | – | – | 0.06 | 27 | 12 |
| Singapore | 4.3 | 7,049 | 80 | 3.5 | 13 | 4 | 1.2 | 100 | 1 | 2 | – | 3 | 0.1 | – | 9.87 | 29,535 | 31,860 |
| Slovak Republic | 5.4 | 113 | 74 | 0.1 | 10 | 9 | 1.3 | 57 | 48 | 33 | 18 | 42 | 9 | 1.20 | 3.64 | 2,364 | 2,216 |
| Slovenia | 1.9 | 96 | 75 | 0.1 | 9 | 9 | 1.3 | 49 | 20 | 10 | 15 | 55 | 2 | 1.80 | 3.72 | 5,130 | 4,611 |
| Solomon Is. | 0.4 | 17 | 72 | 2.9 | 34 | 4 | 4.7 | 20 | 28 | 2 | 1 | 91 | 73 | – | 0.13 | 317 | 344 |
| Somalia | 7.5 | 12 | 47 | 3.5 | 47 | 18 | 7.1 | 27 | 627 | 2 | 69 | 12 | 71 | – | 13.00 | 42 | 25 |
| South Africa | 43.6 | 36 | 48 | 0.1 | 21 | 17 | 2.4 | 57 | 1,221 | 13 | 69 | 7 | 10 | 4.17 | 2.68 | 633 | 707 |
| Spain | 40.0 | 77 | 79 | 0.1 | 9 | 9 | 1.2 | 78 | 499 | 37 | 23 | 29 | 7 | 0.79 | 3.40 | 4,004 | 1,335 |
| Sri Lanka | 19.4 | 300 | 72 | 0.9 | 17 | 6 | 2.0 | 23 | 65 | 29 | 7 | 30 | 46 | 0.06 | 0.24 | 314 | 268 |
| Sudan | 36.0 | 15 | 57 | 2.7 | 38 | 10 | 5.4 | 36 | 2,376 | 7 | 46 | 26 | 61 | 0.25 | 0.05 | 33 | 47 |
| Suriname | 0.4 | 3 | 72 | 0.6 | 21 | 6 | 2.5 | 74 | 156 | 0 | 0 | 90 | 19 | 2.34 | 1.93 | 1,210 | 1,021 |
| Swaziland | 1.1 | 64 | 39 | 1.6 | 40 | 22 | 5.8 | 26 | 17 | 10 | 67 | 30 | 34 | 0.21 | 0.50 | 841 | 798 |
| Sweden | 8.9 | 22 | 80 | 0.1 | 10 | 11 | 1.5 | 83 | 412 | 7 | 1 | 66 | 3 | 3.95 | 6.38 | 9,014 | 10,76 |
| Switzerland | 7.3 | 184 | 80 | 0.2 | 10 | 9 | 1.5 | 67 | 40 | 11 | 29 | 30 | 4 | 2.20 | 4.26 | 12,577 | 12,536 |
| Syria | 16.7 | 91 | 69 | 2.5 | 31 | 5 | 4.0 | 51 | 184 | 30 | 45 | 3 | 28 | 2.21 | 1.24 | 209 | 287 |
| Taiwan | 22.4 | 921 | 77 | 0.8 | 14 | 6 | 1.8 | – | 36 | – | – | – | 67 | 0.55 | 4.25 | 6,259 | 6,633 |
| Tajikistan | 6.6 | 47 | 64 | 2.1 | 33 | 8 | 4.3 | 28 | 141 | 6 | 25 | 3 | 34 | 0.56 | 0.93 | 119 | 116 |
| Tanzania | 36.2 | 41 | 52 | 2.6 | 40 | 13 | 5.4 | 32 | 884 | 5 | 40 | 44 | 80 | 0.02 | 0.04 | 43 | 43 |
| Thailand | 61.8 | 121 | 69 | 0.9 | 17 | 8 | 1.9 | 20 | 511 | 35 | 2 | 29 | 56 | 0.52 | 1.04 | 1,000 | 1,104 |
| Togo | 5.2 | 95 | 54 | 2.5 | 37 | 11 | 5.3 | 33 | 54 | 42 | 18 | 9 | 60 | 0.01 | 0.09 | 88 | 65 |
| Trinidad & Tobago | 1.2 | 228 | 69 | −0.5 | 14 | 8 | 1.8 | 74 | 5 | 24 | 2 | 50 | 9 | 16.85 | 8.78 | 2,564 | 2,735 |
| Tunisia | 9.7 | 63 | 74 | 1.1 | 17 | 5 | 2.0 | 66 | 155 | 33 | 25 | 3 | 25 | 0.64 | 0.76 | 866 | 625 |
| Turkey | 66.5 | 86 | 71 | 1.2 | 18 | 6 | 2.1 | 66 | 770 | 35 | 16 | 13 | 46 | 0.38 | 1.21 | 838 | 405 |
| Turkmenistan | 4.6 | 10 | 61 | 1.8 | 29 | 9 | 3.6 | 45 | 470 | 4 | 65 | 8 | 33 | 11.22 | 2.02 | 358 | 52 |
| Uganda | 24.0 | 122 | 43 | 2.9 | 48 | 18 | 6.9 | 14 | 197 | 35 | 9 | 21 | 80 | 0.02 | 0.03 | 46 | 21 |
| Ukraine | 48.8 | 84 | 66 | −0.7 | 9 | 16 | 1.3 | 68 | 604 | 58 | 14 | 17 | 14 | 1.80 | 3.34 | 308 | 299 |
| United Arab Emirates | 2.4 | 29 | 74 | 1.6 | 18 | 4 | 3.2 | 87 | 83 | 2 | 4 | 4 | 5 | 71.62 | 18.23 | 14,125 | 19,11 |
| United Kingdom | 58.8 | 243 | 78 | 0.2 | 12 | 10 | 1.7 | 89 | 241 | 25 | 47 | 11 | 2 | 4.74 | 4.18 | 5,432 | 4,728 |
| USA | 278.1 | 30 | 77 | 0.9 | 14 | 9 | 2.1 | 77 | 9,159 | 20 | 26 | 25 | 2 | 6.49 | 8.95 | 4,398 | 2,791 |
| Uruguay | 3.4 | 19 | 75 | 0.8 | 17 | 9 | 2.4 | 91 | 175 | 7 | 77 | 7 | 13 | 0.54 | 1.24 | 1,012 | 774 |
| Uzbekistan | 25.2 | 61 | 64 | 1.6 | 26 | 8 | 3.1 | 37 | 414 | 12 | 55 | 5 | 28 | 2.42 | 1.92 | 103 | 115 |
| Venezuela | 23.9 | 27 | 73 | 1.5 | 21 | 5 | 2.5 | 87 | 882 | 4 | 21 | 56 | 8 | 9.42 | 2.87 | 615 | 1,371 |
| Vietnam | 79.9 | 246 | 70 | 1.4 | 21 | 6 | 2.5 | 24 | 325 | 23 | 2 | 30 | 67 | 0.35 | 0.21 | 190 | 179 |
| West Bank (OPT)* | 2.1 | 361 | 72 | 3.4 | 36 | 4 | 4.9 | – | 6 | 36 | 4 | – | 11 | – | – | 765 | 209 |
| Western Sahara | 0.3 | 1 | – | – | – | – | – | 95 | 266 | – | – | – | – | – | 0.25 | – | – |
| Yemen | 18.1 | 34 | 60 | 3.4 | 43 | 10 | 7.0 | 25 | 528 | 3 | 4 | 1 | 51 | 1.28 | 0.19 | 149 | 232 |
| Zambia | 9.8 | 13 | 37 | 1.9 | 41 | 22 | 5.5 | 40 | 743 | 7 | 43 | 42 | 69 | 0.22 | 0.25 | 107 | 95 |
| Zimbabwe | 11.4 | 29 | 37 | 0.1 | 25 | 23 | 3.3 | 35 | 387 | 9 | 23 | 49 | 63 | 0.32 | 0.56 | 114 | 150 |

## NOTES

**OPT***
Occupied Palestinian Territory. Some of the figures for the West Bank and Gaza Strip are combined to summarize the territory as a whole.
**PER CAPITA**
An amount divided by the total population of a country or the amount per person.
**PPP**
Purchasing Power Parity (PPP) is a method used to enable real comparisons to be made between countries when measuring wealth. The UN International Comparison Programme gives estimates of the PPP for each country, so it can be used as an indicator of real price levels for goods and services rather than using currency exchange rates (see GNI and GDP per capita).

**POPULATION TOTAL**
These are estimates of the mid-year total in 2001.
**POPULATION DENSITY**
The total population divided by the total land area (both are recorded in the table above).
**LIFE EXPECTANCY**
The average age that a child born today is expected to live to, if mortality levels of today last throughout its lifetime.
**AVERAGE ANNUAL CHANGE**
These are estimates of the percentage growth or decline of a country's population as a yearly average.
**BIRTH/DEATH RATES**
These are 2001 estimates from the CIA World Factbook.
**FERTILITY RATE**
The average number of children that a woman gives birth to in her lifetime.

**URBAN POPULATION**
The percentage of the total population living in towns and cities (each country will differ with regard to which size or type of town is defined as an urban area).
**LAND AREA**
The total land area of a country, less the area of major lakes and rivers, in square kilometres.
**ARABLE AND PERMANENT CROPS**
The percentage of the total land area that is used for crops and fruit (including temporary fallow land or meadows).
**PERMANENT PASTURE**
The percentage of total land area that has permanent forage crops for cattle or horses, cultivated or wild. Some land may be classified both as permanent pasture or as forest (see Forest), especially areas of scrub or savannah.

**FOREST**
Natural/planted trees including cleared la that will be reforested in the near future a a percentage of the total land area.
**AGRICULTURAL WORKFORCE**
The population working in agriculture (including hunting and fishing) as a percentage of the total working population.
**PRODUCTION AND CONSUMPTION OF ENERGY**
The total amount of commercial energy produced or consumed in a country pe capita (see note). It is expressed in metr tonnes of oil equivalent (an energy unit giving the heating value derived from on tonne of oil).
**IMPORTS AND EXPORTS**
The total value of goods imported into country and exported to other countrie given in US dollars ($) per capita.

| WEALTH | | | | | | | SOCIAL INDICATORS | | | | | | | | | COUNTRY |
|---|---|---|---|---|---|---|---|---|---|---|---|---|---|---|---|---|
| GNI million US$ | GNI per capita (PPP US$) | GDP per capita (PPP US$) | Average annual growth GDP per capita (%) | Agriculture (% of GDP) | Industry (% of GDP) | Services (% of GDP) | HDI, Human Develop. Index (value) | Food supply (calories per capita per day) | Population per doctor | Adults living with HIV/AIDS (% 15–49 year olds) | GDI, Gender Develop. Index (value) | Female illiteracy (% female adults) | Male illiteracy (% male adults) | Aid donated (–) /received (US$ per capita) | Military spending (US$ per capita) | |
| 1999 | 1999 | 2000 | 1990–99 | 1999 | 1999 | 1999 | 2000 | 2000 | 1999 | 1999 | 2000 | 1999 | 1999 | 2000 | 1999 | |
| 33,034 | 5,970 | 5,900 | –0.5 | 14 | 33 | 53 | 0.775 | 3,274 | 543 | 0.1 | 0.773 | 3 | 1 | 19 | 32 | Romania |
| 28,995 | 6,990 | 7,700 | –5.9 | 7 | 34 | 59 | 0.781 | 2,917 | 238 | 0.2 | 0.780 | 1 | 1 | 11 | 314 | Russia |
| 2,041 | 880 | 900 | –0.3 | 40 | 20 | 40 | 0.403 | 2,077 | – | 11.2 | 0.398 | 41 | 27 | 44 | 8 | Rwanda |
| 590 | 5,200 | 4,500 | 0.9 | 11 | 32 | 57 | 0.772 | 2,838 | 2,114 | – | – | – | – | 70 | 31 | St Lucia |
| 39,365 | 11,050 | 10,500 | –1.1 | 6 | 47 | 47 | 0.759 | 2,875 | 602 | 0.1 | 0.731 | 34 | 17 | 1 | 934 | Saudi Arabia |
| 4,685 | 1,400 | 1,600 | 0.6 | 19 | 20 | 61 | 0.431 | 2,257 | 13,333 | 1.8 | 0.421 | 73 | 54 | 41 | 7 | Senegal |
| – | – | 2,300 | – | 20 | 50 | 30 | – | 2,570 | – | 0.1 | – | – | – | – | 71 | Serbia & Montenegro |
| 653 | 440 | 510 | –7.0 | 43 | 26 | 31 | 0.275 | 1,863 | 13,699 | 3.0 | – | – | – | 34 | 11 | Sierra Leone |
| 95,429 | 22,310 | 26,500 | 4.7 | 0 | 30 | 70 | 0.885 | – | 615 | 0.2 | 0.880 | 12 | 4 | 0 | 1,282 | Singapore |
| 20,318 | 10,430 | 10,200 | 1.6 | 5 | 29 | 66 | 0.835 | 3,133 | 283 | 0.1 | 0.833 | 1 | 1 | 21 | 70 | Slovak Republic |
| 19,862 | 16,050 | 12,000 | 2.5 | 4 | 35 | 61 | 0.879 | 3,168 | 439 | 0.1 | 0.877 | 1 | 1 | 32 | 185 | Slovenia |
| 320 | 2,050 | 2,000 | 0.3 | 50 | 4 | 46 | 0.622 | 2,277 | 7,143 | – | – | – | – | 143 | – | Solomon Is. |
| – | – | 600 | – | 60 | 10 | 30 | – | 1,628 | 25,000 | 0.1 | – | 74 | 50 | – | – | Somalia |
| 33,569 | 8,710 | 8,500 | –0.2 | 5 | 30 | 65 | 0.695 | 2,886 | 1,776 | 19.9 | 0.689 | 16 | 14 | 11 | 47 | South Africa |
| 33,082 | 17,850 | 18,000 | 2.0 | 4 | 31 | 65 | 0.913 | 3,352 | 236 | 0.6 | 0.906 | 3 | 2 | –31 | 150 | Spain |
| 15,578 | 3,230 | 3,250 | 4.0 | 21 | 19 | 60 | 0.741 | 2,405 | 2,740 | 0.1 | 0.737 | 11 | 6 | 14 | 38 | Sri Lanka |
| 9,435 | 330 | 1,000 | – | 39 | 17 | 44 | 0.499 | 2,348 | 11,111 | 1.0 | 0.478 | 55 | 31 | 6 | 18 | Sudan |
| 684 | 3,780 | 3,400 | 3.3 | 13 | 22 | 65 | 0.756 | 2,652 | 3,968 | 1.3 | – | – | – | 79 | 21 | Suriname |
| 1,379 | 4,380 | 4,000 | –0.2 | 10 | 46 | 44 | 0.577 | 2,620 | 6,623 | 25.3 | 0.567 | 22 | 20 | 12 | 21 | Swaziland |
| 36,940 | 22,150 | 22,200 | 1.2 | 2 | 28 | 70 | 0.941 | 3,109 | 322 | 0.1 | 0.936 | 1 | 1 | –203 | 562 | Sweden |
| 73,856 | 28,760 | 28,600 | –0.1 | 3 | 31 | 66 | 0.928 | 3,293 | 310 | 0.5 | 0.923 | 1 | 1 | –122 | 431 | Switzerland |
| 15,172 | 3,450 | 3,100 | 2.7 | 29 | 22 | 49 | 0.691 | 3,038 | 694 | 0.1 | 0.669 | 41 | 12 | 9 | 58 | Syria |
| – | – | 17,400 | – | 3 | 33 | 64 | – | – | – | – | – | – | – | – | 360 | Taiwan |
| 1,749 | 280 | 1,140 | – | 20 | 18 | 62 | 0.667 | 1,720 | 498 | 0.1 | 0.664 | 1 | 1 | 22 | 3 | Tajikistan |
| 8,515 | 500 | 710 | –0.1 | 49 | 17 | 34 | 0.440 | 1,906 | 24,390 | 8.1 | 0.436 | 34 | 16 | 29 | 1 | Tanzania |
| 21,051 | 5,950 | 6,700 | 3.8 | 13 | 40 | 47 | 0.762 | 2,506 | 4,167 | 2.2 | 0.760 | 7 | 3 | 10 | 29 | Thailand |
| 1,398 | 1,380 | 1,500 | –0.5 | 42 | 21 | 37 | 0.493 | 2,329 | 13,158 | 6.0 | 0.475 | 60 | 26 | 14 | 6 | Togo |
| 6,142 | 7,690 | 9,500 | 2.0 | 2 | 44 | 54 | 0.805 | 2,777 | 1,269 | 1.1 | 0.798 | 8 | 5 | 1 | 64 | Trinidad & Tobago |
| 19,757 | 5,700 | 6,500 | 2.9 | 14 | 32 | 54 | 0.722 | 3,299 | 1,429 | 0.1 | 0.709 | 41 | 20 | 23 | 38 | Tunisia |
| 36,490 | 6,440 | 6,800 | 2.2 | 15 | 29 | 56 | 0.742 | 3,416 | 826 | 0.1 | 0.734 | 24 | 7 | 5 | 161 | Turkey |
| 3,205 | 3,340 | 4,300 | –9.6 | 25 | 43 | 32 | 0.741 | 2,675 | 333 | 0.1 | – | – | – | 7 | 20 | Turkmenistan |
| 6,794 | 1,160 | 1,100 | 4.0 | 43 | 17 | 40 | 0.444 | 2,359 | – | 8.3 | 0.437 | 45 | 23 | 34 | 4 | Uganda |
| 41,991 | 3,360 | 3,850 | –10.3 | 12 | 26 | 62 | 0.748 | 2,871 | 334 | 1.0 | 0.744 | 1 | 1 | 11 | 10 | Ukraine |
| 48,673 | 19,340 | 22,800 | –1.6 | 3 | 52 | 45 | 0.812 | 3,192 | 552 | 0.2 | 0.798 | 22 | 26 | 2 | 615 | United Arab Emirates |
| 03,843 | 22,220 | 22,800 | 2.1 | 2 | 25 | 73 | 0.928 | 3,334 | 610 | 0.1 | 0.925 | 1 | 1 | –75 | 622 | United Kingdom |
| 79,500 | 31,910 | 36,200 | 2.0 | 2 | 18 | 80 | 0.939 | 3,772 | 358 | 0.6 | 0.937 | 1 | 1 | –36 | 987 | USA |
| 20,604 | 8,750 | 9,300 | 3.0 | 10 | 28 | 62 | 0.831 | 2,879 | 270 | 0.3 | 0.828 | 2 | 3 | 5 | 52 | Uruguay |
| 17,613 | 2,230 | 2,400 | –3.1 | 28 | 21 | 51 | 0.727 | 2,371 | 324 | 0.1 | 0.725 | 16 | 7 | 7 | 8 | Uzbekistan |
| 37,313 | 5,420 | 6,200 | –0.5 | 5 | 24 | 71 | 0.770 | 2,256 | 423 | 0.5 | 0.764 | 8 | 7 | 3 | 39 | Venezuela |
| 28,733 | 1,860 | 1,950 | 6.2 | 25 | 35 | 40 | 0.688 | 2,583 | 2,083 | 0.2 | 0.687 | 9 | 5 | 21 | 8 | Vietnam |
| 5,063 | 1,780 | 1,500 | –0.2 | 9 | 28 | 63 | – | – | – | – | – | – | – | – | – | West Bank (OPT)* |
| – | – | – | – | – | – | – | – | – | – | – | – | – | – | – | – | Western Sahara |
| 6,088 | 730 | 820 | –0.4 | 20 | 42 | 38 | 0.479 | 2,038 | 4,348 | 0.1 | 0.426 | 76 | 33 | 15 | 24 | Yemen |
| 3,222 | 720 | 880 | –2.4 | 18 | 27 | 55 | 0.433 | 1,912 | 14,493 | 20.0 | 0.424 | 30 | 15 | 81 | 8 | Zambia |
| 6,302 | 2,690 | 2,500 | 0.6 | 28 | 32 | 40 | 0.551 | 2,117 | 7,194 | 25.1 | 0.545 | 16 | 8 | 16 | 10 | Zimbabwe |

**NI**
oss National Income: this used be referred to as GNP (Gross tional Product) and is a good ication of a country's wealth. s the income in US dollars from ods and services in a country one year, including income from erseas.

**NI PER CAPITA**
e GNI (see above) divided by the al population by using the PPP thod (see note).

**DP PER CAPITA**
oss Domestic Product using PPP e note) in US dollars per capita. e GDP is the value of all goods d services made in a country in e year, but unlike GNI (see above) loes not include income gained from oad.

**AVERAGE ANNUAL GROWTH IN GDP**
The Gross Domestic Product growth or decline (decline shown as a negative [–] number) per capita, as an average over the ten years from 1990 to 1999.

**AGRICULTURE, INDUSTRY AND SERVICES**
The percentage contributions that each of these three sectors makes to a country's GDP (see note).

**HDI, HUMAN DEVELOPMENT INDEX**
Produced by the UN Development Programme using indicators of life expectancy, knowledge and standards of living to give a value between 0 and 1 for each country. A high value shows a higher human development.

**FOOD INTAKE**
The amount of food (measured in calories) supplied, divided by the total

population. Belgium and Luxembourg are shown as one country.

**ADULTS LIVING WITH HIV/AIDS**
The percentage of all adults (aged 15–49) who have the Human Immunodeficiency Virus or the Acquired Immunodeficiency Syndrome. The total number of adults and children with HIV/AIDS in 2002 was 42 million.

**POPULATION PER DOCTOR**
The total population divided by the number of qualified doctors.

**GDI, GENDER DEVELOPMENT INDEX**
Like the HDI (see note), the GDI uses the same UNDP indicators but gives a value between 0 and 1 to measure the social and economic differences between men and woman. The higher the value, the more equality exists between men and women.

**FEMALE/MALE ILLITERACY**
The percentage of all adult women or men (over 15 years) who cannot read or write simple sentences.

**AID DONATED AND RECEIVED**
Aid defined here is Official Development Assistance (ODA) in US dollars per capita. The OECD Development Assistance Committee uses donations from donor countries and redistributes the money in the form of grants or loans to developing countries on their list of aid recipients. Donations are shown in the table with a negative (–) number. The money is given for economic development and welfare and not for military purposes.

**MILITARY SPENDING**
Government spending on the military or defence in US dollars divided by the total population.

Each topic list is divided into continents and within a continent the items are listed in order of size. The bottom part of many of the lists is selective in order to give examples from as many different countries as possible. The figures are rounded as appropriate.

## WORLD, CONTINENTS, OCEANS

| | km² | miles² | % |
|---|---|---|---|
| The World | 509,450,000 | 196,672,000 | – |
| Land | 149,450,000 | 57,688,000 | 29.3 |
| Water | 360,000,000 | 138,984,000 | 70.7 |
| | | | |
| Asia | 44,500,000 | 17,177,000 | 29.8 |
| Africa | 30,302,000 | 11,697,000 | 20.3 |
| North America | 24,241,000 | 9,357,000 | 16.2 |
| South America | 17,793,000 | 6,868,000 | 11.9 |
| Antarctica | 14,100,000 | 5,443,000 | 9.4 |
| Europe | 9,957,000 | 3,843,000 | 6.7 |
| Australia & Oceania | 8,557,000 | 3,303,000 | 5.7 |
| | | | |
| Pacific Ocean | 179,679,000 | 69,356,000 | 49.9 |
| Atlantic Ocean | 92,373,000 | 35,657,000 | 25.7 |
| Indian Ocean | 73,917,000 | 28,532,000 | 20.5 |
| Arctic Ocean | 14,090,000 | 5,439,000 | 3.9 |

## OCEAN DEPTHS

| Atlantic Ocean | | m | ft |
|---|---|---|---|
| Puerto Rico (Milwaukee) Deep | | 9,220 | 30,249 |
| Cayman Trench | | 7,680 | 25,197 |
| Gulf of Mexico | | 5,203 | 17,070 |
| Mediterranean Sea | | 5,121 | 16,801 |
| Black Sea | | 2,211 | 7,254 |
| North Sea | | 660 | 2,165 |
| | | | |
| Indian Ocean | | m | ft |
| Java Trench | | 7,450 | 24,442 |
| Red Sea | | 2,635 | 8,454 |
| | | | |
| Pacific Ocean | | m | ft |
| Mariana Trench | | 11,022 | 36,161 |
| Tonga Trench | | 10,882 | 35,702 |
| Japan Trench | | 10,554 | 34,626 |
| Kuril Trench | | 10,542 | 34,587 |
| | | | |
| Arctic Ocean | | m | ft |
| Molloy Deep | | 5,608 | 18,399 |

## MOUNTAINS

| Europe | | m | ft |
|---|---|---|---|
| Elbrus | Russia | 5,642 | 18,510 |
| Mont Blanc | France/Italy | 4,807 | 15,771 |
| Monte Rosa | Italy/Switzerland | 4,634 | 15,203 |
| Dom | Switzerland | 4,545 | 14,911 |
| Liskamm | Switzerland | 4,527 | 14,852 |
| Weisshorn | Switzerland | 4,505 | 14,780 |
| Taschorn | Switzerland | 4,490 | 14,730 |
| Matterhorn/Cervino | Italy/Switzerland | 4,478 | 14,691 |
| Mont Maudit | France/Italy | 4,465 | 14,649 |
| Dent Blanche | Switzerland | 4,356 | 14,291 |
| Nadelhorn | Switzerland | 4,327 | 14,196 |
| Grandes Jorasses | France/Italy | 4,208 | 13,806 |
| Jungfrau | Switzerland | 4,158 | 13,642 |
| Grossglockner | Austria | 3,797 | 12,457 |
| Mulhacén | Spain | 3,478 | 11,411 |
| Zugspitze | Germany | 2,962 | 9,718 |
| Olympus | Greece | 2,917 | 9,570 |
| Triglav | Slovenia | 2,863 | 9,393 |
| Gerlachovka | Slovak Republic | 2,655 | 8,711 |
| Galdhöpiggen | Norway | 2,468 | 8,100 |
| Kebnekaise | Sweden | 2,117 | 6,946 |
| Ben Nevis | UK | 1,343 | 4,406 |
| | | | |
| Asia | | m | ft |
| Everest | China/Nepal | 8,850 | 29,035 |
| K2 (Godwin Austen) | China/Kashmir | 8,611 | 28,251 |
| Kanchenjunga | India/Nepal | 8,598 | 28,208 |
| Lhotse | China/Nepal | 8,516 | 27,939 |
| Makalu | China/Nepal | 8,481 | 27,824 |
| Cho Oyu | China/Nepal | 8,201 | 26,906 |
| Dhaulagiri | Nepal | 8,172 | 26,811 |
| Manaslu | Nepal | 8,156 | 26,758 |
| Nanga Parbat | Kashmir | 8,126 | 26,660 |
| Annapurna | Nepal | 8,078 | 26,502 |
| Gasherbrum | China/Kashmir | 8,068 | 26,469 |
| Broad Peak | China/Kashmir | 8,051 | 26,414 |
| Xixabangma | China | 8,012 | 26,286 |
| Kangbachen | India/Nepal | 7,902 | 25,925 |
| Trivor | Pakistan | 7,720 | 25,328 |
| Pik Kommunizma | Tajikistan | 7,495 | 24,590 |
| Demavend | Iran | 5,604 | 18,386 |
| Ararat | Turkey | 5,165 | 16,945 |
| Gunong Kinabalu | Malaysia (Borneo) | 4,101 | 13,455 |
| Fuji-San | Japan | 3,776 | 12,388 |
| | | | |
| Africa | | m | ft |
| Kilimanjaro | Tanzania | 5,895 | 19,340 |
| Mt Kenya | Kenya | 5,199 | 17,057 |
| Ruwenzori | Uganda/Congo (D.R.) | 5,109 | 16,762 |
| Ras Dashan | Ethiopia | 4,620 | 15,157 |
| Meru | Tanzania | 4,565 | 14,977 |
| Karisimbi | Rwanda/Congo (D.R.) | 4,507 | 14,787 |
| Mt Elgon | Kenya/Uganda | 4,321 | 14,176 |
| Batu | Ethiopia | 4,307 | 14,130 |
| Toubkal | Morocco | 4,165 | 13,665 |
| Mt Cameroon | Cameroon | 4,070 | 13,353 |
| | | | |
| Oceania | | m | ft |
| Puncak Jaya | Indonesia | 5,029 | 16,499 |
| Puncak Trikora | Indonesia | 4,750 | 15,584 |

| | | m | ft |
|---|---|---|---|
| Puncak Mandala | Indonesia | 4,702 | 15,427 |
| Mt Wilhelm | Papua New Guinea | 4,508 | 14,790 |
| Mauna Kea | USA (Hawaii) | 4,205 | 13,796 |
| Mauna Loa | USA (Hawaii) | 4,170 | 13,681 |
| Mt Cook (Aoraki) | New Zealand | 3,753 | 12,313 |
| Mt Kosciuszko | Australia | 2,230 | 7,316 |
| | | | |
| North America | | m | ft |
| Mt McKinley (Denali) | USA (Alaska) | 6,194 | 20,321 |
| Mt Logan | Canada | 5,959 | 19,551 |
| Pico de Orizaba | Mexico | 5,610 | 18,405 |
| Mt St Elias | USA/Canada | 5,489 | 18,008 |
| Popocatepetl | Mexico | 5,452 | 17,887 |
| Mt Foraker | USA (Alaska) | 5,304 | 17,401 |
| Ixtaccihuatl | Mexico | 5,286 | 17,342 |
| Lucania | Canada | 5,227 | 17,149 |
| Mt Steele | Canada | 5,073 | 16,644 |
| Mt Bona | USA (Alaska) | 5,005 | 16,420 |
| Mt Whitney | USA | 4,418 | 14,495 |
| Tajumulco | Guatemala | 4,220 | 13,845 |
| Chirripó Grande | Costa Rica | 3,837 | 12,589 |
| Pico Duarte | Dominican Rep. | 3,175 | 10,417 |
| | | | |
| South America | | m | ft |
| Aconcagua | Argentina | 6,962 | 22,841 |
| Bonete | Argentina | 6,872 | 22,546 |
| Ojos del Salado | Argentina/Chile | 6,863 | 22,516 |
| Pissis | Argentina | 6,779 | 22,241 |
| Mercedario | Argentina/Chile | 6,770 | 22,211 |
| Huascaran | Peru | 6,768 | 22,204 |
| Llullaillaco | Argentina/Chile | 6,723 | 22,057 |
| Nudo de Cachi | Argentina | 6,720 | 22,047 |
| Yerupaja | Peru | 6,632 | 21,758 |
| Sajama | Bolivia | 6,542 | 21,463 |
| Chimborazo | Ecuador | 6,267 | 20,561 |
| Pico Colon | Colombia | 5,800 | 19,029 |
| Pico Bolivar | Venezuela | 5,007 | 16,427 |
| | | | |
| Antarctica | | m | ft |
| Vinson Massif | | 4,897 | 16,066 |
| Mt Kirkpatrick | | 4,528 | 14,855 |

## RIVERS

| Europe | | km | miles |
|---|---|---|---|
| Volga | Caspian Sea | 3,700 | 2,300 |
| Danube | Black Sea | 2,850 | 1,770 |
| Ural | Caspian Sea | 2,535 | 1,575 |
| Dnepr (Dnipro) | Black Sea | 2,285 | 1,420 |
| Kama | Volga | 2,030 | 1,260 |
| Don | Volga | 1,990 | 1,240 |
| Petchora | Arctic Ocean | 1,790 | 1,110 |
| Oka | Volga | 1,480 | 920 |
| Dnister (Dniester) | Black Sea | 1,400 | 870 |
| Vyatka | Kama | 1,370 | 850 |
| Rhine | North Sea | 1,320 | 820 |
| N. Dvina | Arctic Ocean | 1,290 | 800 |
| Elbe | North Sea | 1,145 | 710 |
| | | | |
| Asia | | km | miles |
| Yangtze | Pacific Ocean | 6,380 | 3,960 |
| Yenisey–Angara | Arctic Ocean | 5,550 | 3,445 |
| Huang He | Pacific Ocean | 5,464 | 3,395 |
| Ob–Irtysh | Arctic Ocean | 5,410 | 3,360 |
| Mekong | Pacific Ocean | 4,500 | 2,795 |
| Amur | Pacific Ocean | 4,400 | 2,730 |
| Lena | Arctic Ocean | 4,400 | 2,730 |
| Irtysh | Ob | 4,250 | 2,640 |
| Yenisey | Arctic Ocean | 4,090 | 2,540 |
| Ob | Arctic Ocean | 3,680 | 2,285 |
| Indus | Indian Ocean | 3,100 | 1,925 |
| Brahmaputra | Indian Ocean | 2,900 | 1,800 |
| Syrdarya | Aral Sea | 2,860 | 1,775 |
| Salween | Indian Ocean | 2,800 | 1,740 |
| Euphrates | Indian Ocean | 2,700 | 1,675 |
| Amudarya | Aral Sea | 2,540 | 1,575 |
| | | | |
| Africa | | km | miles |
| Nile | Mediterranean | 6,670 | 4,140 |
| Congo | Atlantic Ocean | 4,670 | 2,900 |
| Niger | Atlantic Ocean | 4,180 | 2,595 |
| Zambezi | Indian Ocean | 3,540 | 2,200 |
| Oubangi/Uele | Congo (Dem. Rep.) | 2,250 | 1,400 |
| Kasai | Congo (Dem. Rep.) | 1,950 | 1,210 |
| Shaballe | Indian Ocean | 1,930 | 1,200 |
| Orange | Atlantic Ocean | 1,860 | 1,155 |
| Cubango | Okavango Delta | 1,800 | 1,120 |
| Limpopo | Indian Ocean | 1,600 | 995 |
| Senegal | Atlantic Ocean | 1,600 | 995 |
| | | | |
| Australia | | km | miles |
| Murray–Darling | Indian Ocean | 3,750 | 2,330 |
| Darling | Murray | 3,070 | 1,905 |
| Murray | Indian Ocean | 2,575 | 1,600 |
| Murrumbidgee | Murray | 1,690 | 1,050 |
| | | | |
| North America | | km | miles |
| Mississippi–Missouri | Gulf of Mexico | 6,020 | 3,740 |
| Mackenzie | Arctic Ocean | 4,240 | 2,630 |
| Mississippi | Gulf of Mexico | 3,780 | 2,350 |
| Missouri | Mississippi | 3,780 | 2,350 |
| Yukon | Pacific Ocean | 3,185 | 1,980 |
| Rio Grande | Gulf of Mexico | 3,030 | 1,880 |
| Arkansas | Mississippi | 2,340 | 1,450 |
| Colorado | Pacific Ocean | 2,330 | 1,445 |
| Red | Mississippi | 2,040 | 1,270 |

| | | km | miles |
|---|---|---|---|
| Columbia | Pacific Ocean | 1,950 | 1,210 |
| Saskatchewan | Lake Winnipeg | 1,940 | 1,205 |
| | | | |
| South America | | km | miles |
| Amazon | Atlantic Ocean | 6,450 | 4,010 |
| Paraná–Plate | Atlantic Ocean | 4,500 | 2,800 |
| Purus | Amazon | 3,350 | 2,080 |
| Madeira | Amazon | 3,200 | 1,990 |
| São Francisco | Atlantic Ocean | 2,900 | 1,800 |
| Paraná | Plate | 2,800 | 1,740 |
| Tocantins | Atlantic Ocean | 2,750 | 1,710 |
| Paraguay | Paraná | 2,550 | 1,580 |
| Orinoco | Atlantic Ocean | 2,500 | 1,550 |
| Pilcomayo | Paraná | 2,500 | 1,550 |
| Araguaia | Tocantins | 2,250 | 1,400 |

## LAKES

| Europe | | km² | miles² |
|---|---|---|---|
| Lake Ladoga | Russia | 17,700 | 6,800 |
| Lake Onega | Russia | 9,700 | 3,700 |
| Saimaa system | Finland | 8,000 | 3,100 |
| Vänern | Sweden | 5,500 | 2,100 |
| | | | |
| Asia | | km² | miles² |
| Caspian Sea | Asia | 371,800 | 143,550 |
| Lake Baykal | Russia | 30,500 | 11,780 |
| Aral Sea | Kazakhstan/Uzbekistan | 28,687 | 11,086 |
| Tonlé Sap | Cambodia | 20,000 | 7,700 |
| Lake Balqash | Kazakhstan | 18,500 | 7,100 |
| | | | |
| Africa | | km² | miles² |
| Lake Victoria | East Africa | 68,000 | 26,000 |
| Lake Tanganyika | Central Africa | 33,000 | 13,000 |
| Lake Malawi/Nyasa | East Africa | 29,600 | 11,430 |
| Lake Chad | Central Africa | 25,000 | 9,700 |
| Lake Turkana | Ethiopia/Kenya | 8,500 | 3,300 |
| Lake Volta | Ghana | 8,500 | 3,300 |
| | | | |
| Australia | | km² | miles² |
| Lake Eyre | Australia | 8,900 | 3,400 |
| Lake Torrens | Australia | 5,800 | 2,200 |
| Lake Gairdner | Australia | 4,800 | 1,900 |
| | | | |
| North America | | km² | miles² |
| Lake Superior | Canada/USA | 82,350 | 31,800 |
| Lake Huron | Canada/USA | 59,600 | 23,010 |
| Lake Michigan | USA | 58,000 | 22,400 |
| Great Bear Lake | Canada | 31,800 | 12,280 |
| Great Slave Lake | Canada | 28,500 | 11,000 |
| Lake Erie | Canada/USA | 25,700 | 9,900 |
| Lake Winnipeg | Canada | 24,400 | 9,400 |
| Lake Ontario | Canada/USA | 19,500 | 7,500 |
| Lake Nicaragua | Nicaragua | 8,200 | 3,200 |
| | | | |
| South America | | km² | miles² |
| Lake Titicaca | Bolivia/Peru | 8,300 | 3,200 |
| Lake Poopo | Peru | 2,800 | 1,100 |

## ISLANDS

| Europe | | km² | miles² |
|---|---|---|---|
| Great Britain | UK | 229,880 | 88,700 |
| Iceland | Atlantic Ocean | 103,000 | 39,800 |
| Ireland | Ireland/UK | 84,400 | 32,600 |
| Novaya Zemlya (N.) | Russia | 48,200 | 18,600 |
| Sicily | Italy | 25,500 | 9,800 |
| Corsica | France | 8,700 | 3,400 |
| | | | |
| Asia | | km² | miles² |
| Borneo | South-east Asia | 744,360 | 287,400 |
| Sumatra | Indonesia | 473,600 | 182,860 |
| Honshu | Japan | 230,500 | 88,980 |
| Celebes | Indonesia | 189,000 | 73,000 |
| Java | Indonesia | 126,700 | 48,900 |
| Luzon | Philippines | 104,700 | 40,400 |
| Hokkaido | Japan | 78,400 | 30,300 |
| | | | |
| Africa | | km² | miles² |
| Madagascar | Indian Ocean | 587,040 | 226,660 |
| Socotra | Indian Ocean | 3,600 | 1,400 |
| Réunion | Indian Ocean | 2,500 | 965 |
| | | | |
| Oceania | | km² | miles² |
| New Guinea | Indonesia/Papua NG | 821,030 | 317,000 |
| New Zealand (S.) | Pacific Ocean | 150,500 | 58,100 |
| New Zealand (N.) | Pacific Ocean | 114,700 | 44,300 |
| Tasmania | Australia | 67,800 | 26,200 |
| Hawaii | Pacific Ocean | 10,450 | 4,000 |
| | | | |
| North America | | km² | miles² |
| Greenland | Atlantic Ocean | 2,175,600 | 839,800 |
| Baffin Is. | Canada | 508,000 | 196,100 |
| Victoria Is. | Canada | 212,200 | 81,900 |
| Ellesmere Is. | Canada | 212,000 | 81,800 |
| Cuba | Caribbean Sea | 110,860 | 42,800 |
| Hispaniola | Dominican Rep./Haiti | 76,200 | 29,400 |
| Jamaica | Caribbean Sea | 11,400 | 4,400 |
| Puerto Rico | Atlantic Ocean | 8,900 | 3,400 |
| | | | |
| South America | | km² | miles² |
| Tierra del Fuego | Argentina/Chile | 47,000 | 18,100 |
| Falkland Is. (E.) | Atlantic Ocean | 6,800 | 2,600 |

## How to use the Index

The index contains the names of all the principal places and features shown on the maps. Each name is followed by an additional entry in italics giving the country or region within which it is located. The alphabetical order of names composed of two or more words is governed primarily by the first word and then by the second. This is an example of the rule:

| | | | |
|---|---|---|---|
| Abbeville, *France* | **68 A4** | 50 6N | 1 49 E |
| Abbey Town, *U.K.* | **22 C2** | 54 51N | 3 17W |
| Abbots Bromley, *U.K.* | **23 G5** | 52 50N | 1 52W |
| Abbotsbury, *U.K.* | **24 E3** | 50 40N | 2 37W |

Physical features composed of a proper name (Erie) and a description (Lake) are positioned alphabetically by the proper name. The description is positioned after the proper name and is usually abbreviated:

| | | | |
|---|---|---|---|
| Erie, L., *N. Amer.* | **112 D7** | 42 15N | 81 0W |

Where a description forms part of a settlement or administrative name, however, it is always written in full and put in its true alphabetic position:

| | | | |
|---|---|---|---|
| Mount Isa, *Australia* | **98 E6** | 20 42S | 139 26 E |

Names beginning with M' and Mc are indexed as if they were spelled Mac. Names beginning St. are alphabetized under Saint, but Santa and San are spelt in full and are alphabetized accordingly. If the same place name occurs two or more times in the index and all are in the same country, each is followed by the name of the administrative subdivision in which it is located.

The number in bold type which follows each name in the index refers to the number of the map page where that feature or place will be found. This is usually the largest scale at which the place or feature appears.

The letter and figure which are in bold type immediately after the page number give the grid square on the map page, within which the feature is situated. The letter represents the latitude and the figure the longitude. A lower case letter immediately after the page number refers to an inset map on that page.

In some cases the feature itself may fall within the specified square, while the name is outside. This is usually the case only with features which are larger than a grid square.

The geographical co-ordinates which follow the letter-figure references give the latitude and longitude of each place. The first co-ordinate indicates latitude – the distance north or south of the Equator. The second co-ordinate indicates longitude – the distance east or west of the Greenwich Meridian. Both latitude and longitude are measured in degrees and minutes (there are 60 minutes in a degree).

The latitude is followed by N(orth) or S(outh) and the longitude by E(ast) or W(est).

Rivers are indexed to their mouths or confluences, and carry the symbol → after their names. The following symbols are also used in the index: ■ country, ◪ overseas territory or dependency, □ first order administrative area, △ national park.

## Abbreviations used in the Index

Afghan. – Afghanistan
Ala. – Alabama
Alta. – Alberta
Amer. – America(n)
Arch. – Archipelago
Ariz. – Arizona
Ark. – Arkansas
Atl. Oc. – Atlantic Ocean
B. – Baie, Bahía, Bay, Bucht, Bugt
B.C. – British Columbia
Bangla. – Bangladesh
C. – Cabo, Cap, Cape, Coast
C.A.R. – Central African Republic
Calif. – California
Cent. – Central
Chan. – Channel
Colo. – Colorado
Conn. – Connecticut
Cord. – Cordillera
Cr. – Creek
D.C. – District of Columbia
Del. – Delaware
Dom. Rep. – Dominican Republic
E. – East
El Salv. – El Salvador
Eq. Guin. – Equatorial Guinea
Fla. – Florida
Falk. Is. – Falkland Is.
G. – Golfe, Golfo, Gulf
Ga. – Georgia
Hd. – Head
Hts. – Heights
I.(s). – Île, Ilha, Insel, Isla, Island, Isle(s)
Ill. – Illinois
Ind. – Indiana
Ind. Oc. – Indian Ocean
Ivory C. – Ivory Coast
Kans. – Kansas
Ky. – Kentucky
L. – Lac, Lacul, Lago, Lagoa, Lake, Limni, Loch, Lough
La. – Louisiana
Lux. – Luxembourg
Madag. – Madagascar
Man. – Manitoba
Mass. – Massachusetts
Md. – Maryland
Me. – Maine
Mich. – Michigan
Minn. – Minnesota
Miss. – Mississippi
Mo. – Missouri
Mont. – Montana
Mozam. – Mozambique
Mt.(s) – Mont, Monte, Monti, Montaña, Mountain
N. – Nord, Norte, North, Northern,
N.B. – New Brunswick
N.C. – North Carolina
N. Cal. – New Caledonia
N. Dak. – North Dakota
N.H. – New Hampshire
N.J. – New Jersey
N. Mex. – New Mexico
N.S. – Nova Scotia
N.S.W. – New South Wales
N.W.T. – North West Territory
N.Y. – New York
N.Z. – New Zealand
Nat. Park – National Park
Nebr. – Nebraska
Neths. – Netherlands
Nev. – Nevada
Nfld. – Newfoundland and Labrador
Nic. – Nicaragua
Okla. – Oklahoma
Ont. – Ontario
Oreg. – Oregon
P.E.I. – Prince Edward Island
Pa. – Pennsylvania
Pac. Oc. – Pacific Ocean
Papua N.G. – Papua New Guinea
Pen. – Peninsula, Péninsule
Phil. – Philippines
Pk. – Peak
Plat. – Plateau
Prov. – Province, Provincial
Pt. – Point
Pta. – Ponta, Punta
Pte. – Pointe
Qué. – Québec
Queens. – Queensland
R. – Rio, River
R.I. – Rhode Island
Ra.(s) – Range(s)
Reg. – Region
Rep. – Republic
Res. – Reserve, Reservoir
S. – San, South
Si. Arabia – Saudi Arabia
S.C. – South Carolina
S. Dak. – South Dakota
Sa. – Serra, Sierra
Sask. – Saskatchewan
Scot. – Scotland
Sd. – Sound
Serbia & M. – Serbia & Montenegro
Sib. – Siberia
St. – Saint, Sankt, Sint
Str. – Strait, Stretto
Switz. – Switzerland
Tas. – Tasmania
Tenn. – Tennessee
Tex. – Texas
Trin. & Tob. – Trinidad & Tobago
U.A.E. – United Arab Emirates
U.K. – United Kingdom
U.S.A. – United States of America
Va. – Virginia
Vic. – Victoria
Vol. – Volcano
Vt. – Vermont
W. – West
W. Va. – West Virginia
Wash. – Washington
Wis. – Wisconsin

# A

Aachen, *Germany* **66 C4** 50 45N 6 6 E
Aalst, *Belgium* **65 D4** 50 56N 4 2 E
Aarau, *Switz.* **66 E5** 47 23N 8 4 E
Aare →, *Switz.* **66 E5** 47 33N 8 14 E
Aba, *Nigeria* **94 G7** 5 10N 7 19 E
Ābādān, *Iran* **86 D7** 30 22N 48 20 E
Abakan, *Russia* **79 D11** 53 40N 91 10 E
Abancay, *Peru* **120 D2** 13 35S 72 55W
Abariringa, *Kiribati* **99 A16** 2 50S 171 40W
Abaya, L., *Ethiopia* **88 F2** 6 30N 37 50 E
Abbé, L., *Ethiopia* **88 E3** 11 8N 41 47 E
Abbeville, *France* **68 A4** 50 6N 1 49 E
Abbey Town, *U.K.* **22 C2** 54 51N 3 17W
Abbots Bromley, *U.K.* **23 G5** 52 50N 1 52W
Abbotsbury, *U.K.* **24 E3** 50 40N 2 37W
Abéché, *Chad* **95 F10** 13 50N 20 35 E
Abeokuta, *Nigeria* **94 G6** 7 3N 3 19 E
Aberaeron, *U.K.* **26 C5** 52 15N 4 15W
Aberchirder, *U.K.* **19 G12** 57 34N 2 37W
Aberdare, *U.K.* **24 C2** 51 43N 3 27W
Aberdeen, *U.K.* **19 H13** 57 9N 2 5W
Aberdeen, *S. Dak., U.S.A.* **110 A7** 45 28N 98 29W
Aberdeen, *Wash., U.S.A.* **110 A2** 46 59N 123 50W
Aberdyfi, *U.K.* **26 B5** 52 33N 4 3W
Aberfeldy, *U.K.* **19 J10** 56 37N 3 51W
Aberfoyle, *U.K.* **20 B7** 56 11N 4 23W
Abergavenny, *U.K.* **24 C2** 51 49N 3 1W
Abergele, *U.K.* **26 A6** 53 17N 3 35W
Aberporth, *U.K.* **26 C4** 52 8N 4 33W
Abersoch, *U.K.* **26 B5** 52 49N 4 30W
Abersychan, *U.K.* **24 C2** 51 44N 3 3W
Abert, L., *U.S.A.* **110 B2** 42 38N 120 14W
Abertillery, *U.K.* **24 C2** 51 44N 3 8W
Aberystwyth, *U.K.* **26 C5** 52 25N 4 5W
Abhā, *Si. Arabia* **88 D3** 18 0N 42 34 E
Abidjan, *Ivory C.* **94 G5** 5 26N 3 58W
Abilene, *U.S.A.* **110 D7** 32 28N 99 43W
Abingdon, *U.K.* **24 C6** 51 40N 1 17W
Abitibi, L., *Canada* **109 D12** 48 40N 79 40W
Abkhazia □, *Georgia* **73 F7** 43 12N 41 5 E
Abomey, *Benin* **94 G6** 7 10N 2 5 E
Aboyne, *U.K.* **19 H12** 57 4N 2 47W
Absaroka Range, *U.S.A.* **110 B5** 44 45N 109 50W
Abu Dhabi, *U.A.E.* **87 E8** 24 28N 54 22 E
Abu Hamed, *Sudan* **95 E12** 19 32N 33 13 E
Abuja, *Nigeria* **94 G7** 9 5N 7 32 E
Abunã, *Brazil* **120 C3** 9 40S 65 20W
Abunã →, *Brazil* **120 C3** 9 41S 65 20W
Acaponeta, *Mexico* **114 C3** 22 30N 105 20W
Acapulco, *Mexico* **114 D5** 16 51N 99 56W
Acarai, Serra, *Brazil* **120 B4** 1 50N 57 50W
Accomac, *U.S.A.* **113 G10** 37 43N 75 40W
Accra, *Ghana* **94 G5** 5 35N 0 6W
Accrington, *U.K.* **23 E4** 53 45N 2 22W
Aceh □, *Indonesia* **83 C1** 4 15N 97 30 E
Achill Hd., *Ireland* **28 D1** 53 58N 10 15W
Achill I., *Ireland* **28 D1** 53 58N 10 1W
Acklins I., *Bahamas* **115 C10** 22 30N 74 0W
Acle, *U.K.* **25 A12** 52 39N 1 33 E
Aconcagua, Cerro, *Argentina* **121 F3** 32 39S 70 0W
Acre □, *Brazil* **120 C2** 9 1S 71 0W
Acre →, *Brazil* **120 C3** 8 45S 67 22W
Acton Burnell, *U.K.* **23 G3** 52 37N 2 41W
Ad Dammām, *Si. Arabia* **86 E7** 26 20N 50 5 E
Ad Dīwānīyah, *Iraq* **86 D6** 32 0N 45 0 E
Adair, C., *Canada* **109 A12** 71 30N 71 34W
Adak I., *U.S.A.* **108 C2** 51 45N 176 45W
Adamawa Highlands, *Cameroon* **95 G7** 7 20N 12 20 E
Adam's Bridge, *Sri Lanka* **84 Q11** 9 15N 79 40 E
Adana, *Turkey* **73 G6** 37 0N 35 16 E
Adare, C., *Antarctica* **55 D11** 71 0S 171 0 E
Addis Ababa, *Ethiopia* **88 F2** 9 2N 38 42 E
Adelaide, *Australia* **98 G6** 34 52S 138 30 E
Adelaide I., *Antarctica* **55 C17** 67 15S 68 30W
Adelaide Pen., *Canada* **108 B10** 68 15N 97 30W
Adélie Land, *Antarctica* **55 C10** 68 0S 140 0 E
Aden, *Yemen* **88 E4** 12 45N 45 0 E
Aden, G. of, *Asia* **88 E4** 12 30N 47 30 E
Adigrat, *Ethiopia* **88 E2** 14 20N 39 26 E
Adirondack Mts., *U.S.A.* **113 D10** 44 0N 74 0W
Adjuntas, *Puerto Rico* **115 d** 18 10N 66 43W
Admiralty Is., *Papua N. G.* **102 H6** 2 0S 147 0 E
Adour →, *France* **68 E3** 43 32N 1 32W
Adrar, *Mauritania* **94 D3** 20 30N 7 30 E
Adrar des Iforas, *Algeria* **94 C5** 27 51N 0 11 E
Adrian, *U.S.A.* **112 E5** 41 54N 84 2W
Adriatic Sea, *Medit. S.* **70 C6** 43 0N 16 0 E
Adwick le Street, *U.K.* **23 E6** 53 34N 1 10W
Adygea □, *Russia* **73 F7** 45 0N 40 0 E
Ægean Sea, *Medit. S.* **71 E11** 38 30N 25 0 E
Aerhtai Shan, *Mongolia* **79 E10** 46 40N 92 45 E
Afghanistan ■, *Asia* **84 C4** 33 0N 65 0 E
Africa **90 E6** 10 0N 20 0 E
Afyon, *Turkey* **73 G5** 38 45N 30 33 E
Agadez, *Niger* **94 E7** 16 58N 7 59 E
Agadir, *Morocco* **94 B4** 30 28N 9 55W
Agartala, *India* **85 H17** 23 50N 91 23 E
Agen, *France* **68 D4** 44 12N 0 38 E
Agra, *India* **84 F10** 27 17N 77 58 E
Ağri, *Turkey* **73 G7** 39 44N 43 3 E
Agrigento, *Italy* **70 F5** 37 19N 13 34 E
Agua Prieta, *Mexico* **114 A3** 31 20N 109 32W
Aguadilla, *Puerto Rico* **115 d** 18 26N 67 10W
Aguascalientes, *Mexico* **114 C4** 21 53N 102 12W
Aguila, Punta, *Puerto Rico* **115 d** 17 57N 67 13W
Aguja, C. de la, *Colombia* **116 B3** 11 18N 74 12W
Agujereada, Pta., *Puerto Rico* **115 d** 18 30N 67 8W
Agulhas, C., *S. Africa* **97 L4** 34 52S 20 0 E
Ahmadabad, *India* **84 H8** 23 0N 72 40 E
Ahmadnagar, *India* **84 K9** 19 7N 74 46 E
Ahmadpur, *Pakistan* **84 E7** 29 12N 71 10 E
Ahvāz, *Iran* **86 D7** 31 20N 48 40 E
Ahvenanmaa, *Finland* **63 E8** 60 15N 20 0 E
Aihui, *China* **81 A7** 50 10N 127 30 E
Ailsa Craig, *U.K.* **20 D5** 55 15N 5 6W
Ainsdale, *U.K.* **23 E2** 53 37N 3 2W
Aïr, *Niger* **94 E7** 18 30N 8 0 E
Air Force I., *Canada* **109 B12** 67 58N 74 5W
Airdrie, *Canada* **108 C8** 51 18N 114 2W
Airdrie, *U.K.* **21 C8** 55 52N 3 57W
Aire →, *U.K.* **23 E7** 53 43N 0 55W
Aisgill, *U.K.* **22 D4** 54 23N 2 21W
Aisne →, *France* **68 B5** 49 26N 2 50 E
Aix-en-Provence, *France* **68 E6** 43 32N 5 27 E
Aix-les-Bains, *France* **68 D6** 45 41N 5 53 E
Aizawl, *India* **85 H18** 23 40N 92 44 E
Aizuwakamatsu, *Japan* **82 E6** 37 30N 139 56 E
Ajaccio, *France* **68 F8** 41 55N 8 40 E
Ajaria □, *Georgia* **73 F7** 41 30N 42 0 E
Ajdābiyā, *Libya* **95 B10** 30 54N 20 4 E
'Ajmān, *U.A.E.* **87 E8** 25 25N 55 30 E
Ajmer, *India* **84 F9** 26 28N 74 37 E
Akhisar, *Turkey* **73 G4** 38 56N 27 48 E
Akimiski I., *Canada* **109 C11** 52 50N 81 30W
Akita, *Japan* **82 D7** 39 45N 140 7 E
'Akko, *Israel* **86 C3** 32 55N 35 4 E
Aklavik, *Canada* **108 B6** 68 12N 135 0W
Akola, *India* **84 J10** 20 42N 77 2 E
Akpatok I., *Canada* **109 B13** 60 25N 68 8W
Akranes, *Iceland* **63 B1** 64 19N 22 5W
Akron, *U.S.A.* **112 E7** 41 5N 81 31W
Aksai Chin, *China* **84 B11** 35 15N 79 55 E
Aksaray, *Turkey* **73 G5** 38 25N 34 2 E
Akşehir Gölü, *Turkey* **73 G5** 38 30N 31 25 E
Aksu, *China* **80 B3** 41 5N 80 10 E
Aksum, *Ethiopia* **88 E2** 14 5N 38 40 E
Akure, *Nigeria* **94 G7** 7 15N 5 5 E
Akureyri, *Iceland* **63 A2** 65 40N 18 6W
Al 'Aqabah, *Jordan* **86 D3** 29 31N 35 0 E
Al 'Aramah, *Si. Arabia* **86 E6** 25 30N 46 0 E
Al 'Ayn, *U.A.E.* **87 E8** 24 15N 55 45 E
Al Fāw, *Iraq* **86 D7** 30 0N 48 30 E
Al Ḥillah, *Iraq* **86 C6** 32 30N 44 25 E
Al Hoceïma, *Morocco* **94 A5** 35 8N 3 58W
Al Ḥudaydah, *Yemen* **88 E3** 14 50N 43 0 E
Al Hufūf, *Si. Arabia* **86 E7** 25 25N 49 45 E
Al Jawf, *Libya* **95 D10** 24 10N 23 24 E
Al Jawf, *Si. Arabia* **86 D4** 29 55N 39 40 E
Al Khalīl, *West Bank* **86 D3** 31 32N 35 6 E
Al Khums, *Libya* **95 B8** 32 40N 14 17 E
Al Kufrah, *Libya* **90 D6** 24 17N 23 15 E
Al Kūt, *Iraq* **86 C6** 32 30N 46 0 E
Al Manāmah, *Bahrain* **87 E7** 26 10N 50 30 E
Al Mubarraz, *Si. Arabia* **86 E7** 25 30N 49 40 E
Al Mukallā, *Yemen* **88 E4** 14 33N 49 2 E
Al Musayyib, *Iraq* **86 C6** 32 49N 44 20 E
Al Qāmishlī, *Syria* **86 B5** 37 2N 41 14 E
Al Qaţīf, *Si. Arabia* **86 E7** 26 35N 50 0 E
Alabama □, *U.S.A.* **111 D9** 33 0N 87 0W
Alabama →, *U.S.A.* **111 D9** 31 8N 87 57W
Alagoas □, *Brazil* **122 A3** 9 0S 36 0W
Alagoinhas, *Brazil* **122 B3** 12 7S 38 20W
Alai Range, *Asia* **87 B13** 39 45N 72 0 E
Alamogordo, *U.S.A.* **110 D5** 32 54N 105 57W
Alamosa, *U.S.A.* **110 C5** 37 28N 105 52W
Aland Is. = Ahvenanmaa, *Finland* **63 E8** 60 15N 20 0 E
Alanya, *Turkey* **73 G5** 36 38N 32 0 E
Alaşehir, *Turkey* **73 G4** 38 23N 28 30 E
Alaska □, *U.S.A.* **108 B5** 64 0N 154 0W
Alaska, G. of, *Pac. Oc.* **108 C5** 58 0N 145 0W
Alaska Peninsula, *U.S.A.* **108 C4** 56 0N 159 0W
Alaska Range, *U.S.A.* **108 B4** 62 50N 151 0W
Alba-Iulia, *Romania* **67 E12** 46 8N 23 39 E
Albacete, *Spain* **69 C5** 39 0N 1 50W
Albanel, L., *Canada* **109 C12** 50 55N 73 12W
Albania ■, *Europe* **71 D9** 41 0N 20 0 E
Albany, *Australia* **98 H2** 35 1S 117 58 E
Albany, *Ga., U.S.A.* **111 D10** 31 35N 84 10W
Albany, *N.Y., U.S.A.* **113 D11** 42 39N 73 45W
Albany, *Oreg., U.S.A.* **110 B2** 44 38N 123 6W
Albany →, *Canada* **109 C11** 52 17N 81 31W
Albemarle Sd., *U.S.A.* **111 C11** 36 5N 76 0W
Albert, L., *Africa* **96 D6** 1 30N 31 0 E
Albert Lea, *U.S.A.* **111 B8** 43 39N 93 22W
Albert Nile →, *Uganda* **96 D6** 3 36N 32 2 E
Alberta □, *Canada* **108 C8** 54 40N 115 0W
Albertville, *France* **68 D7** 45 40N 6 22 E
Albi, *France* **68 E5** 43 56N 2 9 E
Albion, *U.S.A.* **112 D5** 42 15N 84 45W
Ålborg, *Denmark* **63 F5** 57 2N 9 54 E
Albrighton, *U.K.* **23 G4** 52 38N 2 16W
Albuquerque, *U.S.A.* **110 C5** 35 5N 106 39W
Albury-Wodonga, *Australia* **98 H8** 36 3S 146 56 E
Alcalá de Henares, *Spain* **69 B4** 40 28N 3 22W
Alcester, *U.K.* **23 H5** 52 14N 1 52W
Alchevsk, *Ukraine* **73 E6** 48 30N 38 45 E
Aldabra Is., *Seychelles* **91 G8** 9 22S 46 28 E
Aldan →, *Russia* **79 C14** 63 28N 129 35 E
Aldborough, *U.K.* **22 D6** 54 5N 1 22W
Aldbourne, *U.K.* **24 D5** 51 29N 1 37W

Aldbrough, *U.K.* **23 E8** 53 49N 0 6W
Aldeburgh, *U.K.* **25 B12** 52 10N 1 37 E
Alderbury, *U.K.* **24 D5** 51 3N 1 44W
Alderley Edge, *U.K.* **23 F4** 53 18N 2 13W
Alderney, *U.K.* **27 H9** 49 42N 2 11W
Aldershot, *U.K.* **25 D7** 51 15N 0 44W
Alegrete, *Brazil* **121 E4** 29 40S 56 0W
Além Paraíba, *Brazil* **122 D2** 21 52S 42 41W
Alençon, *France* **68 B4** 48 27N 0 4 E
Alenuihaha Channel, *U.S.A.* **110 H17** 20 30N 156 0W
Aleppo, *Syria* **86 B4** 36 10N 37 15 E
Alès, *France* **68 D6** 44 9N 4 5 E
Alessándria, *Italy* **68 D8** 44 54N 8 37 E
Ålesund, *Norway* **63 E5** 62 28N 6 12 E
Aleutian Is., *Pac. Oc.* **102 B10** 52 0N 175 0W
Aleutian Trench, *Pac. Oc.* **102 C10** 48 0N 180 0 E
Alexander Arch., *U.S.A.* **108 C6** 56 0N 136 0W
Alexander I., *Antarctica* **55 C17** 69 0S 70 0W
Alexandria, *Egypt* **95 B11** 31 13N 29 58 E
Alexandria, *U.K.* **20 C6** 55 59N 4 35W
Alexandria, *La., U.S.A.* **111 D8** 31 18N 92 27W
Alexandria, *Va., U.S.A.* **112 F9** 38 48N 77 3W
Alford, *Aberds., U.K.* **19 H12** 57 14N 2 41W
Alford, *Lincs., U.K.* **23 F9** 53 15N 0 10 E
Alfreton, *U.K.* **23 F6** 53 6N 1 24W
Alfriston, *U.K.* **25 E9** 50 48N 0 10 E
Algarve, *Portugal* **69 D1** 36 58N 8 20W
Algeciras, *Spain* **69 D3** 36 9N 5 28W
Algeria ■, *Africa* **94 C6** 28 30N 2 0 E
Algiers, *Algeria* **94 A6** 36 42N 3 8 E
Algoa B., *S. Africa* **90 K6** 33 50S 25 45 E
Alicante, *Spain* **69 C5** 38 23N 0 30W
Alice Springs, *Australia* **98 E5** 23 40S 133 50 E
Aligarh, *India* **84 F11** 27 55N 78 10 E
Alipur Duar, *India* **85 F16** 26 30N 89 35 E
Aliquippa, *U.S.A.* **112 E7** 40 37N 80 15W
Alkmaar, *Neths.* **65 B4** 52 37N 4 45 E
Allahabad, *India* **85 G12** 25 25N 81 58 E
Allegan, *U.S.A.* **112 D5** 42 32N 85 51W
Allegheny →, *U.S.A.* **112 E8** 40 27N 80 1W
Allegheny Mts., *U.S.A.* **111 C11** 38 15N 80 10W
Allègre, Pte., *Guadeloupe* **114 b** 16 22N 61 46W
Allen →, *U.K.* **22 C4** 54 58N 2 18W
Allen, Bog of, *Ireland* **31 B9** 53 15N 7 0W
Allen, L., *Ireland* **28 C5** 54 8N 8 4W
Allendale Town, *U.K.* **22 C4** 54 53N 2 14W
Allenheads, *U.K.* **22 C4** 54 49N 2 12W
Allentown, *U.S.A.* **113 E10** 40 37N 75 29W
Alleppey, *India* **84 Q10** 9 30N 76 28 E
Alleynes B., *Barbados* **115 g** 13 13N 59 39W
Alliance, *U.S.A.* **110 B6** 42 6N 102 52W
Allier →, *France* **68 C5** 46 57N 3 4 E
Alligator Pond, *Jamaica* **114 a** 17 52N 77 34W
Alloa, *U.K.* **21 B8** 56 7N 3 47W
Allonby, *U.K.* **22 C2** 54 46N 3 26W
Alluitsup Paa, *Greenland* **109 B15** 60 30N 45 35W
Alma, *U.S.A.* **112 D5** 43 23N 84 39W
Alma Ata, *Kazakhstan* **79 E9** 43 15N 76 57 E
Almelo, *Neths.* **65 B6** 52 22N 6 42 E
Almería, *Spain* **69 D4** 36 52N 2 27W
Almondsbury, *U.K.* **24 C3** 51 32N 2 34W
Aln →, *U.K.* **22 B5** 55 24N 1 37W
Alness, *U.K.* **19 G9** 57 41N 4 16W
Alnmouth, *U.K.* **22 B5** 55 24N 1 37W
Alnwick, *U.K.* **22 B5** 55 24N 1 42W
Alor, *Indonesia* **83 D4** 8 15S 124 30 E
Alor Setar, *Malaysia* **83 C2** 6 7N 100 22 E
Alpena, *U.S.A.* **112 C6** 45 4N 83 27W
Alpes Maritimes, *Europe* **66 F4** 44 10N 7 10 E
Alphington, *U.K.* **24 E1** 50 42N 3 31W
Alpine, *U.S.A.* **110 D6** 30 22N 103 40W
Alps, *Europe* **66 E5** 46 30N 9 30 E
Alrewas, *U.K.* **23 G5** 52 44N 1 44W
Alsace, *France* **68 B7** 48 15N 7 25 E
Alsager, *U.K.* **23 F4** 53 6N 2 18W
Alsask, *Canada* **108 C9** 51 21N 109 59W
Alston, *U.K.* **22 C4** 54 49N 2 25W
Altanbulag, *Mongolia* **80 A5** 50 16N 106 30 E
Altarnun, *U.K.* **27 F4** 50 35N 4 32W
Altay, *China* **80 B3** 47 48N 88 10 E
Alton, *U.K.* **25 D7** 51 9N 0 59W
Alton, *U.S.A.* **111 C8** 38 53N 90 11W
Altoona, *U.S.A.* **112 E8** 40 31N 78 24W
Altrincham, *U.K.* **23 F4** 53 24N 2 21W
Altun Shan, *China* **80 C3** 38 30N 88 0 E
Altus, *U.S.A.* **110 D7** 34 38N 99 20W
Alucra, *Turkey* **73 F6** 40 22N 38 47 E
Alvechurch, *U.K.* **23 H5** 52 21N 1 57W
Alwar, *India* **84 F10** 27 38N 76 34 E
Alwinton, *U.K.* **22 B4** 55 21N 2 7W
Alxa Zuoqi, *China* **80 C5** 38 50N 105 40 E
Alyth, *U.K.* **19 J11** 56 38N 3 13W
Amadjuak L., *Canada* **109 B12** 65 0N 71 8W
Amagasaki, *Japan* **82 F4** 34 42N 135 20 E
Amapá, *Brazil* **120 B4** 2 5N 50 50W
Amapá □, *Brazil* **120 B4** 1 40N 52 0W
Amarillo, *U.S.A.* **110 C6** 35 13N 101 50W
Amasya, *Turkey* **73 F6** 40 40N 35 50 E
Amazon →, *S. Amer.* **120 C4** 0 5S 50 0W
Amazonas □, *Brazil* **120 C3** 5 0S 65 0W
Ambala, *India* **84 D10** 30 23N 76 56 E
Ambato, *Ecuador* **120 C2** 1 5S 78 42W
Ambergris Cay, *Belize* **114 D7** 18 0N 88 0W
Ambikapur, *India* **85 H13** 23 15N 83 15 E
Ambilobé, *Madag.* **97 G9** 13 10S 49 3 E
Amble, *U.K.* **22 B5** 55 20N 1 36W
Ambleside, *U.K.* **22 D3** 54 26N 2 58W
Ambon, *Indonesia* **83 D4** 3 43S 128 12 E
Amchitka I., *U.S.A.* **108 C1** 51 32N 179 0 E
Ameca, *Mexico* **114 C4** 20 30N 104 0W
American Highland, *Antarctica* **55 D6** 73 0S 75 0 E
American Samoa ⧄, *Pac. Oc.* **99 C16** 14 20S 170 40W
Americana, *Brazil* **122 D1** 22 45S 47 20W
Amersfoort, *Neths.* **65 B5** 52 9N 5 23 E
Amersham, *U.K.* **25 C7** 51 40N 0 36W
Ames, *U.S.A.* **111 B8** 42 2N 93 37W
Amesbury, *U.K.* **24 D5** 51 10N 1 46W
Amherst, *Canada* **109 D13** 45 48N 64 8W
Amiens, *France* **68 B5** 49 54N 2 16 E
Amirante Is., *Seychelles* **53 E12** 6 0S 53 0 E
Amlia I., *U.S.A.* **108 C2** 52 4N 173 30W
Amlwch, *U.K.* **26 A5** 53 24N 4 20W
'Ammān, *Jordan* **86 D3** 31 57N 35 52 E
Ammanford, *U.K.* **26 D6** 51 48N 3 59W
Amos, *Canada* **109 D12** 48 35N 78 5W
Ampleforth, *U.K.* **22 D6** 54 13N 1 6W
Ampthill, *U.K.* **25 B8** 52 2N 0 30W
Amravati, *India* **84 J10** 20 55N 77 45 E
Amreli, *India* **84 J7** 21 35N 71 17 E
Amritsar, *India* **84 D9** 31 35N 74 57 E
Amroha, *India* **84 E11** 28 53N 78 30 E
Amsterdam, *Neths.* **65 B4** 52 23N 4 54 E
Amsterdam, *U.S.A.* **113 D10** 42 56N 74 11W
Amsterdam, I., *Ind. Oc.* **53 F13** 38 30S 77 30 E
Amudarya →, *Uzbekistan* **79 E7** 43 58N 59 34 E
Amundsen Gulf, *Canada* **108 A7** 71 0N 124 0W
Amundsen Sea, *Antarctica* **55 D15** 72 0S 115 0W
Amur →, *Russia* **79 D16** 52 56N 141 10 E
An Najaf, *Iraq* **86 C6** 32 3N 44 15 E
An Nāşiriyah, *Iraq* **86 D6** 31 0N 46 15 E
An Uaimh, *Ireland* **29 D8** 53 39N 6 41W
Anaconda, *U.S.A.* **110 A4** 46 8N 112 57W
Anadyr, *Russia* **79 C19** 64 35N 177 20 E
Anadyr, G. of, *Russia* **79 C20** 64 0N 180 0 E
Anaheim, *U.S.A.* **110 D3** 33 50N 117 55W
Anambas, Kepulauan, *Indonesia* **83 C2** 3 20N 106 30 E
Anamur, *Turkey* **73 G5** 36 8N 32 58 E
Anantapur, *India* **84 M10** 14 39N 77 42 E
Anápolis, *Brazil* **122 C1** 16 15S 48 50W
Anār, *Iran* **87 D8** 30 55N 55 13 E
Anatolia, *Turkey* **73 G5** 39 0N 30 0 E
Añatuya, *Argentina* **121 E3** 28 20S 62 50W
Ancaster, *U.K.* **23 G7** 52 59N 0 32W
Ancholme →, *U.K.* **23 E7** 53 40N 0 32W
Anchorage, *U.S.A.* **108 B5** 61 13N 149 54W
Ancohuma, Nevada, *Bolivia* **120 D3** 16 0S 68 50W
Ancona, *Italy* **70 C5** 43 38N 13 30 E
Ancrum, *U.K.* **22 A3** 55 31N 2 35W
Ancud, *Chile* **121 G2** 42 0S 73 50W
Ancud, G. de, *Chile* **121 G2** 42 0S 73 0W
Andalgalá, *Argentina* **121 E3** 27 40S 66 30W
Andalucía □, *Spain* **69 D3** 37 35N 5 0W
Andalusia, *U.S.A.* **111 D9** 31 18N 86 29W
Andaman Is., *Ind. Oc.* **83 B1** 12 30N 92 45 E
Anderson, *Alaska, U.S.A.* **108 B5** 64 25N 149 15W
Anderson, *Ind., U.S.A.* **112 E5** 40 10N 85 41W
Anderson, *S.C., U.S.A.* **111 D10** 34 31N 82 39W
Anderson →, *Canada* **108 B7** 69 42N 129 0W
Andes, Cord. de los, *S. Amer.* **121 E3** 20 0S 68 0W
Andhra Pradesh □, *India* **84 L11** 18 0N 79 0 E
Andijon, *Uzbekistan* **87 A13** 41 10N 72 15 E
Andorra ■, *Europe* **68 E4** 42 30N 1 30 E
Andover, *U.K.* **24 D6** 51 12N 1 29W
Andradina, *Brazil* **120 E4** 20 54S 51 23W
Andreanof Is., *U.S.A.* **108 C2** 51 30N 176 0W
Ándria, *Italy* **70 D7** 41 13N 16 17 E
Andros I., *Bahamas* **115 C9** 24 30N 78 0W
Anegada I., *Br. Virgin Is.* **115 e** 18 45N 64 20W
Aneityum, *Vanuatu* **99 E12** 20 12S 169 45 E
Angara →, *Russia* **79 D11** 58 5N 94 20 E
Angarsk, *Russia* **79 D12** 52 30N 104 0 E
Ånge, *Sweden* **63 E7** 62 31N 15 35 E
Angel Falls, *Venezuela* **120 B3** 5 57N 62 30W
Angeles, *Phil.* **83 B4** 15 9N 120 33 E
Ångermanälven →, *Sweden* **63 E7** 62 40N 18 0 E
Angers, *France* **68 C3** 47 30N 0 35W
Anglesey □, *U.K.* **26 A5** 53 16N 4 18W
Angoche, *Mozam.* **97 H7** 16 8S 39 55 E
Angola ■, *Africa* **97 G3** 12 0S 18 0 E
Angoulême, *France* **68 D4** 45 39N 0 10 E
Angoumois, *France* **68 D3** 45 50N 0 25 E
Angra dos Reis, *Brazil* **122 D2** 23 0S 44 10W
Angren, *Uzbekistan* **87 A12** 41 1N 70 12 E
Anguilla ⧄, *W. Indies* **115 D12** 18 14N 63 5W
Anhui □, *China* **81 C6** 32 0N 117 0 E
Anjou, *France* **68 C3** 47 20N 0 15W
Ankang, *China* **81 C5** 32 40N 109 1 E
Ankara, *Turkey* **73 G5** 39 57N 32 54 E
Ann, C., *U.S.A.* **113 D12** 42 38N 70 35W
Ann Arbor, *U.S.A.* **112 D6** 42 17N 83 45W
Annaba, *Algeria* **94 A7** 36 50N 7 46 E
Annalee →, *Ireland* **28 C7** 54 2N 7 24W
Annan, *U.K.* **21 E9** 54 59N 3 16W
Annan →, *U.K.* **21 E9** 54 58N 3 16W
Annandale, *U.K.* **22 B2** 55 10N 3 25W
Annapolis, *U.S.A.* **112 F9** 38 59N 76 30W
Annapurna, *Nepal* **85 E14** 28 34N 83 50 E
Annecy, *France* **68 D7** 45 55N 6 8 E
Annfield Plain, *U.K.* **22 C5** 54 52N 1 44W
Anning, *China* **80 D5** 24 55N 102 26 E
Anniston, *U.S.A.* **111 D9** 33 39N 85 50W
Annobón, *Atl. Oc.* **90 G4** 1 25S 5 36 E
Annotto Bay, *Jamaica* **114 a** 18 17N 76 45W
Anqing, *China* **81 C6** 30 30N 117 3 E
Anshan, *China* **81 B7** 41 5N 122 58 E
Anshun, *China* **80 D5** 26 18N 105 57 E
Anstey, *U.K.* **23 G6** 52 41N 1 12W
Anstruther, *U.K.* **21 B10** 56 14N 2 41W
Antalya, *Turkey* **73 G5** 36 52N 30 45 E
Antananarivo, *Madag.* **97 H9** 18 55S 47 31 E
Antarctic Pen., *Antarctica* **55 C18** 67 0S 60 0W
Antarctica **55 E3** 90 0S 0 0W
Anti Atlas, *Morocco* **94 C4** 30 0N 8 30W
Antibes, *France* **68 E7** 43 34N 7 6 E
Anticosti, Î. d', *Canada* **109 D13** 49 30N 63 0W
Antigonish, *Canada* **109 D13** 45 38N 61 58W
Antigua & Barbuda ■, *W. Indies* **115 D12** 17 20N 61 48W
Antilles, *Cent. Amer.* **115 E12** 15 0N 65 0W
Antioch, *Turkey* **73 G6** 36 14N 36 10 E
Antioquia, *Colombia* **120 B2** 6 40N 75 55W
Antipodes Is., *Pac. Oc.* **102 M9** 49 45S 178 40 E
Antofagasta, *Chile* **121 E2** 23 50S 70 30W
Antrim, *U.K.* **29 B9** 54 43N 6 14W
Antrim □, *U.K.* **29 B9** 54 56N 6 25W
Antrim, Mts. of, *U.K.* **29 A9** 55 3N 6 14W
Antsirabe, *Madag.* **97 H9** 19 55S 47 2 E
Antsiranana, *Madag.* **97 G9** 12 25S 49 20 E
Antwerp, *Belgium* **65 C4** 51 13N 4 25 E
Anuradhapura, *Sri Lanka* **84 Q12** 8 22N 80 28 E
Anxi, *China* **80 B4** 40 30N 95 43 E
Anyang, *China* **81 C6** 36 5N 114 21 E
Aomori, *Japan* **82 C7** 40 45N 140 45 E
Aoraki Mount Cook, *N.Z.* **99 J13** 43 36S 170 9 E
Aozou Strip, *Chad* **95 D9** 22 0N 19 0 E
Apalachee B., *U.S.A.* **111 E10** 30 0N 84 0W
Apaporis →, *Colombia* **120 C3** 1 23S 69 25W
Apatity, *Russia* **72 A5** 67 34N 33 22 E
Apeldoorn, *Neths.* **65 B5** 52 13N 5 57 E
Apia, *Samoa* **99 C16** 13 50S 171 50W
Apostle Is., *U.S.A.* **111 A8** 47 0N 90 40W
Appalachian Mts., *U.S.A.* **112 G7** 38 0N 80 0W
Appennini, *Italy* **70 B4** 44 0N 10 0 E
Appleby-in-Westmorland, *U.K.* **22 C4** 54 35N 2 29W
Appledore, *Devon, U.K.* **27 E5** 51 3N 4 13W
Appledore, *Kent, U.K.* **25 D10** 51 1N 0 47 E
Appleton, *U.S.A.* **112 C3** 44 16N 88 25W
Apure →, *Venezuela* **120 B3** 7 37N 66 25W
Apurimac →, *Peru* **120 D2** 12 17S 73 56W
Aqaba, G. of, *Red Sea* **86 D3** 28 15N 33 20 E
Aqtöbe, *Kazakhstan* **73 D10** 50 17N 57 10 E
Ar Ramādī, *Iraq* **86 C5** 33 25N 43 20 E
Ara, *India* **85 G14** 25 35N 84 32 E
Arab, Shatt al →, *Asia* **86 D7** 30 0N 48 31 E
Arabia, *Asia* **74 G8** 25 0N 45 0 E
Arabian Desert, *Egypt* **95 C12** 27 30N 32 30 E
Arabian Gulf = Gulf, The, *Asia* **87 E7** 27 0N 50 0 E
Arabian Sea, *Ind. Oc.* **74 H10** 16 0N 65 0 E
Aracaju, *Brazil* **122 B3** 10 55S 37 4W
Aracati, *Brazil* **120 C6** 4 30S 37 44W
Araçatuba, *Brazil* **120 E4** 21 10S 50 30W
Araçuaí, *Brazil* **122 C2** 16 52S 42 4W
Arad, *Romania* **67 E11** 46 10N 21 20 E
Arafura Sea, *E. Indies* **83 D5** 9 0S 135 0 E
Aragón □, *Spain* **69 B5** 41 25N 0 40W
Araguacema, *Brazil* **120 C5** 8 50S 49 20W
Araguaia →, *Brazil* **120 C5** 5 21S 48 41W
Araguari, *Brazil* **122 C1** 18 38S 48 11W
Arāk, *Iran* **86 C7** 34 0N 49 40 E
Arakan Coast, *Burma* **85 K19** 19 0N 94 0 E
Arakan Yoma, *Burma* **85 K19** 20 0N 94 40 E
Araks →, *Asia* **86 A7** 40 5N 48 29 E
Aral, *Kazakhstan* **79 E8** 46 41N 61 45 E
Aral Sea, *Asia* **79 E8** 44 30N 60 0 E
Aran I., *Ireland* **28 B4** 55 0N 8 30W
Aran Is., *Ireland* **30 B3** 53 6N 9 38W
Aransas Pass, *U.S.A.* **111 E7** 27 55N 97 9W
Arapiraca, *Brazil* **122 A3** 9 45S 36 39W
Araraquara, *Brazil* **122 D1** 21 50S 48 0W
Araras, *Brazil* **122 D1** 22 22S 47 23W
Ararat, Mt., *Turkey* **73 G7** 39 50N 44 15 E
Araripe, Chapada do, *Brazil* **120 C5** 7 20S 40 0W
Arauca →, *Venezuela* **120 B3** 7 24N 66 35W
Araxá, *Brazil* **122 C1** 19 35S 46 55W
Arbroath, *U.K.* **21 A10** 56 34N 2 35W
Arcachon, *France* **68 D3** 44 40N 1 10W
Arctic Bay, *Canada* **109 A11** 73 1N 85 7W
Arctic Ocean, *Arctic* **54 B18** 78 0N 160 0W
Ardabīl, *Iran* **86 B7** 38 15N 48 18 E
Ardee, *Ireland* **29 D8** 53 52N 6 33W
Ardennes, *Belgium* **65 E5** 49 50N 5 5 E
Arderin, *Ireland* **31 B7** 53 2N 7 39W
Ardingly, *U.K.* **25 D8** 51 3N 0 4W
Ardivachar Pt., *U.K.* **18 H3** 57 23N 7 26W
Ardmore, *U.S.A.* **111 D7** 34 10N 97 8W
Ardnamurchan, Pt. of, *U.K.* **18 J5** 56 43N 6 14W
Ardnave Pt., *U.K.* **20 C3** 55 53N 6 20W
Ardrossan, *U.K.* **20 C6** 55 39N 4 49W
Ards Pen., *U.K.* **29 B10** 54 33N 5 34W
Arecibo, *Puerto Rico* **115 d** 18 29N 66 43W
Arena, Pt., *U.S.A.* **110 C2** 38 57N 123 44W
Arendal, *Norway* **63 F5** 58 28N 8 46 E
Arequipa, *Peru* **120 D2** 16 20S 71 30W
Argentan, *France* **68 B3** 48 45N 0 1W
Argentina ■, *S. Amer.* **121 F3** 35 0S 66 0W
Argentino, L., *Argentina* **121 H2** 50 10S 73 0W
Århus, *Denmark* **63 F6** 56 8N 10 11 E
Arica, *Chile* **120 D2** 18 32S 70 20W
Arinos →, *Brazil* **116 E5** 10 25S 58 20W
Aripuanã →, *Brazil* **120 C3** 5 7S 60 25W
Arisaig, *U.K.* **18 J6** 56 55N 5 51W
Arizona □, *U.S.A.* **110 D4** 34 0N 112 0W
Arkaig, L., *U.K.* **18 J7** 56 59N 5 10W
Arkansas □, *U.S.A.* **111 D8** 35 0N 92 30W
Arkansas →, *U.S.A.* **111 D8** 33 47N 91 4W
Arkansas City, *U.S.A.* **111 C7** 37 4N 97 2W
Arkhangelsk, *Russia* **72 B7** 64 38N 40 36 E
Arkle →, *U.K.* **22 D5** 54 24N 1 56W
Arklow, *Ireland* **31 C10** 52 48N 6 10W
Arles, *France* **68 E6** 43 41N 4 40 E
Arlington, *U.S.A.* **112 F9** 38 53N 77 7W
Arlon, *Belgium* **65 E5** 49 42N 5 49 E
Armagh, *U.K.* **29 C8** 54 21N 6 39W
Armagh □, *U.K.* **29 C8** 54 18N 6 37W
Armavir, *Russia* **73 E7** 45 2N 41 7 E
Armenia ■, *Asia* **73 F7** 40 20N 45 0 E
Arnaud →, *Canada* **109 B12** 59 59N 69 46W
Arnhem, *Neths.* **65 C5** 51 58N 5 55 E
Arnhem, C., *Australia* **98 C6** 12 20S 137 30 E
Arnhem Land, *Australia* **98 C5** 13 10S 134 30 E
Arnold, *U.K.* **23 F6** 53 1N 1 7W
Arnprior, *Canada* **112 C9** 45 26N 76 21W
Arnside, *U.K.* **22 D3** 54 12N 2 49W
Arran, *U.K.* **20 C5** 55 34N 5 12W
Arras, *France* **68 A5** 50 17N 2 46 E
Arrecife, *Canary Is.* **94 C3** 28 57N 13 37W
Arrow, L., *Ireland* **28 C5** 54 3N 8 19W
Artemovsk, *Ukraine* **73 E6** 48 35N 38 0 E
Artigas, *Uruguay* **121 F4** 30 20S 56 30W
Artois, *France* **68 A5** 50 20N 2 30 E
Artvin, *Turkey* **73 F7** 41 14N 41 44 E
Aru, Kepulauan, *Indonesia* **83 D5** 6 0S 134 30 E
Arua, *Uganda* **96 D6** 3 1N 30 58 E
Aruanã, *Brazil* **120 D4** 14 54S 51 10W
Aruba ⧄, *W. Indies* **115 E11** 12 30N 70 0W
Arun →, *U.K.* **25 E7** 50 49N 0 33W
Arunachal Pradesh □, *India* **85 F19** 28 0N 95 0 E
Arundel, *U.K.* **25 E7** 50 51N 0 33W
Arusha, *Tanzania* **96 E7** 3 20S 36 40 E
Arviat, *Canada* **108 B10** 61 6N 94 3W
Arxan, *China* **81 B6** 47 11N 119 57 E
Arzamas, *Russia* **72 C7** 55 27N 43 55 E
As Sulaymānīyah, *Iraq* **86 C6** 35 35N 45 29 E
As Şuwayrah, *Iraq* **86 C6** 32 55N 45 0 E
Asahigawa, *Japan* **82 B8** 43 46N 142 22 E
Asamankese, *Ghana* **94 G5** 5 50N 0 40W
Asansol, *India* **85 H15** 23 40N 87 1 E
Asbestos, *Canada* **113 C12** 45 47N 71 58W
Asbury Park, *U.S.A.* **113 E10** 40 13N 74 1W
Ascension I., *Atl. Oc.* **52 E9** 7 57S 14 23W
Ascot, *U.K.* **25 D7** 51 25N 0 40W
Aseb, *Eritrea* **88 E3** 13 0N 42 40 E
Asfordby, *U.K.* **23 G7** 52 47N 0 57W
Ash, *Kent, U.K.* **25 D11** 51 16N 1 17 E
Ash, *Surrey, U.K.* **25 D7** 51 15N 0 43W
Ashbourne, *U.K.* **23 F5** 53 2N 1 43W
Ashburton, *U.K.* **27 F6** 50 30N 3 46W
Ashby de la Zouch, *U.K.* **23 G6** 52 46N 1 29W
Ashchurch, *U.K.* **24 C4** 52 0N 2 5W
Ashdown Forest, *U.K.* **25 D9** 51 3N 0 5 E
Asheville, *U.S.A.* **111 C10** 35 36N 82 33W
Ashford, *Derby, U.K.* **23 F5** 53 14N 1 42W
Ashford, *Kent, U.K.* **25 D10** 51 8N 0 53 E
Ashington, *U.K.* **22 B5** 55 11N 1 33W
Ashkhabad, *Turkmenistan* **79 F7** 38 0N 57 50 E
Ashland, *Ky., U.S.A.* **112 F6** 38 28N 82 38W
Ashland, *Ohio, U.S.A.* **112 E6** 40 52N 82 19W
Ashland, *Wis., U.S.A.* **111 A8** 46 35N 90 53W
Ashqelon, *Israel* **86 D3** 31 42N 34 35 E
Ashtabula, *U.S.A.* **112 E7** 41 52N 80 47W
Ashton-in-Makerfield, *U.K.* **23 F3** 53 30N 2 40W
Ashton under Lyne, *U.K.* **23 F4** 53 29N 2 6W
Ashuanipi, L., *Canada* **109 C13** 52 45N 66 15W
Ashwater, *U.K.* **27 F5** 50 43N 4 19W
Ashwick, *U.K.* **24 D3** 51 13N 2 31W
Asia **74 E11** 45 0N 75 0 E
'Asīr □, *Si. Arabia* **88 D3** 18 40N 42 30 E
Asir, Ras, *Somali Rep.* **88 E5** 11 55N 51 10 E
Askrigg, *U.K.* **22 D4** 54 19N 2 6W
Aslackby, *U.K.* **23 G8** 52 53N 0 24W
Asmera, *Eritrea* **88 D2** 15 19N 38 55 E
Aspatria, *U.K.* **22 C2** 54 47N 3 19W
Aspen, *U.S.A.* **110 C5** 39 11N 106 49W
Assam □, *India* **85 G18** 26 0N 93 0 E
Assen, *Neths.* **65 A6** 53 0N 6 35 E
Assiniboia, *Canada* **108 D9** 49 40N 105 59W
Assiniboine →, *Canada* **108 D10** 49 53N 97 8W
Assisi, *Italy* **70 C5** 43 4N 12 37 E
Assynt, L., *U.K.* **18 F7** 58 10N 5 3W
Astana, *Kazakhstan* **79 D9** 51 10N 71 30 E
Asti, *Italy* **68 D8** 44 54N 8 12 E
Astoria, *U.S.A.* **110 A2** 46 11N 123 50W
Astrakhan, *Russia* **73 E8** 46 25N 48 5 E
Asturias □, *Spain* **69 A3** 43 15N 6 0W
Astwood Bank, *U.K.* **23 H5** 52 15N 1 56W
Asunción, *Paraguay* **121 E4** 25 10S 57 30W
Aswân, *Egypt* **95 D12** 24 4N 32 57 E
Aswan Dam, *Egypt* **95 D12** 23 54N 32 54 E
Asyût, *Egypt* **95 C12** 27 11N 31 4 E
Aţ Tā'if, *Si. Arabia* **88 C3** 21 5N 40 27 E
Atacama, Desierto de, *Chile* **121 E3** 24 0S 69 20W
Atatürk Barajı, *Turkey* **73 G6** 37 28N 38 30 E
'Atbara, *Sudan* **95 E12** 17 42N 33 59 E
Atbara →, *Sudan* **95 E12** 17 40N 33 56 E
Atchafalaya B., *U.S.A.* **111 E8** 29 25N 91 25W
Athabasca, *Canada* **108 C8** 54 45N 113 20W
Athabasca →, *Canada* **108 C8** 58 40N 110 50W
Athabasca, L., *Canada* **108 C9** 59 15N 109 15W
Athboy, *Ireland* **29 D8** 53 37N 6 56W
Athenry, *Ireland* **28 E4** 53 18N 8 44W
Athens, *Greece* **71 F10** 37 58N 23 46 E
Athens, *Ga., U.S.A.* **111 D10** 33 57N 83 23W
Athens, *Ohio, U.S.A.* **112 F6** 39 20N 82 6W
Atherstone, *U.K.* **23 G5** 52 35N 1 33W
Atherton, *U.K.* **23 E4** 53 32N 2 30W
Athlone, *Ireland* **28 E6** 53 25N 7 56W
Atholl, Forest of, *U.K.* **19 J10** 56 51N 3 50W
Athy, *Ireland* **31 B8** 53 0N 7 0W
Atikokan, *Canada* **112 A2** 48 45N 91 37W
Atka I., *U.S.A.* **108 C2** 52 7N 174 30W
Atlanta, *U.S.A.* **111 D10** 33 45N 84 23W
Atlantic City, *U.S.A.* **113 F10** 39 21N 74 27W
Atlantic Ocean **52 E9** 0 0 20 0W
Atlin, *Canada* **108 C6** 59 31N 133 41W
Attawapiskat, *Canada* **109 C11** 52 56N 82 24W
Attawapiskat →, *Canada* **109 C11** 52 57N 82 18W
Attleborough, *U.K.* **25 A11** 52 32N 1 1 E
Attu I., *U.S.A.* **108 C1** 52 55N 172 55 E
Atyraū, *Kazakhstan* **73 E9** 47 5N 52 0 E
Au Sable →, *U.S.A.* **112 C6** 44 25N 83 20W
Aube →, *France* **68 B5** 48 34N 3 43 E
Auburn, *Ind., U.S.A.* **112 E5** 41 22N 85 4W
Auburn, *N.Y., U.S.A.* **112 D9** 42 56N 76 34W
Aubusson, *France* **68 D5** 45 57N 2 11 E
Auch, *France* **68 E4** 43 39N 0 36 E
Auchterarder, *U.K.* **21 B8** 56 18N 3 41W
Auchtermuchty, *U.K.* **21 B9** 56 18N 3 13W
Auckland, *N.Z.* **99 H13** 36 52S 174 46 E
Auckland Is., *Pac. Oc.* **102 N8** 50 40S 166 5 E
Aude →, *France* **68 E5** 43 13N 3 14 E
Audlem, *U.K.* **23 G4** 52 59N 2 30W
Aughnacloy, *U.K.* **29 C8** 54 25N 6 59W
Augsburg, *Germany* **66 D6** 48 25N 10 52 E
Augusta, *Australia* **98 G2** 34 19S 115 9 E
Augusta, *Ga., U.S.A.* **111 D10** 33 28N 81 58W
Augusta, *Maine, U.S.A.* **109 D13** 44 19N 69 47W
Aunis, *France* **68 C3** 46 5N 0 50W
Aurangabad, *Bihar, India* **85 G14** 24 45N 84 18 E
Aurangabad, *Maharashtra, India* **84 K9** 19 50N 75 23 E
Aurillac, *France* **68 D5** 44 55N 2 26 E
Aurora, *Colo., U.S.A.* **110 C6** 39 44N 104 52W
Aurora, *Ill., U.S.A.* **112 E3** 41 45N 88 19W
Austin, *U.S.A.* **110 D7** 30 17N 97 45W
Austral Seamount Chain, *Pac. Oc.* **103 K13** 24 0S 150 0W
Australia ■, *Oceania* **98 E3** 23 0S 135 0 E
Australian Capital Territory □, *Australia* **98 H8** 35 30S 149 0 E
Austria ■, *Europe* **66 E8** 47 0N 14 0 E
Autun, *France* **68 C6** 46 58N 4 17 E
Auvergne, *France* **68 D5** 45 20N 3 15 E
Auxerre, *France* **68 C5** 47 48N 3 32 E
Avallon, *France* **68 C5** 47 30N 3 53 E
Avebury, *U.K.* **24 D5** 51 26N 1 50W
Avellaneda, *Argentina* **121 F4** 34 50S 58 10W
Avellino, *Italy* **70 D6** 40 54N 14 47 E
Aveton Gifford, *U.K.* **27 G6** 50 18N 3 50W
Aviemore, *U.K.* **19 H10** 57 12N 3 50W
Avignon, *France* **68 E6** 43 57N 4 50 E
Ávila, *Spain* **69 B3** 40 39N 4 43W
Avoca →, *Ireland* **31 C10** 52 48N 6 10W
Avon →, *Bristol, U.K.* **24 D3** 51 29N 2 41W
Avon →, *Dorset, U.K.* **24 E5** 50 44N 1 46W
Avon →, *Warks., U.K.* **24 B5** 52 0N 2 8W
Avonmouth, *U.K.* **24 C3** 51 30N 2 42W
Avranches, *France* **68 B3** 48 40N 1 20W
Awasa, *Ethiopia* **88 F2** 7 2N 38 28 E
Awash, *Ethiopia* **88 F3** 9 1N 40 10 E
Awe, L., *U.K.* **20 B5** 56 17N 5 16W
Axbridge, *U.K.* **24 D3** 51 17N 2 49W
Axe →, *U.K.* **24 D3** 50 42N 3 4W
Axe Edge, *U.K.* **23 F5** 53 14N 1 57W
Axel Heiberg I., *Canada* **54 B3** 80 0N 90 0W
Axholme, Isle of, *U.K.* **23 E7** 53 32N 0 50W
Axiós →, *Greece* **71 D10** 40 57N 22 35 E
Axminster, *U.K.* **24 E3** 50 46N 3 0W
Axmouth, *U.K.* **24 E2** 50 42N 3 3W
Ayacucho, *Argentina* **121 F4** 37 5S 58 20W
Ayacucho, *Peru* **120 D2** 13 0S 74 0W
Aydın, *Turkey* **73 G4** 37 51N 27 51 E
Ayers Rock, *Australia* **98 F5** 25 23S 131 5 E
Aylesbury, *U.K.* **25 C7** 51 49N 0 49W
Aylesford, *U.K.* **25 D10** 51 18N 0 30 E
Aylmer, L., *Canada* **108 B8** 64 0N 110 8W
Aylsham, *U.K.* **25 A11** 52 48N 1 15 E
Aynho, *U.K.* **24 C6** 52 0N 1 15W
Ayr, *U.K.* **20 D6** 55 28N 4 38W
Ayr →, *U.K.* **20 D6** 55 28N 4 38W
Aysgarth, *U.K.* **22 D4** 54 18N 2 1W
Ayton, *Borders, U.K.* **22 A4** 55 51N 2 6W
Ayton, *N. Yorks., U.K.* **22 D8** 54 15N 0 28W
Ayvalık, *Turkey* **73 G4** 39 20N 26 46 E
Az Zarqā, *Jordan* **86 C4** 32 5N 36 4 E
Az Zāwiyah, *Libya* **95 B8** 32 52N 12 56 E
Azamgarh, *India* **85 F13** 26 5N 83 13 E
Azerbaijan ■, *Asia* **73 F8** 40 20N 48 0 E
Azores, *Atl. Oc.* **52 C8** 38 0N 27 0W
Azov, *Russia* **73 E6** 47 3N 39 25 E
Azov, Sea of, *Europe* **73 E6** 46 0N 36 30 E
Azuero, Pen. de, *Panama* **115 F8** 7 30N 80 30W
Azul, *Argentina* **121 F4** 36 42S 59 43W

# B

Bab el Mandeb, *Red Sea* **88 E3** 12 35N 43 25 E
Bābā, Koh-i-, *Afghan.* **84 B5** 34 30N 67 0 E
Babine L., *Canada* **108 C7** 54 48N 126 0W
Bābol, *Iran* **87 B8** 36 40N 52 50 E
Babruysk, *Belarus* **67 B15** 53 10N 29 15 E
Babuyan Chan., *Phil.* **83 B4** 18 40N 121 30 E
Babylon, *Iraq* **86 C6** 32 34N 44 22 E
Bac Lieu, *Vietnam* **83 C2** 9 17N 105 43 E
Bacău, *Romania* **67 E14** 46 35N 26 55 E

**Back**                                                                 **Bienville, L.**

Back →, Canada ... 108 B9 65 10N 104 0W
Bacolod, Phil. ... 83 B4 10 40N 122 57 E
Bacton, U.K. ... 25 A11 52 51N 1 27 E
Bacup, U.K. ... 23 E4 53 42N 2 11W
Bad Axe, U.S.A. ... 112 D6 43 48N 83 10W
Bad Lands, U.S.A. ... 110 B6 43 40N 102 10W
Badagara, India ... 84 P9 11 35N 75 40 E
Badajoz, Spain ... 69 C2 38 50N 6 59W
Badakhshān □, Afghan. ... 87 B12 36 30N 71 0 E
Badalona, Spain ... 69 B7 41 26N 2 15 E
Baden-Württemberg □, Germany ... 66 D5 48 20N 8 40 E
Bādghīs □, Afghan. ... 87 C10 35 0N 63 0 E
Baffin B., Canada ... 109 A13 72 0N 64 0W
Baffin I., Canada ... 109 B12 68 0N 75 0W
Bafoulabé, Mali ... 94 F3 13 50N 10 55W
Bafoussam, Cameroon ... 96 C2 5 28N 10 25 E
Bafra, Turkey ... 73 F6 41 34N 35 54 E
Bagé, Brazil ... 121 F4 31 20S 54 15W
Baggy Pt., U.K. ... 27 E5 51 8N 4 16W
Baghdād, Iraq ... 86 C6 33 20N 44 30 E
Baghlān, Afghan. ... 87 B12 32 12N 68 46 E
Bagshot, U.K. ... 25 D7 51 22N 0 41W
Baguio, Phil. ... 83 B4 16 26N 120 34 E
Bahamas ■, N. Amer. ... 115 C10 24 0N 75 0W
Baharampur, India ... 85 G16 24 2N 88 27 E
Bahawalpur, Pakistan ... 84 E7 29 24N 71 40 E
Bahía = Salvador, Brazil ... 122 B3 13 0S 38 30W
Bahía □, Brazil ... 122 B2 12 0S 42 0W
Bahía Blanca, Argentina ... 121 F3 38 35S 62 13W
Bahir Dar, Ethiopia ... 88 E2 11 37N 37 10 E
Bahr el Ghazâl □, Sudan ... 95 G11 7 0N 28 0 E
Bahraich, India ... 85 F12 27 38N 81 37 E
Bahrain ■, Asia ... 87 E7 26 0N 50 35 E
Baia Mare, Romania ... 67 E12 47 40N 23 35 E
Baidoa, Somali Rep. ... 88 G3 3 8N 43 30 E
Baie-Comeau, Canada ... 109 D13 49 12N 68 10W
Baie-St-Paul, Canada ... 113 B12 47 28N 70 32W
Baie Verte, Canada ... 109 D14 49 55N 56 12W
Ba'ījī, Iraq ... 86 C5 35 0N 43 30 E
Baikal, L., Russia ... 79 D12 53 0N 108 0 E
Baildon, U.K. ... 23 E5 53 51N 1 46W
Bain →, U.K. ... 23 F8 53 6N 0 12W
Bainbridge, U.K. ... 22 D4 54 18N 2 6W
Baiyin, China ... 80 C5 36 45N 104 14 E
Baja, Pta., Mexico ... 114 B1 29 50N 116 0W
Baja California, Mexico ... 114 A1 31 10N 115 12W
Baker, L., Canada ... 108 B10 64 0N 96 0W
Baker City, U.S.A. ... 110 B3 44 47N 117 50W
Baker I., Pac. Oc. ... 99 A15 0 10N 176 35W
Baker Lake, Canada ... 108 B10 64 20N 96 3W
Bakers Dozen Is., Canada ... 109 C12 56 45N 78 45W
Bakersfield, U.S.A. ... 110 C3 35 23N 119 1W
Bakewell, U.K. ... 23 F5 53 13N 1 40W
Bākhtarān, Iran ... 86 C6 34 23N 47 0 E
Bakony, Hungary ... 67 E9 47 10N 17 30 E
Baku, Azerbaijan ... 73 F8 40 29N 49 56 E
Bala, U.K. ... 26 B6 52 54N 3 36W
Bala, L., U.K. ... 26 B6 52 53N 3 37W
Balabac Str., E. Indies ... 83 C3 7 53N 117 5 E
Balaklava, Ukraine ... 73 F5 44 30N 33 30 E
Balakovo, Russia ... 72 D8 52 4N 47 55 E
Balashov, Russia ... 73 D7 51 30N 43 10 E
Balaton, Hungary ... 67 E9 46 50N 17 40 E
Balbi, Mt., Papua N. G. ... 99 B10 5 55S 154 58 E
Balbriggan, Ireland ... 29 D9 53 37N 6 11W
Balcarce, Argentina ... 121 F4 38 0S 58 10W
Balderton, U.K. ... 23 F7 53 3N 0 46W
Baldock, U.K. ... 25 C8 52 0N 0 11W
Baldwin, U.S.A. ... 112 D5 43 54N 85 51W
Baldy Peak, U.S.A. ... 110 D5 33 54N 109 34W
Balearic Is., Spain ... 69 C7 39 30N 3 0 E
Baleshare, U.K. ... 18 G3 57 31N 7 22W
Baleshwar, India ... 85 J15 21 35N 87 3 E
Bali, Indonesia ... 83 D3 8 20S 115 0 E
Balıkesir, Turkey ... 71 E12 39 39N 27 53 E
Balikpapan, Indonesia ... 83 D3 1 10S 116 55 E
Balkan Mts., Bulgaria ... 71 C10 43 15N 23 0 E
Balkhash, L., Kazakhstan ... 79 E9 46 0N 74 50 E
Ballachulish, U.K. ... 18 J7 56 41N 5 8W
Ballaghaderreen, Ireland ... 28 D4 53 55N 8 34W
Ballantrae, U.K. ... 20 D6 55 6N 4 59W
Ballarat, Australia ... 98 H7 37 33S 143 50 E
Ballater, U.K. ... 19 H11 57 3N 3 3W
Ballenas, B. de, Mexico ... 114 B2 26 45N 113 26W
Balleny Is., Antarctica ... 55 C11 66 30S 163 0 E
Ballina, Ireland ... 28 C3 54 7N 9 9W
Ballinasloe, Ireland ... 28 E5 53 20N 8 13W
Ballinrobe, Ireland ... 28 D3 53 38N 9 13W
Ballinskelligs B., Ireland ... 30 E2 51 48N 10 13W
Ballybunion, Ireland ... 30 C3 52 31N 9 40W
Ballycastle, U.K. ... 29 A9 55 12N 6 15W
Ballyclare, U.K. ... 29 B10 54 46N 6 0W
Ballyhaunis, Ireland ... 28 D4 53 46N 8 46W
Ballymena, U.K. ... 29 B9 54 52N 6 17W
Ballymoney, U.K. ... 29 A8 55 5N 6 31W
Ballymote, Ireland ... 28 C4 54 5N 8 31W
Ballynahinch, U.K. ... 29 C10 54 24N 5 54W
Ballyquintin Pt., U.K. ... 29 C11 54 20N 5 30W
Ballyshannon, Ireland ... 28 B5 54 30N 8 11W
Balrampur, India ... 85 F13 27 30N 82 20 E
Balsas →, Mexico ... 114 D4 17 55N 102 10W
Bălti, Moldova ... 67 E14 47 48N 27 58 E
Baltic Sea, Europe ... 63 F7 57 0N 19 0 E
Baltimore, Ireland ... 30 F4 51 29N 9 22W
Baltimore, U.S.A. ... 112 F9 39 17N 76 37W
Baluchistan □, Pakistan ... 84 F4 27 30N 65 0 E
Bamako, Mali ... 94 F4 12 34N 7 55W
Bambari, C.A.R. ... 96 C4 5 40N 20 35 E
Bamberg, Germany ... 66 D6 49 54N 10 54 E
Bamburgh, U.K. ... 22 A5 55 37N 1 43W
Bamenda, Cameroon ... 96 C2 5 57N 10 11 E
Bamford, U.K. ... 23 F5 53 22N 1 41W
Bāmīān □, Afghan. ... 87 C11 35 0N 67 0 E
Bampton, Devon, U.K. ... 24 E2 50 59N 3 29W
Bampton, Oxon., U.K. ... 24 C5 51 44N 1 32W
Banaba, Kiribati ... 102 H8 0 45S 169 50 E
Bananal, I. do, Brazil ... 120 D4 11 30S 50 30W
Banbridge, U.K. ... 29 C9 54 22N 6 16W
Banbury, U.K. ... 24 B6 52 4N 1 20W
Banchory, U.K. ... 19 H13 57 3N 2 29W
Bancroft, Canada ... 112 C9 45 3N 77 51W
Banda, India ... 84 G12 25 30N 80 26 E
Banda, Kepulauan, Indonesia ... 83 D4 4 37S 129 50 E
Banda Aceh, Indonesia ... 83 C1 5 35N 95 20 E
Banda Sea, Indonesia ... 83 D5 6 0S 130 0 E
Bandar-e Abbās, Iran ... 87 E9 27 15N 56 15 E
Bandar-e Anzali, Iran ... 86 B7 37 30N 49 30 E
Bandar-e Ma'shur, Iran ... 86 D7 30 35N 49 10 E
Bandar-e Torkeman, Iran ... 87 B8 37 0N 54 10 E
Bandar Seri Begawan, Brunei ... 83 C3 4 52N 115 0 E
Bandeira, Pico da, Brazil ... 116 F6 20 26S 41 47W
Bandırma, Turkey ... 73 F4 40 20N 28 0 E
Bandon, Ireland ... 30 E5 51 44N 8 44W
Bandon →, Ireland ... 30 E5 51 43N 8 37W
Bandundu, Dem. Rep. of the Congo ... 96 E3 3 15S 17 22 E

Bandung, Indonesia ... 83 D2 6 54S 107 36 E
Banes, Cuba ... 115 C9 21 0N 75 42W
Banff, Canada ... 108 C8 51 10N 115 34W
Banff, U.K. ... 19 G12 57 40N 2 33W
Bangalore, India ... 84 N10 12 59N 77 40 E
Banggai, Kepulauan, Indonesia ... 83 D4 1 40S 123 30 E
Bangka, Indonesia ... 83 D2 2 0S 105 50 E
Bangkok, Thailand ... 83 B2 13 45N 100 35 E
Bangladesh ■, Asia ... 85 H17 24 0N 90 0 E
Bangor, Down, U.K. ... 29 B10 54 40N 5 40W
Bangor, Gwynedd, U.K. ... 26 A5 53 14N 4 8W
Bangor, U.S.A. ... 109 D13 44 48N 68 46W
Bangui, C.A.R. ... 96 D3 4 23N 18 35 E
Bangweulu, L., Zambia ... 96 G6 11 0S 30 0 E
Bangweulu Swamp, Zambia ... 90 H7 11 20S 30 15 E
Banham, U.K. ... 25 B11 52 27N 1 2 E
Bani, Dom. Rep. ... 115 D10 18 16N 70 22W
Banja Luka, Bos.-H. ... 70 B7 44 49N 17 11 E
Banjarmasin, Indonesia ... 83 D3 3 20S 114 35 E
Banjul, Gambia ... 94 F2 13 28N 16 40W
Bankend, U.K. ... 22 B1 55 1N 3 33W
Banks I., Canada ... 108 A7 73 15N 121 30W
Banks Is., Vanuatu ... 99 C12 13 50S 167 30 E
Bann →, U.K. ... 29 A8 55 8N 6 41W
Bannockburn, U.K. ... 21 B8 56 5N 3 55W
Bannu, Pakistan ... 84 C7 33 0N 70 18 E
Banská Bystrica, Slovak Rep. ... 67 D10 48 46N 19 14 E
Bantry, Ireland ... 30 E4 51 41N 9 27W
Bantry B., Ireland ... 30 E3 51 37N 9 44W
Banwell, U.K. ... 24 D3 51 19N 2 52W
Banyak, Kepulauan, Indonesia ... 83 C1 2 10N 97 10 E
Banyuwangi, Indonesia ... 83 D3 8 13S 114 21 E
Baoding, China ... 81 C6 38 50N 115 28 E
Baoji, China ... 80 C5 34 20N 107 5 E
Baoshan, China ... 80 D4 25 10N 99 5 E
Baotou, China ... 81 B6 40 32N 110 2 E
Ba'qūbah, Iraq ... 86 C6 33 45N 44 50 E
Bar Harbor, U.S.A. ... 113 C13 44 23N 68 13W
Bar-le-Duc, France ... 68 B6 48 47N 5 10 E
Baracoa, Cuba ... 115 C10 20 20N 74 30W
Barahona, Dom. Rep. ... 115 D10 18 13N 71 7W
Barakaldo, Spain ... 69 A4 43 18N 2 59W
Baranavichy, Belarus ... 67 B14 53 10N 26 0 E
Baranof I., U.S.A. ... 108 C6 57 0N 135 0W
Barbacena, Brazil ... 122 D2 21 15S 43 56W
Barbados ■, W. Indies ... 115 g 13 10N 59 30W
Barberton, U.S.A. ... 112 E7 41 0N 81 39W
Barbonneau, St. Lucia ... 115 f 13 59N 60 58W
Barcelona, Spain ... 69 B7 41 21N 2 10 E
Barcelona, Venezuela ... 120 A3 10 10N 64 40W
Barceloneta, Puerto Rico ... 115 d 18 27N 66 32W
Barddhaman, India ... 85 H15 23 14N 87 39 E
Bardney, U.K. ... 23 F8 53 13N 0 19W
Bardsey I., U.K. ... 26 B4 52 45N 4 47W
Bardstown, U.S.A. ... 112 G5 37 49N 85 28W
Bareilly, India ... 84 E11 28 22N 79 27 E
Barents Sea, Arctic ... 54 B9 73 0N 39 0 E
Barford, U.K. ... 23 H5 52 16N 1 35W
Bargoed, U.K. ... 24 C2 51 42N 3 15W
Barham, U.K. ... 25 D11 51 12N 1 11 E
Barhi, India ... 85 G14 24 15N 85 25 E
Bari, Italy ... 70 D7 41 8N 16 51 E
Barim, Yemen ... 90 E8 12 39N 43 25 E
Baring, C., Canada ... 108 B8 70 0N 117 30W
Barisal, Bangla. ... 85 H17 22 45N 90 20 E
Barisal □, Bangla. ... 85 H17 22 40N 90 20 E
Barking and Dagenham □, U.K. ... 25 C9 51 32N 0 10 E
Barkly Tableland, Australia ... 98 D6 17 50S 136 40 E
Barlborough, U.K. ... 23 F6 53 17N 1 17W
Barlby, U.K. ... 23 E6 53 48N 1 2W
Barlee, L., Australia ... 98 F2 29 15S 119 30 E
Barletta, Italy ... 70 D7 41 19N 16 17 E
Barmby Moor, U.K. ... 23 E7 53 56N 0 49W
Barmer, India ... 84 G7 25 45N 71 20 E
Barmoor Castle, U.K. ... 22 A5 55 39N 1 59W
Barmouth, U.K. ... 26 B5 52 44N 4 4W
Barnard Castle, U.K. ... 22 C5 54 33N 1 55W
Barnaul, Russia ... 79 D10 53 20N 83 40 E
Barnby le Wold, U.K. ... 23 E8 53 34N 0 24W
Barnoldswick, U.K. ... 23 E4 53 55N 2 11W
Barnsley, U.K. ... 23 E6 53 34N 1 27W
Barnstaple, U.K. ... 27 E5 51 5N 4 4W
Barotseland, Zambia ... 97 H4 15 0S 24 0 E
Barques, Pt. Aux, U.S.A. ... 112 C6 44 4N 82 58W
Barquísimeto, Venezuela ... 120 A3 10 4N 69 19W
Barra, Brazil ... 122 B2 11 5S 43 10W
Barra, U.K. ... 18 J2 57 0N 7 29W
Barra, Sd. of, U.K. ... 18 H3 57 4N 7 25W
Barra do Pirai, Brazil ... 122 D2 22 30S 43 50W
Barra Hd., U.K. ... 18 J2 56 47N 7 40W
Barra Mansa, Brazil ... 122 D2 22 35S 44 12W
Barrancabermeja, Colombia ... 120 B2 7 0N 73 50W
Barranquilla, Colombia ... 120 A2 11 0N 74 50W
Barre, U.S.A. ... 113 C11 44 12N 72 30W
Barreiras, Brazil ... 122 B2 12 8S 45 0W
Barretos, Brazil ... 122 D1 20 30S 48 35W
Barrie, Canada ... 109 D12 44 24N 79 40W
Barrow, U.S.A. ... 108 A4 71 18N 156 47W
Barrow →, Ireland ... 31 D9 52 25N 6 58W
Barrow-in-Furness, U.K. ... 22 D2 54 7N 3 14W
Barrow upon Humber, U.K. ... 23 E8 53 41N 0 23W
Barrowford, U.K. ... 23 E4 53 51N 2 14W
Barry, U.K. ... 24 D2 51 24N 3 16W
Barry's Bay, Canada ... 112 C9 45 29N 77 41W
Barstow, U.S.A. ... 110 D3 34 54N 117 1W
Bartlesville, U.S.A. ... 111 C7 36 45N 95 59W
Barton, U.K. ... 22 D5 54 29N 1 38W
Barton upon Humber, U.K. ... 23 E8 53 41N 0 25W
Barwell, U.K. ... 23 G6 52 35N 1 21W
Barysaw, Belarus ... 67 A15 54 17N 28 28 E
Bashi Channel, Phil. ... 83 A4 21 15N 122 0 E
Bashkortostan □, Russia ... 72 D10 54 0N 57 0 E
Basildon, U.K. ... 25 C9 51 34N 0 28 E
Basingstoke, U.K. ... 24 D6 51 15N 1 5W
Baskatong, Rés., Canada ... 113 B10 46 46N 75 50W
Basle, Switz. ... 66 E4 47 35N 7 35 E
Basque Provinces = País Vasco □, Spain ... 69 A4 42 50N 2 45W
Basra, Iraq ... 86 D6 30 30N 47 50 E
Bass Str., Australia ... 98 H8 39 15S 146 30 E
Bassas da India, Ind. Oc. ... 97 J7 22 0S 39 0 E
Basse-Pointe, Martinique ... 114 c 14 52N 61 8W
Basse-Terre, Guadeloupe ... 114 b 16 0N 61 44W
Bassein, Burma ... 85 L19 16 45N 94 30 E
Bassenthwaite L., U.K. ... 22 C2 54 40N 3 14W
Basses, Pte. des, Guadeloupe ... 114 b 15 52N 61 17W
Basseterre, St. Kitts & Nevis ... 115 D12 17 17N 62 43W
Basti, India ... 85 F13 26 52N 82 55 E
Bastia, France ... 68 E8 42 40N 9 30 E
Baston, U.K. ... 23 G8 52 43N 0 21W
Batabanó, G. de, Cuba ... 115 C8 22 30N 82 30W
Batangas, Phil. ... 83 B4 13 35N 121 10 E
Batavia, U.S.A. ... 112 D8 43 0N 78 11W

Batdambang, Cambodia ... 83 B2 13 7N 103 12 E
Bath, U.K. ... 24 D4 51 23N 2 22W
Bath, Maine, U.S.A. ... 113 D13 43 55N 69 49W
Bath, N.Y., U.S.A. ... 112 D9 42 20N 77 19W
Bathford, U.K. ... 24 D4 51 24N 2 18W
Bathurst, Australia ... 98 G8 33 25S 149 31 E
Bathurst, Canada ... 109 D13 47 37N 65 43W
Bathurst, C., Canada ... 108 A7 70 34N 128 0W
Bathurst Inlet, Canada ... 108 B9 66 50N 108 1W
Batley, U.K. ... 23 E5 53 43N 1 38W
Batman, Turkey ... 73 G7 37 55N 41 5 E
Batna, Algeria ... 94 A7 35 34N 6 15 E
Baton Rouge, U.S.A. ... 111 D8 30 27N 91 11W
Batticaloa, Sri Lanka ... 84 R12 7 43N 81 45 E
Battle, U.K. ... 25 E9 50 55N 0 30 E
Battle →, Canada ... 108 C9 52 43N 108 15W
Battle Creek, U.S.A. ... 112 D5 42 19N 85 11W
Batu, Kepulauan, Indonesia ... 83 D1 0 30S 98 25 E
Batu Pahat, Malaysia ... 83 C2 1 50N 102 56 E
Batumi, Georgia ... 73 F7 41 39N 41 44 E
Baturité, Brazil ... 120 C6 4 28S 38 45W
Bauld, C., Canada ... 109 C14 51 38N 55 26W
Bauru, Brazil ... 122 D1 22 10S 49 0W
Bavaria = Bayern □, Germany ... 66 D6 48 50N 12 0 E
Bawdsey, U.K. ... 25 B11 52 1N 1 27 E
Bawtry, U.K. ... 23 F6 53 26N 1 2W
Bay City, U.S.A. ... 112 D6 43 36N 83 54W
Bayamo, Cuba ... 115 C9 20 20N 76 40W
Bayamón, Puerto Rico ... 115 d 18 24N 66 10W
Bayan Har Shan, China ... 80 C4 34 0N 98 0 E
Bayanhongor, Mongolia ... 80 B5 46 8N 102 43 E
Bayern □, Germany ... 66 D6 48 50N 12 0 E
Bayeux, France ... 68 B3 49 17N 0 42W
Bayonne, France ... 68 E3 43 30N 1 28W
Bayswater, U.K. ... 24 C3 51 37N 2 39W
Beachley, U.K. ... 25 E9 50 44N 0 15 E
Beachy Hd., U.K. ... 25 E9 50 44N 0 15 E
Beacon, U.S.A. ... 113 E11 41 30N 73 58W
Beaconsfield, U.K. ... 25 C7 51 36N 0 38W
Beadnell, U.K. ... 22 A5 55 33N 1 38W
Beagle, Canal, S. Amer. ... 121 H3 55 0S 68 30W
Beaminster, U.K. ... 24 E3 50 48N 2 44W
Bear →, U.S.A. ... 110 B4 41 30N 112 8W
Bear, I., Ireland ... 30 E3 51 38N 9 50W
Bear L., U.S.A. ... 110 B4 41 59N 111 21W
Beardmore Glacier, Antarctica ... 55 E11 84 30S 170 0 E
Béarn, France ... 68 E3 43 20N 0 30W
Bearsted, U.K. ... 25 D10 51 16N 0 35 E
Beatrice, U.S.A. ... 111 B7 40 16N 96 45W
Beattock, U.K. ... 22 B2 55 20N 3 28W
Beauce, Plaine de la, France ... 68 B4 48 10N 1 45 E
Beaufort Sea, Arctic ... 54 B1 72 0N 140 0W
Beaufort West, S. Africa ... 97 L4 32 18S 22 36 E
Beauharnois, Canada ... 113 C11 45 20N 73 52W
Beaulieu, Canada ... 24 E6 50 48N 1 27W
Beauly, U.K. ... 19 H9 57 30N 4 28W
Beauly →, U.K. ... 19 H9 57 29N 4 27W
Beaumaris, U.K. ... 26 A5 53 16N 4 6W
Beaumont, U.S.A. ... 111 D8 30 5N 94 6W
Beaune, France ... 68 C6 47 2N 4 50 E
Beauvais, France ... 68 B5 49 25N 2 8 E
Beaver →, Canada ... 108 C9 55 26N 107 45W
Beaver Creek, Canada ... 108 B5 63 0N 141 0W
Beaver Falls, U.S.A. ... 112 E7 40 46N 80 20W
Beaver I., U.S.A. ... 112 C5 45 40N 85 33W
Beawar, India ... 84 F9 26 3N 74 18 E
Bebedouro, Brazil ... 122 D1 21 0S 48 25W
Bebington, U.K. ... 23 F3 53 22N 3 0W
Beccles, U.K. ... 25 B12 52 27N 1 35 E
Béchar, Algeria ... 94 B5 31 38N 2 18W
Beckermet, U.K. ... 22 D1 54 27N 3 30W
Beckfoot, U.K. ... 22 C2 54 50N 3 24W
Beckingham, U.K. ... 23 F7 53 24N 0 50W
Beckley, U.S.A. ... 112 G7 37 47N 81 11W
Bedale, U.K. ... 22 D5 54 18N 1 36W
Beddgelert, U.K. ... 26 A5 53 1N 4 6W
Bedford, U.K. ... 25 B8 52 8N 0 28W
Bedford, Ind., U.S.A. ... 112 F4 38 52N 86 29W
Bedford, Va., U.S.A. ... 112 G8 37 20N 79 31W
Bedford Level, U.K. ... 23 G8 52 32N 0 7W
Bedfordshire □, U.K. ... 25 B8 52 4N 0 28W
Bedlington, U.K. ... 22 B5 55 8N 1 35W
Bedworth, U.K. ... 23 H6 52 29N 1 28W
Beef I., Br. Virgin Is. ... 115 e 18 26N 64 30W
Beeford, U.K. ... 23 E8 53 58N 0 17W
Beer, U.K. ... 24 E2 50 41N 3 6W
Be'er Sheva, Israel ... 86 D3 31 15N 34 48 E
Beeston, U.K. ... 23 G6 52 56N 1 14W
Bei Jiang →, China ... 81 D6 23 2N 112 58 E
Bei'an, China ... 81 B7 48 10N 126 20 E
Beighton, U.K. ... 23 F6 53 21N 1 20W
Beihai, China ... 81 D5 21 28N 109 6 E
Beijing, China ... 81 C6 39 55N 116 20 E
Beira, Mozam. ... 97 H6 19 50S 34 52 E
Beirut, Lebanon ... 86 C3 33 53N 35 31 E
Beitbridge, Zimbabwe ... 97 J6 22 12S 30 0 E
Béja, Tunisia ... 95 A7 36 43N 9 12 E
Bejaïa, Algeria ... 94 A7 36 42N 5 2 E
Békéscsaba, Hungary ... 67 E11 46 40N 21 5 E
Bela, Pakistan ... 84 F5 26 12N 66 20 E
Belarus ■, Europe ... 67 B14 53 30N 27 0 E
Belau = Palau ■, Pac. Oc. ... 102 G5 7 30N 134 30 E
Belbroughton, U.K. ... 23 H4 52 24N 2 7W
Belcher Is., Canada ... 109 C12 56 15N 78 45W
Belém, Brazil ... 120 C5 1 20S 48 30W
Belep, Is., N. Cal. ... 99 D11 19 45S 163 40 E
Belet Uen, Somali Rep. ... 88 G4 4 30N 45 5 E
Belfast, U.K. ... 29 B10 54 37N 5 56W
Belfast L., U.K. ... 29 B10 54 40N 5 50W
Belford, U.K. ... 22 A5 55 36N 1 49W
Belfort, France ... 68 C7 47 38N 6 50 E
Belgaum, India ... 84 M9 15 55N 74 35 E
Belgium ■, Europe ... 65 D4 50 30N 5 0 E
Belgorod, Russia ... 73 D6 50 35N 36 35 E
Belgrade, Serbia & M. ... 71 B9 44 50N 20 37 E
Belitung, Indonesia ... 83 D2 3 10S 107 50 E
Belize ■, Cent. Amer. ... 114 D7 17 0N 88 30W
Belize City, Belize ... 114 D7 17 25N 88 0W
Bell Peninsula, Canada ... 109 B11 63 50N 82 0W
Bell Ville, Argentina ... 121 F3 32 40S 62 40W
Bella Coola, Canada ... 108 C7 52 25N 126 40W
Bellaire, U.S.A. ... 112 E7 40 1N 80 45W
Bellary, India ... 84 M10 15 10N 76 56 E
Belle Fourche →, U.S.A. ... 110 B6 44 26N 102 18W
Belle-Île, France ... 68 C2 47 20N 3 10W
Belle Isle, Canada ... 109 C14 51 57N 55 25W
Belle Isle, Str. of, Canada ... 109 C14 51 30N 56 30W
Bellefontaine, U.S.A. ... 112 E6 40 22N 83 46W
Belleplaine, Barbados ... 115 g 13 15N 59 34W
Belleville, Canada ... 109 D12 44 10N 77 23W
Belleville, U.S.A. ... 112 F4 38 31N 89 59W
Bellingham, U.K. ... 22 B4 55 9N 2 16W
Bellingham, U.S.A. ... 110 A2 48 46N 122 29W
Bellingshausen Sea, Antarctica ... 55 C17 66 0S 80 0W
Bellinzona, Switz. ... 66 E5 46 11N 9 1 E
Belmonte, Brazil ... 122 C3 16 0S 39 0W
Belmopan, Belize ... 114 D7 17 18N 88 30W

Belmullet, Ireland ... 28 C2 54 14N 9 58W
Belo Horizonte, Brazil ... 122 C2 19 55S 43 56W
Belomorsk, Russia ... 72 B5 64 35N 34 54 E
Beloretsk, Russia ... 72 D10 53 58N 58 24 E
Beloye, L., Russia ... 72 B6 60 10N 37 35 E
Belper, U.K. ... 23 F6 53 2N 1 29W
Belsay, U.K. ... 22 B5 55 6N 1 51W
Belton, N. Lincs., U.K. ... 23 E7 53 33N 0 48W
Belton, Norfolk, U.K. ... 25 A12 52 35N 1 40 E
Belturbet, Ireland ... 28 C7 54 6N 7 26W
Bembridge, U.K. ... 24 E6 50 41N 1 5W
Bemidji, U.S.A. ... 111 A8 47 28N 94 53W
Ben Cruachan, U.K. ... 20 B5 56 26N 5 8W
Ben Dearg, U.K. ... 19 G8 57 47N 4 56W
Ben Hope, U.K. ... 19 F8 58 25N 4 36W
Ben Lawers, U.K. ... 20 A7 56 32N 4 14W
Ben Lomond, U.K. ... 20 B6 56 11N 4 38W
Ben Macdhui, U.K. ... 19 H10 57 4N 3 40W
Ben Mhor, U.K. ... 18 H3 57 15N 7 18W
Ben More, Arg. & Bute, U.K. ... 20 B3 56 26N 6 1W
Ben More, Stirl., U.K. ... 20 B6 56 23N 4 32W
Ben More Assynt, U.K. ... 19 F8 58 8N 4 52W
Ben Nevis, U.K. ... 18 J7 56 48N 5 1W
Ben Vorlich, U.K. ... 20 B7 56 21N 4 14W
Ben Wyvis, U.K. ... 19 G8 57 40N 4 35W
Benares = Varanasi, India ... 85 G13 25 22N 83 0 E
Benbecula, U.K. ... 18 H3 57 26N 7 21W
Bend, U.S.A. ... 110 B2 44 4N 121 19W
Bendigo, Australia ... 98 H7 36 40S 144 15 E
Benevento, Italy ... 70 D6 41 8N 14 45 E
Bengal, Bay of, Ind. Oc. ... 85 M17 15 0N 90 0 E
Bengbu, China ... 81 C6 32 58N 117 20 E
Benghazi, Libya ... 95 B10 32 11N 20 3 E
Bengkulu, Indonesia ... 83 D2 3 50S 102 12 E
Benguela, Angola ... 97 G2 12 37S 13 25 E
Beni →, Bolivia ... 120 D3 10 23S 65 24W
Beni Mellal, Morocco ... 94 B4 32 21N 6 21W
Beni Suef, Egypt ... 95 C12 29 5N 31 6 E
Benidorm, Spain ... 69 C5 38 33N 0 9W
Benin ■, Africa ... 94 G6 10 0N 2 0 E
Benin, Bight of, W. Afr. ... 94 H6 5 0N 3 0 E
Benin City, Nigeria ... 94 G7 6 20N 5 31 E
Benington, U.K. ... 23 F9 53 0N 0 5 E
Benjamin Constant, Brazil ... 120 C2 4 40S 70 15W
Benoni, S. Africa ... 97 K5 26 11S 28 18 E
Benson, U.K. ... 24 C6 51 37N 1 6W
Bentley, Hants., U.K. ... 25 D7 51 12N 0 52W
Bentley, S. Yorks., U.K. ... 23 E6 53 33N 1 9W
Benton Harbor, U.S.A. ... 112 D4 42 6N 86 27W
Benue →, Nigeria ... 94 G7 7 48N 6 46 E
Benxi, China ... 81 B7 41 20N 123 48 E
Beppu, Japan ... 82 G2 33 15N 131 30 E
Berbera, Somali Rep. ... 88 E4 10 30N 45 2 E
Berbérati, C.A.R. ... 96 D3 4 15N 15 40 E
Berbice →, Guyana ... 120 B4 6 20N 57 32W
Berdyansk, Ukraine ... 73 E6 46 45N 36 50 E
Berdychiv, Ukraine ... 73 E4 49 57N 28 30 E
Bere Alston, U.K. ... 27 G5 50 29N 4 13W
Bere Regis, U.K. ... 24 E4 50 45N 2 14W
Berea, U.S.A. ... 112 G5 37 34N 84 17W
Berens →, Canada ... 108 C10 52 25N 97 2W
Berezina →, Belarus ... 72 D5 52 33N 30 14 E
Bereznik, Russia ... 72 B7 62 51N 42 40 E
Berezniki, Russia ... 72 C10 59 24N 56 46 E
Bérgamo, Italy ... 68 D8 45 41N 9 43 E
Bergen, Norway ... 63 E5 60 20N 5 20 E
Bergen op Zoom, Neths. ... 65 C4 51 28N 4 18 E
Bergerac, France ... 68 D4 44 51N 0 30 E
Bergisch Gladbach, Germany ... 65 D7 50 59N 7 8 E
Bering Sea, Pac. Oc. ... 102 B10 58 0N 171 0 E
Bering Strait, Pac. Oc. ... 108 B3 65 30N 169 0W
Berkeley, U.S.A. ... 24 C4 51 41N 2 27W
Berkhamsted, U.K. ... 25 C7 51 46N 0 33W
Berkner I., Antarctica ... 55 D18 79 30S 50 0W
Berkshire Downs, U.K. ... 24 C6 51 33N 1 29W
Berlin, Germany ... 66 B7 52 30N 13 25 E
Berlin, U.S.A. ... 113 C12 44 28N 71 11W
Bermejo →, Argentina ... 121 E4 26 51S 58 23W
Bermuda ☐, Atl. Oc. ... 52 C6 32 45N 65 0W
Bern, Switz. ... 66 E4 46 57N 7 28 E
Berneray, U.K. ... 18 H3 57 43N 7 11W
Berry, France ... 68 C5 46 50N 2 0 E
Berry Hd., U.K. ... 27 G7 50 24N 3 29W
Bertraghboy B., Ireland ... 28 E2 53 22N 9 54W
Berwick, U.S.A. ... 112 E9 41 3N 76 14W
Berwyn Mts., U.K. ... 23 G2 52 54N 3 26W
Besançon, France ... 68 C7 47 15N 6 2 E
Bessarabiya, Moldova ... 73 E4 47 0N 28 10 E
Bethel, U.S.A. ... 108 B3 60 48N 161 45W
Bethesda, U.K. ... 26 A5 53 10N 4 3W
Bethlehem, S. Africa ... 97 K5 28 14S 28 18 E
Bethlehem, U.S.A. ... 113 E10 40 37N 75 23W
Béthune, France ... 68 A5 50 30N 2 38 E
Bettiah, India ... 85 F14 26 48N 84 33 E
Betul, India ... 84 J10 21 58N 77 59 E
Betws-y-Coed, U.K. ... 26 A6 53 5N 3 48W
Beverley, U.K. ... 23 E8 53 51N 0 26W
Beverly, U.S.A. ... 113 D12 42 33N 70 53W
Bewdley, U.K. ... 23 H4 52 23N 2 19W
Bexhill, U.K. ... 25 E9 50 51N 0 29 E
Bexley □, U.K. ... 25 D9 51 27N 0 9 E
Beyneu, Kazakhstan ... 73 E10 45 18N 55 9 E
Beypazarı, Turkey ... 73 F5 40 10N 31 56 E
Beyşehir Gölü, Turkey ... 73 G5 37 41N 31 33 E
Béziers, France ... 68 E5 43 20N 3 12 E
Bhagalpur, India ... 85 G15 25 10N 87 0 E
Bharatpur, India ... 84 F10 27 15N 77 30 E
Bharuch, India ... 84 J8 21 47N 73 0 E
Bhatpara, India ... 85 H16 22 50N 88 25 E
Bhavnagar, India ... 84 J8 21 45N 72 10 E
Bhilwara, India ... 84 G9 25 25N 74 38 E
Bhima →, India ... 84 L10 16 25N 77 17 E
Bhiwandi, India ... 84 K8 19 20N 73 0 E
Bhiwani, India ... 84 E10 28 50N 76 9 E
Bhopal, India ... 84 H10 23 20N 77 30 E
Bhubaneshwar, India ... 85 J14 20 15N 85 50 E
Bhuj, India ... 84 H6 23 15N 69 49 E
Bhusawal, India ... 84 J9 21 3N 75 46 E
Bhutan ■, Asia ... 85 F17 27 25N 90 30 E
Biała Podlaska, Poland ... 67 B12 52 4N 23 6 E
Białystok, Poland ... 67 B12 53 10N 23 10 E
Biarritz, France ... 68 E3 43 29N 1 33W
Bibury, U.K. ... 24 C5 51 45N 1 49W
Bicester, U.K. ... 24 C6 51 54N 1 9W
Bicton, U.K. ... 23 G3 52 44N 2 48W
Biddeford, U.S.A. ... 113 D12 43 30N 70 28W
Biddulph, U.K. ... 23 F4 53 7N 2 10W
Bideford, U.K. ... 27 E5 51 1N 4 13W
Bideford Bay, U.K. ... 27 E5 51 5N 4 20W
Bidford-on-Avon, U.K. ... 24 B5 52 11N 1 50W
Bié, Planalto de, Angola ... 97 G3 12 0S 16 0 E
Biel, Switz. ... 66 E4 47 8N 7 14 E
Bielefeld, Germany ... 66 B5 52 1N 8 33 E
Bielsko-Biała, Poland ... 67 D10 49 50N 19 2 E
Bien Hoa, Vietnam ... 83 B2 10 57N 106 49 E
Bienville, L., Canada ... 109 C12 55 5N 72 40W

**Big Belt Mts.**                                                                                          **Burns**

Big Belt Mts., U.S.A. 110 A4 46 30N 111 25W
Big Rapids, U.S.A. 112 D5 43 42N 85 29W
Big Sioux →, U.S.A. 111 B7 42 29N 96 27W
Big Spring, U.S.A. 110 D6 32 15N 101 28W
Big Trout L., Canada 109 C11 53 40N 90 0W
Bigbury, U.K. 27 G6 50 18N 3 53W
Bigbury B., U.K. 27 G6 50 16N 3 54W
Biggar, Canada 108 C9 52 4N 108 0W
Biggar, U.K. 21 C8 55 38N 3 32W
Biggleswade, U.K. 25 B8 52 5N 0 14W
Bighorn →, U.S.A. 110 A5 46 10N 107 28W
Bighorn Mts., U.S.A. 110 B5 44 30N 107 30W
Bihar, India 85 G14 25 5N 85 40 E
Bihar □, India 85 G15 25 0N 86 0 E
Bijagós, Arquipélago dos, Guinea-Biss. 94 F2 11 15N 16 10W
Bikaner, India 84 E8 28 2N 73 18 E
Bikini Atoll, Marshall Is. 102 F8 12 0N 167 30 E
Bila Tserkva, Ukraine 67 D16 49 45N 30 10 E
Bilaspur, India 85 H13 22 2N 82 15 E
Bilbao, Spain 69 A4 43 16N 2 56W
Bilecik, Turkey 73 F5 40 5N 30 5 E
Bilhorod-Dnistrovskyy, Ukraine 67 E16 46 11N 30 23 E
Billericay, U.K. 25 C9 51 38N 0 25 E
Billesdon, U.K. 23 G7 52 38N 0 54W
Billingham, U.K. 22 C6 54 36N 1 17W
Billinghay, U.K. 23 F8 53 5N 0 15W
Billings, U.S.A. 110 A5 45 47N 108 30W
Billingshurst, U.K. 25 D8 51 2N 0 27W
Bilma, Niger 95 E8 18 50N 13 30 E
Biloxi, U.S.A. 111 D9 30 24N 88 53W
Bilston, U.K. 23 G4 52 34N 2 4W
Bimini Is., Bahamas 115 B9 25 42N 79 25W
Binbrook, U.K. 23 F8 53 26N 0 10W
Bingham, U.K. 23 G7 52 57N 0 58W
Binghamton, U.S.A. 113 D10 42 6N 75 55W
Bingley, U.K. 23 E5 53 51N 1 50W
Bioko, Eq. Guin. 96 D1 3 30N 8 40 E
Biratnagar, Nepal 85 F15 26 27N 87 17 E
Birchington, U.K. 25 D11 51 22N 1 19 E
Birdlip, U.K. 24 C4 51 50N 2 5W
Birkdale, U.K. 23 E2 53 38N 3 1W
Birkenhead, U.K. 23 F2 53 23N 3 2W
Birmingham, U.K. 23 H5 52 29N 1 52W
Birmingham, U.S.A. 111 D9 33 31N 86 48W
Birr, Ireland 30 B7 53 6N 7 54W
Birtley, Northumberland, U.K. 22 B4 55 6N 2 12W
Birtley, Tyne & W., U.K. 22 C5 54 54N 1 34W
Biscay, B. of, Atl. Oc. 68 D1 45 0N 2 0W
Bishkek, Kyrgyzstan 79 E9 42 54N 74 46 E
Bishop Auckland, U.K. 22 C5 54 39N 1 40W
Bishop's Castle, U.K. 23 H3 52 30N 2 59W
Bishop's Cleeve, U.K. 24 C4 51 57N 2 3W
Bishop's Frome, U.K. 24 B4 52 8N 2 29W
Bishop's Nympton, U.K. 24 E1 51 0N 3 47W
Bishop's Stortford, U.K. 25 C9 51 52N 0 10 E
Bishop's Waltham, U.K. 24 E6 50 57N 1 11W
Bishopsteignton, U.K. 27 F6 50 33N 3 33W
Bishopstoke, U.K. 24 E6 50 58N 1 19W
Biskra, Algeria 94 B7 34 50N 5 44 E
Bismarck, U.S.A. 110 A6 46 48N 100 47W
Bismarck Arch., Papua N. G. 98 A9 2 30S 150 0 E
Bissau, Guinea-Biss. 94 F2 11 45N 15 45W
Bitola, Macedonia 71 D9 41 1N 21 20 E
Bitterfontein, S. Africa 97 L3 31 1S 18 32 E
Bitterroot Range, U.S.A. 110 A4 46 0N 114 20W
Bitton, U.K. 24 D4 51 25N 2 27W
Biwa-Ko, Japan 82 F5 35 15N 136 10 E
Bizerte, Tunisia 95 A7 37 15N 9 50 E
Blaby, U.K. 23 G6 52 35N 1 10W
Black Combe, U.K. 22 D2 54 16N 3 20W
Black Esk →, U.K. 22 B2 55 12N 3 11W
Black Forest = Schwarzwald, Germany 66 D5 48 30N 8 20 E
Black Hd., Ireland 30 B4 53 9N 9 16W
Black Hd., U.K. 27 H3 50 0N 5 7W
Black Hills, U.S.A. 110 B6 44 0N 103 45W
Black Mts., U.K. 24 C2 51 55N 3 7W
Black Range, U.S.A. 110 D5 33 15N 107 50W
Black River, Jamaica 114 a 18 0N 77 50W
Black Rock, Barbados 115 g 13 7N 59 37W
Black Sea, Eurasia 73 F6 43 30N 35 0 E
Blackburn, U.K. 23 E4 53 45N 2 29W
Blackdown Hills, U.K. 24 E2 50 57N 3 15W
Blackmoor Vale, U.K. 24 E4 50 54N 2 28W
Blackpool, U.K. 23 E2 53 49N 3 3W
Blacksburg, U.S.A. 112 G7 37 14N 80 25W
Blacksod B., Ireland 28 C1 54 6N 10 0W
Blackwater →, Meath, Ireland 29 D8 53 39N 6 41W
Blackwater →, Waterford, Ireland 30 D7 52 4N 7 52W
Blackwater →, Arm., U.K. 29 B8 54 31N 6 35W
Blackwater →, Essex, U.K. 25 C10 51 44N 0 53 E
Blaenau Ffestiniog, U.K. 26 B6 53 0N 3 56W
Blaenavon, U.K. 24 C2 51 46N 3 5W
Blagdon, U.K. 24 D3 51 20N 2 43W
Blagoveshchensk, Russia 79 D14 50 20N 127 30 E
Blair Atholl, U.K. 19 J10 56 46N 3 50W
Blairgowrie, U.K. 21 A9 56 35N 3 21W
Blakeney, Gloucs., U.K. 24 C4 51 46N 2 28W
Blakeney, Norfolk, U.K. 25 A11 52 58N 1 1 E
Blanc, Mont, Alps 68 D7 45 48N 6 50 E
Blanca, B., Argentina 121 F3 39 10S 61 30W
Blanca Peak, U.S.A. 110 C5 37 35N 105 29W
Blanco, C., U.S.A. 110 B2 42 51N 124 34W
Blandford Forum, U.K. 24 E4 50 51N 2 9W
Blanquilla, I., Venezuela 115 E12 11 51N 64 37W
Blantyre, Malawi 97 H6 15 45S 35 0 E
Blarney, Ireland 30 E5 51 56N 8 33W
Blaydon, U.K. 22 C5 54 58N 1 42W
Blean, U.K. 25 D11 51 18N 1 3 E
Bleasdale Moors, U.K. 23 E3 53 55N 2 35W
Blenheim, N.Z. 99 J13 41 38S 173 57 E
Bletchingdon, U.K. 24 C6 51 51N 1 15W
Bletchley, U.K. 25 C7 51 59N 0 44W
Blida, Algeria 94 A6 36 30N 2 49 E
Blisworth, U.K. 25 B7 52 10N 0 56W
Blockley, U.K. 24 B5 52 1N 1 46W
Bloemfontein, S. Africa 97 K5 29 6S 26 7 E
Blofield, U.K. 25 A11 52 38N 1 26 E
Blois, France 68 C4 47 35N 1 20 E
Bloody Foreland, Ireland 28 A5 55 10N 8 17W
Bloomington, Ill., U.S.A. 111 B9 40 28N 89 0W
Bloomington, Ind., U.S.A. 112 F4 39 10N 86 32W
Bloomsburg, U.S.A. 112 E9 41 0N 76 27W
Bloxham, U.K. 24 B6 52 1N 1 21W
Blue Mountain Pk., Jamaica 114 a 18 3N 76 36W
Blue Mts., Jamaica 114 a 18 3N 76 36W
Blue Mts., Oreg., U.S.A. 110 A3 45 15N 119 0W
Blue Mts., Pa., U.S.A. 112 E9 40 30N 76 30W
Blue Nile →, Sudan 95 E12 15 38N 32 31 E
Blue Ridge Mts., U.S.A. 111 C10 36 30N 80 15W
Bluefield, U.S.A. 112 G7 37 15N 81 17W
Bluefields, Nic. 115 E8 12 20N 83 50W
Blumenau, Brazil 121 E5 27 0S 49 0W
Blundeston, U.K. 25 A12 52 31N 1 42 E
Blyth, Northumberland, U.K. 22 B5 55 8N 1 31W

Blyth, Notts., U.K. 23 F6 53 22N 1 3W
Blyth →, U.K. 22 B5 55 8N 1 33W
Blyth Bridge, U.K. 22 A2 55 42N 3 22W
Blyton, U.K. 23 F7 53 27N 0 42W
Boa Vista, Brazil 120 B3 2 48N 60 30W
Bobcaygeon, Canada 112 C8 44 33N 78 33W
Bobo-Dioulasso, Burkina Faso 94 F5 11 8N 4 13W
Bôbr →, Poland 66 B8 52 4N 15 4 E
Bochum, Germany 66 C4 51 28N 7 13 E
Boddam, U.K. 18 C15 57 28N 1 47W
Boden, Sweden 63 D8 65 50N 21 42 E
Bodiam, U.K. 25 D10 51 0N 0 34 E
Bodinnick, U.K. 27 G4 50 20N 4 38W
Bodmin, U.K. 27 G4 50 28N 4 43W
Bodmin Moor, U.K. 27 F4 50 33N 4 36W
Bodø, Norway 63 D6 67 17N 14 24 E
Bodrog →, Hungary 67 D11 48 11N 21 22 E
Bodrum, Turkey 73 G4 37 3N 27 30 E
Bogalusa, U.S.A. 111 D9 30 47N 89 52W
Boggeragh Mts., Ireland 30 D5 52 2N 8 55W
Bognor Regis, U.K. 25 E7 50 47N 0 40W
Bogor, Indonesia 83 D2 6 36S 106 48 E
Bogotá, Colombia 120 B2 4 34N 74 0W
Bogra, Bangla. 85 G16 24 51N 89 22 E
Böhmerwald, Germany 66 D7 49 8N 13 14 E
Bohol Sea, Phil. 83 C4 9 0N 124 0 E
Boise, U.S.A. 110 B3 43 37N 116 13W
Bole, China 80 B3 45 11N 81 37 E
Bolivia ■, S. Amer. 120 D3 17 6S 64 0W
Bolivian Plateau, Bolivia 116 E4 17 0S 68 0W
Bollington, U.K. 23 F4 53 18N 2 6W
Bolney, U.K. 25 E8 50 59N 0 12W
Bologna, Italy 70 B4 44 29N 11 20 E
Bologoye, Russia 72 C5 57 55N 34 5 E
Bolsover, U.K. 23 F6 53 14N 1 16W
Bolt Head, U.K. 27 G6 50 12N 3 48W
Bolt Tail, U.K. 27 G6 50 14N 3 52W
Bolton, U.K. 23 E4 53 35N 2 26W
Bolton Abbey, U.K. 23 E5 53 59N 1 53W
Bolton by Bowland, U.K. 23 E4 53 56N 2 20W
Bolton le Sands, U.K. 22 D3 54 6N 2 48W
Bolu, Turkey 73 F5 40 45N 31 35 E
Bolvadin, Turkey 73 G5 38 45N 31 4 E
Bolzano, Italy 70 A4 46 31N 11 22 E
Bom Jesus da Lapa, Brazil 122 B2 13 15S 43 25W
Boma, Dem. Rep. of the Congo 96 F2 5 50S 13 4 E
Bombala, Australia 98 H8 36 56S 149 15 E
Bombay = Mumbai, India 84 K8 18 55N 72 50 E
Bon, C., Tunisia 90 C5 37 1N 11 2 E
Bonaire, Neth. Ant. 115 E11 12 10N 68 15W
Bonar Bridge, U.K. 19 G9 57 54N 4 20W
Bonavista, Canada 109 D14 48 40N 53 5W
Bonchester Bridge, U.K. 22 B3 55 24N 2 39W
Bonchurch, U.K. 24 E6 50 37N 1 11W
Bo'ness, U.K. 21 B8 56 1N 3 37W
Bongor, Chad 95 F9 10 35N 15 20 E
Bonifacio, France 68 F8 41 24N 9 10 E
Bonn, Germany 66 C4 50 46N 7 6 E
Bonnyrigg, U.K. 21 C9 55 53N 3 6W
Boonville, U.S.A. 112 F4 38 3N 87 16W
Boot, U.K. 22 D2 54 24N 3 13W
Boothia, Gulf of, Canada 109 A11 71 0N 90 0W
Boothia Pen., Canada 108 A10 71 0N 94 0W
Bootle, Cumb., U.K. 22 D2 54 18N 3 22W
Bootle, Mersey., U.K. 23 F2 53 28N 3 1W
Borås, Sweden 63 F6 57 43N 12 56 E
Borborema, Planalto da, Brazil 116 D7 7 0S 37 0W
Bordeaux, France 68 D3 44 50N 0 36W
Borden Pen., Canada 109 A11 73 0N 83 0W
Bordon, U.K. 25 D7 51 8N 0 52W
Borehamwood, U.K. 25 C8 51 40N 0 15W
Boreland, U.K. 22 B2 55 13N 3 17W
Borger, U.S.A. 110 C6 35 39N 101 24W
Borhoyn Tal, Mongolia 81 B6 43 50N 111 58 E
Borisoglebsk, Russia 73 D7 51 27N 42 5 E
Borkou, Chad 95 E9 18 15N 18 50 E
Borneo, E. Indies 83 C3 1 0N 115 0 E
Bornholm, Denmark 63 F7 55 10N 15 0 E
Boroughbridge, U.K. 22 D6 54 6N 1 24W
Borovichi, Russia 72 C5 58 25N 33 55 E
Borrowdale, U.K. 22 C2 54 31N 3 10W
Borth, U.K. 26 C5 52 29N 4 2W
Borüjerd, Iran 86 C7 33 55N 48 50 E
Bosaso, Somali Rep. 88 E4 11 12N 49 18 E
Bosbury, U.K. 24 B4 52 5N 2 26W
Boscastle, U.K. 27 F4 50 41N 4 42W
Boscobelle, Barbados 115 g 13 16N 59 34W
Bosham, U.K. 25 E7 50 49N 0 51W
Bosnia-Herzegovina ■, Europe 70 B7 44 0N 18 0 E
Bosporus, Turkey 71 D13 41 10N 29 10 E
Bossangoa, C.A.R. 96 C3 6 35N 17 30 E
Bosten Hu, China 80 B3 41 55N 87 40 E
Boston, U.K. 23 G8 52 59N 0 2W
Boston, U.S.A. 113 D12 42 22N 71 4W
Bothel, U.K. 22 C2 54 45N 3 15W
Bothnia, G. of, Europe 63 E8 63 0N 20 15 E
Botletle →, Botswana 97 J4 20 10S 23 15 E
Botoşani, Romania 67 E14 47 42N 26 41 E
Botswana ■, Africa 97 J4 22 0S 24 0 E
Bottesford, U.K. 23 G7 52 57N 0 47W
Bottrop, Germany 65 C6 51 31N 6 58 E
Botucatu, Brazil 122 D1 22 55S 48 30W
Bouaké, Ivory C. 94 G4 7 40N 5 2W
Bouar, C.A.R. 96 C3 6 0N 15 40 E
Bouârfa, Morocco 94 B5 32 32N 1 58W
Bougainville I., Papua N. G. 99 B10 6 0S 155 0 E
Bouillante, Guadeloupe 114 b 16 8N 61 46W
Boulder, U.S.A. 110 B5 40 1N 105 17W
Boulogne-sur-Mer, France 68 A4 50 42N 1 36 E
Bounty Is., Pac. Oc. 102 M9 48 0S 178 30 E
Bourbonnais, France 68 C5 46 28N 3 0 E
Bourg-en-Bresse, France 68 C6 46 13N 5 12 E
Bourges, France 68 C5 47 9N 2 25 E
Bourgogne, France 68 C6 47 0N 4 50 E
Bourke, Australia 98 G8 30 8S 145 55 E
Bourne, U.K. 23 G8 52 47N 0 22W
Bournemouth, U.K. 24 E5 50 43N 1 52W
Bourton-on-the-Water, U.K. 24 C5 51 52N 1 45W
Bouvet I., Antarctica 53 G10 54 26S 3 24 E
Bovey Tracey, U.K. 27 G6 50 36N 3 41W
Bow →, Canada 108 C8 49 57N 111 41W
Bowes, U.K. 22 C5 54 0N 2 0W
Bowland, Forest of, U.K. 23 E3 54 0N 2 30W
Bowling Green, Ky., U.S.A. 112 G4 36 59N 86 27W
Bowling Green, Ohio, U.S.A. 112 E6 41 23N 83 39W
Bowmore, U.K. 20 C3 55 45N 6 17W
Bowness-on-Solway, U.K. 22 C2 54 57N 3 12W
Bowness-on-Windermere, U.K. 22 D3 54 22N 2 55W
Box, U.K. 24 D4 51 25N 2 15W
Box Hill, U.K. 25 D8 51 15N 0 16W
Boyle, Ireland 28 D5 53 59N 8 18W
Boyne →, Ireland 29 D9 53 43N 6 15W
Boyoma, Chutes, Dem. Rep. of the Congo 90 F6 0 35N 25 23 E
Bozeat, U.K. 25 B7 52 14N 0 40W
Bozeman, U.S.A. 110 A4 45 41N 111 2W
Bozoum, C.A.R. 96 C3 6 25N 16 35 E

Bracadale, L., U.K. 18 H4 57 20N 6 30W
Bracebridge, Canada 112 C8 45 2N 79 19W
Bracebridge Heath, U.K. 23 F7 53 12N 0 32W
Brackley, U.K. 24 B6 52 2N 1 8W
Bracknell, U.K. 25 D7 51 25N 0 43W
Bradenton, U.S.A. 111 E10 27 30N 82 34W
Bradford, U.K. 23 E5 53 47N 1 45W
Bradford, U.S.A. 112 E8 41 58N 78 38W
Bradford on Avon, U.K. 24 D4 51 21N 2 14W
Brading, U.K. 24 E6 50 41N 1 8W
Bradwell-on-Sea, U.K. 25 C10 51 43N 0 56 E
Bradworthy, U.K. 27 F5 50 53N 4 24W
Braga, Portugal 69 B1 41 35N 8 25W
Bragança, Brazil 120 C5 1 0S 47 2W
Bragança Paulista, Brazil 122 D1 22 55S 46 32W
Brahmanbaria, Bangla. 85 H17 23 58N 91 15 E
Brahmapur, India 85 K14 19 15N 84 54 E
Brahmaputra →, Asia 85 H16 23 40N 90 35 E
Braich-y-pwll, U.K. 26 B4 52 47N 4 46W
Brăila, Romania 67 F14 45 19N 27 59 E
Brailsford, U.K. 23 G5 52 58N 1 35W
Brainerd, U.S.A. 111 A8 46 22N 94 12W
Braintree, U.K. 25 C10 51 53N 0 34 E
Bramford, U.K. 25 B11 52 4N 1 7 E
Brampton, Canada 112 D8 43 45N 79 45W
Brampton, Cambs., U.K. 23 H8 52 20N 0 14W
Brampton, Cumb., U.K. 22 C3 54 57N 2 44W
Brancaster, U.K. 25 A10 52 58N 0 38 E
Branco →, Brazil 120 C3 1 20S 61 50W
Brandenburg, Germany 66 B7 52 25N 12 33 E
Brandenburg □, Germany 66 B6 52 50N 13 0 E
Brandon, Canada 108 D10 49 50N 99 57W
Brandon, Durham, U.K. 22 C5 54 46N 1 37W
Brandon, Suffolk, U.K. 25 B10 52 27N 0 38 E
Brandon B., Ireland 30 D2 52 17N 10 8W
Brandon Mt., Ireland 30 D2 52 15N 10 15W
Branston, U.K. 23 F8 53 12N 0 27W
Brantford, Canada 112 D7 43 10N 80 15W
Bras d'Or L., Canada 113 C17 45 50N 60 50W
Brasília, Brazil 122 C1 15 47S 47 55W
Braşov, Romania 67 F13 45 38N 25 35 E
Bratislava, Slovak Rep. 67 D9 48 10N 17 7 E
Bratsk, Russia 79 D12 56 10N 101 30 E
Brattleboro, U.S.A. 113 D11 42 51N 72 34W
Braunschweig, Germany 66 B6 52 15N 10 31 E
Braunton, U.K. 27 E5 51 7N 4 10W
Bray, Ireland 31 B10 53 13N 6 7W
Bray, U.K. 25 D7 51 30N 0 41W
Brazil, U.S.A. 112 F4 39 32N 87 8W
Brazil ■, S. Amer. 120 D4 12 0S 50 0W
Brazilian Highlands, Brazil 116 E6 18 0S 46 30W
Brazos →, U.S.A. 111 E7 28 53N 95 23W
Brazzaville, Congo 96 E3 4 9S 15 12 E
Breage, U.K. 27 G3 50 6N 5 20W
Breamish →, U.K. 22 A4 55 35N 2 2W
Brechin, U.K. 19 J12 56 44N 2 39W
Breckland, U.K. 25 B10 52 30N 0 40 E
Brecon, U.K. 24 C1 51 57N 3 23W
Brecon Beacons, U.K. 24 C2 51 53N 3 26W
Breda, Neths. 65 C4 51 35N 4 45 E
Brede, U.K. 25 E10 50 56N 0 36 E
Bredon Hill, U.K. 24 B4 52 3N 2 2W
Bregenz, Austria 66 E5 47 30N 9 45 E
Breiðafjörður, Iceland 63 A1 65 15N 23 15W
Bremen, Germany 66 B5 53 4N 8 47 E
Bremerhaven, Germany 66 B5 53 33N 8 36 E
Bremerton, U.S.A. 110 A2 47 34N 122 38W
Brendon Hills, U.K. 24 D2 51 6N 3 25W
Brennerpass, Austria 66 E6 47 2N 11 30 E
Brent □, U.K. 25 C8 51 33N 0 16W
Brentwood, U.K. 25 C9 51 37N 0 19 E
Bréscia, Italy 68 D9 45 33N 10 15 E
Bressay, U.K. 18 B15 60 9N 1 6W
Brest, Belarus 67 B12 52 10N 23 40 E
Brest, France 68 B1 48 24N 4 31W
Bretagne, France 68 B2 48 10N 3 0W
Breton Sd., U.S.A. 111 E9 29 35N 89 15W
Brewer, U.S.A. 113 C13 44 48N 68 46W
Brewood, U.K. 23 G4 52 41N 2 9W
Briançon, France 68 D7 44 54N 6 39 E
Bridestowe, U.K. 27 F5 50 41N 4 7W
Bridge, U.K. 25 D11 51 15N 1 8 E
Bridgefield, Barbados 115 g 13 9N 59 36W
Bridgend, U.K. 24 C1 51 30N 3 34W
Bridgeport, U.S.A. 113 E11 41 11N 73 12W
Bridgeton, U.S.A. 113 F10 39 26N 75 14W
Bridgetown, Barbados 115 g 13 5N 59 30W
Bridgewater, Canada 109 D13 44 25N 64 31W
Bridgnorth, U.K. 23 G4 52 32N 2 25W
Bridgwater, U.K. 24 D3 51 8N 2 59W
Bridgwater B., U.K. 24 D2 51 15N 3 15W
Bridlington, U.K. 22 D8 54 5N 0 12W
Bridlington B., U.K. 22 D8 54 4N 0 10W
Bridport, U.K. 24 E3 50 44N 2 45W
Brierfield, U.K. 23 E4 53 49N 2 14W
Brierley Hill, U.K. 23 H4 52 29N 2 6W
Brigg, U.K. 23 E8 53 34N 0 28W
Brigham City, U.S.A. 110 B4 41 31N 112 1W
Brighouse, U.K. 23 E5 53 42N 1 46W
Brighstone, U.K. 24 E6 50 38N 1 23W
Brightlingsea, U.K. 25 C11 51 49N 1 2 E
Brighton, U.K. 25 E8 50 49N 0 7W
Brigstock, U.K. 23 H7 52 27N 0 36W
Brill, U.K. 24 C6 51 49N 1 1W
Brimfield, U.K. 23 H3 52 18N 2 41W
Brindisi, Italy 71 D7 40 39N 17 55 E
Brinklow, U.K. 23 H6 52 25N 1 22W
Brinkworth, U.K. 24 C5 51 33N 1 59W
Brisbane, Australia 98 F9 27 25S 153 2 E
Bristol, U.K. 24 D3 51 26N 2 35W
Bristol, U.S.A. 108 C4 58 0N 160 0W
Bristol B., U.S.A. 27 E5 51 18N 4 30W
Bristol Channel, U.K. 25 A11 52 51N 1 4 E
Briston, U.K. 25 A11 52 51N 1 4 E
British Columbia □, Canada 108 C7 55 0N 125 15W
British Isles, Europe 56 E5 54 0N 4 0W
British Virgin Is. ☑, W. Indies 115 e 18 30N 64 30W
Brittany = Bretagne, France 68 B2 48 10N 3 0W
Brive-la-Gaillarde, France 68 D4 45 10N 1 32 E
Brixham, U.K. 27 G6 50 23N 3 31W
Brixton, U.K. 27 H2 52 20N 0 54W
Brize Norton, U.K. 24 C5 51 46N 1 34W
Brno, Czech Rep. 67 D9 49 10N 16 35 E
Broad B., U.K. 18 F5 58 14N 6 18W
Broad Haven, Ireland 28 C5 51 1N 9 55W
Broad Law, U.K. 21 C9 55 30N 3 21W
Broad Sd., U.K. 27 H1 49 55N 6 20W
Broadclyst, U.K. 27 F7 50 46N 3 27W
Broadhembury, U.K. 24 E2 50 49N 3 18W
Broadstairs, U.K. 25 D11 51 21N 1 27 E
Broadway, U.K. 24 B5 52 2N 1 50W
Broadwindsor, U.K. 24 E3 50 48N 2 47W
Brochet, Canada 108 C9 57 53N 101 40W
Brocken, Germany 66 C6 51 47N 10 37 E
Brockenhurst, U.K. 24 E5 50 49N 1 34W

Brockville, Canada 113 C10 44 35N 75 41W
Brockworth, U.K. 24 C4 51 51N 2 9W
Brodeur Pen., Canada 109 A11 72 30N 88 10W
Brodick, U.K. 20 C5 55 35N 5 9W
Broken Hill, Australia 98 G7 31 58S 141 29 E
Bromfield, U.K. 23 H3 52 24N 2 45W
Bromham, U.K. 24 D4 51 23N 2 1W
Bromley □, U.K. 25 D9 51 24N 0 2 E
Brompton, U.K. 22 D6 54 21N 1 25W
Bromsgrove, U.K. 23 H4 52 21N 2 2W
Bromyard, U.K. 24 B4 52 11N 2 30W
Brookhaven, U.S.A. 111 D8 31 35N 90 26W
Brookings, U.S.A. 111 B7 44 19N 96 48W
Brooks, Canada 108 C8 50 35N 111 55W
Brooks Range, U.S.A. 108 B5 68 0N 152 0W
Broom, L., U.K. 18 G7 57 55N 5 15W
Broome, Australia 98 D3 18 0S 122 15 E
Broomhill, U.K. 22 B5 55 18N 1 36W
Brora, U.K. 19 F10 58 0N 3 52W
Brora →, U.K. 19 F10 58 0N 3 51W
Broseley, U.K. 23 G4 52 37N 2 29W
Brosna →, Ireland 30 B7 53 14N 7 58W
Brothertoft, U.K. 23 F8 53 0N 0 7W
Brotton, U.K. 22 C7 54 35N 0 56W
Brough, Cumb., U.K. 22 C4 54 32N 2 18W
Brough, E. Riding, U.K. 23 E7 53 44N 0 36W
Brough Hd., U.K. 19 D10 59 8N 3 20W
Broughton, Borders, U.K. 22 A2 55 37N 3 24W
Broughton, N. Lincs., U.K. 23 E7 53 34N 0 34W
Broughton, Northants., U.K. 23 H7 52 22N 0 46W
Broughton-in-Furness, U.K. 22 D2 54 17N 3 13W
Brown Willy, U.K. 23 G5 52 39N 1 54W
Brownhills, U.K. 23 G5 52 39N 1 54W
Brownsville, U.S.A. 111 E7 25 54N 97 30W
Brownwood, U.S.A. 110 D7 31 43N 98 59W
Bruay-la-Buissière, France 68 A5 50 29N 2 33 E
Bruce, Mt., Australia 98 E2 22 37S 118 8 E
Brue →, U.K. 24 D3 51 13N 2 59W
Brugge, Belgium 65 C3 51 13N 3 13 E
Brumado, Brazil 122 B2 14 14S 41 40W
Brunei ■, Asia 83 C3 4 50N 115 0 E
Brunswick, Ga., U.S.A. 111 D10 31 10N 81 30W
Brunswick, Maine, U.S.A. 113 D13 43 55N 69 58W
Brunton, U.K. 22 B4 55 2N 2 6W
Brussels, Belgium 65 D4 50 51N 4 21 E
Bruton, U.K. 24 D4 51 7N 2 27W
Bryan, Ohio, U.S.A. 112 E5 41 28N 84 33W
Bryan, Tex., U.S.A. 111 D7 30 40N 96 22W
Bryansk, Russia 72 D4 53 13N 34 25 E
Bryher, U.K. 27 H1 49 57N 6 22W
Brynamman, U.K. 24 C1 51 49N 3 51W
Brynmawr, U.K. 24 C2 51 48N 3 10W
Bucaramanga, Colombia 120 B2 7 0N 73 0W
Buchan, U.K. 19 G13 57 32N 2 21W
Buchan Ness, U.K. 19 H14 57 29N 1 46W
Bucharest, Romania 67 F14 44 27N 26 10 E
Buckden, U.K. 23 H8 52 18N 0 14W
Buckfastleigh, U.K. 27 G6 50 28N 3 46W
Buckhannon, U.S.A. 112 F7 39 0N 80 8W
Buckhaven, U.K. 21 B9 56 11N 3 3W
Buckie, U.K. 19 G12 57 41N 2 58W
Buckingham, Canada 113 C10 45 37N 75 24W
Buckingham, U.K. 25 C7 51 59N 0 57W
Buckinghamshire □, U.K. 25 C7 51 53N 0 55W
Buckland Brewer, U.K. 27 F5 50 58N 4 15W
Buckland Newton, U.K. 24 E4 50 50N 2 26W
Buckley, U.K. 23 F2 53 10N 3 5W
Budapest, Hungary 67 E10 47 29N 19 5 E
Bude, U.K. 27 F4 50 49N 4 34W
Bude B., U.K. 27 F4 50 49N 4 35W
Budle B., U.K. 22 A5 55 37N 1 45W
Budleigh Salterton, U.K. 27 F7 50 37N 3 19W
Buena Vista, U.S.A. 112 G8 37 44N 79 21W
Buenaventura, Colombia 120 B2 3 53N 77 4W
Buenos Aires, Argentina 121 F4 34 30S 58 20W
Buenos Aires, L., Chile 121 G2 46 35S 72 30W
Buffalo, N.Y., U.S.A. 112 D8 42 53N 78 53W
Buffalo, Wyo., U.S.A. 110 B5 44 21N 106 42W
Bug →, Poland 67 B11 52 31N 21 5 E
Bug →, Ukraine 73 E5 46 59N 31 58 E
Bugle, U.K. 27 G4 50 24N 4 47W
Bugulma, Russia 72 D9 54 33N 52 48 E
Bugun Shara, Mongolia 80 B5 49 0N 104 0 E
Buguruslan, Russia 72 D9 53 39N 52 26 E
Builth Wells, U.K. 24 B2 52 9N 3 25W
Buir Nur, Mongolia 81 B6 47 50N 117 42 E
Bujumbura, Burundi 96 E5 3 16S 29 18 E
Bukavu, Dem. Rep. of the Congo 96 E5 2 20S 28 52 E
Bukhoro, Uzbekistan 87 B11 39 48N 64 25 E
Bukittinggi, Indonesia 83 D2 0 20S 100 20 E
Bulawayo, Zimbabwe 97 J5 20 7S 28 32 E
Bulford, U.K. 24 D5 51 11N 1 45W
Bulgaria ■, Europe 71 C11 42 35N 25 30 E
Bullhead City, U.S.A. 110 C4 35 8N 114 32W
Bunbury, Australia 98 G2 33 20S 115 35 E
Bunclody, Ireland 31 C9 52 39N 6 40W
Buncrana, Ireland 28 A7 55 8N 7 27W
Bundaberg, Australia 98 E9 24 54S 152 22 E
Bundi, India 84 G9 25 30N 75 35 E
Bundoran, Ireland 28 C5 54 28N 8 16W
Bungay, U.K. 25 B11 52 27N 1 28 E
Buntingford, U.K. 25 C8 51 56N 0 0W
Bunwell, U.K. 25 A11 52 30N 1 9 E
Buon Ma Thuot, Vietnam 83 B2 12 40N 108 3 E
Bûr Safâga, Egypt 95 C12 26 43N 33 57 E
Burao, Somali Rep. 88 F4 9 32N 45 32 E
Buraydah, Si. Arabia 86 E5 26 20N 43 59 E
Burbage, Derby, U.K. 23 F5 53 15N 1 55W
Burbage, Leics., U.K. 23 G6 52 32N 1 21W
Burbage, Wilts., U.K. 24 D5 51 21N 1 39W
Burdur, Turkey 73 G5 37 45N 30 17 E
Bure →, U.K. 25 A12 52 38N 1 43 E
Burford, U.K. 24 C5 51 49N 1 38W
Burgas, Bulgaria 71 C12 42 33N 27 29 E
Burgess Hill, U.K. 25 E8 50 58N 0 6W
Burgh le Marsh, U.K. 23 F9 53 9N 0 15 E
Burghead, U.K. 19 G11 57 43N 3 30W
Burgos, Spain 69 A4 42 21N 3 41W
Burgundy = Bourgogne, France 68 C6 47 0N 4 50 E
Burhanpur, India 84 J10 21 18N 76 14 E
Burkina Faso ■, Africa 94 F5 12 0N 1 0W
Burley, Hants., U.K. 24 E5 50 49N 1 43W
Burley, W. Yorks., U.K. 23 E5 53 55N 1 46W
Burley, U.S.A. 110 B4 42 32N 113 48W
Burlington, Colo., U.S.A. 110 C6 39 18N 102 16W
Burlington, Iowa, U.S.A. 111 B8 40 49N 91 14W
Burlington, Vt., U.S.A. 113 C11 44 29N 73 12W
Burlington, Wis., U.S.A. 112 D3 42 41N 88 17W
Burma ■, Asia 85 J20 21 0N 96 30 E
Burnham Market, U.K. 25 A10 52 57N 0 44 E
Burnham-on-Crouch, U.K. 25 C10 51 38N 0 49 E
Burnham-on-Sea, U.K. 24 D3 51 14N 3 0W
Burnie, Australia 98 J8 41 4S 145 56 E
Burnley, U.K. 23 E4 53 47N 2 14W
Burnmouth, U.K. 22 A4 55 50N 2 4W
Burns, U.S.A. 110 B3 43 35N 119 3W

**Burnside**

Burnside →, Canada ........ 108 B9 66 51N 108 4W
Burray, U.K. .......... 19 E12 58 51N 2 54W
Burren Nat. Park △, Ireland . 30 B4 53 1N 8 58W
Burrow Hd., U.K. ......... 20 E7 54 41N 4 24W
Burry Port, U.K. ......... 26 D5 51 41N 4 15W
Bursa, Turkey ......... 71 D13 40 15N 29 5 E
Burstwick, U.K. ......... 23 E8 53 44N 0 8W
Burton, U.K. ......... 22 D3 54 11N 2 43W
Burton Agnes, U.K. ....... 22 D8 54 4N 0 18W
Burton Bradstock, U.K. .... 24 E3 50 42N 2 43W
Burton Fleming, U.K. ...... 22 D8 54 8N 0 20W
Burton Latimer, U.K. ...... 23 H7 52 22N 0 41W
Burton upon Stather, U.K. .. 23 E7 53 39N 0 41W
Burton upon Trent, U.K. ... 23 G5 52 48N 1 38W
Buru, Indonesia ......... 83 D4 3 30S 126 30 E
Burundi ■, Africa ......... 96 E5 3 15S 30 0 E
Burwash, U.K. ......... 25 E9 50 59N 0 23 E
Burwell, U.K. ......... 25 B9 52 17N 0 20 E
Burwick, U.K. ......... 19 E12 58 45N 2 58W
Bury, U.K. ......... 23 E4 53 35N 2 17W
Bury St. Edmunds, U.K. .... 25 B10 52 15N 0 43 E
Büshehr, Iran ......... 87 D7 28 55N 50 55 E
Bushey, U.K. ......... 25 C8 51 38N 0 22W
Butaritari, Kiribati ....... 102 G9 3 30N 174 0 E
Bute, U.K. ......... 20 C5 55 48N 5 2W
Butha Qi, China ......... 81 B7 48 0N 122 32 E
Butler, U.S.A. ......... 112 E8 40 52N 79 54W
Buton, Indonesia ......... 83 D4 5 0S 122 45 E
Butte, U.S.A. ......... 110 A4 46 0N 112 32W
Buttermere, U.K. ......... 22 C2 54 32N 3 16W
Butterworth, Malaysia ..... 83 C2 5 24N 100 23 E
Buttevant, Ireland ....... 30 D5 52 14N 8 40W
Butuan, Phil. ......... 83 C4 8 57N 125 33 E
Buxton, U.K. ......... 23 F5 53 16N 1 54W
Buzău, Romania ......... 67 F14 45 10N 26 50 E
Buzuluk, Russia ......... 72 D9 52 48N 52 12 E
Bydgoszcz, Poland ......... 67 B9 53 10N 18 0 E
Byfield, U.K. ......... 24 B6 52 10N 1 14W
Bylot I., Canada ......... 109 A12 73 13N 78 34W
Bytom, Poland ......... 67 C10 50 25N 18 54 E

# C

Ca Mau, Vietnam ......... 83 C2 9 7N 105 8 E
Cabanatuan, Phil. ......... 83 B4 15 30N 120 58 E
Cabedelo, Brazil ......... 120 C6 7 0S 34 50W
Cabimas, Venezuela ......... 120 A2 10 23N 71 25W
Cabinda □, Angola ......... 96 F2 5 0S 12 30 E
Cabo Frio, Brazil ......... 122 D2 22 51S 42 3W
Cabonga, Réservoir, Canada . 109 D12 47 20N 76 40W
Cabot Str., Canada ......... 109 D14 47 15N 59 40W
Čačak, Serbia & M. ......... 71 C9 43 54N 20 20 E
Cáceres, Spain ......... 69 C2 39 26N 6 23W
Cachimbo, Serra do, Brazil .. 120 C4 9 30S 55 30W
Cachoeira, Brazil ......... 122 B3 12 30S 39 0W
Cachoeira do Sul, Brazil .... 121 F4 30 3S 52 53W
Cachoeiro de Itapemirim, Brazil 122 D2 20 51S 41 7W
Cader Idris, U.K. ......... 26 A4 52 42N 3 53W
Cadillac, U.S.A. ......... 112 C5 44 15N 85 24W
Cádiz, Spain ......... 69 D2 36 30N 6 20W
Caen, France ......... 68 B3 49 10N 0 22W
Caenby Corner, U.K. ......... 23 F7 53 24N 0 33W
Caernarfon, U.K. ......... 26 A5 53 8N 4 16W
Caernarfon B., U.K. ......... 26 A4 53 4N 4 40W
Caerphilly, U.K. ......... 24 C2 51 35N 3 13W
Caersws, U.K. ......... 23 G2 52 31N 3 26W
Caetité, Brazil ......... 122 B2 13 50S 42 32W
Cagayan de Oro, Phil. ......... 83 C4 8 30N 124 40 E
Cágliari, Italy ......... 70 E3 39 13N 9 7 E
Caguas, Puerto Rico ......... 115 d 18 14N 66 2W
Caha Mts., Ireland ......... 30 E3 51 45N 9 40W
Caher, Ireland ......... 30 D7 52 22N 7 56W
Caherciveen, Ireland ......... 30 E2 51 56N 10 14W
Cahora Bassa, Reprêsa de, Mozam. ......... 97 H6 15 20S 32 50 E
Cahore Pt., Ireland ......... 31 C10 52 33N 6 12W
Cahors, France ......... 68 D4 44 27N 1 27 E
Cairn Gorm, U.K. ......... 19 H10 57 7N 3 39W
Cairngorm Mts., U.K. ......... 19 H10 57 6N 3 42W
Cairnryan, U.K. ......... 20 E5 54 59N 5 1W
Cairns, Australia ......... 98 D8 16 57S 145 45 E
Cairnsmore of Fleet, U.K. .. 20 E7 54 59N 4 20W
Cairo, Egypt ......... 95 B12 30 1N 31 14 E
Caister-on-Sea, U.K. ......... 25 A12 52 40N 1 43 E
Caistor, U.K. ......... 23 F8 53 30N 0 18W
Caithness, U.K. ......... 19 F10 58 25N 3 35W
Caithness, Ord of, U.K. .... 19 F10 58 8N 3 36W
Caja de Muertos, I., Puerto Rico 115 d 17 54N 66 32W
Cajamarca, Peru ......... 120 C2 7 5S 78 28W
Calabar, Nigeria ......... 94 H7 4 57N 8 20 E
Calábria □, Italy ......... 70 E7 39 0N 16 30 E
Calais, France ......... 68 A4 50 57N 1 56 E
Calais, U.S.A. ......... 113 C14 45 11N 67 17W
Calama, Chile ......... 121 E3 22 30S 68 55W
Calamar, Colombia ......... 120 A2 10 15N 74 55W
Calamian Group, Phil. ..... 83 B3 11 50N 119 55 E
Calapan, Phil. ......... 83 B4 13 25N 121 7 E
Calbayog, Phil. ......... 83 B4 12 4N 124 38 E
Calcutta = Kolkata, India .. 85 H16 22 36N 88 24 E
Caldbeck, U.K. ......... 22 C2 54 45N 3 3W
Calder →, U.K. ......... 23 E6 53 44N 1 22W
Calder Bridge, U.K. ......... 22 D2 54 27N 3 29W
Caldera, Chile ......... 121 E2 27 5S 70 55W
Caldew →, U.K. ......... 22 C3 54 54N 2 56W
Caldwell, U.S.A. ......... 110 B3 43 40N 116 41W
Calgary, Canada ......... 108 C8 51 0N 114 10W
Cali, Colombia ......... 120 B2 3 25N 76 35W
Calicut, India ......... 84 P9 11 15N 75 43 E
California □, U.S.A. ......... 110 C2 37 30N 119 30W
California, G. de, Mexico ... 114 B2 27 0N 111 0W
Callan, Ireland ......... 31 C8 52 32N 7 24W
Callander, U.K. ......... 20 B7 56 15N 4 13W
Callao, Peru ......... 120 D2 12 0S 77 0W
Calne, U.K. ......... 24 D5 51 26N 2 0W
Calshot, U.K. ......... 24 E6 50 48N 1 19W
Calstock, U.K. ......... 27 F5 50 30N 4 13W
Caltanissetta, Italy ......... 70 F6 37 29N 14 4 E
Calvi, France ......... 68 E8 42 34N 8 45 E
Calvinia, S. Africa ......... 97 L3 31 28S 19 45 E
Cam →, U.K. ......... 25 B9 52 21N 0 16 E
Cam Ranh, Vietnam ......... 83 B2 11 54N 109 12 E
Camagüey, Cuba ......... 115 C9 21 20N 78 0W
Camargue, France ......... 68 E6 43 34N 4 34 E
Camberley, U.K. ......... 25 D7 51 20N 0 44W
Cambo, U.K. ......... 22 B5 55 10N 1 57W
Cambodia ■, Asia ......... 83 B2 12 15N 105 0 E
Camborne, U.K. ......... 27 G3 50 12N 5 19W
Cambrai, France ......... 68 A5 50 11N 3 14 E
Cambrian Mts., U.K. ......... 24 B1 52 3N 3 57W
Cambridge, Jamaica ......... 114 a 18 18N 77 54W
Cambridge, U.K. ......... 25 B9 52 12N 0 8 E
Cambridge, Mass., U.S.A. .. 113 D12 42 22N 71 6W
Cambridge, Md., U.S.A. .... 113 F9 38 34N 76 5W

Cambridge, Ohio, U.S.A. ... 112 E7 40 2N 81 35W
Cambridgeshire □, U.K. .... 23 H8 52 25N 0 7W
Camden, Ark., U.S.A. ......... 111 D8 33 35N 92 50W
Camden, N.J., U.S.A. ......... 113 F10 39 56N 75 7W
Camden □, U.K. ......... 25 C8 51 32N 0 8W
Camel →, U.K. ......... 27 F4 50 31N 4 51W
Camelford, U.K. ......... 27 F4 50 37N 4 42W
Cameroon ■, Africa ......... 96 C2 6 0N 12 30 E
Cameroun, Mt., Cameroon .. 96 D1 4 13N 9 10 E
Camocim, Brazil ......... 120 C5 2 55S 40 50W
Campana, Chile ......... 121 G2 48 20S 75 20W
Campánia □, Italy ......... 70 D6 41 0N 14 30 E
Campbell I., Pac. Oc. ......... 102 N8 52 30S 169 0 E
Campbell River, Canada .... 108 C7 50 5N 125 20W
Campbellsville, U.S.A. ..... 112 G5 37 21N 85 20W
Campbellton, Canada ......... 109 D13 47 57N 66 43W
Campbeltown, U.K. ......... 20 D4 55 26N 5 36W
Campeche, Mexico ......... 114 D6 19 50N 90 32W
Campeche, Golfo de, Mexico . 114 D6 19 30N 93 0W
Campina Grande, Brazil .... 120 C6 7 20S 35 47W
Campinas, Brazil ......... 122 D1 22 50S 47 0W
Campo Grande, Brazil ..... 120 E4 20 25S 54 40W
Campos, Brazil ......... 122 D2 21 50S 41 20W
Campos Belos, Brazil ......... 122 B1 13 10S 47 3W
Camrose, Canada ......... 108 C8 53 0N 112 50W
Can Tho, Vietnam ......... 83 B2 10 2N 105 46 E
Canada ■, N. Amer. ......... 108 C10 60 0N 100 0W
Canadian →, U.S.A. ......... 111 C7 35 28N 95 3W
Çanakkale, Turkey ......... 73 F4 40 8N 26 24 E
Canandaigua, U.S.A. ......... 112 D9 42 54N 77 17W
Cananea, Mexico ......... 114 A2 31 0N 110 20W
Canaries, St. Lucia ......... 115 f 13 55N 61 4W
Canary Is., Atl. Oc. ......... 94 C2 28 30N 16 0W
Canaveral, C., U.S.A. ......... 111 E10 28 27N 80 32W
Canavieiras, Brazil ......... 122 C3 15 39S 39 0W
Canberra, Australia ......... 98 H8 35 15S 149 8 E
Cancún, Mexico ......... 114 C7 21 8N 86 44W
Caniapiscau →, Canada ... 109 C13 56 40N 69 30W
Caniapiscau, L. de, Canada . 109 C13 54 10N 69 55W
Çankırı, Turkey ......... 73 F5 40 40N 33 37 E
Canna, U.K. ......... 18 H4 57 3N 6 33W
Cannanore, India ......... 84 P9 11 53N 75 27 E
Cannes, France ......... 68 E7 43 32N 7 1 E
Cannington, U.K. ......... 24 D2 51 9N 3 4W
Cannock, U.K. ......... 23 G4 52 41N 2 1W
Cannock Chase, U.K. ......... 23 G4 52 44N 2 4W
Canoas, Brazil ......... 121 E4 29 56S 51 11W
Canon City, U.S.A. ......... 110 C5 38 27N 105 14W
Canonbie, U.K. ......... 22 B3 55 5N 2 58W
Canora, Canada ......... 108 C9 51 40N 102 30W
Canso, Canada ......... 113 C17 45 20N 61 0W
Cantabria □, Spain ......... 69 A4 43 10N 4 0W
Cantábrica, Cordillera, Spain . 69 A3 43 0N 5 10W
Canterbury, U.K. ......... 25 D11 51 16N 1 6 E
Canton = Guangzhou, China . 81 D6 23 5N 113 10 E
Canton, N.Y., U.S.A. ......... 113 C10 44 36N 75 10W
Canton, Ohio, U.S.A. ......... 112 E7 40 48N 81 23W
Canvey, U.K. ......... 25 C10 51 31N 0 37 E
Cap-Chat, Canada ......... 113 A14 49 6N 66 40W
Cap-de-la-Madeleine, Canada . 113 B11 46 22N 72 31W
Cap-Haïtien, Haiti ......... 115 D10 19 40N 72 20W
Cap Pt., St. Lucia ......... 115 f 14 7N 60 57W
Cape Breton I., Canada .... 109 D14 46 0N 60 30W
Cape Charles, U.S.A. ......... 113 G10 37 16N 76 1W
Cape Coast, Ghana ......... 94 G5 5 5N 1 15W
Cape Dorset, Canada ......... 109 B12 64 14N 76 32W
Cape Fear →, U.S.A. ......... 111 D11 33 53N 78 1W
Cape May, U.S.A. ......... 113 F10 38 56N 74 56W
Cape May Point, U.S.A. .... 111 C12 38 56N 74 58W
Cape Town, S. Africa ......... 97 L3 33 55S 18 22 E
Cape Verde Is. ■, Atl. Oc. .. 52 D8 16 0N 24 0W
Cape York Peninsula, Australia 98 C7 12 0S 142 30 E
Capela, Brazil ......... 122 B3 10 30S 37 0W
Capesterre, Guadeloupe .... 114 b 15 53N 61 14W
Capesterre-Belle-Eau, Guadeloupe ......... 114 b 16 4N 61 36W
Capreol, Canada ......... 112 B7 46 43N 80 56W
Capri, Italy ......... 70 D6 40 33N 14 14 E
Caprivi Strip, Namibia ..... 97 H4 18 0S 23 0 E
Caquetá →, Colombia ..... 120 C3 1 15S 69 15W
Caracas, Venezuela ......... 120 A3 10 30N 66 55W
Caracol, Brazil ......... 122 A2 9 15S 43 22W
Caratasca, L., Honduras .... 115 D8 15 20N 83 40W
Caratinga, Brazil ......... 122 C2 19 50S 42 10W
Caravelas, Brazil ......... 122 C3 17 45S 39 15W
Caravelle, Presqu'île de la, Martinique ......... 114 c 14 46N 60 48W
Carbondale, U.S.A. ......... 113 E10 41 35N 75 30W
Carbonear, Canada ......... 109 D14 47 42N 53 13W
Carcassonne, France ......... 68 E5 43 13N 2 20 E
Carcross, Canada ......... 108 B6 60 13N 134 45W
Cárdenas, Cuba ......... 115 C8 23 0N 81 30W
Cardiff, U.K. ......... 24 D2 51 29N 3 10W
Cardigan, U.K. ......... 26 C4 52 5N 4 40W
Cardigan B., U.K. ......... 26 B4 52 30N 4 30W
Cardington, U.K. ......... 25 B8 52 6N 0 25W
Cardston, Canada ......... 108 D8 49 15N 113 20W
Cariacica, Brazil ......... 122 D2 20 16S 40 25W
Caribbean Sea, W. Indies ... 115 E10 15 0N 75 0W
Cariboo Mts., Canada ......... 108 C7 53 0N 121 0W
Caribou →, Canada ......... 113 B13 46 52N 68 1W
Caribou Mts., Canada ......... 108 C8 59 12N 115 40W
Carinhanha, Brazil ......... 122 B2 14 15S 44 46W
Carinhanha →, Brazil ..... 122 B2 14 20S 43 47W
Carinthia = Kärnten □, Austria 66 E8 46 52N 13 30 E
Carisbrooke, U.K. ......... 24 E6 50 41N 1 19W
Cark, U.K. ......... 22 D3 54 11N 2 58W
Carleton Place, Canada .... 113 C9 45 8N 76 9W
Carleton Rode, U.K. ......... 25 A11 52 30N 1 7 E
Carlingford L., U.K. ......... 29 C9 54 3N 6 9W
Carlisle, U.K. ......... 22 C3 54 54N 2 56W
Carlisle B., Barbados ......... 115 g 13 5N 59 37W
Carlops, U.K. ......... 22 A2 55 47N 3 20W
Carlow, Ireland ......... 31 C9 52 50N 6 56W
Carlow □, Ireland ......... 31 C9 52 43N 6 50W
Carlsbad, U.S.A. ......... 110 D6 32 25N 104 14W
Carlton, U.K. ......... 23 G6 52 59N 1 5W
Carlton Colville, U.K. ......... 25 B12 52 27N 1 43 E
Carlton Miniott, U.K. ......... 22 D6 54 12N 1 22W
Carluke, U.K. ......... 21 C8 55 45N 3 50W
Carmacks, Canada ......... 108 B6 62 5N 136 16W
Carmarthen, U.K. ......... 26 D5 51 52N 4 19W
Carmarthen B., U.K. ......... 26 D5 51 40N 4 30W
Carmaux, France ......... 68 D5 44 3N 2 10 E
Carn Ban, U.K. ......... 18 H9 57 7N 4 15W
Carn Eige, U.K. ......... 18 H8 57 17N 5 8W
Carnarvon, Australia ......... 98 E1 24 51S 113 42 E
Carnarvon, S. Africa ......... 97 L4 30 56S 22 8 E
Carnegie, L., Australia ..... 98 F3 26 5S 122 30 E
Carnforth, U.K. ......... 22 C3 54 7N 2 45W
Carno, U.K. ......... 24 A1 52 34N 3 30W
Carnoustie, U.K. ......... 21 A10 56 30N 2 42W
Carnsore Pt., Ireland ......... 31 D10 52 10N 6 22W
Caro, U.S.A. ......... 112 D6 43 29N 83 24W

Carolina, Puerto Rico ......... 115 d 18 23N 65 58W
Caroline I., Kiribati ......... 103 H12 9 58S 150 13W
Caroline Is., Micronesia .... 102 G7 8 0N 150 0 E
Carondelet, Kiribati ......... 99 B16 5 33S 173 50 E
Caroni →, Venezuela ......... 120 B3 8 21N 62 43W
Carpathians, Europe ......... 67 D11 49 30N 21 0 E
Carpentaria, G. of, Australia . 98 C6 14 0S 139 0 E
Carpentras, France ......... 68 D6 44 3N 5 2 E
Carrauntoohill, Ireland ..... 30 E3 52 0N 9 45W
Carrick-on-Shannon, Ireland . 28 D5 53 57N 8 5W
Carrick-on-Suir, Ireland .... 31 D8 52 21N 7 24W
Carrickfergus, U.K. ......... 29 B10 54 43N 5 49W
Carrickmacross, Ireland .... 29 D8 53 59N 6 43W
Carron →, U.K. ......... 19 G9 57 53N 4 22W
Carron, L., U.K. ......... 18 H6 57 22N 5 35W
Carson City, U.S.A. ......... 110 C3 39 10N 119 46W
Carson Sink, U.S.A. ......... 110 C3 39 50N 118 25W
Cartagena, Colombia ......... 120 A2 10 25N 75 33W
Cartagena, Spain ......... 69 D5 37 38N 0 59W
Cartago, Colombia ......... 120 B2 4 45N 75 55W
Carthage, Tunisia ......... 95 A8 36 50N 10 21 E
Carthage, U.S.A. ......... 111 C8 37 11N 94 19W
Cartmel, U.K. ......... 22 D3 54 12N 2 57W
Cartwright, Canada ......... 109 C14 53 41N 56 58W
Caruaru, Brazil ......... 122 A3 8 15S 35 55W
Carúpano, Venezuela ......... 120 A3 10 39N 63 15W
Casa Grande, U.S.A. ......... 110 D4 32 53N 111 45W
Casablanca, Morocco ......... 94 B4 33 36N 7 36W
Cascade Ra., U.S.A. ......... 110 A2 47 0N 121 30W
Cascavel, Brazil ......... 121 E4 24 57S 53 28W
Cashel, Ireland ......... 30 C7 52 30N 7 53W
Casiquiare →, Venezuela ... 120 B3 2 1N 67 7W
Casper, U.S.A. ......... 110 B5 42 51N 106 19W
Caspian Depression, Eurasia . 73 E8 47 0N 48 0 E
Caspian Sea, Eurasia ......... 73 F9 43 0N 50 0 E
Cassiar Mts., Canada ......... 108 C6 59 30N 130 30W
Castelló de la Plana, Spain .. 69 C5 39 58N 0 3W
Castelsarrasin, France ..... 68 E4 44 2N 1 7 E
Castle Acre, U.K. ......... 25 A10 52 42N 0 42 E
Castle Cary, U.K. ......... 24 D3 51 6N 2 31W
Castle Donington, U.K. ..... 23 G6 52 51N 1 20W
Castle Douglas, U.K. ......... 21 E8 54 56N 3 56W
Castlebar, Ireland ......... 28 D3 53 52N 9 18W
Castleblaney, Ireland ......... 29 C8 54 7N 6 44W
Castlederg, U.K. ......... 28 B6 54 42N 7 35W
Castleford, U.K. ......... 23 E6 53 43N 1 21W
Castlepollard, Ireland ......... 28 D7 53 41N 7 19W
Castlerea, Ireland ......... 28 D5 53 46N 8 29W
Castleton, Derby, U.K. ..... 23 F5 53 22N 1 46W
Castleton, N. Yorks., U.K. .. 22 D7 54 28N 0 57W
Castletown, U.K. ......... 29 C12 54 5N 4 38W
Castletown Bearhaven, Ireland 30 E3 51 39N 9 55W
Castres, France ......... 68 E5 43 37N 2 13 E
Castries, St. Lucia ......... 115 f 14 2N 60 58W
Castro, Chile ......... 121 G2 42 30S 73 50W
Castro Alves, Brazil ......... 122 B3 12 46S 39 33W
Cat I., Bahamas ......... 115 C9 24 30N 75 30W
Cataguases, Brazil ......... 122 D2 21 23S 42 39W
Catalão, Brazil ......... 122 C1 18 10S 47 57W
Cataluña □, Spain ......... 69 B6 41 40N 1 15 E
Catamarca, Argentina ..... 121 E3 28 30S 65 50W
Catanduanes, Phil. ......... 83 B4 13 50N 124 20 E
Catanduva, Brazil ......... 122 D1 21 5S 48 58W
Catánia, Italy ......... 70 F6 37 30N 15 6 E
Catanzaro, Italy ......... 70 E7 38 54N 16 35 E
Catcleugh, U.K. ......... 22 B4 55 20N 2 24W
Caterham, U.K. ......... 25 D8 51 15N 0 4W
Catoche, C., Mexico ......... 114 C7 21 40N 87 8W
Caton, U.K. ......... 22 C4 54 5N 2 42W
Catsfield, U.K. ......... 25 E9 50 54N 0 28 E
Catskill, U.S.A. ......... 113 D11 42 14N 73 52W
Catskill Mts., U.S.A. ......... 113 D10 42 10N 74 25W
Catterick, U.K. ......... 22 D5 54 23N 1 37W
Catterick Camp, U.K. ......... 22 D5 54 22N 1 42W
Catton, U.K. ......... 22 C4 54 55N 2 15W
Cauca →, Colombia ......... 120 B2 8 54N 74 28W
Caucasus Mountains, Eurasia . 73 F7 42 50N 44 0 E
Caulkerbush, U.K. ......... 22 C1 54 54N 3 41W
Caura →, Venezuela ......... 120 B3 7 38N 64 53W
Cauvery →, India ......... 84 P11 11 9N 78 52 E
Cavan, Ireland ......... 28 D7 54 0N 7 22W
Cavan □, Ireland ......... 29 C7 54 1N 7 16W
Caviana, I., Brazil ......... 120 B4 0 10N 50 10W
Cawood, U.K. ......... 23 E6 53 50N 1 8W
Cawston, U.K. ......... 25 A11 52 47N 1 9 E
Caxias, Brazil ......... 120 C5 4 55S 43 20W
Caxias do Sul, Brazil ......... 121 E4 29 10S 51 10W
Cayenne, Fr. Guiana ......... 120 B4 5 5N 52 18W
Cayey, Puerto Rico ......... 115 d 18 7N 66 10W
Cayman Is. ☑, W. Indies ... 115 D8 19 40N 80 30W
Cayuga L., U.S.A. ......... 112 D9 42 41N 76 41W
Ceanannus Mor, Ireland ... 29 D8 53 44N 6 53W
Ceará □, Brazil ......... 120 C6 5 0S 40 0W
Cebu, Phil. ......... 83 B4 10 18N 123 54 E
Cedar City, U.S.A. ......... 110 C4 37 41N 113 4W
Cedar L., Canada ......... 108 C10 53 10N 100 0W
Cedar Rapids, U.S.A. ......... 111 B8 41 59N 91 40W
Cegléd, Hungary ......... 67 E10 47 11N 19 47 E
Celaya, Mexico ......... 114 C4 20 31N 100 37W
Celebes Sea, Indonesia ..... 83 C4 3 0N 123 0 E
Celina, U.S.A. ......... 112 E5 40 33N 84 35W
Celtic Sea, Atl. Oc. ......... 64 F2 50 9N 9 34W
Cemaes, U.K. ......... 26 A5 53 24N 4 27W
Central, Cordillera, Colombia . 120 C2 5 0N 75 0W
Central, Cordillera, Puerto Rico 115 d 18 8N 66 35W
Central African Rep. ■, Africa 96 C4 7 0N 20 0 E
Central Makran Range, Pakistan 84 F4 26 30N 64 15 E
Central Russian Uplands, Europe ......... 56 E13 54 0N 36 0 E
Central Siberian Plateau, Russia 74 C14 65 0N 105 0 E
Centralia, U.S.A. ......... 110 A2 46 43N 122 58W
Cephalonia = Kefallinía, Greece 71 E9 38 15N 20 30 E
Cerignola, Italy ......... 70 D6 41 17N 15 53 E
Cerne Abbas, U.K. ......... 24 E4 50 49N 2 29W
Cerrigydrudion, U.K. ......... 26 A6 53 1N 3 35W
České Budějovice, Czech Rep. . 66 D8 48 55N 14 25 E
Çeşme, Turkey ......... 73 G4 38 20N 26 23 E
Ceuta, N. Afr. ......... 69 E3 35 52N 5 18W
Ceve-i-Ra, Fiji ......... 99 E13 21 46S 174 31 E
Cévennes, France ......... 68 D5 44 10N 3 50 E
Chacewater, U.K. ......... 27 G3 50 15N 5 11W
Chachapoyas, Peru ......... 120 C2 6 15S 77 50W
Chaco Austral, S. Amer. .... 121 E3 27 0S 61 30W
Chaco Boreal, S. Amer. .... 121 E4 22 0S 60 0W
Chaco Central, S. Amer. .... 121 E3 24 0S 61 0W
Chad ■, Africa ......... 95 F8 15 0N 17 15 E
Chad, L., Chad ......... 95 F8 13 30N 14 30 E
Chadron, U.S.A. ......... 110 B6 42 50N 103 0W
Chagford, U.K. ......... 27 F6 50 40N 3 50W
Chaghcharán, Afghan. ..... 84 B4 34 31N 65 15 E
Chah Gay Hills, Afghan. .... 87 D10 29 30N 64 0 E
Chakradharpur, India ..... 85 H14 22 45N 85 40 E
Chaleur B., Canada ......... 113 B15 47 55N 65 30W
Chalisgaon, India ......... 84 J9 20 30N 75 10 E
Chalon-sur-Saône, France .. 68 C6 46 48N 4 50 E

**Cheviot Hills**

Châlons-en-Champagne, France 68 B6 48 58N 4 20 E
Chambal →, India ......... 84 F11 26 29N 79 15 E
Chambersburg, U.S.A. ..... 112 F9 39 56N 77 40W
Chambéry, France ......... 68 D6 45 34N 5 55 E
Champagne, France ......... 68 B6 48 40N 4 20 E
Champaign, U.S.A. ......... 112 E3 40 7N 88 15W
Champlain, L., U.S.A. ......... 113 C11 44 40N 73 20W
Chañaral, Chile ......... 121 E2 26 23S 70 40W
Chancery Lane, Barbados ... 115 g 13 4N 59 30W
Chandigarh, India ......... 84 D10 30 43N 76 47 E
Chandler's Ford, U.K. ......... 24 E6 50 59N 1 22W
Chandpur, Bangla. ......... 85 H17 23 8N 90 45 E
Chandrapur, India ......... 84 K11 19 57N 79 25 E
Changchun, China ......... 81 B7 43 57N 125 17 E
Changde, China ......... 81 D6 29 4N 111 35 E
Changhua, Taiwan ......... 81 D7 24 2N 120 30 E
Changsha, China ......... 81 D6 28 12N 113 0 E
Changzhi, China ......... 81 C6 36 10N 113 6 E
Changzhou, China ......... 81 C6 31 47N 119 58 E
Channel Is., U.K. ......... 27 J9 49 19N 2 24W
Channel Is., U.S.A. ......... 110 D2 33 40N 119 15W
Channel-Port aux Basques, Canada ......... 109 D14 47 30N 59 9W
Chantrey Inlet, Canada ..... 108 B10 67 48N 96 20W
Chaozhou, China ......... 81 D6 23 42N 116 32 E
Chapala, L. de, Mexico ..... 114 C4 20 10N 103 20W
Chapayevsk, Russia ......... 72 D8 53 0N 49 40 E
Chapel en le Frith, U.K. .... 23 F5 53 20N 1 54W
Chapel St. Leonards, U.K. .. 23 F9 53 13N 0 20 E
Chapleau, Canada ......... 109 D11 47 50N 83 24W
Charaña, Bolivia ......... 120 D3 17 30S 69 25W
Chard, U.K. ......... 24 E3 50 52N 2 58W
Chari →, Chad ......... 95 F8 12 58N 14 31 E
Chárikár, Afghan. ......... 84 B6 35 0N 69 10 E
Charing, U.K. ......... 25 D10 51 12N 0 49 E
Chärjew, Turkmenistan ..... 87 B10 39 6N 63 34 E
Charlbury, U.K. ......... 24 C6 51 53N 1 28W
Charleroi, Belgium ......... 65 D4 50 24N 4 27 E
Charles, C., U.S.A. ......... 113 G10 37 7N 75 58W
Charles City, U.S.A. ......... 111 B8 43 4N 92 41W
Charleston, Ill., U.S.A. ..... 112 F3 39 30N 88 10W
Charleston, S.C., U.S.A. .... 111 D11 32 46N 79 56W
Charleston, W. Va., U.S.A. .. 112 F7 38 21N 81 38W
Charlestown, Ireland ......... 28 D4 53 58N 8 48W
Charlestown of Aberlour, U.K. . 19 H11 57 28N 3 14W
Charleville, Australia ......... 98 F8 26 24S 146 15 E
Charleville-Mézières, France . 68 B6 49 44N 4 40 E
Charlevoix, U.S.A. ......... 112 C5 45 19N 85 16W
Charlotte, Mich., U.S.A. .... 112 D5 42 34N 84 50W
Charlotte, N.C., U.S.A. ..... 111 C10 35 13N 80 51W
Charlotte Amalie, U.S. Virgin Is. 115 e 18 21N 64 56W
Charlotte Harbor, U.S.A. ... 111 E10 26 50N 82 10W
Charlottesville, U.S.A. ..... 112 F8 38 2N 78 30W
Charlottetown, Canada ..... 109 D13 46 14N 63 8W
Charlton I., Canada ......... 109 C12 52 0N 79 20W
Charlton Kings, U.K. ......... 24 C5 51 53N 2 3W
Charlwood, U.K. ......... 25 D8 51 9N 0 13W
Charminster, U.K. ......... 24 E4 50 44N 2 28W
Charmouth, U.K. ......... 24 E3 50 44N 2 54W
Charnwood Forest, U.K. .... 23 G6 52 44N 1 17W
Charolles, France ......... 68 C6 46 27N 4 16 E
Charters Towers, Australia .. 98 E8 20 5S 146 13 E
Chartham, U.K. ......... 25 D11 51 14N 1 1 E
Chartres, France ......... 68 B4 48 29N 1 30 E
Chascomús, Argentina ..... 121 F4 35 30S 58 0W
Châteaubriant, France ......... 68 C3 47 43N 1 23W
Châteaulin, France ......... 68 B1 48 11N 4 8W
Châteauroux, France ......... 68 C4 46 50N 1 40 E
Châteaux, Pte. des, Guadeloupe 114 b 16 15N 61 10W
Châtellerault, France ......... 68 C4 46 50N 0 30 E
Chatham, U.K. ......... 25 D10 51 22N 0 32 E
Chatham Is., Pac. Oc. ......... 99 J15 44 0S 176 40W
Chatham-Kent, Canada ..... 112 D5 42 24N 82 11W
Chattanooga, U.S.A. ......... 111 C9 35 3N 85 19W
Chatteris, U.K. ......... 23 H9 52 28N 0 2 E
Chatton, U.K. ......... 22 A5 55 35N 2 0W
Chaumont, France ......... 68 B6 48 7N 5 8 E
Chaykovskiy, Russia ......... 72 C9 56 47N 54 9 E
Cheadle, Gt. Man., U.K. .... 23 F4 53 23N 2 12W
Cheadle, Staffs., U.K. ......... 23 G5 52 59N 1 58W
Cheb, Czech Rep. ......... 66 C7 50 9N 12 28 E
Cheboksary, Russia ......... 72 C8 56 8N 47 12 E
Cheboygan, U.S.A. ......... 112 C5 45 39N 84 29W
Chechenia □, Russia ......... 73 F8 43 30N 45 29 E
Chedabucto B., Canada .... 113 C17 45 25N 61 8W
Cheddar, U.K. ......... 24 D3 51 17N 2 46W
Cheddleton, U.K. ......... 23 F4 53 4N 2 2W
Cheduba I., Burma ......... 85 K18 18 45N 93 40 E
Chegutu, Zimbabwe ......... 97 H6 18 10S 30 14 E
Cheju do, S. Korea ......... 81 C7 33 29N 126 34 E
Cheleken, Turkmenistan .... 73 G9 39 34N 53 16 E
Chełm, Poland ......... 67 C12 51 8N 23 30 E
Chelmsford, U.K. ......... 25 C10 51 44N 0 30 E
Chelmsford, U.K. ......... 25 C9 51 44N 0 29 E
Cheltenham, U.K. ......... 24 C5 51 54N 2 4W
Chelyabinsk, Russia ......... 79 D8 55 10N 61 24 E
Chelyuskin, C., Russia ..... 79 B12 77 30N 103 0 E
Chemnitz, Germany ......... 66 C7 50 51N 12 54 E
Chenab →, Pakistan ......... 84 D7 30 23N 71 2 E
Chengde, China ......... 81 B6 40 59N 117 58 E
Chengdu, China ......... 80 C5 30 38N 104 2 E
Chengjiang, China ......... 80 D5 24 39N 103 0 E
Chennai, India ......... 84 N12 13 8N 80 19 E
Chepstow, U.K. ......... 24 C3 51 38N 2 41W
Cher →, France ......... 68 C4 47 21N 0 29 E
Cherbourg, France ......... 68 B3 49 39N 1 40W
Cherepovets, Russia ......... 72 C6 59 5N 37 55 E
Cheriton, U.K. ......... 24 E6 51 3N 1 8W
Cheriton Fitzpaine, U.K. .... 24 E1 50 51N 3 35W
Cherkasy, Ukraine ......... 73 E5 49 27N 32 4 E
Cherkessk, Russia ......... 73 F7 44 15N 42 5 E
Chernihiv, Ukraine ......... 72 D5 51 28N 31 20 E
Chernivtsi, Ukraine ......... 67 D13 48 15N 25 52 E
Chernobyl, Ukraine ......... 67 C16 51 20N 30 15 E
Cherokee, U.S.A. ......... 111 B7 42 45N 95 33W
Cherrapunji, India ......... 85 G17 25 17N 91 47 E
Cherski Ra., Russia ......... 79 C16 65 0N 143 0 E
Chertsey, U.K. ......... 25 D7 51 23N 0 30W
Chervonohrad, Ukraine ..... 73 D3 50 25N 24 10 E
Cherwell →, U.K. ......... 24 C6 51 44N 1 14W
Chesapeake B., U.S.A. ..... 112 F9 38 0N 76 10W
Chesha B., Russia ......... 72 A8 67 20N 47 0 E
Chesham, U.K. ......... 25 C7 51 43N 0 36W
Cheshire □, U.K. ......... 23 F4 53 14N 2 30W
Cheshunt, U.K. ......... 25 C8 51 43N 0 1W
Chesil Beach, U.K. ......... 24 E3 50 37N 2 33W
Chester, U.K. ......... 23 F3 53 12N 2 53W
Chester, U.S.A. ......... 113 F10 39 51N 75 22W
Chester-le-Street, U.K. ..... 22 C5 54 51N 1 34W
Chesterfield, U.K. ......... 23 F6 53 15N 1 25W
Chesterfield, Îs., N. Cal. .... 99 D10 19 52S 158 15 E
Chesterfield Inlet, Canada ... 108 B10 63 30N 90 45W
Chetumal, Mexico ......... 114 D7 18 30N 88 20W
Chetwynd, Canada ......... 108 C7 55 45N 121 36W
Cheviot, The, U.K. ......... 22 B4 55 29N 2 9W
Cheviot Hills, U.K. ......... 22 B3 55 20N 2 30W

**Chew Bahir**      **Culm**

Chew Bahir, Ethiopia 88 G2 4 40N 36 50 E
Chew Magna, U.K. 24 D3 51 22N 2 37W
Cheyenne, U.S.A. 110 B6 41 8N 104 49W
Cheyenne →, U.S.A. 110 B6 44 41N 101 18W
Chhapra, India 85 G14 25 48N 84 44 E
Chhattisgarh □, India 85 J12 22 0N 82 0 E
Chi →, Thailand 83 B2 15 11N 104 43 E
Chiai, Taiwan 81 D7 23 29N 120 25 E
Chiang Mai, Thailand 83 B1 18 47N 98 59 E
Chiba, Japan 82 F7 35 30N 140 7 E
Chibougamau, Canada 109 D12 49 56N 74 24W
Chibougamau, L., Canada 113 A10 49 50N 74 20W
Chicago, U.S.A. 112 E4 41 53N 87 38W
Chichagof I., U.S.A. 108 C6 57 30N 135 30W
Chichester, U.K. 25 E7 50 50N 0 47W
Chickasha, U.S.A. 110 C7 35 3N 97 58W
Chiclayo, Peru 120 C2 6 42S 79 50W
Chico, U.S.A. 110 C2 39 44N 121 50W
Chico →, Chubut, Argentina 121 G3 44 0S 67 0W
Chico →, Santa Cruz, Argentina 121 G3 50 0S 68 30W
Chicopee, U.S.A. 113 D11 42 9N 72 37W
Chicoutimi, Canada 109 D12 48 28N 71 5W
Chiddingfold, U.K. 25 D7 51 7N 0 37W
Chidley, C., Canada 109 B13 60 23N 64 26W
Chieti, Italy 70 C6 42 21N 14 10 E
Chihli, G. of, China 81 C6 39 0N 119 0 E
Chihuahua, Mexico 114 B3 28 40N 106 3W
Chilapa, Mexico 114 D5 17 40N 99 11W
Chilaw, Sri Lanka 84 R11 7 30N 79 50 E
Childress, U.S.A. 110 D6 34 25N 100 13W
Chile ■, S. Amer. 121 F2 35 0S 72 0W
Chile Rise, Pac. Oc. 103 L18 38 0S 92 0W
Chilham, U.K. 25 D10 51 15N 0 59 E
Chililabombwe, Zambia 97 G5 12 18S 27 43 E
Chilka L., India 85 K14 19 40N 85 25 E
Chillán, Chile 121 F2 36 40S 72 10W
Chillicothe, U.S.A. 112 F6 39 20N 82 59W
Chilliwack, Canada 108 D7 49 10N 121 54W
Chiloé, I. de, Chile 121 G2 42 30S 73 50W
Chilpancingo, Mexico 114 D5 17 30N 99 30W
Chiltern Hills, U.K. 25 C7 51 40N 0 53W
Chilton, U.S.A. 112 C3 44 2N 88 10W
Chilung, Taiwan 81 D7 25 3N 121 45 E
Chilwa, L., Malawi 97 H7 15 15S 35 40 E
Chimborazo, Ecuador 120 C2 1 29S 78 55W
Chimbote, Peru 120 C2 9 0S 78 35W
Chimkent, Kazakhstan 79 E8 42 18N 69 36 E
Chin □, Burma 85 J18 22 0N 93 0 E
China ■, Asia 81 C6 30 0N 110 0 E
Chinandega, Nic. 114 E7 12 35N 87 12W
Chincha Alta, Peru 120 D2 13 25S 76 7W
Chindwin →, Burma 85 J19 21 26N 95 15 E
Chingola, Zambia 97 G5 12 31S 27 53 E
Chinhoyi, Zimbabwe 97 H6 17 20S 30 8 E
Chiniot, Pakistan 84 D8 31 45N 73 0 E
Chinon, France 68 C4 47 10N 0 15 E
Chios, Greece 71 E12 38 27N 26 9 E
Chipata, Zambia 97 G6 13 38S 32 28 E
Chipman, Canada 113 B15 46 6N 65 53W
Chippenham, U.K. 24 D5 51 27N 2 6W
Chipping Campden, U.K. 24 B5 52 3N 1 45W
Chipping Norton, U.K. 24 C5 51 56N 1 32W
Chipping Ongar, U.K. 25 C9 51 42N 0 15 E
Chipping Sodbury, U.K. 24 C4 51 33N 2 23W
Chirbury, U.K. 23 G2 52 35N 3 4W
Chiredzi, Zimbabwe 97 J6 21 0S 31 38 E
Chirnside, U.K. 22 A4 55 48N 2 12W
Chisasibi, Canada 109 C12 53 50N 79 0W
Chiseldon, U.K. 24 C5 51 31N 1 44W
Chistopol, Russia 72 C9 55 25N 50 38 E
Chita, Russia 79 D13 52 0N 113 35 E
Chitral, Pakistan 84 B7 35 50N 71 56 E
Chittagong, Bangla. 85 H17 22 19N 91 48 E
Chittagong □, Bangla. 85 G17 24 5N 91 0 E
Chitungwiza, Zimbabwe 97 H6 18 0S 31 6 E
Choiseul, St. Lucia 115 f 13 47N 61 3W
Choiseul, Solomon Is. 99 B10 7 0S 156 40 E
Cholet, France 68 C3 47 4N 0 52W
Chollerton, U.K. 22 B4 55 4N 2 7W
Cholsey, U.K. 24 C6 51 35N 1 8W
Choluteca, Honduras 114 E7 13 20N 87 14W
Chon Buri, Thailand 83 B2 13 21N 101 1 E
Chŏngjin, N. Korea 81 B7 41 47N 129 50 E
Chongqing, China 80 D5 29 35N 106 25 E
Chongqing Shi □, China 80 C5 30 0N 108 0 E
Chŏnju, S. Korea 81 C7 35 50N 127 4 E
Chonos, Arch. de los, Chile 121 G2 45 0S 75 0W
Chorley, U.K. 23 E3 53 39N 2 38W
Chorzów, Poland 67 C10 50 18N 18 57 E
Choybalsan, Mongolia 81 B6 48 4N 114 30 E
Christchurch, N.Z. 99 J13 43 33S 172 47 E
Christchurch, U.K. 24 E5 50 44N 1 47W
Christmas I., Ind. Oc. 83 E2 10 30S 105 40 E
Chu →, Kazakhstan 74 E10 45 0N 67 44 E
Chubut →, Argentina 121 G3 43 20S 65 5W
Chudleigh, U.K. 27 F6 50 36N 3 36W
Chudskoye, L., Russia 56 D11 58 13N 27 30 E
Chukot Ra., Russia 79 C19 68 0N 175 0 E
Chulmleigh, U.K. 24 E1 50 54N 3 51W
Ch'unch'ŏn, S. Korea 81 C7 37 58N 127 44 E
Chuquicamata, Chile 121 E3 22 15S 69 0W
Chur, Switz. 66 E5 46 52N 9 32 E
Church Stretton, U.K. 23 G3 52 32N 2 48W
Churchdown, U.K. 24 C4 51 52N 2 9W
Churchill, Canada 108 C10 58 47N 94 11W
Churchill →, Man., Canada 108 C10 58 47N 94 12W
Churchill →, Nfld. & L., Canada 109 C13 53 19N 60 10W
Churchill, C., Canada 108 C10 58 46N 93 12W
Churchill Falls, Canada 109 C13 53 36N 64 19W
Churchill L., Canada 108 C9 55 55N 108 20W
Churchill Pk., Canada 108 C7 58 10N 125 10W
Churu, India 84 E9 28 20N 74 50 E
Chuska Mts., U.S.A. 110 C5 36 15N 108 50W
Chusovoy, Russia 72 C10 58 22N 57 50 E
Chuvashia □, Russia 72 C8 55 30N 47 0 E
Cicero, U.S.A. 112 E4 41 51N 87 45W
Ciechanów, Poland 67 B11 52 52N 20 38 E
Ciego de Avila, Cuba 115 C8 21 50N 78 50W
Cienfuegos, Cuba 115 C8 22 10N 80 30W
Cilo Dağı, Turkey 73 G7 37 28N 43 55 E
Cimarron →, U.S.A. 111 C7 36 10N 96 17W
Cincinnati, U.S.A. 112 F5 39 6N 84 31W
Cinderford, U.K. 24 C3 51 49N 2 30W
Cinto, Mte., France 68 E8 42 24N 8 54 E
Circle, U.S.A. 108 B5 65 50N 144 4W
Circleville, U.S.A. 112 F6 39 36N 82 57W
Cirebon, Indonesia 83 D2 6 45S 108 32 E
Cirencester, U.K. 24 C5 51 43N 1 57W
Ciudad Bolívar, Venezuela 120 B3 8 5N 63 36W
Ciudad del Carmen, Mexico 114 D6 18 38N 91 50W
Ciudad Guayana, Venezuela 120 B3 8 0N 62 30W
Ciudad Guzmán, Mexico 114 D4 19 40N 103 30W
Ciudad Juárez, Mexico 114 A3 31 40N 106 28W
Ciudad Madero, Mexico 114 C5 22 19N 97 50W
Ciudad Mante, Mexico 114 C5 22 50N 99 0W
Ciudad Obregón, Mexico 114 B3 27 28N 109 59W
Ciudad Real, Spain 69 C4 38 59N 3 55W

Ciudad Victoria, Mexico 114 C5 23 41N 99 9W
Cizre, Turkey 73 G7 37 19N 42 10 E
Clacton-on-Sea, U.K. 25 C11 51 47N 1 11 E
Claire, L., Canada 108 C8 58 35N 112 5W
Clara, Ireland 28 E6 53 21N 7 37W
Clare, U.K. 25 B10 52 4N 0 34 E
Clare □, Ireland 30 C4 52 45N 9 0W
Clare →, Ireland 28 E3 53 20N 9 2W
Clare I., Ireland 28 D1 53 49N 10 0W
Claremont, U.S.A. 113 D11 43 23N 72 20W
Clark Fork →, U.S.A. 110 A3 48 9N 116 15W
Clarksburg, U.S.A. 112 F7 39 17N 80 30W
Clarksdale, U.S.A. 111 D8 34 12N 90 35W
Clarksville, U.S.A. 111 C9 36 32N 87 21W
Claverley, U.K. 23 G4 52 32N 2 18W
Claydon, U.K. 25 B11 52 7N 1 8 E
Clay Cross, U.K. 23 F6 53 10N 1 25W
Clear, C., Ireland 30 F3 51 25N 9 32W
Clear I., Ireland 30 F4 51 26N 9 30W
Clearfield, U.S.A. 112 E8 41 2N 78 27W
Clearwater, U.S.A. 111 E10 27 58N 82 48W
Cleator Moor, U.K. 22 C2 54 32N 3 30W
Clee Hills, U.K. 23 H3 52 26N 2 35W
Cleethorpes, U.K. 23 E8 53 33N 0 3W
Cleeve Cloud, U.K. 24 C5 51 56N 2 0W
Clent Hills, U.K. 23 H4 52 25N 2 4W
Cleobury Mortimer, U.K. 23 H4 52 22N 2 28W
Clevedon, U.K. 24 D3 51 26N 2 52W
Cleveland, Miss., U.S.A. 111 D8 33 45N 90 43W
Cleveland, Ohio, U.S.A. 112 E7 41 30N 81 42W
Cleveland Hills, U.K. 22 D6 54 25N 1 11W
Clew B., Ireland 28 D2 53 50N 9 49W
Cley, U.K. 25 A11 52 57N 1 2 E
Clifden, Ireland 28 E1 53 29N 10 1W
Cliffe, U.K. 25 D10 51 28N 0 31 E
Clifford, U.K. 24 B2 52 7N 3 6W
Clinton, Iowa, U.S.A. 111 B8 41 51N 90 12W
Clinton, Okla., U.S.A. 110 C7 35 31N 98 58W
Clinton Colden L., Canada 108 B9 63 58N 107 27W
Clipperton, I., Pac. Oc. 103 F17 10 18N 109 13W
Clipston, U.K. 23 H7 52 27N 0 58W
Clitheroe, U.K. 23 E4 53 53N 2 22W
Clogher Hd., Ireland 29 D9 53 48N 6 14W
Clonakilty, Ireland 30 E5 51 37N 8 53W
Clonakilty B., Ireland 30 E5 51 35N 8 51W
Cloncurry →, Australia 98 E7 18 37S 140 40 E
Clondalkin, Ireland 29 E9 53 19N 6 25W
Clones, Ireland 29 C7 54 11N 7 15W
Clonmel, Ireland 31 D7 52 21N 7 42W
Cloughton, U.K. 22 D8 54 20N 0 26W
Clovelly, U.K. 27 F5 51 0N 4 25W
Clovis, U.S.A. 110 D6 34 24N 103 12W
Clowne, U.K. 23 F6 53 16N 1 17W
Cluj-Napoca, Romania 67 E12 46 47N 23 38 E
Clun Forest, U.K. 23 H2 52 27N 3 7W
Clunbury, U.K. 23 H3 52 25N 2 55W
Clwyd →, U.K. 26 A6 53 19N 3 31W
Clyde →, U.K. 20 C6 55 55N 4 30W
Clyde, Firth of, U.K. 20 D5 55 22N 5 1W
Clyde River, Canada 109 A13 70 30N 68 30W
Clydebank, U.K. 20 C7 55 54N 4 23W
Coalbrookdale, U.K. 23 G3 52 39N 2 30W
Coalisland, U.K. 29 B8 54 33N 6 42W
Coalville, U.K. 23 G6 52 44N 1 23W
Coamo, Puerto Rico 115 d 18 5N 66 22W
Coast Mts., Canada 108 C7 55 0N 129 20W
Coast Ranges, U.S.A. 110 B2 39 0N 123 0W
Coatbridge, U.K. 20 C7 55 52N 4 6W
Coaticook, Canada 113 C12 45 10N 71 46W
Coats I., Canada 109 B11 62 30N 83 0W
Coats Land, Antarctica 55 D1 77 0S 25 0W
Coatzacoalcos, Mexico 114 D6 18 7N 94 25W
Cobán, Guatemala 114 D6 15 30N 90 21W
Cobar, Australia 98 G8 31 27S 145 48 E
Cóbh, Ireland 30 E6 51 51N 8 17W
Cobija, Bolivia 120 D3 11 0S 68 50W
Cobourg, Canada 112 D8 43 58N 78 10W
Cochabamba, Bolivia 120 D3 17 26S 66 10W
Cochin, India 84 Q10 9 58N 76 20 E
Cochrane, Canada 109 D11 49 0N 81 0W
Cockburn, Canal, Chile 121 H2 54 30S 72 0W
Cockburn I., Canada 112 C6 45 55N 83 22W
Cockerham, U.K. 23 E3 53 58N 2 49W
Cockermouth, U.K. 22 C2 54 40N 3 22W
Cockfield, U.K. 25 B10 52 10N 0 48 E
Cockpit Country, The, Jamaica 114 a 18 15N 77 45W
Coco →, Cent. Amer. 115 E8 15 0N 83 8W
Coco, I. del, Pac. Oc. 103 G19 5 25N 87 55W
Cocos Is., Ind. Oc. 83 E1 12 10S 96 55 E
Cod, C., U.S.A. 111 B12 42 5N 70 10W
Coddenham, U.K. 25 B11 52 9N 1 8 E
Codó, Brazil 120 C5 4 30S 43 55W
Cody, U.S.A. 110 B5 44 32N 109 3W
Cœur d'Alene, U.S.A. 110 A3 47 45N 116 51W
Coggeshall, U.K. 25 C10 51 52N 0 42 E
Cognac, France 68 D3 45 41N 0 20W
Coigeach, Rubha, U.K. 18 F7 58 6N 5 26W
Coimbatore, India 84 P10 11 2N 76 59 E
Coimbra, Portugal 69 B1 40 15N 8 27W
Colatina, Brazil 122 C2 19 32S 40 37W
Colchester, U.K. 25 C10 51 54N 0 55 E
Cold Fell, U.K. 22 C3 54 53N 2 36W
Coldstream, U.K. 21 C11 55 39N 2 15W
Colebrook, U.S.A. 113 C12 44 54N 71 30W
Colebrooke, U.K. 24 E1 50 47N 3 44W
Coleford, U.K. 24 C3 51 47N 2 36W
Coleraine, U.K. 29 A8 55 8N 6 41W
Coleshill, U.K. 23 G5 52 30N 1 41W
Colima, Mexico 114 D4 19 14N 103 43W
Coll, U.K. 18 J4 56 39N 6 34W
Collier Law, U.K. 22 C5 54 47N 1 59W
Collin, U.K. 22 B1 54 58N 3 31W
Collingbourne Kingston, U.K. 24 D5 51 18N 1 40W
Collingham, U.K. 23 F7 53 8N 0 46W
Collingwood, Canada 112 C7 44 29N 80 13W
Collooney, Ireland 28 C5 54 11N 8 29W
Colmar, France 68 B7 48 5N 7 20 E
Colne, U.K. 23 E4 53 51N 2 9W
Colne →, Bucks., U.K. 25 D7 51 27N 0 32W
Colne →, Essex, U.K. 25 C10 51 51N 0 58 E
Cologne, Germany 66 C4 50 56N 6 57 E
Colombia ■, S. Amer. 120 B2 3 45N 73 0W
Colombo, Sri Lanka 84 R11 6 56N 79 58 E
Colón, Arch. de, Ecuador 103 H18 0 0N 91 0W
Colonsay, U.K. 20 B3 56 5N 6 12W
Colorado □, U.S.A. 110 C5 39 30N 105 30W
Colorado →, Argentina 121 F3 39 50S 62 8W
Colorado →, N. Amer. 110 D4 31 45N 114 40W
Colorado →, U.S.A. 111 E7 28 36N 95 59W
Colorado Plateau, U.S.A. 110 C4 37 0N 111 0W
Colorado Springs, U.S.A. 110 C6 38 50N 104 49W
Colsterworth, U.K. 23 G7 52 49N 0 37W
Coltishall, U.K. 25 A11 52 44N 1 21 E
Columbia, Mo., U.S.A. 111 C8 38 57N 92 20W
Columbia, S.C., U.S.A. 111 D10 34 0N 81 2W
Columbia, Tenn., U.S.A. 111 C9 35 37N 87 2W

Columbia →, N. Amer. 110 A2 46 15N 124 5W
Columbia, District of □, U.S.A. 112 F9 38 55N 77 0W
Columbus, Ga., U.S.A. 111 D10 32 28N 84 59W
Columbus, Ind., U.S.A. 112 F5 39 13N 85 55W
Columbus, Miss., U.S.A. 111 D9 33 30N 88 25W
Columbus, Nebr., U.S.A. 111 B7 41 26N 97 22W
Columbus, Ohio, U.S.A. 112 F6 39 58N 83 0W
Colville →, U.S.A. 108 A4 70 25N 150 30W
Colwell, U.K. 22 B4 55 5N 2 4W
Colwich, U.K. 23 G5 52 48N 1 58W
Colwyn Bay, U.K. 26 A6 53 18N 3 44W
Colyton, U.K. 24 E2 50 44N 3 5W
Combe Martin, U.K. 27 E5 51 12N 4 3W
Comber, U.K. 29 B10 54 33N 5 45W
Comeragh Mts., Ireland 31 D7 52 18N 7 34W
Comilla, Bangla. 85 H17 23 28N 91 10 E
Committee B., Canada 109 B11 68 30N 86 30W
Communism Pk., Tajikistan 79 F9 39 0N 72 2 E
Como, Italy 68 D8 45 47N 9 5 E
Como, Lago di, Italy 68 D8 46 0N 9 11 E
Comodoro Rivadavia, Argentina 121 G3 45 50S 67 40W
Comorin, C., India 84 Q10 8 3N 77 40 E
Comoros ■, Ind. Oc. 91 H8 12 10S 44 15 E
Compass Mt., S. Africa 90 K6 31 45S 24 32 E
Compiègne, France 68 B5 49 24N 2 50 E
Conakry, Guinea 94 G3 9 29N 13 49W
Conceição da Barra, Brazil 122 C3 18 35S 39 45W
Concepción, Chile 121 F2 36 50S 73 0W
Concepción, Paraguay 121 E4 23 22S 57 26W
Concepción, Est. de, Chile 121 H2 50 30S 74 55W
Concepción del Oro, Mexico 114 C4 24 40N 101 30W
Concepción del Uruguay, Argentina 121 F4 32 35S 58 20W
Conception, Pt., U.S.A. 110 D2 34 27N 120 28W
Conchos →, Mexico 114 B4 29 32N 105 0W
Concord, U.S.A. 113 D12 43 12N 71 32W
Concordia, Argentina 121 F4 31 20S 58 2W
Concordia, U.S.A. 110 C7 39 34N 97 40W
Condeúba, Brazil 122 B2 14 52S 42 0W
Condover, U.K. 23 G3 52 39N 2 44W
Congleton, U.K. 23 F4 53 10N 2 13W
Congo ■, Africa 96 E3 1 0S 16 0 E
Congo →, Africa 96 F2 6 4S 12 24 E
Congo, Dem. Rep. of the ■, Africa 96 E4 3 0S 23 0 E
Congo Basin, Africa 96 E4 0 10S 24 30 E
Congresbury, U.K. 24 D3 51 22N 2 48W
Coningsby, U.K. 23 F8 53 7N 0 10W
Conisbrough, U.K. 23 F6 53 29N 1 14W
Coniston, Canada 112 B7 46 29N 80 51W
Coniston, U.K. 22 D2 54 22N 3 5W
Coniston Water, U.K. 22 D2 54 20N 3 5W
Conn, L., Ireland 28 C3 54 3N 9 15W
Connacht □, Ireland 28 D3 53 43N 9 12W
Connah's Quay, U.K. 23 F2 53 13N 3 4W
Connecticut □, U.S.A. 112 E7 41 57N 80 34W
Connecticut →, U.S.A. 113 E11 41 16N 72 20W
Connellsville, U.S.A. 112 E8 40 1N 79 35W
Connemara, Ireland 28 E2 53 29N 9 45W
Connemara Nat. Park △, Ireland 28 D2 53 32N 9 52W
Connersville, U.S.A. 112 F5 39 39N 85 8W
Conselheiro Lafaiete, Brazil 122 D2 20 40S 43 48W
Consett, U.K. 22 C5 54 51N 1 50W
Constance, L., Europe 66 E5 47 35N 9 25 E
Constanța, Romania 67 F15 44 14N 28 38 E
Constantine, Algeria 94 A7 36 25N 6 42 E
Constitución, Chile 121 F2 35 20S 72 30W
Contas →, Brazil 122 B3 14 17S 39 1W
Contwoyto L., Canada 108 B8 65 42N 110 50W
Conway, Ark., U.S.A. 111 C8 35 5N 92 26W
Conwy, U.K. 26 A6 53 17N 3 50W
Conwy →, U.K. 26 A6 53 17N 3 50W
Coober Pedy, Australia 98 F6 29 1S 134 43 E
Cook Inlet, U.S.A. 108 C4 60 0N 152 0W
Cook Is., Pac. Oc. 103 J12 17 0S 160 0W
Cook Strait, N.Z. 99 J13 41 15S 174 29 E
Cookstown, U.K. 29 B8 54 39N 6 45W
Cooktown, Australia 98 D8 15 30S 145 16 E
Coondapoor, India 84 N9 13 42N 74 40 E
Coos Bay, U.S.A. 110 B2 43 22N 124 13W
Cootehill, Ireland 29 C7 54 4N 7 5W
Copenhagen, Denmark 63 F6 55 41N 12 34 E
Copiapó, Chile 121 E2 27 30S 70 20W
Copper Harbor, U.S.A. 112 B4 47 28N 87 53W
Coppermine →, Canada 108 B8 67 49N 116 4W
Coquet →, U.K. 22 B5 55 20N 1 32W
Coquet I., U.K. 22 B5 55 20N 1 36W
Coquimbo, Chile 121 E2 30 0S 71 20W
Coracora, Peru 120 D2 15 5S 73 45W
Coral Harbour, Canada 109 B11 64 8N 83 10W
Coral Sea, Pac. Oc. 98 C9 15 0S 150 0 E
Corbin, U.S.A. 112 G5 36 57N 84 6W
Corbridge, U.K. 22 C5 54 58N 2 0W
Corby, U.K. 23 G7 52 30N 0 41W
Corby Glen, U.K. 23 G7 52 49N 0 30W
Corcaigh = Cork, Ireland 30 E5 51 54N 8 29W
Córdoba, Argentina 121 F3 31 20S 64 10W
Córdoba, Mexico 114 D5 18 50N 97 0W
Córdoba, Spain 69 D3 37 50N 4 50W
Córdoba, Sierra de, Argentina 121 F3 31 10S 64 25W
Cordova, U.S.A. 108 B5 60 33N 145 45W
Corfe Castle, U.K. 24 E4 50 38N 2 3W
Corfe Mullen, U.K. 24 E4 50 46N 2 1W
Corfu, Greece 71 E8 39 38N 19 50 E
Corinth, U.S.A. 111 D9 34 56N 88 31W
Corinth, G. of, Greece 71 E10 38 16N 22 30 E
Corinto, Brazil 122 C2 18 20S 44 30W
Cork, Ireland 30 E6 51 54N 8 29W
Cork □, Ireland 30 E5 51 57N 8 40W
Cork Harbour, Ireland 30 E6 51 47N 8 16W
Corner Brook, Canada 109 D14 48 57N 57 58W
Corning, U.S.A. 112 D9 42 9N 77 3W
Cornwall, Canada 109 D12 45 2N 74 44W
Cornwall □, U.K. 27 G4 50 26N 4 40W
Cornwall, C., U.K. 27 G2 50 8N 5 43W
Coro, Venezuela 120 A3 11 25N 69 41W
Corocoro, Bolivia 120 D3 17 15S 68 28W
Coromandel Coast, India 84 N12 12 30N 81 0 E
Coronation Gulf, Canada 108 B8 68 25N 110 0W
Coronel Pringles, Argentina 121 F3 38 0S 61 30W
Coronel Suárez, Argentina 121 F3 37 30S 61 52W
Coropuna, Nevado, Peru 120 D2 15 30S 72 41W
Corpus Christi, U.S.A. 110 E7 27 47N 97 24W
Corrain Pen., Ireland 28 D2 53 54N 9 54W
Corrib, L., Ireland 28 E3 53 27N 9 16W
Corrientes, Argentina 121 E4 27 30S 58 45W
Corrientes →, Colombia 120 B2 5 30N 77 34W
Corrientes, C., Mexico 114 C3 20 25N 105 42W
Corringham, U.K. 23 F7 53 25N 0 41W
Corse, France 68 E8 42 0N 9 0 E
Corse, C., France 68 E8 43 1N 9 25 E
Corsham, U.K. 24 D4 51 27N 2 10W
Corsica, France 68 F8 42 0N 9 0 E
Corsicana, U.S.A. 111 D7 32 6N 96 28W
Corsley, U.K. 24 D4 51 13N 2 14W

Corte, France 68 E8 42 19N 9 11 E
Cortez, U.S.A. 110 C5 37 21N 108 35W
Cortland, U.S.A. 113 D9 42 36N 76 11W
Corton, U.K. 25 A12 52 31N 1 45 E
Çorum, Turkey 73 F5 40 30N 34 57 E
Corumbá, Brazil 120 D4 19 0S 57 30W
Corunna = La Coruña, Spain 69 A1 43 20N 8 25W
Corvallis, U.S.A. 110 B2 44 34N 123 16W
Corve →, U.K. 23 H3 52 22N 2 43W
Corwen, U.K. 23 G4 52 59N 3 21W
Cosenza, Italy 70 E7 39 18N 16 15 E
Cosham, U.K. 24 E6 50 51N 1 2W
Coshocton, U.S.A. 112 E7 40 16N 81 51W
Costa Blanca, Spain 69 C5 38 25N 0 10W
Costa Brava, Spain 69 B7 41 30N 3 0 E
Costa del Sol, Spain 69 D3 36 30N 4 30W
Costa Dorada, Spain 69 B6 41 12N 1 15 E
Costa Rica ■, Cent. Amer. 115 F8 10 0N 84 0W
Costessey, U.K. 25 A11 52 40N 1 13 E
Cotabato, Phil. 83 C4 7 14N 124 15 E
Côte d'Azur, France 68 E7 43 25N 7 10 E
Côte-d'Ivoire = Ivory Coast ■, Africa 94 G4 7 30N 5 0W
Cotentin, France 68 B3 49 15N 1 30W
Cotherstone, U.K. 22 C5 54 35N 1 59W
Cotonou, Benin 94 G6 6 20N 2 25 E
Cotopaxi, Ecuador 120 C2 0 40S 78 30W
Cotswold Hills, U.K. 24 C4 51 42N 2 10W
Cottbus, Germany 66 C8 51 45N 14 20 E
Cottenham, U.K. 23 H9 52 18N 0 9 E
Coudersport, U.S.A. 112 E8 41 46N 78 1W
Council Bluffs, U.S.A. 111 B7 41 16N 95 52W
Courantyne →, S. Amer. 120 B4 5 55N 57 5W
Courtenay, Canada 108 D7 49 45N 125 0W
Coventry, U.K. 23 H6 52 25N 1 28W
Cover →, U.K. 22 D5 54 17N 1 47W
Coverack, U.K. 27 G3 50 1N 5 7W
Covington, U.S.A. 112 F5 39 5N 84 31W
Cowbridge, U.K. 24 D2 51 27N 3 27W
Cowdenbeath, U.K. 21 B9 56 7N 3 21W
Cowes, U.K. 24 E6 50 45N 1 18W
Cowfold, U.K. 25 E8 50 59N 0 16W
Cowpen, U.K. 22 B5 55 8N 1 32W
Cox's Bazar, Bangla. 85 J17 21 26N 91 59 E
Cozumel, Isla, Mexico 114 C7 20 30N 86 40W
Crabhill, Barbados 115 g 13 19N 59 38W
Cradock, S. Africa 97 L5 32 8S 25 36 E
Craig, U.S.A. 110 B5 40 31N 107 33W
Craigavon, U.K. 29 C9 54 27N 6 23W
Craiova, Romania 67 F12 44 21N 23 48 E
Cramlington, U.K. 22 B5 55 6N 1 34W
Cranborne, U.K. 24 E5 50 55N 1 54W
Cranborne Chase, U.K. 24 E4 50 56N 2 6W
Cranbrook, Canada 108 D8 49 30N 115 46W
Cranbrook, U.K. 25 D10 51 6N 0 34 E
Cranleigh, U.K. 25 D8 51 8N 0 29W
Cranwell, U.K. 23 F8 53 3N 0 27W
Crateús, Brazil 120 C5 5 10S 40 39W
Crato, Brazil 120 C6 7 10S 39 25W
Craven Arms, U.K. 23 H3 52 26N 2 50W
Crawfordsville, U.S.A. 112 E4 40 2N 86 54W
Crawley, U.K. 25 D8 51 7N 0 11W
Credenhill, U.K. 24 B3 52 5N 2 48W
Crediton, U.K. 24 E1 50 47N 3 39W
Cree →, Canada 108 C9 58 57N 105 47W
Cree →, U.K. 20 E7 54 55N 4 25W
Cree L., Canada 108 C9 57 30N 106 30W
Cremona, Italy 68 D9 45 7N 10 2 E
Crete, Greece 71 G11 35 15N 25 0 E
Creuse →, France 68 C4 47 0N 0 34 E
Crewe, U.K. 23 F4 53 6N 2 26W
Crewkerne, U.K. 24 E3 50 53N 2 48W
Crianlarich, U.K. 20 B6 56 24N 4 37W
Criccieth, U.K. 26 B5 52 55N 4 13W
Crick, U.K. 23 H6 52 22N 1 8W
Crickhowell, U.K. 24 C2 51 52N 3 8W
Cricklade, U.K. 24 C5 51 38N 1 50W
Crieff, U.K. 21 B8 56 22N 3 50W
Criffell, U.K. 22 C1 54 56N 3 50W
Crimea □, Ukraine 73 E5 45 30N 33 10 E
Crimean Pen., Ukraine 73 F5 45 0N 34 0 E
Crișul Alb →, Romania 67 E11 46 42N 21 17 E
Crișul Negru →, Romania 67 E11 46 42N 21 16 E
Croagh Patrick, Ireland 28 D2 53 46N 9 40W
Croatia ■, Europe 66 F9 45 20N 16 0 E
Croglin, U.K. 22 C3 54 50N 2 39W
Crohy Hd., Ireland 28 B5 54 55N 8 26W
Croker, C., Australia 98 C5 10 58S 132 35 E
Cromarty, U.K. 19 G9 57 40N 4 2W
Cromer, U.K. 25 A11 52 56N 1 17 E
Crondall, U.K. 25 D7 51 14N 0 51W
Crook, U.K. 22 C5 54 43N 1 45W
Crooked I., Bahamas 115 C10 22 50N 74 10W
Crooklands, U.K. 22 D3 54 16N 2 42W
Crosby, Cumb., U.K. 22 C2 54 45N 3 25W
Crosby, Mersey., U.K. 23 F2 53 30N 3 3W
Crosby Ravensworth, U.K. 22 C3 54 33N 2 35W
Cross Fell, U.K. 22 C4 54 43N 2 28W
Cross Sound, U.S.A. 108 C6 58 0N 135 0W
Crosshaven, Ireland 30 E6 51 47N 8 17W
Crossmaglen, U.K. 29 C8 54 5N 6 36W
Crouch →, U.K. 25 C10 51 37N 0 53 E
Crow Hd., Ireland 30 E2 51 35N 10 9W
Crow Sound, U.K. 27 H1 49 56N 6 16W
Crowborough, U.K. 25 D9 51 3N 0 11 E
Crowland, U.K. 23 G8 52 41N 0 10W
Crowle, U.K. 23 E7 53 36N 0 49W
Crowsnest Pass, Canada 108 D8 49 40N 114 40W
Croyde, U.K. 27 E5 51 7N 4 14W
Croydon □, U.K. 25 D8 51 22N 0 5W
Crozet, Is., Ind. Oc. 53 G12 46 27S 52 0 E
Crudgington, U.K. 23 G3 52 46N 2 32W
Crummock Water, U.K. 22 C2 54 33N 3 18W
Cruz Bay, U.S. Virgin Is. 115 e 18 20N 64 48W
Cruzeiro, Brazil 122 D1 22 33S 45 0W
Cruzeiro do Sul, Brazil 120 C2 7 35S 72 35W
Crystal Falls, U.S.A. 112 B3 46 5N 88 20W
Cuando →, Angola 97 H4 17 30S 23 15 E
Cuango = Kwango →, Angola 96 F2 9 21S 13 9 E
Cuauhtémoc, Mexico 114 B3 28 25N 106 52W
Cuba ■, W. Indies 115 C9 22 0N 79 0W
Cubango →, Africa 97 H4 18 50S 22 25 E
Cuckfield, U.K. 25 D8 51 1N 0 8W
Cúcuta, Colombia 120 B2 7 54N 72 31W
Cuddalore, India 84 P11 11 46N 79 45 E
Cuenca, Ecuador 120 C2 2 50S 79 9W
Cuenca, Spain 69 B4 40 5N 2 10W
Cuernavaca, Mexico 114 D5 18 55N 99 15W
Cuiabá, Brazil 120 D4 15 30S 56 0W
Cuillin Hills, U.K. 18 H5 57 13N 6 15W
Cuillin Sd., U.K. 18 H5 57 4N 6 20W
Cuito →, Angola 97 H4 18 1S 20 48 E
Culebra, Isla de, Puerto Rico 115 d 18 19N 65 18W
Culiacán, Mexico 114 C3 24 50N 107 23W
Cullen, U.K. 19 G12 57 42N 2 49W
Cullompton, U.K. 24 E2 50 51N 3 24W
Culm →, U.K. 24 E1 50 46N 3 31W

Culpeper, U.S.A. ............ 112 F9 38 30N 78 0W
Cumaná, Venezuela ......... 120 A3 10 30N 64 5W
Cumberland, U.S.A. ........ 112 F8 39 39N 78 46W
Cumberland →, U.S.A. ..... 111 C9 36 15N 87 0W
Cumberland Pen., Canada . 109 B13 67 0N 64 0W
Cumberland Plateau, U.S.A. 111 C10 36 0N 85 0W
Cumberland Sd., Canada ... 109 B13 65 30N 66 0W
Cumbernauld, U.K. ......... 21 C8 55 57N 3 58W
Cumbria □, U.K. ........... 22 C3 54 42N 2 52W
Cumbrian Mts., U.K. ....... 22 D2 54 30N 3 0W
Cummertrees, U.K. ......... 22 C2 54 59N 3 20W
Cumnock, U.K. ............. 20 D7 55 28N 4 17W
Cumnor, U.K. .............. 24 C6 51 44N 1 19W
Cumwhinton, U.K. .......... 22 C3 54 52N 2 50W
Cunene →, Angola .......... 97 H2 17 20S 11 50 E
Cúneo, Italy .............. 68 D7 44 23N 7 32 E
Cunnamulla, Australia ..... 98 F8 28 2S 145 38 E
Cupar, U.K. ............... 21 B9 56 19N 3 1W
Curaçao, Neth. Ant. ....... 115 E11 12 10N 69 0W
Curicó, Chile ............. 121 F2 34 55S 71 20W
Curitiba, Brazil .......... 122 E1 25 20S 49 10W
Curry Rivel, U.K. ......... 24 D3 51 1N 2 52W
Curvelo, Brazil ........... 122 C2 18 45S 44 27W
Cuttack, India ............ 85 J14 20 25N 85 57 E
Cuxhaven, Germany ......... 66 B5 53 51N 8 41 E
Cuyahoga Falls, U.S.A. .... 112 E7 41 8N 81 29W
Cuyuni →, Guyana .......... 120 B4 6 23N 58 41W
Cuzco, Peru ............... 120 D2 13 32S 72 0W
Cwmbran, U.K. ............. 24 C2 51 39N 3 2W
Cyclades, Greece .......... 71 F11 37 0N 24 30 E
Cynthiana, U.S.A. ......... 112 F5 38 23N 84 18W
Cyprus ■, Asia ............ 86 C3 35 0N 33 0 E
Cyrenaica, Libya .......... 95 C10 27 0N 23 0 E
Czech Rep. ■, Europe ...... 66 D8 50 0N 15 0 E
Częstochowa, Poland ....... 67 C10 50 49N 19 7 E

D
Da Hinggan Ling, China .... 81 B7 48 0N 121 0 E
Da Lat, Vietnam ........... 83 B2 11 56N 108 25 E
Da Nang, Vietnam .......... 83 B2 16 4N 108 13 E
Da Qaidam, China .......... 80 C4 37 50N 95 15 E
Daba Shan, China .......... 81 C5 32 0N 109 0 E
Dadra & Nagar Haveli □, India 84 J8 20 5N 73 0 E
Dadu, Pakistan ............ 84 F5 26 45N 67 45 E
Dagestan □, Russia ........ 73 F8 42 30N 47 0 E
Dagupan, Phil. ............ 83 B4 16 3N 120 20 E
Dahod, India .............. 84 H9 22 50N 74 15 E
Daingean, Ireland ......... 28 E7 53 18N 7 17W
Dajarra, Australia ........ 98 E6 21 42S 139 30 E
Dakar, Senegal ............ 94 F2 14 34N 17 29W
Dakhla, W. Sahara ......... 94 D2 23 50N 15 53W
Dalandzadgad, Mongolia .... 80 B5 43 27N 104 30 E
Dalap-Uliga-Darrit, Marshall Is. 102 G9 7 7N 171 24 E
Dalbeattie, U.K. .......... 21 E8 54 56N 3 50W
Dalhart, U.S.A. ........... 110 C6 36 4N 102 31W
Dalhousie, Canada ......... 113 A14 48 5N 66 26W
Dali, China ............... 80 D5 25 40N 100 10 E
Dalian, China ............. 81 C7 38 50N 121 40 E
Daliang Shan, China ....... 80 D5 28 0N 102 45 E
Dalkeith, U.K. ............ 21 C9 55 54N 3 4W
Dallas, U.S.A. ............ 111 D7 32 47N 96 49W
Dalmatia, Croatia ......... 70 C7 43 20N 17 0 E
Dalmellington, U.K. ....... 20 D7 55 19N 4 23W
Daloa, Ivory C. ........... 94 G4 7 0N 6 30W
Dalry, U.K. ............... 20 C6 55 42N 4 43W
Dalton, Dumf. & Gall., U.K. 22 B2 55 4N 3 24W
Dalton, N. Yorks., U.K. ... 22 D5 54 28N 1 32W
Dalton-in-Furness, U.K. ... 22 D2 54 10N 3 11W
Daly Waters, Australia .... 98 D5 16 15S 133 24 E
Daman, India .............. 84 J8 20 25N 72 57 E
Damaraland, Namibia ....... 97 H2 20 0S 15 0 E
Damascus, Syria ........... 86 C4 33 30N 36 18 E
Damerham, U.K. ............ 24 E5 50 56N 1 51W
Dampier, Australia ........ 98 E2 20 41S 116 42 E
Danakil Desert, Ethiopia .. 88 E3 12 45N 41 0 E
Danbury, U.S.A. ........... 113 E11 41 24N 73 28W
Dandong, China ............ 81 B7 40 10N 124 20 E
Danube →, Europe .......... 67 F15 45 20N 29 40 E
Danville, Ill., U.S.A. .... 112 E4 40 8N 87 37W
Danville, Ky., U.S.A. ..... 112 G5 37 39N 84 46W
Danville, Va., U.S.A. ..... 111 C11 36 36N 79 23W
Dar Banda, Africa ......... 90 F6 8 0N 23 0 E
Dar es Salaam, Tanzania ... 96 F7 6 50S 39 12 E
Darbhanga, India .......... 85 F14 26 15N 85 55 E
Dardanelles, Turkey ....... 71 D12 40 17N 26 32 E
Darent →, U.K. ............ 25 D9 51 28N 0 14 E
Dârfûr, Sudan ............. 95 F10 13 40N 24 0 E
Darién, G. del, Colombia .. 120 B2 9 0N 77 0W
Darjiling, India .......... 85 F16 27 3N 88 18 E
Darling →, Australia ...... 98 G7 34 4S 141 54 E
Darling Ra., Australia .... 98 G2 32 30S 116 0 E
Darlington, U.K. .......... 22 C5 54 32N 1 33W
Darmstadt, Germany ........ 66 D5 49 51N 8 39 E
Darnah, Libya ............. 95 B10 32 45N 22 45 E
Darnley, C., Antarctica ... 55 C6 68 0S 69 0 E
Darnley B., Canada ........ 108 B7 69 30N 123 30W
Dart →, U.K. .............. 27 G6 50 24N 3 39W
Dartford, U.K. ............ 25 D9 51 26N 0 13 E
Dartington, U.K. .......... 27 G6 50 27N 3 43W
Dartmoor, U.K. ............ 27 F6 50 38N 3 57W
Dartmouth, Canada ......... 109 D13 44 40N 63 30W
Dartmouth, U.K. ........... 27 G6 50 21N 3 36W
Darton, U.K. .............. 23 E5 53 35N 1 31W
Darwen, U.K. .............. 23 E4 53 42N 2 29W
Darwin, Australia ......... 98 C5 12 25S 130 51 E
Dashen, Ras, Ethiopia ..... 88 E2 13 8N 38 26 E
Dashhowuz, Turkmenistan ... 87 A9 41 49N 59 58 E
Dasht →, Pakistan ......... 84 G2 25 10N 61 40 E
Datong, China ............. 81 B6 40 6N 113 18 E
Daugavpils, Latvia ........ 72 C4 55 53N 26 32 E
Dauphin, Canada ........... 108 C9 51 9N 100 5W
Dauphiné, France .......... 68 D6 45 15N 5 25 E
Davangere, India .......... 84 M9 14 25N 75 55 E
Davao, Phil. .............. 83 C4 7 0N 125 40 E
Davenport, U.S.A. ......... 111 B8 41 32N 90 35W
Daventry, U.K. ............ 23 H6 52 16N 1 10W
Davis Str., N. Amer. ...... 109 B14 65 0N 58 0W
Dawlish, U.K. ............. 27 G6 50 35N 3 28W
Dawna Ra., Burma .......... 85 L21 16 30N 98 30 E
Dawros Hd., Ireland ....... 28 B4 54 50N 8 33W
Dawson, Canada ............ 108 B6 64 10N 139 30W
Dawson Creek, Canada ...... 108 C7 55 45N 120 15W
Dax, France ............... 68 E3 43 44N 1 3W
Daxian, China ............. 80 C5 31 15N 107 23 E
Daxue Shan, China ......... 80 C5 30 30N 101 30 E
Dayr az Zawr, Syria ....... 86 C5 35 20N 40 5 E
Dayton, U.S.A. ............ 112 F5 39 45N 84 12W
Daytona Beach, U.S.A. ..... 111 E10 29 13N 81 1W
De Aar, S. Africa ......... 97 L4 30 39S 24 0 E
De Pere, U.S.A. ........... 112 C3 44 27N 88 4W
De Ridder, U.S.A. ......... 111 D8 30 51N 93 17W
Dead Sea, Asia ............ 86 D3 31 30N 35 30 E

Deal, U.K. ................ 25 D11 51 13N 1 25 E
Dean, Forest of, U.K. ..... 24 C3 51 45N 2 33W
Dearham, U.K. ............. 22 C2 54 44N 3 25W
Dease →, Canada ........... 108 C7 59 56N 128 32W
Dease Lake, Canada ........ 108 C6 58 25N 130 6W
Death Valley, U.S.A. ...... 110 C3 36 15N 116 50W
Deben →, U.K. ............. 25 B11 52 0N 1 25 E
Debenham, U.K. ............ 25 B11 52 14N 1 12 E
Debre Markos, Ethiopia .... 88 E2 10 20N 37 40 E
Debre Tabor, Ethiopia ..... 88 E2 11 50N 38 26 E
Debrecen, Hungary ......... 67 E11 47 33N 21 42 E
Decatur, Ala., U.S.A. ..... 111 D9 34 36N 86 59W
Decatur, Ill., U.S.A. ..... 111 C9 39 51N 88 57W
Decatur, Ind., U.S.A. ..... 112 E5 40 50N 84 56W
Deccan, India ............. 84 L11 18 0N 79 0 E
Deddington, U.K. .......... 24 C6 51 59N 1 18W
Dee →, Aberds., U.K. ...... 19 H13 57 9N 2 5W
Dee →, Dumf. & Gall., U.K. 20 E7 54 51N 4 3W
Dee →, Wales, U.K. ........ 23 F2 53 22N 3 17W
Deeping Fen, U.K. ......... 23 G8 52 45N 0 15W
Deeping St. Nicholas, U.K. 23 G8 52 44N 0 12W
Deer Lake, Canada ......... 109 D14 49 11N 57 27W
Defiance, U.S.A. .......... 112 E5 41 17N 84 22W
Dehra Dun, India .......... 84 D11 30 20N 78 4 E
Del Rio, U.S.A. ........... 110 E6 29 22N 100 54W
Delabole, U.K. ............ 27 F4 50 37N 4 46W
Delaware, U.S.A. .......... 112 E6 40 18N 83 4W
Delaware □, U.S.A. ........ 113 F10 39 0N 75 20W
Delaware →, U.S.A. ........ 113 F10 39 15N 75 20W
Delaware B., U.S.A. ....... 111 C12 39 0N 75 10W
Delft, Neths. ............. 65 B4 52 1N 4 22 E
Delfzijl, Neths. .......... 65 A6 53 20N 6 55 E
Delgado, C., Mozam. ....... 96 G8 10 45S 40 40 E
Delhi, India .............. 84 E10 28 38N 77 17 E
Delice, Turkey ............ 73 G5 39 54N 34 2 E
Delicias, Mexico .......... 114 B3 28 10N 105 30W
Déline, Canada ............ 108 B7 65 11N 123 25W
Delphos, U.S.A. ........... 112 E5 40 51N 84 21W
Delta Junction, U.S.A. .... 108 B5 64 2N 145 44W
Demavend, Iran ............ 87 C8 35 56N 52 10 E
Deming, U.S.A. ............ 110 D5 32 16N 107 46W
Demopolis, U.S.A. ......... 111 D9 32 31N 87 50W
Den Helder, Neths. ........ 65 B4 52 57N 4 45 E
Denbigh, U.K. ............. 23 F2 53 12N 3 25W
Denby Dale, U.K. .......... 23 E5 53 34N 1 40W
Denham, Mt., Jamaica ...... 114 a 18 13N 77 32W
Denizli, Turkey ........... 73 G4 37 42N 29 2 E
Denmark ■, Europe ......... 63 F6 55 45N 10 0 E
Denmark Str., Atl. Oc. .... 54 C6 66 0N 30 0W
Dennery, St. Lucia ........ 115 f 13 55N 60 54W
Denny, U.K. ............... 21 B8 56 1N 3 55W
Denpasar, Indonesia ....... 83 D3 8 39S 115 13 E
Dent, U.K. ................ 22 D4 54 17N 2 27W
Denton, Gt. Man., U.K. .... 23 F4 53 27N 2 9W
Denton, Lincs., U.K. ...... 23 G7 52 53N 0 43W
Denton, U.S.A. ............ 111 D7 33 13N 97 8W
Denver, U.S.A. ............ 110 C5 39 44N 104 59W
Deoghar, India ............ 85 G15 24 30N 86 42 E
Deolali, India ............ 84 K8 19 58N 73 50 E
Dera Ghazi Khan, Pakistan  84 D7 30 5N 70 43 E
Dera Ismail Khan, Pakistan 84 D7 31 50N 70 50 E
Derbent, Russia ........... 73 F8 42 5N 48 15 E
Derby, Australia .......... 98 D3 17 18S 123 38 E
Derby, U.K. ............... 23 G6 52 56N 1 28W
Derg →, U.K. .............. 28 B7 54 44N 7 26W
Derg, L., Ireland ......... 30 C6 53 0N 8 20W
Derryveagh Mts., Ireland .. 28 B5 54 56N 8 11W
Derwent →, Derby, U.K. .... 23 G6 52 57N 1 28W
Derwent →, N. Yorks., U.K. 23 E7 53 45N 0 58W
Derwent →, Tyne & W., U.K. 22 C5 54 58N 1 41W
Derwent Water, U.K. ....... 22 C2 54 35N 3 9W
Des Moines, U.S.A. ........ 111 B8 41 35N 93 37W
Des Moines →, U.S.A. ...... 111 B8 40 23N 91 25W
Desborough, U.K. .......... 23 H7 52 27N 0 49W
Deschutes →, U.S.A. ....... 110 A2 45 38N 120 55W
Dese, Ethiopia ........... 88 E2 11 5N 39 40 E
Deseado →, Argentina ...... 121 G3 47 45S 65 54W
Desford, U.K. ............. 23 G6 52 37N 1 17W
Desolación, I., Chile ..... 121 H2 53 0S 74 0W
Dessau, Germany ........... 66 C7 51 51N 12 14 E
Detour, Pt., U.S.A. ....... 112 C4 45 40N 86 40W
Detroit, U.S.A. ........... 112 D6 42 20N 83 3W
Deutsche Bucht, Germany ... 66 A5 54 15N 8 0 E
Deventer, Neths. .......... 65 B6 52 15N 6 10 E
Deveron →, U.K. ........... 19 G12 57 41N 2 32W
Devils Lake, U.S.A. ....... 110 A7 48 7N 98 52W
Devizes, U.K. ............. 24 D5 51 22N 1 58W
Devon □, U.K. ............. 24 E1 50 50N 3 40W
Devon I., Canada .......... 54 B3 75 10N 85 0W
Devonport, U.K. ........... 27 G5 50 22N 4 11W
Dewey, Puerto Rico ........ 115 d 18 18N 65 18W
Dewsbury, U.K. ............ 23 E5 53 42N 1 37W
Dezfûl, Iran .............. 86 C7 32 20N 48 30 E
Dezhneva, C., Russia ...... 79 C20 66 5N 169 40W
Dhahran, Si. Arabia ....... 86 E7 26 10N 50 7 E
Dhaka, Bangla. ........... 85 H17 23 43N 90 26 E
Dhaka □, Bangla. .......... 85 G17 24 25N 90 25 E
Dhamtari, India ........... 85 J12 20 42N 81 35 E
Dhanbad, India ............ 85 H15 23 50N 86 30 E
Dharwad, India ............ 84 M9 15 30N 75 4 E
Dhaulagiri, Nepal ......... 85 E13 28 39N 83 28 E
Dhenkanal, India .......... 85 J14 20 45N 85 35 E
Dhubri, India ............. 85 F16 26 2N 89 59 E
Dhule, India .............. 84 J9 20 58N 74 50 E
Diamantina, Brazil ........ 122 C2 18 17S 43 40W
Diamantina →, Australia ... 98 F6 26 45S 139 10 E
Diamantino, Brazil ........ 120 D4 14 30S 56 30W
Dibrugarh, India .......... 85 F19 27 29N 94 55 E
Dickinson, U.S.A. ......... 110 A6 46 53N 102 47W
Didcot, U.K. .............. 24 C6 51 36N 1 14W
Diefenbaker, L., Canada ... 108 C9 51 0N 106 55W
Diego Garcia, Ind. Oc. .... 53 E13 7 50S 72 50 E
Dieppe, France ............ 68 B4 49 54N 1 4 E
Digby, Canada ............. 109 D13 44 38N 65 50W
Digne-les-Bains, France ... 68 D7 44 5N 6 12 E
Dijon, France ............. 68 C6 47 20N 5 3 E
Dili, E. Timor ............ 83 D4 8 39S 125 34 E
Dillingham, U.S.A. ........ 108 C4 59 3N 158 28W
Dimitrovgrad, Bulgaria .... 71 C11 42 5N 25 35 E
Dimitrovgrad, Russia ...... 72 D8 54 14N 49 39 E
Dinajpur, Bangla. ......... 85 G16 25 33N 88 43 E
Dinan, France ............. 68 B2 48 28N 2 2W
Dinant, Belgium ........... 65 D4 50 16N 4 55 E
Dinaric Alps, Croatia ..... 70 C7 44 0N 16 30 E
Dingle, Ireland ........... 30 D2 52 9N 10 17W
Dingle B., Ireland ........ 30 D2 52 3N 10 20W
Dingwall, U.K. ............ 19 G9 57 36N 4 26W
Dire Dawa, Ethiopia ....... 88 F3 9 35N 41 45 E
Dirranbandi, Australia .... 98 F8 28 33S 148 17 E
Disappointment, C., U.S.A. 110 A2 46 18N 124 5W
Disappointment, L., Australia 98 E3 23 20S 122 40 E
Diss, U.K. ................ 25 B11 52 23N 1 7 E
Distington, U.K. .......... 22 C1 54 36N 3 32W
Distrito Federal □, Brazil 122 C1 15 45S 47 45W
Ditchingham, U.K. ......... 25 B11 52 28N 1 28 E
Ditchling Beacon, U.K. .... 25 E8 50 54N 0 6W

Dittisham, U.K. ........... 27 G6 50 22N 3 37W
Ditton Priors, U.K. ....... 23 H3 52 30N 2 34W
Diu, India ................ 84 J7 20 45N 70 58 E
Divinópolis, Brazil ....... 122 D2 20 10S 44 54W
Dixon Entrance, U.S.A. .... 108 C6 54 30N 132 0W
Diyarbakır, Turkey ........ 73 G7 37 55N 40 18 E
Dizzard Pt., U.K. ......... 27 F4 50 44N 4 40W
Djerba, I. de, Tunisia .... 95 B8 33 50N 10 48 E
Djerid, Chott, Tunisia .... 94 B7 33 42N 8 30 E
Djibouti, Djibouti ........ 88 E3 11 30N 43 5 E
Djibouti ■, Africa ........ 88 E3 12 0N 43 0 E
Dnepropetrovsk, Ukraine ... 73 E6 48 30N 35 0 E
Dnieper →, Ukraine ........ 73 E5 46 30N 32 18 E
Dniester →, Europe ........ 67 E16 46 18N 30 17 E
Dniprodzerzhynsk, Ukraine  73 E5 48 32N 34 37 E
Doba, Chad ................ 95 G9 8 40N 16 50 E
Dobrich, Bulgaria ......... 71 C12 43 37N 27 49 E
Docking, U.K. ............. 25 A10 52 54N 0 38 E
Doddington, Cambs., U.K. .. 23 H9 52 30N 0 3 E
Doddington, Northumberland,
  U.K. .................... 22 A5 55 33N 1 54W
Dodecanese, Greece ........ 71 F12 36 35N 27 0 E
Dodge City, U.S.A. ........ 110 C6 37 45N 100 1W
Dodman Pt., U.K. .......... 27 G4 50 13N 4 48W
Dodoma, Tanzania .......... 96 F7 6 8S 35 45 E
Doha, Qatar ............... 87 E7 25 15N 51 35 E
Dolbeau-Mistassini, Canada 109 D12 48 53N 72 14W
Dole, France .............. 68 C6 47 7N 5 31 E
Dolgarrog, U.K. ........... 26 A6 53 11N 3 50W
Dolgellau, U.K. ........... 24 A1 52 45N 3 53W
Dolo, Ethiopia ............ 88 G3 4 11N 42 3 E
Dolomites, Italy .......... 70 A4 46 23N 11 51 E
Dolores, Argentina ........ 121 F4 36 20S 57 40W
Dolphin and Union Str., Canada 108 B8 69 5N 114 45W
Dolphinton, U.K. .......... 22 A2 55 42N 3 25W
Dolton, U.K. .............. 27 F5 50 53N 4 2W
Dominica ■, W. Indies ..... 115 D12 15 20N 61 20W
Dominican Rep. ■, W. Indies 115 D10 19 0N 70 30W
Don →, Russia ............. 73 E6 47 4N 39 18 E
Don →, Aberds., U.K. ...... 19 H13 57 11N 2 5W
Don →, S. Yorks., U.K. .... 23 E7 53 41N 0 52W
Don Figuero Mts., Jamaica  114 a 18 5N 77 36W
Donaghadee, U.K. .......... 29 B10 54 39N 5 33W
Doncaster, U.K. ........... 23 E6 53 32N 1 6W
Dondra Head, Sri Lanka .... 84 S12 5 55N 80 40 E
Donegal, Ireland .......... 28 B5 54 39N 8 5W
Donegal □, Ireland ........ 28 B5 54 53N 8 0W
Donegal B., Ireland ....... 28 B4 54 31N 8 49W
Donets →, Russia .......... 73 E7 47 33N 40 55 E
Donetsk, Ukraine .......... 73 E6 48 0N 37 45 E
Dong Hoi, Vietnam ......... 83 B2 17 29N 106 36 E
Dongola, Sudan ............ 95 E12 19 9N 30 22 E
Dongting Hu, China ........ 81 D6 29 18N 112 45 E
Donhead, U.K. ............. 24 D4 51 1N 2 7W
Donington, U.K. ........... 23 G8 52 54N 0 12W
Donna Nook, U.K. .......... 23 F9 53 29N 0 8 E
Donostia-San Sebastián, Spain 69 A5 43 17N 1 58W
Doon →, U.K. .............. 20 D6 55 27N 4 39W
Dorchester, Dorset, U.K. .. 24 E4 50 42N 2 27W
Dorchester, Oxon., U.K. ... 24 C6 51 39N 1 10W
Dorchester, C., Canada .... 109 B12 65 27N 77 27W
Dordogne →, France ........ 68 D3 45 2N 0 36W
Dordrecht, Neths. ......... 65 C4 51 48N 4 39 E
Dorking, U.K. ............. 25 D8 51 14N 0 19W
Dornie, U.K. .............. 18 H6 57 17N 5 31W
Dornoch, U.K. ............. 19 G9 57 53N 4 2W
Dornoch Firth, U.K. ....... 19 G9 57 51N 4 4W
Dörgön Nuur, Mongolia ..... 80 B4 48 0N 93 0 E
Dorset □, U.K. ............ 24 E4 50 45N 2 26W
Dorstone, U.K. ............ 24 B3 52 3N 2 59W
Dortmund, Germany ......... 66 C4 51 30N 7 28 E
Dos Bahías, C., Argentina  121 G3 44 58S 65 32W
Dothan, U.S.A. ............ 111 D9 31 13N 85 24W
Douai, France ............. 68 A5 50 21N 3 4 E
Douala, Cameroon .......... 96 D1 4 0N 9 45 E
Doubs →, France ........... 68 C6 46 53N 5 1 E
Douglas, U.K. ............. 29 C13 54 10N 4 28W
Douglas, U.S.A. ........... 110 D5 31 21N 109 33W
Dounreay, U.K. ............ 19 E10 58 35N 3 44W
Dourados, Brazil .......... 120 E4 22 9S 54 50W
Douro →, Europe ........... 69 B1 41 8N 8 40W
Dove →, Derby, U.K. ....... 23 G5 52 51N 1 36W
Dove →, N. Yorks., U.K. ... 22 D7 54 15N 0 55W
Dove Dale, U.K. ........... 23 F5 53 7N 1 46W
Dover, U.K. ............... 25 D11 51 7N 1 19 E
Dover, Del., U.S.A. ....... 113 F10 39 10N 75 32W
Dover, N.H., U.S.A. ....... 113 D12 43 12N 70 56W
Dover, Str. of, Europe .... 64 F7 51 0N 1 30 E
Dover-Foxcroft, U.S.A. .... 113 C13 45 11N 69 13W
Doveridge, U.K. ........... 23 G5 52 54N 1 49W
Dovey →, U.K. ............. 29 C9 54 23N 6 2W
Downham, U.K. ............. 23 B9 52 26N 0 14 E
Downham Market, U.K. ...... 25 A9 52 37N 0 23 E
Downpatrick, U.K. ......... 29 C10 54 20N 5 43W
Downpatrick Hd., Ireland .. 28 C3 54 20N 9 21W
Downton, U.K. ............. 24 E5 50 59N 1 44W
Draguignan, France ........ 68 E7 43 32N 6 27 E
Drake Passage, S. Ocean ... 55 B17 58 0S 68 0W
Drakensberg, S. Africa .... 97 L5 31 0S 28 0 E
Drammen, Norway ........... 63 F6 59 42N 10 12 E
Drava →, Croatia .......... 71 B8 45 33N 18 55 E
Drenthe □, Neths. ......... 65 B6 52 52N 6 40 E
Dresden, Germany .......... 66 C7 51 3N 13 44 E
Dreux, France ............. 68 B4 48 44N 1 23 E
Driffield, U.K. ........... 23 D8 54 0N 0 26W
Drina →, Bos.-H. .......... 71 B8 44 53N 19 21 E
Drobeta-Turnu Severin,
  Romania ................. 67 F12 44 39N 22 41 E
Drogheda, Ireland ......... 29 D9 53 43N 6 22W
Drohobych, Ukraine ........ 73 E3 49 20N 23 30 E
Droichead Nua, Ireland .... 31 B9 53 11N 6 48W
Droitwich, U.K. ........... 23 H4 52 16N 2 8W
Dromore, U.K. ............. 24 E6 54 31N 7 28W
Dromore West, Ireland ..... 28 C4 54 15N 8 52W
Dronfield, U.K. ........... 23 F6 53 19N 1 27W
Drummond I., Canada ....... 112 B5 46 1N 83 39W
Drummondville, Canada ..... 113 C11 45 55N 72 25W
Druridge B., U.K. ......... 22 B5 55 17N 1 32W
Dry Harbour Mts., Jamaica  114 a 18 19N 77 24W
Dryden, Canada ............ 108 D10 49 47N 92 50W
Drygalski I., Antarctica .. 55 C7 66 0S 92 0 E
Du Bois, U.S.A. ........... 112 E8 41 8N 78 46W
Dubai, U.A.E. ............. 87 E8 25 18N 55 20 E
Dubawnt →, Canada ......... 108 B9 64 33N 100 6W
Dubawnt L., Canada ........ 108 B9 63 4N 101 42W
Dubbo, Australia .......... 98 G8 32 11S 148 35 E
Dublin, Ireland ........... 31 B10 53 21N 6 15W
Dublin, U.S.A. ............ 111 D10 32 32N 82 54W
Dublin □, Ireland ......... 31 B10 53 24N 6 20W
Dubrovnik, Croatia ........ 71 C8 42 39N 18 6 E
Dubuque, U.S.A. ........... 111 B8 42 30N 90 41W
Ducie I., Pac. Oc. ........ 103 K15 24 40S 124 48W
Duddington, U.K. .......... 23 G7 52 36N 0 32W
Duddon →, U.K. ............ 22 D2 54 12N 3 15W
Dudinka, Russia ........... 79 C10 69 30N 86 13 E

Dudley, U.K. .............. 23 G4 52 31N 2 5W
Duffield, U.K. ............ 23 G6 52 59N 1 29W
Dufftown, U.K. ............ 19 H11 57 27N 3 8W
Duisburg, Germany ......... 66 C4 51 26N 6 45 E
Dukinfield, U.K. .......... 23 F4 53 28N 2 6W
Dulce →, Argentina ........ 121 F3 30 32S 62 33W
Duluth, U.S.A. ............ 111 A8 46 47N 92 6W
Dulverton, U.K. ........... 24 D1 51 2N 3 33W
Dumbarton, U.K. ........... 20 C6 55 57N 4 33W
Dumfries, U.K. ............ 21 D8 55 4N 3 37W
Dumfries & Galloway □, U.K. 21 D8 55 9N 3 58W
Dumyât, Egypt ............. 95 B12 31 24N 31 48 E
Dún Laoghaire, Ireland .... 31 B10 53 17N 6 8W
Dunbar, U.K. .............. 21 B10 56 0N 2 31W
Dunblane, U.K. ............ 21 B8 56 11N 3 58W
Duncan, U.S.A. ............ 110 D7 34 30N 97 57W
Duncansby Head, U.K. ...... 19 E11 58 38N 3 1W
Dunchurch, U.K. ........... 23 H6 52 21N 1 17W
Dundalk, Ireland .......... 29 C9 54 1N 6 24W
Dundalk Bay, Ireland ...... 29 D9 53 55N 6 15W
Dundee, U.K. .............. 21 B10 56 28N 2 59W
Dundrum, U.K. ............. 29 C10 54 16N 5 52W
Dundrum B., U.K. .......... 29 C10 54 13N 5 47W
Dunedin, N.Z. ............. 99 K13 45 50S 170 33 E
Dunfermline, U.K. ......... 21 B9 56 5N 3 27W
Dungannon, U.K. ........... 29 B8 54 31N 6 46W
Dungarvan, Ireland ........ 31 D7 52 5N 7 37W
Dungarvan Harbour, Ireland 31 D7 52 4N 7 35W
Dungeness, U.K. ........... 25 E10 50 54N 0 59 E
Dunhuang, China ........... 80 B4 40 8N 94 36 E
Dunkeld, U.K. ............. 21 A8 56 34N 3 35W
Dunkerque, France ......... 68 A5 51 2N 2 20 E
Dunkery Beacon, U.K. ...... 24 D1 51 9N 3 36W
Dunkirk, U.S.A. ........... 112 D8 42 29N 79 20W
Dunleer, Ireland .......... 29 D9 53 50N 6 24W
Dunmanway, Ireland ........ 30 E4 51 43N 9 6W
Dunmore, U.S.A. ........... 113 E10 41 25N 75 38W
Dunnet Hd., U.K. .......... 19 E11 58 40N 3 21W
Dunoon, U.K. .............. 20 C6 55 57N 4 56W
Duns, U.K. ................ 21 C11 55 47N 2 20W
Dunsford, U.K. ............ 24 E1 50 41N 3 41W
Dunstable, U.K. ........... 25 C7 51 53N 0 32W
Dunster, U.K. ............. 24 D2 51 11N 3 27W
Dunston, U.K. ............. 23 G4 52 46N 2 7W
Dunvegan, U.K. ............ 18 H4 57 27N 6 35W
Duque de Caxias, Brazil ... 122 D2 22 45S 43 19W
Durance →, France ......... 68 E6 43 55N 4 45 E
Durango, Mexico ........... 114 C4 24 3N 104 39W
Durango, U.S.A. ........... 110 C5 37 16N 107 53W
Durant, U.S.A. ............ 111 D7 33 59N 96 25W
Durazno, Uruguay .......... 121 F4 33 25S 56 31W
Durban, S. Africa ......... 97 K6 29 49S 31 1 E
Düren, Germany ............ 66 C4 50 48N 6 29 E
Durg, India ............... 85 J12 21 15N 81 22 E
Durgapur, India ........... 85 H15 23 30N 87 20 E
Durham, U.K. .............. 22 C5 54 47N 1 34W
Durham, U.S.A. ............ 111 C11 35 59N 78 54W
Durham □, U.K. ............ 22 C5 54 42N 1 45W
Durlston Hd., U.K. ........ 24 E5 50 36N 1 57W
Durness, U.K. ............. 19 E8 58 34N 4 45W
Durrës, Albania ........... 71 D8 41 19N 19 28 E
Durrington, U.K. .......... 24 D5 51 12N 1 47W
Durrow, Ireland ........... 31 C8 52 51N 7 24W
Dursey I., Ireland ........ 30 E2 51 36N 10 12W
Dursley, U.K. ............. 24 C4 51 40N 2 21W
Dushanbe, Tajikistan ...... 79 F8 38 33N 68 48 E
Düsseldorf, Germany ....... 66 C4 51 14N 6 47 E
Dutch Harbor, U.S.A. ...... 108 C3 53 53N 166 32W
Duyun, China .............. 80 D5 26 18N 107 29 E
Dvina, N. →, Russia ....... 72 B7 64 32N 40 30 E
Dwarka, India ............. 84 H6 22 18N 69 8 E
Dyce, U.K. ................ 19 H13 57 13N 2 12W
Dyer, C., Canada .......... 109 B13 66 37N 61 16W
Dyersburg, U.S.A. ......... 111 C9 36 3N 89 23W
Dyfi →, U.K. .............. 26 B5 52 32N 4 3W
Dymchurch, U.K. ........... 25 D11 51 1N 1 0 E
Dymock, U.K. .............. 24 C3 51 59N 2 26W
Dzerzhinsk, Russia ........ 72 C7 56 14N 43 30 E
Dzhankoy, Ukraine ......... 73 E5 45 40N 34 20 E
Dzhugdzhur Ra., Russia .... 79 D15 57 30N 138 0 E
Dzuumod, Mongolia ......... 80 B5 47 45N 106 58 E

E
Eagle, U.S.A. ............. 108 B5 64 47N 141 12W
Eagle L., U.S.A. .......... 113 B13 46 20N 69 22W
Eagle Pass, U.S.A. ........ 110 E6 28 43N 100 30W
Eaglesfield, U.K. ......... 22 B2 55 4N 3 12W
Eakring, U.K. ............. 23 F7 53 9N 0 58W
Ealing □, U.K. ............ 25 C8 51 31N 0 20W
Earby, U.K. ............... 23 E4 53 55N 2 7W
Eardisley, U.K. ........... 24 B2 52 8N 3 1W
Earith, U.K. .............. 23 H9 52 22N 0 2 E
Earl Shilton, U.K. ........ 23 G6 52 35N 1 18W
Earl Soham, U.K. .......... 25 B11 52 14N 1 18 E
Earls Barton, U.K. ........ 23 H7 52 16N 0 45W
Earl's Colne, U.K. ........ 25 C10 51 56N 0 43 E
Earlston, U.K. ............ 22 A3 55 39N 2 40W
Earn →, U.K. .............. 21 B9 56 21N 3 18W
Earn, L., U.K. ............ 20 B7 56 23N 4 13W
Earsdon, U.K. ............. 22 B6 55 3N 1 29W
Easebourne, U.K. .......... 25 E7 51 0N 0 43W
Easington, Durham, U.K. ... 22 C6 54 47N 1 21W
Easington, E. Riding, U.K. 23 E9 53 39N 0 6 E
Easington Colliery, U.K. .. 22 C6 54 48N 1 19W
Easingwold, U.K. .......... 22 D6 54 8N 1 11W
East Bengal, Bangla. ...... 85 H17 24 0N 90 0 E
East Bergholt, U.K. ....... 25 C11 51 59N 1 3 E
East Beskids, Europe ...... 67 D11 49 20N 22 0 E
East Brent, U.K. .......... 24 D3 51 15N 2 56W
East China Sea, Asia ...... 81 D7 30 0N 126 0 E
East Cowes, U.K. .......... 24 E6 50 45N 1 16W
East Dereham, U.K. ........ 25 A10 52 41N 0 57 E
East Falkland, Falk. Is. .. 121 H4 51 30S 58 30W
East Fen, U.K. ............ 23 F9 53 4N 0 5 E
East Grinstead, U.K. ...... 25 D9 51 7N 0 0W
East Harling, U.K. ........ 25 B10 52 26N 0 56 E
East Ilsley, U.K. ......... 24 C6 51 31N 1 16W
East Indies, Asia ......... 74 K15 0 0N 120 0 E
East Kilbride, U.K. ....... 20 C7 55 47N 4 11W
East Lansing, U.S.A. ...... 112 D5 42 44N 84 29W
East London, S. Africa .... 97 L5 33 0S 27 55 E
East Markham, U.K. ........ 23 F7 53 15N 0 53W
East Moor, U.K. ........... 23 F5 53 16N 1 34W
East Pacific Ridge, Pac. Oc. 103 J17 15 0S 110 0W
East Pt., Br. Virgin Is. .. 115 e 18 40N 64 18W
East Retford = Retford, U.K. 23 B17 46 27N 1 16W
East Sea = Japan, Sea of, Asia 81 C7 40 0N 135 0 E
East Siberian Sea, Russia  79 B18 73 0N 160 0 E
East Sussex □, U.K. ....... 25 E9 50 56N 0 19 E
East Timor ■, Asia ........ 83 D4 8 50S 126 0 E
East Wittering, U.K. ...... 25 E7 50 46N 0 52W
East Woodhay, U.K. ........ 24 D6 51 21N 1 25W

**Eastbourne**                                          **Franklin D. Roosevelt L.**

Eastbourne, *U.K.* ............... 25 E9   50 46N   0 18 E
Eastchurch, *U.K.* .............. 25 D10  51 24N   0 53 E
Easter I., *Chile* ............... 103 K17  27  7S 109 23W
Eastern Ghats, *India* .......... 84 N11  14  0N  78 50 E
Eastern Group, *Fiji* ........... 99 D15  17  0S 178 30W
Eastleigh, *U.K.* ............... 24 E6   50 58N   1 21W
Eastmain, *Canada* .............. 109 C12  52 10N  78 30W
Eastmain →, *Canada* ............ 109 C12  52 27N  78 26W
Eastnor, *U.K.* ................. 24 B4   52  2N   2 23W
Easton, *Dorset, U.K.* .......... 24 E4   50 33N   2 26W
Easton, *Northants., U.K.* ...... 23 G7   52 37N   0 31W
Easton, *Md., U.S.A.* ........... 113 F9   38 47N  76  5W
Easton, *Pa., U.S.A.* ........... 113 E10  40 41N  75 13W
Easton-in-Gordano, *U.K.* ....... 24 D3   51 28N   2 42W
Eastport, *U.S.A.* .............. 113 C14  44 56N  67  0W
Eastry, *U.K.* .................. 25 D11  51 14N   1 19 E
Eastwood, *U.K.* ................ 23 F6   53  1N   1 18W
Eaton, *U.K.* ................... 23 G7   52 51N   0 49W
Eaton Socon, *U.K.* ............. 23 H8   52 14N   0 17W
Eau Claire, *U.S.A.* ............ 111 B8   44 49N  91 30W
Eau Claire, L. à l', *Canada* ... 109 C12  56 10N  74 25W
Ebberston, *U.K.* ............... 22 D7   54 14N   0 37W
Ebbw Vale, *U.K.* ............... 24 C2   51 46N   3 12W
Ebetsu, *Japan* ................. 82 B7   43  7N 141 34 E
Ebro →, *Spain* ................. 69 B6   40 43N   0 54 E
Ecclefechan, *U.K.* ............. 22 B5   55  4N   3 16W
Eccleshall, *U.K.* .............. 23 G4   52 52N   2 15W
Ech Chéliff, *Algeria* .......... 94 A6   36 10N   1 20 E
Echo Bay, *Canada* .............. 108 B8   66  5N 117 55W
Eckington, *U.K.* ............... 23 F6   53 18N   1 22W
Eclipse Sd., *Canada* ........... 109 A11  72 38N  79  0W
Ecuador ■, *S. Amer.* ........... 120 C2    2  0S  78  0W
Ed Damazin, *Sudan* ............. 95 F12  11 46N  34 21 E
Edam, *Neths.* .................. 65 B5   52 31N   5  3 E
Eday, *U.K.* .................... 19 D12  59 11N   2 47W
Eddrachillis B., *U.K.* ......... 18 F7   58 17N   5 14W
Eddystone, *U.K.* ............... 27 G5   50 11N   4 16W
Eden →, *U.K.* .................. 22 C2   54 57N   3  1W
Edenbridge, *U.K.* .............. 25 D9   51 12N   0  5 E
Edenderry, *Ireland* ............ 29 E7   53 21N   7  4W
Edge Hill, *U.K.* ............... 24 B6   52  8N   1 26W
Edinburgh, *U.K.* ............... 21 C9   55 57N   3 13W
Edington, *U.K.* ................ 24 D4   51 17N   2  5W
Edirne, *Turkey* ................ 73 F4   41 40N  26 34 E
Edmonton, *Canada* .............. 108 C8   53 30N 113 30W
Edmundbyers, *U.K.* ............. 22 C5   54 50N   1 58W
Edmundston, *Canada* ............ 109 D13  47 23N  68 20W
Edremit, *Turkey* ............... 86 B1   39 34N  27  0 E
Edson, *Canada* ................. 108 C8   53 35N 116 28W
Edward, *L., Africa* ............ 96 E5    0 25S  29 40 E
Edward VII Land, *Antarctica* ... 55 E13  80  0S 150  0W
Edwards Plateau, *U.S.A.* ....... 110 D6   30 45N 101 20W
Effingham, *U.S.A.* ............. 112 F3   39  7N  88 33W
Eganville, *Canada* ............. 112 C9   45 32N  77  5W
Eger, *Hungary* ................. 67 E11  47 53N  20 27 E
Egham, *U.K.* ................... 25 D7   51 25N   0 32W
Egremont, *U.K.* ................ 22 D1   54 29N   3 32W
Eğridir, *Turkey* ............... 73 G5   37 52N  30 51 E
Eğridir Gölü, *Turkey* .......... 73 G5   37 53N  30 50 E
Egton, *U.K.* ................... 22 D7   54 28N   0 44W
Egypt ■, *Africa* ............... 95 C12  28  0N  31  0 E
Eifel, *Germany* ................ 66 C4   50 15N   6 50 E
Eigg, *U.K.* .................... 18 J5   56 54N   6 10W
Eil, L., *U.K.* ................. 18 J7   56 51N   5 16W
Eindhoven, *Neths.* ............. 65 C5   51 26N   5 28 E
Eire = Ireland ■, *Europe* ...... 64 E2   53 50N   7 52W
Eivissa, *Spain* ................ 69 C6   38 54N   1 26 E
El Aaiún, *W. Sahara* ........... 94 C3   27  9N  13 12W
El 'Alamein, *Egypt* ............ 95 B11  30 48N  28 58 E
El Centro, *U.S.A.* ............. 110 D3   32 48N 115 34W
El Dorado, *U.S.A.* ............. 111 D8   33 12N  92 40W
El Faiyûm, *Egypt* .............. 95 C12  29 19N  30 50 E
El Fâsher, *Sudan* .............. 95 F11  13 33N  25 26 E
El Fuerte, *Mexico* ............. 114 B3   26 30N 108 40W
El Gîza, *Egypt* ................ 95 C12  30  0N  31 10 E
El Istiwa'iya, *Sudan* .......... 95 G11   5  0N  28  0 E
El Jadida, *Morocco* ............ 94 B4   33 11N   8 17W
El Khârga, *Egypt* .............. 95 C12  25 30N  30 33 E
El Mahalla el Kubra, *Egypt* .... 95 B12  31  0N  31  0 E
El Mansûra, *Egypt* ............. 95 B12  31  0N  31 19 E
El Minyâ, *Egypt* ............... 95 C12  28  7N  30 33 E
El Obeid, *Sudan* ............... 95 F12  13  8N  30 10 E
El Oued, *Algeria* .............. 94 B7   33 20N   6 58 E
El Paso, *U.S.A.* ............... 110 D5   31 45N 106 29W
El Reno, *U.S.A.* ............... 110 C7   35 32N  97 57W
El Salvador ■, *Cent. Amer.* .... 114 E7   13 50N  89  0W
El Tigre, *Venezuela* ........... 120 B3    8 44N  64 15W
Elat, *Israel* .................. 86 D3   29 30N  34 56 E
Elazığ, *Turkey* ................ 73 G6   38 37N  39 14 E
Elba, *Italy* ................... 70 C4   42 46N  10 17 E
Elbasan, *Albania* .............. 71 D9   41  9N  20  9 E
Elbe →, *Europe* ................ 66 B5   53 50N   9  0 E
Elbert, Mt., *U.S.A.* ........... 110 C5   39  7N 106 27W
Elbeuf, *France* ................ 68 B4   49 17N   1  2 E
Elbląg, *Poland* ................ 67 A10  54 10N  19 25 E
Elbrus, *Russia* ................ 73 F7   43 21N  42 30 E
Elburz Mts., *Iran* ............. 87 B8   36  0N  52  0 E
Elche, *Spain* .................. 69 C5   38 15N   0 42W
Eldoret, *Kenya* ................ 96 D7    0 30N  35 17 E
Elektrostal, *Russia* ........... 72 C6   55 41N  38 32 E
Elephant Butte Reservoir,
 *U.S.A.* ....................... 110 D5   33  9N 107 11W
Elephant I., *Antarctica* ....... 55 C18  61  0S  55  0W
Elephants →, *Africa* ........... 97 J6   24 10S  32 40 E
Eleuthera, *Bahamas* ............ 115 C9   25  0N  76 20W
Elgin, *U.K.* ................... 19 G11  57 39N   3  9W
Elgin, *U.S.A.* ................. 112 D3   42  2N  88 17W
Elgon, Mt., *Africa* ............ 96 D6    1 10N  34 30 E
Elham, *U.K.* ................... 25 D11  51  9N   1  8 E
Elishaw, *U.K.* ................. 22 B4   55 15N   2  6W
Elista, *Russia* ................ 73 E7   46 16N  44 14 E
Elizabeth, *U.S.A.* ............. 113 E10  40 40N  74 13W
Elizabeth City, *U.S.A.* ........ 111 C11  36 18N  76 14W
Elizabethtown, *U.S.A.* ......... 112 G5   37 42N  85 52W
Elkhart, *U.S.A.* ............... 112 E3   41 41N  85 58W
Elkins, *U.S.A.* ................ 112 F8   38 55N  79 51W
Elko, *U.S.A.* .................. 110 B3   40 50N 115 46W
Elland, *U.K.* .................. 23 E5   53 41N   1 50W
Ellen →, *U.K.* ................. 22 C2   54 44N   3 30W
Ellensburg, *U.S.A.* ............ 110 A2   46 59N 120 34W
Ellerton, *Barbados* ............ 115 g   13  7N  59 33W
Ellesmere, *U.K.* ............... 23 G3   52 55N   2 53W
Ellesmere I., *Canada* .......... 54 B4   79 30N  80  0W
Ellesmere Port, *U.K.* .......... 23 F3   53 17N   2 54W
Ellington, *U.K.* ............... 22 B5   55 14N   1 33W
Elliot Lake, *Canada* ........... 109 D11  46 25N  82 35W
Ellon, *U.K.* ................... 19 H13  57 22N   2  4W
Ellsworth Land, *Antarctica* .... 55 D16  76  0S   89  0W
Elmalı, *Turkey* ................ 73 G4   36 44N  29 56 E
Elmira, *U.S.A.* ................ 112 D9   42  6N  76 48W
Elmswell, *U.K.* ................ 25 B10  52 15N   0 55 E
Eluru, *India* .................. 85 L12  16 48N  81  8 E
Ely, *U.K.* ..................... 25 B9   52 24N   0 16 E
Ely, *U.S.A.* ................... 110 C4   39 15N 114 54W
Elyria, *U.S.A.* ................ 112 E6   41 22N  82  7W
Emāmrūd, *Iran* ................. 87 B8   36 30N  55  0 E

Embarcación, *Argentina* ........ 121 E3   23 10S  64  0W
Embleton, *U.K.* ................ 22 B5   55 29N   1 38W
Emden, *Germany* ................ 66 B4   53 21N   7 12 E
Emerald, *Australia* ............ 98 E8   37 56S 145 29 E
Emmeloord, *Neths.* ............. 65 B5   52 44N   5 46 E
Emmen, *Neths.* ................. 65 B6   52 48N   6 57 E
Emmonak, *U.S.A.* ............... 108 B3   62 46N 164 30W
Empalme, *Mexico* ............... 114 B2   28  1N 110 49W
Empangeni, *S. Africa* .......... 97 K6   28 50S  31 52 E
Empedrado, *Argentina* .......... 121 E4   28  0S  58 46W
Emperor Seamount Chain,
 *Pac. Oc.* ..................... 102 D9   40  0N 170  0 E
Emporia, *U.S.A.* ............... 111 C7   38 25N  96 11W
Emporium, *U.S.A.* .............. 112 E8   41 31N  78 14W
Empty Quarter = Rub' al Khâli,
 *Si. Arabia* ................... 88 D4   19  0N  48  0 E
Ems →, *Germany* ................ 66 B4   53 20N   7 12 E
Enard B., *U.K.* ................ 18 F7   58  5N   5 20W
Encarnación, *Paraguay* ......... 121 E4   27 15S  55 50W
Encounter B., *Australia* ....... 98 H6   35 45S 138 45 E
Ende, *Indonesia* ............... 83 D4    8 45S 121 40 E
Enderby I., *Kiribati* .......... 102 H10   3  8S 171  5W
Enderby, *U.K.* ................. 23 G6   52 36N   1 13W
Enderby Land, *Antarctica* ...... 55 C5   66  0S  53  0 E
Endicott, *U.S.A.* .............. 113 D9   42  6N  76  4W
Enewetak Atoll, *Marshall Is.* .. 102 F8   11 30N 162 15 E
Enez, *Turkey* .................. 73 F4   40 45N  26  5 E
Enfer, Pte. d', *Martinique* .... 114 c   14 22N  60 54W
Enfield □, *U.K.* ............... 25 C8   51 38N   0  4W
Engadin, *Switz.* ............... 66 E6   46 45N  10 10 E
Engels, *Russia* ................ 73 D8   51 28N  46  6 E
Enggano, *Indonesia* ............ 83 D2    5 20S 102 40 E
England □, *U.K.* ............... 64 E6   53  0N   2  0W
English →, *Canada* ............. 108 C10  49 12N  91  5W
English Channel, *Europe* ....... 64 F6   50  0N   2  0W
Enid, *U.S.A.* .................. 110 C7   36 24N  97 53W
Ennadai L., *Canada* ............ 108 B9   60 58N 101 20W
Ennedi, *Chad* .................. 95 E10  17 15N  22  0 E
Ennerdale Water, *U.K.* ......... 22 C2   54 32N   3 24W
Ennis, *Ireland* ................ 30 C5   52 51N   8 59W
Enniscorthy, *Ireland* .......... 31 D9   52 30N   6 34W
Enniskillen, *U.K.* ............. 28 C6   54 21N   7 39W
Ennistimon, *Ireland* ........... 30 C4   52 57N   9 17W
Enns →, *Austria* ............... 66 D8   48 14N  14 32 E
Enschede, *Neths.* .............. 65 B6   52 13N   6 53 E
Ensenada, *Mexico* .............. 114 A1   31 50N 116 50W
Enstone, *U.K.* ................. 24 C6   51 55N   1 27W
Entebbe, *Uganda* ............... 96 D6    0  4N  32 28 E
Entre Rios, *Argentina* ......... 116 G5   30 30S  58 30W
Enugu, *Nigeria* ................ 94 G7    6 30N   7 30 E
Épernay, *France* ............... 68 B5   49  3N   3 56 E
Épinal, *France* ................ 68 B7   48 10N   6 27 E
Epping, *U.K.* .................. 25 C9   51 41N   0  7 E
Epping Forest, *U.K.* ........... 25 C9   51 40N   0  5 E
Epsom, *U.K.* ................... 25 D8   51 19N   0 16W
Epworth, *U.K.* ................. 23 E7   53 32N   0 48W
Equatorial Guinea ■, *Africa* ... 96 E1    2  0N   8  0 E
Er Rachidia, *Morocco* .......... 94 B5   31 58N   4 20W
Ercıyaş Dağı, *Turkey* .......... 86 B3   38 30N  35 30 E
Erebus, Mt., *Antarctica* ....... 55 D11  77 35S 167  0 E
Ereğli, *Konya, Turkey* ......... 73 G5   37 31N  34  4 E
Ereğli, *Zonguldak, Turkey* ..... 73 F5   41 15N  31 24 E
Erfurt, *Germany* ............... 66 C6   50 58N  11  2 E
Eriboll, L., *U.K.* ............. 19 E8   58 30N   4 42W
Erie, *U.S.A.* .................. 112 D7   42  8N  80  5W
Erie, L., *N. Amer.* ............ 112 D7   42 15N  81  0W
Eriskay, *U.K.* ................. 18 H3   57  4N   7  8W
Eritrea ■, *Africa* ............. 88 D2   14  0N  38 30 E
Erlangen, *Germany* ............. 66 D6   49 36N  11  0 E
Ernakulam, *India* .............. 84 Q10   9 59N  76 22 E
Erne →, *Ireland* ............... 28 C5   54 30N   8 16W
Erne, Lower L., *U.K.* .......... 28 C6   54 28N   7 47W
Erne, Upper L., *U.K.* .......... 28 C6   54 14N   7 32W
Erode, *India* .................. 84 P10  11 24N  77 45 E
Errigal, *Ireland* .............. 28 A5   55  2N   8  6W
Erris Hd., *Ireland* ............ 28 C1   54 19N  10  0W
Erromango, *Vanuatu* ............ 99 D12  18 45S 169  5 E
Erzgebirge, *Germany* ........... 66 C7   50 27N  12 55 E
Erzincan, *Turkey* .............. 73 G6   39 46N  39 30 E
Erzurum, *Turkey* ............... 73 G7   39 57N  41 15 E
Esbjerg, *Denmark* .............. 63 F5   55 29N   8 29 E
Escanaba, *U.S.A.* .............. 112 C4   45 45N  87  4W
Esch-sur-Alzette, *Lux.* ........ 65 E6   49 32N   6  0 E
Escrick, *U.K.* ................. 23 E6   53 53N   1  2W
Escuinapa, *Mexico* ............. 114 C3   22 50N 105 50W
Escuintla, *Guatemala* .......... 114 E6   14 20N  90 48W
Eşfahân, *Iran* ................. 87 C7   32 39N  51 43 E
Esha Ness, *U.K.* ............... 18 B14  60 29N   1 38W
Esk →, *Cumb., U.K.* ............ 21 E9   54 58N   3  2W
Esk →, *Cumb., U.K.* ............ 22 D2   54 20N   3 24W
Esk →, *N. Yorks., U.K.* ........ 22 D7   54 30N   0 37W
Eskdale, *U.K.* ................. 22 B2   55 12N   3  4W
Esker, *Canada* ................. 109 C13  53 53N  66 25W
Eskilstuna, *Sweden* ............ 63 F7   59 22N  16 32 E
Eskişehir, *Turkey* ............. 73 G5   39 50N  30 30 E
Eslâmâbâd-e Gharb, *Iran* ....... 86 C6   34 10N  46 30 E
Esperance, *Australia* .......... 98 G3   33 45S 121 55 E
Esperance B., *St. Lucia* ....... 115 f   14  4N  60 55W
Esperanza, *Puerto Rico* ........ 115 d   18  6N  65 28W
Espinhaço, Serra do, *Brazil* ... 122 C2   17 30S  43 30W
Espírito Santo □, *Brazil* ...... 122 C2   20  0S  40 45W
Espiritu Santo, *Vanuatu* ....... 99 D12  15 15S 166 50 E
Espoo, *Finland* ................ 63 E8   60 12N  24 40 E
Essaouira, *Morocco* ............ 94 B4   31 32N   9 42W
Essen, *Germany* ................ 66 C4   51 28N   7  2 E
Essequibo →, *Guyana* ........... 120 B4    6 50N  58 30W
Essex □, *U.K.* ................. 25 C9   51 54N   0 27 E
Estância, *Brazil* .............. 122 B3   11 16S  37 26W
Estevan, *Canada* ............... 108 D9   49 10N 102 59W
Eston, *U.K.* ................... 22 C6   54 34N   1  8W
Estonia ■, *Europe* ............. 72 C4   58 30N  25 30 E
Estrela, Serra da, *Portugal* ... 69 B2   40 10N   7 45W
Estrondo, Serra do, *Brazil* .... 120 C5    7 20S  48  0W
Etawah, *India* ................. 84 F11  26 48N  79  6 E
Etchingham, *U.K.* .............. 25 D9   51  0N   0 26 E
Ethiopia ■, *Africa* ............ 88 F3    8  0N  40  0 E
Ethiopian Highlands, *Ethiopia* . 74 J7   10  0N  37  0 E
Etive, L., *U.K.* ............... 20 B5   56 29N   5 10W
Etna, *Italy* ................... 70 F6   37 50N  14 55 E
Eton, *U.K.* .................... 25 C7   51 30N   0 36W
Etosha Pan, *Namibia* ........... 97 H3   18 40S  16 30 E
Ettington, *U.K.* ............... 24 B5   52  8N   1 35W
Ettrick Forest, *U.K.* .......... 21 C10  55 31N   2 55W
Ettrick Water →, *U.K.* ......... 21 C10  55 31N   2 55W
Euclid, *U.S.A.* ................ 112 E7   41 34N  81 32W
Eugene, *U.S.A.* ................ 110 B2   44  5N 123  4W
Euphrates →, *Asia* ............. 110 B2   40 47N 124  9W
Europa, Île, *Ind. Oc.* ......... 97 J8   22 20S  40 22 E
Europe .......................... 56 E10  50  0N  20  0 E
Euxton, *U.K.* .................. 23 E3   53 41N   2  4W
Evanston, *Ill., U.S.A.* ........ 112 D4   42  3N  87 41W
Evanston, *Wyo., U.S.A.* ........ 110 B4   41 16N 110 58W
Evansville, *U.S.A.* ............ 112 G4   37 58N  87 35W
Evercreech, *U.K.* .............. 24 D4   51  9N   2 30W
Everest, Mt., *Nepal* ........... 85 E15  28  5N  86 58 E
Everett, *U.S.A.* ............... 110 A2   47 59N 122 12W

Everglades, The, *U.S.A.* ....... 111 E10  25 50N  81  0W
Evesham, *U.K.* ................. 24 B5   52  6N   1 56W
Évora, *Portugal* ............... 69 C2   38 33N   7 57W
Évreux, *France* ................ 68 B4   49  3N   1  8 E
Évvoia, *Greece* ................ 71 E11  38 30N  24  0 E
Ewe, L., *U.K.* ................. 18 G6   57 49N   5 38W
Ewell, *U.K.* ................... 25 D8   51 20N   0 14W
Ewhurst, *U.K.* ................. 25 D8   51  9N   0 25W
Exe →, *U.K.* ................... 24 E2   50 41N   3 29W
Exeter, *U.K.* .................. 24 E1   50 43N   3 31W
Exminster, *U.K.* ............... 24 E2   50 40N   3 29W
Exmoor, *U.K.* .................. 24 D1   51 12N   3 45W
Exmouth, *U.K.* ................. 24 E2   50 37N   3 25W
Exton, *U.K.* ................... 23 G7   52 42N   0 38W
Extremadura □, *Spain* .......... 69 C2   39 30N   6  5W
Eyam, *U.K.* .................... 23 F5   53 17N   1 40W
Eyasi, L., *Tanzania* ........... 96 E6    3 30S  35  0 E
Eye, *Cambs., U.K.* ............. 23 G8   52 37N   0 11W
Eye, *Suffolk, U.K.* ............ 25 B11  52 19N   1  9 E
Eye Pen., *U.K.* ................ 18 F5   58 13N   6 10W
Eyemouth, *U.K.* ................ 21 C11  55 52N   2  5W
Eynsham, *U.K.* ................. 24 C6   51 47N   1 22W
Eyre, L., *Australia* ........... 98 F6   29 30S 137 26 E
Eyre Pen., *Australia* .......... 98 G6   33 30S 136 17 E

## F

F.Y.R.O.M. = Macedonia ■,
 *Europe* ....................... 71 D9   41 53N  21 40 E
Fair Hd., *U.K.* ................ 29 A9   55 14N   6  9W
Fair Isle, *U.K.* ............... 64 B6   59 30N   1 40W
Fairbanks, *U.S.A.* ............. 108 B5   64 51N 147 43W
Fairfield, *U.S.A.* ............. 112 F3   38 23N  88 22W
Fairford, *U.K.* ................ 24 C5   51 43N   1 46W
Fairlight, *U.K.* ............... 25 E10  50 52N   0 40 E
Fairmont, *U.S.A.* .............. 112 F7   39 29N  80  9W
Fairweather, Mt., *U.S.A.* ...... 108 C6   58 55N 137 32W
Faisalabad, *Pakistan* .......... 84 D8   31 30N  73  5 E
Faizabad, *India* ............... 85 F13  26 45N  82 10 E
Fajardo, *Puerto Rico* .......... 115 d   18 20N  65 39W
Fakenham, *U.K.* ................ 25 A10  52 51N   0 51 E
Falcon Reservoir, *U.S.A.* ...... 110 E7   26 34N  99 10W
Faldingworth, *U.K.* ............ 23 F8   53 21N   0 24W
Falkirk, *U.K.* ................. 21 C8   56  0N   3 47W
Falkland, *U.K.* ................ 21 B9   56  3N   3 12W
Falkland Is. ☑, *Atl. Oc.* ...... 121 H4   51 30S  59  0W
Fall River, *U.S.A.* ............ 113 E12  41 43N  71 10W
Falmouth, *Jamaica* ............. 114 a   18 30N  77 40W
Falmouth, *U.K.* ................ 27 G3   50  9N   5  5W
Falmouth B., *U.K.* ............. 27 G3   50  6N   5  5W
Falstone, *U.K.* ................ 22 B4   55 11N   2 26W
Falun, *Sweden* ................. 63 E7   60 37N  15 37 E
Famagusta, *Cyprus* ............. 86 C3   35  8N  33 55 E
Fanad Hd., *Ireland* ............ 28 A6   55 17N   7 38W
Fannich, L., *U.K.* ............. 19 G8   57 38N   4 59W
Far East, *Asia* ................ 74 E16  40  0N 130  0 E
Farâh, *Afghan.* ................ 84 C3   32 20N  62  7 E
Farasan, *Si. Arabia* ........... 88 D3   16 45N  41 55 E
Fareham, *U.K.* ................. 24 E6   50 51N   1 11W
Farewell C., *Greenland* ........ 109 C15  59 48N  43 55W
Fargo, *U.S.A.* ................. 111 A7   46 53N  96 48W
Faridabad, *India* .............. 84 E10  28 26N  77 19 E
Faringdon, *U.K.* ............... 24 C5   51 39N   1 34W
Farmington, *U.S.A.* ............ 110 C5   36 44N 108 12W
Farmville, *U.S.A.* ............. 112 G8   37 18N  78 24W
Farnborough, *U.K.* ............. 25 D7   51 16N   0 45W
Farne Is., *U.K.* ............... 22 A5   55 38N   1 37W
Farnham, *U.K.* ................. 25 D7   51 13N   0 47W
Farnworth, *U.K.* ............... 23 E4   53 34N   2 25W
Faro, *Portugal* ................ 108 B6   62 11N 133 22W
Faroe Is., *Atl. Oc.* ........... 57 C4   62  0N   7  0W
Fârs □, *Iran* .................. 87 D8   29 30N  55  0 E
Fâryâb □, *Afghan.* ............. 87 B11  36  0N  65  0 E
Fataka, *Solomon Is.* ........... 99 C12  11 55S 170 12 E
Fatehgarh, *India* .............. 84 F11  27 25N  79 35 E
Fatehpur, *Raj., India* ......... 84 F9   28  0N  74 40 E
Fatehpur, *Ut. P., India* ....... 85 G12  25 56N  81 13 E
Faversham, *U.K.* ............... 25 D10  51 19N   0 56 E
Fawley, *U.K.* .................. 24 E6   50 50N   1 20W
Fayetteville, *Ark., U.S.A.* .... 111 C8   36  4N  94 10W
Fayetteville, *N.C., U.S.A.* .... 111 D11  35  3N  78 53W
Fazeley, *U.K.* ................. 23 G5   52 37N   1 40W
Fazilka, *India* ................ 84 D9   30 27N  74  2 E
Fdérik, *Mauritania* ............ 94 D3   22 40N  12 45W
Feale →, *Ireland* .............. 30 D3   52 27N   9 37W
Fear, C., *U.S.A.* .............. 111 D11  33 50N  77 58W
Fécamp, *France* ................ 68 B4   49 45N   0 22 E
Fehmarn, *Germany* .............. 66 A6   54 27N  11  7 E
Feira de Santana, *Brazil* ...... 122 B3   12 15S  38 57W
Felipe Carrillo Puerto, *Mexico* 114 D7   19 38N  88  3W
Felixstowe, *U.K.* .............. 25 C11  51 58N   1 23 E
Felton, *U.K.* .................. 22 B5   55 18N   1 42W
Feltwell, *U.K.* ................ 25 B10  52 30N   0 32 E
Fenny Bentley, *U.K.* ........... 23 F5   53  3N   1 45W
Fenny Compton, *U.K.* ........... 24 B6   52 10N   1 23W
Fenny Stratford, *U.K.* ......... 25 C7   52  0N   0 44W
Fens, The, *U.K.* ............... 23 G8   52 38N   0  2W
Fenyang, *China* ................ 81 C6   37 18N 111 48 E
Feodosiya, *Ukraine* ............ 73 E6   45 2N   35 16 E
Fergus Falls, *U.S.A.* .......... 111 A7   46 17N  96  4W
Ferkéssédougou, *Ivory C.* ...... 94 G4    9 35N   5  6W
Fermanagh □, *U.K.* ............. 28 C6   54 21N   7 40W
Fermont, *Canada* ............... 109 C13  52 47N  67  5W
Fermoy, *Ireland* ............... 30 D6   52  9N   8 16W
Fernhurst, *U.K.* ............... 25 D7   51  3N   0 43W
Ferrara, *Italy* ................ 70 B4   44 50N  11 35 E
Ferret, C., *France* ............ 68 D3   44 38N   1 15W
Ferryhill, *U.K.* ............... 22 C5   54 41N   1 33W
Fès, *Morocco* .................. 94 B5   34  0N   5  0W
Fethiye, *Turkey* ............... 73 G4   36 36N  29  6 E
Fetlar, *U.K.* .................. 18 A16  60 36N   0 52W
Feuilles →, *Canada* ............ 109 C12  58 47N  70  4W
Feyzâbâd, *Afghan.* ............. 87 B12  37  7N  70 33 E
Fezzan, *Libya* ................. 95 C8   27  0N  13  0 E
Ffestiniog, *U.K.* .............. 26 B6   52 57N   3 55W
Fianarantsoa, *Madag.* .......... 97 J9   21 26S  47  5 E
Fife □, *U.K.* .................. 21 B9   56 16N   3  1W
Fife Ness, *U.K.* ............... 21 B10  56 17N   2 35W
Figeac, *France* ................ 68 D5   44 37N   2  2 E
Fiji ■, *Pac. Oc.* .............. 99 D14  17 20S 179  0 E
Filby, *U.K.* ................... 25 A12  52 40N   1 39 E
Filey, *U.K.* ................... 22 D8   54 12N   0 18W
Filey B., *U.K.* ................ 22 D8   54 12N   0 15W
Filton, *U.K.* .................. 24 C3   51 30N   2 34W
Fincham, *U.K.* ................. 25 A9   52 38N   0 30 E
Findhorn, *U.K.* ................ 19 G10  57 38N   3 38W
Findhorn →, *U.K.* .............. 19 G10  57 38N   3 38W
Findlay, *U.S.A.* ............... 112 E6   41  2N  83 39W
Finedon, *U.K.* ................. 23 H7   52 21N   0 39W
Finike, *Turkey* ................ 86 B2   36 21N  30 10 E
Finland ■, *Europe* ............. 63 E9   63  0N  27  0 E
Finland, G. of, *Europe* ........ 63 F9   60  0N  26  0 E
Finlay →, *Canada* .............. 108 C7   57  0N 125 10W
Finn →, *Ireland* ............... 28 B7   54 51N   7 28W

Firozabad, *India* .............. 84 F11  27 10N  78 25 E
Firozpur, *India* ............... 84 D9   30 55N  74 40 E
Fish →, *Namibia* ............... 97 K3   28  7S  17 10 E
Fishguard, *U.K.* ............... 26 D4   52  0N   4 58W
Fishtoft, *U.K.* ................ 23 G9   52 58N   0  1 E
Fisterra, C., *Spain* ........... 69 A1   42 50N   9  1W
Fitchburg, *U.S.A.* ............. 113 D12  42 35N  71 48W
Flagstaff, *U.S.A.* ............. 110 C4   35 12N 111 39W
Flamborough, *U.K.* ............. 22 D8   54  7N   0  5W
Flamborough Hd., *U.K.* ......... 22 D8   54  7N   0  5W
Flandre, *Europe* ............... 65 D2   50 50N   2 30 E
Flathead L., *U.S.A.* ........... 110 A4   47 54N 114  3W
Flattery, C., *U.S.A.* .......... 110 A2   48 23N 124 29W
Fleet, *U.K.* ................... 25 D7   51 17N   0 50W
Fleetwood, *U.K.* ............... 23 E2   53 55N   3  1W
Flensburg, *Germany* ............ 66 A5   54 47N   9 27 E
Flers, *France* ................. 68 B3   48 47N   0 33W
Flimby, *U.K.* .................. 22 C2   54 42N   3 30W
Flin Flon, *Canada* ............. 108 C9   54 46N 101 53W
Flinders →, *Australia* ......... 98 D7   17 36S 140 36 E
Flinders Ranges, *Australia* .... 98 G6   31 30S 138 30 E
Flint, *U.K.* ................... 23 F2   53 15N   3  8W
Flint, *U.S.A.* ................. 112 D6   43  1N  83 41W
Flint →, *U.S.A.* ............... 111 D10  30 57N  84 34W
Flint I., *Kiribati* ............ 103 J12  11 26S 151 48W
Flitwick, *U.K.* ................ 25 C8   52  0N   0 30W
Flodden, *U.K.* ................. 22 A4   55 37N   2  8W
Flora, *U.S.A.* ................. 112 F3   38 40N  88 29W
Florence, *Italy* ............... 70 C4   43 46N  11 15 E
Florence, *U.S.A.* .............. 111 D11  34 12N  79 46W
Florencia, *Colombia* ........... 120 B2    1 36N  75 36W
Flores, *Indonesia* ............. 83 D4    8 35S 121  0 E
Flores Sea, *Indonesia* ......... 83 D4    6 30S 120  0 E
Florianópolis, *Brazil* ......... 121 E5   27 30S  48 30W
Florida, *Uruguay* .............. 121 F4   34  7S  56 10W
Florida □, *U.S.A.* ............. 111 E10  28  0N  82  0W
Florida, Straits of, *U.S.A.* ... 115 C9   25  0N  80  0W
Florida Keys, *U.S.A.* .......... 111 F10  24 40N  81  0W
Florø, *Norway* ................. 63 E5   61 35N   5  1 E
Fly →, *Papua N. G.* ............ 98 B7    8 25S 143  0 E
Fochabers, *U.K.* ............... 19 G11  57 37N   3  6W
Focșani, *Romania* .............. 67 F14  45 41N  27 15 E
Fóggia, *Italy* ................. 70 D6   41 27N  15 34 E
Foix, *France* .................. 68 E4   42 58N   1 38 E
Folkestone, *U.K.* .............. 25 D11  51 5N   1 12 E
Fond-du-Lac, *Canada* ........... 108 C9   59 19N 107 12W
Fongafale, *Tuvalu* ............. 99 B14   8 31S 179 13 E
Fontainebleau, *France* ......... 68 B5   48 24N   2 40 E
Fontenay-le-Comte, *France* ..... 68 C3   46 28N   0 48W
Fordham, *U.K.* ................. 25 B9   52 19N   0 23 E
Fordingbridge, *U.K.* ........... 24 E5   50 56N   1 47W
Forel, Mt., *Greenland* ......... 54 C6   66 52N  36 55W
Forest Row, *U.K.* .............. 25 D9   51  5N   0  3 E
Forfar, *U.K.* .................. 19 J12  56 39N   2 53W
Forlì, *Italy* .................. 70 B5   44 13N  12  3 E
Formby, *U.K.* .................. 23 E2   53 34N   3  4W
Formby Pt., *U.K.* .............. 23 E2   53 33N   3  6W
Formiga, *Brazil* ............... 122 D1   20 27S  45 25W
Formosa, *Argentina* ............ 121 E4   26 15S  58 10W
Formosa, *Brazil* ............... 122 C1   15 32S  47 20W
Forres, *U.K.* .................. 19 G10  57 37N   3 37W
Forsayth, *Australia* ........... 98 D7   18 33S 143 34 E
Fort Albany, *Canada* ........... 109 C11  52 15N  81 35W
Fort Augustus, *U.K.* ........... 19 H8   57  9N   4 42W
Fort Chipewyan, *Canada* ........ 108 C8   58 42N 111  8W
Fort Collins, *U.S.A.* .......... 110 B5   40 35N 105  5W
Fort-Coulonge, *Canada* ......... 112 C9   45 50N  76 45W
Fort-de-France, *Martinique* .... 114 c   14 36N  61  2W
Fort Dodge, *U.S.A.* ............ 111 B8   42 30N  94 11W
Fort Good Hope, *Canada* ........ 108 B7   66 14N 128 40W
Fort Kent, *U.S.A.* ............. 113 B13  47 15N  68 36W
Fort Lauderdale, *U.S.A.* ....... 111 E10  26  7N  80  8W
Fort Liard, *Canada* ............ 108 B7   60 14N 123 30W
Fort MacKay, *Canada* ........... 108 C8   57 12N 111 41W
Fort Macleod, *Canada* .......... 108 D8   49 45N 113 30W
Fort McMurray, *Canada* ......... 108 C8   56 44N 111  7W
Fort McPherson, *Canada* ........ 108 B6   67 30N 134 55W
Fort Morgan, *U.S.A.* ........... 110 B6   40 15N 103 48W
Fort Myers, *U.S.A.* ............ 111 E10  26 39N  81 52W
Fort Nelson, *Canada* ........... 108 C7   58 50N 122 44W
Fort Nelson →, *Canada* ......... 108 C7   59 32N 124  0W
Fort Peck L., *U.S.A.* .......... 110 A5   48 0N  106 26W
Fort Providence, *Canada* ....... 108 B8   61  3N 117 40W
Fort Resolution, *Canada* ....... 108 B8   61 10N 113 40W
Fort St. John, *Canada* ......... 108 C7   56 15N 120 50W
Fort Scott, *U.S.A.* ............ 111 C8   37 50N  94 42W
Fort Shevchenko, *Kazakhstan* ... 73 F9   44 30N  50 23 E
Fort Simpson, *Canada* .......... 108 B7   61 45N 121 15W
Fort Smith, *Canada* ............ 108 B8   60  0N 111 51W
Fort Smith, *U.S.A.* ............ 111 C8   35 23N  94 25W
Fort Stockton, *U.S.A.* ......... 110 D6   30 53N 102 53W
Fort Wayne, *U.S.A.* ............ 112 E5   41  4N  85  9W
Fort William, *U.K.* ............ 18 J7   56 49N   5  7W
Fort Worth, *U.S.A.* ............ 111 D7   32 45N  97 18W
Fort Yukon, *U.S.A.* ............ 108 B5   66 34N 145 16W
Fortaleza, *Brazil* ............. 120 C6    3 45S  38 35W
Forth, Firth of, *U.K.* ......... 21 B10  56  5N   2 55W
Fortrose, *U.K.* ................ 19 G9   57 35N   4  9W
Foshan, *China* ................. 81 D6   23  4N 113  5 E
Fostoria, *U.S.A.* .............. 112 E6   41 10N  83 25W
Fothergill, *U.K.* .............. 22 C2   54 43N   3 29W
Fotheringhay, *U.K.* ............ 23 G8   52 32N   0 27W
Fougères, *France* .............. 68 B3   48 21N   1 14W
Foula, *U.K.* ................... 64 A5   60 10N   2  5W
Foulness I., *U.K.* ............. 25 C10  51 36N   0 55 E
Foulness Pt., *U.K.* ............ 25 C10  51 37N   0 58 E
Foulsham, *U.K.* ................ 25 A10  52 48N   0 59 E
Foulweather, C., *U.S.A.* ....... 110 B2   44 50N 124  5W
Fountainhall, *U.K.* ............ 22 A3   55 44N   2 53W
Fouta Djalon, *Guinea* .......... 94 F3   11 20N  12 10W
Fovant, *U.K.* .................. 24 D5   51  4N   2  0W
Fowey, *U.K.* ................... 27 G4   50 20N   4 39W
Fownhope, *U.K.* ................ 24 B3   52  0N   2 37W
Foxe Basin, *Canada* ............ 109 B12  66  0N  77  0W
Foxe Chan., *Canada* ............ 109 B11  65  0N  80  0W
Foxe Pen., *Canada* ............. 109 B12  65  0N  76  0W
Foyle, Lough, *U.K.* ............ 29 A7   55  7N   7  4W
Foynes, *Ireland* ............... 30 C4   52 37N   9  7W
Foz do Iguaçu, *Brazil* ......... 121 E4   25 30S  54 30W
Fraddon, *U.K.* ................. 27 G4   50 23N   4 58W
Framlingham, *U.K.* ............. 25 B11  52 14N   1 21 E
Franca, *Brazil* ................ 122 D1   20 33S  47 30W
France ■, *Europe* .............. 68 C5   47  0N   3  0 E
Franceville, *Gabon* ............ 96 E2    1 40S  13 32 E
Franche-Comté, *France* ......... 68 C6   46 50N   5 55 E
Francis Case, L., *U.S.A.* ...... 110 B7   43  4N  98 34W
Francistown, *Botswana* ......... 97 J5   21  7S  27 33 E
Frankfort, *Ind., U.S.A.* ....... 108 C7   54  0N 125 30W
Frankfort, *Ky., U.S.A.* ........ 112 F5   38 12N  84 52W
Frankfurt, *Brandenburg,
 Germany* ....................... 66 B8   52 20N  14 32 E
Frankfurt, *Hessen, Germany* .... 66 C5   50  7N   8 41 E
Franklin, *N.H., U.S.A.* ........ 113 D12  43 27N  71 39W
Franklin, *Pa., U.S.A.* ......... 112 E7   41 24N  79 50W
Franklin B., *Canada* ........... 108 B7   69 45N 126  0W
Franklin D. Roosevelt L., *U.S.A.* 110 A3   48 18N 118  9W

**Franklin L.**  **Grudziądz**

Franklin L., U.S.A. ... 110 B3 40 25N 115 22W
Franklin Mts., Canada ... 108 B7 65 0N 125 0W
Franklin Str., Canada ... 108 A10 72 0N 96 0W
Frant, U.K. ... 25 D9 51 5N 0 16 E
Franz Josef Land, Russia ... 79 A7 82 0N 55 0 E
Fraser →, Canada ... 108 D7 49 7N 123 11W
Fraserburgh, U.K. ... 19 G13 57 42N 2 1W
Frederick, U.S.A. ... 112 F9 39 25N 77 25W
Fredericksburg, U.S.A. ... 112 F9 38 18N 77 28W
Fredericton, Canada ... 109 D13 45 57N 66 40W
Frederikshavn, Denmark ... 63 F6 57 28N 10 31 E
Fredonia, U.S.A. ... 112 D8 42 26N 79 20W
Fredrikstad, Norway ... 63 F6 59 13N 10 57 E
Free State □, S. Africa ... 97 K5 28 30S 27 0 E
Freeport, Bahamas ... 115 B9 26 30N 78 47W
Freeport, U.S.A. ... 111 E7 28 57N 95 21W
Freetown, S. Leone ... 94 G3 8 30N 13 17W
Freiburg, Germany ... 66 E4 47 59N 7 51 E
Fremont, U.S.A. ... 112 E6 41 21N 83 7W
French Creek →, U.S.A. ... 112 E8 41 24N 79 50W
French Guiana ☑, S. Amer. ... 120 B4 4 0N 53 0W
French Polynesia ☑, Pac. Oc. ... 103 K13 20 0S 145 0W
Frenchman Cr. →, N. Amer. ... 110 A5 48 31N 107 10W
Freshwater, U.K. ... 24 E5 50 41N 1 31W
Fresnillo, Mexico ... 114 C4 23 10N 103 0W
Fresno, U.S.A. ... 110 C3 36 44N 119 47W
Fria, C., Namibia ... 90 H5 18 0S 12 0 E
Fridaythorpe, U.K. ... 22 D7 54 2N 0 39W
Friesland □, Neths. ... 65 A5 53 5N 5 50 E
Frimley, U.K. ... 25 D7 51 19N 0 44W
Frinton-on-Sea, U.K. ... 25 C11 51 49N 1 15 E
Frio, C., Brazil ... 116 F6 22 50S 41 50W
Frizington, U.K. ... 22 C2 54 33N 3 28W
Frobisher B., Canada ... 109 B13 62 30N 66 0W
Frobisher L., Canada ... 108 C9 56 20N 108 15W
Frodsham, U.K. ... 23 F3 53 18N 2 43W
Frome, U.K. ... 24 D4 51 14N 2 19W
Frome →, U.K. ... 24 E4 50 41N 2 6W
Front Range, U.S.A. ... 110 C5 40 25N 105 45W
Front Royal, U.S.A. ... 112 F8 38 55N 78 12W
Frutal, Brazil ... 122 C1 20 0S 49 0W
Frýdek-Místek, Czech Rep. ... 67 D10 49 40N 18 20 E
Fuchū, Japan ... 82 F3 34 34N 133 14 E
Fuerte →, Mexico ... 114 B3 25 50N 109 25W
Fuerteventura, Canary Is. ... 94 C3 28 30N 14 0W
Fuhai, China ... 80 B3 47 2N 87 25 E
Fuji, Japan ... 82 F6 35 9N 138 39 E
Fuji-San, Japan ... 82 F6 35 22N 138 44 E
Fujian □, China ... 81 D6 26 0N 118 0 E
Fukui, Japan ... 82 E5 36 5N 136 10 E
Fukuoka, Japan ... 82 G2 33 39N 130 21 E
Fukushima, Japan ... 82 E7 37 44N 140 28 E
Fukuyama, Japan ... 82 F3 34 35N 133 20 E
Fulda, Germany ... 66 C5 50 32N 9 40 E
Fulda →, Germany ... 66 C5 51 25N 9 39 E
Fulton, U.S.A. ... 112 D9 43 19N 76 25W
Fulwood, U.K. ... 23 E3 53 47N 2 40W
Funabashi, Japan ... 82 F7 35 45N 140 0 E
Funchal, Madeira ... 94 B2 32 38N 16 54W
Fundy, B. of, Canada ... 109 D13 45 0N 66 0W
Furnas, Reprêsa de, Brazil ... 122 D1 20 50S 45 30W
Furneaux Group, Australia ... 98 J8 40 10S 147 50 E
Fürth, Germany ... 66 D6 49 28N 10 59 E
Fury and Hecla Str., Canada ... 109 B11 69 56N 84 0W
Fushun, China ... 81 B7 41 50N 123 56 E
Fustic, Barbados ... 115 g 13 16N 59 38W
Futuna, Wall. & F. Is. ... 102 J9 14 25S 178 20W
Fuxin, China ... 81 B7 42 5N 121 48 E
Fuzhou, China ... 81 D6 26 5N 119 16 E
Fylingdales Moor, U.K. ... 22 D7 54 25N 0 41W
Fyn, Denmark ... 63 F6 55 20N 10 30 E
Fyne, L., U.K. ... 20 C5 55 59N 5 23W

**G**

Gabès, Tunisia ... 95 B8 33 53N 10 2 E
Gabès, G. de, Tunisia ... 95 B8 34 0N 10 30 E
Gabon ■, Africa ... 96 E2 0 10S 10 0 E
Gaborone, Botswana ... 97 J5 24 45S 25 57 E
Gabrovo, Bulgaria ... 71 C11 42 52N 25 19 E
Gachsārān, Iran ... 87 D7 30 15N 50 45 E
Gadarwara, India ... 84 H11 22 50N 78 50 E
Gadsden, U.S.A. ... 111 D9 34 1N 86 1W
Gafsa, Tunisia ... 95 B7 34 24N 8 43 E
Gagnoa, Ivory C. ... 94 G4 6 56N 5 16W
Gagnon, Canada ... 109 C13 51 50N 68 5W
Gainesville, Fla., U.S.A. ... 111 E10 29 40N 82 20W
Gainesville, Ga., U.S.A. ... 111 D10 34 18N 83 50W
Gainford, U.K. ... 22 C5 54 34N 1 43W
Gainsborough, U.K. ... 23 F7 53 24N 0 46W
Gairdner, L., Australia ... 98 G6 31 30S 136 0 E
Gairloch, U.K. ... 18 G6 57 43N 5 41W
Gairloch, L., U.K. ... 18 G6 57 43N 5 45W
Galashiels, U.K. ... 21 C10 55 37N 2 49W
Galați, Romania ... 67 F15 45 27N 28 2 E
Galdhøpiggen, Norway ... 63 E5 61 38N 8 18 E
Galena, U.S.A. ... 108 B4 64 44N 156 56W
Galesburg, U.S.A. ... 111 B8 40 57N 90 22W
Galgate, U.K. ... 23 E3 53 59N 2 46W
Galicia □, Spain ... 69 A2 42 43N 7 45W
Galilee, Sea of, Israel ... 86 C3 32 45N 35 35 E
Galina Pt., Jamaica ... 114 a 18 24N 76 58W
Gallan Hd., U.K. ... 18 F3 58 15N 7 2W
Galle, Sri Lanka ... 84 R12 6 5N 80 10 E
Galley Hd., Ireland ... 30 E5 51 32N 8 55W
Gallinas, Pta., Colombia ... 120 A2 12 28N 71 40W
Gallipolis, U.S.A. ... 112 F6 38 49N 82 12W
Gällivare, Sweden ... 63 D8 67 9N 20 40 E
Galloway, U.K. ... 20 D7 55 1N 4 29W
Galloway, Mull of, U.K. ... 20 E6 54 39N 4 52W
Gallup, U.S.A. ... 110 C5 35 32N 108 45W
Galmpton, U.K. ... 27 G6 50 23N 3 35W
Galty Mts., Ireland ... 30 D6 52 22N 8 10W
Galtymore, Ireland ... 30 D6 52 21N 8 11W
Galveston, U.S.A. ... 111 E8 29 18N 94 48W
Galway, Ireland ... 28 E3 53 17N 9 3W
Galway □, Ireland ... 28 E3 53 22N 9 1W
Galway B., Ireland ... 28 E3 53 13N 9 10W
Gambia ■, W. Afr. ... 94 F2 13 25N 16 0W
Gambia →, W. Afr. ... 94 F2 13 28N 16 34W
Gamlingay, U.K. ... 25 B8 52 10N 0 11W
Gan Jiang →, China ... 81 D6 29 15N 116 0 E
Gananoque, Canada ... 113 C9 44 20N 76 10W
Gäncä, Azerbaijan ... 73 F8 40 45N 46 20 E
Gandak →, India ... 85 G14 25 39N 85 13 E
Gander, Canada ... 109 D14 48 58N 54 35W
Gandhi Sagar, India ... 84 E8 24 40N 75 40 E
Ganganagar, India ... 84 E8 29 56N 73 56 E
Ganges →, India ... 85 H17 23 20N 90 30 E
Gangtok, India ... 85 F16 27 20N 88 37 E
Gannett Peak, U.S.A. ... 110 E9 43 11N 109 39W
Gansu □, China ... 80 C5 36 0N 104 0 E
Ganzhou, China ... 81 D6 25 51N 114 56 E

Gao, Mali ... 94 E5 16 15N 0 5W
Gap, France ... 68 D7 44 33N 6 5 E
Gar, China ... 80 C2 32 10N 79 58 E
Garanhuns, Brazil ... 122 A3 8 50S 36 30W
Garboldisham, U.K. ... 25 B10 52 23N 0 57 E
Garda, L. di, Italy ... 70 B4 45 40N 10 41 E
Garden City, U.S.A. ... 110 C6 37 58N 100 53W
Gardēz, Afghan. ... 84 C6 33 37N 69 9 E
Garforth, U.K. ... 23 E6 53 47N 1 24W
Gargrave, U.K. ... 23 E4 53 59N 2 1W
Garissa, Kenya ... 96 E7 0 25S 39 40 E
Garoe, Somali Rep. ... 88 F4 8 25N 48 33 E
Garonne →, France ... 68 D3 45 2N 0 36W
Garoua, Cameroon ... 95 G8 9 19N 13 21 E
Garron Pt., U.K. ... 29 A10 55 3N 5 59W
Garry →, U.K. ... 19 J10 56 44N 3 47W
Garry, L., Canada ... 108 B9 65 58N 100 18W
Garsdale Head, U.K. ... 22 D4 54 20N 2 20W
Garstang, U.K. ... 23 E3 53 55N 2 46W
Gary, U.S.A. ... 112 E4 41 36N 87 20W
Garzê, China ... 80 C5 31 38N 100 1 E
Gascogne, France ... 68 E4 43 45N 0 20 E
Gascogne, G. de, Europe ... 68 D2 44 0N 2 0W
Gaspé, Canada ... 109 D13 48 52N 64 30W
Gaspé, C., Canada ... 113 A15 48 48N 64 7W
Gaspésie, Pén. de la, Canada ... 109 D13 48 45N 65 40W
Gatehouse of Fleet, U.K. ... 20 E7 54 53N 4 12W
Gateshead, U.K. ... 22 C5 54 57N 1 35W
Gatineau →, Canada ... 113 C10 45 27N 75 42W
Gatley, U.K. ... 23 F4 53 24N 2 15W
Gävle, Sweden ... 63 E7 60 40N 17 9 E
Gawthwaite, U.K. ... 22 D2 54 16N 3 8W
Gaxun Nur, China ... 80 B5 42 22N 100 30 E
Gaya, India ... 85 G14 24 47N 85 4 E
Gaylord, U.S.A. ... 112 C5 45 2N 84 41W
Gayton, U.K. ... 25 A10 52 45N 0 36 E
Gaywood, U.K. ... 25 A9 52 46N 0 26 E
Gaza, Gaza Strip ... 86 D3 31 30N 34 28 E
Gaza Strip ☑, Asia ... 86 D3 31 29N 34 25 E
Gaziantep, Turkey ... 73 G6 37 6N 37 23 E
Gdańsk, Poland ... 67 A10 54 22N 18 40 E
Gdynia, Poland ... 67 A10 54 35N 18 33 E
Gebze, Turkey ... 73 F4 40 47N 29 25 E
Gedaref, Sudan ... 95 F13 14 2N 35 28 E
Gedney, U.K. ... 23 G9 52 48N 0 4 E
Gedser, Denmark ... 63 G6 54 35N 11 55 E
Geelong, Australia ... 98 H7 38 10S 144 22 E
Gejiu, China ... 80 D5 23 20N 103 10 E
Gelderland □, Neths. ... 65 B6 52 5N 6 10 E
Gelibolu, Turkey ... 71 D12 40 28N 26 43 E
Gelsenkirchen, Germany ... 64 C6 51 32N 7 6 E
General Acha, Argentina ... 121 F3 37 20S 64 38W
General Alvear, Argentina ... 121 F3 35 0S 67 40W
General Pico, Argentina ... 121 F3 35 45S 63 50W
General Santos, Phil. ... 83 C4 6 5N 125 14 E
Geneva, U.S.A. ... 112 D9 42 52N 76 59W
Geneva, Switz. ... 66 E4 46 12N 6 9 E
Geneva, L. = Léman, L., Europe ... 66 E4 46 26N 6 30 E
Genk, Belgium ... 65 D5 50 58N 5 32 E
Gennargentu, Mti. del, Italy ... 70 D3 40 1N 9 19 E
Genoa, Italy ... 70 B3 44 25N 8 57 E
Gent, Belgium ... 65 C3 51 2N 3 42 E
George, S. Africa ... 97 L4 33 58S 22 29 E
George →, Canada ... 109 C13 58 49N 66 10W
George, L., U.S.A. ... 111 E10 29 17N 81 36W
George Town, Malaysia ... 83 C2 5 25N 100 20 E
George V Land, Antarctica ... 55 C10 69 0S 148 0 E
Georgetown, Guyana ... 120 B4 6 50N 58 12W
Georgetown, Ky., U.S.A. ... 112 F5 38 13N 84 33W
Georgetown, S.C., U.S.A. ... 111 D11 33 23N 79 17W
Georgia □, U.S.A. ... 111 D10 32 50N 83 15W
Georgia ■, Asia ... 73 F7 42 0N 43 0 E
Georgian B., Canada ... 109 D11 45 15N 81 0W
Georgiyevsk, Russia ... 73 F7 44 12N 43 28 E
Gera, Germany ... 66 C7 50 53N 12 4 E
Geraldton, Australia ... 98 F1 28 48S 114 32 E
Geraldton, Canada ... 112 A4 49 44N 86 59W
Germany ■, Europe ... 66 C6 51 0N 10 0 E
Germiston, S. Africa ... 97 K5 26 15S 28 10 E
Gerrans B., U.K. ... 27 G4 50 12N 4 57W
Gerrards Cross, U.K. ... 25 C7 51 35N 0 33W
Getafe, Spain ... 69 B4 40 18N 3 44W
Ghaghara →, India ... 85 G14 25 45N 84 40 E
Ghana ■, W. Afr. ... 94 G5 8 0N 1 0W
Ghardaïa, Algeria ... 94 B6 32 20N 3 37 E
Gharyān, Libya ... 95 B8 32 10N 13 0 E
Ghazal, Bahr el →, Chad ... 95 F9 13 0N 15 47 E
Ghazâl, Bahr el →, Sudan ... 95 G12 9 31N 30 25 E
Ghaziabad, India ... 84 E10 28 42N 77 26 E
Ghazipur, India ... 85 G13 25 38N 83 35 E
Ghazni, Afghan. ... 84 C6 33 30N 68 28 E
Ghent = Gent, Belgium ... 65 C3 51 2N 3 42 E
Ghowr □, Afghan. ... 87 C11 34 0N 64 20 E
Ghudāmis, Libya ... 95 B7 30 11N 9 29 E
Giants Causeway, U.K. ... 29 A9 55 16N 6 29W
Gibraltar ☑, Europe ... 69 D3 36 7N 5 22W
Gibraltar, Str. of, Medit. S. ... 69 E3 35 55N 5 40W
Gibraltar Pt., U.K. ... 23 F9 53 6N 0 19 E
Gibson Desert, Australia ... 98 E4 24 0S 126 0 E
Gifu, Japan ... 82 F5 35 30N 136 45 E
Giggleswick, U.K. ... 22 D4 54 5N 2 17W
Gigha, U.K. ... 20 D4 55 42N 5 44W
Gijón, Spain ... 69 A3 43 32N 5 42W
Gila →, U.S.A. ... 110 D4 32 43N 114 33W
Gilbert Is., Kiribati ... 102 G9 1 0N 172 0 E
Gilgit, India ... 84 B9 35 50N 74 15 E
Gillette, U.S.A. ... 110 B5 44 18N 105 30W
Gillingham, Dorset, U.K. ... 24 D4 51 2N 2 18W
Gillingham, Medway, U.K. ... 25 D10 51 23N 0 33 E
Gilsland, U.K. ... 22 C3 55 0N 2 34W
Gimie, Mt, St. Lucia ... 115 f 13 54N 61 0W
Girdle Ness, U.K. ... 19 H13 57 9N 2 3W
Giresun, Turkey ... 73 F6 40 55N 38 30 E
Girona, Spain ... 69 B7 41 58N 2 46 E
Gironde →, France ... 68 D3 45 32N 1 7W
Girvan, U.K. ... 20 D6 55 14N 4 51W
Gisborne, N.Z. ... 99 H14 38 39S 178 5 E
Gisburn, U.K. ... 23 E4 53 56N 2 16W
Gitega, Burundi ... 96 E5 3 26S 29 56 E
Gizhiga, Russia ... 79 C18 62 3N 160 30 E
Gjoa Haven, Canada ... 108 B10 68 38N 95 53W
Glace Bay, Canada ... 109 D14 46 11N 59 58W
Glacier Nat. Park △, U.S.A. ... 110 A4 48 59N 113 47W
Gladstone, Australia ... 98 E9 23 52S 151 16 E
Gladstone, U.S.A. ... 112 C4 45 51N 87 1W
Gladwin, U.S.A. ... 112 D5 43 59N 84 29W
Glanton, U.K. ... 22 B5 55 26N 1 54W
Glasgow, U.K. ... 20 C7 55 51N 4 15W
Glasgow, Ky., U.S.A. ... 112 G5 37 0N 85 55W
Glasgow, Mont., U.S.A. ... 110 A5 48 12N 106 38W
Glastonbury, U.K. ... 24 D3 51 9N 2 43W
Glazov, Russia ... 72 C9 58 9N 52 40 E
Glemsford, U.K. ... 25 B9 52 6N 0 40 E
Glen →, U.K. ... 23 G8 52 51N 0 7W
Glen Affric, U.K. ... 18 H7 57 17N 5 1W

Glen Coe, U.K. ... 18 J6 56 40N 5 0W
Glen Garry, U.K. ... 18 H7 57 3N 5 7W
Glen Mor, U.K. ... 19 H8 57 9N 4 37W
Glen Moriston, U.K. ... 19 H8 57 11N 4 52W
Glen Spean, U.K. ... 19 J8 56 53N 4 40W
Glendale, Ariz., U.S.A. ... 110 D4 33 32N 112 11W
Glendale, Calif., U.S.A. ... 110 D3 34 9N 118 15W
Glendive, U.S.A. ... 110 A6 47 7N 104 43W
Glengarriff, Ireland ... 30 E3 51 45N 9 34W
Glenkens, The, U.K. ... 20 D7 55 12N 4 12W
Glenluce, U.K. ... 20 E6 54 52N 4 48W
Glennallen, U.S.A. ... 108 B5 62 7N 145 33W
Glennamaddy, Ireland ... 28 D4 53 37N 8 33W
Glenrothes, U.K. ... 21 B9 56 12N 3 10W
Glens Falls, U.S.A. ... 113 D11 43 19N 73 39W
Glenties, Ireland ... 28 B5 54 49N 8 16W
Glenveagh Nat. Park △, Ireland ... 28 A5 55 3N 8 1W
Gliwice, Poland ... 67 C10 50 22N 18 41 E
Globe, U.S.A. ... 110 D4 33 24N 110 47W
Głogów, Poland ... 66 C9 51 37N 16 5 E
Glomma →, Norway ... 63 F6 59 12N 10 57 E
Glossop, U.K. ... 23 F5 53 27N 1 56W
Gloucester, U.K. ... 24 C4 51 53N 2 15W
Gloucestershire □, U.K. ... 24 C5 51 46N 2 15W
Gloversville, U.S.A. ... 113 D10 43 3N 74 21W
Gniezno, Poland ... 67 B9 52 30N 17 35 E
Gnosall, U.K. ... 23 G4 52 48N 2 14W
Goa, India ... 84 M8 15 33N 73 59 E
Goa □, India ... 84 M8 15 33N 73 59 E
Goat Fell, U.K. ... 20 C5 55 38N 5 11W
Gobi, Asia ... 81 B5 44 0N 110 0 E
Godalming, U.K. ... 25 D7 51 11N 0 36W
Godavari →, India ... 85 L13 16 25N 82 18 E
Goderich, Canada ... 112 D7 43 45N 81 41W
Godhra, India ... 84 H8 22 49N 73 40 E
Godmanchester, U.K. ... 23 H8 52 20N 0 11W
Gods →, Canada ... 108 C10 56 22N 92 51W
Gods L., Canada ... 108 C10 54 40N 94 15W
Godshill, U.K. ... 24 E6 50 38N 1 15W
Godstone, U.K. ... 25 D8 51 14N 0 3W
Gogama, Canada ... 112 B7 47 35N 81 43W
Goiânia, Brazil ... 122 C1 16 43S 49 20W
Goiás, Brazil ... 120 D4 15 55S 50 10W
Goiás □, Brazil ... 122 C1 12 10S 48 0W
Goio-Erê, Brazil ... 121 E4 24 12S 53 1W
Gold Coast, Australia ... 98 F9 28 0S 153 25 E
Gold Coast, W. Afr. ... 94 H5 4 0N 1 40W
Golden Vale, Ireland ... 30 C6 52 33N 8 17W
Goldsboro, U.S.A. ... 111 C11 35 23N 77 59W
Golspie, U.K. ... 19 G10 57 58N 3 59W
Goma, Dem. Rep. of the Congo ... 96 E5 1 37S 29 10 E
Gomel, Belarus ... 67 B16 52 28N 31 0 E
Gomera, Canary Is. ... 94 C2 28 7N 17 14W
Gómez Palacio, Mexico ... 114 B4 25 40N 104 0W
Gonābād, Iran ... 87 C9 34 15N 58 45 E
Gonaïves, Haiti ... 115 D10 19 20N 72 42W
Gonbad-e Kāvūs, Iran ... 87 B8 37 20N 55 25 E
Gonda, India ... 85 F12 27 9N 81 58 E
Gonder, Ethiopia ... 88 E2 12 39N 37 30 E
Gonghe, China ... 80 C5 36 18N 100 32 E
Good Hope, C. of, S. Africa ... 97 L3 34 24S 18 30 E
Goodrich, U.K. ... 24 C3 51 52N 2 37W
Goodwood, U.K. ... 25 E7 50 53N 0 44W
Goole, U.K. ... 23 E7 53 42N 0 53W
Goose →, Canada ... 110 B2 41 56N 120 26W
Gorakhpur, India ... 85 F13 26 47N 83 23 E
Gordon, U.K. ... 22 A3 55 41N 2 34W
Gore, Ethiopia ... 88 F2 8 12N 35 32 E
Gorebridge, U.K. ... 22 A2 55 50N 3 2W
Gorey, Ireland ... 31 C10 52 41N 6 18W
Gorgān, Iran ... 87 B8 36 55N 54 30 E
Goring, U.K. ... 24 C6 51 31N 1 7W
Goring-by-Sea, U.K. ... 25 E8 50 49N 0 24W
Gorleston, U.K. ... 25 A12 52 35N 1 44 E
Görlitz, Germany ... 66 C8 51 9N 14 58 E
Gorontalo, Indonesia ... 83 C4 0 35N 123 5 E
Gort, Ireland ... 30 B5 53 3N 8 49W
Gorzów Wielkopolski, Poland ... 66 B8 52 43N 15 15 E
Gosberton, U.K. ... 23 G8 52 53N 0 9W
Gosforth, U.K. ... 22 D2 54 26N 3 27W
Gosier, Guadeloupe ... 114 b 16 12N 61 30W
Gosport, U.K. ... 24 E6 50 48N 1 9W
Göta kanal, Sweden ... 63 F7 58 30N 15 58 E
Göteborg, Sweden ... 63 F6 57 43N 11 59 E
Gotha, Germany ... 66 C6 50 56N 10 42 E
Gothenburg = Göteborg, Sweden ... 63 F6 57 43N 11 59 E
Gotland, Sweden ... 63 F7 57 30N 18 33 E
Gotō-Rettō, Japan ... 82 G1 32 55N 129 5 E
Göttingen, Germany ... 66 C5 51 31N 9 55 E
Gouda, Neths. ... 65 B4 52 1N 4 42 E
Goudhurst, U.K. ... 25 D9 51 6N 0 29 E
Gough I., Atl. Oc. ... 52 G8 40 10S 9 45W
Gouin, Rés., Canada ... 109 D12 48 35N 74 40W
Goulburn, Australia ... 98 G8 34 44S 149 44 E
Goulimine, Morocco ... 94 C3 28 56N 10 0W
Gourock, U.K. ... 20 C6 55 57N 4 49W
Governador Valadares, Brazil ... 122 C2 18 15S 41 57W
Gower, U.K. ... 27 D5 51 35N 4 10W
Gowna, L., Ireland ... 28 D6 53 51N 7 34W
Goya, Argentina ... 121 E4 29 10S 59 10W
Gozo, Malta ... 70 a 36 3N 14 15 E
Graaff-Reinet, S. Africa ... 97 L4 32 13S 24 32 E
Gracias a Dios, C., Honduras ... 115 E8 15 0N 83 10W
Grafham Water, U.K. ... 23 H8 52 19N 0 18W
Grafton, Australia ... 98 F9 29 38S 152 58 E
Grafton, U.S.A. ... 111 A7 48 25N 97 25W
Graham Land, Antarctica ... 55 C17 65 0S 64 0W
Grahamstown, S. Africa ... 97 L5 33 19S 26 31 E
Grain Coast, W. Afr. ... 94 H3 4 20N 10 0W
Grainthorpe, U.K. ... 23 F9 53 27N 0 5 E
Grampian Mts., U.K. ... 19 J9 56 50N 4 0W
Gran Canaria, Canary Is. ... 94 C2 27 55N 15 35W
Gran Chaco, S. Amer. ... 121 E3 25 0S 61 0W
Gran Sasso d'Itália, Italy ... 70 C5 42 27N 13 42 E
Granada, Nic. ... 114 E7 11 58N 86 0W
Granada, Spain ... 69 D4 37 10N 3 35W
Granard, Ireland ... 28 D6 53 47N 7 30W
Granby, Canada ... 109 D12 45 25N 72 45W
Grand →, U.S.A. ... 110 A6 45 40N 100 45W
Grand Bahama, Bahamas ... 115 B9 26 40N 78 30W
Grand-Bourg, Guadeloupe ... 114 b 15 53N 61 19W
Grand Canyon, U.S.A. ... 110 C4 36 3N 112 9W
Grand Canyon Nat. Park △, U.S.A. ... 110 C4 36 15N 112 30W
Grand Cayman, Cayman Is. ... 115 D8 19 20N 81 20W
Grand Falls, Canada ... 109 D13 47 3N 67 44W
Grand Falls-Windsor, Canada ... 109 D14 48 56N 55 40W
Grand Forks, U.S.A. ... 111 A7 47 55N 97 3W
Grand Haven, U.S.A. ... 112 D4 43 4N 86 13W
Grand Island, U.S.A. ... 110 B7 40 55N 98 21W
Grand Junction, U.S.A. ... 110 C5 39 4N 108 33W
Grand L., Canada ... 113 C14 45 57N 66 7W
Grand Manan I., Canada ... 113 C14 44 45N 66 52W
Grand-Mère, Canada ... 113 B11 46 36N 72 40W
Grand Rapids, Canada ... 108 C10 53 12N 99 19W

Grand Rapids, U.S.A. ... 112 D4 42 58N 85 40W
Grand St.-Bernard, Col du, Europe ... 66 F4 45 50N 7 10 E
Grand Teton, U.S.A. ... 110 B4 43 54N 111 50W
Grand-Vigie, Pte. de la, Guadeloupe ... 114 b 16 32N 61 27W
Grande →, Bolivia ... 120 D3 15 51S 64 39W
Grande →, Brazil ... 122 B2 11 30S 44 30W
Grande, B., Argentina ... 121 H3 50 30S 68 20W
Grande, Rio →, U.S.A. ... 111 E7 25 58N 97 9W
Grande Baleine, R. de la →, Canada ... 109 C12 55 16N 77 47W
Grande Prairie, Canada ... 108 C8 55 10N 118 50W
Grande-Terre, I., Guadeloupe ... 114 b 16 20N 61 25W
Grange-over-Sands, U.K. ... 22 D3 54 12N 2 54W
Grangemouth, U.K. ... 21 B8 56 1N 3 42W
Grangeville, U.S.A. ... 110 A3 45 56N 116 7W
Grantham, U.K. ... 23 G7 52 55N 0 38W
Grantown-on-Spey, U.K. ... 19 H10 57 20N 3 36W
Grants Pass, U.S.A. ... 110 B2 42 26N 123 19W
Granville, U.S.A. ... 113 D11 43 24N 73 16W
Grasmere, U.K. ... 22 D2 54 28N 3 1W
Grasse, France ... 68 E7 43 38N 6 56 E
Grassington, U.K. ... 22 D5 54 5N 1 59W
Graulhet, France ... 68 E4 43 45N 1 59 E
Gravesend, U.K. ... 25 D9 51 26N 0 22 E
Grayling, U.S.A. ... 112 C5 44 40N 84 43W
Grayrigg, U.K. ... 22 D3 54 23N 2 39W
Grays, U.K. ... 25 D9 51 28N 0 21 E
Graz, Austria ... 66 E8 47 4N 15 27 E
Great Abaco I., Bahamas ... 115 B9 26 25N 77 10W
Great Australian Bight, Australia ... 98 G5 33 30S 130 0 E
Great Ayton, U.K. ... 22 D6 54 30N 1 8W
Great Baddow, U.K. ... 25 C10 51 43N 0 31 E
Great Barrier Reef, Australia ... 98 D8 18 0S 146 50 E
Great Basin, U.S.A. ... 110 B3 40 0N 117 0W
Great Bear →, Canada ... 108 B7 65 0N 124 0W
Great Bear L., Canada ... 108 B8 65 30N 120 0W
Great Bend, U.S.A. ... 110 C7 38 22N 98 46W
Great Bentley, U.K. ... 25 C11 51 51N 1 4 E
Great Blasket I., Ireland ... 30 D1 52 6N 10 32W
Great Britain, Europe ... 56 E5 54 0N 2 15W
Great Broughton, U.K. ... 22 D6 54 26N 1 9W
Great Camanoe, Br. Virgin Is. ... 115 e 18 30N 64 35W
Great Chesterford, U.K. ... 25 B9 52 4N 0 13 E
Great Clifton, U.K. ... 22 C2 54 39N 3 29W
Great Dividing Ra., Australia ... 98 E8 23 0S 146 0 E
Great Dunmow, U.K. ... 25 C9 51 52N 0 23 E
Great Exuma I., Bahamas ... 115 C9 23 30N 75 50W
Great Falls, U.S.A. ... 110 A4 47 30N 111 17W
Great Harwood, U.K. ... 23 E4 53 47N 2 24W
Great Inagua I., Bahamas ... 115 C10 21 0N 73 20W
Great Karoo, S. Africa ... 97 L4 31 55S 21 0 E
Great Malvern, U.K. ... 24 B4 52 7N 2 18W
Great Massingham, U.K. ... 25 A10 52 47N 0 40 E
Great Missenden, U.K. ... 25 C7 51 42N 0 41W
Great Ormes Head, U.K. ... 26 A6 53 20N 3 52W
Great Ouse →, U.K. ... 23 G9 52 48N 0 21 E
Great Pedro Bluff, Jamaica ... 114 a 17 51N 77 44W
Great Plains, N. Amer. ... 110 A6 47 0N 105 0W
Great Salt L., U.S.A. ... 110 B4 41 15N 112 40W
Great Salt Lake Desert, U.S.A. ... 110 B4 40 50N 113 30W
Great Sandy Desert, Australia ... 98 E3 21 0S 124 0 E
Great Shefford, U.K. ... 24 D6 51 28N 1 28W
Great Shelford, U.K. ... 25 B9 52 9N 0 8 E
Great Shunner Fell, U.K. ... 22 D4 54 22N 2 14W
Great Skellig, Ireland ... 30 E1 51 47N 10 33W
Great Slave L., Canada ... 108 B8 61 23N 115 38W
Great Snow Mt., Canada ... 108 C7 57 26N 124 0W
Great Torrington, U.K. ... 27 F5 50 57N 4 9W
Great Victoria Desert, Australia ... 98 F4 29 30S 126 30 E
Great Wall, China ... 81 C6 38 30N 109 30 E
Great Waltham, U.K. ... 25 C9 51 47N 0 28 E
Great Whernside, U.K. ... 22 D5 54 10N 1 58W
Great Yarmouth, U.K. ... 25 A12 52 37N 1 44 E
Greater Antilles, W. Indies ... 115 D10 17 40N 74 0W
Greater London □, U.K. ... 25 C8 51 31N 0 6W
Greater Manchester □, U.K. ... 23 E4 53 30N 2 15W
Greater Sunda Is., Indonesia ... 83 D3 7 0S 112 0 E
Greatham, U.K. ... 22 C6 54 39N 1 14W
Greece ■, Europe ... 71 E9 40 0N 23 0 E
Greeley, U.S.A. ... 110 B6 40 25N 104 42W
Green →, Ky., U.S.A. ... 112 G4 37 54N 87 30W
Green →, Utah, U.S.A. ... 110 C5 38 11N 109 53W
Green B., U.S.A. ... 112 C4 45 0N 87 30W
Green Bay, U.S.A. ... 112 C4 44 31N 88 0W
Green Hammerton, U.K. ... 23 D6 54 1N 1 18W
Green River, U.S.A. ... 110 B5 41 32N 109 28W
Greencastle, U.S.A. ... 112 F4 39 38N 86 52W
Greenfield, Ind., U.S.A. ... 112 F5 39 47N 85 46W
Greenfield, Mass., U.S.A. ... 113 D11 42 35N 72 36W
Greenhead, U.K. ... 22 C3 54 59N 2 30W
Greenland ☑, N. Amer. ... 54 C5 66 0N 45 0W
Greenland Sea, Arctic ... 54 B7 73 0N 10 0W
Greenlaw, U.K. ... 22 A4 55 43N 2 27W
Greenock, U.K. ... 20 C6 55 57N 4 46W
Greenodd, U.K. ... 22 D2 54 14N 3 4W
Greenore, Ireland ... 29 C9 54 2N 6 8W
Greenore Pt., Ireland ... 31 D10 52 14N 6 19W
Greensboro, U.S.A. ... 111 C11 36 4N 79 48W
Greensburg, Ind., U.S.A. ... 112 F5 39 20N 85 29W
Greensburg, Pa., U.S.A. ... 112 E8 40 18N 79 33W
Greenstone Pt., U.K. ... 18 G6 57 55N 5 37W
Greenville, Ala., U.S.A. ... 111 D9 31 50N 86 38W
Greenville, Maine, U.S.A. ... 113 C13 45 28N 69 35W
Greenville, Mich., U.S.A. ... 112 D5 43 11N 85 15W
Greenville, Miss., U.S.A. ... 111 D8 33 24N 91 4W
Greenville, Ohio, U.S.A. ... 112 E5 40 6N 84 38W
Greenville, S.C., U.S.A. ... 111 D10 34 51N 82 24W
Greenwich □, U.K. ... 25 D9 51 29N 0 1 E
Greenwood, U.S.A. ... 111 D8 33 31N 90 11W
Gremikha, Russia ... 72 A6 67 59N 39 47 E
Grenada ■, W. Indies ... 115 E12 12 10N 61 40W
Grenoble, France ... 68 D6 45 12N 5 42 E
Greta →, Australia ... 22 D3 54 9N 2 37W
Gretna, U.K. ... 21 E9 55 0N 3 3W
Gretna Green, U.K. ... 22 B2 55 1N 3 3W
Gretton, U.K. ... 23 G7 52 33N 0 40W
Grey Ra., Australia ... 98 F7 27 0S 143 30 E
Greymouth, N.Z. ... 99 J13 42 29S 171 13 E
Greystoke, U.K. ... 22 C3 54 41N 2 51W
Greystones, Ireland ... 31 B10 53 9N 6 5W
Griffith, Australia ... 98 G8 34 18S 146 2 E
Grimsay, U.K. ... 18 H3 57 29N 7 14W
Grimsby, U.K. ... 23 E8 53 34N 0 5W
Gris-Nez, C., France ... 68 A4 50 52N 1 35 E
Grizebeck, U.K. ... 22 D2 54 16N 3 10W
Groningen, Neths. ... 65 A6 53 15N 6 35 E
Groote Eylandt, Australia ... 98 C6 14 0S 136 40 E
Gros Islet, St. Lucia ... 115 f 14 5N 60 58W
Gros Piton, St. Lucia ... 115 f 13 49N 61 5W
Gros Piton Pt., St. Lucia ... 115 f 13 49N 61 5W
Grossglockner, Austria ... 66 E7 47 5N 12 40 E
Groundhog →, Canada ... 112 A6 48 45N 82 58W
Groznyy, Russia ... 73 F8 43 20N 45 45 E
Grudziądz, Poland ... 67 B10 53 30N 18 47 E

**Gruinard B.**                                                 **Hrodna**

Gruinard B., U.K. 18 G6 57 56N 5 35W
Guadalajara, Mexico 114 C4 20 40N 103 20W
Guadalajara, Spain 69 B4 40 37N 3 12W
Guadalcanal, Solomon Is. 99 B11 9 32S 160 12 E
Guadalete →, Spain 69 D2 36 35N 6 13W
Guadalquivir →, Spain 69 D2 36 47N 6 22W
Guadarrama, Sierra de, Spain 69 B4 41 0N 4 0W
Guadeloupe ☑, W. Indies 114 b 16 20N 61 40W
Guadiana →, Portugal 69 D2 37 14N 7 22W
Guadix, Spain 69 D4 37 18N 3 11W
Guafo, Boca del, Chile 121 G2 43 35S 74 0W
Guajará-Mirim, Brazil 120 D3 10 50S 65 20W
Guajira, Pen. de la, Colombia 120 A2 12 0N 72 0W
Gualeguaychú, Argentina 121 F4 33 3S 59 31W
Guam ☑, Pac. Oc. 102 F6 13 27N 144 45 E
Guamúchil, Mexico 114 B3 25 25N 108 3W
Guana I., Br. Virgin Is. 115 e 18 30N 64 30W
Guanajuato, Mexico 114 C4 21 0N 101 20W
Guane, Cuba 115 C8 22 10N 84 7W
Guangdong ☐, China 81 D6 23 0N 113 0 E
Guangxi Zhuang ☐, China 81 D5 24 0N 109 0 E
Guangzhou, China 81 D6 23 5N 113 10 E
Guanica, Puerto Rico 115 d 17 59N 66 55W
Guantánamo, Cuba 115 C9 20 10N 75 14W
Guaporé →, Brazil 120 D3 11 55S 65 4W
Guaqui, Bolivia 120 D3 16 41S 68 54W
Guarapuava, Brazil 121 E4 25 20S 51 30W
Guaratinguetá, Brazil 122 D1 22 49S 45 9W
Guarulhos, Brazil 122 D1 23 29S 46 33W
Guarus, Brazil 122 D2 21 44S 41 20W
Guatemala, Guatemala 114 E6 14 40N 90 22W
Guatemala ■, Cent. Amer. 114 D6 15 40N 90 30W
Guaviare →, Colombia 120 B3 4 3N 67 44W
Guaxupé, Brazil 122 D1 21 10S 47 5W
Guayama, Puerto Rico 115 d 17 59N 66 7W
Guayaquil, Ecuador 120 C2 2 15S 79 52W
Guayaquil, G. de, Ecuador 120 C1 3 10S 81 0W
Guaymas, Mexico 114 B2 27 59N 110 54W
Gubkin, Russia 73 D6 51 17N 37 32 E
Guelph, Canada 112 D7 43 35N 80 20W
Guéret, France 68 C4 46 11N 1 51 E
Guernsey ☐, U.K. 27 J8 49 26N 2 35W
Guestling Green, U.K. 25 E10 50 53N 0 39 E
Guiana Highlands, S. Amer. 116 C4 5 10N 60 40W
Guildford, U.K. 25 D7 51 14N 0 34W
Guilin, China 81 D6 25 18N 110 15 E
Guinea, Africa 90 F4 8 0N 8 0 E
Guinea ■, W. Afr. 94 F3 10 20N 11 30W
Guinea, Gulf of, Atl. Oc. 90 F4 3 0N 2 30 E
Guinea-Bissau ■, Africa 94 F3 12 0N 15 0W
Güines, Cuba 115 C8 22 50N 82 0W
Guingamp, France 68 B2 48 34N 3 10W
Guisborough, U.K. 22 C6 54 33N 1 4W
Guiyang, China 80 D5 26 32N 106 40 E
Guizhou ☐, China 80 D5 27 0N 107 0 E
Gujarat ☐, India 84 H7 23 20N 71 0 E
Gujranwala, Pakistan 84 C9 32 10N 74 12 E
Gujrat, Pakistan 84 C9 32 40N 74 2 E
Gulbarga, India 84 L10 17 20N 76 50 E
Gulf, The, Asia 87 E7 27 0N 50 0 E
Gulfport, U.S.A. 111 D9 30 22N 89 6W
Guna, India 84 G10 24 40N 77 19 E
Gunnison →, U.S.A. 110 C5 39 4N 108 35W
Guntur, India 85 L12 16 23N 80 30 E
Gurgueia →, Brazil 120 C5 6 50S 43 24W
Gurkha, Nepal 85 E14 28 5N 84 40 E
Gurnard's Hd., U.K. 27 G2 50 11N 5 37W
Gürün, Turkey 73 G6 38 43N 37 15 E
Gurupi, Brazil 122 B1 11 43S 49 4W
Gurupi →, Brazil 120 C5 1 13S 46 6W
Gusau, Nigeria 94 F7 12 12N 6 40 E
Gushgy, Turkmenistan 87 C10 35 20N 62 18 E
Guwahati, India 85 F17 26 10N 91 45 E
Guyana ■, S. Amer. 120 B4 5 0N 59 0W
Guyenne, France 68 D4 44 30N 0 40 E
Gwädar, Pakistan 84 G3 25 10N 62 18 E
Gwalchmai, U.K. 26 A5 53 16N 4 25W
Gwalior, India 84 F11 26 12N 78 10 E
Gwanda, Zimbabwe 97 J5 20 55S 29 0 E
Gweebarra B., Ireland 28 B5 54 51N 8 23W
Gweedore, Ireland 28 A5 55 3N 8 13W
Gweek, U.K. 27 G3 50 5N 5 13W
Gwennap, U.K. 27 G3 50 12N 5 11W
Gweru, Zimbabwe 97 H5 19 28S 29 45 E
Gyaring Hu, China 80 C4 34 50N 97 40 E
Gympie, Australia 98 F9 26 11S 152 38 E
Győr, Hungary 67 E9 47 41N 17 40 E
Gyumri, Armenia 73 F7 40 47N 43 50 E
Gyzylarbat, Turkmenistan 87 B9 39 4N 56 23 E

**H**

Ha Tinh, Vietnam 83 B2 18 20N 105 54 E
Ha'apai Group, Tonga 99 D16 19 47S 174 27W
Haarlem, Neths. 65 B4 52 23N 4 39 E
Hachinohe, Japan 82 C7 40 30N 141 29 E
Hackney ☐, U.K. 25 C8 51 33N 0 3W
Hackthorpe, U.K. 22 C3 54 34N 2 42W
Ḥadd, Ra's al, Oman 87 F9 22 35N 59 50 E
Haddenham, U.K. 25 C7 51 46N 0 55W
Haddington, U.K. 21 C10 55 57N 2 47W
Hadleigh, U.K. 25 B10 52 3N 0 58 E
Hadlow, U.K. 25 D9 51 13N 0 22 E
Hadramawt, Yemen 88 D4 15 30N 49 30 E
Haeju, N. Korea 81 C7 38 3N 125 45 E
Hafizabad, Pakistan 84 C8 32 5N 73 40 E
Hagen, Germany 64 C4 51 21N 7 27 E
Hagerstown, U.S.A. 112 F9 39 39N 77 43W
Hags Hd., Ireland 30 C4 52 57N 9 28W
Hague, C. de la, France 68 B3 49 44N 1 56W
Hague, The, Neths. 65 B4 52 7N 4 17 E
Haguenau, France 68 B7 48 49N 7 47 E
Haifa, Israel 86 C3 32 46N 35 0 E
Haikou, China 81 D6 20 1N 110 16 E
Ḥā'il, Si. Arabia 86 E5 27 28N 41 45 E
Hailar, China 81 B6 49 10N 119 38 E
Hailey, U.S.A. 110 B4 43 31N 114 19W
Haileybury, Canada 112 B8 47 30N 79 38W
Hailsham, U.K. 25 E9 50 52N 0 16 E
Hainan ☐, China 81 E5 19 0N 109 30 E
Haines Junction, Canada 108 B6 60 45N 137 30W
Hainton, U.K. 23 F8 53 21N 0 14W
Haiphong, Vietnam 80 D5 20 47N 106 41 E
Haiti ■, W. Indies 115 D10 19 0N 72 30W
Hakodate, Japan 82 C7 41 45N 140 44 E
Halberstadt, Germany 66 C6 51 54N 11 3 E
Halberton, U.K. 24 E2 50 54N 3 25W
Halden, Norway 63 F6 59 9N 11 23 E
Haldia, India 85 H16 22 5N 88 3 E
Haldwani, India 84 E11 29 31N 79 30 E
Halesowen, U.K. 23 H4 52 27N 2 3W
Halesworth, U.K. 25 B12 52 20N 1 31 E
Halifax, Canada 109 D13 44 38N 63 35W

Halifax, U.K. 23 E5 53 43N 1 52W
Halkirk, U.K. 19 E11 58 30N 3 29W
Hall Pen., Canada 109 B13 63 30N 66 0W
Halle, Germany 66 C6 51 30N 11 56 E
Hallow, U.K. 23 H4 52 14N 2 15W
Halls Creek, Australia 98 D4 18 16S 127 38 E
Hallworthy, U.K. 27 F4 50 39N 4 35W
Halmahera, Indonesia 83 C4 0 40N 128 0 E
Halmstad, Sweden 63 F6 56 41N 12 52 E
Halstead, U.K. 25 C10 51 57N 0 40 E
Haltwhistle, U.K. 22 C4 54 58N 2 26W
Hamadán, Iran 86 C7 34 52N 48 32 E
Hamāh, Syria 86 C4 35 5N 36 40 E
Hamamatsu, Japan 82 F5 34 45N 137 45 E
Hamar, Norway 63 E6 60 48N 11 7 E
Hambantota, Sri Lanka 84 R12 6 10N 81 10 E
Hambledon, U.K. 24 E6 50 55N 1 5W
Hambleton Hills, U.K. 22 D6 54 17N 1 12W
Hamburg, Germany 66 B5 53 33N 9 59 E
Hämeenlinna, Finland 63 E8 61 0N 24 28 E
Hameln, Germany 66 B5 52 6N 9 21 E
Hamersley Ra., Australia 98 E2 22 0S 117 45 E
Hami, China 80 B4 42 55N 93 25 E
Hamilton, Canada 109 D12 43 15N 79 50W
Hamilton, N.Z. 99 H14 37 47S 175 19 E
Hamilton, U.K. 20 C7 55 46N 4 2W
Hamilton, U.S.A. 112 F5 39 24N 84 34W
Hamm, Germany 64 C4 51 40N 7 50 E
Hammerfest, Norway 63 C8 70 39N 23 41 E
Hammersmith and Fulham ☐, U.K. 25 D8 51 30N 0 14W
Hammond, U.S.A. 112 E4 41 38N 87 30W
Hammonton, U.S.A. 113 F10 39 39N 74 48W
Hampshire ☐, U.K. 24 D6 51 7N 1 23W
Hampshire Downs, U.K. 24 D6 51 15N 1 10W
Hampton in Arden, U.K. 23 H5 52 26N 1 41W
Hancock, U.S.A. 112 B3 47 8N 88 35W
Handan, China 81 C6 36 35N 114 28 E
Hanford, U.S.A. 110 C3 36 20N 119 39W
Hangayn Nuruu, Mongolia 80 B4 47 30N 99 0 E
Hangzhou, China 81 C7 30 18N 120 11 E
Hangzhou Wan, China 81 C7 30 15N 120 45 E
Hanna, Canada 108 C8 51 40N 111 54W
Hannibal, U.S.A. 111 C8 39 42N 91 22W
Hanningfield Res., U.K. 25 C10 51 40N 0 31 E
Hannover, Germany 66 B5 52 22N 9 46 E
Hanoi, Vietnam 80 D5 21 5N 105 55 E
Hanover, U.K. 112 F9 39 48N 76 59W
Hanover, I., Chile 121 H2 51 0S 74 50W
Hans Lollik I., U.S. Virgin Is. 115 e 18 24N 64 53W
Hanzhong, China 80 C5 33 10N 107 1 E
Haora, India 85 H16 22 37N 88 20 E
Haparanda, Sweden 63 D8 65 52N 24 8 E
Happy Valley-Goose Bay, Canada 109 C13 53 15N 60 20W
Har Hu, China 80 C4 38 20N 97 38 E
Har Us Nuur, Mongolia 80 B4 48 0N 92 0 E
Ḥaraḍ, Si. Arabia 86 E7 24 22N 49 0 E
Harare, Zimbabwe 97 H6 17 43S 31 2 E
Harbin, China 81 B7 45 48N 126 40 E
Harbor Beach, U.S.A. 112 D6 43 51N 82 39W
Hardangerfjorden, Norway 63 E5 60 5N 6 0 E
Hardy, Pte., St. Lucia 115 f 14 6N 60 56W
Harer, Ethiopia 88 F3 9 20N 42 8 E
Harewood, U.K. 23 E6 53 54N 1 30W
Hargeisa, Somali Rep. 88 F3 9 30N 44 2 E
Haridwar, India 84 E11 29 58N 78 9 E
Haringey ☐, U.K. 25 C8 51 34N 0 5W
Haringhata →, Bangla. 85 J16 22 0N 89 58 E
Harirūd →, Asia 87 B10 37 24N 60 38 E
Harlech, U.K. 26 B5 52 52N 4 6W
Harleston, U.K. 25 B11 52 24N 1 18 E
Harlingen, Neths. 65 A5 53 11N 5 25 E
Harlingen, U.S.A. 110 E7 26 12N 97 42W
Harlow, U.K. 25 C9 51 46N 0 8 E
Harney L., U.S.A. 110 B3 43 14N 119 8W
Härnösand, Sweden 63 E7 62 38N 17 55 E
Haroldswick, U.K. 18 A16 60 48N 0 50W
Harpenden, U.K. 25 C8 51 49N 0 21W
Harricana →, Canada 109 C12 50 56N 79 32W
Harrietsham, U.K. 25 D10 51 14N 0 41 E
Harrington, U.K. 22 C1 54 37N 3 33W
Harris, U.K. 18 G4 57 50N 6 55W
Harris, Sd. of, U.K. 18 G3 57 44N 7 6W
Harrisburg, U.S.A. 112 E9 40 16N 76 53W
Harrison →, Canada 109 C14 54 55N 57 55W
Harrisonburg, U.S.A. 112 F8 38 27N 78 52W
Harrisville, U.S.A. 112 C6 44 39N 83 17W
Harrogate, U.K. 23 D5 54 0N 1 33W
Harrow ☐, U.K. 25 C8 51 35N 0 21W
Hart, U.S.A. 112 D4 43 42N 86 22W
Hartest, U.K. 25 B10 52 8N 0 40 E
Hartford, Conn., U.S.A. 113 E11 41 46N 72 41W
Hartford, Ky., U.S.A. 112 G4 37 27N 86 55W
Hartland, U.K. 27 F5 50 59N 4 29W
Hartland Pt., U.K. 27 E4 51 1N 4 32W
Hartlebury, U.K. 23 H4 52 20N 2 14W
Hartlepool, U.K. 22 C6 54 42N 1 13W
Hartley, U.K. 22 B6 55 5N 1 28W
Hartpury, U.K. 24 C4 51 55N 2 17W
Harvey, U.S.A. 112 E4 41 36N 87 50W
Harwell, U.K. 24 C5 51 36N 1 17W
Harwich, U.K. 25 C11 51 56N 1 17 E
Haryana ☐, India 84 E10 29 0N 76 10 E
Harz, Germany 66 C6 51 38N 10 44 E
Hasa □, Si. Arabia 86 E7 25 60N 49 0 E
Haslemere, U.K. 25 D7 51 5N 0 43W
Haslingden, U.K. 23 E4 53 42N 2 19W
Hasselt, Belgium 65 D5 50 56N 5 21 E
Hastings, U.K. 25 E10 50 51N 0 35 E
Hastings, U.S.A. 110 B7 40 35N 98 23W
Hat Yai, Thailand 83 C2 7 1N 100 27 E
Hatfield, U.K. 25 C8 51 46N 0 13W
Hatgal, Mongolia 80 A5 50 26N 100 9 E
Hatherleigh, U.K. 27 F5 50 49N 4 5W
Hathersage, U.K. 23 F5 53 20N 1 39W
Hathras, India 84 F11 27 36N 78 6 E
Hatia, Bangla. 85 H17 22 30N 91 5 E
Hatteras, C., U.S.A. 111 C11 35 14N 75 32W
Hattiesburg, U.S.A. 111 D9 31 20N 89 17W
Haugesund, Norway 63 F5 59 23N 5 13 E
Haughley, U.K. 25 B10 52 13N 0 57 E
Havana, Cuba 115 C8 23 8N 82 22W
Havant, U.K. 25 E7 50 51N 0 58W
Havasu, L., U.S.A. 110 D4 34 18N 114 28W
Havel →, Germany 66 B7 52 50N 12 3 E
Haverfordwest, U.K. 26 D3 51 48N 4 58W
Haverhill, U.K. 25 B9 52 5N 0 28 E
Haverhill, U.S.A. 113 D12 42 47N 71 5W
Haverigg, U.K. 22 D2 54 12N 3 17W
Havering ☐, U.K. 25 C9 51 34N 0 14 E
Havre, U.S.A. 110 A5 48 33N 109 41W
Havre-St.-Pierre, Canada 109 C13 50 18N 63 33W
Hawaii ☐, U.S.A. 110 H16 19 30N 156 30W
Hawaii I., Pac. Oc. 103 E12 20 30N 156 0W
Hawaiian Is., Pac. Oc. 103 E12 20 30N 156 0W
Hawaiian Ridge, Pac. Oc. 103 E11 24 0N 165 0W

Hawes, U.K. 22 D4 54 19N 2 12W
Haweswater, U.K. 22 C3 54 31N 2 47W
Hawick, U.K. 21 D10 55 26N 2 47W
Hawkchurch, U.K. 24 E3 50 48N 2 56W
Hawkesbury, Canada 113 C10 45 37N 74 37W
Hawkesbury Upton, U.K. 24 C4 51 35N 2 19W
Hawkhurst, U.K. 25 D10 51 2N 0 32 E
Hawkshead, U.K. 22 D3 54 23N 2 59W
Haworth, U.K. 23 E5 53 50N 1 58W
Hawsker, U.K. 22 D7 54 27N 0 34W
Haxby, U.K. 23 D6 54 1N 1 4W
Hay →, Australia 98 G8 24 50S 138 0 E
Hay →, Canada 108 B8 60 50N 116 26W
Hay-on-Wye, U.K. 24 B2 52 5N 3 8W
Hay River, Canada 108 B8 60 51N 115 44W
Hayes →, Canada 108 C10 57 3N 92 12W
Hayle, U.K. 27 G3 50 11N 5 26W
Hays, U.S.A. 110 C7 38 53N 99 20W
Hayton, U.K. 22 C3 54 55N 2 45W
Haywards Heath, U.K. 25 E8 51 0N 0 5W
Hazard, U.S.A. 112 G6 37 15N 83 12W
Hazaribag, India 85 H14 23 58N 85 26 E
Heacham, U.K. 25 A9 52 54N 0 29 E
Headcorn, U.K. 25 D10 51 10N 0 38 E
Heanor, U.K. 23 F6 53 1N 1 21W
Heard I., Ind. Oc. 53 G13 53 0S 74 0 E
Hearst, Canada 109 D11 49 40N 83 41W
Heath, Pte., Canada 113 A17 49 8N 61 40W
Heathfield, U.K. 25 E9 50 58N 0 16 E
Hebburn, U.K. 22 C5 54 59N 1 32W
Hebden Bridge, U.K. 23 E5 53 45N 2 0W
Hebei ☐, China 81 C6 39 0N 116 0 E
Hebrides, U.K. 56 D4 57 30N 7 0W
Hebrides, Sea of the, U.K. 18 H4 57 5N 7 0W
Hebron, Canada 109 C13 58 5N 62 30W
Hecate Str., Canada 108 C6 53 10N 130 30W
Hechi, China 80 D5 24 40N 108 2 E
Hechuan, China 80 C5 30 2N 106 12 E
Heckington, U.K. 23 G8 52 59N 0 17W
Hednesford, U.K. 23 G5 52 43N 1 59W
Hedon, U.K. 23 E8 53 44N 0 12W
Heerlen, Neths. 65 D5 50 55N 5 58 E
Hefei, China 81 C6 31 52N 117 18 E
Hegang, China 81 B8 47 20N 130 19 E
Heidelberg, Germany 66 D5 49 24N 8 42 E
Heilbronn, Germany 66 D5 49 9N 9 13 E
Heilongjiang ☐, China 81 B7 48 0N 126 0 E
Hekou, China 80 D5 22 30N 103 59 E
Helena, U.S.A. 110 A4 46 36N 112 2W
Helensburgh, U.K. 20 B6 56 1N 4 43W
Helgoland, Germany 66 A4 54 10N 7 53 E
Hellifield, U.K. 23 D4 54 1N 2 12W
Helmand →, Afghan. 84 D2 31 12N 61 34 E
Helmond, Neths. 65 C5 51 29N 5 41 E
Helmsdale, U.K. 19 F10 58 7N 3 39W
Helmsley, U.K. 22 D6 54 15N 1 3W
Helperby, U.K. 22 D6 54 8N 1 19W
Helsby, U.K. 23 F3 53 17N 2 46W
Helsingborg, Sweden 63 F6 56 3N 12 42 E
Helsinki, Finland 63 E9 60 15N 25 3 E
Helston, U.K. 27 G3 50 6N 5 17W
Helvellyn, U.K. 22 C2 54 32N 3 1W
Helwân, Egypt 95 C12 29 50N 31 20 E
Hemel Hempstead, U.K. 25 C8 51 44N 0 28W
Hempton, U.K. 25 A10 52 50N 0 50 E
Hemsworth, U.K. 23 E6 53 37N 1 21W
Hemyock, U.K. 24 E2 50 54N 3 15W
Henan ☐, China 81 C6 34 0N 114 0 E
Henderson, Ky., U.S.A. 112 G4 37 50N 87 35W
Henderson, Nev., U.S.A. 110 C3 36 2N 114 59W
Henfield, U.K. 25 E8 50 56N 0 16W
Hengelo, Neths. 65 B6 52 16N 6 48 E
Hengyang, China 81 D6 26 59N 112 22 E
Henley-in-Arden, U.K. 23 H5 52 18N 1 46W
Henley-on-Thames, U.K. 25 C7 51 32N 0 54W
Henlopen, C., U.S.A. 113 F10 38 48N 75 6W
Henlow, U.K. 25 B8 52 2N 0 17W
Henrietta Maria, C., Canada 109 C11 55 9N 82 20W
Henstridge, U.K. 24 E4 50 58N 2 24W
Hentiyn Nuruu, Mongolia 81 B5 48 30N 108 30 E
Herät, Afghan. 84 B3 34 20N 62 7 E
Hereford, U.K. 24 B3 52 4N 2 43W
Herford, Germany 66 B5 52 7N 8 39 E
Hermosillo, Mexico 114 B2 29 10N 111 0W
Hernád →, Hungary 67 D11 47 56N 21 8 E
Herne, Germany 65 C7 51 32N 7 14 E
Herne Bay, U.K. 25 D11 51 21N 1 8 E
Herstmonceux, U.K. 25 E9 50 53N 0 20 E
Hertford, U.K. 25 C8 51 48N 0 4W
Hertfordshire ☐, U.K. 25 C8 51 51N 0 5W
's-Hertogenbosch, Neths. 65 C5 51 42N 5 17 E
Hessen ☐, Germany 66 C5 50 30N 9 0 E
Hessle, U.K. 23 E8 53 44N 0 24W
Hethersett, U.K. 25 A11 52 36N 1 10 E
Hetton-le-Hole, U.K. 22 C6 54 50N 1 26W
Hexham, U.K. 22 C4 54 58N 2 4W
Heybridge, U.K. 25 C10 51 45N 0 42 E
Heysham, U.K. 22 D3 54 3N 2 53W
Heytesbury, U.K. 24 D4 51 11N 2 6W
Heywood, U.K. 23 E4 53 35N 2 12W
Hibbing, U.S.A. 111 A8 47 25N 92 56W
Hidalgo del Parral, Mexico 114 B3 26 58N 105 40W
Hierro, Canary Is. 94 C2 27 44N 18 0W
Higashiōsaka, Japan 82 F4 34 40N 135 37 E
High Atlas, Morocco 94 B4 32 30N 5 0W
High Bentham, U.K. 22 D4 54 7N 2 28W
High Ercall, U.K. 23 G3 52 45N 2 35W
High Hesket, U.K. 22 C3 54 48N 2 49W
High Level, Canada 108 C8 58 31N 117 8W
High Pike, U.K. 22 C2 54 42N 3 4W
High Plateaux, Algeria 90 C4 35 0N 1 0 E
High Prairie, Canada 108 C8 55 30N 116 30W
High River, Canada 108 C8 50 30N 113 50W
High Veld, Africa 90 J6 27 0S 27 0 E
High Willhays, U.K. 27 F5 50 40N 4 0W
High Wycombe, U.K. 25 C7 51 37N 0 45W
Higham Ferrers, U.K. 23 H7 52 19N 0 35W
Highbridge, U.K. 24 D3 51 13N 2 58W
Highclere, U.K. 24 D6 51 20N 1 21W
Highland ☐, U.K. 19 H9 57 17N 4 21W
Highley, U.K. 23 H4 52 27N 2 23W
Highworth, U.K. 24 C5 51 37N 1 43W
Hiiumaa, Estonia 72 C3 58 50N 22 45 E
Ḥijāz ☐, Si. Arabia 86 E4 24 0N 40 0 E
Hildesheim, Germany 66 B5 52 9N 9 56 E
Hilgay, U.K. 25 A9 52 34N 0 24 E
Hillaby, Mt., Barbados 115 g 13 12N 59 35W
Hillcrest, Barbados 115 g 13 13N 59 32W
Hillingdon ☐, U.K. 25 C8 51 32N 0 27W
Hillsborough, U.K. 29 C9 54 28N 6 5W
Hillsdale, U.S.A. 112 E5 41 56N 84 38W
Hilo, U.S.A. 110 J17 19 44N 155 5W
Hilpsford Pt., U.K. 22 D2 54 4N 3 12W
Hilversum, Neths. 65 B5 52 14N 5 10 E
Himachal Pradesh ☐, India 84 D10 31 30N 77 0 E

Himalaya, Asia 85 E14 29 0N 84 0 E
Himeji, Japan 82 F4 34 50N 134 40 E
Hinckley, U.K. 23 G6 52 33N 1 22W
Hinderwell, U.K. 22 C7 54 32N 0 45W
Hindhead, U.K. 25 D7 51 7N 0 43W
Hindley, U.K. 23 E3 53 33N 2 35W
Hindu Kush, Asia 84 B7 36 0N 71 0 E
Hingham, U.K. 25 A10 52 35N 1 0 E
Hingoli, India 84 K10 19 41N 77 15 E
Hinkley Pt., U.K. 24 D2 51 12N 3 8W
Hinstock, U.K. 23 G4 52 50N 2 27W
Hinton, U.S.A. 112 G7 37 40N 80 54W
Hirosaki, Japan 82 C7 40 34N 140 28 E
Hiroshima, Japan 82 F3 34 24N 132 30 E
Hisar, India 84 E9 29 12N 75 45 E
Hispaniola, W. Indies 115 D10 19 0N 71 0W
Histon, U.K. 23 H9 52 16N 0 7 E
Hitachi, Japan 82 E7 36 36N 140 39 E
Hitchin, U.K. 25 C8 51 58N 0 16W
Hjälmaren, Sweden 63 F7 59 18N 15 40 E
Hkakabo Razi, Burma 85 E20 28 25N 97 23 E
Ho Chi Minh City, Vietnam 83 B2 10 58N 106 40 E
Hoare B., Canada 109 B13 65 17N 62 30W
Hobart, Australia 98 J8 42 50S 147 21 E
Hobbs, U.S.A. 110 D6 32 42N 103 8W
Hodder →, U.K. 23 E4 53 57N 2 27W
Hoddesdon, U.K. 25 C8 51 45N 0 1W
Hodge →, U.K. 22 D7 54 16N 0 56W
Hodgson, Canada 108 C10 51 13N 97 36W
Hódmezóvásárhely, Hungary 67 E11 46 28N 20 22 E
Hoff, U.K. 22 C3 54 34N 2 31W
Hōfu, Japan 82 F2 34 3N 131 34 E
Hoggar, Algeria 94 D7 23 0N 6 30 E
Hog's Back, U.K. 25 D7 51 13N 0 38W
Hoher Rhön, Germany 66 C5 50 24N 9 58 E
Hohhot, China 81 B6 40 52N 111 40 E
Hokkaidō ☐, Japan 82 B8 43 30N 143 0 E
Holbeach, U.K. 23 G9 52 48N 0 1 E
Holbeach Marsh, U.K. 23 G9 52 52N 0 5 E
Holderness, U.K. 23 E8 53 45N 0 5W
Holetown, Barbados 115 g 13 11N 59 38W
Holguín, Cuba 115 C9 20 50N 76 20W
Holkham, U.K. 25 A10 52 57N 0 48 E
Holland, U.S.A. 112 D4 42 47N 86 7W
Holland Fen, U.K. 23 G8 53 0N 0 8W
Holland on Sea, U.K. 25 C11 51 48N 1 13 E
Holman, Canada 108 A8 70 44N 117 44W
Holme, U.K. 23 E7 53 50N 0 46W
Holmes Chapel, U.K. 23 F4 53 12N 2 21W
Holmfirth, U.K. 23 E5 53 35N 1 46W
Holsworthy, U.K. 27 F5 50 48N 4 22W
Holt, U.K. 25 A11 52 55N 1 6 E
Holy I., Angl., U.K. 26 A4 53 17N 4 37W
Holy I., Northumberland, U.K. 22 A5 55 40N 1 47W
Holyhead, U.K. 26 A4 53 18N 4 38W
Home B., Canada 109 B13 68 40N 67 10W
Homer, U.S.A. 108 C4 59 39N 151 33W
Homs, Syria 86 C4 34 40N 36 45 E
Honduras ■, Cent. Amer. 114 E7 14 40N 86 30W
Honduras, G. de, Caribbean 114 D7 16 50N 87 0W
Honey L., U.S.A. 110 B2 40 15N 120 19W
Hong Kong ☐, China 81 D6 22 11N 114 14 E
Hongjiang, China 81 D5 27 7N 109 59 E
Hongshui He →, China 81 D5 23 48N 109 30 E
Hongze Hu, China 81 C6 33 15N 118 35 E
Honiara, Solomon Is. 99 B10 9 27S 159 57 E
Honington, U.K. 23 G7 52 59N 0 35W
Honiton, U.K. 24 E2 50 47N 3 11W
Honolulu, U.S.A. 103 E12 21 19N 157 52W
Honshū, Japan 82 F6 36 0N 138 0 E
Hoo, U.K. 25 D10 51 25N 0 35 E
Hood, Mt., U.S.A. 110 A2 45 23N 121 42W
Hoogeveen, Neths. 65 B6 52 44N 6 28 E
Hook, U.K. 25 D7 51 17N 0 57W
Hook Hd., Ireland 31 D9 52 7N 6 56W
Hooper Bay, U.S.A. 108 B3 61 32N 166 6W
Hoopeston, U.S.A. 112 E4 40 28N 87 40W
Hoorn, Neths. 65 B5 52 38N 5 4 E
Hoover Dam, U.S.A. 110 C4 36 1N 114 44W
Hope, U.K. 111 D8 33 40N 93 36W
Hopedale, Canada 109 C13 55 28N 60 13W
Hopetown, S. Africa 97 K4 29 34S 24 3 E
Hopkinsville, U.S.A. 112 G4 36 52N 87 29W
Horden, U.K. 22 C6 54 46N 1 19W
Horley, U.K. 25 D8 51 10N 0 10W
Horlivka, Ukraine 73 E6 48 19N 38 5 E
Hormozgān ☐, Iran 87 E9 27 30N 56 0 E
Hormuz, Str. of, The Gulf 87 E9 26 30N 56 30 E
Horn, C. = Hornos, C. de, Chile 121 H3 55 50S 67 30W
Horn, Is., Wall. & F. Is. 99 C15 14 16S 178 6W
Horn Head, Ireland 28 A6 55 14N 8 0W
Hornavan, Sweden 63 D7 66 15N 17 30 E
Horncastle, U.K. 23 F8 53 13N 0 7W
Horndean, U.K. 24 E6 50 55N 1 1W
Hornell, U.S.A. 112 D9 42 20N 77 40W
Hornepayne, Canada 112 A5 49 14N 84 48W
Horningsham, U.K. 24 D4 51 10N 2 16W
Hornos, C. de, Chile 121 H3 55 50S 67 30W
Hornsea, U.K. 23 E8 53 55N 0 11W
Horqin Youyi Qianqi, China 81 B7 46 5N 122 3 E
Horsforth, U.K. 23 E5 53 50N 1 39W
Horsham, Australia 98 H7 36 44S 142 13 E
Horsham, U.K. 25 D8 51 4N 0 20W
Horsham St. Faith, U.K. 25 A11 52 43N 1 14 E
Horsted Keynes, U.K. 25 D8 51 2N 0 1W
Horton →, Canada 108 B7 69 56N 126 52W
Horton in Ribblesdale, U.K. 22 D4 54 9N 2 17W
Horwich, U.K. 23 E3 53 36N 2 33W
Hoste, I., Chile 121 H3 55 0S 69 0W
Hot Springs, Ark., U.S.A. 111 D8 34 31N 93 3W
Hot Springs, S. Dak., U.S.A. 110 B6 43 26N 103 29W
Hotan, China 80 C2 37 25N 79 55 E
Houghton, U.S.A. 112 B3 47 7N 88 34W
Houghton-le-Spring, U.K. 22 C6 54 51N 1 28W
Houghton Regis, U.K. 25 C8 51 54N 0 32W
Houlton, U.S.A. 113 B14 46 8N 67 51W
Houma, U.S.A. 111 E8 29 36N 90 43W
Hounslow ☐, U.K. 25 D8 51 28N 0 21W
Houston, U.S.A. 111 E7 29 46N 95 22W
Hovd, Mongolia 80 B4 48 2N 91 37 E
Hove, U.K. 25 E8 50 50N 0 10W
Hoveton, U.K. 25 A11 52 43N 1 25 E
Hovingham, U.K. 22 D6 54 10N 0 58W
Hövsgöl Nuur, Mongolia 80 A5 51 0N 100 30 E
Howden, U.K. 23 E7 53 45N 0 52W
Howe, C., Australia 98 H9 37 30S 150 0 E
Howell, U.S.A. 112 D6 42 36N 83 56W
Howland I., Pac. Oc. 102 G10 0 48N 176 38W
Howth Hd., Ireland 29 B10 53 22N 6 4W
Hoxne, U.K. 25 B11 52 21N 1 12 E
Hoy, U.K. 19 E11 58 50N 3 15W
Høyanger, Norway 63 E5 61 13N 6 4 E
Hoylake, U.K. 23 E2 53 24N 3 10W
Hradec Králové, Czech Rep. 66 C8 50 15N 15 50 E
Hrodna, Belarus 67 B12 53 42N 23 52 E

**Hron**                                                                                           **Kansas City**

Hron →, Slovak Rep. ......... 67 E10 47 49N 18 45 E
Hsinchu, Taiwan ............ 81 D7 24 48N 120 58 E
Huacho, Peru .............. 120 D2 11 10S 77 35W
Huai He →, China ........... 81 C6 33 0N 118 30 E
Huainan, China ............ 81 C6 32 38N 116 58 E
Huallaga →, Peru ........... 120 C2 5 15S 75 30W
Huambo, Angola ............ 97 G3 12 42S 15 54 E
Huancavelica, Peru ......... 120 D2 12 50S 75 5W
Huancayo, Peru ............ 120 D2 12 5S 75 12W
Huangshan, China .......... 81 D6 29 42N 118 25 E
Huangshi, China ........... 81 C6 30 10N 115 3 E
Huánuco, Peru ............. 120 C2 9 55S 76 15W
Huaraz, Peru .............. 120 C2 9 30S 77 32W
Huascarán, Peru ........... 120 C2 9 8S 77 36W
Huasco, Chile ............. 121 E2 28 30S 71 15W
Huatabampo, Mexico ........ 114 B3 26 50N 109 50W
Hubei □, China ............ 81 C6 31 0N 112 0 E
Hucknall, U.K. ............. 23 F6 53 3N 1 13W
Huddersfield, U.K. .......... 23 E5 53 39N 1 47W
Hudiksvall, Sweden ......... 63 E7 61 43N 17 10 E
Hudson →, U.S.A. ........... 113 E10 40 42N 74 2W
Hudson Bay, Canada ........ 109 C11 60 0N 86 0W
Hudson Falls, U.S.A. ........ 113 D11 43 18N 73 35W
Hudson Str., Canada ........ 109 B13 62 0N 70 0W
Hue, Vietnam .............. 83 B2 16 30N 107 35 E
Huelva, Spain ............. 69 D2 37 18N 6 57W
Huesca, Spain ............. 69 A5 42 8N 0 25W
Hugh Town, U.K. ........... 27 H1 49 55N 6 19W
Hughenden, Australia ....... 98 E7 20 52S 144 10 E
Hugli →, India ............. 85 J16 21 56N 88 4 E
Huila, Nevado del, Colombia . 120 B2 3 0N 76 0W
Huize, China .............. 80 D5 26 24N 103 15 E
Hull = Kingston upon Hull, U.K. . 23 E8 53 45N 0 21W
Hull, Canada .............. 109 D12 45 25N 75 44W
Hull →, U.K. .............. 23 E8 53 44N 0 20W
Hullavington, U.K. .......... 24 C4 51 32N 2 8W
Hulme End, U.K. ........... 23 F5 53 8N 1 50W
Hulun Nur, China .......... 81 B6 49 0N 117 30 E
Humacao, Puerto Rico ....... 115 d 18 9N 65 50W
Humaitá, Brazil ............ 120 C3 7 35S 63 1W
Humber →, U.K. ........... 23 E8 53 42N 0 27W
Humber, Mouth of the, U.K. .. 23 E9 53 32N 0 8 E
Humberside □, U.K. ......... 23 E7 53 48N 0 47W
Humboldt, Canada .......... 108 C9 52 15N 105 9W
Humboldt →, U.S.A. ........ 110 B3 39 59N 118 36W
Humphreys Peak, U.S.A. ..... 110 C4 35 21N 111 41W
Humshaugh, U.K. ........... 22 B4 55 3N 2 8W
Hunan □, China ........... 81 D6 27 30N 112 0 E
Hungary ■, Europe ........ 67 E10 47 20N 19 20 E
Hungary, Plain of, Europe ... 56 F10 47 0N 20 0 E
Hungerford, U.K. ........... 24 D5 51 25N 1 31W
Hŭngnam, N. Korea ........ 81 C7 39 49N 127 45 E
Hunmanby, U.K. ........... 22 D8 54 10N 0 20W
Hunsrück, Germany ......... 66 D4 49 56N 7 27 E
Hunstanton, U.K. ........... 25 A9 52 56N 0 29 E
Huntingdon, U.K. ........... 23 H8 52 20N 0 11W
Huntington, Ind., U.S.A. ..... 112 E5 40 53N 85 30W
Huntington, W. Va., U.S.A. ... 112 F6 38 25N 82 27W
Huntly, U.K. .............. 19 H12 57 27N 2 47W
Huntsville, Canada ......... 109 D12 45 20N 79 14W
Huntsville, Ala., U.S.A. ...... 111 D9 34 44N 86 35W
Huntsville, Tex., U.S.A. ...... 111 D7 30 43N 95 33W
Huron, U.S.A. ............. 110 B7 44 22N 98 13W
Huron, L., U.S.A. .......... 112 C6 44 30N 82 40W
Hursley, U.K. ............. 24 D6 51 2N 1 23W
Hurstbourne Tarrant, U.K. ... 24 D6 51 17N 1 26W
Hurstpierpoint, U.K. ........ 25 E8 50 56N 0 11W
Húsavík, Iceland ........... 63 A2 66 3N 17 21W
Husband's Bosworth, U.K. ... 23 H6 52 28N 1 4W
Hutchinson, U.S.A. ......... 110 C7 38 5N 97 56W
Huyton, U.K. .............. 23 F3 53 25N 2 51W
Hwang-ho →, China ........ 81 C6 37 55N 118 50 E
Hwange, Zimbabwe ......... 97 H5 18 18S 26 30 E
Hyargas Nuur, Mongolia ..... 80 B4 49 0N 93 0 E
Hyde, U.K. ............... 23 F4 53 27N 2 4W
Hyderabad, India .......... 84 L11 17 22N 78 29 E
Hyderabad, Pakistan ........ 84 G6 25 23N 68 24 E
Hyères, France ............ 68 E7 43 8N 6 9 E
Hyères, Is. d', France ...... 68 E7 43 0N 6 20 E
Hyndman Peak, U.S.A. ...... 110 B4 43 45N 114 8W
Hythe, U.K. .............. 25 D11 51 4N 1 5 E

# I

Ialomița →, Romania ........ 67 F14 44 42N 27 51 E
Iași, Romania ............. 67 E14 47 10N 27 40 E
Ibadan, Nigeria ........... 94 G6 7 22N 3 58 E
Ibagué, Colombia .......... 120 B2 4 20N 75 20W
Ibarra, Ecuador ........... 120 B2 0 21N 78 7W
Iberian Peninsula, Europe ... 56 H5 40 0N 5 0W
Ibiá, Brazil ............... 122 C1 19 30S 46 30W
Ibiapaba, Sa. da, Brazil ..... 120 C5 4 0S 41 30W
Ibiza = Eivissa, Spain ...... 69 C6 38 54N 1 26 E
Ibotirama, Brazil .......... 122 B2 12 13S 43 12W
Ibstock, U.K. ............. 23 G6 52 42N 1 24W
Ica, Peru ................ 120 D2 14 0S 75 48W
Içá →, Brazil ............. 120 C3 2 55S 67 58W
Iceland ■, Europe ......... 63 B2 64 45N 19 0W
Ichihara, Japan ........... 82 F7 35 28N 140 5 E
Ichinomiya, Japan ......... 82 F5 35 18N 136 48 E
Idaho □, U.S.A. ........... 110 B4 45 0N 115 0W
Idaho Falls, U.S.A. ......... 110 B4 43 30N 112 2W
Idar-Oberstein, Germany .... 66 D4 49 43N 7 16 E
Idle →, U.K. ............. 23 F7 53 27N 0 49W
Idlib, Syria .............. 86 C4 35 55N 36 36 E
Idmiston, U.K. ............ 24 D5 51 9N 1 42W
Ieper, Belgium ............ 65 D2 50 51N 2 53 E
Ife, Nigeria .............. 94 G6 7 30N 4 31 E
Igarapava, Brazil .......... 122 D1 20 3S 47 47W
Iglésias, Italy ............ 70 E3 39 19N 8 32 E
Igloolik, Canada .......... 109 B11 69 20N 81 49W
Ignace, Canada ........... 112 A2 49 30N 91 40W
Iguaçu →, Brazil .......... 121 E4 25 36S 54 36W
Iguaçu Falls, Brazil ........ 121 E4 25 41S 54 26W
Iguala, Mexico ............ 114 D5 18 20N 99 40W
Iguatu, Brazil ............. 120 C6 6 20S 39 18W
Iisalmi, Finland ........... 63 E9 63 32N 27 10 E
IJsselmeer, Neths. ......... 65 B5 52 45N 5 20 E
Ikaluktutiak, Canada ....... 108 B9 69 10N 105 0W
Ikeda, Japan ............. 82 F3 34 1N 133 48 E
Ilagan, Phil. ............. 83 B4 17 7N 121 53 E
Ilām, Iran ............... 86 C6 33 36N 46 36 E
Ilchester, U.K. ........... 24 D3 51 0N 2 41W
Île-de-France □, France ..... 68 B5 49 0N 2 20 E
Ilebo, Dem. Rep. of the Congo . 96 E4 4 17S 20 55 E
Ilesha, Nigeria ........... 94 G6 7 37N 4 40 E
Ilfracombe, U.K. .......... 27 E5 51 12N 4 8W
Ilhéus, Brazil ............ 122 B3 14 49S 39 2W
Ili →, Kazakhstan ......... 79 E9 45 53N 77 10 E
Iliamna L., U.S.A. ......... 108 C4 59 30N 155 0W
Iligan, Phil. ............. 83 C4 8 12N 124 13 E
Ilkeston, U.K. ............ 23 G6 52 58N 1 19W
Ilkley, U.K. ............. 23 E5 53 56N 1 48W

Illapel, Chile ............. 121 F2 32 0S 71 10W
Iller →, Germany .......... 66 D6 48 23N 9 58 E
Illimani, Nevado, Bolivia .... 120 D3 16 30S 67 50W
Illinois □, U.S.A. .......... 111 B9 40 15N 89 30W
Illinois →, U.S.A. ......... 111 C8 38 58N 90 28W
Ilmen, L., Russia .......... 72 C5 58 15N 31 10 E
Ilminster, U.K. ........... 24 E3 50 55N 2 55W
Iloilo, Phil. .............. 83 B4 10 45N 122 33 E
Ilorin, Nigeria ........... 94 G6 8 30N 4 35 E
Imabari, Japan ........... 82 F3 34 4N 133 0 E
Imandra, L., Russia ........ 72 A5 67 30N 33 0 E
Immingham, U.K. .......... 23 E8 53 37N 0 13W
Imperatriz, Brazil ......... 120 C5 5 30S 47 29W
Imphal, India ............ 85 G18 24 48N 93 56 E
In Salah, Algeria .......... 94 C6 27 10N 2 32 E
Inari, Finland ............ 63 D9 68 54N 27 5 E
Inarijärvi, Finland ......... 63 D9 69 0N 28 0 E
Ince Burun, Turkey ........ 73 F5 42 7N 34 56 E
Inch'ŏn, S. Korea ......... 81 C7 37 27N 126 40 E
Incomáti →, Mozam. ....... 97 K6 25 46S 32 43 E
Indalsälven →, Sweden ..... 63 E7 62 36N 17 30 E
India ■, Asia ............ 84 K11 20 0N 78 0 E
Indian Ocean ............ 53 E13 5 0S 75 0 E
Indiana, U.S.A. ........... 112 E8 40 37N 79 9W
Indiana □, U.S.A. ......... 112 E4 40 0N 86 0W
Indianapolis, U.S.A. ....... 112 F4 39 46N 86 9W
Indigirka →, Russia ....... 79 B16 70 48N 148 54 E
Indira Gandhi Canal, India ... 84 F8 28 0N 72 0 E
Indo-China, Asia .......... 74 H14 15 0N 102 0 E
Indonesia ■, Asia ......... 83 D3 5 0S 115 0 E
Indore, India ............ 84 H9 22 42N 75 53 E
Indre →, France .......... 68 C4 47 16N 0 11 E
Indus →, Pakistan ......... 84 G5 24 20N 67 47 E
İnebolu, Turkey ........... 73 F5 41 55N 33 40 E
Ingatestone, U.K. ......... 25 C9 51 40N 0 24 E
Ingleborough, U.K. ........ 22 D4 54 10N 2 22W
Ingleton, U.K. ............ 22 D4 54 10N 2 27W
Ingoldmells Pt., U.K. ....... 23 F9 53 11N 0 21 E
Ingolstadt, Germany ....... 66 D6 48 46N 11 26 E
Ingraj Bazar, India ........ 85 G16 24 58N 88 10 E
Ingushetia □, Russia ....... 73 F8 43 20N 44 50 E
Inishbofin, Ireland ........ 28 D1 53 37N 10 13W
Inisheer, Ireland .......... 30 B3 53 3N 9 32W
Inishfree B., Ireland ....... 28 A5 55 4N 8 23W
Inishkea North, Ireland ..... 28 C1 54 9N 10 11W
Inishkea South, Ireland ..... 28 C1 54 7N 10 12W
Inishmaan, Ireland ........ 30 B3 53 5N 9 35W
Inishmore, Ireland ........ 30 B3 53 8N 9 45W
Inishowen Pen., Ireland .... 29 A7 55 14N 7 15W
Inishshark, Ireland ........ 28 D1 53 37N 10 16W
Inishturk, Ireland ......... 28 D1 53 42N 10 7W
Inishvickillane, Ireland ..... 30 D1 52 3N 10 37W
Inkberrow, U.K. .......... 23 H5 52 13N 1 58W
Inland Sea, Japan ......... 82 F3 34 20N 133 30 E
Inn →, Austria ........... 66 D7 48 35N 13 28 E
Inner Hebrides, U.K. ....... 18 J4 57 0N 6 30W
Inner Mongolia, China ...... 81 B6 42 0N 112 0 E
Inner Sound, U.K. ......... 18 H6 57 30N 5 55W
Innerleithen, U.K. ......... 22 A2 55 37N 3 4W
Innsbruck, Austria ........ 66 E6 47 16N 11 23 E
Inowrocław, Poland ........ 67 B10 52 50N 18 12 E
Insein, Burma ............ 85 L20 16 50N 96 5 E
Inta, Russia .............. 72 A11 66 5N 60 8 E
Interlaken, Switz. ......... 66 E4 46 41N 7 50 E
Inukjuak, Canada ......... 109 C12 58 25N 78 15W
Inuvik, Canada ........... 108 B6 68 16N 133 40W
Inveraray, U.K. ........... 20 B5 56 14N 5 5W
Inverbervie, U.K. ......... 19 J13 56 51N 2 17W
Invercargill, N.Z. .......... 99 K12 46 24S 168 24 E
Invergordon, U.K. ......... 19 G9 57 41N 4 10W
Inverness, U.K. ........... 19 H9 57 29N 4 13W
Inverurie, U.K. ........... 19 H13 57 17N 2 23W
Iona, U.K. ............... 20 B3 56 20N 6 25W
Ionia, U.S.A. ............. 112 D5 42 59N 85 4W
Ionian Is., Greece ......... 71 E9 38 40N 20 0 E
Ionian Sea, Medit. S. ....... 71 E7 37 30N 17 30 E
Iowa □, U.S.A. ........... 111 B8 42 18N 93 30W
Iowa City, U.S.A. .......... 111 B8 41 40N 91 32W
Ipameri, Brazil ........... 122 C1 17 44S 48 9W
Ipatinga, Brazil ........... 122 C2 19 32S 42 30W
Ipoh, Malaysia ........... 83 C2 4 35N 101 5 E
Ipswich, Australia ......... 98 F9 27 35S 152 40 E
Ipswich, U.K. ............ 25 B11 52 4N 1 10 E
Iqaluit, Canada ........... 109 B13 63 44N 68 31W
Iquique, Chile ............ 120 E2 20 19S 70 5W
Iquitos, Peru ............. 120 C2 3 45S 73 10W
Iráklion, Greece .......... 71 G11 35 20N 25 12 E
Iran ■, Asia ............. 87 C8 33 0N 53 0 E
Iran, Pegunungan, Asia ..... 74 F9 32 0N 55 0 E
Irapuato, Mexico .......... 114 C4 20 40N 101 30W
Iraq ■, Asia ............. 86 C5 33 0N 44 0 E
Irbil, Iraq ............... 86 B6 36 15N 44 5 E
Irchester, U.K. ........... 23 H7 52 18N 0 39W
Ireland ■, Europe ........ 64 E2 53 50N 7 52W
Iringa, Tanzania .......... 96 F7 7 48S 35 43 E
Irish Sea, U.K. ........... 64 E4 53 38N 4 48W
Irkutsk, Russia ........... 79 D12 52 18N 104 20 E
Irlam, U.K. .............. 23 F4 53 26N 2 26W
Iron Gate, Europe ......... 67 F12 44 44N 22 30 E
Iron Mountain, U.S.A. ...... 112 C3 45 49N 88 4W
Ironbridge, U.K. .......... 23 G3 52 38N 2 30W
Ironton, U.S.A. ........... 112 F6 38 32N 82 41W
Ironwood, U.S.A. ......... 111 A8 46 27N 90 9W
Irrawaddy →, Burma ....... 85 M19 15 50N 95 6 E
Irt →, U.K. .............. 22 D2 54 25N 3 26W
Irthlingborough, U.K. ...... 23 H7 52 20N 0 37W
Irtysh →, Russia .......... 79 C8 61 4N 68 52 E
Irvine, U.S.A. ............ 20 C6 55 37N 4 41W
Irvinestown, U.K. ......... 28 C6 54 28N 7 39W
Isabela, Puerto Rico ....... 115 d 18 30N 67 2W
Ísafjörður, Iceland ........ 63 A1 66 5N 23 9W
Isar →, Germany .......... 66 D7 48 48N 12 57 E
Ise, Japan .............. 82 F5 34 25N 136 45 E
Ishinomaki, Japan ......... 82 E7 38 32N 141 20 E
Ishpeming, U.S.A. ......... 112 B4 46 29N 87 40W
İskenderun, Turkey ........ 73 G6 36 32N 36 10 E
Isla →, U.K. ............. 21 A9 56 32N 3 20W
Islamabad, Pakistan ....... 84 C8 33 40N 73 10 E
Island L., Canada ......... 108 C10 53 47N 94 25W
Island Pond, U.S.A. ....... 113 C12 44 49N 71 53W
Islay, U.K. .............. 20 C3 55 46N 6 10W
Isle →, France ........... 68 D3 44 55N 0 15W
Isleham, U.K. ............ 25 B9 52 21N 0 25 E
Islip, U.K. ............... 24 C6 51 50N 1 12W
Ismâ'ilîya, Egypt .......... 95 B12 30 37N 32 18 E
Isparta, Turkey .......... 73 G5 37 47N 30 30 E
Israel ■, Asia ............ 86 C3 32 0N 34 50 E
Issoire, France ........... 68 D5 45 32N 3 15 E
Istanbul, Turkey .......... 71 D13 41 0N 29 0 E
Istra, Croatia ............ 66 F7 45 10N 14 0 E
Istres, France ............ 68 E6 43 31N 4 59 E
Itaberaba, Brazil .......... 122 B2 12 32S 40 18W
Itabira, Brazil ............ 122 C2 19 37S 43 13W
Itabuna, Brazil ........... 122 B3 14 48S 39 16W
Itacaotiara, Brazil ........ 120 C4 3 8S 58 25W
Itajaí, Brazil ............. 121 E5 27 50S 48 39W
Itajubá, Brazil ............ 122 D1 22 24S 45 30W
Italy ■, Europe ........... 70 C5 42 0N 13 0 E

Itaperuna, Brazil .......... 122 D2 21 10S 41 54W
Itapetinga, Brazil ......... 122 C2 15 15S 40 15W
Itapetininga, Brazil ........ 122 D1 23 36S 48 7W
Itapicuru →, Brazil ........ 122 B3 11 47S 37 32W
Itararé, Brazil ............ 122 D1 24 6S 49 23W
Itaúna, Brazil ............ 122 D2 20 4S 44 34W
Itchen →, U.K. ........... 24 E6 50 55N 1 22W
Ithaca, U.S.A. ............ 112 D9 42 27N 76 30W
Ivanava, Belarus .......... 67 B13 52 7N 25 29 E
Ivano-Frankivsk, Ukraine ... 67 D13 48 40N 24 40 E
Ivanovo, Russia .......... 72 C7 57 5N 41 0 E
Ivinghoe, U.K. ........... 25 C7 51 50N 0 37W
Ivory Coast ■, Africa ...... 94 G4 7 30N 5 0W
Ivujivik, Canada .......... 109 B12 62 24N 77 55W
Ivybridge, U.K. ........... 27 G6 50 23N 3 56W
Iwaki, Japan ............. 82 E7 37 3N 140 55 E
Iwakuni, Japan ........... 82 F3 34 15N 132 8 E
Iwo, Nigeria ............. 94 G6 7 39N 4 9 E
Ixworth, U.K. ............ 25 B10 52 18N 0 51 E
Iyssyk Kul, Kyrgyzstan ..... 74 E11 42 25N 77 15 E
Izhevsk, Russia ........... 72 C9 56 51N 53 14 E
Izmayil, Ukraine .......... 73 E4 45 22N 28 46 E
İzmir, Turkey ............ 71 E12 38 25N 27 8 E
İznik Gölü, Turkey ......... 73 F4 40 27N 29 30 E
Izumi-Sano, Japan ........ 82 F4 34 23N 135 18 E

# J

Jabalpur, India ........... 84 H11 23 9N 79 58 E
Jaboatão, Brazil .......... 120 C6 8 7S 35 1W
Jaboticabal, Brazil ........ 122 D1 21 15S 48 17W
Jackson, Barbados ......... 115 g 13 7N 59 36W
Jackson, Ky., U.S.A. ....... 112 G6 37 33N 83 23W
Jackson, Mich., U.S.A. ..... 112 D5 42 15N 84 24W
Jackson, Miss., U.S.A. ...... 111 D8 32 18N 90 12W
Jackson, Tenn., U.S.A. ..... 111 C9 35 37N 88 49W
Jacksonville, U.S.A. ....... 111 D10 30 20N 81 39W
Jacmel, Haiti ............ 115 D10 18 14N 72 32W
Jacobabad, Pakistan ....... 84 E6 28 20N 68 29 E
Jacobina, Brazil .......... 122 B2 11 11S 40 30W
Jaén, Spain .............. 69 D4 37 44N 3 43W
Jaffna, Sri Lanka ......... 84 Q12 9 45N 80 2 E
Jahrom, Iran ............. 87 D8 28 30N 53 31 E
Jaipur, India ............. 84 F9 27 0N 75 50 E
Jakarta, Indonesia ........ 83 D2 6 9S 106 49 E
Jalalabad, Afghan. ........ 84 B7 34 30N 70 29 E
Jalgaon, India ........... 84 J9 21 0N 75 42 E
Jalna, India ............. 84 K9 19 48N 75 38 E
Jalpaiguri, India .......... 85 F16 26 32N 88 46 E
Jaluit I., Marshall Is. ...... 102 G8 6 0N 169 30 E
Jamaica ■, W. Indies ...... 114 a 18 10N 77 30W
Jamalpur, Bangla. ......... 85 G16 24 52N 89 56 E
Jamalpur, India .......... 85 G15 25 18N 86 28 E
Jambi, Indonesia ......... 83 D2 1 38S 103 30 E
James →, U.S.A. ......... 111 B7 42 52N 97 18W
James B., Canada ......... 109 C11 54 0N 80 0W
Jamestown, N. Dak., U.S.A. .. 110 A7 46 54N 98 42W
Jamestown, N.Y., U.S.A. .... 112 D8 42 6N 79 14W
Jammu, India ............ 84 C9 32 43N 74 54 E
Jammu & Kashmir □, India .. 84 B10 34 25N 77 0 E
Jamnagar, India .......... 84 H7 22 30N 70 6 E
Jamshedpur, India ........ 85 H15 22 44N 86 12 E
Jan Mayen, Arctic ........ 54 B7 71 0N 9 0W
Janaúba, Brazil ........... 122 C2 15 48S 43 19W
Janesville, U.S.A. ......... 111 B9 42 41N 89 1W
Januária, Brazil .......... 122 C2 15 25S 44 25W
Jaora, India ............. 84 H9 23 40N 75 10 E
Japan ■, Asia ............ 82 F5 36 0N 136 0 E
Japan, Sea of, Asia ........ 82 D4 40 0N 135 0 E
Japan Trench, Pac. Oc. ..... 102 D6 32 0N 142 0 E
Japurá →, Brazil .......... 120 C3 3 8S 65 46W
Jari →, Brazil ............ 120 C4 1 9S 51 54W
Jarrow, U.K. ............. 22 C6 54 59N 1 28W
Jarvis I., Pac. Oc. ......... 103 H12 0 15S 160 5W
Jäsk, Iran ............... 87 E9 25 38N 57 45 E
Jasper, Canada ........... 108 C8 52 55N 118 5W
Jauja, Peru .............. 120 D2 11 45S 75 15W
Jaunpur, India ........... 85 G13 25 46N 82 44 E
Java, Indonesia .......... 83 D3 7 0S 110 0 E
Java Sea, Indonesia ....... 83 D2 4 35S 107 15 E
Java Trench, Indonesia ..... 83 D2 9 0S 105 0 E
Jaya, Puncak, Indonesia .... 83 D5 3 57S 137 17 E
Jebel, Bahr el →, Sudan .... 95 G12 9 30N 30 25 E
Jedburgh, U.K. ........... 21 D10 55 29N 2 33W
Jedda, Si. Arabia ......... 86 F4 21 29N 39 10 E
Jeffersonville, U.S.A. ...... 112 F5 38 17N 85 44W
Jelenia Góra, Poland ...... 66 C8 50 50N 15 45 E
Jelgava, Latvia ........... 72 C3 56 41N 23 49 E
Jena, Germany ........... 66 C6 50 54N 11 35 E
Jequié, Brazil ............ 122 B2 13 51S 40 5W
Jequitinhonha, Brazil ...... 122 C2 16 30S 41 0W
Jequitinhonha →, Brazil .... 122 C3 15 51S 38 53W
Jérémie, Haiti ............ 115 D10 18 40N 74 10W
Jerez de la Frontera, Spain .. 69 D2 36 41N 6 7W
Jersey, U.K. ............. 27 J9 49 11N 2 7W
Jersey City, U.S.A. ........ 113 E10 40 44N 74 4W
Jerusalem, Israel ......... 86 D3 31 47N 35 10 E
Jervaulx, U.K. ........... 22 D5 54 16N 1 43W
Jessore, Bangla. .......... 85 H16 23 10N 89 10 E
Jhang Maghiana, Pakistan .. 84 D8 31 15N 72 22 E
Jhansi, India ............ 84 G11 25 30N 78 36 E
Jharkhand □, India ........ 85 H14 24 0N 85 50 E
Jhelum, Pakistan ......... 84 C8 33 0N 73 45 E
Jhelum →, Pakistan ....... 84 D8 31 20N 72 10 E
Jiamusi, China ........... 81 B8 46 40N 130 26 E
Ji'an, China ............. 81 D6 27 6N 114 59 E
Jiangmen, China ......... 81 D6 22 32N 113 0 E
Jiangsu □, China ......... 81 C7 33 0N 120 0 E
Jiangxi □, China .......... 81 D6 27 30N 116 0 E
Jiaxing, China ........... 81 C7 30 49N 120 45 E
Jihlava →, Czech Rep. ...... 67 D9 48 55N 16 36 E
Jilin, China ............. 81 B7 43 44N 126 30 E
Jilin □, China ............ 81 B7 44 0N 127 0 E
Jima, Ethiopia ........... 88 F2 7 40N 36 47 E
Jiménez, Mexico .......... 114 B4 27 10N 104 54W
Jinan, China ............ 81 C6 36 38N 117 1 E
Jinchang, China .......... 80 C5 38 30N 102 10 E
Jingdezhen, China ........ 81 D6 29 20N 117 11 E
Jinggu, China ........... 80 D5 23 35N 100 41 E
Jinhua, China ........... 81 D6 29 8N 119 38 E
Jining, Nei Monggol Zizhiqu, China ............. 81 B6 41 5N 113 0 E
Jining, Shandong, China .... 81 C6 35 22N 116 34 E
Jinja, Uganda ............ 96 D6 0 25N 33 12 E
Jinzhou, China ........... 81 B7 41 5N 121 3 E
Jiujiang, China .......... 81 D6 29 42N 115 58 E
Jixi, China .............. 81 B8 45 20N 130 50 E
Jizzakh, Uzbekistan ....... 87 A11 40 6N 67 50 E
João Pessoa, Brazil ....... 120 C6 7 10S 34 52W
Jodhpur, India ........... 84 F8 26 23N 73 8 E
John Crow Mts., Jamaica ... 114 a 18 5N 76 25W
John Day →, U.S.A. ....... 110 A2 45 44N 120 39W

John o' Groats, U.K. ....... 19 E11 58 38N 3 4W
Johnson City, N.Y., U.S.A. ... 113 D10 42 7N 75 58W
Johnson City, Tenn., U.S.A. .. 111 C10 36 19N 82 21W
Johnston I., Pac. Oc. ....... 103 F11 17 10N 169 8W
Johnstown, U.S.A. ......... 112 E8 40 20N 78 55W
Johor Baharu, Malaysia ..... 83 C2 1 28N 103 46 E
Joinville, Brazil ........... 121 E5 26 15S 48 55W
Joliet, U.S.A. ............ 112 E3 41 32N 88 5W
Joliette, Canada .......... 109 D12 46 3N 73 24W
Jolo, Phil. .............. 83 C4 6 0N 121 0 E
Jonesboro, U.S.A. ......... 111 C8 35 50N 90 42W
Jönköping, Sweden ........ 63 F6 57 45N 14 8 E
Jonquière, Canada ........ 109 D12 48 27N 71 14W
Joplin, U.S.A. ............ 111 C8 37 6N 94 31W
Jordan ■, Asia ........... 86 D4 31 0N 36 0 E
Jordan →, Asia ........... 86 D3 31 48N 35 32 E
Jos, Nigeria ............. 94 G7 9 53N 8 51 E
Joseph Bonaparte G., Australia 98 C4 14 35S 128 50 E
Jost Van Dyke, Br. Virgin Is. . 115 e 18 29N 64 47W
Jotunheimen, Norway ...... 63 E6 61 35N 8 25 E
Jowzjan □, Afghan. ........ 87 B11 36 10N 66 0 E
Juan de Fuca Str., Canada ... 110 A2 48 15N 124 0W
Juan Fernández, Arch. de, Pac. Oc. ............ 103 L20 33 50S 80 0W
Juàzeiro, Brazil .......... 122 A2 9 30S 40 30W
Juàzeiro do Norte, Brazil ... 120 C6 7 10S 39 18W
Juba, Somali Rep. ......... 88 G3 1 30N 42 35 E
Juba →, Sudan ........... 95 H12 4 50N 31 35 E
Juchitán, Mexico ......... 114 D5 16 27N 95 5W
Juiz de Fora, Brazil ....... 122 D2 21 43S 43 19W
Juliaca, Peru ............ 120 D2 15 25S 70 10W
Julianatop, Suriname ...... 120 B4 3 40N 56 30W
Jullundur, India .......... 84 D9 31 20N 75 40 E
Junagadh, India .......... 84 J7 21 30N 70 30 E
Jundiaí, Brazil ........... 122 D1 24 30S 47 0W
Juneau, U.S.A. ........... 108 C6 58 18N 134 25W
Junggar Pendi, China ...... 80 B3 44 30N 86 0 E
Junín, Argentina .......... 121 F3 34 33S 60 57W
Jupiter →, Canada ........ 113 A16 49 29N 63 37W
Jura, Europe ............. 66 E4 46 40N 6 5 E
Jura, U.K. ............... 20 C4 56 0N 5 50W
Jura, Sd. of, U.K. ......... 20 C4 55 57N 5 45W
Juruá →, Brazil .......... 120 C3 2 37S 65 44W
Juruena →, Brazil ........ 120 C4 7 20S 58 3W
Jutland, Denmark ......... 63 F5 56 25N 9 30 E
Juventud, I. de la, Cuba .... 115 C8 21 40N 82 40W
Jyväskylä, Finland ........ 63 E9 62 14N 25 50 E

# K

K2, Pakistan ............. 84 B10 35 58N 76 32 E
Kabardino-Balkaria □, Russia . 73 F7 43 30N 43 30 E
Kābul, Afghan. ........... 84 B6 34 28N 69 11 E
Kabwe, Zambia ........... 97 G5 14 30S 28 29 E
Kachchh, Gulf of, India ..... 84 H6 22 50N 69 15 E
Kachchh, Rann of, India .... 84 H7 24 0N 70 0 E
Kachin □, Burma ......... 85 G20 26 0N 97 30 E
Kaçkar, Turkey ........... 73 F7 40 45N 41 10 E
Kadavu, Fiji ............. 99 E14 19 0S 178 15 E
Kadoma, Zimbabwe ....... 97 H5 18 20S 29 52 E
Kaduna, Nigeria .......... 94 F7 10 30N 7 21 E
Kaesŏng, N. Korea ........ 81 C7 37 58N 126 35 E
Kafue →, Zambia ......... 97 H5 15 30S 29 0 E
Kaga Bandoro, C.A.R. ...... 96 C3 7 0N 19 10 E
Kagoshima, Japan ........ 82 H2 31 35N 130 33 E
Kahoolawe, U.S.A. ........ 110 H16 20 33N 156 37W
Kahramanmaraş, Turkey .... 73 G6 37 37N 36 53 E
Kai, Kepulauan, Indonesia ... 83 D5 5 55S 132 45 E
Kaieteur Falls, Guyana ..... 120 B4 5 1N 59 10W
Kaifeng, China ........... 81 C6 34 48N 114 21 E
Kailua Kona, U.S.A. ........ 110 J17 19 39N 155 59W
Kainji Res., Nigeria ........ 94 F6 10 1N 4 40 E
Kairouan, Tunisia ......... 95 A8 35 45N 10 5 E
Kaiserslautern, Germany .... 66 D4 49 26N 7 45 E
Kaitaia, N.Z. ............. 99 H13 35 8S 173 17 E
Kajaani, Finland .......... 63 E9 64 17N 27 46 E
Kajabbi, Australia ......... 98 E7 20 0S 140 1 E
Kakamega, Kenya ......... 96 D6 0 20N 34 46 E
Kakinada, India .......... 85 L13 16 57N 82 11 E
Kalaallit Nunaat = Greenland □, N. Amer. ............ 54 C5 66 0N 45 0W
Kalahari, Africa .......... 97 J4 24 0S 21 30 E
Kalamazoo, U.S.A. ........ 112 D5 42 17N 85 35W
Kalamazoo →, U.S.A. ...... 112 D4 42 40N 86 10W
Kalemie, Dem. Rep. of the Congo ............ 96 F5 5 55S 29 9 E
Kalgoorlie-Boulder, Australia . 98 G3 30 40S 121 22 E
Kalimantan, Indonesia ..... 83 D3 0 0 114 0 E
Kaliningrad, Russia ....... 72 D3 54 42N 20 32 E
Kalispell, U.S.A. .......... 110 A4 48 12N 114 19W
Kalisz, Poland ........... 67 C10 51 45N 18 8 E
Kalkaska, U.S.A. .......... 112 C5 44 44N 85 11W
Kalmar, Sweden .......... 63 F7 56 40N 16 20 E
Kalmykia □, Russia ........ 73 E8 46 5N 46 1 E
Kaluga, Russia ........... 72 D6 54 35N 36 10 E
Kalutara, Sri Lanka ....... 84 R12 6 35N 80 0 E
Kalyan, India ............ 84 K8 19 15N 73 9 E
Kama →, Russia .......... 72 C9 55 45N 52 0 E
Kamchatka Pen., Russia .... 79 D18 57 0N 160 0 E
Kamina, Dem. Rep. of the Congo ............ 96 F5 8 45S 25 0 E
Kamloops, Canada ........ 108 C7 50 40N 120 20W
Kampala, Uganda ......... 96 D6 0 20N 32 30 E
Kampong Saom, Cambodia .. 83 B2 10 38N 103 30 E
Kamyanets-Podilskyy, Ukraine 67 D14 48 45N 26 40 E
Kamyshin, Russia ......... 73 D8 50 10N 45 24 E
Kananaupscow, Canada ..... 109 C12 53 39N 77 9W
Kananga, Dem. Rep. of the Congo ............ 96 F4 5 55S 22 18 E
Kanash, Russia ........... 72 C8 55 30N 47 32 E
Kanawha →, U.S.A. ....... 112 F6 38 50N 82 9W
Kanazawa, Japan ......... 82 E5 36 30N 136 38 E
Kanchenjunga, Nepal ...... 85 F16 27 50N 88 10 E
Kanchipuram, India ....... 84 N11 12 52N 79 45 E
Kandalaksha, Russia ....... 72 A5 67 9N 32 30 E
Kandanghaur, Indonesia .... 83 D2 6 21S 108 6 E
Kandi, Benin ............. 94 F6 11 7N 2 55 E
Kandy, Sri Lanka ......... 84 R12 7 18N 80 43 E
Kane, U.S.A. ............. 112 E8 41 40N 78 49W
Kaneohe, U.S.A. .......... 110 H16 21 25N 157 48W
Kangaroo I., Australia ...... 98 H6 35 45S 137 0 E
Kangiqsualujjuaq, Canada ... 109 C13 58 30N 65 59W
Kangiqsujuaq, Canada ...... 109 B12 61 30N 72 0W
Kangirsuk, Canada ........ 109 B13 60 0N 70 0W
Kanin Pen., Russia ........ 72 A8 68 0N 45 0 E
Kankakee, U.S.A. ......... 112 E4 41 7N 87 52W
Kankakee →, U.S.A. ....... 112 E3 41 23N 88 15W
Kankan, Guinea .......... 94 F4 10 23N 9 15W
Kano, Nigeria ............ 94 F7 12 2N 8 30 E
Kanpur, India ............ 84 F12 26 28N 80 20 E
Kansas □, U.S.A. ......... 110 C7 38 30N 99 0W
Kansas →, U.S.A. ........ 111 C8 39 7N 94 37W
Kansas City, U.S.A. ....... 111 C8 39 6N 94 35W

**Kanturk** ⸱ ⸱ ⸱ ⸱ **La Palma**

| | | | |
|---|---|---|---|
| Kanturk, Ireland | 30 D5 | 52 11N | 8 54W |
| Kaohsiung, Taiwan | 81 D7 | 22 35N 120 16 E | |
| Kaolack, Senegal | 94 F2 | 14 5N | 16 8W |
| Kapaa, U.S.A. | 110 G15 | 22 5N 159 19W | |
| Kapiri Mposhi, Zambia | 97 G5 | 13 59S | 28 43 E |
| Kápisá □, Afghan. | 87 C12 | 35 0N | 69 20 E |
| Kaposvár, Hungary | 67 E9 | 46 25N | 17 47 E |
| Kaptai L., Bangla. | 85 H18 | 22 40N | 92 20 E |
| Kapuas →, Indonesia | 83 D2 | 0 25S 109 20 E | |
| Kapuskasing, Canada | 112 A6 | 49 25N | 82 30W |
| Kara Bogaz Gol, Turkmenistan | 73 F9 | 41 0N | 53 30 E |
| Kara Kum, Turkmenistan | 87 B9 | 39 30N | 60 0 E |
| Kara Sea, Russia | 79 B8 | 75 0N | 70 0 E |
| Karabük, Turkey | 73 F5 | 41 12N | 32 37 E |
| Karachey-Cherkessia □, Russia | 73 F7 | 43 40N | 41 30 E |
| Karachi, Pakistan | 84 G5 | 24 53N | 67 0 E |
| Karaganda, Kazakhstan | 79 E9 | 49 50N | 73 10 E |
| Karagiye Depression, Kazakhstan | 73 F9 | 43 27N | 51 45 E |
| Karakalpakstan □, Uzbekistan | 87 A9 | 43 0N | 58 0 E |
| Karakoram, Pakistan | 84 B10 | 35 30N | 77 0 E |
| Karaman, Turkey | 73 G5 | 37 14N | 33 13 E |
| Karamay, China | 80 B3 | 45 30N | 84 58 E |
| Karawang, Indonesia | 83 D2 | 6 30S 107 15 E | |
| Karayazı, Turkey | 73 G7 | 39 41N | 42 9 E |
| Karbalā', Iraq | 86 C6 | 32 36N | 44 3 E |
| Karelia □, Russia | 72 A5 | 65 30N | 32 30 E |
| Kariba, L., Zimbabwe | 97 H5 | 16 40S | 28 25 E |
| Kariba Dam, Zimbabwe | 97 H5 | 16 30S | 28 35 E |
| Karimata, Str. of, Indonesia | 83 D2 | 2 0S 108 40 E | |
| Karlskrona, Sweden | 63 F7 | 56 10N | 15 35 E |
| Karlsruhe, Germany | 66 D5 | 49 0N | 8 23 E |
| Karlstad, Sweden | 63 F6 | 59 23N | 13 30 E |
| Karnak, Egypt | 95 C12 | 25 43N | 32 39 E |
| Karnal, India | 84 E10 | 29 42N | 77 2 E |
| Karnataka □, India | 84 N10 | 13 15N | 77 0 E |
| Kärnten □, Austria | 66 E8 | 46 52N | 13 30 E |
| Kars, Turkey | 73 F7 | 40 40N | 43 5 E |
| Karwar, India | 84 M9 | 14 55N | 74 13 E |
| Kasai →, Dem. Rep. of the Congo | 96 E3 | 3 30S | 16 10 E |
| Kasaragod, India | 84 N9 | 12 30N | 74 58 E |
| Kasba L., Canada | 108 B9 | 60 20N 102 10W | |
| Kāshān, Iran | 87 C7 | 34 5N | 51 30 E |
| Kashi, China | 80 C2 | 39 30N | 76 2 E |
| Kasongo, Dem. Rep. of the Congo | 96 E5 | 4 30S | 26 33 E |
| Kassalâ, Sudan | 95 E13 | 15 30N | 36 0 E |
| Kassel, Germany | 66 C5 | 51 18N | 9 26 E |
| Kastamonu, Turkey | 73 F5 | 41 25N | 33 43 E |
| Kasur, Pakistan | 84 D9 | 31 5N | 74 25 E |
| Katanga □, Dem. Rep. of the Congo | 96 F4 | 8 0S | 25 0 E |
| Katherine →, Australia | 98 C5 | 14 40S 131 42 E | |
| Kathiar, India | 85 G15 | 25 34N | 87 36 E |
| Katima Mulilo, Zambia | 97 H4 | 17 28S | 24 13 E |
| Katmandu, Nepal | 85 F14 | 27 45N | 85 20 E |
| Katowice, Poland | 67 C10 | 50 17N | 19 5 E |
| Katrine, L., U.K. | 20 B7 | 56 15N | 4 30W |
| Katsina, Nigeria | 94 F7 | 13 0N | 7 32 E |
| Kattegat, Denmark | 63 F6 | 56 40N | 11 20 E |
| Kauai, U.S.A. | 110 H15 | 22 3N 159 30W | |
| Kauai Channel, U.S.A. | 110 H15 | 21 45N 158 50W | |
| Kaukauna, U.S.A. | 112 C3 | 44 17N | 88 17W |
| Kaunakakai, U.S.A. | 110 H16 | 21 6N 157 1W | |
| Kaunas, Lithuania | 72 D3 | 54 54N | 23 54 E |
| Kavála, Greece | 71 D11 | 40 57N | 24 28 E |
| Kavieng, Papua N. G. | 98 A9 | 2 36S 150 51 E | |
| Kavir, Dasht-e, Iran | 87 C8 | 34 30N | 55 0 E |
| Kawagoe, Japan | 82 F6 | 35 55N 139 29 E | |
| Kawaguchi, Japan | 82 F6 | 35 52N 139 45 E | |
| Kawardha, India | 85 J12 | 22 0N | 81 17 E |
| Kawasaki, Japan | 82 F6 | 35 31N 139 43 E | |
| Kayah □, Burma | 85 K20 | 19 15N | 97 15 E |
| Kayes, Mali | 94 F3 | 14 25N | 11 30W |
| Kayin □, Burma | 85 L20 | 18 0N | 97 30 E |
| Kayseri, Turkey | 73 G6 | 38 45N | 35 30 E |
| Kazakhstan ■, Asia | 79 E9 | 50 0N | 70 0 E |
| Kazan, Russia | 72 C8 | 55 50N | 49 10 E |
| Kazan-Rettō, Pac. Oc. | 102 E6 | 25 0N 141 0 E | |
| Kea, U.S.A. | 27 G3 | 50 14N | 5 6W |
| Keady, U.K. | 29 C8 | 54 15N | 6 42W |
| Kearney, U.S.A. | 110 B7 | 40 42N | 99 5W |
| Keban, Turkey | 73 G6 | 38 50N | 38 50 E |
| Keban Baraji, Turkey | 73 G6 | 38 41N | 38 33 E |
| Kebnekaise, Sweden | 63 D7 | 67 53N | 18 33 E |
| Kebri Dehar, Ethiopia | 88 F3 | 6 45N | 44 17 E |
| Kebumen, Indonesia | 83 D2 | 7 42S 109 40 E | |
| Kecskemét, Hungary | 67 E10 | 46 57N | 19 42 E |
| Kediri, Indonesia | 83 D3 | 7 51S 112 1 E | |
| Keeley L., Canada | 23 E8 | 53 35N | 0 16W |
| Keele, U.K. | 23 F4 | 53 0N | 2 17W |
| Keene, U.S.A. | 113 D11 | 42 56N | 72 17W |
| Keeper Hill, Ireland | 30 C6 | 52 45N | 8 16W |
| Keetmanshoop, Namibia | 97 K3 | 26 35S | 18 8 E |
| Kefallinia, Greece | 71 E9 | 38 15N | 20 30 E |
| Keflavík, Iceland | 63 B1 | 64 2N | 22 35W |
| Kegworth, U.K. | 23 G6 | 52 50N | 1 17W |
| Keighley, U.K. | 23 E5 | 53 52N | 1 54W |
| Keith, U.K. | 19 G12 | 57 32N | 2 57W |
| Kelang, Malaysia | 83 C2 | 3 2N 101 26 E | |
| Keld, U.K. | 22 D4 | 54 24N | 2 10W |
| Kelkit →, Turkey | 73 F6 | 40 45N | 36 32 E |
| Kellogg, U.S.A. | 110 A3 | 47 32N 116 7W | |
| Kells, Rhinns of, U.K. | 29 A13 | 55 7N | 4 19W |
| Kelowna, Canada | 108 D8 | 49 50N 119 25W | |
| Kelsale, U.K. | 25 B12 | 52 14N | 1 31 E |
| Kelsall, U.K. | 23 F3 | 53 13N | 2 43W |
| Kelso, U.K. | 21 C11 | 55 36N | 2 26W |
| Keluang, Malaysia | 83 C2 | 2 3N 103 18 E | |
| Kelvedon, U.K. | 25 C10 | 51 50N | 0 43 E |
| Kem, Russia | 72 B5 | 65 0N | 34 38 E |
| Kemble, U.K. | 24 C5 | 51 40N | 1 59W |
| Kemerovo, Russia | 79 D10 | 55 20N | 86 5 E |
| Kemi, Finland | 63 D8 | 65 44N | 24 34 E |
| Kemijoki →, Finland | 63 D8 | 65 47N | 24 32 E |
| Kemp Land, Antarctica | 55 C5 | 69 0S | 55 0 E |
| Kempsey, U.K. | 24 B5 | 52 8N | 2 12W |
| Kempston, U.K. | 25 B7 | 52 7N | 0 30W |
| Kenai, U.S.A. | 108 B4 | 60 33N 151 16W | |
| Kendal, U.K. | 22 D3 | 54 20N | 2 44W |
| Kendari, Indonesia | 83 D4 | 3 50S 122 30 E | |
| Kenilworth, U.K. | 23 H5 | 52 21N | 1 34W |
| Kenitra, Morocco | 94 B4 | 34 15N | 6 40W |
| Kenmare, Ireland | 30 E3 | 51 53N | 9 36W |
| Kenmare River, Ireland | 30 E3 | 51 48N | 9 51W |
| Kennet →, U.K. | 24 C6 | 51 27N | 0 57W |
| Kennewick, U.S.A. | 110 A3 | 46 12N 119 7W | |
| Kenninghall, U.K. | 25 B11 | 52 26N | 1 0 E |
| Kenogami →, Canada | 109 C11 | 51 6N | 84 28W |
| Kenora, Canada | 108 D10 | 49 47N | 94 29W |
| Kenosha, U.S.A. | 112 D4 | 42 35N | 87 49W |
| Kent, U.K. | 25 D10 | 51 12N | 0 40 E |
| Kent □, U.K. | 25 D10 | 51 12N | 0 40 E |
| Kent Pen., Canada | 108 B9 | 68 30N 107 0W | |
| Kentisbeare, U.K. | 24 E2 | 50 51N | 3 20W |
| Kenton, U.S.A. | 112 E6 | 40 39N | 83 37W |
| Kentucky □, U.S.A. | 112 G5 | 37 0N | 84 0W |
| Kentucky →, U.S.A. | 112 F5 | 38 41N | 85 11W |
| Kentville, Canada | 109 D13 | 45 6N | 64 29W |
| Kenya ■, Africa | 96 D7 | 1 0N | 38 0 E |
| Kenya, Mt., Kenya | 96 E7 | 0 10S | 37 18 E |
| Kerala □, India | 84 P10 | 11 0N | 76 15 E |
| Kerch, Ukraine | 73 E6 | 45 20N | 36 20 E |
| Kerguelen, Ind. Oc. | 53 G13 | 49 15S | 69 10 E |
| Kericho, Kenya | 96 E7 | 0 22S | 35 15 E |
| Kerinci, Indonesia | 83 D2 | 1 40S 101 15 E | |
| Kermadec Is., Pac. Oc. | 99 G15 | 30 0S 178 15W | |
| Kermadec Trench, Pac. Oc. | 99 G15 | 30 30S 176 0W | |
| Kermān, Iran | 87 D9 | 30 15N | 57 1 E |
| Kerrera, U.K. | 20 B4 | 56 24N | 5 33W |
| Kerrobert, Canada | 108 C9 | 51 56N 109 8W | |
| Kerry □, Ireland | 30 D3 | 52 7N | 9 35W |
| Kerry Hd., Ireland | 30 D3 | 52 25N | 9 56W |
| Kerulen →, Asia | 81 B6 | 48 48N 117 0 E | |
| Kessingland, U.K. | 25 B12 | 52 26N | 1 43 E |
| Keswick, U.K. | 22 C2 | 54 36N | 3 8W |
| Ketchikan, U.S.A. | 108 C6 | 55 21N 131 39W | |
| Kettering, U.K. | 23 H7 | 52 24N | 0 43W |
| Kettle Ness, U.K. | 22 C7 | 54 33N | 0 42W |
| Kettlewell, U.K. | 22 D4 | 54 9N | 2 3W |
| Kewaunee, U.S.A. | 112 C4 | 44 27N | 87 31W |
| Keweenaw B., U.S.A. | 112 B3 | 47 0N | 88 15W |
| Keweenaw Pen., U.S.A. | 112 B3 | 47 30N | 88 0W |
| Keweenaw Pt., U.S.A. | 112 B4 | 47 25N | 87 43W |
| Kexby, U.K. | 23 F7 | 53 22N | 0 42W |
| Key West, U.S.A. | 111 F10 | 24 33N | 81 48W |
| Keyingham, U.K. | 23 E8 | 53 43N | 0 7W |
| Keymer, U.K. | 25 E8 | 50 55N | 0 7W |
| Keynsham, U.K. | 24 D4 | 51 24N | 2 29W |
| Keyser, U.S.A. | 112 F8 | 39 26N | 78 59W |
| Keyworth, U.K. | 23 G6 | 52 52N | 1 5W |
| Khabarovsk, Russia | 79 E15 | 48 30N 135 5 E | |
| Khairpur, Pakistan | 84 F6 | 27 32N | 68 49 E |
| Khambhat, India | 84 H8 | 22 23N | 72 33 E |
| Khambhat, G. of, India | 84 J8 | 20 45N | 72 30 E |
| Khanewal, Pakistan | 84 D8 | 30 20N | 71 55 E |
| Khaniá, Greece | 71 G11 | 35 30N | 24 4 E |
| Kharagpur, India | 85 H15 | 22 20N | 87 25 E |
| Kharg, Iran | 86 D7 | 29 15N | 50 28 E |
| Kharkiv, Ukraine | 73 E6 | 49 58N | 36 20 E |
| Khartoum, Sudan | 95 E12 | 15 31N | 32 35 E |
| Khaskovo, Bulgaria | 71 D11 | 41 56N | 25 30 E |
| Khayelitsha, S. Africa | 97 L3 | 34 5S | 18 42 E |
| Khemisset, Morocco | 94 B4 | 33 50N | 6 1W |
| Kherson, Ukraine | 73 E5 | 46 35N | 32 35 E |
| Khmelnytskyy, Ukraine | 67 D14 | 49 23N | 27 0 E |
| Khojak Pass, Afghan. | 84 D5 | 30 51N | 66 34 E |
| Kholm, Afghan. | 87 B11 | 36 45N | 67 40 E |
| Khon Kaen, Thailand | 83 B2 | 16 30N 102 47 E | |
| Khorāsān □, Iran | 87 C9 | 34 0N | 58 0 E |
| Khorramābād, Iran | 86 C7 | 33 30N | 48 25 E |
| Khorramshahr, Iran | 86 D7 | 30 29N | 48 15 E |
| Khouribga, Morocco | 94 B4 | 32 58N | 6 57W |
| Khudzhand, Tajikistan | 87 B12 | 40 17N | 69 37 E |
| Khulna, Bangla. | 85 H16 | 22 45N | 89 34 E |
| Khulna □, Bangla. | 85 H16 | 22 25N | 89 35 E |
| Khushab, Pakistan | 84 C8 | 32 20N | 72 20 E |
| Khuzdar, Pakistan | 84 F5 | 27 52N | 66 30 E |
| Khvoy, Iran | 86 B6 | 38 35N | 45 0 E |
| Khyber Pass, Afghan. | 84 B7 | 34 10N | 71 8 E |
| Kibworth Beauchamp, U.K. | 23 G7 | 52 33N | 0 59W |
| Kicking Horse Pass, Canada | 108 C8 | 51 28N 116 16W | |
| Kidderminster, U.K. | 23 H4 | 52 24N | 2 15W |
| Kidlington, U.K. | 24 C6 | 51 50N | 1 15W |
| Kidsgrove, U.K. | 23 F4 | 53 5N | 2 14W |
| Kidstones, U.K. | 22 D4 | 54 13N | 2 2W |
| Kidwelly, U.K. | 26 D5 | 51 44N | 4 18W |
| Kiel, Germany | 66 A6 | 54 19N | 10 8 E |
| Kiel Canal = Nord-Ostsee-Kanal, Germany | 66 A5 | 54 12N | 9 32 E |
| Kielce, Poland | 67 C11 | 50 52N | 20 42 E |
| Kielder, U.K. | 22 B3 | 55 14N | 2 35W |
| Kieler Bucht, Germany | 66 A6 | 54 35N | 10 25 E |
| Kiev, Ukraine | 67 C16 | 50 30N | 30 28 E |
| Kigali, Rwanda | 96 E6 | 1 59S | 30 4 E |
| Kigoma-Ujiji, Tanzania | 96 E5 | 4 55S | 29 36 E |
| Kihei, U.S.A. | 110 H16 | 20 47N 156 28W | |
| Kikwit, Dem. Rep. of the Congo | 96 E3 | 5 0S | 18 45 E |
| Kilauea Crater, U.S.A. | 110 J17 | 19 25N 155 17W | |
| Kilbrannan Sd., U.K. | 20 C5 | 55 37N | 5 26W |
| Kildare, Ireland | 31 B9 | 53 9N | 6 55W |
| Kildare □, Ireland | 31 B9 | 53 10N | 6 50W |
| Kilfinnane, Ireland | 30 D6 | 52 21N | 8 28W |
| Kilham, U.K. | 22 D8 | 54 4N | 0 23W |
| Kilimanjaro, Tanzania | 96 E7 | 3 7S | 37 20 E |
| Kilkee, Ireland | 30 C3 | 52 41N | 9 39W |
| Kilkeel, U.K. | 29 C10 | 54 4N | 6 0W |
| Kilkenny, Ireland | 31 C8 | 52 39N | 7 15W |
| Kilkenny □, Ireland | 31 C8 | 52 35N | 7 15W |
| Kilkhampton, U.K. | 27 F4 | 50 52N | 4 31W |
| Kilkieran B., Ireland | 28 E2 | 53 20N | 9 41W |
| Killala, Ireland | 28 C3 | 54 13N | 9 12W |
| Killala B., Ireland | 28 C3 | 54 16N | 9 8W |
| Killaloe, Ireland | 30 C6 | 52 48N | 8 28W |
| Killarney, Ireland | 30 D3 | 52 4N | 9 30W |
| Killarney Nat. Park △, Ireland | 30 E3 | 52 0N | 9 33W |
| Killary Harbour, Ireland | 28 D2 | 53 38N | 9 52W |
| Killeen, U.S.A. | 110 D7 | 31 7N | 97 44W |
| Killin, U.K. | 20 B7 | 56 28N | 4 19W |
| Killinghall, U.K. | 23 D5 | 54 2N | 1 33W |
| Killorglin, Ireland | 30 D3 | 52 6N | 9 47W |
| Killybegs, Ireland | 28 B5 | 54 38N | 8 26W |
| Kilmarnock, U.K. | 20 C7 | 55 37N | 4 29W |
| Kilrush, Ireland | 30 C4 | 52 38N | 9 29W |
| Kilsby, U.K. | 23 H6 | 52 20N | 1 10W |
| Kilwinning, U.K. | 20 C6 | 55 39N | 4 43W |
| Kimberley, Australia | 98 D4 | 16 20S 127 0 E | |
| Kimberley, S. Africa | 97 K4 | 28 43S | 24 46 E |
| Kimbolton, U.K. | 23 H8 | 52 18N | 0 24W |
| Kimmirut, Canada | 109 B13 | 62 50N | 69 50W |
| Kinabalu, Gunong, Malaysia | 83 C3 | 6 3N 116 14 E | |
| Kincardine, Canada | 112 C7 | 44 10N | 81 40W |
| Kinder Scout, U.K. | 23 F5 | 53 24N | 1 52W |
| Kindersley, Canada | 108 C9 | 51 30N 109 10W | |
| Kindia, Guinea | 94 F3 | 10 0N | 12 52W |
| Kindu, Dem. Rep. of the Congo | 96 E5 | 2 55S | 25 50 E |
| Kineshma, Russia | 72 C7 | 57 30N | 42 5 E |
| Kineton, U.K. | 24 B5 | 52 10N | 1 31W |
| King George I., Antarctica | 55 C18 | 60 0S | 60 0W |
| King George Is., Canada | 109 C11 | 57 20N | 80 30W |
| King I., Australia | 98 H7 | 39 50S 144 0 E | |
| King William I., Canada | 108 B10 | 69 10N | 97 25W |
| Kingman, U.S.A. | 110 C4 | 35 12N 114 4W | |
| King's Lynn, U.K. | 23 G9 | 52 45N | 0 24 E |
| King's Sutton, U.K. | 24 B6 | 52 1N | 1 16W |
| King's Worthy, U.K. | 24 D6 | 51 6N | 1 17W |
| Kingsbridge, U.K. | 27 G6 | 50 17N | 3 47W |
| Kingsbury, U.K. | 23 G5 | 52 34N | 1 40W |
| Kingsclere, U.K. | 24 D6 | 51 20N | 1 14W |
| Kingscourt, Ireland | 28 D8 | 53 55N | 6 48W |
| Kingskerswell, U.K. | 27 G6 | 50 29N | 3 35W |
| Kingsland, U.K. | 23 H3 | 52 15N | 2 48W |
| Kingsteignton, U.K. | 27 F6 | 50 33N | 3 36W |
| Kingston, Canada | 109 D12 | 44 14N | 76 30W |
| Kingston, Jamaica | 114 a | 18 0N | 76 50W |
| Kingston, N.Y., U.S.A. | 113 E10 | 41 56N | 73 59W |
| Kingston, Pa., U.S.A. | 113 E10 | 41 16N | 75 54W |
| Kingston upon Hull, U.K. | 23 E8 | 53 45N | 0 21W |
| Kingston-upon-Thames □, U.K. | 25 D8 | 51 24N | 0 17W |
| Kingstown, St. Vincent | 115 E12 | 13 10N | 61 10W |
| Kingsville, U.S.A. | 110 E7 | 27 31N | 97 52W |
| Kingswear, U.K. | 27 G6 | 50 21N | 3 35W |
| Kingswood, U.K. | 24 D3 | 51 27N | 2 31W |
| Kington, U.K. | 23 H2 | 52 13N | 3 1W |
| Kingussie, U.K. | 19 H9 | 57 6N | 4 2W |
| Kinlochleven, U.K. | 18 J6 | 56 43N | 5 0W |
| Kinnairds Hd., U.K. | 19 G13 | 57 43N | 2 1W |
| Kinross, U.K. | 21 B9 | 56 13N | 3 25W |
| Kinsale, Ireland | 30 E5 | 51 42N | 8 31W |
| Kinsale, Old Hd. of, Ireland | 30 E5 | 51 37N | 8 33W |
| Kinshasa, Dem. Rep. of the Congo | 96 E3 | 4 20S | 15 15 E |
| Kintore, U.K. | 19 H13 | 57 14N | 2 20W |
| Kintyre, U.K. | 20 D4 | 55 30N | 5 35W |
| Kintyre, Mull of, U.K. | 20 D4 | 55 17N | 5 47W |
| Kippure, Ireland | 31 B10 | 53 11N | 6 21W |
| Kirensk, Russia | 79 D12 | 57 50N 107 55 E | |
| Kirghizia = Kyrgyzstan ■, Asia | 79 E9 | 42 0N | 75 0 E |
| Kiribati ■, Pac. Oc. | 102 H10 | 5 0S 180 0 E | |
| Kiritimati, Kiribati | 103 G12 | 1 58N 157 27W | |
| Kırıkkale, Turkey | 73 G5 | 39 51N | 33 32 E |
| Kirkbean, U.K. | 22 C1 | 54 55N | 3 36W |
| Kirkbride, U.K. | 22 C2 | 54 54N | 3 12W |
| Kirkburton, U.K. | 23 E5 | 53 37N | 1 42W |
| Kirkby, U.K. | 23 F3 | 53 30N | 2 54W |
| Kirkby-in-Ashfield, U.K. | 23 F6 | 53 6N | 1 14W |
| Kirkby Lonsdale, U.K. | 22 D3 | 54 12N | 2 36W |
| Kirkby Malzeard, U.K. | 22 D5 | 54 10N | 1 37W |
| Kirkby Stephen, U.K. | 22 C4 | 54 29N | 2 21W |
| Kirkby Thore, U.K. | 22 C3 | 54 37N | 2 32W |
| Kirkbymoorside, U.K. | 22 D7 | 54 17N | 0 56W |
| Kirkcaldy, U.K. | 21 B9 | 56 7N | 3 9W |
| Kirkcudbright, U.K. | 20 E7 | 54 50N | 4 2W |
| Kirkham, U.K. | 23 E3 | 53 47N | 2 53W |
| Kirkintilloch, U.K. | 20 C7 | 55 56N | 4 8W |
| Kirkland Lake, Canada | 109 D11 | 48 9N | 80 2W |
| Kirklareli, Turkey | 86 A1 | 41 44N | 27 15 E |
| Kirkoswald, U.K. | 22 C3 | 54 46N | 2 41W |
| Kirksville, U.S.A. | 111 B8 | 40 12N | 92 35W |
| Kirkūk, Iraq | 86 C6 | 35 30N | 44 21 E |
| Kirkwall, U.K. | 19 E12 | 58 59N | 2 58W |
| Kirkwhelpington, U.K. | 22 B5 | 55 9N | 1 59W |
| Kirov, Russia | 72 C8 | 58 35N | 49 40 E |
| Kirovohrad, Ukraine | 73 E5 | 48 35N | 32 20 E |
| Kirriemuir, U.K. | 19 J11 | 56 41N | 3 1W |
| Kırşehir, Turkey | 73 G5 | 39 14N | 34 5 E |
| Kirtling, U.K. | 25 B9 | 52 12N | 0 28 E |
| Kirtlington, U.K. | 24 C6 | 51 53N | 1 15W |
| Kirton, U.K. | 23 G8 | 52 56N | 0 3W |
| Kirton in Lindsey, U.K. | 23 F7 | 53 29N | 0 34W |
| Kiruna, Sweden | 63 D8 | 67 52N | 20 15 E |
| Kiryū, Japan | 82 E6 | 36 24N 139 20 E | |
| Kisangani, Dem. Rep. of the Congo | 96 D5 | 0 35N | 25 15 E |
| Kishanganj, India | 85 F16 | 26 3N | 88 14 E |
| Kishinev, Moldova | 67 E15 | 47 2N | 28 50 E |
| Kisii, Kenya | 96 E6 | 0 40S | 34 45 E |
| Kislovodsk, Russia | 73 F7 | 43 50N | 42 45 E |
| Kismayu, Somali Rep. | 91 G8 | 0 22S | 42 32 E |
| Kisumu, Kenya | 96 E6 | 0 3S | 34 45 E |
| Kitakyūshū, Japan | 82 G2 | 33 50N 130 50 E | |
| Kitale, Kenya | 96 D7 | 1 0N | 35 0 E |
| Kitami, Japan | 82 B8 | 43 48N 143 54 E | |
| Kitchener, Canada | 109 D11 | 43 27N | 80 29W |
| Kithira, Greece | 71 F10 | 36 8N | 23 0 E |
| Kitimat, Canada | 108 C6 | 54 3N 128 38W | |
| Kittanning, U.S.A. | 112 E8 | 40 49N | 79 31W |
| Kitwe, Zambia | 97 G5 | 12 54S | 28 13 E |
| Kivu, L., Dem. Rep. of the Congo | 96 E5 | 1 48S | 29 0 E |
| Kizil Irmak →, Turkey | 73 F6 | 41 44N | 35 58 E |
| Kizlyar, Russia | 73 F8 | 43 51N | 46 40 E |
| Kladno, Czech Rep. | 66 C8 | 50 10N | 14 7 E |
| Klagenfurt, Austria | 66 E8 | 46 38N | 14 20 E |
| Klaipėda, Lithuania | 72 C3 | 55 43N | 21 10 E |
| Klamath →, U.S.A. | 110 B2 | 41 33N 124 5W | |
| Klamath Falls, U.S.A. | 110 B2 | 42 13N 121 46W | |
| Klarälven →, Sweden | 63 E6 | 59 23N | 13 32 E |
| Klerksdorp, S. Africa | 97 K5 | 26 53S | 26 38 E |
| Kluane L., Canada | 108 B6 | 61 15N 138 40W | |
| Klyuchevskaya, Russia | 79 D18 | 55 50N 160 30 E | |
| Knaresborough, U.K. | 23 D6 | 54 1N | 1 28W |
| Knebworth, U.K. | 25 C8 | 51 52N | 0 11W |
| Knighton, U.K. | 23 H2 | 52 21N | 3 3W |
| Knock, Ireland | 28 D4 | 53 48N | 8 55W |
| Knockmealdown Mts., Ireland | 30 D7 | 52 14N | 7 56W |
| Knossós, Greece | 71 G11 | 35 16N | 25 10 E |
| Knottingley, U.K. | 23 E6 | 53 43N | 1 16W |
| Knowle, U.K. | 23 H5 | 52 24N | 1 44W |
| Knoxville, U.S.A. | 111 C10 | 35 58N | 83 55W |
| Knutsford, U.K. | 23 F4 | 53 18N | 2 21W |
| Kōbe, Japan | 82 F4 | 34 45N 135 10 E | |
| Koblenz, Germany | 66 C4 | 50 21N | 7 36 E |
| Kocaeli, Turkey | 73 F4 | 40 45N | 29 50 E |
| Koch Bihar, India | 85 F16 | 26 22N | 89 29 E |
| Kōchi, Japan | 82 G3 | 33 30N 133 35 E | |
| Kodiak, U.S.A. | 108 C4 | 57 47N 152 24W | |
| Kodiak I., U.S.A. | 108 C4 | 57 30N 152 45W | |
| Koforidua, Ghana | 94 G5 | 6 3N | 0 17W |
| Kōfu, Japan | 82 F6 | 35 40N 138 30 E | |
| Kohat, Pakistan | 84 C8 | 33 40N | 71 29 E |
| Kohima, India | 85 G19 | 25 35N | 94 10 E |
| Kohtla-Järve, Estonia | 72 C4 | 59 20N | 27 20 E |
| Kokkola, Finland | 63 E8 | 63 50N | 23 8 E |
| Koko Kyunzu, Burma | 85 M18 | 14 10N | 93 25 E |
| Kokomo, U.S.A. | 112 E4 | 40 29N | 86 8W |
| Kökshetaū, Kazakhstan | 79 D8 | 53 20N | 69 25 E |
| Koksoak →, Canada | 109 C13 | 58 30N | 68 10W |
| Kola Pen., Russia | 72 A6 | 67 30N | 38 0 E |
| Kolar Gold Fields, India | 84 N11 | 12 58N | 78 16 E |
| Kolguyev, Russia | 72 A8 | 69 20N | 48 30 E |
| Kolhapur, India | 84 L9 | 16 43N | 74 15 E |
| Kolkata, India | 85 H16 | 22 36N | 88 24 E |
| Kolomna, Russia | 72 C6 | 55 8N | 38 45 E |
| Kolomyya, Ukraine | 73 E4 | 48 31N | 25 2 E |
| Kolpino, Russia | 72 C5 | 59 44N | 30 39 E |
| Kolwezi, Dem. Rep. of the Congo | 96 G5 | 10 40S | 25 25 E |
| Kolyma →, Russia | 79 C18 | 69 30N 161 0 E | |
| Kolyma Ra., Russia | 79 C17 | 63 0N 157 0 E | |
| Komandorskiye Is., Russia | 79 D18 | 55 0N 167 0 E | |
| Komatsu, Japan | 82 E5 | 36 25N 136 30 E | |
| Komi □, Russia | 72 B10 | 64 0N | 55 0 E |
| Kompong Cham, Cambodia | 83 B2 | 12 0N 105 30 E | |
| Komsomolsk, Russia | 79 D15 | 50 30N 137 0 E | |
| Konarhā □, Afghan. | 87 C12 | 34 30N | 71 3 E |
| Konin, Poland | 67 B10 | 52 12N | 18 15 E |
| Konosha, Russia | 72 B7 | 61 0N | 40 5 E |
| Konotop, Ukraine | 73 D5 | 51 12N | 33 7 E |
| Konya, Turkey | 73 G5 | 37 52N | 32 35 E |
| Kootenay L., Canada | 108 D8 | 49 45N 116 50W | |
| Kopet Dagh, Asia | 87 B9 | 38 0N | 58 0 E |
| Korçë, Albania | 71 D9 | 40 37N | 20 50 E |
| Kordofân, Sudan | 95 F11 | 13 0N | 29 0 E |
| Korea, North ■, Asia | 81 C7 | 40 0N 127 0 E | |
| Korea, South ■, Asia | 81 C7 | 36 0N 128 0 E | |
| Korea Bay, Korea | 81 C7 | 39 0N 124 0 E | |
| Korea Strait, Asia | 81 C7 | 34 0N 129 30 E | |
| Korhogo, Ivory C. | 94 G4 | 9 29N | 5 28W |
| Kōriyama, Japan | 82 E7 | 37 24N 140 23 E | |
| Koror, Palau | 102 G5 | 7 20N 134 28 E | |
| Körös →, Hungary | 67 E11 | 46 43N | 20 12 E |
| Korosten, Ukraine | 73 D4 | 50 54N | 28 36 E |
| Kortrijk, Belgium | 65 D3 | 50 50N | 3 17 E |
| Kos, Greece | 71 F12 | 36 50N | 27 15 E |
| Kosciuszko, Mt., Australia | 98 H8 | 36 27S 148 16 E | |
| Košice, Slovak Rep. | 67 D11 | 48 42N | 21 15 E |
| Kosovo □, Serbia & M. | 71 C9 | 42 30N | 21 0 E |
| Kôsti, Sudan | 95 F12 | 13 8N | 32 43 E |
| Kostroma, Russia | 72 C7 | 57 50N | 40 58 E |
| Koszalin, Poland | 66 A9 | 54 11N | 16 8 E |
| Kota, India | 84 G9 | 25 14N | 75 49 E |
| Kota Baharu, Malaysia | 83 C2 | 6 7N 102 14 E | |
| Kota Kinabalu, Malaysia | 83 C3 | 6 0N 116 4 E | |
| Kotabumi, Indonesia | 83 D2 | 4 49S 104 54 E | |
| Kotelnich, Russia | 72 C8 | 58 22N | 48 24 E |
| Kotka, Finland | 63 E9 | 60 28N | 26 58 E |
| Kotlas, Russia | 72 B8 | 61 17N | 46 43 E |
| Kotri, Pakistan | 84 G6 | 25 22N | 68 22 E |
| Kotuy →, Russia | 79 B12 | 71 54N 102 6 E | |
| Kotzebue, U.S.A. | 108 B3 | 66 53N 162 39W | |
| Kovel, Ukraine | 72 D3 | 51 11N | 24 38 E |
| Kovrov, Russia | 72 C7 | 56 25N | 41 25 E |
| Kra, Isthmus of, Thailand | 83 B1 | 10 15N | 99 30 E |
| Kragujevac, Serbia & M. | 71 B9 | 44 2N | 20 56 E |
| Krajina, Bos.-H. | 70 B7 | 44 45N | 16 35 E |
| Krakatau, Indonesia | 83 D2 | 6 10S 105 20 E | |
| Kraków, Poland | 67 C10 | 50 4N | 19 57 E |
| Kramatorsk, Ukraine | 73 E6 | 48 50N | 37 30 E |
| Krasnodar, Russia | 73 E6 | 45 5N | 39 0 E |
| Krasnokamsk, Russia | 72 C10 | 58 4N | 55 48 E |
| Krasnoturinsk, Russia | 72 C11 | 59 46N | 60 12 E |
| Krasnoyarsk, Russia | 79 D11 | 56 8N | 93 0 E |
| Krasnyy Luch, Ukraine | 73 E6 | 48 13N | 39 0 E |
| Krefeld, Germany | 66 C4 | 51 20N | 6 33 E |
| Kremenchuk, Ukraine | 73 E5 | 49 5N | 33 25 E |
| Krishna →, India | 85 M12 | 15 57N | 80 59 E |
| Kristiansand, Norway | 63 F5 | 58 8N | 8 1 E |
| Kristiansund, Norway | 63 E5 | 63 7N | 7 45 E |
| Krivoy Rog, Ukraine | 73 E5 | 47 51N | 33 20 E |
| Kronshtadt, Russia | 72 B4 | 59 57N | 29 51 E |
| Kroonstad, S. Africa | 97 K5 | 27 43S | 27 19 E |
| Kropotkin, Russia | 73 E7 | 45 28N | 40 28 E |
| Krosno, Poland | 67 D11 | 49 42N | 21 46 E |
| Kruševac, Serbia & M. | 71 C9 | 43 35N | 21 28 E |
| Ksar el Kebir, Morocco | 94 B4 | 35 0N | 6 0W |
| Kuala Belait, Malaysia | 83 C3 | 4 35N 114 11 E | |
| Kuala Lumpur, Malaysia | 83 C2 | 3 9N 101 41 E | |
| Kuala Terengganu, Malaysia | 83 C2 | 5 20N 103 8 E | |
| Kuantan, Malaysia | 83 C2 | 3 49N 103 20 E | |
| Kuching, Malaysia | 83 C3 | 1 33N 110 25 E | |
| Kudymkar, Russia | 72 C9 | 59 1N | 54 39 E |
| Kugluktuk, Canada | 108 B8 | 67 50N 115 5W | |
| Kūlob, Tajikistan | 87 B12 | 37 55N | 69 50 E |
| Kulsary, Kazakhstan | 73 E9 | 46 59N | 54 1 E |
| Kuma →, Russia | 73 F8 | 44 55N | 47 0 E |
| Kumagaya, Japan | 82 E6 | 36 9N 139 22 E | |
| Kumamoto, Japan | 82 G2 | 32 45N 130 45 E | |
| Kumanovo, Macedonia | 71 C9 | 42 9N | 21 42 E |
| Kumasi, Ghana | 94 G5 | 6 41N | 1 38W |
| Kumbakonam, India | 84 P11 | 10 58N | 79 25 E |
| Kumertau, Russia | 72 D10 | 52 45N | 55 57 E |
| Kungur, Russia | 72 C10 | 57 25N | 56 57 E |
| Kunlun Shan, Asia | 80 C3 | 36 0N | 86 30 E |
| Kunming, China | 80 D5 | 25 1N 102 41 E | |
| Kuopio, Finland | 63 E9 | 62 53N | 27 35 E |
| Kupang, Indonesia | 83 E4 | 10 19S 123 39 E | |
| Kuqa, China | 80 B3 | 41 35N | 82 30 E |
| Kür →, Azerbaijan | 73 G8 | 39 29N | 49 15 E |
| Kurdistan, Asia | 86 B5 | 37 20N | 43 30 E |
| Kure, Japan | 82 F3 | 34 14N 132 32 E | |
| Kurgan, Russia | 79 D8 | 55 26N | 65 18 E |
| Kuril Is., Russia | 79 E17 | 45 0N 150 0 E | |
| Kuril Trench, Pac. Oc. | 102 C7 | 44 0N 153 0 E | |
| Kurnool, India | 84 M11 | 15 45N | 78 0 E |
| Kursk, Russia | 72 D6 | 51 42N | 36 11 E |
| Kuruktag, China | 80 B3 | 41 0N | 89 0 E |
| Kurume, Japan | 82 G2 | 33 15N 130 30 E | |
| Kushiro, Japan | 82 B9 | 43 0N 144 25 E | |
| Kushtia, Bangla. | 85 H16 | 23 55N | 89 5 E |
| Kuskokwim B., U.S.A. | 108 C3 | 59 45N 162 25W | |
| Kütahya, Turkey | 73 G5 | 39 30N | 30 2 E |
| Kutaisi, Georgia | 73 F7 | 42 19N | 42 40 E |
| Kuujjuaq, Canada | 109 C13 | 58 6N | 68 15W |
| Kuujjuarapik, Canada | 109 C12 | 55 20N | 77 35W |
| Kuwait, Kuwait | 86 D7 | 29 30N | 48 0 E |
| Kuwait ■, Asia | 86 D6 | 29 30N | 47 30 E |
| Kuybyshev Res., Russia | 72 C8 | 55 2N | 49 30 E |
| Kuznetsk, Russia | 72 D8 | 53 12N | 46 40 E |
| Kuzomen, Russia | 72 A6 | 66 22N | 36 50 E |
| KwaMashu, S. Africa | 97 K6 | 29 45S | 30 58 E |
| Kwangju, S. Korea | 81 C7 | 35 9N 126 54 E | |
| Kwango →, Dem. Rep. of the Congo | 96 E3 | 3 14S | 17 22 E |
| KwaZulu Natal □, S. Africa | 97 K6 | 29 0S | 30 0 E |
| Kwekwe, Zimbabwe | 97 H5 | 18 58S | 29 48 E |
| Kyle of Lochalsh, U.K. | 18 H6 | 57 17N | 5 44W |
| Kyoga, L., Uganda | 96 D6 | 1 35N | 33 0 E |
| Kyōto, Japan | 82 F4 | 35 0N 135 45 E | |
| Kyrenia, Cyprus | 86 C3 | 35 20N | 33 20 E |
| Kyrgyzstan ■, Asia | 79 E9 | 42 0N | 75 0 E |
| Kyūshū, Japan | 82 G2 | 33 0N 131 0 E | |
| Kyzyl Kum, Uzbekistan | 87 A10 | 42 30N | 65 0 E |
| Kyzyl-Orda, Kazakhstan | 79 E8 | 44 48N | 65 28 E |

**L**

| | | | |
|---|---|---|---|
| La Ceiba, Honduras | 114 D7 | 15 40N | 86 50W |
| La Coruña, Spain | 69 A1 | 43 20N | 8 25W |
| La Crosse, U.S.A. | 111 B8 | 43 48N | 91 15W |
| La Désirade, Guadeloupe | 114 b | 16 18N | 61 3W |
| La Grande →, Canada | 109 C12 | 53 50N | 79 0W |
| La Grange, U.S.A. | 111 D10 | 33 2N | 85 2W |
| La Junta, U.S.A. | 110 C6 | 37 59N 103 33W | |
| La Loche, Canada | 108 C9 | 56 29N 109 26W | |
| La Louvière, Belgium | 65 D4 | 50 27N | 4 10 E |
| La Mancha, Spain | 69 C4 | 39 10N | 2 54W |
| La Oroya, Peru | 120 D2 | 11 32S | 75 54W |
| La Palma, Canary Is. | 94 C2 | 28 40N | 17 50W |

**La Paz** · · · **Lugwardine**

La Paz, Bolivia ............. 120 D3 16 20S 68 10W
La Paz, Mexico ............. 114 C2 24 10N 110 20W
La Perouse Str., Asia ...... 102 C6 45 40N 142 0 E
La Plata, Argentina ........ 121 F4 35 0S 57 55W
La Porte, U.S.A. ........... 112 E4 41 36N 86 43W
La Quiaca, Argentina ....... 121 E3 22 5S 65 35W
La Rioja, Argentina ........ 121 E3 29 20S 67 0W
La Rioja □, Spain .......... 69 A4 42 20N 2 20W
La Roche-sur-Yon, France ... 68 C3 46 40N 1 25W
La Rochelle, France ........ 68 C3 46 10N 1 9W
La Romana, Dom. Rep. ....... 115 D11 18 27N 68 57W
La Ronge, Canada ........... 108 C9 55 5N 105 20W
La Sarre, Canada ........... 112 A8 48 45N 79 15W
La Serena, Chile ........... 121 E2 29 55S 71 10W
La Spézia, Italy ........... 68 D8 44 7N 9 50 E
La Tortuga, Venezuela ...... 120 A3 11 0N 65 22W
La Trinité, Martinique ..... 114 c 14 43N 60 58W
La Tuque, Canada ........... 109 D12 47 30N 72 50W
La Vega, Dom. Rep. ......... 115 D10 19 20N 70 30W
Labé, Guinea ............... 94 F3 11 24N 12 16W
Labinsk, Russia ............ 73 F7 44 40N 40 48 E
Laborie, St. Lucia ......... 115 f 13 45N 61 2W
Labrador, Canada ........... 109 C13 53 20N 61 0W
Labrador City, Canada ...... 109 C13 52 57N 66 55W
Labrador Sea, Atl. Oc. ..... 109 C14 57 0N 54 0W
Lac La Biche, Canada ....... 108 C8 54 45N 111 58W
Lac-Mégantic, Canada ....... 113 C12 45 35N 70 53W
Laccadive Is. = Lakshadweep
  Is., India ............... 74 H11 10 0N 72 30 E
Laceby, U.K. ............... 23 E8 53 33N 0 10W
Lachine, Canada ............ 113 C11 45 30N 73 40W
Lacock, U.K. ............... 24 D4 51 24N 2 7W
Lacombe, Canada ............ 108 C8 52 30N 113 44W
Laconia, U.S.A. ............ 113 D12 43 32N 71 28W
Ladock, U.K. ............... 27 G4 50 19N 4 58W
Ladoga, L., Russia ......... 72 B5 61 15N 30 30 E
Ladysmith, S. Africa ....... 97 K5 28 32S 29 46 E
Lae, Papua N. G. ........... 98 B8 6 40S 147 2 E
Lafayette, Ind., U.S.A. .... 112 E4 40 25N 86 54W
Lafayette, La., U.S.A. ..... 111 D8 30 14N 92 1W
Lafia, Nigeria ............. 94 G7 8 30N 8 34 E
Lagan →, U.K. .............. 29 B10 54 36N 5 55W
Laghmán □, Afghan. ......... 87 C12 34 20N 70 0 E
Laghouat, Algeria .......... 94 B6 33 50N 2 59 E
Lagos, Nigeria ............. 94 G6 6 25N 3 27 E
Lagos, Portugal ............ 69 D1 37 5N 8 41W
Lahn →, Germany ............ 66 C4 50 19N 7 37 E
Lahore, Pakistan ........... 84 D9 31 32N 74 22 E
Lahti, Finland ............. 63 E9 60 58N 25 40 E
Lairg, U.K. ................ 19 F9 58 2N 4 24W
Laizhou, China ............. 81 C6 37 8N 119 57 E
Lake Charles, U.S.A. ....... 111 D8 30 14N 93 13W
Lake City, U.S.A. .......... 111 D10 30 11N 82 38W
Lake District Nat. Park △, U.K. .... 22 C2 54 30N 3 21W
Lake Havasu City, U.S.A. ... 110 D4 34 27N 114 22W
Lakeland, U.S.A. ........... 111 E10 28 3N 81 57W
Lakenheath, U.K. ........... 25 B10 52 25N 0 32 E
Lakewood, U.S.A. ........... 112 E7 41 29N 81 48W
Lakshadweep Is., India ..... 74 H11 10 0N 72 30 E
Lamar, U.S.A. .............. 110 C6 38 5N 102 37W
Lambaréné, Gabon ........... 96 E2 0 41S 10 12 E
Lambay I., Ireland ......... 29 E9 53 29N 6 1W
Lamberhurst, U.K. .......... 25 D9 51 5N 0 24 E
Lambeth □, U.K. ............ 25 D8 51 28N 0 6W
Lambley, U.K. .............. 22 C4 54 56N 2 30W
Lambourn, U.K. ............. 24 C5 51 30N 1 32W
Lamesa, U.S.A. ............. 110 D6 32 44N 101 58W
Lammermuir, U.K. ........... 22 A4 55 50N 2 25W
Lammermuir Hills, U.K. ..... 21 C10 55 50N 2 40W
Lamon B., Phil. ............ 83 B4 14 30N 122 20 E
Lampeter, U.K. ............. 26 C5 52 7N 4 4W
Lanark, U.K. ............... 21 C8 55 40N 3 47W
Lancashire □, U.K. ......... 23 E3 53 50N 2 48W
Lancaster, U.K. ............ 22 D3 54 3N 2 48W
Lancaster, Calif., U.S.A. .. 110 D3 34 42N 118 8W
Lancaster, N.H., U.S.A. .... 113 C12 44 29N 71 34W
Lancaster, Pa., U.S.A. ..... 112 E9 40 2N 76 19W
Lancaster Sd., Canada ...... 109 A11 74 13N 84 0W
Lanchester, U.K. ........... 22 C5 54 50N 1 44W
Lancing, U.K. .............. 25 E8 50 49N 0 19W
Landes, France ............. 68 D3 44 0N 1 0W
Landkey, U.K. .............. 27 E6 51 3N 4 0W
Land's End, U.K. ........... 27 G2 50 4N 5 44W
Langholm, U.K. ............. 21 D10 55 9N 3 0W
Langport, U.K. ............. 24 D3 51 2N 2 50W
Langres, France ............ 68 C6 47 52N 5 20 E
Langres, Plateau de, France .. 68 C6 47 45N 5 3 E
Langsa, Indonesia .......... 83 C1 4 30N 97 57 E
Langstrothdale Chase, U.K. .. 22 D4 54 14N 2 13W
Langtoft, U.K. ............. 23 G8 52 42N 0 20W
Langtree, U.K. ............. 27 F5 50 55N 4 13W
Languedoc, France .......... 68 E5 43 58N 3 55 E
Lannion, France ............ 68 B2 48 46N 3 29W
L'Annonciation, Canada ..... 113 B10 46 25N 74 55W
L'Anse, U.S.A. ............. 112 B3 46 45N 88 27W
L'Anse la Raye, St. Lucia .. 115 f 13 55N 61 19W
Lansing, U.S.A. ............ 112 D4 42 44N 84 33W
Lanzarote, Canary Is. ...... 94 C3 29 0N 13 40W
Lanzhou, China ............. 80 C5 36 1N 103 52 E
Laoag, Phil. ............... 83 A4 18 7N 120 34 E
Laois □, Ireland ........... 31 C7 52 57N 7 36W
Laon, France ............... 68 B5 49 33N 3 35 E
Laos ■, Asia ............... 83 B2 17 45N 105 0 E
Lapeer, U.S.A. ............. 112 D6 43 3N 83 19W
Lapford, U.K. .............. 24 E1 50 51N 3 48W
Lapland, Europe ............ 63 D8 68 7N 24 0 E
Laptev Sea, Russia ......... 79 B14 76 0N 125 0 E
Laramie, U.S.A. ............ 110 B5 41 19N 105 35W
Laramie Mts., U.S.A. ....... 110 B5 42 0N 105 30W
Laredo, U.S.A. ............. 110 E7 27 30N 99 30W
Largs, U.K. ................ 20 C6 55 47N 4 52W
Lárisa, Greece ............. 71 E10 39 36N 22 27 E
Larnaca, Cyprus ............ 86 C3 34 55N 33 38 E
Larne, U.K. ................ 29 B10 54 51N 5 51W
Larne L., U.K. ............. 29 B10 54 50N 5 48W
Larrimah, Australia ........ 98 D5 15 35S 133 12 E
Larvik, Norway ............. 63 F6 59 4N 10 2 E
Las Cruces, U.S.A. ......... 110 D5 32 19N 106 47W
Las Palmas, Canary Is. ..... 94 C2 28 7N 15 26W
Las Vegas, N. Mex., U.S.A. . 110 C5 35 36N 105 13W
Las Vegas, Nev., U.S.A. .... 110 C3 36 10N 115 9W
Lashio, Burma .............. 85 H20 22 56N 97 45 E
Lassen Pk., U.S.A. ......... 110 B2 40 29N 121 31W
Lastoursville, Gabon ....... 96 E2 0 55S 12 38 E
Latacunga, Ecuador ......... 120 C2 0 50S 78 35W
Latakia, Syria ............. 86 C3 35 30N 35 45 E
Latina, Italy .............. 70 D5 41 28N 12 52 E
Latvia ■, Europe ........... 72 C3 56 50N 24 0 E
Lauder, U.K. ............... 22 A3 55 43N 2 43W
Lauderdale, U.K. ........... 22 A3 55 44N 2 41W
Launceston, Australia ...... 98 J8 41 24S 147 8 E
Launceston, U.K. ........... 27 F5 50 38N 4 22W
Laune →, Ireland ........... 30 D2 52 7N 9 47W
Laurel, U.S.A. ............. 111 D9 31 41N 89 8W
Laurencekirk, U.K. ......... 19 J13 56 50N 2 28W
Lausanne, Switz. ........... 66 E4 46 32N 6 38 E
Lauzon, Canada ............. 113 B12 46 48N 71 10W

Lavagh More, Ireland ....... 28 B5 54 46N 8 6W
Laval, France .............. 68 B3 48 4N 0 48W
Lavendon, U.K. ............. 25 B7 52 11N 0 39W
Lavenham, U.K. ............. 25 B10 52 6N 0 48 E
Lavras, Brazil ............. 122 D2 21 20S 45 0W
Lawrence, Kans., U.S.A. .... 111 C7 38 58N 95 14W
Lawrence, Mass., U.S.A. .... 113 D12 42 43N 71 10W
Lawton, U.S.A. ............. 110 D7 34 37N 98 25W
Laxey, U.K. ................ 29 C13 54 14N 4 23W
Laxfield, U.K. ............. 25 B11 52 18N 1 22 E
Laxford, L., U.K. .......... 18 F7 58 24N 5 6W
Lazio, Italy ............... 70 C5 42 10N 12 30 E
Lazonby, U.K. .............. 22 C3 54 46N 2 42W
Le Creusot, France ......... 68 C6 46 48N 4 24 E
Le François, Martinique .... 114 c 14 38N 60 57W
Le Havre, France ........... 68 B4 49 30N 0 5 E
Le Lamentin, Martinique .... 114 c 14 35N 61 2W
Le Mans, France ............ 68 C4 48 0N 0 10 E
Le Marin, Martinique ....... 114 c 14 27N 60 55W
Le Prêcheur, Martinique .... 114 c 14 50N 61 12W
Le Puy-en-Velay, France .... 68 D5 45 3N 3 52 E
Le Robert, Martinique ...... 114 c 14 40N 60 56W
Le St-Esprit, Martinique ... 114 c 14 34N 60 56W
Lea, U.K. .................. 23 F7 53 22N 0 45W
Lea →, U.K. ................ 25 C9 51 31N 0 1 E
Leadenham, U.K. ............ 23 F7 53 3N 0 35W
Leamington, Canada ......... 112 D6 42 3N 82 36W
Leane, L., Ireland ......... 30 D3 52 2N 9 32W
Leatherhead, U.K. .......... 25 D8 51 18N 0 20W
Leavenworth, U.S.A. ........ 111 C8 39 19N 94 55W
Lebanon, Ind., U.S.A. ...... 112 E4 40 3N 86 28W
Lebanon, Ky., U.S.A. ....... 112 G5 37 34N 85 15W
Lebanon, Mo., U.S.A. ....... 111 C8 37 41N 92 40W
Lebanon, Pa., U.S.A. ....... 112 E9 40 20N 76 26W
Lebanon ■, Asia ............ 86 C3 34 0N 36 0 E
Lebu, Chile ................ 121 F2 37 40S 73 47W
Lecce, Italy ............... 71 D8 40 23N 18 11 E
Lechlade, U.K. ............. 24 C5 51 42N 1 41W
Ledbury, U.K. .............. 24 B4 52 2N 2 25W
Lee →, Ireland ............. 30 E5 51 53N 8 56W
Lee-on-the-Solent, U.K. .... 24 E6 50 48N 1 12W
Leech L., U.S.A. ........... 111 A8 47 10N 94 24W
Leeds, U.K. ................ 23 E5 53 48N 1 33W
Leek, U.K. ................. 23 F4 53 7N 2 1W
Leeuwarden, Neths. ......... 65 A5 53 15N 5 48 E
Leeuwin, C., Australia ..... 98 G2 34 20S 115 9 E
Leeward Is., Atl. Oc. ...... 115 D12 16 30N 63 30W
Leganés, Spain ............. 69 B4 40 19N 3 45W
Legazpi, Phil. ............. 83 B4 13 10N 123 45 E
Legnica, Poland ............ 66 C9 51 12N 16 10 E
Leicester, U.K. ............ 23 G6 52 38N 1 8W
Leicestershire □, U.K. ..... 23 G6 52 41N 1 17W
Leiden, Neths. ............. 65 B4 52 9N 4 30 E
Leigh, Gt. Man., U.K. ...... 23 E3 53 30N 2 32W
Leigh, Hereford, U.K. ...... 24 B4 52 11N 2 20W
Leighton Buzzard, U.K. ..... 25 C7 51 54N 0 38W
Leine →, Germany ........... 66 B5 52 43N 9 36 E
Leinster □, Ireland ........ 31 B8 53 3N 7 8W
Leinster, Mt., Ireland ..... 31 C9 52 37N 6 46W
Leipzig, Germany ........... 66 C7 51 18N 12 22 E
Leiston, U.K. .............. 25 B12 52 12N 1 36 E
Leith, U.K. ................ 21 C9 55 59N 3 11W
Leith Hill, U.K. ........... 25 D8 51 11N 0 22W
Leitholm, U.K. ............. 22 A4 55 42N 2 20W
Leitrim, Ireland ........... 28 C5 54 0N 8 5W
Leitrim □, Ireland ......... 28 C5 54 8N 8 0W
Leizhou Bandao, China ...... 81 D6 21 0N 110 0 E
Lek →, Neths. .............. 65 C4 51 54N 4 35 E
Lelant, U.K. ............... 27 G3 50 11N 5 28W
Lelystad, Neths. ........... 65 B5 52 30N 5 25 E
Léman, L., Europe .......... 66 E4 46 26N 6 30 E
Lena →, Russia ............. 79 B14 72 52N 126 40 E
Lenham, U.K. ............... 25 D10 51 14N 0 44 E
Lens, France ............... 68 A5 50 26N 2 50 E
Leominster, U.K. ........... 24 B3 52 14N 2 43W
Leominster, U.S.A. ......... 113 D12 42 32N 71 46W
León, Mexico ............... 114 C4 21 7N 101 40W
León, Nic. ................. 114 E7 12 20N 86 51W
León, Spain ................ 69 A3 42 38N 5 34W
Leonora, Australia ......... 98 F3 28 49S 121 19 E
Leopoldina, Brazil ......... 122 D2 21 28S 42 40W
Lerwick, U.K. .............. 18 B15 60 9N 1 9W
Les Cayes, Haiti ........... 115 D10 18 15N 73 46W
Les Sables-d'Olonne, France .. 68 C3 46 30N 1 45W
Lesbury, U.K. .............. 22 B5 55 25N 1 36W
Leskovac, Serbia & M. ...... 71 C9 43 0N 21 58 E
Lesotho ■, Africa .......... 97 K5 29 40S 28 0 E
Lesser Antilles, W. Indies . 115 E12 15 0N 61 0W
Lesser Slave L., Canada .... 108 C8 55 30N 115 25W
Lesser Sunda Is., Indonesia .. 83 D4 8 0S 120 0 E
Lésvos, Greece ............. 71 E12 39 10N 26 20 E
Leszno, Poland ............. 67 C9 51 50N 16 30 E
Letchworth, U.K. ........... 25 C8 51 59N 0 13W
Lethbridge, Canada ......... 108 D8 49 45N 112 45W
Leti, Kepulauan, Indonesia . 83 D4 8 10S 128 0 E
Leticia, Colombia .......... 120 C2 4 9S 70 0W
Letterkenny, Ireland ....... 28 B6 54 57N 7 45W
Leuchars, U.K. ............. 21 B10 56 24N 2 53W
Leuven, Belgium ............ 65 D4 50 52N 4 42 E
Levelland, U.S.A. .......... 110 D6 33 35N 102 23W
Leven, E. Riding, U.K. ..... 23 E8 53 53N 0 18W
Leven, Fife, U.K. .......... 21 B10 56 12N 3 0W
Leven →, U.K. .............. 22 C6 54 31N 1 19W
Leven, L., U.K. ............ 21 B9 56 12N 3 22W
Lévis, Canada .............. 109 D12 46 48N 71 9W
Levkás, Greece ............. 71 E9 38 40N 20 43 E
Lewes, U.K. ................ 25 E9 50 52N 0 1 E
Lewis, U.K. ................ 18 F4 58 9N 6 40W
Lewis, Butt of, U.K. ....... 18 E5 58 31N 6 16W
Lewisham □, U.K. ........... 25 D8 51 27N 0 1W
Lewisporte, Canada ......... 109 D14 49 15N 55 3W
Lewiston, Idaho, U.S.A. .... 110 A3 46 25N 117 1W
Lewiston, Maine, U.S.A. .... 113 C12 44 6N 70 13W
Lewistown, Mont., U.S.A. ... 110 A5 47 4N 109 26W
Lewistown, Pa., U.S.A. ..... 112 E9 40 36N 77 34W
Lexington, U.S.A. .......... 112 F5 38 3N 84 30W
Lexington Park, U.S.A. ..... 112 F9 38 16N 76 27W
Leyburn, U.K. .............. 22 D5 54 19N 1 48W
Leyland, U.K. .............. 23 E3 53 42N 2 43W
Leysdown on Sea, U.K. ...... 25 D10 51 24N 0 56 E
Leyte, Phil. ............... 83 B4 11 0N 125 0 E
Lhasa, China ............... 80 D4 29 25N 90 58 E
Lhazê, China ............... 80 D3 29 5N 87 38 E
L'Hospitalet de Llobregat, Spain .. 69 B7 41 21N 2 6 E
Lianyungang, China ......... 81 C6 34 40N 119 11 E
Liaoning □, China .......... 81 B7 41 40N 122 30 E
Liaoyuan, China ............ 81 B7 42 58N 125 2 E
Liard →, Canada ............ 108 B7 61 51N 121 18W
Liberal, U.S.A. ............ 110 C6 37 3N 100 55W
Liberec, Czech Rep. ........ 66 C8 50 47N 15 7 E
Liberia ■, W. Afr. ......... 94 G4 6 30N 9 30W
Libourne, France ........... 68 D3 44 55N 0 14W
Libreville, Gabon .......... 96 D1 0 25N 9 26 E
Libya ■, N. Afr. ........... 95 C9 27 0N 17 0 E
Libyan Desert, Africa ...... 95 C10 25 0N 25 0 E
Lichfield, U.K. ............ 23 G5 52 41N 1 49W

Liechtenstein ■, Europe .... 66 E5 47 8N 9 35 E
Liège, Belgium ............. 65 D5 50 38N 5 35 E
Liepāja, Latvia ............ 72 C3 56 30N 21 0 E
Liffey →, Ireland .......... 31 B10 53 21N 6 13W
Lifford, Ireland ........... 28 B7 54 51N 7 29W
Liguria □, Italy ........... 68 D8 44 30N 8 50 E
Ligurian Sea, Medit. S. .... 70 C3 43 20N 9 0 E
Lihue, U.S.A. .............. 110 H15 21 59N 159 23W
Lijiang, China ............. 80 D5 26 55N 100 20 E
Likasi, Dem. Rep. of the Congo .. 96 G5 10 55S 26 48 E
Lille, France .............. 68 A5 50 38N 3 3 E
Lillehammer, Norway ........ 63 E6 61 8N 10 30 E
Lilleshall, U.K. ........... 23 G4 52 44N 2 23W
Lilongwe, Malawi ........... 97 G6 14 0S 33 48 E
Lima, Peru ................. 120 D2 12 0S 77 0W
Lima, U.S.A. ............... 112 E5 40 44N 84 6W
Limassol, Cyprus ........... 86 C3 34 42N 33 1 E
Limavady, U.K. ............. 29 A8 55 3N 6 56W
Limay →, Argentina ......... 121 F3 39 0S 68 0W
Limbe, Cameroon ............ 96 D1 4 1N 9 10 E
Limburg □, Neths. .......... 65 C5 51 20N 5 55 E
Limeira, Brazil ............ 122 D1 22 35S 47 28W
Limerick, Ireland .......... 30 C5 52 40N 8 37W
Limerick □, Ireland ........ 30 C5 52 30N 8 50W
Limfjorden, Denmark ........ 63 F5 56 55N 9 0 E
Limnos, Greece ............. 71 E11 39 50N 25 5 E
Limoges, France ............ 68 D4 45 50N 1 15 E
Limón, Costa Rica .......... 115 F8 10 0N 83 2W
Limousin, France ........... 68 D4 45 30N 1 30 E
Limoux, France ............. 68 E5 43 4N 2 12 E
Limpopo →, Africa .......... 97 K6 25 5S 33 30 E
Linares, Chile ............. 121 F2 35 50S 71 40W
Linares, Mexico ............ 114 C5 24 50N 99 40W
Linares, Spain ............. 69 C4 38 10N 3 40W
Lincoln, U.K. .............. 23 F7 53 14N 0 32W
Lincoln, Maine, U.S.A. ..... 113 C13 45 22N 68 30W
Lincoln, Nebr., U.S.A. ..... 111 B7 40 49N 96 41W
Lincoln Sea, Arctic ........ 54 A5 84 0N 55 0W
Lincolnshire Wolds, U.K. ... 23 F8 53 26N 0 13W
Lindale, U.K. .............. 22 D3 54 14N 2 53W
Lindesnes, Norway .......... 63 F5 57 58N 7 3 E
Lindsay, Canada ............ 112 C8 44 22N 78 43W
Lingfield, U.K. ............ 25 D8 51 11N 0 0W
Lingga, Kepulauan, Indonesia .. 83 D2 0 10S 104 30 E
Linhai, China .............. 81 D7 28 50N 121 8 E
Linhares, Brazil ........... 122 C2 19 25S 40 4W
Linkinhorne, U.K. .......... 27 F5 50 32N 4 24W
Linköping, Sweden .......... 63 F7 58 28N 15 36 E
Linnhe, L., U.K. ........... 20 A5 56 36N 5 25W
Linslade, U.K. ............. 25 C7 51 54N 0 41W
Linstead, Jamaica .......... 114 a 18 8N 77 2W
Linton, U.K. ............... 25 B9 52 6N 0 17 E
Linxi, China ............... 81 B6 43 36N 118 2 E
Linxia, China .............. 80 C5 35 36N 103 10 E
Linz, Austria .............. 66 D8 48 18N 14 18 E
Lion, G. du, France ........ 68 E6 43 10N 4 0 E
Lipa, Phil. ................ 83 B4 13 57N 121 10 E
Lipetsk, Russia ............ 72 D6 52 37N 39 35 E
Lippe →, Germany ........... 66 C4 51 39N 6 58 E
Liquillo, Sierra de, Puerto Rico .. 115 d 18 20N 65 47W
Lisbon, Portugal ........... 69 C1 38 42N 9 10W
Lisburn, U.K. .............. 29 B9 54 31N 6 3W
Liscannor B., Ireland ...... 30 C4 52 55N 9 24W
Lisianski I., Pac. Oc. ..... 102 E10 26 2N 174 0W
Lisieux, France ............ 68 B4 49 10N 0 12 E
Liskeard, U.K. ............. 27 G5 50 27N 4 29W
Liski, Russia .............. 73 D6 51 3N 39 30 E
Lismore, Australia ......... 98 F9 28 44S 153 21 E
Lismore, Ireland ........... 30 D7 52 8N 7 55W
Liss, U.K. ................. 25 D7 51 3N 0 54W
Listowel, Canada ........... 112 D7 43 44N 80 58W
Listowel, Ireland .......... 30 D4 52 27N 9 29W
Litani →, Lebanon .......... 86 C3 33 20N 35 15 E
Litcham, U.K. .............. 25 A10 52 44N 0 47 E
Litherland, U.K. ........... 23 F3 53 29N 2 59W
Lithuania ■, Europe ........ 72 C3 55 30N 24 0 E
Little Current, Canada ..... 112 C7 45 55N 82 0W
Little Minch, U.K. ......... 18 G7 57 35N 6 45W
Little Missouri →, U.S.A. .. 110 A6 47 36N 102 25W
Little Ouse →, U.K. ........ 25 B11 52 22N 1 12 E
Little Rock, U.S.A. ........ 111 D8 34 45N 92 17W
Little Walsingham, U.K. .... 25 A10 52 54N 0 52 E
Littlehampton, U.K. ........ 25 E7 50 49N 0 32W
Littleport, U.K. ........... 25 B9 52 27N 0 19 E
Littlestone-on-Sea, U.K. ... 25 E10 50 58N 0 58 E
Liuwa Plain, Zambia ........ 97 G4 14 20S 22 30 E
Liuzhou, China ............. 81 D5 24 22N 109 22 E
Liverpool, Canada .......... 109 D13 44 5N 64 41W
Liverpool, U.K. ............ 23 F3 53 25N 3 0W
Livingston, U.K. ........... 21 C9 55 54N 3 30W
Livingston, U.S.A. ......... 110 A4 45 40N 110 34W
Livingstone, Zambia ........ 97 H5 17 46S 25 52 E
Livonia, U.S.A. ............ 112 D6 42 23N 83 23W
Livorno, Italy ............. 70 C4 43 33N 10 19 E
Lizard, U.K. ............... 27 H3 49 58N 5 13W
Lizard Pt., U.K. ........... 27 H3 49 57N 5 13W
Ljubljana, Slovenia ........ 66 E8 46 4N 14 33 E
Llandeilo, U.K. ............ 26 D6 51 53N 3 59W
Llandovery, U.K. ........... 24 C1 51 59N 3 48W
Llandrindod Wells, U.K. .... 23 H2 52 14N 3 22W
Llandudno, U.K. ............ 26 A6 53 19N 3 50W
Llanelli, U.K. ............. 26 D5 51 41N 4 10W
Llanerchymedd, U.K. ........ 26 A5 53 20N 4 23W
Llanfair Caereinion, U.K. .. 23 G2 52 39N 3 20W
Llanfair Talhaiarn, U.K. ... 26 A6 53 13N 3 37W
Llanfairfechan, U.K. ....... 26 A6 53 15N 3 58W
Llangefni, U.K. ............ 26 A5 53 15N 4 18W
Llangollen, U.K. ........... 23 G2 52 58N 3 11W
Llanidloes, U.K. ........... 24 B1 52 27N 3 31W
Llanllyfni, U.K. ........... 26 A5 53 2N 4 17W
Llano Estacado, U.S.A. ..... 110 D6 33 30N 103 0W
Llanos, S. Amer. ........... 116 C3 5 0N 71 35W
Llanquihue, L., Chile ...... 121 G2 41 10S 72 50W
Llanrhystyd, U.K. .......... 26 C5 52 19N 4 7W
Llantrisant, U.K. .......... 24 C2 51 32N 3 22W
Llantwit-Major, U.K. ....... 24 D2 51 24N 3 29W
Llanwrtyd Wells, U.K. ...... 24 B1 52 7N 3 38W
Llanyblodwel, U.K. ......... 23 G2 52 48N 3 8W
Llanymynech, U.K. .......... 23 G2 52 47N 3 5W
Lleida, Spain .............. 69 B6 41 37N 0 39 E
Lleyn Peninsula, U.K. ...... 26 B4 52 51N 4 36W
Lloret de Mar, Spain ....... 69 B7 41 41N 2 53 E
Lloydminster, Canada ....... 108 C9 53 17N 110 0W
Llullaillaco, Volcán, S. Amer. .. 121 E3 24 43S 68 30W
Lobatse, Botswana .......... 97 K5 25 12S 25 40 E
Lobito, Angola ............. 97 G2 12 18S 13 35 E
Lochaber, U.K. ............. 18 J7 56 59N 5 1W
Lochboisdale, U.K. ......... 18 H3 57 9N 7 20W
Loches, France ............. 68 C4 47 7N 1 0 E
Lochgilphead, U.K. ......... 20 B5 56 2N 5 26W
Lochinver, U.K. ............ 18 F7 58 9N 5 14W
Lochmaben, U.K. ............ 22 B2 55 8N 3 27W
Lochmaddy, U.K. ............ 18 G3 57 36N 7 10W
Lochnagar, U.K. ............ 19 J11 56 57N 3 15W
Lochy, L., U.K. ............ 19 J8 57 0N 4 53W
Lock Haven, U.S.A. ......... 112 E9 41 8N 77 28W

Lockerbie, U.K. ............ 21 D9 55 7N 3 21W
Loddon, U.K. ............... 25 A12 52 32N 1 31 E
Łódź, Poland ............... 67 C10 51 45N 19 27 E
Lofoten, Norway ............ 63 D6 68 30N 14 0 E
Loftus, U.K. ............... 22 C7 54 34N 0 53W
Logan, Ohio, U.S.A. ........ 112 F6 39 32N 82 25W
Logan, Utah, U.S.A. ........ 110 B4 41 44N 111 50W
Logan, W. Va., U.S.A. ...... 112 G7 37 51N 81 59W
Logan, Mt., Canada ......... 108 B5 60 34N 140 23W
Logansport, U.S.A. ......... 112 E4 40 45N 86 22W
Logroño, Spain ............. 69 A4 42 28N 2 27W
Lohardaga, India ........... 85 H14 23 27N 84 45 E
Loir →, France ............. 68 C3 47 33N 0 32W
Loire →, France ............ 68 C2 47 16N 2 10W
Loja, Ecuador .............. 120 C2 3 59S 79 16W
Lombárdia □, Italy ......... 68 D8 45 40N 9 30 E
Lomblen, Indonesia ......... 83 D4 8 30S 123 32 E
Lombok, Indonesia .......... 83 D3 8 45S 116 30 E
Lomé, Togo ................. 94 G6 6 9N 1 20 E
Lomond, L., U.K. ........... 20 B6 56 8N 4 38W
Łomża, Poland .............. 67 B12 53 10N 22 2 E
London, Canada ............. 109 D11 42 59N 81 15W
London, U.K. ............... 25 D8 51 30N 0 3W
Londonderry, U.K. .......... 28 A7 55 0N 7 20W
Londonderry □, U.K. ........ 28 B7 55 0N 7 20W
Londonderry, C., Australia . 98 C4 13 45S 126 55 E
Londrina, Brazil ........... 121 E4 23 18S 51 10W
Long Beach, U.S.A. ......... 110 D3 33 47N 118 11W
Long Bennington, U.K. ...... 23 G7 52 59N 0 44W
Long Branch, U.S.A. ........ 113 E11 40 18N 74 0W
Long Clawson, U.K. ......... 23 G7 52 51N 0 55W
Long Crendon, U.K. ......... 25 C7 51 46N 0 59W
Long Eaton, U.K. ........... 23 G6 52 53N 1 15W
Long I., Bahamas ........... 115 C9 23 20N 75 10W
Long I., Ireland ........... 30 F3 51 30N 9 34W
Long I., U.S.A. ............ 113 E11 40 45N 73 30W
Long Itchington, U.K. ...... 23 H6 52 16N 1 22W
Long Melford, U.K. ......... 25 B10 52 4N 0 45 E
Long Mynd, The, U.K. ....... 23 G3 52 35N 2 50W
Long Preston, U.K. ......... 22 D4 54 2N 2 14W
Long Sutton, U.K. .......... 23 G9 52 48N 0 7 E
Long Xuyen, Vietnam ........ 83 B2 10 19N 105 28 E
Longford, Ireland .......... 28 D6 53 43N 7 49W
Longford, U.K. ............. 24 C4 51 54N 2 14W
Longford □, Ireland ........ 28 D6 53 42N 7 45W
Longframlington, U.K. ...... 22 B5 55 18N 1 47W
Longhoughton, U.K. ......... 22 B5 55 26N 1 37W
Longlac, Canada ............ 109 D11 49 45N 86 25W
Longreach, Australia ....... 98 E7 23 28S 144 14 E
Longridge, U.K. ............ 23 E3 53 50N 2 35W
Longton, U.K. .............. 23 E3 53 44N 2 48W
Longtown, Cumb., U.K. ...... 22 B3 55 1N 2 58W
Longtown, Hereford, U.K. ... 24 C3 51 58N 2 59W
Longview, Tex., U.S.A. ..... 111 D8 32 30N 94 44W
Longview, Wash., U.S.A. .... 110 A2 46 8N 122 57W
Lons-le-Saunier, France .... 68 C6 46 40N 5 31 E
Looe, U.K. ................. 27 G5 50 22N 4 28W
Loop Hd., Ireland .......... 30 C3 52 34N 9 56W
Lop Nur, China ............. 80 B4 40 20N 90 10 E
Lopez, C., Gabon ........... 90 G4 0 47S 8 40 E
Lorain, U.S.A. ............. 112 E6 41 28N 82 11W
Loralai, Pakistan .......... 84 D6 30 20N 68 41 E
Lorca, Spain ............... 69 D5 37 41N 1 42W
Lord Howe I., Pac. Oc. ..... 99 G10 31 33S 159 6 E
Lord Howe Ridge, Pac. Oc. .. 99 H12 30 0S 162 30 E
Lordsburg, U.S.A. .......... 110 D5 32 21N 108 43W
Lorestān □, Iran ........... 86 C6 33 20N 47 0 E
Lorient, France ............ 68 C2 47 45N 3 23W
Lorn, U.K. ................. 20 B5 56 26N 5 10W
Lorn, Firth of, U.K. ....... 20 B4 56 20N 5 40W
Lorraine, France ........... 68 B7 48 53N 6 0 E
Los Alamos, U.S.A. ......... 110 C5 35 53N 106 19W
Los Andes, Chile ........... 121 F2 32 50S 70 40W
Los Angeles, Chile ......... 121 F2 37 28S 72 23W
Los Angeles, U.S.A. ........ 110 D3 34 4N 118 15W
Los Mochis, Mexico ......... 114 B3 25 45N 108 57W
Los Roques Is., Venezuela .. 120 A3 11 50N 66 45W
Lossiemouth, U.K. .......... 19 G11 57 42N 3 17W
Lostwithiel, U.K. .......... 27 G4 50 24N 4 32W
Lot →, France .............. 68 D4 44 18N 0 20 E
Lota, Chile ................ 121 F2 37 5S 73 10W
Loughborough, U.K. ......... 23 G6 52 47N 1 11W
Loughrea, Ireland .......... 30 B5 53 12N 8 33W
Loughros More B., Ireland .. 28 B4 54 48N 8 32W
Louis Trichardt, S. Africa . 97 J5 23 1S 29 43 E
Louis XIV, Pte., Canada .... 109 C12 54 37N 79 45W
Louisa, U.S.A. ............. 112 F6 38 7N 82 36W
Louiseville, Canada ........ 113 B11 46 20N 72 56W
Louisiade Arch., Papua N. G. .. 98 C9 11 10S 153 0 E
Louisiana □, U.S.A. ........ 111 D8 30 50N 92 0W
Louisville, U.S.A. ......... 112 F5 38 15N 85 46W
Lourdes, France ............ 68 E3 43 6N 0 3W
Louth, Ireland ............. 29 D8 53 58N 6 32W
Louth, U.K. ................ 23 F8 53 22N 0 1W
Louth □, Ireland ........... 29 D8 53 56N 6 34W
Lowell, U.S.A. ............. 113 D12 42 38N 71 19W
Lower Beeding, U.K. ........ 25 D8 51 2N 0 15W
Lower Saxony =
  Niedersachsen □, Germany .. 66 B5 52 50N 9 0 E
Lower Tunguska →, Russia ... 79 C10 65 48N 88 4 E
Lowestoft, U.K. ............ 25 B12 52 29N 1 45 E
Lowick, U.K. ............... 22 A5 55 39N 1 58W
Lowville, U.S.A. ........... 113 D10 43 47N 75 29W
Loyauté, Îs., N. Cal. ...... 99 E12 20 50S 166 30 E
Lualaba →, Dem. Rep. of
  the Congo ................ 96 D5 0 26N 25 30 E
Luanda, Angola ............. 96 F2 8 50S 13 15 E
Luang Prabang, Laos ........ 83 B2 19 52N 102 10 E
Luangwa →, Zambia .......... 97 G6 14 25S 30 25 E
Luanshya, Zambia ........... 97 G5 13 3S 28 28 E
Luapula →, Africa .......... 96 F5 9 26S 28 33 E
Luarca, Spain .............. 69 A2 43 32N 6 32W
Lubbock, U.S.A. ............ 110 D6 33 35N 101 51W
Lübeck, Germany ............ 66 B6 53 52N 10 40 E
Lublin, Poland ............. 67 C12 51 12N 22 38 E
Lubumbashi, Dem. Rep. of
  the Congo ................ 97 G5 11 40S 27 28 E
Lucania, Mt., Canada ....... 108 B5 61 1N 140 27W
Luce Bay, U.K. ............. 20 E6 54 45N 4 48W
Lucea, Jamaica ............. 114 a 18 25N 78 10W
Lucena, Phil. .............. 83 B4 13 56N 121 37 E
Lucknow, India ............. 85 F12 26 50N 81 0 E
Lüda = Dalian, China ....... 81 C7 38 50N 121 40 E
Lüderitz, Namibia .......... 97 K3 26 41S 15 8 E
Ludgershall, U.K. .......... 24 D5 51 15N 1 37W
Ludgvan, U.K. .............. 27 G2 50 9N 5 30W
Ludhiana, India ............ 84 D9 30 57N 75 56 E
Ludington, U.S.A. .......... 112 D4 43 57N 86 27W
Ludlow, U.K. ............... 23 H3 52 22N 2 42W
Ludwigshafen, Germany ...... 66 D5 49 29N 8 26 E
Lufkin, U.S.A. ............. 111 D8 31 21N 94 44W
Luga, Russia ............... 72 C4 58 40N 29 55 E
Lugano, Switz. ............. 66 E5 46 1N 8 57 E
Lugansk, Ukraine ........... 73 E6 48 38N 39 15 E
Lugnaquilla, Ireland ....... 31 C10 52 58N 6 28W
Lugo, Spain ................ 69 A2 43 2N 7 35W
Lugwardine, U.K. ........... 24 B3 52 4N 2 39W

Luing · Mende

Luing, U.K. .......... 20 B4 56 14N 5 39W
Lule älv →, Sweden .... 63 D8 65 35N 22 10 E
Luleå, Sweden ........ 63 D8 65 35N 22 10 E
Lundy, U.K. .......... 27 E4 51 10N 4 41W
Lune →, U.K. ......... 23 D3 54 0N 2 51W
Lüneburger Heide, Germany 66 B6 53 10N 10 12 E
Lunéville, France ..... 68 B7 48 36N 6 30 E
Luni →, India ........ 84 G7 24 41N 71 14 E
Luofu, Dem. Rep. of the Congo 96 E5 0 10S 29 15 E
Luoyang, China ....... 81 C6 34 40N 112 26 E
Luray, U.S.A. ........ 112 F8 38 40N 78 28W
Lurgan, U.K. ......... 29 C9 54 28N 6 19W
Lusaka, Zambia ....... 97 H5 15 28S 28 16 E
Lūt, Dasht-e, Iran .... 87 D9 31 30N 58 0 E
Luton, U.K. .......... 25 C8 51 53N 0 24W
Łutselk'e, Canada .... 108 B8 62 24N 110 44W
Lutsk, Ukraine ....... 67 C13 50 50N 25 15 E
Lutterworth, U.K. ..... 23 H6 52 28N 1 12W
Luvua →, Dem. Rep. of the Congo 96 G6 6 50S 27 30 E
Luxembourg, Lux. ..... 65 E6 49 37N 6 9 E
Luxembourg ■, Europe 65 E6 49 45N 6 0 E
Luxor, Egypt ......... 95 C12 25 41N 32 38 E
Luzern, Switz. ....... 66 E5 47 3N 8 18 E
Luzhou, China ....... 80 D5 28 52N 105 20 E
Luziânia, Brazil ...... 122 C1 16 20S 48 0W
Luzon, Phil. ......... 83 B4 16 0N 121 0 E
Lvov, Ukraine ....... 67 D13 49 50N 24 0 E
Lyakhov Is., Russia ... 79 B16 73 40N 141 0 E
Lybster, U.K. ........ 19 F11 58 18N 3 15W
Lydd, U.K. .......... 25 E10 50 57N 0 55 E
Lydford, U.K. ........ 27 F5 50 38N 4 8W
Lydham, U.K. ........ 23 G3 52 31N 2 58W
Lyme B., U.K. ........ 24 E3 50 42N 2 53W
Lyme Regis, U.K. ..... 24 E3 50 43N 2 57W
Lyminge, U.K. ....... 25 D11 51 7N 1 6 E
Lymington, U.K. ...... 24 E5 50 45N 1 32W
Lymm, U.K. .......... 23 F4 53 23N 2 29W
Lympne, U.K. ........ 25 D11 51 4N 1 2 E
Lynchburg, U.S.A. .... 112 G8 37 25N 79 9W
Lyndhurst, U.K. ...... 24 E5 50 52N 1 35W
Lyneham, U.K. ....... 24 C5 51 30N 1 58W
Lynmouth, U.K. ...... 27 D3 51 13N 3 49W
Lynn Lake, Canada ... 108 C9 56 51N 101 3W
Lynton, U.K. ......... 24 D1 51 13N 3 50W
Lyonnais, France ..... 68 D6 45 45N 4 15 E
Lyons, France ........ 68 D6 45 46N 4 50 E
Lysva, Russia ........ 72 C10 58 7N 57 49 E
Lysychansk, Ukraine .. 73 E6 48 55N 38 30 E
Lytchett Minster, U.K. . 24 E4 50 44N 2 4W
Lytham St. Anne's, U.K. 23 E2 53 45N 3 0W
Lythe, U.K. .......... 22 C7 54 31N 0 41W
Lyubertsy, Russia .... 72 C6 55 39N 37 50 E

M

Ma'ān, Jordan ....... 86 D3 30 12N 35 44 E
Ma'anshan, China .... 81 C6 31 44N 118 29 E
Maas →, Neths. ...... 65 C4 51 45N 4 32 E
Maastricht, Neths. .... 65 D5 50 50N 5 40 E
Mablethorpe, U.K. .... 23 F9 53 20N 0 15 E
Macaé, Brazil ........ 122 D2 22 20S 41 43W
McAlester, U.S.A. .... 111 D7 34 56N 95 46W
McAllen, U.S.A. ...... 110 E7 26 12N 98 14W
MacAlpine L., Canada . 108 B9 66 32N 102 45W
Macapá, Brazil ....... 120 B4 0 5N 51 4W
Macau, Brazil ........ 120 C6 5 15S 36 40W
Macau, China ........ 81 D6 22 12N 113 33 E
Macclesfield, U.K. .... 23 F4 53 15N 2 8W
M'Clintock Chan., Canada 108 A9 72 0N 102 0W
M'Clure Str., Canada . 54 B2 75 0N 119 0W
McComb, U.S.A. ...... 111 D8 31 15N 90 27W
McCook, U.S.A. ...... 110 B6 40 12N 100 38W
McDonald Is., Ind. Oc. 53 G13 53 0S 73 0 E
MacDonnell Ranges, Australia 98 E5 23 40S 133 0 E
Macduff, U.K. ........ 19 G12 57 40N 2 31W
Macedonia, Greece ... 71 D10 40 39N 22 0 E
Macedonia ■, Europe . 71 D9 41 53N 21 40 E
Maceió, Brazil ....... 122 A3 9 40S 35 41W
Macgillycuddy's Reeks, Ireland 30 E3 51 58N 9 45W
Mach, Pakistan ...... 84 E5 29 50N 67 20 E
Machakos, Kenya ..... 96 E7 1 30S 37 15 E
Machala, Ecuador .... 120 C2 3 20S 79 57W
Machars, The, U.K. ... 20 E6 54 46N 4 30W
Machias, U.S.A. ...... 113 C14 44 43N 67 28W
Machilipatnam, India . 85 L12 16 12N 81 8 E
Machrihanish, U.K. ... 20 D4 55 25N 5 43W
Machynlleth, U.K. .... 24 A1 52 35N 3 50W
Mackay, Australia .... 98 E8 21 8S 149 11 E
Mackay, L., Australia .. 98 E4 22 30S 129 0 E
McKeesport, U.S.A. ... 112 E8 40 21N 79 52W
Mackenzie, Canada ... 108 C7 55 20N 123 5W
Mackenzie →, Canada . 108 B6 69 10N 134 20W
Mackenzie Mts., Canada 108 B6 64 0N 130 0W
Mackinaw City, U.S.A. 112 C5 45 47N 84 44W
McKinley, Mt., U.S.A. . 108 B4 63 4N 151 0W
McKinley Sea, Arctic .. 54 A7 82 0N 0 0W
McMinnville, U.S.A. ... 110 A2 45 13N 123 12W
McMurdo Sd., Antarctica 55 D11 77 0S 170 0 E
Mâcon, France ....... 68 C6 46 19N 4 50 E
Macon, U.S.A. ....... 111 D10 32 51N 83 38W
McPherson, U.S.A. ... 110 C7 38 22N 97 40W
Macquarie Is., Pac. Oc. 102 N7 54 36S 158 55 E
Macroom, Ireland .... 30 E5 51 54N 8 57W
Madagascar ■, Africa . 97 J9 20 0S 47 0 E
Madang, Papua N. G. . 98 B8 5 12S 145 49 E
Madeira, Atl. Oc. ..... 94 B2 32 50N 17 0W
Madeira →, Brazil .... 120 C4 3 22S 58 45W
Madeley, U.K. ....... 23 F4 53 0N 2 20W
Madhya Pradesh □, India 84 J11 22 50N 78 0 E
Madison, Ind., U.S.A. . 112 F5 38 44N 85 23W
Madison, S. Dak., U.S.A. 111 B7 44 0N 97 7W
Madison, Wis., U.S.A. . 111 B9 43 4N 89 24W
Madisonville, U.S.A. .. 112 G4 37 20N 87 30W
Madiun, Indonesia ... 83 D3 7 38S 111 32 E
Madley, U.K. ......... 24 B3 52 2N 2 51W
Madras = Chennai, India 84 N12 13 8N 80 19 E
Madre de Dios →, Bolivia 120 D3 10 59S 66 8W
Madre de Dios, I., Chile 121 H2 50 20S 75 10W
Madre Occidental, Sierra, Mexico 114 B3 27 0N 107 0W
Madre Oriental, Sierra, Mexico 114 C5 25 0N 100 0W
Madrid, Spain ....... 69 B4 40 25N 3 45W
Madura, Indonesia ... 83 D3 7 30S 114 0 E
Madurai, India ....... 84 Q11 9 55N 78 10 E
Maebashi, Japan ..... 82 E6 36 24N 139 4 E
Maesteg, U.K. ....... 24 C1 51 36N 3 40W
Mafia I., Tanzania .... 96 F7 7 45S 39 50 E
Magadan, Russia .... 79 D17 59 38N 150 50 E
Magangué, Colombia . 120 B2 9 14N 74 45W
Magdalen Is., Canada 109 D13 47 30N 61 40W
Magdalena →, Colombia 120 A2 11 6N 74 51W
Magdeburg, Germany . 66 B6 52 7N 11 38 E

Magee, I., U.K. ...... 29 B10 54 48N 5 43W
Magelang, Indonesia . 83 D3 7 29S 110 13 E
Magellan's Str., Chile . 121 H2 52 30S 75 0W
Maggiore, Lago, Italy . 68 D8 45 57N 8 39 E
Maggotty, Jamaica ... 114 a 18 9N 77 46W
Magherafelt, U.K. .... 29 B8 54 45N 6 37W
Maghreb, N. Afr. ..... 90 C3 32 0N 5 0W
Maghull, U.K. ........ 23 E3 53 31N 2 57W
Magnetic Pole (North), Canada 54 A2 80 30N 107 0W
Magnetic Pole (South), Antarctica 55 C9 64 8S 138 8 E
Magnitogorsk, Russia . 72 D10 53 27N 59 4 E
Magog, Canada ...... 113 C11 45 18N 72 9W
Magwe, Burma ....... 85 J19 20 10N 95 0 E
Mahābād, Iran ....... 86 B6 36 50N 45 45 E
Mahajanga, Madag. .. 97 H9 15 40S 46 25 E
Mahakam →, Indonesia 83 D3 0 35S 117 17 E
Mahalapye, Botswana 97 J5 23 1S 26 51 E
Mahanadi →, India ... 85 J15 20 20N 86 25 E
Maharashtra □, India . 84 J9 20 30N 75 30 E
Mahdia, Tunisia ..... 95 A8 35 28N 11 0 E
Mahesana, India ..... 84 H8 23 39N 72 26 E
Mahilyow, Belarus ... 67 B16 53 55N 30 18 E
Mai-Ndombe, L., Dem. Rep. of the Congo 96 E3 2 0S 18 20 E
Maiden Bradley, U.K. . 24 D4 51 9N 2 17W
Maiden Newton, U.K. . 24 E3 50 46N 2 34W
Maidenhead, U.K. .... 25 C7 51 31N 0 42W
Maidstone, U.K. ...... 25 D10 51 16N 0 32 E
Maiduguri, Nigeria ... 95 F8 12 0N 13 20 E
Maijdi, Bangla. ...... 85 H17 22 48N 91 10 E
Main →, Germany .... 66 C5 50 0N 8 18 E
Main →, U.K. ........ 29 B9 54 48N 6 18W
Maine, France ....... 68 C3 48 20N 0 15W
Maine □, U.S.A. ..... 113 C13 45 20N 69 0W
Maine →, Ireland .... 30 D3 52 9N 9 45W
Mainland, Orkney, U.K. 19 E11 58 59N 3 8W
Mainland, Shet., U.K. 18 B15 60 15N 1 22W
Mainz, Germany ..... 66 C5 50 1N 8 14 E
Maiquetía, Venezuela 120 A3 10 36N 66 57W
Majorca = Mallorca, Spain 69 C7 39 30N 3 0 E
Makale, Indonesia .... 83 D3 3 6S 119 51 E
Makasar, Str. of, Indonesia 83 D3 1 0S 118 20 E
Makgadikgadi Salt Pans, Botswana 97 J5 20 40S 25 45 E
Makhachkala, Russia . 73 F8 43 0N 47 30 E
Makran Coast Range, Pakistan 84 G4 25 40N 64 0 E
Makurdi, Nigeria ..... 94 G7 7 43N 8 35 E
Mal B., Ireland ...... 30 C4 52 50N 9 30W
Malabar Coast, India . 84 P9 11 0N 75 0 E
Malacca, Str. of, Indonesia 83 C2 3 0N 101 0 E
Málaga, Spain ....... 69 D3 36 43N 4 23W
Malahide, Ireland .... 29 E9 53 26N 6 9W
Malaita, Solomon Is. . 99 B11 9 0S 161 0 E
Malakâl, Sudan ...... 95 G12 9 33N 31 40 E
Malakula, Vanuatu ... 99 D12 16 15S 167 30 E
Malang, Indonesia ... 83 D3 7 59S 112 45 E
Malanje, Angola ..... 96 F3 9 36S 16 17 E
Mälaren, Sweden .... 63 F7 59 30N 17 10 E
Malatya, Turkey ...... 73 G6 38 25N 38 20 E
Malawi ■, Africa ..... 97 G6 11 55S 34 0 E
Malay Pen., Asia ..... 74 J14 7 25N 100 0 E
Malāyer, Iran ........ 86 C7 34 19N 48 51 E
Malaysia ■, Asia ..... 83 C4 5 0N 110 0 E
Malden I., Kiribati ... 103 H12 4 3S 155 1W
Maldives ■, Ind. Oc. . 74 J11 5 0N 73 0 E
Maldon, U.K. ........ 25 C10 51 44N 0 42 E
Maldonado, Uruguay . 121 F4 34 59S 55 0W
Malegaon, India ..... 84 J9 20 30N 74 38 E
Malham Tarn, U.K. ... 22 C4 54 6N 2 10W
Malheur L., U.S.A. ... 110 B3 43 20N 118 48W
Mali ■, Africa ....... 94 E5 17 0N 3 0W
Malin Hd., Ireland ... 28 A7 55 23N 7 23W
Malin Pen., Ireland .. 29 A7 55 20N 7 17W
Malindi, Kenya ...... 96 E8 3 12S 40 5 E
Mallaig, U.K. ........ 18 H6 57 0N 5 50W
Mallorca, Spain ...... 69 C7 39 30N 3 0 E
Mallow, Ireland ...... 30 D5 52 8N 8 39W
Malmesbury, U.K. .... 24 C4 51 35N 2 5W
Malmö, Sweden ...... 63 F6 55 36N 12 59 E
Malone, U.S.A. ...... 113 C10 44 51N 74 18W
Malpas, U.K. ........ 23 F3 53 1N 2 45W
Malpelo, I. de, Colombia 103 G19 3 3N 81 35W
Malta ■, Europe ..... 70 a 35 55N 14 26 E
Maltby, U.K. ........ 23 F6 53 25N 1 12W
Malton, U.K. ........ 22 D7 54 8N 0 49W
Malvinas, Is. = Falkland Is. ☒, Atl. Oc. 121 H4 51 30S 59 0W
Mamoré →, Bolivia .. 120 D3 10 23S 65 53W
Mamoudzou, Mayotte 91 H8 12 48S 45 14 E
Man, Ivory C. ....... 94 G4 7 30N 7 40W
Man, I. of, U.K. ..... 29 C12 54 15N 4 30W
Manacles, The, U.K. . 27 G3 50 1N 5 5W
Manado, Indonesia ... 83 C4 1 29N 124 51 E
Managua, Nic. ...... 114 E7 12 6N 86 20W
Manas, China ....... 80 B3 44 17N 85 56 E
Manati, Puerto Rico .. 115 d 18 26N 66 29W
Manaus, Brazil ...... 120 C3 3 0S 60 0W
Manby, U.K. ......... 23 F9 53 21N 0 6 E
Manchester, U.K. .... 23 F4 53 29N 2 12W
Manchester, U.S.A. .. 113 D12 42 59N 71 28W
Manchuria, China .... 81 B7 45 0N 125 0 E
Manchurian Plain, China 74 E16 47 0N 124 0 E
Mandal, Norway ..... 63 F5 58 2N 7 25 E
Mandalay, Burma .... 85 J20 22 0N 96 4 E
Mandan, U.S.A. ..... 110 A6 46 50N 100 54W
Mandeville, Jamaica . 114 a 18 2N 77 31W
Mandla, India ....... 85 H12 22 39N 80 30 E
Mandsaur, India ..... 84 G9 24 3N 75 8 E
Mandvi, India ........ 84 H6 22 51N 69 22 E
Manea, U.K. ......... 23 H9 52 29N 0 10 E
Manebeiras, Chapada das, Brazil 122 B1 10 0S 46 30W
Mangalore, India .... 84 N9 12 55N 74 47 E
Mangnai, China ...... 80 C4 37 52N 91 43 E
Mangole, Indonesia .. 83 D4 1 50S 125 55 E
Mangotsfield, U.K. ... 24 D4 51 29N 2 30W
Manhattan, U.S.A. ... 111 C7 39 11N 96 35W
Manica, Mozam. ..... 97 H6 18 58S 32 59 E
Manicoré, Brazil ..... 120 C3 5 48S 61 16W
Manicouagan →, Canada 109 D13 49 30N 68 30W
Manicouagan, Rés., Canada 109 C13 51 5N 68 40W
Manihiki, Cook Is. ... 103 J11 10 24S 161 1W
Manila, Phil. ........ 83 B4 14 40N 121 3 E
Manipur □, India ..... 85 G19 25 0N 94 0 E
Manisa, Turkey ...... 73 G4 38 38N 27 30 E
Manistee, U.S.A. .... 112 C4 44 15N 86 19W
Manistee →, U.S.A. .. 112 C4 44 15N 86 21W
Manistique, U.S.A. ... 112 C4 45 57N 86 15W
Manitoba □, Canada . 108 C10 53 30N 97 0W
Manitoba, L., Canada 108 C10 51 0N 98 45W
Manitou Is., U.S.A. .. 112 C4 45 8N 86 0W
Manitoulin I., Canada 109 D11 45 40N 82 30W
Manitowoc, U.S.A. ... 112 C4 44 5N 87 40W
Manizales, Colombia . 120 B2 5 5N 75 32W
Mankato, U.S.A. ..... 111 B8 44 10N 94 0W

Mannar, Sri Lanka ... 84 Q11 9 1N 79 54 E
Mannar, G. of, Asia .. 84 Q11 8 30N 79 0 E
Mannheim, Germany . 66 D5 49 29N 8 29 E
Manning, Canada .... 108 C8 56 53N 117 39W
Manningtree, U.K. .... 25 C11 51 56N 1 5 E
Manokwari, Indonesia 83 D5 0 54S 134 0 E
Manosque, France ... 68 E6 43 49N 5 47 E
Manresa, Spain ...... 69 B11 61 20N 80 0W
Mansel I., Canada ... 109 B11 62 0N 80 0W
Mansfield, U.K. ...... 23 F6 53 9N 1 11W
Mansfield, U.S.A. .... 112 E6 40 45N 82 31W
Mansfield Woodhouse, U.K. 23 F6 53 11N 1 12W
Manta, Ecuador ...... 120 C1 1 0S 80 40W
Mantes-la-Jolie, France 68 B4 48 58N 1 41 E
Mantiqueira, Serra da, Brazil 116 F6 22 0S 44 0W
Manton, U.K. ........ 23 G7 52 38N 0 41W
Manton, U.S.A. ...... 112 C5 44 25N 85 24W
Mántova, Italy ....... 70 B4 45 9N 10 48 E
Manuel Alves →, Brazil 122 B1 11 19S 48 28W
Manzai, Pakistan .... 84 C7 32 12N 70 15 E
Manzanillo, Cuba .... 115 C9 20 20N 77 31W
Manzanillo, Mexico .. 114 D4 19 0N 104 20W
Manzhouli, China .... 81 B6 49 35N 117 25 E
Maoming, China ..... 81 D6 21 50N 110 54 E
Mapam Yumco, China 80 C3 30 45N 81 28 E
Maputo, Mozam. ..... 97 K6 25 58S 32 32 E
Maputo, B. de, Mozam. 90 J7 25 50S 32 45 E
Maquinchao, Argentina 121 G3 41 15S 68 50W
Mar, Serra do, Brazil 116 F6 25 30S 49 0W
Mar Chiquita, L., Argentina 121 F3 30 40S 62 50W
Mar del Plata, Argentina 121 F4 38 0S 57 30W
Marabá, Brazil ....... 120 C5 5 20S 49 5W
Maracá, I. de, Brazil . 120 B4 2 10N 50 30W
Maracaibo, Venezuela 120 A2 10 40N 71 37W
Maracaibo, L. de, Venezuela 120 B2 9 40N 71 30W
Maracay, Venezuela .. 120 A3 10 15N 67 28W
Maradi, Niger ........ 94 F7 13 29N 7 20 E
Marajó, I. de, Brazil .. 120 C5 1 0S 49 30W
Maranhão □, Brazil .. 120 C5 5 0S 46 0W
Marañón →, Peru .... 120 C2 4 30S 73 35W
Marazion, U.K. ....... 27 G3 50 7N 5 29W
Marbella, Spain ...... 69 D3 36 30N 4 57W
March, U.K. ......... 23 G9 52 33N 0 5 E
Marche, France ...... 68 C4 46 5N 1 20 E
Marcus I., Pac. Oc. .. 102 E7 24 20N 153 58 E
Marcus Necker Ridge, Pac. Oc. 102 F9 20 0N 175 0 E
Mardan, Pakistan .... 84 B8 34 20N 72 0 E
Marden, U.K. ........ 24 B3 52 7N 2 42W
Mardin, Turkey ...... 73 G7 37 20N 40 43 E
Maree, L., U.K. ...... 18 G7 57 40N 5 26W
Mareham le Fen, U.K. 23 F8 53 7N 0 5W
Marfleet, U.K. ....... 23 E8 53 45N 0 17W
Margarita, I. de, Venezuela 120 A3 11 0N 64 0W
Margate, U.K. ....... 25 D11 51 23N 1 23 E
Margilan, Uzbekistan . 87 A12 40 27N 71 42 E
Märgow, Dasht-e, Afghan. 87 D10 30 40N 62 30 E
Mari El □, Russia .... 72 C8 56 30N 48 0 E
Mariana Trench, Pac. Oc. 102 F6 13 0N 145 0 E
Maribor, Slovenia .... 66 E8 46 36N 15 40 E
Marie Byrd Land, Antarctica 55 D14 79 30S 125 0W
Marie-Galante, Guadeloupe 114 b 15 56N 61 16W
Mariental, Namibia .. 97 J3 24 36S 18 0 E
Marietta, U.S.A. ..... 112 F7 39 25N 81 27W
Marília, Brazil ....... 120 E4 22 13S 50 0W
Marinette, U.S.A. .... 112 C4 45 6N 87 38W
Marion, Ill., U.S.A. ... 111 C9 37 44N 88 56W
Marion, Ind., U.S.A. . 112 E5 40 32N 85 40W
Marion, Ohio, U.S.A. . 112 E6 40 35N 83 8W
Mariupol, Ukraine ... 73 E6 47 5N 37 31 E
Market Bosworth, U.K. 23 G6 52 38N 1 24W
Market Deeping, U.K. 23 G8 52 41N 0 19W
Market Drayton, U.K. 23 G4 52 54N 2 29W
Market Harborough, U.K. 23 H7 52 29N 0 55W
Market Lavington, U.K. 24 D5 51 17N 1 58W
Market Rasen, U.K. .. 23 F8 53 24N 0 20W
Market Weighton, U.K. 23 E7 53 52N 0 40W
Markfield, U.K. ...... 23 G6 52 42N 1 17W
Markham, Mt., Antarctica 55 E11 83 0S 164 0 E
Marks Tey, U.K. ..... 25 C10 51 52N 0 49 E
Marlborough, U.K. ... 24 D5 51 25N 1 43W
Marlborough Downs, U.K. 24 D5 51 27N 1 53W
Marlow, U.K. ........ 25 C7 51 34N 0 46W
Marmara, Sea of, Turkey 71 D13 40 45N 28 15 E
Marmaris, Turkey .... 86 B2 36 50N 28 14 E
Marmora, Canada .... 112 C9 44 28N 77 41W
Marne →, France .... 68 B5 48 48N 2 24 E
Marnhull, U.K. ....... 24 E4 50 57N 2 19W
Maroua, Cameroon ... 95 F8 10 40N 14 20 E
Marple, U.K. ........ 23 F4 53 24N 2 4W
Marquesas Is., Pac. Oc. 103 H14 9 30S 140 0W
Marquette, U.S.A. ... 112 B4 46 33N 87 24W
Marquis, St. Lucia ... 115 f 14 2N 60 54W
Marrakesh, Morocco . 94 B4 31 9N 8 0W
Marree, Australia .... 98 F6 29 39S 138 1 E
Marsá Matrûh, Egypt 95 B11 31 19N 27 9 E
Marseilles, France ... 68 E6 43 18N 5 23 E
Marsh I., U.S.A. ..... 111 E8 29 34N 91 53W
Marshall, U.S.A. ..... 111 D7 32 33N 94 23W
Marshall Is. ■, Pac. Oc. 102 G9 9 0N 171 0 E
Marshfield, U.K. ..... 24 D4 51 28N 2 19W
Marske by the Sea, U.K. 22 C7 54 36N 1 0W
Marston Moor, U.K. .. 23 E6 53 58N 1 17W
Martaban, Burma .... 85 L20 16 30N 97 35 E
Martaban, G. of, Burma 85 L20 16 5N 96 30 E
Martham, U.K. ....... 25 A12 52 42N 1 38 E
Martha's Vineyard, U.S.A. 113 E12 41 25N 70 38W
Martigues, France ... 68 E6 43 24N 5 4 E
Martinique ☒, W. Indies 114 c 14 40N 61 0W
Martin's Bay, Barbados 115 g 13 12N 59 29W
Martinsburg, U.S.A. .. 112 F9 39 27N 77 58W
Martinsville, U.S.A. .. 112 F4 39 26N 86 25W
Martley, U.K. ........ 23 H4 52 15N 2 21W
Martock, U.K. ....... 24 E3 50 58N 2 46W
Marwar, India ........ 84 G8 25 43N 73 45 E
Mary, Turkmenistan .. 87 B10 37 40N 61 50 E
Maryborough, Australia 98 F9 25 31S 152 37 E
Maryland □, U.S.A. .. 112 F9 39 0N 76 30W
Maryport, U.K. ...... 22 C2 54 44N 3 28W
Marystown, Canada .. 109 D14 47 10N 55 10W
Marytavy, U.K. ...... 27 F5 50 36N 4 7W
Marzūq, Libya ....... 95 C8 25 53N 13 57 E
Masan, S. Korea ..... 81 C7 35 11N 128 32 E
Masandam, Ra's, Oman 88 B6 26 30N 56 30 E
Masaya, Nic. ........ 114 E7 12 0N 86 7W
Masbate, Phil. ....... 83 B4 12 21N 123 36 E
Mascara, Algeria ..... 94 A6 35 26N 0 6 E
Maseru, Lesotho ..... 97 K5 29 18S 27 30 E
Masham, U.K. ....... 22 D5 54 14N 1 39W
Mashhad, Iran ....... 87 B9 36 20N 59 35 E
Mashonaland, Zimbabwe 97 H6 16 30S 31 0 E
Maşīrah, Oman ...... 88 C6 21 0N 58 50 E
Masjed Soleyman, Iran 86 D7 31 55N 49 18 E
Mask, L., Ireland .... 28 D3 53 36N 9 22W
Mason City, U.S.A. .. 111 B8 43 9N 93 12W
Massachusetts □, U.S.A. 113 D11 42 30N 72 0W
Massawa, Eritrea .... 89 D2 15 35N 39 53 E
Massena, U.S.A. ..... 113 C10 44 56N 74 54W
Massiah Street, Barbados 115 g 13 9N 59 29W

Massif Central, France 68 D5 44 55N 3 0 E
Massillon, U.S.A. .... 112 E7 40 48N 81 32W
Masurian Lakes, Poland 67 B11 53 50N 21 0 E
Masvingo, Zimbabwe . 97 J6 20 8S 30 49 E
Mata Utu, Wall. & F. Is. 99 C15 13 17S 176 8W
Matabeleland, Zimbabwe 97 H5 18 0S 27 0 E
Matadi, Dem. Rep. of the Congo 96 F2 5 52S 13 31 E
Matagalpa, Nic. ...... 114 E7 13 0N 85 58W
Matagami, Canada ... 109 D12 49 45N 77 34W
Matagami, L., Canada 109 D12 49 50N 77 40W
Matagorda I., U.S.A. . 111 E7 28 15N 96 30W
Matamoros, Coahuila, Mexico 114 B5 25 33N 103 15W
Matamoros, Tamaulipas, Mexico 114 B5 25 50N 97 30W
Matane, Canada ..... 109 D13 48 50N 67 33W
Matanzas, Cuba ..... 115 C8 23 0N 81 40W
Matara, Sri Lanka .... 84 S12 5 58N 80 30 E
Mataró, Spain ....... 69 B7 41 32N 2 29 E
Matehuala, Mexico ... 114 C4 23 40N 100 40W
Matera, Italy ........ 70 D7 40 40N 16 36 E
Mathura, India ...... 84 F10 27 30N 77 40 E
Mati, Phil. .......... 83 C4 6 55N 126 15 E
Matlock, U.K. ....... 23 F5 53 9N 1 33W
Mato Grosso □, Brazil 120 D4 14 0S 55 0W
Mato Grosso, Planalto do, Brazil 120 D4 15 0S 55 0W
Mato Grosso do Sul □, Brazil 120 D4 18 0S 55 0W
Maţruḥ, Oman ....... 87 F9 23 37N 58 30 E
Matsue, Japan ....... 82 F3 35 25N 133 10 E
Matsumoto, Japan ... 82 E6 36 15N 138 0 E
Matsusaka, Japan ... 82 F5 34 34N 136 32 E
Matsuyama, Japan ... 82 G3 33 45N 132 45 E
Mattagami →, Canada 109 C11 50 43N 81 29W
Mattancheri, India ... 84 Q10 9 50N 76 15 E
Mattawa, Canada .... 112 B8 46 20N 78 45W
Matterhorn, Switz. ... 66 F4 45 58N 7 39 E
Matthew, I., N. Cal. .. 99 E13 22 29S 171 15 E
Maturín, Venezuela .. 120 B3 9 45N 63 11W
Maubeuge, France ... 68 A6 50 17N 3 57 E
Maudin Sun, Burma . 85 M19 16 0N 94 30 E
Maumee →, U.S.A. .. 112 E6 41 42N 83 28W
Maun, Botswana ..... 97 H4 20 0S 23 26 E
Mauna Kea, U.S.A. .. 110 J17 19 50N 155 28W
Mauna Loa, U.S.A. .. 110 J17 19 30N 155 35W
Mauritania ■, Africa . 94 E3 20 50N 10 0W
Mauritius ■, Ind. Oc. 91 J9 20 0S 57 0 E
Mawgan, U.K. ....... 27 G3 50 4N 5 13W
Maxwellheugh, U.K. . 22 A4 55 35N 2 26W
May Pen, Jamaica ... 114 a 17 58N 77 15W
Mayaguana, Bahamas 115 C10 22 30N 72 44W
Mayagüez, Puerto Rico 115 d 18 12N 67 9W
Maybole, U.K. ....... 20 D6 55 21N 4 42W
Mayfield, E. Susx., U.K. 25 D9 51 1N 0 17 E
Mayfield, Staffs., U.K. 23 F5 53 1N 1 47W
Mayfield, U.S.A. ..... 112 G3 36 44N 88 38W
Maykop, Russia ...... 73 F7 44 35N 40 10 E
Maynooth, Ireland ... 29 E8 53 23N 6 34W
Mayo, Canada ....... 108 B6 63 38N 135 57W
Mayo □, Ireland ..... 28 D3 53 53N 9 3W
Mayon Volcano, Phil. 83 B4 13 15N 123 41 E
Mayotte, Ind. Oc. .... 97 G9 12 50S 45 10 E
Maysville, U.S.A. .... 112 F6 38 39N 83 46W
Māzandarān □, Iran .. 87 B8 36 30N 52 0 E
Mazār-e Sharif, Afghan. 87 B11 36 41N 67 0 E
Mazaruni →, Guyana 120 B4 6 25N 58 35W
Mazatlán, Mexico .... 114 C3 23 13N 106 25W
Mazyr, Belarus ...... 72 D4 51 59N 29 15 E
Mbabane, Swaziland . 97 K6 26 18S 31 6 E
Mbaïki, C.A.R. ....... 96 D3 3 53N 18 1 E
Mbala, Zambia ...... 96 F6 8 46S 31 24 E
Mbale, Uganda ...... 96 D6 1 8N 34 12 E
Mbandaka, Dem. Rep. of the Congo 96 D3 0 1N 18 18 E
Mbanza Ngungu, Dem. Rep. of the Congo 96 F2 5 12S 14 53 E
Mbeya, Tanzania ..... 96 F6 8 54S 33 29 E
Mbuji-Mayi, Dem. Rep. of the Congo 96 F4 6 9S 23 40 E
Mdantsane, S. Africa 97 L5 32 56S 27 46 E
Mead, L., U.S.A. .... 110 C4 36 1N 114 44W
Meadow Lake, Canada 108 C9 54 10N 108 26W
Meadville, U.S.A. .... 112 E7 41 39N 80 9W
Meaford, Canada .... 112 C7 44 36N 80 35W
Mealsgate, U.K. ..... 22 C2 54 47N 3 13W
Measham, U.K. ...... 23 G5 52 43N 1 31W
Meath □, Ireland .... 29 D8 53 40N 6 57W
Meaux, France ...... 68 B5 48 58N 2 50 E
Mecca, Si. Arabia .... 86 F4 21 30N 39 54 E
Mechelen, Belgium ... 65 C4 51 2N 4 29 E
Mecklenburg, Germany 66 B6 53 33N 11 40 E
Medan, Indonesia .... 83 C1 3 40N 98 38 E
Médéa, Algeria ...... 94 A6 36 12N 2 50 E
Medellín, Colombia .. 120 B2 6 15N 75 35W
Medford, U.S.A. ..... 110 B2 42 19N 122 52W
Medicine Hat, Canada 108 D8 50 0N 110 45W
Medina, Si. Arabia ... 86 E4 24 35N 39 52 E
Mediterranean Sea, Europe 90 C5 35 0N 15 0 E
Médoc, France ...... 68 D3 45 10N 0 50W
Medstead, U.K. ...... 24 D6 51 8N 1 3W
Medvezhyegorsk, Russia 72 B5 63 0N 34 25 E
Medway →, U.K. .... 25 D10 51 27N 0 46 E
Meekatharra, Australia 98 F2 26 32S 118 29 E
Meerut, India ........ 84 E10 29 1N 77 42 E
Meghalaya □, India .. 85 G17 25 50N 91 0 E
Meghna →, Bangla. .. 85 H17 22 50N 90 50 E
Meizhou, China ...... 86 B2 36 30N 34 3 E
Mektila, Burma ...... 85 J19 20 53N 95 54 E
Meizhou, China ...... 81 D6 24 16N 116 6 E
Mejillones, Chile .... 121 E2 23 10S 70 30W
Mekele, Ethiopia ..... 88 E2 13 33N 39 30 E
Mekhtar, Pakistan ... 84 D6 30 30N 69 15 E
Meknès, Morocco .... 94 B4 33 57N 5 33W
Mekong →, Asia ..... 83 C2 9 30N 106 15 E
Melaka, Malaysia .... 83 C2 2 15N 102 15 E
Melanesia, Pac. Oc. . 102 H7 4 0S 155 0 E
Melbourn, U.K. ...... 25 B9 52 4N 0 1 E
Melbourne, Australia 98 H8 37 50S 145 0 E
Melbourne, U.K. ..... 23 G6 52 50N 1 25W
Mélèzes →, Canada .. 109 C12 57 40N 69 29W
Melfort, Canada ..... 108 C9 52 50N 104 37W
Melilla, N. Afr. ...... 94 A5 35 21N 2 57W
Melitopol, Ukraine ... 73 E6 46 50N 35 22 E
Melksham, U.K. ..... 24 C4 51 23N 2 8W
Melmerby, U.K. ...... 22 C3 54 45N 2 35W
Melrose, U.K. ....... 22 C4 55 36N 2 43W
Melsonby, U.K. ...... 22 D5 54 29N 1 42W
Melton Constable, U.K. 25 A11 52 52N 1 1 E
Melton Mowbray, U.K. 23 G7 52 47N 0 54W
Melun, France ....... 68 B5 48 32N 2 39 E
Melville, Canada ..... 108 C9 50 55N 102 50W
Melville, I., Australia . 98 C5 11 30S 131 0 E
Melville I., Canada ... 54 B2 75 30N 112 0W
Melville Pen., Canada 109 B11 68 0N 84 0W
Memphis, U.S.A. ..... 111 C9 35 8N 90 3W
Menai Bridge, U.K. .. 26 A5 53 14N 4 10W
Menai Strait, U.K. ... 26 A5 53 11N 4 13W
Mende, France ...... 68 D5 44 31N 3 30 E

**Mendip Hills**                                                                 **Nashville**

| | | | | |
|---|---|---|---|---|
| Mendip Hills, *U.K.* | 24 D3 | 51 17N | 2 40W |
| Mendlesham, *U.K.* | 25 B11 | 52 16N | 1 6 E |
| Mendocino, C., *U.S.A.* | 110 B2 | 40 26N | 124 25W |
| Mendoza, *Argentina* | 121 F3 | 32 50S | 68 52W |
| Mengzi, *China* | 80 D5 | 23 20N | 103 22 E |
| Menominee, *U.S.A.* | 112 C4 | 45 6N | 87 37W |
| Menominee →, *U.S.A.* | 112 C4 | 45 6N | 87 36W |
| Menorca, *Spain* | 69 C8 | 40 0N | 4 0 E |
| Mentawai, Kepulauan, *Indonesia* | 83 D1 | 2 0S | 99 0 E |
| Merca, *Somali Rep.* | 88 G3 | 1 48N | 44 50 E |
| Merced, *U.S.A.* | 110 C2 | 37 18N | 120 29W |
| Mercedes, Corrientes, *Argentina* | 121 E4 | 29 10S | 58 5W |
| Mercedes, San Luis, *Argentina* | 121 F3 | 33 40S | 65 21W |
| Mercedes, *Uruguay* | 121 F4 | 33 12S | 58 0W |
| Mercy, C., *Canada* | 109 B13 | 65 0N | 63 30W |
| Mere, *U.K.* | 24 D4 | 51 6N | 2 16W |
| Mergui, *Burma* | 83 B1 | 12 26N | 98 34 E |
| Mérida, *Mexico* | 114 C7 | 20 58N | 89 37W |
| Mérida, *Venezuela* | 120 B2 | 8 24N | 71 8W |
| Mérida, Cord. de, *Venezuela* | 116 C3 | 9 0N | 71 0W |
| Meriden, *U.K.* | 23 H5 | 52 26N | 1 38W |
| Meriden, *U.S.A.* | 113 E11 | 41 32N | 72 48W |
| Meridian, *U.S.A.* | 111 D9 | 32 22N | 88 42W |
| Merrick, *U.K.* | 20 D7 | 55 8N | 4 28W |
| Merrill, *U.S.A.* | 111 A9 | 45 11N | 89 41W |
| Merritt, *Canada* | 108 C7 | 50 10N | 120 45W |
| Merse, *U.K.* | 22 A4 | 55 43N | 2 16W |
| Mersea I., *U.K.* | 25 C10 | 51 47N | 0 58 E |
| Mersey →, *U.K.* | 23 F2 | 53 25N | 3 1W |
| Merseyside □, *U.K.* | 23 E2 | 53 31N | 3 2W |
| Mersin, *Turkey* | 73 G5 | 36 51N | 34 36 E |
| Merthyr Tydfil, *U.K.* | 24 C2 | 51 45N | 3 22W |
| Merton □, *U.K.* | 25 D8 | 51 25N | 0 11W |
| Meru, *Kenya* | 96 D7 | 0 3N | 37 40 E |
| Mesa, *U.S.A.* | 110 D4 | 33 25N | 111 50W |
| Mesopotamia, *Iraq* | 86 C5 | 33 30N | 44 0 E |
| Messina, *Italy* | 70 E6 | 38 11N | 15 34 E |
| Messina, Str. di, *Italy* | 70 F6 | 38 15N | 15 35 E |
| Meta →, *S. Amer.* | 120 B3 | 6 12N | 67 28W |
| Meta Incognita Pen., *Canada* | 109 B13 | 62 45N | 68 30W |
| Metheringham, *U.K.* | 23 F8 | 53 9N | 0 23W |
| Methwold, *U.K.* | 25 A10 | 52 32N | 0 33 E |
| Metlakatla, *U.S.A.* | 108 C6 | 55 8N | 131 35W |
| Metz, *France* | 68 B7 | 49 8N | 6 10 E |
| Meuse →, *Europe* | 65 D5 | 50 45N | 5 41 E |
| Mevagissey, *U.K.* | 27 G4 | 50 6N | 4 48W |
| Mevagissey B., *U.K.* | 27 G4 | 50 17N | 4 47W |
| Mexborough, *U.K.* | 23 E6 | 53 30N | 1 15W |
| Mexiana, I., *Brazil* | 120 B5 | 0 0 | 49 30W |
| Mexicali, *Mexico* | 114 A1 | 32 40N | 115 30W |
| México, *Mexico* | 114 D5 | 19 20N | 99 10W |
| Mexico, *U.S.A.* | 111 C4 | 25 0N | 105 0W |
| Mexico, G. of, *Cent. Amer.* | 114 C7 | 25 0N | 90 0W |
| Meymaneh, *Afghan.* | 84 B4 | 35 53N | 64 38 E |
| Mezen →, *Russia* | 72 A7 | 65 44N | 44 22 E |
| Miami, *U.S.A.* | 111 E10 | 25 47N | 80 11W |
| Miändowāb, *Iran* | 86 B6 | 37 0N | 46 5 E |
| Miāneh, *Iran* | 86 B6 | 37 30N | 47 40 E |
| Mianwali, *Pakistan* | 84 C7 | 32 38N | 71 28 E |
| Miass, *Russia* | 72 D11 | 54 59N | 60 6 E |
| Micheldever, *U.K.* | 24 D6 | 51 9N | 1 14W |
| Michigan □, *U.S.A.* | 111 B9 | 44 0N | 85 0W |
| Michigan, L., *U.S.A.* | 112 D4 | 44 0N | 87 0W |
| Michipicoten I., *Canada* | 112 B5 | 47 40N | 85 40W |
| Michurinsk, *Russia* | 72 D7 | 52 58N | 40 27 E |
| Mickle Fell, *U.K.* | 22 C4 | 54 37N | 2 18W |
| Mickleover, *U.K.* | 23 G5 | 52 55N | 1 33W |
| Mickleton, *U.K.* | 22 C4 | 54 36N | 2 2W |
| Micoud, *St. Lucia* | 115 f | 13 49N | 60 54W |
| Micronesia, *Pac. Oc.* | 102 G7 | 11 0N | 160 0 E |
| Micronesia, Federated States of ■, *Pac. Oc.* | 102 G7 | 9 0N | 150 0 E |
| Middelburg, *Neths.* | 65 C3 | 51 30N | 3 36 E |
| Middelburg, *S. Africa* | 97 L5 | 31 30S | 25 0 E |
| Middle Atlas, *Morocco* | 94 B4 | 33 0N | 5 0W |
| Middle East, *Asia* | 74 F7 | 38 0N | 40 0 E |
| Middleham, *U.K.* | 22 D5 | 54 17N | 1 48W |
| Middlemarsh, *U.K.* | 24 E4 | 50 51N | 2 28W |
| Middlesbrough, *U.K.* | 22 C6 | 54 35N | 1 13W |
| Middleton, Gt. Man., *U.K.* | 23 E4 | 53 33N | 2 12W |
| Middleton, Norfolk, *U.K.* | 25 A9 | 52 43N | 0 29 E |
| Middleton Cheney, *U.K.* | 24 B6 | 52 5N | 1 16W |
| Middleton in Teesdale, *U.K.* | 22 C4 | 54 38N | 2 4W |
| Middleton on the Wolds, *U.K.* | 23 E7 | 53 56N | 0 35W |
| Middletown, *U.K.* | 29 C8 | 54 17N | 6 51W |
| Middletown, N.Y., *U.S.A.* | 113 E10 | 41 27N | 74 25W |
| Middletown, Ohio, *U.S.A.* | 112 F5 | 39 31N | 84 24W |
| Middlewich, *U.K.* | 23 F4 | 53 12N | 2 28W |
| Middlezoy, *U.K.* | 24 D3 | 51 5N | 2 54W |
| Midhurst, *U.K.* | 25 E7 | 50 59N | 0 44W |
| Midi, Canal du, *France* | 68 E4 | 43 45N | 1 21 E |
| Midland, *Canada* | 112 C8 | 44 45N | 79 50W |
| Midland, Mich., *U.S.A.* | 112 D5 | 43 37N | 84 14W |
| Midland, Tex., *U.S.A.* | 110 D6 | 32 0N | 102 3W |
| Midleton, *Ireland* | 30 E6 | 51 55N | 8 10W |
| Midsomer Norton, *U.K.* | 24 D4 | 51 17N | 2 28W |
| Midway Is., *Pac. Oc.* | 102 E10 | 28 13N | 177 22W |
| Midwest, *U.S.A.* | 111 C9 | 42 0N | 90 0W |
| Mieres, *Spain* | 69 A3 | 43 18N | 5 48W |
| Mikhaylovka, *Russia* | 73 D7 | 50 3N | 43 5 E |
| Milan, *Italy* | 68 D8 | 45 28N | 9 12 E |
| Milborne Port, *U.K.* | 24 E4 | 50 58N | 2 28W |
| Mildenhall, *U.K.* | 25 B10 | 52 21N | 0 32 E |
| Mildura, *Australia* | 98 G7 | 34 13S | 142 9 E |
| Miles City, *U.S.A.* | 110 A5 | 46 25N | 105 51W |
| Milford, *U.S.A.* | 113 F10 | 38 55N | 75 26W |
| Milford Haven, *U.K.* | 26 D3 | 51 42N | 5 7W |
| Milford on Sea, *U.K.* | 24 E5 | 50 43N | 1 35W |
| Milk →, *U.S.A.* | 110 A5 | 48 4N | 106 19W |
| Millau, *France* | 68 D5 | 44 8N | 3 4 E |
| Millbrook, *U.K.* | 27 G5 | 50 20N | 4 14W |
| Millet, *St. Lucia* | 115 f | 13 55N | 60 59W |
| Millinocket, *U.S.A.* | 113 C13 | 45 39N | 68 43W |
| Millom, *U.K.* | 22 D2 | 54 13N | 3 16W |
| Milltown Malbay, *Ireland* | 30 C4 | 52 52N | 9 24W |
| Millville, *U.S.A.* | 113 F10 | 39 24N | 75 2W |
| Milnthorpe, *U.K.* | 22 D3 | 54 14N | 2 45W |
| Milton Abbot, *U.K.* | 27 F5 | 50 35N | 4 16W |
| Milton Keynes, *U.K.* | 25 B7 | 52 1N | 0 44W |
| Milverton, *U.K.* | 24 D2 | 51 1N | 3 16W |
| Milwaukee, *U.S.A.* | 112 D4 | 43 2N | 87 55W |
| Min Jiang →, Fujian, *China* | 81 D6 | 26 0N | 119 35 E |
| Min Jiang →, Sichuan, *China* | 80 D5 | 28 45N | 104 40 E |
| Minas, *Uruguay* | 121 F4 | 34 20S | 55 10W |
| Minas Gerais □, *Brazil* | 122 C1 | 18 50S | 46 0W |
| Minatitlán, *Mexico* | 114 D6 | 17 59N | 94 31W |
| Minchinhampton, *U.K.* | 24 C4 | 51 42N | 2 11W |
| Mindanao, *Phil.* | 83 C4 | 8 0N | 125 0 E |
| Mindanao Trench, *Pac. Oc.* | 83 B4 | 12 0N | 126 6 E |
| Mindoro, *Phil.* | 83 B4 | 13 0N | 121 0 E |
| Mindoro Str., *Phil.* | 83 B4 | 12 30N | 120 30 E |
| Minehead, *U.K.* | 24 D2 | 51 12N | 3 29W |
| Mineral Wells, *U.S.A.* | 110 D7 | 32 48N | 98 7W |
| Minna, *Nigeria* | 94 G7 | 9 37N | 6 30 E |
| Minneapolis, *U.S.A.* | 111 B8 | 44 59N | 93 16W |
| Minnesota □, *U.S.A.* | 111 A8 | 46 0N | 94 15W |
| Minorca = Menorca, *Spain* | 69 C8 | 40 0N | 4 0 E |
| Minot, *U.S.A.* | 110 A6 | 48 14N | 101 18W |
| Minsk, *Belarus* | 67 B14 | 53 52N | 27 30 E |
| Minster, Kent, *U.K.* | 25 D11 | 51 20N | 1 20 E |
| Minster, Kent, *U.K.* | 25 D10 | 51 25N | 0 50 E |
| Minsterley, *U.K.* | 23 G3 | 52 39N | 2 54W |
| Minto, L., *Canada* | 109 C12 | 57 13N | 75 0W |
| Miramichi, *Canada* | 109 D13 | 47 2N | 65 28W |
| Miramichi B., *Canada* | 113 B15 | 47 15N | 65 0W |
| Mirim, L., *S. Amer.* | 121 F4 | 32 45S | 52 50W |
| Mirpur Khas, *Pakistan* | 84 G6 | 25 30N | 69 0 E |
| Mirzapur, *India* | 85 G13 | 25 10N | 82 34 E |
| Mishan, *China* | 81 B8 | 45 37N | 131 48 E |
| Mishawaka, *U.S.A.* | 112 E4 | 41 40N | 86 11W |
| Miskolc, *Hungary* | 67 D11 | 48 7N | 20 50 E |
| Misool, *Indonesia* | 83 D5 | 1 52S | 130 10 E |
| Mişrātah, *Libya* | 95 B9 | 32 24N | 15 3 E |
| Missinaibi →, *Canada* | 109 C11 | 50 43N | 81 29W |
| Mississippi □, *U.S.A.* | 111 D9 | 33 0N | 90 0W |
| Mississippi →, *U.S.A.* | 111 E9 | 29 9N | 89 15W |
| Mississippi River Delta, *U.S.A.* | 111 E9 | 29 10N | 89 15W |
| Missoula, *U.S.A.* | 110 A4 | 46 52N | 114 1W |
| Missouri □, *U.S.A.* | 111 C8 | 38 25N | 92 30W |
| Missouri →, *U.S.A.* | 111 C8 | 38 49N | 90 7W |
| Mistassini, L., *Canada* | 109 C12 | 51 0N | 73 30W |
| Misterton, Notts., *U.K.* | 23 F7 | 53 27N | 0 50W |
| Misterton, Somst., *U.K.* | 24 E3 | 50 52N | 2 47W |
| Mitcheldean, *U.K.* | 24 C4 | 51 51N | 2 28W |
| Mitchell, *U.K.* | 110 B7 | 43 43N | 98 2W |
| Mitchell →, *Australia* | 98 D7 | 15 12S | 141 35 E |
| Mitchelstown, *Ireland* | 30 D6 | 52 15N | 8 16W |
| Mito, *Japan* | 82 E7 | 36 20N | 140 30 E |
| Mitú, *Colombia* | 120 B2 | 1 15N | 70 13W |
| Mitumba, Mts., Dem. Rep. of the Congo | 96 F5 | 7 0S | 27 30 E |
| Miyakonojō, *Japan* | 82 H2 | 31 40N | 131 5 E |
| Miyazaki, *Japan* | 82 H2 | 31 56N | 131 30 E |
| Mizen Hd., Cork, *Ireland* | 30 F3 | 51 27N | 9 50W |
| Mizen Hd., Wicklow, *Ireland* | 31 C10 | 52 51N | 6 4W |
| Mizoram □, *India* | 85 H18 | 23 30N | 92 40 E |
| Mjøsa, *Norway* | 63 E6 | 60 40N | 11 0 E |
| Mo i Rana, *Norway* | 63 D6 | 66 20N | 14 7 E |
| Moab, *U.S.A.* | 110 C5 | 38 35N | 109 33W |
| Moate, *Ireland* | 28 E6 | 53 24N | 7 44W |
| Mobaye, *C.A.R.* | 96 D4 | 4 25N | 21 5 E |
| Moberly, *U.S.A.* | 111 C8 | 39 25N | 92 26W |
| Mobile, *U.S.A.* | 111 D9 | 30 41N | 88 3W |
| Mobridge, *U.S.A.* | 110 A6 | 45 32N | 100 26W |
| Moçâmbique, *Mozam.* | 97 H8 | 15 3S | 40 42 E |
| Mocoa, *Colombia* | 120 B2 | 1 7N | 76 35W |
| Modbury, *U.K.* | 27 G6 | 50 21N | 3 55W |
| Módena, *Italy* | 70 B4 | 44 40N | 10 55 E |
| Modesto, *U.S.A.* | 110 C2 | 37 39N | 121 0W |
| Moffat, *U.K.* | 21 D9 | 55 21N | 3 27W |
| Mogadishu, *Somali Rep.* | 88 G4 | 2 2N | 45 25 E |
| Mogi das Cruzes, *Brazil* | 122 D1 | 23 31S | 46 11W |
| Mogi-Mirim, *Brazil* | 122 D1 | 22 29S | 47 0W |
| Mohammedia, *Morocco* | 94 B4 | 33 44N | 7 21W |
| Moher, Cliffs of, *Ireland* | 30 C4 | 52 58N | 9 27W |
| Moidart, L., *U.K.* | 18 J6 | 56 47N | 5 52W |
| Moisie →, *Canada* | 109 C13 | 50 14N | 66 5W |
| Mojave Desert, *U.S.A.* | 110 D3 | 35 0N | 116 30W |
| Mold, *U.K.* | 23 F2 | 53 9N | 3 8W |
| Molde, *Norway* | 63 E5 | 62 45N | 7 9 E |
| Moldova ■, *Europe* | 67 E15 | 47 0N | 28 0 E |
| Mole →, *U.K.* | 25 D8 | 51 24N | 0 21W |
| Mollendo, *Peru* | 120 D2 | 17 0S | 72 0W |
| Molokai, *U.S.A.* | 110 H16 | 21 8N | 157 0W |
| Molopo →, *Africa* | 97 K4 | 28 30S | 20 12 E |
| Molucca Sea, *Indonesia* | 83 D4 | 0 0 | 125 0 E |
| Moluccas, *Indonesia* | 83 D4 | 1 0S | 127 0 E |
| Mombasa, *Kenya* | 96 E7 | 4 2S | 39 43 E |
| Mompós, *Colombia* | 120 B2 | 9 14N | 74 26W |
| Mon □, *Burma* | 85 L20 | 16 0N | 97 30 E |
| Mona Passage, *W. Indies* | 115 D11 | 18 30N | 67 45W |
| Monaco ■, *Europe* | 68 E7 | 43 46N | 7 23 E |
| Monadhliath Mts., *U.K.* | 19 H9 | 57 10N | 4 4W |
| Monaghan, *Ireland* | 29 C8 | 54 15N | 6 57W |
| Monaghan □, *Ireland* | 29 C8 | 54 11N | 6 56W |
| Monar, L., *U.K.* | 18 H7 | 57 26N | 5 8W |
| Monasterevin, *Ireland* | 31 B8 | 53 8N | 7 4W |
| Mönchengladbach, *Germany* | 66 C4 | 51 11N | 6 27 E |
| Monclova, *Mexico* | 114 B4 | 26 50N | 101 30W |
| Moncton, *Canada* | 109 D13 | 46 7N | 64 51W |
| Moneague, *Jamaica* | 114 a | 18 16N | 77 7W |
| Moneymore, *U.K.* | 29 B8 | 54 41N | 6 40W |
| Mongolia ■, *Asia* | 80 B5 | 47 0N | 103 0 E |
| Mongu, *Zambia* | 97 H4 | 15 16S | 23 12 E |
| Monifieth, *U.K.* | 21 B10 | 56 30N | 2 48W |
| Monmouth, *U.K.* | 24 C3 | 51 48N | 2 42W |
| Monnow →, *U.K.* | 24 C3 | 51 49N | 2 38W |
| Monroe, La., *U.S.A.* | 111 D8 | 32 30N | 92 7W |
| Monroe, Mich., *U.S.A.* | 112 E6 | 41 55N | 83 24W |
| Monrovia, *Liberia* | 94 G3 | 6 18N | 10 47W |
| Mons, *Belgium* | 65 D3 | 50 27N | 3 58 E |
| Mont-de-Marsan, *France* | 68 E3 | 43 54N | 0 31W |
| Mont-Laurier, *Canada* | 109 D12 | 46 35N | 75 30W |
| Montaña, *Peru* | 120 C2 | 6 0S | 73 0W |
| Montana □, *U.S.A.* | 110 A5 | 47 0N | 110 0W |
| Montargis, *France* | 68 C5 | 47 59N | 2 43 E |
| Montauban, *France* | 68 D4 | 44 2N | 1 21 E |
| Montbéliard, *France* | 68 C7 | 47 31N | 6 48 E |
| Montceau-les-Mines, *France* | 68 C6 | 46 40N | 4 23 E |
| Monte Azul, *Brazil* | 122 C2 | 15 9S | 42 53W |
| Monte-Carlo, *Monaco* | 66 G4 | 43 46N | 7 23 E |
| Monte Caseros, *Argentina* | 121 F4 | 30 10S | 57 50W |
| Monte Cristi, *Dom. Rep.* | 115 D10 | 19 52N | 71 39W |
| Montego Bay, *Jamaica* | 114 a | 18 30N | 78 0W |
| Montélimar, *France* | 68 D6 | 44 33N | 4 45 E |
| Montemorelos, *Mexico* | 114 B5 | 25 11N | 99 42W |
| Montenegro □, Serbia & M. | 71 C8 | 42 40N | 19 20 E |
| Monterey, *U.S.A.* | 110 C2 | 36 37N | 121 55W |
| Montería, *Colombia* | 120 B2 | 8 46N | 75 53W |
| Monterrey, *Mexico* | 114 B4 | 25 40N | 100 30W |
| Montes Claros, *Brazil* | 122 C2 | 16 30S | 43 50W |
| Montevideo, *Uruguay* | 121 F4 | 34 50S | 56 11W |
| Montgomery, *U.K.* | 23 G2 | 52 34N | 3 8W |
| Montgomery, *U.S.A.* | 111 D9 | 32 23N | 86 19W |
| Monticello, *U.S.A.* | 112 E4 | 40 45N | 86 46W |
| Montluçon, *France* | 68 C5 | 46 22N | 2 36 E |
| Montmagny, *Canada* | 113 B12 | 46 58N | 70 34W |
| Montpelier, Idaho, *U.S.A.* | 110 B4 | 42 19N | 111 18W |
| Montpelier, Vt., *U.S.A.* | 113 C11 | 44 16N | 72 35W |
| Montpellier, *France* | 68 E5 | 43 37N | 3 52 E |
| Montréal, *Canada* | 109 D12 | 45 31N | 73 34W |
| Montreux, *Switz.* | 66 E4 | 46 26N | 6 55 E |
| Montrose, *U.K.* | 19 J13 | 56 44N | 2 27W |
| Montrose, *U.S.A.* | 110 C5 | 38 29N | 107 53W |
| Montserrat ☑, *W. Indies* | 115 D12 | 16 40N | 62 10W |
| Monywa, *Burma* | 85 H19 | 22 7N | 95 11 E |
| Monze, C., *Pakistan* | 84 G5 | 24 47N | 66 37 E |
| Moorfoot Hills, *U.K.* | 21 C9 | 55 44N | 3 8W |
| Moose →, *Canada* | 108 C9 | 50 48N | 105 30W |
| Moose Jaw, *Canada* | 108 C9 | 50 24N | 105 30W |
| Moosehead L., *U.S.A.* | 113 C13 | 45 38N | 69 40W |
| Moosomin, *Canada* | 108 C9 | 50 9N | 101 40W |
| Moosonee, *Canada* | 109 C11 | 51 17N | 80 39W |
| Mopti, *Mali* | 94 F5 | 14 30N | 4 0W |
| Mora, *Sweden* | 63 E6 | 61 2N | 14 38 E |
| Moradabad, *India* | 84 E11 | 28 50N | 78 50 E |
| Morant Bay, *Jamaica* | 114 a | 17 53N | 76 25W |
| Morant Pt., *Jamaica* | 114 a | 17 55N | 76 12W |
| Morar, L., *U.K.* | 18 J6 | 56 57N | 5 40W |
| Moratuwa, *Sri Lanka* | 84 R11 | 6 45N | 79 55 E |
| Morava →, Serbia & M. | 71 B9 | 44 36N | 21 4 E |
| Morava →, Slovak Rep. | 67 D9 | 48 10N | 16 59 E |
| Moray Firth, *U.K.* | 19 G10 | 57 40N | 3 52W |
| Morden, *Canada* | 108 D10 | 49 15N | 98 10W |
| Mordvinia □, *Russia* | 72 D7 | 54 20N | 44 30 E |
| Morea, *Greece* | 56 H10 | 37 45N | 22 10 E |
| Moreau →, *U.S.A.* | 110 A6 | 45 18N | 100 43W |
| Morebattle, *U.K.* | 22 A4 | 55 31N | 2 22W |
| Morecambe, *U.K.* | 22 D3 | 54 5N | 2 52W |
| Morecambe B., *U.K.* | 22 D3 | 54 7N | 3 0W |
| Moree, *Australia* | 98 F9 | 29 28S | 149 54 E |
| Morehead, *U.S.A.* | 112 F6 | 38 11N | 83 26W |
| Morelia, *Mexico* | 114 D4 | 19 42N | 101 7W |
| Morena, Sierra, *Spain* | 69 C3 | 38 20N | 4 0W |
| Moresby I., *Canada* | 108 C6 | 52 30N | 131 40W |
| Moreton-in-Marsh, *U.K.* | 24 C5 | 51 59N | 1 41W |
| Moretonhampstead, *U.K.* | 27 F6 | 50 39N | 3 46W |
| Morgan City, *U.S.A.* | 111 E8 | 29 42N | 91 12W |
| Morgantown, *U.S.A.* | 112 F8 | 39 38N | 79 57W |
| Morioka, *Japan* | 82 D7 | 39 45N | 141 8 E |
| Morlaix, *France* | 68 B2 | 48 36N | 3 52W |
| Morley, *U.K.* | 23 E5 | 53 45N | 1 36W |
| Morocco ■, N. Afr. | 94 B4 | 32 0N | 5 50W |
| Morogoro, *Tanzania* | 96 F7 | 6 50S | 37 40 E |
| Morón, *Cuba* | 115 C9 | 22 8N | 78 39W |
| Moroni, *Comoros Is.* | 91 H8 | 11 40S | 43 16 E |
| Morotai, *Indonesia* | 83 C4 | 2 10N | 128 30 E |
| Morpeth, *U.K.* | 22 B5 | 55 10N | 1 41W |
| Morphou, *Cyprus* | 86 C3 | 35 12N | 32 59 E |
| Morrinhos, *Brazil* | 122 C1 | 17 45S | 49 10W |
| Morris, *U.S.A.* | 112 E3 | 41 22N | 88 26W |
| Morte Bay, *U.K.* | 27 E5 | 51 9N | 4 14W |
| Morte Pt., *U.K.* | 27 E5 | 51 11N | 4 14W |
| Mortehoe, *U.K.* | 27 E5 | 51 11N | 4 12W |
| Mortimer's Cross, *U.K.* | 23 H3 | 52 16N | 2 50W |
| Morton Fen, *U.K.* | 23 G8 | 52 45N | 0 20W |
| Morvern, *U.K.* | 18 J6 | 56 38N | 5 44W |
| Morwenstow, *U.K.* | 27 F4 | 50 54N | 4 33W |
| Moscos Is., *Burma* | 85 N20 | 14 0N | 97 30 E |
| Moscow, *Russia* | 72 C6 | 55 45N | 37 35 E |
| Moscow, *U.S.A.* | 110 A3 | 46 44N | 117 0W |
| Mosel →, *Europe* | 66 C4 | 50 22N | 7 36 E |
| Moses Lake, *U.S.A.* | 110 A3 | 47 8N | 119 17W |
| Moshi, *Tanzania* | 96 E7 | 3 22S | 37 18 E |
| Mosselbaai, S. Africa | 97 L4 | 34 11S | 22 8 E |
| Mossley, *U.K.* | 23 E4 | 53 33N | 2 1W |
| Mossoró, *Brazil* | 120 C6 | 5 10S | 37 15W |
| Most, Czech Rep. | 66 C7 | 50 31N | 13 38 E |
| Mostaganem, *Algeria* | 94 A6 | 35 54N | 0 5 E |
| Mostar, Bos.-H. | 71 C7 | 43 22N | 17 50 E |
| Mosul, *Iraq* | 86 B5 | 36 15N | 43 5 E |
| Motcombe, *U.K.* | 24 D4 | 51 1N | 2 13W |
| Motherwell, *U.K.* | 21 C8 | 55 47N | 3 58W |
| Motihari, *India* | 85 F14 | 26 30N | 84 55 E |
| Mottisfont, *U.K.* | 24 D5 | 51 2N | 1 32W |
| Moule, *Guadeloupe* | 114 b | 16 20N | 61 21W |
| Moule à Chique, C., St. Lucia | 115 f | 13 43N | 60 57W |
| Moulins, *France* | 68 C5 | 46 35N | 3 19 E |
| Moulmein, *Burma* | 85 L20 | 16 30N | 97 40 E |
| Moulouya, O. →, Morocco | 94 B5 | 35 5N | 2 25W |
| Moulton, *U.K.* | 23 H7 | 52 17N | 0 51W |
| Moundou, *Chad* | 95 G9 | 8 40N | 16 10 E |
| Moundsville, *U.S.A.* | 112 F7 | 39 55N | 80 44W |
| Mount Carmel, *U.S.A.* | 112 F4 | 38 25N | 87 46W |
| Mount Desert I., *U.S.A.* | 113 C13 | 44 21N | 68 20W |
| Mount Gambier, *Australia* | 98 H7 | 37 50S | 140 46 E |
| Mount Hagen, Papua N. G. | 98 B7 | 5 52S | 144 16 E |
| Mount Isa, *Australia* | 98 E6 | 20 42S | 139 26 E |
| Mount Magnet, *Australia* | 98 F2 | 28 2S | 117 47 E |
| Mount Pleasant, U.S.A. | 112 D5 | 43 36N | 84 46W |
| Mount Sterling, *U.S.A.* | 112 F6 | 38 4N | 83 56W |
| Mount Vernon, Ill., *U.S.A.* | 111 C9 | 38 17N | 88 57W |
| Mount Vernon, N.Y., *U.S.A.* | 113 E11 | 40 55N | 73 50W |
| Mount Vernon, Ohio, *U.S.A.* | 112 E6 | 40 23N | 82 29W |
| Mountain Ash, *U.K.* | 24 C2 | 51 40N | 3 23W |
| Mountain Home, *U.S.A.* | 110 B3 | 43 8N | 115 41W |
| Mountain View, *U.S.A.* | 110 J17 | 19 33N | 155 7W |
| Mountmellick, *Ireland* | 31 B8 | 53 7N | 7 20W |
| Mountrath, *Ireland* | 31 C8 | 53 0N | 7 28W |
| Mount's Bay, *U.K.* | 27 G2 | 50 5N | 5 31W |
| Mountsorrel, *U.K.* | 23 G6 | 52 44N | 1 8W |
| Mourne →, *U.K.* | 28 B7 | 54 52N | 7 26W |
| Mourne Mts., *U.K.* | 29 C9 | 54 10N | 6 0W |
| Mouscron, *Belgium* | 65 D3 | 50 45N | 3 12 E |
| Moville, *Ireland* | 29 A7 | 55 11N | 7 3W |
| Moy →, *Ireland* | 28 C3 | 54 8N | 9 8W |
| Mozambique ■, Africa | 97 H7 | 19 0S | 35 0 E |
| Mozambique Chan., Africa | 90 H8 | 17 30S | 42 30 E |
| Mozdok, *Russia* | 73 F7 | 43 45N | 44 48 E |
| Mpanda, *Tanzania* | 96 F6 | 6 23S | 31 1 E |
| Mtwara-Mikindani, *Tanzania* | 96 G8 | 10 20S | 40 20 E |
| Mu Us Shamo, *China* | 81 C5 | 39 0N | 109 0 E |
| Muar, *Malaysia* | 83 C2 | 2 3N | 102 34 E |
| Much Dewchurch, *U.K.* | 24 C3 | 51 58N | 2 45W |
| Much Marcle, *U.K.* | 24 C4 | 51 59N | 2 29W |
| Much Wenlock, *U.K.* | 23 G3 | 52 35N | 2 33W |
| Muck, *U.K.* | 18 J5 | 56 50N | 6 15W |
| Muckle Flugga, *U.K.* | 18 A16 | 60 51N | 0 54W |
| Mucuri, *Brazil* | 122 C3 | 18 0S | 39 36W |
| Mudanjiang, *China* | 81 B7 | 44 38N | 129 30 E |
| Mufulira, *Zambia* | 97 G5 | 12 32S | 28 15 E |
| Muğla, *Turkey* | 73 G4 | 37 15N | 28 22 E |
| Muine Bheag, *Ireland* | 31 C9 | 52 42N | 6 58W |
| Muir of Ord, *U.K.* | 18 D9 | 57 32N | 4 28W |
| Muktsar, *India* | 84 D9 | 30 30N | 74 30 E |
| Mulde →, *Germany* | 66 C7 | 51 53N | 12 15 E |
| Mulhacén, *Spain* | 69 D4 | 37 4N | 3 20W |
| Mulhouse, *France* | 68 C7 | 47 40N | 7 20 E |
| Mull, *U.K.* | 20 A4 | 56 25N | 5 56W |
| Mull, Sound of, *U.K.* | 20 A4 | 56 30N | 5 50W |
| Mullet Pen., *Ireland* | 28 C1 | 54 13N | 10 2W |
| Mullingar, *Ireland* | 28 D7 | 53 31N | 7 21W |
| Mullion, *U.K.* | 27 G3 | 50 1N | 5 16W |
| Mulroy B., *Ireland* | 28 A6 | 55 15N | 7 46W |
| Multan, *Pakistan* | 84 D7 | 30 15N | 71 36 E |
| Mumbai, *India* | 84 K8 | 18 55N | 72 50 E |
| Mumbles, The, *U.K.* | 27 D6 | 51 34N | 3 59W |
| Muna, *Indonesia* | 83 D4 | 5 0S | 122 30 E |
| Muncie, *U.S.A.* | 112 E5 | 40 12N | 85 23W |
| Mundesley, *U.K.* | 25 A11 | 52 53N | 1 25 E |
| Mundo Novo, *Brazil* | 122 B2 | 11 50S | 40 29W |
| Munger, *India* | 85 G15 | 25 23N | 86 30 E |
| Munich, *Germany* | 66 D6 | 48 8N | 11 34 E |
| Munising, *U.S.A.* | 112 B4 | 46 25N | 86 40W |
| Münster, *Germany* | 66 C4 | 51 58N | 7 37 E |
| Munster □, *Ireland* | 30 D5 | 52 18N | 8 44W |
| Murashi, *Russia* | 72 C8 | 59 30N | 49 0 E |
| Murat →, *Turkey* | 73 G7 | 38 46N | 40 0 E |
| Murchison →, *Australia* | 98 F1 | 27 45S | 114 0 E |
| Murcia, *Spain* | 69 D5 | 38 5N | 1 10W |
| Mureş →, *Romania* | 67 E11 | 46 15N | 20 13 E |
| Muriaé, *Brazil* | 122 D2 | 21 8S | 42 23W |
| Müritz, *Germany* | 66 B7 | 53 25N | 12 42 E |
| Murmansk, *Russia* | 72 A5 | 68 57N | 33 10 E |
| Murom, *Russia* | 72 C7 | 55 35N | 42 3 E |
| Muroran, *Japan* | 82 B7 | 42 25N | 141 0 E |
| Murray →, *U.S.A.* | 112 G3 | 36 37N | 88 19W |
| Murray →, *Australia* | 98 H6 | 35 20S | 139 22 E |
| Murton, *U.K.* | 22 C6 | 54 50N | 1 22W |
| Mururoa, Pac. Oc. | 103 K14 | 21 52S | 138 55W |
| Murwara, *India* | 85 K12 | 23 46N | 80 28 E |
| Muş, *Turkey* | 73 G7 | 38 45N | 41 30 E |
| Muscat, *Oman* | 87 F9 | 23 37N | 58 36 E |
| Musgrave Ranges, *Australia* | 98 F5 | 26 0S | 132 0 E |
| Musina, S. Africa | 97 J6 | 22 20S | 30 5 E |
| Muskegon, *U.S.A.* | 112 D4 | 43 14N | 86 16W |
| Muskegon →, *U.S.A.* | 112 D4 | 43 14N | 86 21W |
| Muskegon Heights, *U.S.A.* | 112 D4 | 43 12N | 86 16W |
| Muskogee, *U.S.A.* | 111 C7 | 35 45N | 95 22W |
| Musselburgh, *U.K.* | 21 C9 | 55 57N | 3 2W |
| Musselshell →, *U.S.A.* | 110 A5 | 47 21N | 107 57W |
| Mutare, *Zimbabwe* | 97 H6 | 18 58S | 32 38 E |
| Mutton I., *Ireland* | 30 C3 | 52 49N | 9 32W |
| Muynak, *Uzbekistan* | 87 A9 | 43 44N | 59 10 E |
| Muzaffarnagar, *India* | 84 E10 | 29 26N | 77 40 E |
| Mwanza, *Tanzania* | 96 E6 | 2 30S | 32 58 E |
| Mweelrea, *Ireland* | 28 D2 | 53 39N | 9 49W |
| Mweru, L., *Zambia* | 96 F5 | 9 0S | 28 40 E |
| My Tho, *Vietnam* | 83 B2 | 10 29N | 106 23 E |
| Myanmar = Burma ■, Asia | 85 J20 | 21 0N | 96 30 E |
| Myddle, *U.K.* | 23 G3 | 52 49N | 2 47W |
| Myingyan, *Burma* | 85 J19 | 21 30N | 95 20 E |
| Myitkyina, *Burma* | 85 G20 | 25 24N | 97 26 E |
| Mymensingh, *Bangla.* | 85 G17 | 24 45N | 90 24 E |
| Mynydd Du, *U.K.* | 24 C1 | 51 52N | 3 50W |
| Mynydd Prescelly, *U.K.* | 26 D4 | 51 57N | 4 48W |
| Mysore, *India* | 84 N10 | 12 17N | 76 41 E |
| Mytishchi, *Russia* | 72 C6 | 55 50N | 37 50 E |

## N

| | | | | |
|---|---|---|---|---|
| Naab →, *Germany* | 66 D6 | 49 1N | 12 2 E |
| Naas, *Ireland* | 31 B9 | 53 12N | 6 40W |
| Naberezhnyye Chelny, *Russia* | 72 C9 | 55 42N | 52 19 E |
| Nabeul, *Tunisia* | 95 A8 | 36 30N | 10 44 E |
| Nābulus, West Bank | 86 C3 | 32 14N | 35 15 E |
| Nacala, *Mozam.* | 97 G8 | 14 31S | 40 34 E |
| Nacogdoches, *U.S.A.* | 111 D8 | 31 36N | 94 39W |
| Nacozari, *Mexico* | 114 A3 | 30 24N | 109 39W |
| Nadiad, *India* | 84 H8 | 22 41N | 72 56 E |
| Nador, *Morocco* | 94 B5 | 35 14N | 2 58W |
| Nafferton, *U.K.* | 23 D8 | 54 1N | 0 23W |
| Nafud Desert, Si. Arabia | 86 D5 | 28 15N | 41 0 E |
| Naga, *Phil.* | 83 B4 | 13 38N | 123 15 E |
| Nagaland □, *India* | 85 G19 | 26 0N | 94 30 E |
| Nagano, *Japan* | 82 E6 | 36 40N | 138 10 E |
| Nagaoka, *Japan* | 82 E6 | 37 27N | 138 51 E |
| Nagappattinam, *India* | 84 P11 | 10 46N | 79 51 E |
| Nagasaki, *Japan* | 82 G1 | 32 47N | 129 50 E |
| Nagaur, *India* | 84 F8 | 27 15N | 73 45 E |
| Nagercoil, *India* | 84 Q10 | 8 12N | 77 26 E |
| Nagorno-Karabakh □, *Azerbaijan* | 73 F8 | 39 55N | 46 45 E |
| Nagoya, *Japan* | 82 F5 | 35 10N | 136 50 E |
| Nagpur, *India* | 84 J11 | 21 8N | 79 10 E |
| Naguabo, Puerto Rico | 115 d | 18 13N | 65 44W |
| Naha, *Japan* | 81 D7 | 26 13N | 127 42 E |
| Nailsea, *U.K.* | 24 D3 | 51 26N | 2 44W |
| Nailsworth, *U.K.* | 24 C4 | 51 41N | 2 14W |
| Nain, *Canada* | 109 C13 | 56 34N | 61 40W |
| Nairn, *U.K.* | 19 G10 | 57 35N | 3 53W |
| Nairobi, *Kenya* | 96 E7 | 1 17S | 36 48 E |
| Najafābād, *Iran* | 86 C7 | 32 40N | 51 15 E |
| Najd, Si. Arabia | 86 E5 | 26 30N | 42 0 E |
| Najibabad, *India* | 84 E11 | 29 40N | 78 20 E |
| Najran, Si. Arabia | 88 D3 | 17 34N | 44 18 E |
| Nakhodka, *Russia* | 82 B3 | 42 53N | 132 54 E |
| Nakhon Ratchasima, *Thailand* | 83 B2 | 14 59N | 102 12 E |
| Nakhon Sawan, *Thailand* | 83 B2 | 15 35N | 100 10 E |
| Nakhon Si Thammarat, *Thailand* | 83 C2 | 8 29N | 100 0 E |
| Nakina, *Canada* | 109 C11 | 50 10N | 86 40W |
| Nakuru, *Kenya* | 96 E7 | 0 15S | 36 4 E |
| Nalchik, *Russia* | 73 F7 | 43 30N | 43 33 E |
| Nam Co, *China* | 80 C4 | 30 30N | 90 45 E |
| Nam Dinh, *Vietnam* | 83 A2 | 20 25N | 106 5 E |
| Namak, Daryācheh-ye, *Iran* | 87 C8 | 34 30N | 52 0 E |
| Namaland, *Namibia* | 97 K3 | 26 0S | 17 0 E |
| Namangan, *Uzbekistan* | 87 A12 | 41 0N | 71 40 E |
| Namib Desert, *Namibia* | 97 J3 | 22 30S | 15 0 E |
| Namibe, *Angola* | 97 H2 | 15 7S | 12 11 E |
| Namibia ■, *Africa* | 97 J3 | 22 0S | 18 9 E |
| Nampa, *U.S.A.* | 110 B3 | 43 34N | 116 34W |
| Namp'o, N. Korea | 81 C7 | 38 52N | 125 10 E |
| Nampula, *Mozam.* | 97 H7 | 15 6S | 39 15 E |
| Namumea, *Tuvalu* | 99 B14 | 5 41S | 176 9 E |
| Namur, *Belgium* | 65 D4 | 50 27N | 4 52 E |
| Nan-ch'ang, *China* | 81 D6 | 28 42N | 115 55 E |
| Nanaimo, *Canada* | 108 D7 | 49 10N | 124 0W |
| Nanchong, *China* | 80 C5 | 30 43N | 106 2 E |
| Nancy, *France* | 68 B7 | 48 42N | 6 12 E |
| Nanda Devi, *India* | 84 D11 | 30 23N | 79 59 E |
| Nanded, *India* | 84 K10 | 19 10N | 77 20 E |
| Nandurbar, *India* | 84 J9 | 21 20N | 74 15 E |
| Nanga Parbat, *Pakistan* | 84 B9 | 35 10N | 74 35 E |
| Nangarhār □, Afghan. | 87 C12 | 34 20N | 70 0 E |
| Nanjing, *China* | 81 C6 | 32 2N | 118 47 E |
| Nanning, *China* | 80 D5 | 22 48N | 108 20 E |
| Nanping, *China* | 81 D6 | 26 38N | 118 10 E |
| Nantes, *France* | 68 C3 | 47 12N | 1 33W |
| Nantucket I., *U.S.A.* | 111 B13 | 41 16N | 70 5W |
| Nantwich, *U.K.* | 23 F3 | 53 4N | 2 31W |
| Nanuque, *Brazil* | 122 C2 | 17 50S | 40 21W |
| Nanyang, *China* | 81 C6 | 33 11N | 112 30 E |
| Nanyuki, *Kenya* | 96 D7 | 0 2N | 37 4 E |
| Napa, *U.S.A.* | 110 C2 | 38 18N | 122 17W |
| Napier, N.Z. | 99 H14 | 39 30S | 176 56 E |
| Naples, *Italy* | 70 D6 | 40 50N | 14 15 E |
| Napo →, *Peru* | 120 C2 | 3 20S | 72 40W |
| Narayanganj, *Bangla.* | 85 H17 | 23 40N | 90 33 E |
| Narberth, *U.K.* | 26 D4 | 51 47N | 4 44W |
| Narbonne, *France* | 68 E5 | 43 11N | 3 0 E |
| Narborough, *U.K.* | 23 G6 | 52 34N | 1 12W |
| Narmada →, *India* | 84 J8 | 21 38N | 72 36 E |
| Narodnaya, *Russia* | 72 A10 | 65 5N | 59 58 E |
| Narva, *Estonia* | 72 C4 | 59 23N | 28 12 E |
| Narvik, *Norway* | 63 D7 | 68 28N | 17 26 E |
| Naryan-Mar, *Russia* | 72 A9 | 67 42N | 53 12 E |
| Naseby, *U.K.* | 23 H7 | 52 24N | 0 59W |
| Nashua, *U.S.A.* | 113 D12 | 42 45N | 71 28W |
| Nashville, *U.S.A.* | 111 C9 | 36 10N | 86 47W |

**Nasik**          **Onny**

Nasik, India . . . . . . . . . . . 84 K8 19 58N 73 50 E
Nasirabad, India . . . . . . . . 84 F9 26 15N 74 45 E
Nassau, Bahamas . . . . . . . 115 B9 25 5N 77 20W
Nasser, L., Egypt . . . . . . . 95 D12 23 0N 32 30 E
Natal, Brazil . . . . . . . . . . 120 C6 5 47S 35 13W
Natashquan, Canada . . . . . 109 C13 50 14N 61 46W
Natashquan →, Canada . . . 109 C13 50 7N 61 50W
Natchez, U.S.A. . . . . . . . . 111 D8 31 34N 91 24W
Natchitoches, U.S.A. . . . . . 111 D8 31 46N 93 5W
Nathdwara, India . . . . . . . 84 G8 24 55N 73 50 E
Natitingou, Benin . . . . . . . 94 F6 10 20N 1 26 E
Natron, L., Tanzania . . . . . 96 E7 2 20S 36 0 E
Natuna Besar, Kepulauan, Indonesia . . . . . . . . . . 83 C2 4 0N 108 15 E
Nauru ■, Pac. Oc. . . . . . . 102 H8 1 0S 166 0 E
Navarino, Chile . . . . . . . . 121 H3 55 0S 67 40W
Navarra □, Spain . . . . . . . 69 A5 42 40N 1 40W
Navenby, U.K. . . . . . . . . . 23 F7 53 6N 0 31W
Naver →, U.K. . . . . . . . . . 19 E9 58 32N 4 14W
Navojoa, Mexico . . . . . . . 114 B3 27 0N 109 30W
Navsari, India . . . . . . . . . 84 J8 20 57N 72 59 E
Nawabshah, Pakistan . . . . 84 F6 26 15N 68 25 E
Naxçivan □, Azerbaijan . . . 73 G8 39 25N 45 26 E
Náxos, Greece . . . . . . . . . 71 F11 37 8N 25 25 E
Nazaré, Brazil . . . . . . . . . 122 B3 13 2S 39 0W
Nazas →, Mexico . . . . . . . 114 B4 25 35N 103 25W
Nazca, Peru . . . . . . . . . . 120 D2 14 50S 74 57W
Naze, The, U.K. . . . . . . . . 25 C11 51 53N 1 18 E
Ndjamena, Chad . . . . . . . 95 F8 12 10N 14 59 E
Ndola, Zambia . . . . . . . . 97 G5 13 0S 28 34 E
Neagh, Lough, U.K. . . . . . . 29 B9 54 37N 6 25W
Near Is., U.S.A. . . . . . . . . 108 C1 52 30N 174 0 E
Neath, U.K. . . . . . . . . . . 24 C1 51 39N 3 48W
Nebitdag, Turkmenistan . . . 87 B8 39 30N 54 22 E
Nebraska □, U.S.A. . . . . . 110 B7 41 30N 99 30W
Neckar →, Germany . . . . . 66 D5 49 27N 8 29 E
Necochea, Argentina . . . . 121 F4 38 30S 58 50W
Needham Market, U.K. . . . 25 B11 52 9N 1 4 E
Needles, The, U.K. . . . . . . 24 E5 50 39N 1 35W
Neenah, U.S.A. . . . . . . . . 112 C3 44 11N 88 28W
Neepawa, Canada . . . . . . 108 C10 50 15N 99 30W
Neftekumsk, Russia . . . . . 73 F7 44 46N 44 50 E
Negaunee, U.S.A. . . . . . . 112 B4 46 30N 87 36W
Negele, Ethiopia . . . . . . . 88 F2 5 20N 39 36 E
Negombo, Sri Lanka . . . . . 84 R11 7 12N 79 50 E
Negra, Pta., Peru . . . . . . . 116 D2 6 6S 81 10W
Negril, Jamaica . . . . . . . . 114 a 18 22N 78 20W
Negro →, Argentina . . . . . 121 G3 41 2S 62 47W
Negro →, Brazil . . . . . . . . 120 C3 3 0S 60 0W
Negros, Phil. . . . . . . . . . 83 C4 9 30N 122 40 E
Neijiang, China . . . . . . . . 80 D5 29 35N 104 55 E
Neisse →, Europe . . . . . . . 66 B8 52 4N 14 46 E
Neiva, Colombia . . . . . . . 120 B2 2 56N 75 18W
Nellore, India . . . . . . . . . 84 M11 14 27N 79 59 E
Nelson, Canada . . . . . . . . 108 D8 49 30N 117 20W
Nelson, N.Z. . . . . . . . . . 99 J13 41 18S 173 16 E
Nelson, U.K. . . . . . . . . . 23 C5 53 50N 2 13W
Nelson →, Canada . . . . . . 108 C10 54 33N 98 2W
Neman →, Lithuania . . . . . 72 C3 55 25N 21 10 E
Nenagh, Ireland . . . . . . . 30 C6 52 52N 8 11W
Nene →, U.K. . . . . . . . . . 23 G9 52 49N 0 11 E
Nenjiang, China . . . . . . . . 81 B7 49 10N 125 10 E
Neosho →, U.S.A. . . . . . . 111 C7 36 48N 95 18W
Nepal ■, Asia . . . . . . . . . 85 F14 28 0N 84 30 E
Nephi, U.S.A. . . . . . . . . . 110 C4 39 43N 111 50W
Nephin, Ireland . . . . . . . . 28 C3 54 1N 9 22W
Neryungri, Russia . . . . . . 79 D14 57 38N 124 28 E
Ness, L., U.K. . . . . . . . . . 19 H8 57 15N 4 32W
Neston, U.K. . . . . . . . . . 23 F2 53 17N 3 4W
Netherbury, U.K. . . . . . . . 24 E3 50 46N 2 45W
Netherlands ■, Europe . . . 65 C5 52 0N 5 30 E
Netherlands Antilles ☑, W. Indies . . . . . . . . . . 115 E11 12 15N 69 0W
Netley, U.K. . . . . . . . . . . 24 E6 50 52N 1 20W
Nettilling L., Canada . . . . . 109 B12 66 30N 71 0W
Nettlebed, U.K. . . . . . . . . 25 C7 51 34N 0 59W
Nettleham, U.K. . . . . . . . . 23 F8 53 16N 0 29W
Neuchâtel, Switz. . . . . . . 66 E4 47 0N 6 55 E
Neuchâtel, Lac de, Switz. . . 66 E4 46 53N 6 50 E
Neuquén, Argentina . . . . . 121 F3 38 55S 68 0W
Neusiedler See, Austria . . . 67 E9 47 50N 16 47 E
Neva →, Russia . . . . . . . . 72 C5 59 50N 30 30 E
Nevada □, U.S.A. . . . . . . 110 C3 39 0N 117 0W
Nevers, France . . . . . . . . 68 C5 47 0N 3 9 E
Nevinnomyssk, Russia . . . . 73 F7 44 40N 42 0 E
New Abbey, U.K. . . . . . . . 22 C1 54 59N 3 37W
New Alresford, U.K. . . . . . 24 D6 51 5N 1 8W
New Amsterdam, Guyana . . 120 B4 6 15N 57 36W
New Bedford, U.S.A. . . . . 113 E12 41 38N 70 56W
New Britain, Papua N. G. . . 98 B9 5 50S 150 20 E
New Britain, U.S.A. . . . . . 113 E11 41 40N 72 47W
New Brunswick, U.S.A. . . . 113 E10 40 30N 74 27W
New Brunswick □, Canada . 109 D13 46 50N 66 30W
New Caledonia ☑, Pac. Oc. . 99 E12 21 0S 165 0 E
New Castle, Ind., U.S.A. . . 112 F5 39 55N 85 22W
New Castle, Pa., U.S.A. . . . 112 E7 41 0N 80 21W
New Delhi, India . . . . . . . 84 E10 28 37N 77 13 E
New England □, U.S.A. . . . 111 B12 46 32N 102 52W
New Forest, U.K. . . . . . . . 24 E5 50 53N 1 34W
New Galloway, U.K. . . . . . 20 D7 55 5N 4 9W
New Georgia Is., Solomon Is. . 99 B10 8 15S 157 30 E
New Glasgow, Canada . . . . 109 D13 45 35N 62 36W
New Guinea, Oceania . . . . 98 B7 4 0S 136 0 E
New Hampshire □, U.S.A. . 113 D12 44 0N 71 30W
New Haven, U.S.A. . . . . . 113 E11 41 18N 72 55W
New Hebrides = Vanuatu ■, Pac. Oc. . . . . . . . . . . 99 D12 15 0S 168 0 E
New Holland, U.K. . . . . . . 23 E8 53 42N 0 21W
New Iberia, U.S.A. . . . . . . 111 D8 30 1N 91 49W
New Ireland, Papua N. G. . . 98 A9 3 20S 151 50 E
New Jersey □, U.S.A. . . . . 113 E10 40 0N 74 30W
New Lexington, U.S.A. . . . 112 F6 39 43N 82 13W
New Liskeard, Canada . . . . 109 D12 47 31N 79 41W
New London, U.S.A. . . . . . 113 E11 41 22N 72 6W
New Mexico □, U.S.A. . . . 110 D5 34 30N 106 0W
New Mills, U.K. . . . . . . . . 23 F5 53 23N 2 0W
New Milton, U.K. . . . . . . . 24 E5 50 45N 1 40W
New Orleans, U.S.A. . . . . 111 E8 29 58N 90 4W
New Philadelphia, U.S.A. . . 112 E7 40 30N 81 27W
New Plymouth, N.Z. . . . . . 99 H13 39 4S 174 5 E
New Providence I., Bahamas . 115 B9 25 25N 78 35W
New Quay, U.K. . . . . . . . . 26 C5 52 13N 4 21W
New Radnor, U.K. . . . . . . 23 H2 52 15N 3 9W
New Romney, U.K. . . . . . . 25 E10 50 59N 0 57 E
New Ross, Ireland . . . . . . 31 D9 52 23N 6 57W
New Rossington, U.K. . . . . 23 F6 53 29N 1 4W
New Siberian Is., Russia . . 79 B15 75 0N 142 0 E
New South Wales □, Australia . 98 G8 33 0S 146 0 E
New York, U.S.A. . . . . . . 113 E11 40 45N 74 0W
New York □, U.S.A. . . . . . 113 D9 43 0N 75 0W
New Zealand ■, Oceania . . 99 J14 40 0S 176 0 E
Newark, Del., U.S.A. . . . . 113 F10 39 41N 75 46W
Newark, N.J., U.S.A. . . . . 113 E10 40 44N 74 10W
Newark, N.Y., U.S.A. . . . . 112 D9 43 3N 77 6W
Newark, Ohio, U.S.A. . . . . 112 E6 40 3N 82 24W
Newark-on-Trent, U.K. . . . 23 F7 53 5N 0 48W
Newberry, U.S.A. . . . . . . 112 B5 46 21N 85 30W

Newbiggin-by-the-Sea, U.K. . 22 B5 55 11N 1 31W
Newbigging, U.K. . . . . . . . 22 A1 55 42N 3 34W
Newburgh, U.S.A. . . . . . . 113 E10 41 30N 74 1W
Newburn, U.K. . . . . . . . . 22 C5 54 59N 1 43W
Newbury, U.K. . . . . . . . . 24 D6 51 24N 1 20W
Newburyport, U.S.A. . . . . 113 D12 42 49N 70 53W
Newby Bridge, U.K. . . . . . 22 D3 54 17N 2 57W
Newcastle, Australia . . . . . 98 G9 33 0S 151 46 E
Newcastle, Canada . . . . . . 113 B15 47 1N 65 38W
Newcastle, U.K. . . . . . . . 29 C10 54 13N 5 54W
Newcastle Emlyn, U.K. . . . 26 C5 52 2N 4 28W
Newcastle-under-Lyme, U.K. . 23 F4 53 1N 2 14W
Newcastle-upon-Tyne, U.K. . 22 C5 54 58N 1 36W
Newcastle West, Ireland . . 30 D4 52 27N 9 3W
Newcastleton, U.K. . . . . . 22 B3 55 11N 2 49W
Newent, U.K. . . . . . . . . . 24 C4 51 56N 2 24W
Newfoundland & Labrador □, Canada . . . . . . . . . . 109 C14 53 0N 58 0W
Newham □, U.K. . . . . . . . 25 C9 51 31N 0 3 E
Newhaven, U.K. . . . . . . . 25 E9 50 47N 0 3 E
Newington, Kent, U.K. . . . 25 D11 51 21N 0 41 E
Newington, Kent, U.K. . . . 25 D11 51 5N 1 7 E
Newlyn, U.K. . . . . . . . . . 27 G2 50 6N 5 34W
Newlyn East, U.K. . . . . . . 27 G3 50 22N 5 5W
Newman, Australia . . . . . . 98 E2 23 18S 119 45 E
Newmarket, Ireland . . . . . 30 D5 52 13N 9 0W
Newmarket, U.K. . . . . . . . 25 B9 52 15N 0 25 E
Newnham, U.K. . . . . . . . . 24 C4 51 48N 2 27W
Newport, Ireland . . . . . . . 28 D2 53 53N 9 33W
Newport, Essex, U.K. . . . . 25 C9 51 59N 0 14 E
Newport, I. of W., U.K. . . . 24 E6 50 42N 1 17W
Newport, Newp., U.K. . . . . 24 C3 51 35N 3 0W
Newport, Pembs., U.K. . . . 26 C4 52 1N 4 51W
Newport, Telford & Wrekin, U.K. . . . . . . . . . . 23 G4 52 46N 2 22W
Newport, Ark., U.S.A. . . . . 111 C8 35 37N 91 16W
Newport, Ky., U.S.A. . . . . 112 F5 39 5N 84 30W
Newport, R.I., U.S.A. . . . . 113 E12 41 29N 71 19W
Newport, Vt., U.S.A. . . . . . 113 C11 44 56N 72 13W
Newport News, U.S.A. . . . 111 C11 36 59N 76 25W
Newport Pagnell, U.K. . . . 25 B7 52 5N 0 43W
Newquay, U.K. . . . . . . . . 27 G3 50 25N 5 6W
Newry, U.K. . . . . . . . . . . 29 C9 54 11N 6 21W
Newton Abbot, U.K. . . . . . 27 F6 50 32N 3 37W
Newton Arlosh, U.K. . . . . . 22 C2 54 53N 3 14W
Newton Aycliffe, U.K. . . . . 22 C5 54 37N 1 34W
Newton Ferrers, U.K. . . . . 27 G5 50 19N 4 3W
Newton le Willows, U.K. . . 23 F3 53 28N 2 38W
Newton St. Cyres, U.K. . . . 24 E1 50 46N 3 36W
Newton Stewart, U.K. . . . . 20 E6 54 57N 4 30W
Newtonmore, U.K. . . . . . . 19 H9 57 4N 4 8W
Newtown, U.K. . . . . . . . . 23 G2 52 31N 3 19W
Newtown St. Boswells, U.K. . 22 A3 55 34N 2 39W
Newtownabbey, U.K. . . . . 29 B10 54 40N 5 56W
Newtownards, U.K. . . . . . 29 B10 54 36N 5 42W
Newtownstewart, U.K. . . . 28 B7 54 43N 7 23W
Neyshābūr, Iran . . . . . . . 87 B9 36 10N 58 50 E
Ngaoundéré, Cameroon . . . 96 C2 7 15N 13 35 E
Ngoring Hu, China . . . . . . 80 C4 34 55N 97 5 E
Nha Trang, Vietnam . . . . . 83 B2 12 16N 109 10 E
Nhamundá →, Brazil . . . . . 120 C4 2 12S 56 41W
Niagara Falls, Canada . . . . 109 D12 43 7N 79 5W
Niagara Falls, U.S.A. . . . . 112 D8 43 5N 79 4W
Niamey, Niger . . . . . . . . . 94 F6 13 27N 2 6 E
Nias, Indonesia . . . . . . . . 83 C1 1 0N 97 30 E
Nicaragua ■, Cent. Amer. . . 114 E7 11 40N 85 30W
Nicaragua, L. de, Nic. . . . . 114 E7 12 0N 85 30W
Nice, France . . . . . . . . . . 68 E7 43 42N 7 14 E
Nicholasville, U.S.A. . . . . 112 G5 37 53N 84 34W
Nicobar Is., Ind. Oc. . . . . . 83 C1 8 0N 93 30 E
Nicosia, Cyprus . . . . . . . . 86 C3 35 10N 33 25 E
Nicoya, Pen. de, Costa Rica . 114 F7 9 45N 85 40W
Nidd →, U.K. . . . . . . . . . 23 E6 53 59N 1 23W
Nidderdale, U.K. . . . . . . . 22 D5 54 5N 1 46W
Niedersachsen □, Germany . 66 B5 52 50N 9 0 E
Nieuw Nickerie, Suriname . . 120 B4 6 0N 56 59W
Niğde, Turkey . . . . . . . . . 86 B3 37 58N 34 40 E
Niger ■, W. Afr. . . . . . . . . 94 E7 17 30N 10 0 E
Niger →, W. Afr. . . . . . . . 94 G7 5 33N 6 33 E
Nigeria ■, W. Afr. . . . . . . . 94 G7 8 30N 8 0 E
Niigata, Japan . . . . . . . . . 82 E6 37 58N 139 0 E
Niihau, U.S.A. . . . . . . . . . 110 H14 21 54N 160 9W
Nijmegen, Neths. . . . . . . . 65 C5 51 50N 5 52 E
Nikolayev, Ukraine . . . . . . 73 E5 46 58N 32 0 E
Nikolayevsk-na-Amur, Russia . 79 D16 53 8N 140 44 E
Nikopol, Ukraine . . . . . . . 73 E5 47 35N 34 25 E
Nile, Africa . . . . . . . . . . 95 B12 30 10N 31 6 E
Nimach, India . . . . . . . . . 84 G9 24 30N 74 56 E
Nîmes, France . . . . . . . . . 68 E6 43 50N 4 23 E
Nimrūz □, Afghan. . . . . . . 87 D10 30 0N 62 0 E
Ninawá, Iraq . . . . . . . . . . 86 B5 36 25N 43 10 E
Ninfield, U.K. . . . . . . . . . 25 E9 50 53N 0 26 E
Ningbo, China . . . . . . . . . 81 D7 29 51N 121 28 E
Ningxia Hui □, China . . . . . 80 C5 38 0N 106 0 E
Niobrara →, U.S.A. . . . . . . 110 B7 42 46N 98 3W
Niort, France . . . . . . . . . 68 C3 46 19N 0 29W
Nipawin, Canada . . . . . . . 108 C9 53 20N 104 0W
Nipigon, Canada . . . . . . . 112 A3 49 0N 88 17W
Nipigon, L., Canada . . . . . 109 D11 49 50N 88 30W
Nipissing, L., Canada . . . . 109 D12 46 20N 80 0W
Niquelândia, Brazil . . . . . . 122 B1 14 33S 48 23W
Niš, Serbia & M. . . . . . . . 71 C9 43 19N 21 58 E
Niterói, Brazil . . . . . . . . . 122 D2 22 52S 43 0W
Nith →, U.K. . . . . . . . . . . 21 D8 55 14N 3 33W
Niton, U.K. . . . . . . . . . . 24 E6 50 35N 1 17W
Nitra, Slovak Rep. . . . . . . 67 D10 48 19N 18 4 E
Nitra →, Slovak Rep. . . . . 67 E10 47 46N 18 10 E
Niuafo'ou, Tonga . . . . . . . 99 D15 15 30S 175 58W
Niue, Cook Is. . . . . . . . . . 99 D17 19 2S 169 54W
Nivernais, France . . . . . . . 68 C5 47 15N 3 30 E
Nizamabad, India . . . . . . . 84 K11 18 45N 78 7 E
Nizhnekamsk, Russia . . . . 72 C9 55 38N 51 49 E
Nizhnevartovsk, Russia . . . 79 C9 60 56N 76 38 E
Nizhniy Novgorod, Russia . . 72 C7 56 20N 44 0 E
Nizhniy Tagil, Russia . . . . 72 C10 57 55N 59 57 E
Nizhyn, Ukraine . . . . . . . 73 D5 51 5N 31 55 E
Nkongsamba, Cameroon . . 96 D1 4 55N 9 55 E
Nobeoka, Japan . . . . . . . 82 G2 32 36N 131 41 E
Noblesville, U.S.A. . . . . . 112 E5 40 3N 86 1W
Nogales, Mexico . . . . . . . 114 A2 31 20N 110 56W
Nogales, U.S.A. . . . . . . . . 110 D4 31 20N 110 56W
Noirmoutier, Î. de, France . . 68 C2 46 58N 2 10W
Nola, C.A.R. . . . . . . . . . . 96 D3 3 35N 16 4 E
Nome, U.S.A. . . . . . . . . . 108 B3 64 30N 165 25W
Nord-Ostsee-Kanal, Germany . 66 A5 54 12N 9 32 E
Nordelph, U.K. . . . . . . . . 23 G9 52 35N 0 17 E
Nordfriesische Inseln, Germany . 66 A5 54 40N 8 20 E
Nordkapp, Norway . . . . . . 63 C9 71 10N 25 50 E
Nordrhein-Westfalen □, Germany . . . . . . . . . . 66 C4 51 45N 7 30 E
Nore →, Ireland . . . . . . . . 31 D9 52 25N 6 58W
Norfolk, Nebr., U.S.A. . . . . 111 B7 42 2N 97 25W
Norfolk, Va., U.S.A. . . . . . 111 C11 36 51N 76 17W
Norfolk □, U.K. . . . . . . . . 25 A10 52 39N 0 54 E
Norfolk I., Pac. Oc. . . . . . . 99 F12 28 58S 168 3 E
Norham, U.K. . . . . . . . . . 22 A4 55 43N 2 9W
Norilsk, Russia . . . . . . . . 79 C10 69 20N 88 6 E

Norman, U.S.A. . . . . . . . . 110 C7 35 13N 97 26W
Norman Wells, Canada . . . 108 B7 65 17N 126 51W
Normandie, France . . . . . . 68 B4 48 45N 0 10 E
Normanton, Australia . . . . 98 D7 17 40S 141 10 E
Normanton, U.K. . . . . . . . 23 E6 53 42N 1 24W
Norristown, U.S.A. . . . . . . 113 E10 40 7N 75 21W
Norrköping, Sweden . . . . . 63 F7 58 37N 16 11 E
Norrland, Sweden . . . . . . 63 E7 62 15N 15 45 E
Norseman, Australia . . . . . 98 G3 32 8S 121 43 E
Norte, Serra do, Brazil . . . 120 D4 11 20S 59 0W
North, C., Canada . . . . . . 109 D13 47 2N 60 20W
North Battleford, Canada . . 108 C9 52 50N 108 17W
North Bay, Canada . . . . . . 109 D12 46 20N 79 30W
North Berwick, U.K. . . . . . 21 B10 56 4N 2 42W
North C., Canada . . . . . . . 113 B15 47 5N 64 0W
North C., N.Z. . . . . . . . . . 99 G13 34 23S 173 4 E
North Canadian →, U.S.A. . 110 C7 35 16N 95 31W
North Carolina □, U.S.A. . . 111 C11 35 30N 80 0W
North Cerney, U.K. . . . . . . 24 C5 51 45N 1 57W
North Channel, Canada . . . 112 B6 46 0N 83 0W
North Channel, U.K. . . . . . 20 D4 55 13N 5 52W
North Dakota □, U.S.A. . . . 110 A7 47 30N 100 15W
North Dorset Downs, U.K. . 24 E4 50 51N 2 30W
North Downs, U.K. . . . . . . 25 D9 51 19N 0 21 E
North Esk →, U.K. . . . . . . 19 J13 56 46N 2 24W
North European Plain, Europe . 56 E10 55 0N 25 0 E
North Foreland, U.K. . . . . . 25 D11 51 22N 1 28 E
North Hill, U.K. . . . . . . . . 27 F5 50 33N 4 27W
North Hykeham, U.K. . . . . 23 F7 53 11N 0 35W
North I., N.Z. . . . . . . . . . 99 H14 38 0S 175 0 E
North Korea ■, Asia . . . . . 81 C7 40 0N 127 0 E
North Magnetic Pole, Canada . 54 A2 85 0N 107 0W
North Minch, U.K. . . . . . . 18 F6 58 5N 5 55W
North Molton, U.K. . . . . . . 24 D1 51 3N 3 49W
North Ossetia □, Russia . . 73 F7 43 30N 44 30 E
North Petherton, U.K. . . . . 24 D2 51 5N 3 1W
North Platte, U.S.A. . . . . . 110 B6 41 8N 100 46W
North Platte →, U.S.A. . . . 110 B6 41 7N 100 42W
North Pole, Arctic . . . . . . 54 A 90 0N 0 0W
North Pt., Barbados . . . . . 115 g 13 20N 59 37W
North Ronaldsay, U.K. . . . . 19 D13 59 22N 2 26W
North Saskatchewan →, Canada . . . . . . . . . . 108 C9 53 15N 105 5W
North Sea, Europe . . . . . . 64 C7 56 0N 4 0 E
North Sea Canal = Nord-Ostsee-Kanal, Germany . . . . 66 A5 54 12N 9 32 E
North Somercotes, U.K. . . . 23 F9 53 27N 0 8 E
North Sunderland, U.K. . . . 22 A5 55 34N 1 40W
North Tawton, U.K. . . . . . 27 F6 50 48N 3 54W
North Thompson →, Canada . 108 C7 50 40N 120 20W
North Thoresby, U.K. . . . . 23 F8 53 28N 0 4W
North Tidworth, U.K. . . . . . 24 D5 51 15N 1 40W
North Tyne →, U.K. . . . . . 22 C4 55 0N 2 8W
North Uist, U.K. . . . . . . . . 18 G3 57 40N 7 15W
North Vernon, U.S.A. . . . . 112 F5 39 0N 85 38W
North Walsham, U.K. . . . . 25 A11 52 50N 1 22 E
North West C., Australia . . . 98 E1 21 45S 114 9 E
North West Christmas I. Ridge, Pac. Oc. . . . . . . . . 103 G11 6 30N 165 0W
North West Frontier □, Pakistan . 84 C7 34 0N 72 0 E
North West Highlands, U.K. . 19 G8 57 33N 4 58W
North West River, Canada . 109 C13 53 30N 60 10W
North York Moors, U.K. . . . 22 D7 54 23N 0 53W
North Yorkshire □, U.K. . . . 22 D6 54 15N 1 25W
Northallerton, U.K. . . . . . . 22 D6 54 20N 1 26W
Northam, Australia . . . . . . 98 G2 31 35S 116 42 E
Northam, U.K. . . . . . . . . . 27 E5 51 2N 4 13W
Northampton, U.K. . . . . . . 25 B7 52 15N 0 53W
Northampton, U.S.A. . . . . 113 D11 42 19N 72 38W
Northamptonshire □, U.K. . 23 H7 52 16N 0 55W
Northern Areas □, Pakistan . 84 B9 36 30N 73 0 E
Northern Circars, India . . . 85 L13 17 30N 82 30 E
Northern Ireland □, U.K. . . 29 B8 54 45N 7 0W
Northern Marianas ☑, Pac. Oc. . 102 F6 17 0N 145 0 E
Northern Territory □, Australia . 98 D5 20 0S 133 0 E
Northfleet, U.K. . . . . . . . . 25 D9 51 26N 0 20 E
Northiam, U.K. . . . . . . . . 25 E10 50 59N 0 36 E
Northleach, U.K. . . . . . . . 24 C5 51 49N 1 50W
Northrepps, U.K. . . . . . . . 25 A11 52 54N 1 21 E
Northumberland □, U.K. . . 22 B4 55 12N 2 0W
Northumberland Str., Canada . 109 D13 46 20N 64 0W
Northwest Territories □, Canada . . . . . . . . . . 108 B9 63 0N 118 0W
Northwich, U.K. . . . . . . . . 23 F3 53 15N 2 31W
Northwold, U.K. . . . . . . . . 25 A10 52 33N 0 36 E
Norton, N. Yorks., U.K. . . . 22 D7 54 8N 0 47W
Norton, Suffolk, U.K. . . . . 25 B10 52 16N 0 52 E
Norton Fitzwarren, U.K. . . . 24 D2 51 1N 3 8W
Norton Sd., U.S.A. . . . . . . 108 B3 63 50N 164 0W
Norwalk, U.S.A. . . . . . . . . 112 E6 41 15N 82 37W
Norway ■, Europe . . . . . . 63 E6 63 0N 11 0 E
Norway House, Canada . . . 108 C10 53 59N 97 50W
Norwegian Sea, Atl. Oc. . . 54 C8 66 0N 1 0 E
Norwich, U.K. . . . . . . . . . 25 A11 52 38N 1 18 E
Norwich, U.S.A. . . . . . . . . 113 D10 42 32N 75 32W
Noss Hd., U.K. . . . . . . . . 19 F11 58 28N 3 4W
Nossob →, S. Africa . . . . . 97 K4 26 55S 20 45 E
Notre Dame B., Canada . . . 109 D14 49 45N 55 30W
Nottaway →, Canada . . . . . 109 C12 51 22N 78 55W
Nottingham, U.K. . . . . . . . 23 G6 52 58N 1 10W
Nottingham I., Canada . . . . 109 B12 63 20N 77 55W
Nottinghamshire □, U.K. . . 23 F6 53 10N 1 3W
Nouâdhibou, Mauritania . . 94 D2 20 54N 17 0W
Nouâdhibou, Ras, Mauritania . 94 D2 20 50N 17 0W
Nouakchott, Mauritania . . . 94 E2 18 9N 15 58W
Nouméa, N. Cal. . . . . . . . 99 E12 22 17S 166 30 E
Nova Casa Nova, Brazil . . . 122 A2 9 25S 41 5W
Nova Friburgo, Brazil . . . . 122 D2 22 16S 42 30W
Nova Iguaçu, Brazil . . . . . 122 D2 22 45S 43 28W
Nova Lima, Brazil . . . . . . . 122 D2 19 59S 43 51W
Nova Scotia □, Canada . . . 109 D13 45 10N 63 0W
Nova Venécia, Brazil . . . . 122 C2 18 45S 40 24W
Novara, Italy . . . . . . . . . 68 D8 45 28N 8 38 E
Novaya Zemlya, Russia . . . 79 B7 75 0N 56 0 E
Novgorod, Russia . . . . . . 72 C5 58 30N 31 25 E
Novi Sad, Serbia & M. . . . 71 B8 45 18N 19 52 E
Novo Remanso, Brazil . . . . 122 A2 9 41S 42 4W
Novocherkassk, Russia . . . 73 E7 47 27N 40 15 E
Novokuybyshevsk, Russia . . 72 D8 53 7N 49 58 E
Novokuznetsk, Russia . . . . 79 D10 53 45N 87 10 E
Novomoskovsk, Russia . . . 72 D6 54 5N 38 15 E
Novorossiysk, Russia . . . . 73 F6 44 43N 37 46 E
Novoshakhtinsk, Russia . . . 73 E7 47 46N 39 58 E
Novosibirsk, Russia . . . . . 79 D10 55 0N 83 5 E
Novotroitsk, Russia . . . . . 72 D10 51 10N 58 15 E
Nowy Sącz, Poland . . . . . . 67 D11 49 40N 20 41 E
Nubia, Africa . . . . . . . . . 90 D7 21 0N 32 0 E
Nubian Desert, Sudan . . . . 95 D12 21 30N 33 30 E
Nueces →, U.S.A. . . . . . . . 110 E7 27 51N 97 30W
Nueltin L., Canada . . . . . . 108 B10 60 30N 99 30W
Nueva Rosita, Mexico . . . . 114 B4 28 0N 101 11W
Nuevitas, Cuba . . . . . . . . 115 C9 21 30N 77 20W
Nuevo Laredo, Mexico . . . 114 B5 27 30N 99 30W
Nuku'alofa, Tonga . . . . . . 99 E16 21 10S 174 0W
Nukulaelae, Tuvalu . . . . . 99 B14 9 23S 179 52 E
Nukus, Uzbekistan . . . . . . 87 A9 42 27N 59 41 E
Nullarbor Plain, Australia . . 98 G4 31 10S 129 0 E

Numazu, Japan . . . . . . . . 82 F6 35 7N 138 51 E
Nunavut □, Canada . . . . . 109 D8 66 0N 85 0W
Nuneaton, U.K. . . . . . . . . 23 G6 52 32N 1 27W
Nunivak I., U.S.A. . . . . . . 108 B3 60 10N 166 30W
Nunney, U.K. . . . . . . . . . 24 D4 51 12N 2 22W
Nuremberg, Germany . . . . 66 D6 49 27N 11 3 E
Nusaybin, Turkey . . . . . . . 73 G7 37 3N 41 10 E
Nuuk, Greenland . . . . . . . 109 B14 64 10N 51 35W
Nyahururu, Kenya . . . . . . 96 D7 0 2N 36 27 E
Nyainqentanglha Shan, China . 80 D4 30 0N 90 0 E
Nyâlâ, Sudan . . . . . . . . . 95 F10 12 2N 24 58 E
Nyasa, L., Africa . . . . . . . 97 G6 12 30S 34 30 E
Nyíregyháza, Hungary . . . . 67 E11 47 58N 21 47 E
Nysa, Poland . . . . . . . . . 67 C9 50 30N 17 22 E

## O

Oa, Mull of, U.K. . . . . . . . 20 C3 55 35N 6 20W
Oadby, U.K. . . . . . . . . . . 23 G6 52 36N 1 5W
Oahe, L., U.S.A. . . . . . . . 110 A6 44 27N 100 24W
Oahu, U.S.A. . . . . . . . . . 110 H16 21 28N 157 58W
Oak Hill, U.S.A. . . . . . . . . 112 G7 37 59N 81 9W
Oak Ridge, U.S.A. . . . . . . 111 C10 36 1N 84 16W
Oakengates, U.K. . . . . . . . 23 G4 52 41N 2 26W
Oakham, U.K. . . . . . . . . . 23 G7 52 40N 0 43W
Oakland, U.S.A. . . . . . . . . 110 C2 37 49N 122 16W
Oates Land, Antarctica . . . 55 C11 69 0S 160 0 E
Oaxaca, Mexico . . . . . . . . 114 D5 17 2N 96 40W
Ob →, Russia . . . . . . . . . 79 C8 66 45N 69 30 E
Ob, G. of, Russia . . . . . . . 79 C9 69 0N 73 0 E
Oba, Canada . . . . . . . . . 109 D11 49 4N 84 7W
Oban, U.K. . . . . . . . . . . . 20 B5 56 25N 5 29W
Oberhausen, Germany . . . 66 C4 51 28N 6 51 E
Obi, Indonesia . . . . . . . . . 83 D4 1 23S 127 45 E
Óbidos, Brazil . . . . . . . . . 120 C4 1 50S 55 30W
Obihiro, Japan . . . . . . . . . 82 B8 42 56N 143 12 E
Obozerskiy, Russia . . . . . . 72 B7 63 34N 40 21 E
Obshchi Syrt, Russia . . . . 56 E16 52 0N 53 0 E
Ocala, U.S.A. . . . . . . . . . 111 E10 29 11N 82 8W
Occidental, Cordillera, Colombia . . . . . . . . . . 116 C3 5 0N 76 0W
Ocean City, U.S.A. . . . . . . 113 F10 39 17N 74 35W
Oceanside, U.S.A. . . . . . . 110 D3 33 12N 117 23W
Ochil Hills, U.K. . . . . . . . . 21 B8 56 14N 3 40W
Ocho Rios, Jamaica . . . . . 114 a 18 24N 77 6W
Oconto, U.S.A. . . . . . . . . 112 C4 44 53N 87 52W
Odawara, Japan . . . . . . . 82 F6 35 20N 139 6 E
Odense, Denmark . . . . . . 63 F6 55 22N 10 23 E
Oder →, Europe . . . . . . . . 66 B8 53 33N 14 38 E
Odessa, Ukraine . . . . . . . 73 E5 46 30N 30 45 E
Odessa, U.S.A. . . . . . . . . 110 D6 31 52N 102 23W
Odiham, U.K. . . . . . . . . . 25 D7 51 15N 0 56W
Odintsovo, Russia . . . . . . 72 C6 55 39N 37 15 E
Offa, Nigeria . . . . . . . . . . 94 G6 8 13N 4 42 E
Offaly □, Ireland . . . . . . . 31 B8 53 15N 7 30W
Offenbach, Germany . . . . . 66 C5 50 6N 8 44 E
Ogaden, Ethiopia . . . . . . . 88 F3 7 30N 45 30 E
Ōgaki, Japan . . . . . . . . . 82 F5 35 21N 136 37 E
Ogasawara Gunto, Pac. Oc. . 102 E6 27 0N 142 0 E
Ogbomosho, Nigeria . . . . . 94 G6 8 1N 4 11 E
Ogden, U.S.A. . . . . . . . . . 110 B4 41 13N 111 58W
Ogdensburg, U.S.A. . . . . . 113 C10 44 42N 75 30W
Ogooué →, Gabon . . . . . . 96 E1 1 0S 9 0 E
Ohio □, U.S.A. . . . . . . . . 112 E5 40 15N 82 45W
Ohio →, U.S.A. . . . . . . . . 111 C9 36 59N 89 8W
Ohře →, Czech Rep. . . . . . 66 C8 50 30N 14 10 E
Ohrid, L., Macedonia . . . . 71 D9 41 8N 20 52 E
Oil City, U.S.A. . . . . . . . . 112 E8 41 26N 79 42W
Oise →, France . . . . . . . . 68 B5 49 0N 2 4 E
Oistins, Barbados . . . . . . 115 g 13 4N 59 33W
Oistins B., Barbados . . . . . 115 g 13 4N 59 33W
Ōita, Japan . . . . . . . . . . 82 G2 33 14N 131 36 E
Ojos del Salado, Cerro, Argentina . . . . . . . . . 121 E3 27 0S 68 40W
Oka →, Russia . . . . . . . . . 72 C7 56 20N 43 59 E
Okara, Pakistan . . . . . . . . 84 D8 30 50N 73 31 E
Okavango Delta, Botswana . 97 H4 18 45S 22 45 E
Okayama, Japan . . . . . . . 82 F3 34 40N 133 54 E
Okazaki, Japan . . . . . . . . 82 F5 34 57N 137 10 E
Okeechobee, L., U.S.A. . . . 111 E10 27 0N 80 50W
Okehampton, U.K. . . . . . . 27 F5 50 44N 4 0W
Okhotsk, Russia . . . . . . . 79 D16 59 20N 143 10 E
Okhotsk, Sea of, Asia . . . . 79 D16 55 0N 145 0 E
Oki-Shotō, Japan . . . . . . . 82 E3 36 5N 133 15 E
Okinawa-Jima, Japan . . . . 81 D7 26 32N 128 0 E
Oklahoma □, U.S.A. . . . . . 110 C7 35 20N 97 30W
Oklahoma City, U.S.A. . . . 110 C7 35 30N 97 30W
Oktyabrsk, Kazakhstan . . . 73 E10 49 28N 57 25 E
Oktyabrskiy, Russia . . . . . 72 D9 54 28N 53 28 E
Öland, Sweden . . . . . . . . 63 F7 56 45N 16 38 E
Olavarría, Argentina . . . . . 121 F3 36 55S 60 20W
Old Basing, U.K. . . . . . . . 24 D6 51 16N 1 3W
Old Crow, Canada . . . . . . 108 B6 67 30N 139 55W
Old Fletton, U.K. . . . . . . . 23 G8 52 33N 0 14W
Old Leake, U.K. . . . . . . . . 23 F9 53 2N 0 6 E
Old Town, U.S.A. . . . . . . . 113 C13 44 56N 68 39W
Oldbury, U.K. . . . . . . . . . 24 C3 51 38N 2 33W
Oldcastle, Ireland . . . . . . 29 D7 53 46N 7 10W
Oldenburg, Germany . . . . 66 B5 53 9N 8 13 E
Oldham, U.K. . . . . . . . . . 23 E4 53 33N 2 7W
Oldmeldrum, U.K. . . . . . . 19 H13 57 20N 2 19W
Olean, U.S.A. . . . . . . . . . 112 D8 42 5N 78 26W
Olekminsk, Russia . . . . . . 79 C14 60 25N 120 30 E
Olenek →, Russia . . . . . . . 79 B14 73 0N 120 10 E
Oléron, Î. d', France . . . . . 68 D3 45 55N 1 15W
Oliveira, Brazil . . . . . . . . 122 D2 20 39S 44 50W
Ollagüe, Chile . . . . . . . . . 120 E3 21 15S 68 10W
Ollerton, U.K. . . . . . . . . . 23 F6 53 12N 1 1W
Olney, U.K. . . . . . . . . . . 25 B7 52 10N 0 41W
Olney, U.S.A. . . . . . . . . . 112 F3 38 44N 88 5W
Olomouc, Czech Rep. . . . . 67 D9 49 38N 17 12 E
Olsztyn, Poland . . . . . . . . 67 B11 53 48N 20 29 E
Olt →, Romania . . . . . . . . 67 G13 43 43N 24 51 E
Olympia, Greece . . . . . . . 71 F9 37 39N 21 39 E
Olympia, U.S.A. . . . . . . . . 110 A2 47 3N 122 53W
Olympus, Mt., Greece . . . . 71 D10 40 6N 22 23 E
Olympus, Mt., U.S.A. . . . . 110 A2 47 48N 123 43W
Omagh, U.K. . . . . . . . . . 28 B7 54 36N 7 19W
Omaha, U.S.A. . . . . . . . . 111 B7 41 17N 95 58W
Oman ■, Asia . . . . . . . . . 88 C6 23 0N 58 0 E
Oman, G. of, Asia . . . . . . 87 E8 24 30N 58 30 E
Ombersley, U.K. . . . . . . . 23 H4 52 16N 2 13W
Omdurmân, Sudan . . . . . . 95 E12 15 40N 32 28 E
Ometepec, Mexico . . . . . . 114 D5 16 39N 98 23W
Omsk, Russia . . . . . . . . . 79 D9 55 0N 73 12 E
Ōmuta, Japan . . . . . . . . . 82 G2 33 5N 130 26 E
Ondangwa, Namibia . . . . . 97 H3 17 57S 16 4 E
Onega →, Russia . . . . . . . 72 B6 63 58N 38 2 E
Onega, G. of, Russia . . . . 72 B6 64 24N 36 38 E
Onega, L., Russia . . . . . . 72 B6 61 44N 35 22 E
O'Neill, U.S.A. . . . . . . . . 110 B7 42 27N 98 39W
Oneonta, U.S.A. . . . . . . . 113 D10 42 27N 75 4W
Onitsha, Nigeria . . . . . . . 94 G7 6 6N 6 42 E
Onny →, U.K. . . . . . . . . . 23 H3 52 24N 2 47W

Onslow B., U.S.A. ... 111 D11 34 20N 77 15W
Ontario, U.S.A. ... 110 B3 44 2N 116 58W
Ontario □, Canada ... 109 C11 48 0N 83 0W
Ontario, L., N. Amer. ... 112 D8 43 20N 78 0W
Ontonagon, U.S.A. ... 112 B3 46 52N 89 19W
Oostende, Belgium ... 65 C2 51 15N 2 54 E
Opava, Czech Rep. ... 67 D9 49 57N 17 58 E
Opole, Poland ... 67 C9 50 42N 17 58 E
Oradea, Romania ... 67 E11 47 2N 21 58 E
Öræfajökull, Iceland ... 63 B2 64 2N 16 39W
Oral, Kazakhstan ... 73 D9 51 20N 51 20 E
Oran, Algeria ... 94 A5 35 45N 0 39W
Orange, Australia ... 98 G8 33 15S 149 7 E
Orange, France ... 68 D6 44 8N 4 47 E
Orange, U.S.A. ... 112 F8 38 15N 78 7W
Orange →, S. Africa ... 97 K3 28 41S 16 28 E
Orange, C., Brazil ... 120 B4 4 20N 51 30W
Orangeburg, U.S.A. ... 111 D10 33 30N 80 52W
Orangeville, Canada ... 112 D7 43 55N 80 5W
Ordu, Turkey ... 73 F6 40 55N 37 53 E
Örebro, Sweden ... 63 F7 59 20N 15 18 E
Oregon □, U.S.A. ... 110 B2 44 0N 121 0W
Orekhovo-Zuyevo, Russia ... 72 C6 55 50N 38 55 E
Orel, Russia ... 72 D6 52 57N 36 3 E
Orem, U.S.A. ... 110 B4 40 19N 111 42W
Orenburg, Russia ... 72 D10 51 45N 55 6 E
Orford, U.K. ... 25 B12 52 6N 1 33 E
Orford Ness, U.K. ... 25 B12 52 5N 1 35 E
Orhon Gol →, Mongolia ... 80 A5 50 21N 106 0 E
Oriental, Cordillera, Colombia ... 116 C3 6 0N 73 0W
Orinoco →, Venezuela ... 120 B3 9 15N 61 30W
Orissa □, India ... 85 K14 20 0N 84 0 E
Oristano, Italy ... 70 E3 39 54N 8 36 E
Orizaba, Mexico ... 114 D5 18 51N 97 6W
Orizaba, Pico de, Mexico ... 114 D5 19 0N 97 20W
Orkney □, U.K. ... 19 D11 59 2N 3 13W
Orlando, U.S.A. ... 111 E10 28 33N 81 23W
Orléanais, France ... 68 C5 48 0N 2 0 E
Orléans, France ... 68 C4 47 54N 1 52 E
Orléans, Î. d', Canada ... 113 B12 46 54N 70 58W
Ormara, Pakistan ... 84 G4 25 16N 64 33 E
Ormesby St. Margaret, U.K. ... 25 A12 52 41N 1 41 E
Ormoc, Phil. ... 83 B4 11 0N 124 37 E
Ormskirk, U.K. ... 23 E3 53 35N 2 54W
Örnsköldsvik, Sweden ... 63 E7 63 17N 18 40 E
Oronsay, U.K. ... 20 B3 56 1N 6 15W
Orsha, Belarus ... 72 D5 54 30N 30 25 E
Orsk, Russia ... 79 D7 51 12N 58 34 E
Oruro, Bolivia ... 120 D3 18 0S 67 9W
Oruzgān □, Afghan. ... 87 C11 33 30N 66 0 E
Orwell →, U.K. ... 25 C11 51 59N 1 18 E
Ōsaka, Japan ... 82 F4 34 40N 135 30 E
Osh, Kyrgyzstan ... 87 A13 40 37N 72 49 E
Oshakati, Namibia ... 97 H3 17 45S 15 40 E
Oshawa, Canada ... 109 D12 43 50N 78 50W
Oshogbo, Nigeria ... 94 G6 7 48N 4 37 E
Osijek, Croatia ... 71 B8 45 34N 18 41 E
Osizweni, S. Africa ... 97 K6 27 49S 30 7 E
Oskaloosa, U.S.A. ... 111 B8 41 18N 92 39W
Oskarshamn, Sweden ... 63 F7 57 15N 16 27 E
Öskemen, Kazakhstan ... 79 D10 50 0N 82 36 E
Oslo, Norway ... 63 F6 59 55N 10 45 E
Oslofjorden, Norway ... 63 F6 59 20N 10 35 E
Osmaniye, Turkey ... 73 G6 37 5N 36 10 E
Osmotherley, U.K. ... 22 D6 54 22N 1 18W
Osnabrück, Germany ... 66 B5 52 17N 8 3 E
Osorno, Chile ... 121 G2 40 25S 73 0W
Ossa, Mt., Australia ... 98 J8 41 52S 146 3 E
Ossett, U.K. ... 23 E5 53 41N 1 34W
Ostend = Oostende, Belgium ... 65 C2 51 15N 2 54 E
Österdalälven, Sweden ... 63 E6 61 30N 13 45 E
Östersund, Sweden ... 63 E6 63 10N 14 38 E
Ostfriesische Inseln, Germany ... 66 B4 53 42N 7 0 E
Ostrava, Czech Rep. ... 67 D10 49 51N 18 18 E
Ostrołęka, Poland ... 67 B11 53 4N 21 32 E
Ostrów Wielkopolski, Poland ... 67 C9 51 36N 17 44 E
Ostrowiec-Świętokrzyski, Poland ... 67 C11 50 55N 21 22 E
Oswaldtwistle, U.K. ... 23 E4 53 43N 2 26W
Oswego, U.S.A. ... 112 D9 43 27N 76 31W
Oswestry, U.K. ... 23 G2 52 57N 3 3W
Otaru, Japan ... 82 B7 43 10N 141 0 E
Otjiwarongo, Namibia ... 97 J3 20 30S 16 33 E
Otley, U.K. ... 23 E5 53 54N 1 41W
Otranto, Italy ... 71 D8 40 9N 18 28 E
Otranto, Str. of, Italy ... 71 D8 40 15N 18 40 E
Ōtsu, Japan ... 82 F4 35 0N 135 50 E
Ottawa, Canada ... 109 D12 45 27N 75 42W
Ottawa Is., Canada ... 109 C11 59 35N 80 10W
Otter →, U.K. ... 27 F7 50 38N 3 19W
Otterburn, U.K. ... 22 B4 55 14N 2 11W
Ottery St. Mary, U.K. ... 24 E2 50 44N 3 17W
Ottumwa, U.S.A. ... 111 B8 41 1N 92 25W
Ouachita →, U.S.A. ... 111 D8 31 38N 91 49W
Ouachita Mts., U.S.A. ... 111 D8 34 40N 94 25W
Ouagadougou, Burkina Faso ... 94 F5 12 25N 1 30W
Oubangi →, Dem. Rep. of the Congo ... 96 E3 0 30S 17 50 E
Oudtshoorn, S. Africa ... 97 L4 33 35S 22 14 E
Ouezzane, Morocco ... 94 B4 34 51N 5 35W
Oughterard, Ireland ... 28 E3 53 26N 9 18W
Oujda, Morocco ... 94 B5 34 41N 1 55W
Oulton, U.K. ... 25 B12 52 30N 1 43 E
Oulton Broad, U.K. ... 25 B12 52 28N 1 42 E
Oulu, Finland ... 63 D9 65 1N 25 29 E
Oulujärvi, Finland ... 63 E9 64 25N 27 15 E
Oulujoki →, Finland ... 63 D9 65 1N 25 30 E
Oundle, U.K. ... 23 H8 52 29N 0 28W
Ourense, Spain ... 69 A2 42 19N 7 55W
Ouro Prêto, Brazil ... 122 D2 20 20S 43 30W
Ouse →, E. Susx., U.K. ... 25 E9 50 47N 0 4 E
Ouse →, N. Yorks., U.K. ... 23 E7 53 44N 0 55W
Outaouais →, Canada ... 109 D12 45 27N 74 8W
Outer Hebrides, U.K. ... 18 H2 57 30N 7 40W
Outjo, Namibia ... 97 J3 20 5S 16 7 E
Outwell, U.K. ... 23 G9 52 37N 0 14 E
Ovalle, Chile ... 121 F2 30 33S 71 18W
Ovamboland, Namibia ... 97 H3 18 30S 16 0 E
Over Wallop, U.K. ... 24 D5 51 9N 1 36W
Overton, U.K. ... 24 D6 51 15N 1 15W
Oviedo, Spain ... 69 A3 43 25N 5 50W
Owatonna, U.S.A. ... 111 B8 44 5N 93 14W
Owen Sound, Canada ... 109 D11 44 35N 80 55W
Owen Stanley Ra., Papua N. G. ... 98 B8 8 30S 147 0 E
Owens →, U.S.A. ... 110 C3 36 32N 117 59W
Owensboro, U.S.A. ... 112 G4 37 46N 87 7W
Owo, Nigeria ... 94 G7 7 10N 5 39 E
Owosso, U.S.A. ... 112 D5 43 0N 84 10W
Owston Ferry, U.K. ... 23 F7 53 29N 0 47W
Owyhee →, U.S.A. ... 110 B3 43 49N 117 2W
Oxford, U.K. ... 24 C6 51 46N 1 15W
Oxnard, U.S.A. ... 110 D3 34 12N 119 11W
Oyama, Japan ... 82 E6 36 18N 139 48 E
Oykel →, U.K. ... 19 G9 57 56N 4 26W
Oyo, Nigeria ... 94 G6 7 46N 3 56 E
Ozark Plateau, U.S.A. ... 111 C8 37 20N 91 40W
Ozarks, L. of the, U.S.A. ... 111 C8 38 12N 92 38W

# P

Paamiut, Greenland ... 109 B15 62 0N 49 43W
Paarl, S. Africa ... 97 L3 33 45S 18 56 E
Pabbay, U.K. ... 18 G3 57 46N 7 14W
Pabna, Bangla. ... 85 G16 24 1N 89 18 E
Pacaraima, Sa., S. Amer. ... 120 B3 4 0N 62 30W
Pacasmayo, Peru ... 120 C2 7 20S 79 35W
Pachuca, Mexico ... 114 C5 20 10N 98 40W
Pacific-Antarctic Ridge, Pac. Oc. ... 103 M16 43 0S 115 0W
Pacific Ocean, Pac. Oc. ... 103 G14 10 0N 140 0W
Padang, Indonesia ... 83 D2 1 0S 100 20 E
Padangsidempuan, Indonesia ... 83 C1 1 30N 99 15 E
Paddock Wood, U.K. ... 25 D9 51 11N 0 24 E
Paderborn, Germany ... 66 C5 51 42N 8 45 E
Padiham, U.K. ... 23 E4 53 48N 2 18W
Padre I., U.S.A. ... 111 E7 27 10N 97 25W
Padstow, U.K. ... 27 F4 50 33N 4 58W
Padstow B., U.K. ... 27 F4 50 34N 4 57W
Padua, Italy ... 70 B4 45 25N 11 53 E
Paducah, U.S.A. ... 112 G3 37 5N 88 37W
Pagadian, Phil. ... 83 C4 7 55N 123 30 E
Page, U.S.A. ... 110 C4 36 57N 111 27W
Pahala, U.S.A. ... 110 J17 19 12N 155 29W
Paignton, U.K. ... 27 G6 50 26N 3 35W
Painesville, U.S.A. ... 112 E7 41 43N 81 15W
Painswick, U.K. ... 24 C4 51 47N 2 10W
Painted Desert, U.S.A. ... 110 C4 36 0N 111 0W
Paintsville, U.S.A. ... 112 G6 37 49N 82 48W
País Vasco □, Spain ... 69 A4 42 50N 2 45W
Paisley, U.K. ... 20 C7 55 50N 4 25W
Paita, Peru ... 120 C1 5 11S 81 9W
Pakistan ■, Asia ... 84 E7 30 0N 70 0 E
Paktīā □, Afghan. ... 87 C12 33 30N 69 15 E
Pakxe, Laos ... 83 B2 15 5N 105 52 E
Palanpur, India ... 84 G8 24 10N 72 25 E
Palapye, Botswana ... 97 J5 22 30S 27 7 E
Palau ■, Pac. Oc. ... 83 C5 7 30N 134 30 E
Palawan, Phil. ... 83 C3 9 30N 118 30 E
Palembang, Indonesia ... 83 D2 3 0S 104 50 E
Palencia, Spain ... 69 A3 42 1N 4 34W
Palermo, Italy ... 70 E5 38 7N 13 22 E
Palestine, U.S.A. ... 111 D7 31 46N 95 38W
Palghat, India ... 84 P10 10 46N 76 42 E
Palgrave, U.K. ... 25 B11 52 22N 1 6 E
Pali, India ... 84 G8 25 50N 73 20 E
Palikir, Micronesia ... 102 G7 6 55N 158 9 E
Palk Strait, Asia ... 84 Q11 10 0N 79 45 E
Palm Springs, U.S.A. ... 110 D3 33 50N 116 33W
Palma de Mallorca, Spain ... 69 C7 39 35N 2 39 E
Palmares, Brazil ... 122 A3 8 41S 35 28W
Palmas, C., Liberia ... 94 H4 4 27N 7 46W
Palmeira dos Índios, Brazil ... 122 A3 9 25S 36 37W
Palmer, U.S.A. ... 108 B5 61 36N 149 7W
Palmer Land, Antarctica ... 55 D18 73 0S 63 0W
Palmerston North, N.Z. ... 99 J14 40 21S 175 39 E
Palmira, Colombia ... 120 B2 3 32N 76 16W
Palmyra, Syria ... 86 C4 34 36N 38 15 E
Palmyra Is., Pac. Oc. ... 103 G11 5 52N 162 5W
Palopo, Indonesia ... 83 D4 3 0S 120 16 E
Palu, Indonesia ... 83 D3 1 0S 119 52 E
Palu, Turkey ... 73 G7 38 45N 40 0 E
Pamiers, France ... 68 E4 43 7N 1 39 E
Pamir, Tajikistan ... 87 B13 37 40N 73 0 E
Pamlico Sd., U.S.A. ... 111 C11 35 20N 76 0W
Pampa, U.S.A. ... 110 C6 35 32N 100 58W
Pampas, Argentina ... 121 F3 35 0S 63 0W
Pamplona, Spain ... 69 A5 42 48N 1 38W
Panaji, India ... 84 M8 15 25N 73 50 E
Panamá, Panama ... 115 F9 9 0N 79 25W
Panama ■, Cent. Amer. ... 115 F8 8 48N 79 55W
Panamá, G. de, Panama ... 115 F9 8 4N 79 20W
Panama Canal, Panama ... 115 F9 9 10N 79 37W
Panama City, U.S.A. ... 111 D9 30 10N 85 40W
Panay, Phil. ... 83 B4 11 10N 122 30 E
Pančevo, Serbia & M. ... 71 B9 44 52N 20 41 E
Panevėžys, Lithuania ... 72 C3 55 42N 24 25 E
Pangbourne, U.K. ... 24 D6 51 29N 1 6W
Pangkalpinang, Indonesia ... 83 D2 2 0S 106 0 E
Pangnirtung, Canada ... 109 B13 66 8N 65 54W
Pantar, Indonesia ... 83 D4 8 28S 124 10 E
Pantelleria, Italy ... 70 F4 36 50N 11 57 E
Papa Stour, U.K. ... 18 B14 60 20N 1 42W
Papa Westray, U.K. ... 19 D12 59 20N 2 55W
Papantla, Mexico ... 114 C5 20 30N 97 30W
Papeete, Tahiti ... 103 J13 17 32S 149 34W
Paphos, Cyprus ... 86 C3 34 46N 32 25 E
Papua □, Indonesia ... 83 D5 4 0S 137 0 E
Papua, G. of, Papua N. G. ... 98 B7 9 0S 144 50 E
Papua New Guinea ■, Oceania ... 98 B7 8 0S 145 0 E
Pará □, Brazil ... 120 C4 3 20S 52 0W
Paracatu, Brazil ... 122 C1 17 10S 46 50W
Paracel Is., S. China Sea ... 83 B3 15 50N 112 0 E
Paragould, U.S.A. ... 111 C8 36 3N 90 29W
Paraguaçu →, Brazil ... 122 B3 12 45S 38 54W
Paraguaná, Pen. de, Venezuela ... 120 A3 12 0N 70 0W
Paraguarí, Paraguay ... 121 E4 25 36S 57 0W
Paraguay ■, S. Amer. ... 121 E4 23 0S 57 0W
Paraguay →, Paraguay ... 121 E4 27 18S 58 38W
Paraíba □, Brazil ... 120 C6 7 0S 36 0W
Parakou, Benin ... 94 G6 9 25N 2 40 E
Paramaribo, Suriname ... 120 B4 5 50N 55 10W
Paraná, Argentina ... 121 F3 31 45S 60 30W
Paraná □, Brazil ... 122 B1 12 30S 47 48W
Paraná □, Brazil ... 121 F4 24 30S 51 0W
Paraná →, Brazil ... 121 F4 33 43S 59 15W
Paranaguá, Brazil ... 122 E1 25 30S 48 30W
Paranaíba, Brazil ... 120 E4 19 40S 51 4W
Paranapanema →, Brazil ... 121 E4 22 40S 53 9W
Parbhani, India ... 84 K10 19 8N 76 52 E
Pardo →, Brazil ... 122 C3 15 40S 39 0W
Pardubice, Czech Rep. ... 66 C8 50 3N 15 45 E
Parecis, Serra dos, Brazil ... 120 D4 13 0S 60 0W
Parepare, Indonesia ... 83 D3 4 0S 119 40 E
Parima, Serra, S. Amer. ... 120 B3 2 30N 64 0W
Pariñas, Pta., S. Amer. ... 116 D2 4 30S 81 20W
Parintins, Brazil ... 120 C4 2 40S 56 50W
Pariparit Kyun, Burma ... 85 M18 14 55N 93 45 E
Paris, France ... 68 B5 48 50N 2 20 E
Paris, U.S.A. ... 111 D7 33 40N 95 33W
Parkersburg, U.S.A. ... 112 F7 39 16N 81 34W
Parma, Italy ... 68 D9 44 48N 10 20 E
Parnaguá, Brazil ... 122 B2 10 10S 44 38W
Parnaíba, Brazil ... 120 C5 2 54S 41 47W
Parnaíba →, Brazil ... 120 C5 3 0S 41 50W
Pärnu, Estonia ... 72 C3 58 28N 24 33 E
Parracombe, U.K. ... 27 E6 51 11N 3 56W
Parrett →, U.K. ... 24 D2 51 12N 3 1W
Parry Is., Canada ... 54 B2 77 0N 110 0W
Parry Sound, Canada ... 109 D12 45 20N 80 0W
Parsons, U.S.A. ... 111 C7 37 20N 95 16W
Partney, U.K. ... 23 F9 53 12N 0 7 E
Parton, U.K. ... 22 C1 54 35N 3 33W
Paru →, Brazil ... 120 C4 1 33S 52 38W
Parvān □, Afghan. ... 87 C12 35 0N 69 0 E

Pasadena, Calif., U.S.A. ... 110 D3 34 9N 118 9W
Pasadena, Tex., U.S.A. ... 111 E7 29 43N 95 13W
Pasco, Cerro de, Peru ... 120 D2 10 45S 76 10W
Paso Robles, U.S.A. ... 110 C2 35 38N 120 41W
Passage West, Ireland ... 30 E6 51 52N 8 21W
Passau, Germany ... 66 D7 48 34N 13 28 E
Passo Fundo, Brazil ... 121 B4 28 10S 52 20W
Passos, Brazil ... 122 C1 20 45S 46 37W
Pastaza →, Peru ... 120 C2 4 50S 76 52W
Pasto, Colombia ... 120 B2 1 13N 77 17W
Patagonia, Argentina ... 121 G3 45 0S 69 0W
Patan, India ... 84 H8 23 54N 72 14 E
Pateley Bridge, U.K. ... 22 D5 54 5N 1 44W
Paterson, U.S.A. ... 113 E10 40 55N 74 11W
Pathankot, India ... 84 C9 32 18N 75 45 E
Pathfinder Reservoir, U.S.A. ... 110 B5 42 28N 106 51W
Patna, India ... 85 G14 25 35N 85 12 E
Patos, Brazil ... 120 C6 6 55S 37 16W
Patos, L. dos, Brazil ... 121 F4 31 20S 51 0W
Patos de Minas, Brazil ... 122 C1 18 35S 46 32W
Patras, Greece ... 71 E9 38 14N 21 47 E
Patrington, U.K. ... 23 E8 53 41N 0 1W
Patrocínio, Brazil ... 122 C1 18 57S 47 0W
Patten, U.S.A. ... 113 C13 46 0N 68 38W
Patterdale, U.K. ... 22 C3 54 32N 2 56W
Pau, France ... 68 E3 43 19N 0 25W
Paulatuk, Canada ... 108 B7 69 25N 124 0W
Paulistana, Brazil ... 122 A2 8 9S 41 9W
Paull, U.K. ... 23 E8 53 44N 0 14W
Paulo Afonso, Brazil ... 122 A3 9 21S 38 15W
Pavia, Italy ... 68 D8 45 7N 9 8 E
Pavlodar, Kazakhstan ... 79 D9 52 33N 77 0 E
Pavlohrad, Ukraine ... 73 E6 48 30N 35 52 E
Pavlovo, Russia ... 72 C7 55 58N 43 5 E
Pawtucket, U.S.A. ... 113 E12 41 53N 71 23W
Paxton, U.S.A. ... 112 E3 40 27N 88 6W
Payakumbuh, Indonesia ... 83 D2 0 20S 100 35 E
Payette, U.S.A. ... 110 B5 44 5N 116 56W
Payne L., Canada ... 109 C12 59 30N 74 30W
Payson, U.S.A. ... 110 C4 34 14N 111 20W
Paz, B. de la, Mexico ... 114 C2 24 15N 110 25W
Pazardzhik, Bulgaria ... 71 C11 42 12N 24 20 E
Peace →, Canada ... 108 C8 59 0N 111 25W
Peace River, Canada ... 108 C8 56 15N 117 18W
Peacehaven, U.K. ... 25 E8 50 48N 0 0W
Pearl City, U.S.A. ... 110 H16 21 24N 157 59W
Pearl Harbor, U.S.A. ... 110 H16 21 21N 157 57W
Peasenhall, U.K. ... 25 B11 52 16N 1 27 E
Peawanuck, Canada ... 109 C11 55 0N 85 12W
Pechenga, Russia ... 72 A5 69 29N 31 4 E
Pechora, Russia ... 72 A10 65 10N 57 11 E
Pechora →, Russia ... 72 A9 68 13N 54 15 E
Pechora B., Russia ... 72 A9 68 40N 54 0 E
Pecos, U.S.A. ... 110 D6 31 26N 103 30W
Pecos →, U.S.A. ... 110 E6 29 42N 101 22W
Pécs, Hungary ... 67 E10 46 5N 18 15 E
Pedra Azul, Brazil ... 122 C2 16 2S 41 17W
Pedro Afonso, Brazil ... 122 A1 9 0S 48 10W
Peebles, U.K. ... 21 C9 55 40N 3 11W
Peel, U.K. ... 29 C12 54 13N 4 40W
Peel →, Canada ... 108 B6 67 0N 135 0W
Peel Fell, U.K. ... 22 B3 55 18N 2 34W
Peel Sd., Canada ... 108 A10 73 0N 96 0W
Pegswood, U.K. ... 22 B5 55 11N 1 39W
Pegu, Burma ... 85 L20 17 20N 96 29 E
Pegu Yoma, Burma ... 85 K20 19 0N 96 0 E
Pegwell Bay, U.K. ... 25 D11 51 18N 1 24 E
Peixe, Brazil ... 122 B1 12 0S 48 40W
Pekalongan, Indonesia ... 83 D2 6 53S 109 40 E
Pekanbaru, Indonesia ... 83 C2 0 30N 101 15 E
Pekin, U.S.A. ... 111 B9 40 35N 89 40W
Peking = Beijing, China ... 81 C6 39 55N 116 20 E
Pelée, Mt., Martinique ... 114 c 14 48N 61 10W
Peleng, Indonesia ... 83 D4 1 20S 123 30 E
Pelly →, Canada ... 108 B6 62 47N 137 19W
Pelly Bay, Canada ... 109 B11 68 38N 89 50W
Peloponnese, Greece ... 71 F10 37 10N 22 0 E
Pelotas, Brazil ... 121 F4 31 42S 52 23W
Pelvoux, Massif du, France ... 68 D7 44 52N 6 20 E
Pematangsiantar, Indonesia ... 83 C1 2 57N 99 5 E
Pemba, Mozam. ... 97 G8 12 58S 40 30 E
Pemba I., Tanzania ... 96 F7 5 0S 39 45 E
Pembridge, U.K. ... 23 H3 52 13N 2 52W
Pembroke, Canada ... 109 D12 45 50N 77 7W
Pembroke, U.K. ... 26 D4 51 41N 4 55W
Pembury, U.K. ... 25 D9 51 8N 0 20 E
Pen-y-Ghent, U.K. ... 22 C4 54 10N 2 14W
Penarth, U.K. ... 24 D2 51 26N 3 11W
Peñas, G. de, Chile ... 121 G2 47 0S 75 0W
Pend Oreille, L., U.S.A. ... 110 A3 48 10N 116 21W
Pendle Hill, U.K. ... 23 E4 53 52N 2 19W
Pendleton, U.S.A. ... 110 A3 45 40N 118 47W
Penedo, Brazil ... 122 B3 10 15S 36 36W
Penetanguishene, Canada ... 112 C8 44 50N 79 55W
Penicuik, U.K. ... 21 C9 55 50N 3 13W
Peninsular Malaysia □, Malaysia ... 83 C2 4 0N 102 0 E
Penistone, U.K. ... 23 E5 53 31N 1 37W
Penkridge, U.K. ... 23 G4 52 44N 2 6W
Penmarch, Pte. de, France ... 68 C1 47 48N 4 22W
Penn Yan, U.S.A. ... 112 D9 42 40N 77 3W
Pennines, U.K. ... 22 C4 54 45N 2 27W
Pennsylvania □, U.S.A. ... 112 E8 40 45N 77 30W
Penong, Australia ... 98 G5 31 56S 133 1 E
Penrith, U.K. ... 22 C3 54 40N 2 45W
Penryn, U.K. ... 27 G3 50 9N 5 7W
Pensacola, U.S.A. ... 111 D9 30 25N 87 13W
Pensacola Mts., Antarctica ... 55 E1 84 0S 40 0W
Penshurst, U.K. ... 25 D9 51 10N 0 12 E
Penticton, Canada ... 108 D8 49 30N 119 38W
Pentire Pt., U.K. ... 27 F4 50 35N 4 56W
Pentland Firth, U.K. ... 19 E11 58 43N 3 10W
Pentland Hills, U.K. ... 21 C9 55 48N 3 25W
Penwortham, U.K. ... 23 E3 53 45N 2 46W
Penygroes, U.K. ... 26 A5 53 3N 4 17W
Penza, Russia ... 72 D8 53 15N 45 5 E
Penzance, U.K. ... 27 G2 50 7N 5 33W
Peoria, U.S.A. ... 111 B9 40 42N 89 36W
Perabumulih, Indonesia ... 83 D2 3 27S 104 15 E
Perdido, Mte., Spain ... 69 A6 42 40N 0 5 E
Pereira, Colombia ... 120 B2 4 49N 75 43W
Pergamino, Argentina ... 121 F3 33 52S 60 30W
Péribonka →, Canada ... 109 D12 48 45N 72 5W
Périgueux, France ... 68 D4 45 10N 0 42 E
Perm, Russia ... 72 C10 58 0N 56 10 E
Pernambuco □, Brazil ... 120 C6 8 0S 37 0W
Pernik, Bulgaria ... 71 C10 42 35N 23 2 E
Perpignan, France ... 68 E5 42 42N 2 53 E
Perranporth, U.K. ... 27 G3 50 20N 5 11W
Perranzabuloe, U.K. ... 27 G3 50 18N 5 9W
Perryton, U.S.A. ... 110 C6 36 24N 100 48W
Persepolis, Iran ... 87 D8 29 55N 52 50 E
Pershore, U.K. ... 24 B4 52 7N 2 4W
Persian Gulf = Gulf, The, Asia ... 87 E7 27 0N 50 0 E
Perth, Australia ... 98 G2 31 57S 115 52 E
Perth, Canada ... 112 C9 44 55N 76 15W

Perth, U.K. ... 21 B9 56 24N 3 26W
Peru, U.S.A. ... 112 E4 40 45N 86 4W
Peru ■, S. Amer. ... 120 C2 4 0S 75 0W
Peru Basin, Pac. Oc. ... 103 J18 20 0S 95 0W
Peru-Chile Trench, Pac. Oc. ... 103 K20 20 0S 72 0W
Perúgia, Italy ... 70 C5 43 7N 12 23 E
Pervomaysk, Ukraine ... 73 E5 48 10N 30 46 E
Pervouralsk, Russia ... 72 C10 56 59N 59 59 E
Pescara, Italy ... 70 C6 42 28N 14 13 E
Peshawar, Pakistan ... 84 B7 34 2N 71 37 E
Pesqueira, Brazil ... 122 A3 8 20S 36 42W
Petah Tiqwa, Israel ... 86 C3 32 6N 34 53 E
Peter I., Br. Virgin Is. ... 115 e 18 22N 64 32W
Peterborough, Canada ... 109 D12 44 20N 78 20W
Peterborough, U.K. ... 23 G8 52 35N 0 15W
Peterchurch, U.K. ... 24 B3 52 2N 2 56W
Peterculter, U.K. ... 19 H13 57 6N 2 16W
Peterhead, U.K. ... 19 G14 57 31N 1 48W
Peterlee, U.K. ... 22 C6 54 47N 1 20W
Petersburg, Alaska, U.S.A. ... 108 C6 56 48N 132 58W
Petersburg, Va., U.S.A. ... 112 G9 37 14N 77 24W
Petersfield, U.K. ... 25 D7 51 1N 0 56W
Petit-Canal, Guadeloupe ... 114 b 16 25N 61 31W
Petit Piton, St. Lucia ... 115 f 13 51N 61 5W
Petite Terre, Îles de la, Guadeloupe ... 114 b 16 13N 61 9W
Petitot →, Canada ... 108 B7 60 14N 123 29W
Petitsikapau L., Canada ... 109 C13 54 37N 66 25W
Peto, Mexico ... 114 C7 20 10N 88 53W
Petoskey, U.S.A. ... 112 C5 45 22N 84 57W
Petra, Jordan ... 86 D3 30 20N 35 22 E
Petrolândia, Brazil ... 122 A3 9 5S 38 20W
Petrolina, Brazil ... 122 A2 9 24S 40 30W
Petropavlovsk-Kamchatskiy, Russia ... 79 D17 53 3N 158 43 E
Petrópolis, Brazil ... 122 D2 22 33S 43 9W
Petrozavodsk, Russia ... 72 B5 61 41N 34 20 E
Petworth, U.K. ... 25 E7 51 0N 0 36W
Pevensey, U.K. ... 25 E9 50 49N 0 23 E
Pevensey Levels, U.K. ... 25 E9 50 50N 0 20 E
Pewsey, U.K. ... 24 D5 51 20N 1 45W
Pewsey, Vale of, U.K. ... 24 D5 51 22N 1 40W
Pforzheim, Germany ... 66 D5 48 52N 8 41 E
Phalodi, India ... 84 F8 27 12N 72 24 E
Phan Rang, Vietnam ... 83 B2 11 34N 109 0 E
Phan Thiet, Vietnam ... 83 B2 11 1N 108 9 E
Philadelphia, U.S.A. ... 113 E10 39 57N 75 10W
Philippine Sea, Pac. Oc. ... 74 H16 18 0N 125 0 E
Philippines ■, Asia ... 83 B4 12 0N 123 0 E
Phitsanulok, Thailand ... 83 B2 16 50N 100 12 E
Phnom Penh, Cambodia ... 83 B2 11 33N 104 55 E
Phoenix, U.S.A. ... 110 D4 33 27N 112 4W
Phoenix Is., Kiribati ... 99 A16 3 30S 172 0W
Phra Nakhon Si Ayutthaya, Thailand ... 83 B2 14 25N 100 30 E
Phuket, Thailand ... 83 C1 7 53N 98 24 E
Piacenza, Italy ... 68 D8 45 1N 9 40 E
Piatra Neamţ, Romania ... 67 E14 46 56N 26 21 E
Piauí □, Brazil ... 120 C5 7 0S 43 0W
Piauí →, Brazil ... 120 C5 6 38S 42 42W
Picardie, France ... 68 B5 49 50N 3 0 E
Pichilemu, Chile ... 121 F2 34 22S 72 0W
Pickering, U.K. ... 22 D7 54 15N 0 46W
Pickering, Vale of, U.K. ... 22 D7 54 14N 0 45W
Picton, Canada ... 112 C9 44 1N 77 9W
Pidley, U.K. ... 23 H8 52 23N 0 2W
Pidurutalagala, Sri Lanka ... 84 R12 7 10N 80 50 E
Piedmont, Italy ... 68 D7 45 0N 8 0 E
Piedmont, U.S.A. ... 111 D10 34 0N 81 30W
Piedras Negras, Mexico ... 114 B4 28 42N 100 31W
Pierre, U.S.A. ... 110 B6 44 22N 100 21W
Pietermaritzburg, S. Africa ... 97 K6 29 35S 30 25 E
Pikes Peak, U.S.A. ... 110 C5 38 50N 105 3W
Pikeville, U.S.A. ... 112 G6 37 29N 82 31W
Pilar, Paraguay ... 121 E4 26 50S 58 20W
Pilcomayo →, Paraguay ... 121 E4 25 21S 57 42W
Pilibhit, India ... 84 E11 28 40N 79 50 E
Pilica →, Poland ... 67 C11 51 52N 21 17 E
Pilling, U.K. ... 23 E3 53 56N 2 54W
Pilton, U.K. ... 24 D2 51 10N 2 35W
Pimentel, Peru ... 120 C2 6 45S 79 55W
Pinar del Río, Cuba ... 115 C8 22 26N 83 40W
Pinatubo, Mt., Phil. ... 83 B4 15 8N 120 21 E
Pinchbeck, U.K. ... 23 G8 52 50N 0 9W
Pindus Mts., Greece ... 71 E9 40 0N 21 0 E
Pine Bluff, U.S.A. ... 111 D8 34 13N 92 1W
Pine Point, Canada ... 108 B8 60 50N 114 28W
Pinega →, Russia ... 72 B8 64 30N 44 19 E
Pingdong, Taiwan ... 81 D7 22 39N 120 30 E
Pingliang, China ... 80 C5 35 35N 106 31 E
Pingxiang, China ... 80 D5 22 6N 106 46 E
Pinhoe, U.K. ... 24 E2 50 44N 3 28W
Pinsk, Belarus ... 72 D4 52 10N 26 1 E
Piotrków Trybunalski, Poland ... 67 C10 51 23N 19 43 E
Pipmuacan, Rés., Canada ... 113 A12 49 45N 70 30W
Piracicaba, Brazil ... 122 D1 22 45S 47 40W
Piraiévs, Greece ... 71 F10 37 57N 23 42 E
Pirapora, Brazil ... 122 C2 17 20S 44 56W
Pirmasens, Germany ... 66 D4 49 12N 7 36 E
Pisa, Italy ... 70 C4 43 43N 10 23 E
Pisagua, Chile ... 120 D2 19 40S 70 15W
Pishan, China ... 80 C2 37 30N 78 33 E
Pistóia, Italy ... 70 C4 43 56N 10 54 E
Pitcairn I., Pac. Oc. ... 103 K14 25 5S 130 5W
Piteå, Sweden ... 63 D8 65 20N 21 25 E
Piteşti, Romania ... 67 F13 44 52N 24 54 E
Pitlochry, U.K. ... 19 J10 56 42N 3 44W
Pittsburg, U.S.A. ... 111 C8 37 25N 94 42W
Pittsburgh, U.S.A. ... 112 E8 40 26N 80 1W
Pittsfield, U.S.A. ... 113 D11 42 27N 73 15W
Piura, Peru ... 120 C1 5 15S 80 38W
Placentia, Canada ... 109 D14 47 20N 54 0W
Placentia B., Canada ... 109 D14 47 0N 54 40W
Placetas, Cuba ... 115 C9 22 15N 79 44W
Plainview, U.S.A. ... 110 D6 34 11N 101 43W
Plata, Río de la, S. Amer. ... 121 F4 34 45S 57 30W
Platte →, U.S.A. ... 111 C8 39 16N 94 50W
Plattsburgh, U.S.A. ... 113 C11 44 42N 73 28W
Plauen, Germany ... 66 C7 50 30N 12 8 E
Plenty, B. of, N.Z. ... 99 H14 37 45S 177 0 E
Plessisville, Canada ... 113 B12 46 14N 71 47W
Pleven, Bulgaria ... 71 C11 43 26N 24 37 E
Płock, Poland ... 67 B10 52 32N 19 40 E
Ploiești, Romania ... 67 F14 44 57N 26 5 E
Plovdiv, Bulgaria ... 71 C11 42 8N 24 44 E
Plymouth, Ind., U.S.A. ... 112 E4 41 21N 86 19W
Plymouth, Wis., U.S.A. ... 112 D4 43 45N 87 59W
Plymouth, U.K. ... 27 G4 50 22N 4 10W
Plympton, U.K. ... 27 G5 50 23N 4 5W
Plymstock, U.K. ... 27 G5 50 21N 4 7W
Plzeň, Czech Rep. ... 66 D7 49 45N 13 22 E
Po →, Italy ... 70 B5 44 57N 12 4 E
Pocatello, U.S.A. ... 110 B4 42 52N 112 27W
Pocklington, U.K. ... 23 E7 53 56N 0 46W
Poços de Caldas, Brazil ... 122 D1 21 50S 46 33W
Podgorica, Serbia & M. ... 71 C8 42 30N 19 19 E

**Podolsk**

Podolsk, Russia . . . . . . . . . . . . 72 C6 55 25N 37 30 E
Pohnpei, Micronesia . . . . . . . . 102 G7 6 55N 158 10 E
Point Hope, U.S.A. . . . . . . . . . 108 B3 68 21N 166 47W
Point L., Canada . . . . . . . . . . 108 B9 65 15N 113 4W
Point Pleasant, U.S.A. . . . . . . 112 F6 38 51N 82 8W
Pointe-à-Pitre, Guadeloupe . . 114 b 16 10N 61 32W
Pointe-Noire, Congo . . . . . . . . 96 E2 4 48S 11 53 E
Pointe Noire, Guadeloupe . . . 114 b 16 14N 61 47W
Poitiers, France . . . . . . . . . . . 68 C4 46 35N 0 20 E
Poitou, France . . . . . . . . . . . . 68 C3 46 40N 0 10W
Poland ■, Europe . . . . . . . . . . 67 C10 52 0N 20 0 E
Polatsk, Belarus . . . . . . . . . . . 72 C4 55 30N 28 50 E
Polden Hills, U.K. . . . . . . . . . . 24 D3 51 7N 2 50W
Polegate, U.K. . . . . . . . . . . . . 25 E9 50 49N 0 16 E
Polesworth, U.K. . . . . . . . . . . 23 G5 52 37N 1 36W
Polevskoy, Russia . . . . . . . . . 72 C11 56 26N 60 11 E
Polperro, U.K. . . . . . . . . . . . . 27 G4 50 20N 4 32W
Polruan, U.K. . . . . . . . . . . . . . 27 G4 50 19N 4 38W
Poltava, Ukraine . . . . . . . . . . 73 E5 49 35N 34 35 E
Polynesia, Pac. Oc. . . . . . . . . 103 J11 10 0S 162 0W
Ponca City, U.S.A. . . . . . . . . . 111 C7 36 42N 97 5W
Ponce, Puerto Rico . . . . . . . . 115 d 18 1N 66 37W
Pond Inlet, Canada . . . . . . . . 109 A12 72 40N 77 0W
Pondicherry, India . . . . . . . . . 84 P11 11 59N 79 50 E
Ponta Grossa, Brazil . . . . . . . 121 E4 25 7S 50 10W
Pontardawe, U.K. . . . . . . . . . 24 C1 51 43N 3 51W
Pontardulais, U.K. . . . . . . . . . 26 D5 51 43N 4 3W
Pontarlier, France . . . . . . . . . 68 C7 46 54N 6 20 E
Ponte Nova, Brazil . . . . . . . . 122 D2 20 25S 42 54W
Pontefract, U.K. . . . . . . . . . . 23 E6 53 42N 1 18W
Ponteland, U.K. . . . . . . . . . . . 22 B5 55 3N 1 45W
Pontevedra, Spain . . . . . . . . . 69 A1 42 26N 8 40W
Pontiac, U.S.A. . . . . . . . . . . . 112 D6 42 38N 83 18W
Pontianak, Indonesia . . . . . . . 83 D2 0 3S 109 15 E
Pontine Mts., Turkey . . . . . . . 73 F6 41 30N 35 0 E
Pontivy, France . . . . . . . . . . . 68 B2 48 5N 2 58W
Pontrilas, U.K. . . . . . . . . . . . . 24 C3 51 56N 2 52W
Pontypool, U.K. . . . . . . . . . . . 24 C2 51 42N 3 2W
Pontypridd, U.K. . . . . . . . . . . 24 C2 51 36N 3 20W
Poole, U.K. . . . . . . . . . . . . . . 24 E5 50 43N 1 59W
Poole Harbour, U.K. . . . . . . . 24 E5 50 41N 2 0W
Pooley Bridge, U.K. . . . . . . . . 22 C3 54 37N 2 48W
Poopó, L. de, Bolivia . . . . . . . 120 D3 18 30S 67 35W
Popayán, Colombia . . . . . . . . 120 B2 2 27N 76 36W
Poplar Bluff, U.S.A. . . . . . . . . 111 C8 36 46N 90 24W
Popocatépetl, Volcán, Mexico . 114 D5 19 2N 98 38W
Porbandar, India . . . . . . . . . . 84 J6 21 44N 69 43 E
Porcupine →, U.S.A. . . . . . . . 108 B5 66 34N 145 19W
Pori, Finland . . . . . . . . . . . . . 63 E8 61 29N 21 48 E
Porlock, U.K. . . . . . . . . . . . . . 24 D1 51 13N 3 35W
Port Alberni, Canada . . . . . . . 108 D7 49 14N 124 50W
Port Antonio, Jamaica . . . . . . 114 a 18 10N 76 30W
Port Arthur, U.S.A. . . . . . . . . 111 E8 29 54N 93 56W
Port-au-Prince, Haiti . . . . . . . 115 D10 18 40N 72 20W
Port Augusta, Australia . . . . . 98 G6 32 30S 137 50 E
Port Carlisle, U.K. . . . . . . . . . 22 C2 54 57N 3 11W
Port-Cartier, Canada . . . . . . . 109 C13 50 2N 66 50W
Port-de-Paix, Haiti . . . . . . . . . 115 D10 19 50N 72 50W
Port Elgin, Canada . . . . . . . . 112 C7 44 25N 81 25W
Port Elizabeth, S. Africa . . . . . 97 L5 33 58S 25 40 E
Port Ellen, U.K. . . . . . . . . . . . 20 C3 55 38N 6 11W
Port Erin, U.K. . . . . . . . . . . . . 29 C12 54 5N 4 45W
Port Glasgow, U.K. . . . . . . . . 20 C6 55 56N 4 41W
Port Harcourt, Nigeria . . . . . . 94 H7 4 40N 7 10 E
Port Hawkesbury, Canada . . . 109 D13 45 36N 61 22W
Port Hedland, Australia . . . . . 98 E2 20 25S 118 35 E
Port Hope Simpson, Canada . 109 C14 52 33N 56 18W
Port Huron, U.S.A. . . . . . . . . . 112 D6 42 58N 82 26W
Port Isaac, U.K. . . . . . . . . . . . 27 F4 50 35N 4 50W
Port Isaac B., U.K. . . . . . . . . . 27 F4 50 36N 4 50W
Port Laoise, Ireland . . . . . . . . 31 B8 53 2N 7 18W
Port Lincoln, Australia . . . . . . 98 G6 34 42S 135 52 E
Port-Louis, Guadeloupe . . . . 114 b 16 28N 61 32W
Port Louis, Mauritius . . . . . . . 91 H9 20 10S 57 30 E
Port McNeill, Canada . . . . . . . 108 C7 50 35N 127 6W
Port Macquarie, Australia . . . 98 G9 31 25S 152 25 E
Port Maria, Jamaica . . . . . . . . 114 a 18 25N 76 55W
Port Morant, Jamaica . . . . . . . 114 a 17 54N 76 19W
Port Moresby, Papua N. G. . . 98 B8 9 24S 147 8 E
Port Nolloth, S. Africa . . . . . . 97 K3 29 17S 16 52 E
Port of Spain, Trin. & Tob. . . . 120 A3 10 40N 61 31W
Port Pirie, Australia . . . . . . . . 98 G6 33 10S 138 1 E
Port Said, Egypt . . . . . . . . . . 95 B12 31 16N 32 18 E
Port St. Mary, U.K. . . . . . . . . 29 C12 54 5N 4 44W
Port Shepstone, S. Africa . . . . 97 L6 30 44S 30 28 E
Port Sudan, Sudan . . . . . . . . . 95 E13 19 32N 37 9 E
Port Talbot, U.K. . . . . . . . . . . 24 C1 51 35N 3 47W
Port Vila, Vanuatu . . . . . . . . . 99 D12 17 45S 168 18 E
Port Washington, U.S.A. . . . . . 112 D4 43 23N 87 53W
Port William, U.K. . . . . . . . . . 20 E6 54 46N 4 35W
Portadown, U.K. . . . . . . . . . . 29 C9 54 25N 6 27W
Portaferry, U.K. . . . . . . . . . . . 29 C10 54 23N 5 33W
Portage la Prairie, Canada . . . 108 D10 49 58N 98 18W
Portarlington, Ireland . . . . . . 31 B8 53 9N 7 14W
Porthcawl, U.K. . . . . . . . . . . . 24 D1 51 29N 3 42W
Porthleven, U.K. . . . . . . . . . . 27 G3 50 4N 5 19W
Porthmadog, U.K. . . . . . . . . . 26 B5 52 55N 4 8W
Portishead, U.K. . . . . . . . . . . 24 D3 51 29N 2 46W
Portknockie, U.K. . . . . . . . . . 19 G12 57 42N 2 51W
Portland, Maine, U.S.A. . . . . . 109 D12 43 39N 70 16W
Portland, Oreg., U.S.A. . . . . . 110 A2 45 32N 122 37W
Portland, I. of, U.K. . . . . . . . . 24 E4 50 33N 2 26W
Portland Bight, Jamaica . . . . . 114 a 17 52N 77 5W
Portland Bill, U.K. . . . . . . . . . 27 F9 50 31N 2 28W
Portland Pt., Jamaica . . . . . . . 114 a 17 42N 77 11W
Portmore, Jamaica . . . . . . . . . 114 a 17 53N 77 33W
Porto, Portugal . . . . . . . . . . . 69 B1 41 8N 8 40W
Pôrto Alegre, Brazil . . . . . . . . 121 F4 30 5S 51 10W
Pôrto Esperança, Brazil . . . . . 120 D4 19 37S 57 29W
Pôrto Nacional, Brazil . . . . . . 122 B1 10 40S 48 30W
Porto-Novo, Benin . . . . . . . . 94 G6 6 23N 2 42 E
Pôrto Seguro, Brazil . . . . . . . 122 C3 16 26S 39 5W
Porto-Vecchio, France . . . . . . 68 F8 41 35N 9 16 E
Pôrto Velho, Brazil . . . . . . . . 120 C3 8 46S 63 54W
Porton, U.K. . . . . . . . . . . . . . 24 D5 51 8N 1 43W
Portpatrick, U.K. . . . . . . . . . . 20 E5 54 51N 5 7W
Portree, U.K. . . . . . . . . . . . . . 18 H5 57 25N 6 12W
Portrush, U.K. . . . . . . . . . . . . 29 A8 55 12N 6 40W
Portslade, U.K. . . . . . . . . . . . 25 E8 50 50N 0 12W
Portsmouth, U.K. . . . . . . . . . . 24 E6 50 48N 1 6W
Portsmouth, N.H., U.S.A. . . . . 113 D12 43 5N 70 45W
Portsmouth, Ohio, U.S.A. . . . . 112 F6 38 44N 82 57W
Portsoy, U.K. . . . . . . . . . . . . . 19 G12 57 41N 2 41W
Portstewart, U.K. . . . . . . . . . 29 A8 55 11N 6 43W
Porttipahtan tekojärvi, Finland 63 D9 68 5N 26 40 E
Portugal ■, Europe . . . . . . . . 69 C1 40 0N 8 0W
Portumna, Ireland . . . . . . . . . 30 B6 53 6N 8 14W
Posadas, Argentina . . . . . . . . 121 E4 27 30S 55 50W
Posse, Brazil . . . . . . . . . . . . . 122 B1 14 4S 46 18W
Postmasburg, S. Africa . . . . . 97 K4 28 18S 23 5 E
Potchefstroom, S. Africa . . . . 97 K5 26 41S 27 7 E
Potenza, Italy . . . . . . . . . . . . 70 D6 40 38N 15 48 E
Poti, Georgia . . . . . . . . . . . . . 73 F7 42 10N 41 38 E
Potomac →, U.S.A. . . . . . . . . 112 F9 38 0N 76 23W

Potosí, Bolivia . . . . . . . . . . . 120 D3 19 38S 65 50W
Potsdam, Germany . . . . . . . . 66 B7 52 25N 13 4 E
Potsdam, U.S.A. . . . . . . . . . . 113 C10 44 40N 74 59W
Potter Heigham, U.K. . . . . . . . 25 A12 52 42N 1 34 E
Potterne, U.K. . . . . . . . . . . . . 24 D4 51 20N 2 0W
Potters Bar, U.K. . . . . . . . . . . 25 C8 51 42N 0 11W
Potterspury, U.K. . . . . . . . . . . 25 B7 52 5N 0 52W
Pottstown, U.S.A. . . . . . . . . . 113 E10 40 15N 75 39W
Pottsville, U.S.A. . . . . . . . . . . 113 E9 40 41N 76 12W
Pottuvil, Sri Lanka . . . . . . . . . 84 R12 6 55N 81 50 E
Poughkeepsie, U.S.A. . . . . . . 113 E11 41 42N 73 56W
Poulaphouca Res., Ireland . . . 31 B10 53 8N 6 30W
Poulton-le-Fylde, U.K. . . . . . . 23 E3 53 51N 2 58W
Poundstock, U.K. . . . . . . . . . . 27 F4 50 44N 4 35W
Pouso Alegre, Brazil . . . . . . . 122 D1 22 14S 45 57W
Powder →, U.S.A. . . . . . . . . . 110 A5 46 45N 105 26W
Powell, L., U.S.A. . . . . . . . . . . 110 C4 36 57N 111 29W
Powell River, Canada . . . . . . . 108 D7 49 50N 124 35W
Powers, U.S.A. . . . . . . . . . . . 112 C4 45 41N 87 32W
Powick, U.K. . . . . . . . . . . . . . 24 B4 52 10N 2 14W
Powys □, U.K. . . . . . . . . . . . . 23 H2 52 20N 3 20W
Poyang Hu, China . . . . . . . . . 81 D6 29 5N 116 20 E
Poza Rica, Mexico . . . . . . . . . 114 C5 20 33N 97 27W
Poznań, Poland . . . . . . . . . . . 67 B9 52 25N 16 55 E
Prado, Brazil . . . . . . . . . . . . . 122 C3 17 20S 39 13W
Prague, Czech Rep. . . . . . . . . 66 C8 50 5N 14 22 E
Praia, C. Verde Is. . . . . . . . . . 91 E1 15 2N 23 34W
Prata, Brazil . . . . . . . . . . . . . 122 C1 19 25S 48 54W
Prato, Italy . . . . . . . . . . . . . . 70 C4 43 53N 11 6 E
Pratt, U.S.A. . . . . . . . . . . . . . 110 C7 37 39N 98 44W
Prawle Pt., U.K. . . . . . . . . . . . 27 G6 50 12N 3 44W
Praya, Indonesia . . . . . . . . . . 83 D3 8 39S 116 17 E
Prees, U.K. . . . . . . . . . . . . . . 23 G3 52 54N 2 40W
Preesall, U.K. . . . . . . . . . . . . 23 E3 53 55N 2 57W
Prescott, Canada . . . . . . . . . . 113 C10 44 45N 75 30W
Prescott, U.S.A. . . . . . . . . . . . 110 D4 34 33N 112 28W
Presidencia Roque Saenz Peña,
  Argentina . . . . . . . . . . . . . . 121 E3 26 45S 60 30W
Presidente Prudente, Brazil . . 120 E4 22 5S 51 25W
Presidio, U.S.A. . . . . . . . . . . . 110 E6 29 34N 104 22W
Prespa, L., Macedonia . . . . . . 71 D9 40 55N 21 0 E
Presque Isle, U.S.A. . . . . . . . 113 B13 46 41N 68 1W
Prestatyn, U.K. . . . . . . . . . . . 23 F2 53 20N 3 24W
Prestbury, U.K. . . . . . . . . . . . 24 C4 51 54N 2 2W
Presteigne, U.K. . . . . . . . . . . 23 H2 52 17N 3 0W
Preston, Borders, U.K. . . . . . . 22 A4 55 49N 2 19W
Preston, Dorset, U.K. . . . . . . . 24 E4 50 38N 2 26W
Preston, Lancs., U.K. . . . . . . . 23 E3 53 46N 2 42W
Preston, U.S.A. . . . . . . . . . . . 110 B4 42 6N 111 53W
Prestonpans, U.K. . . . . . . . . . 23 E4 55 33N 2 17W
Prestwich, U.K. . . . . . . . . . . . 23 E4 53 32N 2 17W
Prestwick, U.K. . . . . . . . . . . . 20 D6 55 29N 4 37W
Pretoria, S. Africa . . . . . . . . . 97 K5 25 44S 28 12 E
Pribilof Is., U.S.A. . . . . . . . . . 108 C2 57 0N 170 0W
Price, U.S.A. . . . . . . . . . . . . . 110 C4 39 36N 110 49W
Prieska, S. Africa . . . . . . . . . . 97 K4 29 40S 22 42 E
Prince Albert, Canada . . . . . . 108 C9 53 15N 105 50W
Prince Albert Pen., Canada . . 108 A8 72 30N 116 0W
Prince Albert Sd., Canada . . . 108 A8 70 25N 115 0W
Prince Charles I., Canada . . . . 109 B12 67 47N 76 12W
Prince Charles Mts., Antarctica 55 D6 72 0S 67 0 E
Prince Edward I. □, Canada . . 109 D13 46 20N 63 20W
Prince Edward Is., Ind. Oc. . . 53 G11 46 35S 38 0 E
Prince George, Canada . . . . . 108 C7 53 55N 122 50W
Prince of Wales I., Canada . . . 108 A10 73 0N 99 0W
Prince of Wales I., U.S.A. . . . . 108 C6 55 47N 132 50W
Prince Patrick I., Canada . . . . 54 B2 77 0N 120 0W
Prince Rupert, Canada . . . . . . 108 C6 54 20N 130 20W
Princes Risborough, U.K. . . . . 25 C7 51 43N 0 49W
Princeton, Ind., U.S.A. . . . . . . 112 F4 38 21N 87 34W
Princeton, Ky., U.S.A. . . . . . . 112 G4 37 7N 87 53W
Princeton, W. Va., U.S.A. . . . . 112 G7 37 22N 81 6W
Princetown, U.K. . . . . . . . . . . 27 F5 50 33N 4 0W
Principe, I. de, Atl. Oc. . . . . . 90 F4 1 37N 7 27 E
Pripet →, Europe . . . . . . . . . 67 C16 51 20N 30 15 E
Pripet Marshes, Europe . . . . . 67 B15 52 10N 28 10 E
Priština, Serbia & M. . . . . . . . 71 C9 42 40N 21 13 E
Privas, France . . . . . . . . . . . . 68 D6 44 45N 4 37 E
Prizren, Serbia & M. . . . . . . . 71 C9 42 13N 20 45 E
Probolinggo, Indonesia . . . . . 83 D3 7 46S 113 13 E
Probus, U.K. . . . . . . . . . . . . . 27 G4 50 17N 4 58W
Progreso, Mexico . . . . . . . . . 114 C7 21 20N 89 40W
Prome, Burma . . . . . . . . . . . . 85 K19 18 49N 95 13 E
Proprià, Brazil . . . . . . . . . . . . 122 B3 10 13S 36 51W
Provence, France . . . . . . . . . . 68 E6 43 40N 5 46 E
Providence, U.S.A. . . . . . . . . . 113 E12 41 49N 71 24W
Providencia, I. de, Colombia . 115 E8 13 25N 81 26W
Provins, France . . . . . . . . . . . 68 B5 48 33N 3 15 E
Provo, U.S.A. . . . . . . . . . . . . 110 B4 40 14N 111 39W
Prudhoe, U.K. . . . . . . . . . . . . 22 C5 54 57N 1 52W
Prudhoe Bay, U.S.A. . . . . . . . 108 A5 70 18N 148 22W
Prut →, Romania . . . . . . . . . . 67 F15 45 28N 28 10 E
Pryluky, Ukraine . . . . . . . . . . 73 D5 50 30N 32 24 E
Przemyśl, Poland . . . . . . . . . . 67 D12 49 50N 22 45 E
Pskov, Russia . . . . . . . . . . . . 72 C4 57 50N 28 25 E
Puddletown, U.K. . . . . . . . . . . 24 E4 50 44N 2 20W
Pudsey, U.K. . . . . . . . . . . . . . 23 E5 53 47N 1 40W
Puebla, Mexico . . . . . . . . . . . 114 D5 19 3N 98 12W
Pueblo, U.S.A. . . . . . . . . . . . . 110 C6 38 16N 104 37W
Puerca, Pta., Puerto Rico . . . 115 d 18 13N 65 36W
Puerto Aisén, Chile . . . . . . . . 121 G2 45 27S 73 0W
Puerto Barrios, Guatemala . . . 114 D7 15 40N 88 32W
Puerto Cabello, Venezuela . . 120 A3 10 28N 68 1W
Puerto Cabezas, Nic. . . . . . . . 115 E8 14 0N 83 30W
Puerto Carreño, Colombia . . . 120 B3 6 12N 67 22W
Puerto Cortés, Honduras . . . . 114 D7 15 51N 88 0W
Puerto Deseado, Argentina . . 121 G3 47 55S 66 0W
Puerto La Cruz, Venezuela . . 120 A3 10 13N 64 38W
Puerto Madryn, Argentina . . . 121 G3 42 48S 65 4W
Puerto Maldonado, Peru . . . . 120 D3 12 30S 69 10W
Puerto Montt, Chile . . . . . . . . 121 G2 41 28S 73 0W
Puerto Plata, Dom. Rep. . . . . 115 D10 19 48N 70 45W
Puerto Princesa, Phil. . . . . . . 83 C3 9 46N 118 45 E
Puerto Rico ☑, W. Indies . . . . 115 d 18 15N 66 45W
Puerto San Julián, Argentina . 121 G3 49 18S 67 43W
Puerto Suárez, Bolivia . . . . . . 120 D4 18 58S 57 52W
Puerto Wilches, Colombia . . . 120 B2 7 21N 73 54W
Puffin I., Ireland . . . . . . . . . . . 30 E2 51 50N 10 24W
Puget Sound, U.S.A. . . . . . . . 110 A2 47 50N 122 30W
Pukapuka, Cook Is. . . . . . . . . 103 J11 10 53S 165 49W
Pulacayo, Bolivia . . . . . . . . . . 120 E3 20 25S 66 41W
Pulaski, U.S.A. . . . . . . . . . . . . 111 C10 37 3N 80 47W
Pulborough, U.K. . . . . . . . . . . 25 E8 50 58N 0 30W
Pulham Market, U.K. . . . . . . . 25 B11 52 26N 1 13 E
Pulham St. Mary, U.K. . . . . . . 25 B11 52 26N 1 16 E
Pullman, U.S.A. . . . . . . . . . . . 110 A3 46 44N 117 10W
Pumlumon Fawr, U.K. . . . . . . 24 B1 52 28N 3 46W
Pune, India . . . . . . . . . . . . . . 84 K8 18 29N 73 57 E
Punjab □, India . . . . . . . . . . . 84 D10 31 0N 76 0 E
Punjab □, Pakistan . . . . . . . . 84 E9 32 0N 72 30 E
Puno, Peru . . . . . . . . . . . . . . 120 D2 15 55S 70 3W
Punta, Cerro de, Puerto Rico . 115 d 18 10N 66 37W
Punta Arenas, Chile . . . . . . . . 121 H2 53 10S 71 0W
Punxsatawney, U.S.A. . . . . . . 112 E8 40 57N 78 59W
Purbeck, Isle of, U.K. . . . . . . . 24 E5 50 39N 1 59W
Purfleet, U.K. . . . . . . . . . . . . . 25 D9 51 29N 0 16 E
Puri, India . . . . . . . . . . . . . . . 85 K14 19 50N 85 58 E
Purley on Thames, U.K. . . . . . 24 D6 51 29N 1 3W

Purnia, India . . . . . . . . . . . . . 85 G15 25 45N 87 31 E
Puruliya, India . . . . . . . . . . . . 85 H15 23 17N 86 24 E
Purus →, Brazil . . . . . . . . . . . 120 C3 3 42S 61 28W
Pusan, S. Korea . . . . . . . . . . . 81 C7 35 5N 129 0 E
Puttalam, Sri Lanka . . . . . . . . 84 Q11 8 1N 79 55 E
Putumayo →, S. Amer. . . . . . 120 C3 3 7S 67 58W
Puvirnituq, Canada . . . . . . . . 109 B12 60 2N 77 10W
Puy-de-Dôme, France . . . . . . 68 D5 45 46N 2 57 E
Pwllheli, U.K. . . . . . . . . . . . . . 26 B5 52 53N 4 25W
Pyatigorsk, Russia . . . . . . . . . 73 F7 44 2N 43 6 E
P'yŏngyang, N. Korea . . . . . . 81 C7 39 0N 125 30 E
Pyramid L., U.S.A. . . . . . . . . . 110 C3 40 1N 119 35W
Pyrénées, Europe . . . . . . . . . 68 E4 42 45N 0 18 E

## Q

Qaanaaq, Greenland . . . . . . . 54 B4 77 40N 69 0W
Qá'emshahr, Iran . . . . . . . . . . 87 B8 36 30N 52 53 E
Qaidam Basin, China . . . . . . . 80 C4 37 0N 95 0 E
Qandahār, Afghan. . . . . . . . . 84 D4 31 32N 65 43 E
Qaqortoq, Greenland . . . . . . 109 B6 60 43N 46 0W
Qarqan He →, China . . . . . . . 80 C3 39 30N 88 30 E
Qarshi, Uzbekistan . . . . . . . . 87 B11 38 53N 65 48 E
Qatar ■, Asia . . . . . . . . . . . . 87 E7 25 30N 51 15 E
Qattâra Depression, Egypt . . 95 C11 29 30N 27 30 E
Qazvin, Iran . . . . . . . . . . . . . 86 B7 36 15N 50 0 E
Qena, Egypt . . . . . . . . . . . . . 95 C12 26 10N 32 43 E
Qeqertarsuaq, Greenland . . . 109 B5 69 45N 53 30W
Qeqertarsuaq, Greenland . . . 109 B14 69 15N 53 38W
Qeshm, Iran . . . . . . . . . . . . . 87 E9 26 55N 56 10 E
Qikiqtarjuaq, Canada . . . . . . . 109 B13 67 33N 63 0W
Qilian Shan, China . . . . . . . . . 80 C4 38 30N 96 0 E
Qingdao, China . . . . . . . . . . . 81 C7 36 5N 120 20 E
Qinghai □, China . . . . . . . . . . 80 C4 36 0N 98 0 E
Qinghai Hu, China . . . . . . . . . 80 C5 36 40N 100 10 E
Qinhuangdao, China . . . . . . . 81 C6 39 56N 119 30 E
Qinzhou, China . . . . . . . . . . . 80 D5 21 58N 108 38 E
Qiqihar, China . . . . . . . . . . . . 81 B7 47 26N 124 0 E
Qitai, China . . . . . . . . . . . . . . 80 B3 44 2N 89 35 E
Qom, Iran . . . . . . . . . . . . . . . 87 C7 34 40N 51 0 E
Qondūz, Afghan. . . . . . . . . . . 87 B12 36 50N 68 50 E
Quadring, U.K. . . . . . . . . . . . 23 G8 52 54N 0 10W
Quang Ngai, Vietnam . . . . . . 83 B2 15 13N 108 58 E
Quanzhou, China . . . . . . . . . . 81 D6 24 55N 118 34 E
Quaqtaq, Canada . . . . . . . . . 109 B13 60 55N 69 40W
Québec, Canada . . . . . . . . . . 109 C13 46 52N 71 13W
Québec □, Canada . . . . . . . . 109 C13 48 0N 74 0W
Queen Charlotte Is., Canada . 108 C6 53 20N 132 10W
Queen Charlotte Sd., Canada . 108 C7 51 0N 128 0W
Queen Elizabeth Is., Canada . 52 A5 76 0N 95 0W
Queen Maud G., Canada . . . . 108 B9 68 15N 102 30W
Queenborough, U.K. . . . . . . . 25 D10 51 25N 0 46 E
Queensbury, U.K. . . . . . . . . . 23 E5 53 46N 1 50W
Queensland □, Australia . . . . 98 E7 22 0S 142 0 E
Queenstown, N.Z. . . . . . . . . . 99 K12 45 1S 168 40 E
Queenstown, S. Africa . . . . . . 97 L5 31 52S 26 52 E
Queimadas, Brazil . . . . . . . . . 122 B3 11 0S 39 38W
Quelimane, Mozam. . . . . . . . 97 H7 17 53S 36 58 E
Querétaro, Mexico . . . . . . . . . 114 C4 20 36N 100 23W
Quesnel, Canada . . . . . . . . . . 108 C7 53 0N 122 30W
Quesnel L., Canada . . . . . . . . 108 C7 52 30N 121 20W
Quetta, Pakistan . . . . . . . . . . 84 D5 30 15N 66 55 E
Quezaltenango, Guatemala . . 114 E6 14 50N 91 30W
Quezon City, Phil. . . . . . . . . . 83 B4 14 38N 121 0 E
Qui Nhon, Vietnam . . . . . . . . 83 B2 13 40N 109 13 E
Quibdo, Colombia . . . . . . . . . 120 B2 5 42N 76 40W
Quilán, C., Chile . . . . . . . . . . 121 G2 43 15S 74 30W
Quilon, India . . . . . . . . . . . . . 84 Q10 8 50N 76 38 E
Quilpie, Australia . . . . . . . . . . 98 F7 26 35S 144 11 E
Quimper, France . . . . . . . . . . 68 B1 48 0N 4 9W
Quincy, Ill., U.S.A. . . . . . . . . . 111 C8 39 56N 91 23W
Quincy, Mass., U.S.A. . . . . . . 113 D12 42 14N 71 0W
Quinte West, Canada . . . . . . . 112 C9 44 10N 77 34W
Quito, Ecuador . . . . . . . . . . . 120 C2 0 15S 78 35W
Qŭnghirot, Uzbekistan . . . . . . 87 A9 43 6N 58 54 E
Quorndon, U.K. . . . . . . . . . . . 23 G6 52 46N 1 10W
Qŭqon, Uzbekistan . . . . . . . . 87 A12 40 30N 70 57 E
Quseir, Egypt . . . . . . . . . . . . 95 C12 26 7N 34 16 E
Quzhou, China . . . . . . . . . . . . 81 D6 28 57N 118 54 E

## R

Raahe, Finland . . . . . . . . . . . 63 E8 64 40N 24 28 E
Raasay, U.K. . . . . . . . . . . . . . 18 H5 57 25N 6 4W
Raasay, Sd. of, U.K. . . . . . . . . 18 H5 57 30N 6 8W
Raba, Indonesia . . . . . . . . . . . 83 D3 8 36S 118 55 E
Rabat, Morocco . . . . . . . . . . . 94 B4 34 2N 6 48W
Rabaul, Papua N. G. . . . . . . . 98 A9 4 24S 152 18 E
Rābigh, Si. Arabia . . . . . . . . . 88 C2 22 50N 39 5 E
Race, C., Canada . . . . . . . . . . 109 D14 46 40N 53 5W
Rach Gia, Vietnam . . . . . . . . . 83 B2 10 5N 105 5 E
Racine, U.S.A. . . . . . . . . . . . . 112 D4 42 41N 87 51W
Rackheath, U.K. . . . . . . . . . . . 25 A11 52 40N 1 22 E
Radcliffe, U.K. . . . . . . . . . . . . 23 E4 53 34N 2 18W
Radcliffe-on-Trent, U.K. . . . . . 23 G6 52 57N 1 2W
Radford, U.S.A. . . . . . . . . . . . 112 G7 37 8N 80 34W
Radley, U.K. . . . . . . . . . . . . . 24 C6 51 41N 1 14W
Radnor Forest, U.K. . . . . . . . . 23 H2 52 17N 3 10W
Radom, Poland . . . . . . . . . . . 67 C11 51 23N 21 12 E
Radstock, U.K. . . . . . . . . . . . . 24 D4 51 17N 2 26W
Rae, Canada . . . . . . . . . . . . . 108 B8 62 50N 116 3W
Rae Bareli, India . . . . . . . . . . 85 F12 26 18N 81 20 E
Rae Isthmus, Canada . . . . . . . 109 B11 66 40N 87 30W
Rafaela, Argentina . . . . . . . . . 121 F3 31 10S 61 30W
Rafsanjān, Iran . . . . . . . . . . . 87 D9 30 30N 56 5 E
Ragged Pt., Barbados . . . . . . 115 g 13 10N 59 10W
Ragusa, Italy . . . . . . . . . . . . . 70 F6 36 55N 14 44 E
Rahimyar Khan, Pakistan . . . . 84 E7 28 30N 70 25 E
Raichur, India . . . . . . . . . . . . 84 L10 16 10N 77 20 E
Raigarh, India . . . . . . . . . . . . 85 J13 21 56N 83 25 E
Rainbow Lake, Canada . . . . . 108 C8 58 30N 119 23W
Rainham, U.K. . . . . . . . . . . . . 25 D10 51 22N 0 37 E
Rainier, Mt., U.S.A. . . . . . . . . 110 A2 46 52N 121 46W
Rainworth, U.K. . . . . . . . . . . . 23 F6 53 7N 1 7W
Rainy L., Canada . . . . . . . . . . 108 D10 48 42N 93 10W
Raipur, India . . . . . . . . . . . . . 85 J12 21 17N 81 45 E
Raj Nandgaon, India . . . . . . . 85 J12 21 5N 81 5 E
Rajahmundry, India . . . . . . . . 85 L12 17 1N 81 48 E
Rajapalaiyam, India . . . . . . . . 84 Q10 9 25N 77 35 E
Rajasthan □, India . . . . . . . . . 84 F8 26 45N 73 30 E
Rajkot, India . . . . . . . . . . . . . 84 H7 22 15N 70 56 E
Rajshahi, Bangla. . . . . . . . . . 85 G16 24 22N 88 39 E
Rajshahi □, Bangla. . . . . . . . . 85 G16 25 0N 89 0 E
Raleigh, U.S.A. . . . . . . . . . . . 111 C11 35 47N 78 39W
Rame Head, U.K. . . . . . . . . . . 27 G5 50 19N 4 13W
Ramgarh, India . . . . . . . . . . . 85 H14 23 40N 85 35 E
Râmnicu Vâlcea, Romania . . . 67 F13 45 9N 24 21 E
Rampside, U.K. . . . . . . . . . . . 22 D2 54 6N 3 9W
Rampur, India . . . . . . . . . . . . 84 E11 28 50N 79 5 E

Ramree I., Burma . . . . . . . . . 85 K19 19 0N 93 40 E
Ramsbottom, U.K. . . . . . . . . . 23 E4 53 38N 2 19W
Ramsbury, U.K. . . . . . . . . . . . 24 D5 51 26N 1 36W
Ramsey, Cambs., U.K. . . . . . . 23 H8 52 27N 0 7W
Ramsey, Essex, U.K. . . . . . . . 25 C11 51 55N 1 13 E
Ramsey, I. of M., U.K. . . . . . . 29 C13 54 20N 4 22W
Ramsgate, U.K. . . . . . . . . . . . 25 D11 51 20N 1 25 E
Rancagua, Chile . . . . . . . . . . 121 F2 34 10S 70 50W
Ranchi, India . . . . . . . . . . . . . 85 H14 23 19N 85 27 E
Randalstown, U.K. . . . . . . . . . 29 B9 54 45N 6 19W
Randers, Denmark . . . . . . . . . 63 F6 56 29N 10 1 E
Rangoon, Burma . . . . . . . . . . 85 L20 16 45N 96 20 E
Rangpur, Bangla. . . . . . . . . . 85 G16 25 42N 89 22 E
Rankin Inlet, Canada . . . . . . . 108 B10 62 30N 93 0W
Rannoch, L., U.K. . . . . . . . . . 19 J9 56 41N 4 20W
Rannoch Moor, U.K. . . . . . . . 19 J8 56 38N 4 48W
Rantoul, U.S.A. . . . . . . . . . . . 112 E3 40 19N 88 9W
Rapa, Pac. Oc. . . . . . . . . . . . 103 K13 27 35S 144 20W
Raper, C., Canada . . . . . . . . . 109 B13 69 44N 67 6W
Rapid City, U.S.A. . . . . . . . . . 110 B6 44 5N 103 14W
Rarotonga, Cook Is. . . . . . . . 103 K12 21 30S 160 0W
Ra's al Khaymah, U.A.E. . . . . 87 E9 25 50N 55 59 E
Rasht, Iran . . . . . . . . . . . . . . 86 B7 37 20N 49 40 E
Rat Islands, U.S.A. . . . . . . . . . 108 C1 52 0N 178 0 E
Ratangarh, India . . . . . . . . . . 84 E9 28 5N 74 35 E
Rath Luirc, Ireland . . . . . . . . . 30 D5 52 21N 8 40W
Rathdrum, Ireland . . . . . . . . . 31 C10 52 56N 6 14W
Rathkeale, Ireland . . . . . . . . . 30 C5 52 32N 8 56W
Rathlin I., U.K. . . . . . . . . . . . . 29 A9 55 18N 6 14W
Rathmelton, Ireland . . . . . . . 28 A6 55 2N 7 38W
Ratlam, India . . . . . . . . . . . . . 84 H9 23 20N 75 0 E
Ratnagiri, India . . . . . . . . . . . 84 L8 16 57N 73 18 E
Raton, U.S.A. . . . . . . . . . . . . 110 C6 36 54N 104 24W
Rattray Hd., U.K. . . . . . . . . . . 19 G14 57 38N 1 50W
Raunds, U.K. . . . . . . . . . . . . . 23 H7 52 21N 0 32W
Raurkela, India . . . . . . . . . . . 85 H14 22 14N 84 50 E
Ravenglass, U.K. . . . . . . . . . . 22 D2 54 22N 3 24W
Ravenna, Italy . . . . . . . . . . . . 70 B5 44 25N 12 12 E
Ravenstonedale, U.K. . . . . . . 22 D4 54 26N 2 25W
Ravi →, Pakistan . . . . . . . . . . 84 D7 30 35N 71 49 E
Rawalpindi, Pakistan . . . . . . . 84 C8 33 38N 73 8 E
Rawāndūz, Iraq . . . . . . . . . . . 86 B6 36 40N 44 30 E
Rawlins, U.S.A. . . . . . . . . . . . 110 B5 41 47N 107 14W
Rawmarsh, U.K. . . . . . . . . . . . 23 F6 53 27N 1 21W
Rawson, Argentina . . . . . . . . 121 G3 43 15S 65 5W
Rawtenstall, U.K. . . . . . . . . . . 23 E4 53 42N 2 17W
Ray, C., Canada . . . . . . . . . . 109 D14 47 33N 59 15W
Rayleigh, U.K. . . . . . . . . . . . . 25 C10 51 36N 0 37 E
Rayong, Thailand . . . . . . . . . 83 B2 12 40N 101 20 E
Raz, Pte. du, France . . . . . . . 68 C1 48 2N 4 47W
Ré, Î. de, France . . . . . . . . . . 68 C3 46 12N 1 30W
Reading, U.K. . . . . . . . . . . . . 25 D7 51 27N 0 58W
Reading, U.S.A. . . . . . . . . . . . 113 E10 40 20N 75 56W
Reay Forest, U.K. . . . . . . . . . 19 F8 58 22N 4 55W
Recife, Brazil . . . . . . . . . . . . . 122 A3 8 0S 35 0W
Reconquista, Argentina . . . . . 121 E4 29 10S 59 45W
Red →, La., U.S.A. . . . . . . . . 111 D8 31 1N 91 45W
Red →, N. Dak., U.S.A. . . . . . 108 C10 49 0N 97 15W
Red Bluff, U.S.A. . . . . . . . . . . 110 B2 40 11N 122 15W
Red Deer, Canada . . . . . . . . . 108 C8 52 20N 113 50W
Red Dial, U.K. . . . . . . . . . . . . 22 C2 54 49N 3 10W
Red Lake, Canada . . . . . . . . . 108 C10 51 3N 93 49W
Red Oak, U.S.A. . . . . . . . . . . 111 B7 41 1N 95 14W
Red Sea, Asia . . . . . . . . . . . . 88 C2 25 0N 36 0 E
Red Wing, U.S.A. . . . . . . . . . . 111 B8 44 34N 92 31W
Redbridge □, U.K. . . . . . . . . . 25 C9 51 35N 0 7 E
Redcar, U.K. . . . . . . . . . . . . . 22 C6 54 37N 1 4W
Redding, U.S.A. . . . . . . . . . . . 110 B2 40 35N 122 24W
Redditch, U.K. . . . . . . . . . . . . 23 H5 52 18N 1 55W
Rede →, U.K. . . . . . . . . . . . . 22 B4 55 9N 2 13W
Redesmouth, U.K. . . . . . . . . . 22 B4 55 8N 2 13W
Redhill, U.K. . . . . . . . . . . . . . 25 D8 51 14N 0 9W
Redlynch, U.K. . . . . . . . . . . . . 24 E5 50 59N 1 41W
Redmile, U.K. . . . . . . . . . . . . 23 G7 52 54N 0 48W
Redmire, U.K. . . . . . . . . . . . . 22 D5 54 19N 1 55W
Redon, France . . . . . . . . . . . . 68 C2 47 40N 2 6W
Redruth, U.K. . . . . . . . . . . . . 27 G3 50 14N 5 14W
Ree, L., Ireland . . . . . . . . . . . 28 D6 53 35N 8 0W
Reedham, U.K. . . . . . . . . . . . 25 A12 52 34N 1 34 E
Reepham, U.K. . . . . . . . . . . . 25 A11 52 46N 1 6 E
Reese →, U.S.A. . . . . . . . . . . 110 B3 40 48N 117 4W
Reeth, U.K. . . . . . . . . . . . . . . 22 D5 54 23N 1 56W
Regensburg, Germany . . . . . . 66 D7 49 1N 12 6 E
Réggio di Calábria, Italy . . . . 70 E6 38 6N 15 39 E
Réggio nell'Emília, Italy . . . . . 70 B4 44 43N 10 36 E
Regina, Canada . . . . . . . . . . . 108 C9 50 27N 104 35W
Reichenbach, Germany . . . . . 66 C7 50 37N 12 17 E
Reigate, U.K. . . . . . . . . . . . . . 25 D8 51 14N 0 12W
Reims, France . . . . . . . . . . . . 68 B6 49 15N 4 1 E
Reina Adelaida, Arch., Chile . 121 H2 52 20S 74 0W
Reindeer L., Canada . . . . . . . 108 C9 57 15N 102 15W
Remscheid, Germany . . . . . . 65 C7 51 11N 7 12 E
Renfrew, Canada . . . . . . . . . . 112 C9 45 30N 76 40W
Rennell, Solomon Is. . . . . . . . 99 C11 11 40S 160 10 E
Rennes, France . . . . . . . . . . . 68 B3 48 7N 1 41W
Reno, U.S.A. . . . . . . . . . . . . . 110 C3 39 31N 119 48W
Repton, U.K. . . . . . . . . . . . . . 23 G5 52 50N 1 33W
Republican →, U.S.A. . . . . . . 111 C7 39 4N 96 48W
Repulse Bay, Canada . . . . . . . 109 B11 66 30N 86 30W
Resistencia, Argentina . . . . . . 121 E4 27 30S 59 0W
Resolution I., Canada . . . . . . 109 B13 61 30N 65 0W
Reston, U.K. . . . . . . . . . . . . . 22 A4 55 51N 2 10W
Retford, U.K. . . . . . . . . . . . . . 23 F7 53 19N 0 56W
Réthimnon, Greece . . . . . . . . 71 G11 35 18N 24 30 E
Réunion ☑, Ind. Oc. . . . . . . . 91 J9 21 0S 56 0 E
Revda, Russia . . . . . . . . . . . . 72 C10 56 48N 59 57 E
Revelstoke, Canada . . . . . . . . 108 C8 51 0N 118 10W
Revillagigedo, Is. de, Pac. Oc. 103 F16 18 40N 112 0W
Rewa, India . . . . . . . . . . . . . . 85 G12 24 33N 81 25 E
Rexburg, U.S.A. . . . . . . . . . . 110 B4 43 49N 111 47W
Rey Malabo, Eq. Guin. . . . . . . 96 D1 3 45N 8 50 E
Reykjavik, Iceland . . . . . . . . . 63 B1 64 10N 21 57W
Reynosa, Mexico . . . . . . . . . . 114 B5 26 5N 98 18W
Rēzekne, Latvia . . . . . . . . . . . 72 C4 56 30N 27 17 E
Rhayader, U.K. . . . . . . . . . . . 24 B2 52 18N 3 29W
Rheidol →, U.K. . . . . . . . . . . 26 C5 52 25N 4 5W
Rheine, Germany . . . . . . . . . . 66 B4 52 17N 7 26 E
Rheinland-Pfalz, Germany . . . 66 C4 50 0N 7 0 E
Rhine →, Europe . . . . . . . . . 65 C6 51 52N 6 2 E
Rhinelander, U.S.A. . . . . . . . . 111 A9 45 38N 89 25W
Rhinns Pt., U.K. . . . . . . . . . . . 20 C3 55 40N 6 29W
Rhins, The, U.K. . . . . . . . . . . 20 E5 54 52N 5 3W
Rhode Island □, U.S.A. . . . . . 113 E12 41 40N 71 30W
Rhodes, Greece . . . . . . . . . . . 71 F13 36 15N 28 10 E
Rhodope Mts., Bulgaria . . . . . 71 D11 41 40N 24 20 E
Rhondda, U.K. . . . . . . . . . . . . 24 C1 51 39N 3 31W
Rhône →, France . . . . . . . . . 68 E6 43 28N 4 42 E
Rhoslanerchrugog, U.K. . . . . 23 F2 53 1N 3 3W
Rhossili, U.K. . . . . . . . . . . . . . 27 D5 51 34N 4 17W
Rhum, U.K. . . . . . . . . . . . . . . 18 J5 57 0N 6 20W
Rhyl, U.K. . . . . . . . . . . . . . . . 23 G5 53 20N 3 29W
Rhymney, U.K. . . . . . . . . . . . 24 C2 51 46N 3 17W
Riau, Kepulauan, Indonesia . . 23 E4 53 52N 2 25W
Ribble →, U.K. . . . . . . . . . . . 23 E4 53 52N 2 25W
Ribeirão Prêto, Brazil . . . . . . . 122 D1 21 10S 47 50W
Riberalta, Bolivia . . . . . . . . . . 120 D3 11 0S 66 0W
Riccall, U.K. . . . . . . . . . . . . . . 23 E6 53 50N 1 3W

**Richards Bay**　　　　　　　　　　　　　　　　　　　　　　　　　　**San Juan**

Richards Bay, S. Africa ..... 97 K6 28 48S 32 6 E
Richfield, U.S.A. ..... 110 C4 38 46N 112 5W
Richland, U.S.A. ..... 110 A3 46 17N 119 18W
Richlands, U.S.A. ..... 112 G7 37 6N 81 48W
Richmond, U.K. ..... 22 D5 54 25N 1 43W
Richmond, Ind., U.S.A. ..... 112 F5 39 50N 84 53W
Richmond, Ky., U.S.A. ..... 112 G5 37 45N 84 18W
Richmond, Va., U.S.A. ..... 112 G9 37 33N 77 27W
Richmond-upon-Thames □, U.K. ..... 25 D8 51 27N 0 17W
Rickmansworth, U.K. ..... 25 C8 51 38N 0 29W
Ridgecrest, U.S.A. ..... 110 C3 35 38N 117 40W
Ridgway, U.S.A. ..... 112 E8 41 25N 78 44W
Ridsdale, U.K. ..... 22 B4 55 9N 2 9W
Rievaulx, U.K. ..... 22 D6 54 16N 1 7W
Rift Valley, Africa ..... 90 G7 7 0N 30 0 E
Riga, Latvia ..... 72 C3 56 53N 24 8 E
Riga, G. of, Latvia ..... 72 C3 57 40N 23 45 E
Rigestān, Afghan. ..... 87 D11 30 15N 65 0 E
Rigolet, Canada ..... 109 C14 54 10N 58 23W
Rijeka, Croatia ..... 66 F8 45 20N 14 21 E
Rillington, U.K. ..... 22 D7 54 9N 0 42W
Rimini, Italy ..... 70 B5 44 3N 12 33 E
Rimouski, Canada ..... 109 D13 48 27N 68 30W
Ringmer, U.K. ..... 25 E9 50 53N 0 5 E
Ringwood, U.K. ..... 24 E5 50 50N 1 47W
Rio Branco, Brazil ..... 120 C3 9 58S 67 49W
Rio Claro, Brazil ..... 122 D1 22 19S 47 35W
Rio Cuarto, Argentina ..... 121 F3 33 10S 64 25W
Rio de Janeiro, Brazil ..... 122 D2 23 0S 43 12W
Rio de Janeiro □, Brazil ..... 122 D2 22 50S 43 0W
Rio Gallegos, Argentina ..... 121 H3 51 35S 69 15W
Rio Grande, Brazil ..... 121 F4 32 0S 52 20W
Rio Grande, Nic. ..... 115 E8 12 54N 83 33W
Rio Grande, Puerto Rico ..... 115 d 18 23N 65 50W
Rio Grande de Santiago →, Mexico ..... 114 C3 21 36N 105 26W
Rio Grande do Norte □, Brazil ..... 120 C6 5 40S 36 0W
Rio Grande do Sul □, Brazil ..... 121 E4 30 0S 53 0W
Rio Muni □, Eq. Guin. ..... 96 D2 1 30N 10 0 E
Riobamba, Ecuador ..... 120 C2 1 50S 78 45W
Riohacha, Colombia ..... 120 A2 11 33N 72 55W
Ripley, Derby, U.K. ..... 23 F6 53 3N 1 24W
Ripley, N. Yorks., U.K. ..... 22 D5 54 3N 1 34W
Ripon, U.K. ..... 22 D5 54 9N 1 31W
Ripon, U.S.A. ..... 112 D3 43 51N 88 50W
Risca, U.K. ..... 24 C2 51 37N 3 5W
Rishton, U.K. ..... 23 E4 53 46N 2 26W
Rivera, Uruguay ..... 121 F4 31 0S 55 50W
Riverhead, U.S.A. ..... 113 E11 40 55N 72 40W
Riverside, U.S.A. ..... 110 D3 33 59N 117 22W
Riverton, U.S.A. ..... 110 B5 43 2N 108 23W
Rivière-du-Loup, Canada ..... 109 D13 47 50N 69 30W
Rivière-Pilote, Martinique ..... 114 c 14 26N 60 53W
Rivière-Salée, Martinique ..... 114 c 14 31N 60 58W
Rivne, Ukraine ..... 67 C14 50 40N 26 10 E
Riyadh, Si. Arabia ..... 86 E6 24 41N 46 42 E
Rize, Turkey ..... 73 F7 41 0N 40 30 E
Road Town, Br. Virgin Is. ..... 115 e 18 27N 64 37W
Roade, U.K. ..... 25 B7 52 9N 0 53W
Roanne, France ..... 68 C6 46 3N 4 4 E
Roanoke, U.S.A. ..... 112 G8 37 16N 79 56W
Roanoke →, U.S.A. ..... 111 C11 35 57N 76 42W
Roberton, U.K. ..... 22 B3 55 25N 2 54W
Roberval, Canada ..... 109 D12 48 32N 72 15W
Robin Hood's Bay, U.K. ..... 22 D7 54 27N 0 32W
Robson, Mt., Canada ..... 108 C8 53 10N 119 10W
Roca, C. da, Portugal ..... 69 C1 38 40N 9 31W
Rocester, U.K. ..... 23 G5 52 57N 1 50W
Rocha, Uruguay ..... 121 F4 34 30S 54 25W
Rochdale, U.K. ..... 23 E4 53 38N 2 9W
Roche, U.K. ..... 27 G4 50 24N 4 50W
Rochefort, France ..... 68 D3 45 56N 0 57W
Rochester, Medway, U.K. ..... 25 D10 51 23N 0 31 E
Rochester, Northumberland, U.K. ..... 22 B4 55 17N 2 17W
Rochester, Ind., U.S.A. ..... 112 E4 41 4N 86 13W
Rochester, Minn., U.S.A. ..... 111 B8 44 1N 92 28W
Rochester, N.H., U.S.A. ..... 113 D12 43 18N 70 59W
Rochester, N.Y., U.S.A. ..... 112 D9 43 10N 77 37W
Rochford, U.K. ..... 25 C10 51 34N 0 43 E
Rock Hill, U.S.A. ..... 111 D10 34 56N 81 1W
Rock Island, U.S.A. ..... 111 B8 41 30N 90 34W
Rock Springs, U.S.A. ..... 110 B5 41 35N 109 14W
Rockall, Atl. Oc. ..... 56 D3 57 37N 13 42W
Rockcliffe, U.K. ..... 22 C3 54 57N 3 0W
Rockford, U.S.A. ..... 111 B9 42 16N 89 6W
Rockhampton, Australia ..... 98 E9 23 22S 150 32 E
Rockingham, U.K. ..... 23 G7 52 31N 0 43W
Rockingham Forest, U.K. ..... 23 H7 52 29N 0 42W
Rockland, U.S.A. ..... 113 C13 44 6N 69 7W
Rocky Mount, U.S.A. ..... 111 C11 35 57N 77 48W
Rocky Mts., N. Amer. ..... 108 C7 49 0N 115 0W
Rodez, France ..... 68 D5 44 21N 2 33 E
Roding →, U.K. ..... 25 C9 51 31N 0 6 E
Rodriguez, Ind. Oc. ..... 53 E13 19 45S 63 20 E
Roe →, U.K. ..... 29 A8 55 6N 6 59W
Roermond, Neths. ..... 65 C6 51 12N 6 0 E
Roes Welcome Sd., Canada ..... 109 B11 65 0N 87 0W
Roeselare, Belgium ..... 65 D3 50 57N 3 7 E
Rogans Seat, U.K. ..... 22 D4 54 26N 2 7W
Rogate, U.K. ..... 25 D7 51 0N 0 49W
Rogers City, U.S.A. ..... 112 C6 45 25N 83 49W
Rohri, Pakistan ..... 84 F6 27 45N 68 51 E
Rojo, C., Mexico ..... 114 C5 21 33N 97 20W
Rolla, U.S.A. ..... 111 C8 37 57N 91 46W
Roma, Australia ..... 98 F8 26 32S 148 49 E
Romaine →, Canada ..... 109 C13 50 18N 63 47W
Romania ■, Europe ..... 67 F12 46 0N 25 0 E
Romans-sur-Isère, France ..... 68 D6 45 3N 5 3 E
Rome, Italy ..... 70 D5 41 54N 12 29 E
Rome, Ga., U.S.A. ..... 111 D9 34 15N 85 10W
Rome, N.Y., U.S.A. ..... 113 D10 43 13N 75 27W
Romney, U.S.A. ..... 112 F8 39 21N 78 45W
Romney Marsh, U.K. ..... 25 D10 51 2N 0 54 E
Romorantin-Lanthenay, France ..... 68 C4 47 21N 1 45 E
Romsey, U.K. ..... 24 E6 51 0N 1 29W
Rona, U.K. ..... 18 G6 57 34N 5 59W
Roncador, Serra do, Brazil ..... 120 D4 12 30S 52 30W
Rondônia □, Brazil ..... 120 D3 11 0S 63 0W
Ronge, L. la, Canada ..... 108 C9 55 6N 105 17W
Ronne Ice Shelf, Antarctica ..... 55 D18 78 0S 60 0W
Ronse, Belgium ..... 65 D3 50 45N 3 35 E
Roosendaal, Neths. ..... 65 C4 51 32N 4 29 E
Roosevelt →, U.S.A. ..... 116 D4 7 35S 60 20W
Roosevelt I., Antarctica ..... 55 D12 79 30S 162 0W
Ropsley, U.K. ..... 23 G8 52 54N 0 30W
Roraima □, Brazil ..... 120 B3 2 0N 61 30W
Roraima, Mt., Venezuela ..... 120 B3 5 10N 60 40W
Rosario, Argentina ..... 121 F3 33 0S 60 40W
Rosario, Mexico ..... 114 C3 23 0N 105 52W
Rosario de la Frontera, Argentina ..... 121 E3 25 50S 65 0W
Roscommon, Ireland ..... 28 D5 53 38N 8 11W
Roscommon □, Ireland ..... 28 D5 53 49N 8 23W
Roscrea, Ireland ..... 30 C7 52 57N 7 49W
Roseau, Domin. ..... 115 D12 15 20N 61 24W

Roseburg, U.S.A. ..... 110 B2 43 13N 123 20W
Rosedale Abbey, U.K. ..... 22 D7 54 21N 0 52W
Rosehearty, U.K. ..... 19 G13 57 42N 2 7W
Rosenheim, Germany ..... 66 E7 47 51N 12 7 E
Rosetown, Canada ..... 108 C9 51 35N 107 59W
Roseville, U.S.A. ..... 110 C2 38 45N 121 17W
Roslavl, Russia ..... 72 D5 53 57N 32 55 E
Ross Ice Shelf, Antarctica ..... 55 E12 80 0S 180 0 E
Ross-on-Wye, U.K. ..... 24 C3 51 54N 2 34W
Ross River, Canada ..... 108 B6 62 30N 131 30W
Ross Sea, Antarctica ..... 55 D11 74 0S 178 0 E
Rossall Pt., U.K. ..... 23 E2 53 55N 3 3W
Rossan Pt., Ireland ..... 28 B4 54 42N 8 47W
Rosses, The, Ireland ..... 28 A5 55 2N 8 20W
Rossignol L., Canada ..... 113 C15 44 12N 65 10W
Rosslare, Ireland ..... 31 D10 52 17N 6 24W
Rosslare Harbour, Ireland ..... 31 D10 52 15N 6 20W
Rossosh, Russia ..... 73 D6 50 15N 39 28 E
Rostock, Germany ..... 66 A7 54 5N 12 8 E
Rostov, Russia ..... 73 E6 47 15N 39 45 E
Roswell, U.S.A. ..... 110 D6 33 24N 104 32W
Rothbury, U.K. ..... 22 B5 55 19N 1 58W
Rothbury Forest, U.K. ..... 22 B5 55 19N 1 50W
Rother →, U.K. ..... 25 E10 50 59N 0 45 E
Rotherham, U.K. ..... 23 F6 53 26N 1 20W
Rothes, U.K. ..... 19 G11 57 32N 3 13W
Rothesay, U.K. ..... 20 C5 55 50N 5 3W
Rothwell, Northants., U.K. ..... 23 H7 52 25N 0 48W
Rothwell, W. Yorks., U.K. ..... 23 E6 53 45N 1 28W
Rotorua, N.Z. ..... 99 H14 38 9S 176 16 E
Rotterdam, Neths. ..... 65 C4 51 55N 4 30 E
Rottingdean, U.K. ..... 25 E8 50 48N 0 4W
Rotuma, Fiji ..... 99 C14 12 25S 177 5 E
Roubaix, France ..... 68 A5 50 40N 3 10 E
Rouen, France ..... 68 B4 49 27N 1 4 E
Round Mt., Australia ..... 98 G9 30 26S 152 16 E
Rousay, U.K. ..... 19 D11 59 10N 3 2W
Roussillon, France ..... 68 E5 42 30N 2 35 E
Rouyn-Noranda, Canada ..... 109 D12 48 20N 79 0W
Rovaniemi, Finland ..... 63 D9 66 29N 25 41 E
Rowanburn, U.K. ..... 22 B3 55 5N 2 55W
Roxas, Phil. ..... 83 B4 11 36N 122 49 E
Roxburgh, U.K. ..... 22 A4 55 35N 2 28W
Roxby, U.K. ..... 23 E7 53 38N 0 38W
Royal Canal, Ireland ..... 29 E7 53 30N 7 13W
Royal Leamington Spa, U.K. ..... 23 H5 52 18N 1 31W
Royal Tunbridge Wells, U.K. ..... 25 D9 51 7N 0 16 E
Royale, Isle, U.S.A. ..... 111 A9 48 0N 88 54W
Royan, France ..... 68 D3 45 37N 1 2W
Royston, U.K. ..... 25 B8 52 3N 0 0W
Royton, U.K. ..... 23 E4 53 34N 2 8W
Rub' al Khālī, Si. Arabia ..... 88 D4 19 0N 48 0 E
Rubery, U.K. ..... 23 H4 52 24N 2 1W
Rubh a' Mhail, U.K. ..... 20 C3 55 56N 6 8W
Rubha Hunish, U.K. ..... 18 G5 57 42N 6 20W
Ruby L., U.S.A. ..... 110 B3 40 10N 115 28W
Rudston, U.K. ..... 22 D8 54 6N 0 20W
Rufford, U.K. ..... 23 E3 53 38N 2 50W
Rufiji →, Tanzania ..... 96 F7 7 50S 39 15 E
Rufling Pt., Br. Virgin Is. ..... 115 e 18 44N 64 27W
Rugby, U.K. ..... 23 H6 52 23N 1 16W
Rugeley, U.K. ..... 23 G5 52 46N 1 55W
Rügen, Germany ..... 66 A7 54 22N 13 24 E
Ruhr →, Germany ..... 66 C4 51 27N 6 43 E
Rumania = Romania ■, Europe ..... 67 F12 46 0N 25 0 E
Rumford, U.S.A. ..... 113 C12 44 33N 70 33W
Runaway Bay, Jamaica ..... 114 a 18 27N 77 20W
Runcorn, U.K. ..... 23 F3 53 21N 2 44W
Rundu, Namibia ..... 97 H3 17 52S 19 43 E
Rungwe, Tanzania ..... 90 G7 9 11S 33 32 E
Ruoqiang, China ..... 80 C3 38 55N 88 10 E
Rupert →, Canada ..... 110 B4 42 37N 113 41W
Rupert →, Canada ..... 109 C12 51 29N 78 45W
Ruse, Bulgaria ..... 71 C12 43 48N 25 59 E
Rush, Ireland ..... 29 D9 53 31N 6 6W
Rushden, U.K. ..... 23 H7 52 18N 0 35W
Rushville, U.S.A. ..... 112 F5 39 37N 85 27W
Ruskington, U.K. ..... 23 F8 53 3N 0 22W
Russellville, U.S.A. ..... 111 C8 35 17N 93 8W
Russia ■, Eurasia ..... 79 C12 62 0N 105 0 E
Rustavi, Georgia ..... 73 F8 41 30N 45 0 E
Rustenburg, S. Africa ..... 97 K5 25 41S 27 14 E
Ruthin, U.K. ..... 23 F2 52 0N 3 19W
Ruthwell, U.K. ..... 22 C2 55 0N 3 24W
Ruvuma →, Tanzania ..... 96 G8 10 29S 40 28 E
Ruwenzori, Africa ..... 96 D5 0 30N 29 55 E
Rwanda ■, Africa ..... 96 E5 2 0S 30 0 E
Ryan, L., U.K. ..... 20 E5 55 0N 5 2W
Ryazan, Russia ..... 72 D6 54 40N 39 40 E
Rybinsk, Russia ..... 72 C6 58 5N 38 50 E
Rybinsk Res., Russia ..... 72 C6 58 30N 38 25 E
Rydal, U.K. ..... 22 D3 54 27N 2 59W
Ryde, U.K. ..... 24 E6 50 43N 1 9W
Rye, U.K. ..... 25 E10 50 57N 0 45 E
Rye →, U.K. ..... 22 D7 54 11N 0 44W
Rye Bay, U.K. ..... 25 E10 50 52N 0 49 E
Ryhope, U.K. ..... 22 C6 54 53N 1 21W
Ryton, U.K. ..... 23 H6 52 22N 1 25W
Ryukyu Is., Japan ..... 81 D7 26 0N 126 0 E
Rzeszów, Poland ..... 67 C11 50 5N 21 58 E
Rzhev, Russia ..... 72 C5 56 20N 34 20 E

## S

Saale →, Germany ..... 66 C6 51 56N 11 54 E
Saar →, Europe ..... 65 E6 49 41N 6 32 E
Saarbrücken, Germany ..... 66 D4 49 14N 6 59 E
Saaremaa, Estonia ..... 72 C3 58 30N 22 30 E
Sabadell, Spain ..... 69 B7 41 28N 2 7 E
Sabah □, Malaysia ..... 83 C3 6 0N 117 0 E
Sabhah, Libya ..... 95 C8 27 9N 14 29 E
Sabinas, Mexico ..... 114 B4 27 50N 101 10W
Sabinas Hidalgo, Mexico ..... 114 B4 26 33N 100 10W
Sabine →, U.S.A. ..... 111 E8 29 59N 93 47W
Sable, C., Canada ..... 109 D13 43 29N 65 38W
Sable, C., U.S.A. ..... 111 E10 25 9N 81 8W
Sable I., Canada ..... 109 D14 44 0N 60 0W
Sachsen, Germany ..... 66 C7 50 55N 13 10 E
Sachsen-Anhalt □, Germany ..... 66 C7 52 0N 12 0 E
Saco, U.S.A. ..... 113 D12 43 30N 70 27W
Sacramento, U.S.A. ..... 110 C2 38 35N 121 29W
Sacramento →, U.S.A. ..... 110 C2 38 3N 121 56W
Sacramento Mts., U.S.A. ..... 110 D5 32 30N 105 30W
Sado, Japan ..... 82 E6 38 0N 138 25 E
Safford, U.S.A. ..... 110 D5 32 50N 109 43W
Saffron Walden, U.K. ..... 25 B9 52 1N 0 16 E
Safi, Morocco ..... 94 B4 32 18N 9 20W
Saga, Japan ..... 82 G2 33 15N 130 16 E
Sagar, India ..... 84 H11 23 50N 78 44 E
Saginaw, U.S.A. ..... 112 D6 43 26N 83 56W
Saginaw →, U.S.A. ..... 112 D6 43 39N 83 51W
Sagua la Grande, Cuba ..... 115 C8 22 50N 80 10W
Saguenay →, Canada ..... 113 A12 48 22N 71 0W

Sahara, Africa ..... 94 D6 23 0N 5 0 E
Saharan Atlas, Algeria ..... 94 B6 33 30N 1 0 E
Saharanpur, India ..... 84 E10 29 58N 77 33 E
Sahel, Africa ..... 94 E5 16 0N 5 0 E
Sahiwal, Pakistan ..... 84 D8 30 45N 73 8 E
Saidpur, Bangla. ..... 85 G16 25 48N 89 0 E
St. Abb's Head, U.K. ..... 21 C11 55 55N 2 8W
St. Agnes, Corn., U.K. ..... 27 G3 50 18N 5 13W
St. Agnes Hd., U.K. ..... 27 G3 50 19N 5 15W
St. Albans, U.K. ..... 25 C8 51 45N 0 19W
St. Albans, Vt., U.S.A. ..... 113 C11 44 49N 73 5W
St. Albans, W. Va., U.S.A. ..... 112 F7 38 23N 81 50W
St. Alban's Head, U.K. ..... 24 E4 50 34N 2 4W
St. Andrews, U.K. ..... 21 B10 56 20N 2 47W
St. Ann's, U.K. ..... 22 B2 55 14N 3 28W
St. Ann's Bay, Jamaica ..... 114 a 18 26N 77 15W
St. Anthony, Canada ..... 109 C14 51 22N 55 35W
St. Asaph, U.K. ..... 23 F2 53 15N 3 27W
St-Augustin, Canada ..... 109 C14 51 13N 58 38W
St. Augustine, U.S.A. ..... 111 E10 29 54N 81 19W
St. Austell, U.K. ..... 27 G4 50 20N 4 47W
St. Bees, U.K. ..... 22 C1 54 30N 3 35W
St. Bees Hd., U.K. ..... 22 C1 54 31N 3 38W
St. Blazey, U.K. ..... 27 G4 50 22N 4 43W
St. Brides B., U.K. ..... 26 D3 51 49N 5 9W
St-Brieuc, France ..... 68 B2 48 30N 2 46W
St. Buryan, U.K. ..... 27 G2 50 4N 5 37W
St. Catharines, Canada ..... 112 D8 43 10N 79 15W
St. Catherine's Pt., U.K. ..... 24 E6 50 34N 1 18W
St. Clair, L., Canada ..... 112 D6 42 30N 82 45W
St. Clears, U.K. ..... 26 D4 51 49N 4 31W
St. Cloud, U.S.A. ..... 111 A8 45 34N 94 10W
St. Columb Major, U.K. ..... 27 G4 50 26N 4 56W
St. Croix, U.S. Virgin Is. ..... 115 D12 17 45N 64 45W
St. David's, U.K. ..... 26 D3 51 53N 5 16W
St. David's Head, U.K. ..... 26 D3 51 54N 5 19W
St. Dennis, U.K. ..... 27 G4 50 23N 4 53W
St-Dizier, France ..... 68 B6 48 38N 4 56 E
St. Dominick, U.K. ..... 27 G5 50 29N 4 16W
St. Elias, Mt., U.S.A. ..... 108 B5 60 18N 140 56W
St. Elias Mts., N. Amer. ..... 108 C6 60 33N 139 28W
St. Enoder, U.K. ..... 27 G4 50 22N 4 59W
St. Erth, U.K. ..... 27 G3 50 9N 5 26W
St-Étienne, France ..... 68 D6 45 27N 4 22 E
St-Félicien, Canada ..... 113 A11 48 40N 72 25W
St-Flour, France ..... 68 D5 45 2N 3 6 E
St. Gallen, Switz. ..... 66 E5 47 26N 9 22 E
St-Gaudens, France ..... 68 E4 43 6N 0 44 E
St. George, Canada ..... 110 C4 37 6N 113 35W
St-Georges, Canada ..... 113 B12 46 8N 70 40W
St. George's, Grenada ..... 115 E12 12 5N 61 43W
St. George's Channel, Europe ..... 31 E11 52 0N 6 0W
St. Germans, U.K. ..... 27 G5 50 23N 4 19W
St. Helena, Atl. Oc. ..... 52 E9 15 58S 5 42W
St. Helens, U.K. ..... 23 F3 53 27N 2 44W
St. Helens, U.S.A. ..... 110 A2 45 52N 122 48W
St. Helens, Mt., U.S.A. ..... 110 A2 46 12N 122 12W
St. Helier, U.K. ..... 27 J9 49 10N 2 7W
St-Hyacinthe, Canada ..... 109 D12 45 40N 72 58W
St. Ignace, U.S.A. ..... 112 C5 45 52N 84 44W
St. Issey, U.K. ..... 27 G4 50 30N 4 57W
St. Ives, Cambs., U.K. ..... 23 H8 52 20N 0 4W
St. Ives, Corn., U.K. ..... 27 G3 50 12N 5 30W
St. Ives B., U.K. ..... 27 G3 50 13N 5 27W
St-Jean, L., Canada ..... 109 D12 48 40N 72 0W
St-Jean-sur-Richelieu, Canada ..... 113 C11 45 20N 73 20W
St-Jérôme, Canada ..... 113 C11 45 47N 74 0W
St. John, Canada ..... 109 D13 45 20N 66 8W
St. John I., U.S. Virgin Is. ..... 115 e 18 20N 64 42W
St. John's, Antigua & B. ..... 115 D12 17 6N 61 51W
St. John's, Canada ..... 109 D14 47 35N 52 40W
St. Johns, U.S.A. ..... 112 D5 43 0N 84 33W
St. Johns →, U.S.A. ..... 111 D10 30 24N 81 24W
St. John's Pt., Ireland ..... 28 B5 54 34N 8 27W
St. Johnsbury, U.S.A. ..... 113 C11 44 25N 72 1W
St. Joseph, Martinique ..... 114 c 14 39N 61 4W
St. Joseph, Mich., U.S.A. ..... 112 D4 42 6N 86 29W
St. Joseph, Mo., U.S.A. ..... 111 C8 39 46N 94 50W
St. Joseph, L., Canada ..... 109 C10 51 10N 90 35W
St. Just, U.K. ..... 27 G2 50 7N 5 42W
St. Keverne, U.K. ..... 27 G3 50 3N 5 6W
St. Kilda, U.K. ..... 64 C2 57 49N 8 34W
St. Kitts & Nevis ■, W. Indies ..... 115 D12 17 20N 62 40W
St. Lawrence →, Canada ..... 109 D13 49 30N 66 0W
St. Lawrence, Gulf of, Canada ..... 109 D13 48 25N 62 0W
St. Lawrence I., U.S.A. ..... 108 B3 63 30N 170 30W
St. Levan, U.K. ..... 27 G2 50 2N 5 41W
St-Lô, France ..... 68 B3 49 7N 1 5W
St-Louis, Guadeloupe ..... 114 b 15 56N 61 19W
St. Louis, Senegal ..... 94 E2 16 8N 16 27W
St. Louis, U.S.A. ..... 111 C8 38 37N 90 12W
St. Lucia ■, W. Indies ..... 115 f 14 0N 60 50W
St. Mabyn, U.K. ..... 27 F4 50 30N 4 46W
St. Magnus B., U.K. ..... 18 B14 60 25N 1 35W
St-Malo, France ..... 68 B2 48 39N 2 1W
St-Marc, Haiti ..... 115 D10 19 10N 72 41W
St. Margaret's-at-Cliffe, U.K. ..... 25 D11 51 9N 1 23 E
St-Martin, W. Indies ..... 115 D12 18 0N 63 0W
St-Martin, C., Martinique ..... 114 c 14 52N 61 14W
St. Martins, Barbados ..... 115 g 13 5N 59 28W
St. Martin's, U.K. ..... 27 H1 49 58N 6 17W
St. Mary Bourne, U.K. ..... 24 D6 51 15N 1 24W
St. Mary's, Corn., U.K. ..... 27 H1 49 55N 6 18W
St. Mary's, Orkney, U.K. ..... 19 E12 58 54N 2 54W
St. Marys, U.S.A. ..... 112 E8 41 26N 78 34W
St. Mary's Sd., U.K. ..... 27 H1 49 54N 6 20W
St. Matthew I., U.S.A. ..... 108 B2 60 24N 172 42W
St. Mawes, U.K. ..... 27 G3 50 10N 5 1W
St. Merryn, U.K. ..... 27 F3 50 32N 5 1W
St. Michael's Mount, U.K. ..... 27 G3 50 7N 5 29W
St. Minver, U.K. ..... 27 F4 50 33N 4 53W
St. Moritz, Switz. ..... 66 E5 46 30N 9 50 E
St-Nazaire, France ..... 68 C2 47 17N 2 12W
St. Neots, U.K. ..... 23 H8 52 14N 0 15W
St-Niklaas, Belgium ..... 65 C4 51 10N 4 8 E
St-Omer, France ..... 68 A5 50 45N 2 15 E
St. Osyth, U.K. ..... 25 C11 51 47N 1 5 E
St. Paul, U.S.A. ..... 111 B8 44 57N 93 6W
St. Paul, I., Ind. Oc. ..... 53 F13 38 55S 77 34 E
St. Peter Port, U.K. ..... 27 J8 49 26N 2 33W
St. Petersburg, Russia ..... 72 C5 59 55N 30 20 E
St. Petersburg, U.S.A. ..... 111 E10 27 46N 82 39W
St-Pierre, Martinique ..... 114 c 14 45N 61 10W
St-Pierre et Miquelon □, N. Amer. ..... 109 D14 46 55N 56 10W
St-Quentin, France ..... 68 B5 49 50N 3 16 E
St. Stephen, Canada ..... 113 C14 45 16N 67 17W
St. Stephen, U.K. ..... 27 G4 50 21N 4 48W
St. Teath, U.K. ..... 27 F4 50 35N 4 45W
St. Thomas, Canada ..... 112 D7 42 45N 81 10W
St. Thomas I., U.S. Virgin Is. ..... 115 e 18 20N 64 55W
St-Tropez, France ..... 68 E7 43 17N 6 38 E
St. Tudy, U.K. ..... 27 F4 50 33N 4 45W
St. Vincent, G., Australia ..... 98 G6 35 0S 138 0 E
St. Vincent & the Grenadines ■, W. Indies ..... 115 E12 13 0N 61 10W

Ste-Anne, Guadeloupe ..... 114 b 16 13N 61 24W
Ste-Marie, Canada ..... 113 B12 46 26N 71 0W
Ste-Marie, Martinique ..... 114 c 14 48N 61 1W
Ste-Rose, Guadeloupe ..... 114 b 16 20N 61 45W
Saintes, France ..... 68 D3 45 45N 0 37W
Saintes, I. des, Guadeloupe ..... 114 b 15 50N 61 35W
Saintfield, U.K. ..... 29 C10 54 28N 5 49W
Saintonge, France ..... 68 D3 45 40N 0 50W
Saipan, Pac. Oc. ..... 102 F6 15 12N 145 45 E
Sajama, Bolivia ..... 120 D3 18 7S 69 0W
Sakakawea, L., U.S.A. ..... 110 A6 47 30N 101 25W
Sakarya, Turkey ..... 73 F5 40 48N 30 25 E
Sakata, Japan ..... 82 D6 38 55N 139 50 E
Sakhalin, Russia ..... 79 D16 51 0N 143 0 E
Sala, Sweden ..... 63 F7 59 58N 16 35 E
Sala-y-Gómez, Pac. Oc. ..... 103 K17 26 28S 105 28W
Salado →, La Pampa, Argentina ..... 121 F3 37 30S 67 0W
Salado →, Santa Fe, Argentina ..... 121 F3 31 40S 60 41W
Salālah, Oman ..... 88 D5 16 56N 53 59 E
Salamanca, Spain ..... 69 B3 40 58N 5 39W
Salamanca, U.S.A. ..... 112 D8 42 10N 78 43W
Salar de Uyuni, Bolivia ..... 120 E3 20 30S 67 45W
Salavat, Russia ..... 72 D10 53 21N 55 55 E
Salaverry, Peru ..... 120 C2 8 15S 79 0W
Salayar, Indonesia ..... 83 D4 6 7S 120 30 E
Salcombe, U.K. ..... 27 G6 50 14N 3 47W
Saldanha, S. Africa ..... 97 L3 33 0S 17 58 E
Sale, Australia ..... 98 H8 38 6S 147 6 E
Salé, Morocco ..... 94 B4 34 3N 6 48W
Sale, U.K. ..... 23 F4 53 26N 2 19W
Salekhard, Russia ..... 79 C8 66 30N 66 35 E
Salem, India ..... 84 P11 11 40N 78 11 E
Salem, Ind., U.S.A. ..... 112 F4 38 36N 86 6W
Salem, Mass., U.S.A. ..... 113 D12 42 31N 70 53W
Salem, Ohio, U.S.A. ..... 112 E7 40 54N 80 52W
Salem, Oreg., U.S.A. ..... 110 B2 44 56N 123 2W
Salem, Va., U.S.A. ..... 112 G7 37 18N 80 3W
Salerno, Italy ..... 70 D6 40 41N 14 47 E
Salford, U.K. ..... 23 F4 53 30N 2 18W
Salford Priors, U.K. ..... 24 B5 52 10N 1 53W
Salida, U.S.A. ..... 110 C5 38 32N 106 0W
Salina, U.S.A. ..... 110 C7 38 50N 97 37W
Salina Cruz, Mexico ..... 114 D5 16 10N 95 10W
Salinas, U.S.A. ..... 110 C2 36 40N 121 39W
Salinas →, U.S.A. ..... 110 C2 36 45N 121 48W
Salinas Grandes, Argentina ..... 121 E3 30 0S 65 0W
Salisbury, U.K. ..... 24 D5 51 4N 1 47W
Salisbury, U.S.A. ..... 113 F10 38 22N 75 36W
Salisbury I., Canada ..... 109 B12 63 30N 77 0W
Salisbury Plain, U.K. ..... 24 D5 51 14N 1 55W
Salmon, U.S.A. ..... 110 A4 45 11N 113 54W
Salmon →, U.S.A. ..... 110 A3 45 51N 116 47W
Salmon Arm, Canada ..... 108 C8 50 40N 119 15W
Salmon River Mts., U.S.A. ..... 110 B4 45 0N 114 30W
Salon-de-Provence, France ..... 68 E6 43 39N 5 6 E
Salsk, Russia ..... 73 E7 46 28N 41 30 E
Salt →, U.S.A. ..... 110 D4 33 23N 112 19W
Salt Lake City, U.S.A. ..... 110 B4 40 45N 111 53W
Salta, Argentina ..... 121 E3 24 57S 65 25W
Saltash, U.K. ..... 27 G5 50 24N 4 14W
Saltburn by the Sea, U.K. ..... 22 C7 54 35N 0 58W
Saltcoats, U.K. ..... 20 C6 55 38N 4 47W
Saltee Is., Ireland ..... 31 D9 52 7N 6 37W
Saltfleet, U.K. ..... 23 F9 53 25N 0 11 E
Saltfleetby, U.K. ..... 23 F9 53 23N 0 10 E
Saltillo, Mexico ..... 114 B4 25 25N 101 0W
Salton Sea, U.S.A. ..... 110 D3 33 15N 115 45W
Saltwood, U.K. ..... 25 D11 51 4N 1 2 E
Salvador, Brazil ..... 122 B3 13 0S 38 30W
Salween →, Burma ..... 85 L20 16 31N 97 37 E
Salyan, Azerbaijan ..... 73 G8 39 33N 48 59 E
Salzburg, Austria ..... 66 E7 47 48N 13 2 E
Salzgitter, Germany ..... 66 B6 52 9N 10 19 E
Samangān □, Afghan. ..... 87 B12 36 15N 68 3 E
Samar, Phil. ..... 83 B4 12 0N 125 0 E
Samara, Russia ..... 72 D9 53 8N 50 6 E
Samarinda, Indonesia ..... 83 D3 0 30S 117 9 E
Samarkand, Uzbekistan ..... 79 F8 39 40N 66 55 E
Sambalpur, India ..... 85 J14 21 28N 84 4 E
Sambhal, India ..... 84 E11 28 35N 78 37 E
Sambhar, India ..... 84 F9 26 52N 75 6 E
Samoa ■, Pac. Oc. ..... 99 C16 14 0S 172 0W
Sámos, Greece ..... 71 F12 37 45N 26 50 E
Sampford Courtenay, U.K. ..... 27 F6 50 47N 3 58W
Samsun, Turkey ..... 73 F6 41 15N 36 22 E
San →, Poland ..... 67 C11 50 45N 21 51 E
San Ambrosio, Pac. Oc. ..... 103 K20 26 28S 79 53W
San Andrés, I. de, Caribbean ..... 115 E8 12 42N 81 46W
San Andres Mts., U.S.A. ..... 110 D5 33 0N 106 30W
San Andrés Tuxtla, Mexico ..... 114 D5 18 27N 95 13W
San Angelo, U.S.A. ..... 110 D6 31 28N 100 26W
San Antonio, Chile ..... 121 F2 33 40S 71 40W
San Antonio, U.S.A. ..... 110 E7 29 25N 98 30W
San Antonio →, U.S.A. ..... 111 E7 28 30N 96 54W
San Antonio Oeste, Argentina ..... 121 G3 40 40S 65 0W
San Bernardino, U.S.A. ..... 110 D3 34 7N 117 19W
San Bernardino Str., Phil. ..... 83 B4 13 0N 125 0 E
San Bernardo, Chile ..... 121 F2 33 40S 70 50W
San Blas, C., U.S.A. ..... 111 E9 29 40N 85 21W
San Carlos, Phil. ..... 83 B4 10 29N 123 25 E
San Carlos de Bariloche, Argentina ..... 121 G2 41 10S 71 25W
San Carlos de Bolivar, Argentina ..... 121 F3 36 15S 61 6W
San Cristóbal, Argentina ..... 121 F3 30 20S 61 10W
San Cristóbal, Solomon Is. ..... 99 C11 10 30S 161 0 E
San Cristóbal, Venezuela ..... 120 B2 7 46N 72 14W
San Cristóbal de la Casas, Mexico ..... 114 D6 16 50N 92 33W
San Diego, U.S.A. ..... 110 D3 32 43N 117 9W
San Felipe, Venezuela ..... 120 A3 10 20N 68 44W
San Félix, Pac. Oc. ..... 103 K20 26 23S 80 0W
San Fernando, Chile ..... 121 F2 34 30S 71 0W
San Fernando de Apure, Venezuela ..... 120 B3 7 54N 67 15W
San Francisco, U.S.A. ..... 110 C2 37 47N 122 25W
San Francisco de Macorís, Dom. Rep. ..... 115 D10 19 19N 70 15W
San Francisco Solano, Pta., Colombia ..... 116 C3 6 18N 77 29W
San German, Puerto Rico ..... 115 d 18 4N 67 4W
San Gottardo, P. del, Switz. ..... 66 E5 46 33N 8 33 E
San Ignacio, Bolivia ..... 120 D3 16 20N 60 55W
San Joaquin →, U.S.A. ..... 110 C2 38 4N 121 51W
San Jorge, G., Argentina ..... 121 G3 46 0S 66 0W
San José, Costa Rica ..... 115 F8 9 55N 84 2W
San Jose, Phil. ..... 83 B4 12 27N 121 4 E
San Jose, U.S.A. ..... 110 C2 37 20N 121 53W
San José de Chiquitos, Bolivia ..... 120 D3 17 53S 60 50W
San José de Jáchal, Argentina ..... 121 F3 30 15S 68 46W
San José de Mayo, Uruguay ..... 121 F4 34 27S 56 40W
San Juan, Argentina ..... 121 F3 31 30S 68 30W
San Juan, Dom. Rep. ..... 115 D10 18 49N 71 12W
San Juan, Puerto Rico ..... 115 d 18 28N 66 7W

San Juan

Skowhegan

San Juan →, Nic. .......... 115 E8   10 56N  83 42W
San Juan →, U.S.A. ....... 110 C4   37 16N 110 26W
San Juan de los Morros,
  Venezuela ............... 120 B3    9 55N  67 21W
San Juan Mts., U.S.A. .... 110 C5   37 30N 107  0W
San Lorenzo, Mte., Argentina  121 G2  47 40S  72 20W
San Lucas, C., Mexico ..... 114 C3   22 50N 110  0W
San Luis, Argentina ....... 121 F3   33 20S  66 20W
San Luis Obispo, U.S.A. ... 110 C2   35 17N 120 40W
San Luis Potosí, Mexico ... 114 C4   22  9N 100 59W
San Marcos, U.S.A. ........ 110 E7   29 53N  97 56W
San Marino ■, Europe ..... 70 C5    43 56N  12 25 E
San Matías, G., Argentina . 121 G3   41 30S  64  0W
San Miguel, El Salv. ...... 114 E7   13 30N  88 12W
San Miguel de Tucumán,
  Argentina ............... 121 E3   26 50S  65 20W
San Nicolás de los Arroyos,
  Argentina ............... 121 F3   33 25S  60 10W
San Pedro de las Colonias,
  Mexico .................. 114 B4   25 50N 102 59W
San Pedro de Macorís,
  Dom. Rep. ............... 115 D11  18 30N  69 18W
San Pedro Sula, Honduras . 114 D7   15 30N  88  0W
San Rafael, Argentina ..... 121 F3   34 40S  68 21W
San Remo, Italy ........... 68 E7    43 49N   7 46 E
San Salvador, El Salv. ..... 114 E7   13 40N  89 10W
San Salvador de Jujuy,
  Argentina ............... 121 E3   24 10S  64 48W
San Salvador I., Bahamas . 115 C10  24  0N  74 40W
San Sebastián, Puerto Rico  115 d   18 20N  66 59W
San Valentín, Mte., Chile . 121 G2   46 30S  73 30W
Sana', Yemen ............. 88 D3    15 27N  44 12 E
Sanandaj, Iran ............ 86 C6    35 18N  47  1 E
Sancti Spíritus, Cuba ...... 115 C9   21 52N  79 33W
Sancy, Puy de, France ..... 68 D5    45 32N   2 50 E
Sandakan, Malaysia ....... 83 C3     5 53N 118  4 E
Sanday, U.K. .............. 19 D12  59 16N   2 31W
Sandbach, U.K. ............ 23 F4    53  9N   2 21W
Sandgate, U.K. ............ 25 D11  51  4N   1 10 E
Sandhurst, U.K. ........... 25 D7   51 21N   0 48W
Sandown, U.K. ............. 24 E6   50 40N   1 10W
Sandpoint, U.S.A. ......... 110 A3   48 17N 116 33W
Sandray, U.K. ............. 18 J2    56 53N   7 31W
Sandringham, U.K. ......... 25 A10  52 51N   0 31 E
Sandusky, U.S.A. .......... 112 E6   41 27N  82 42W
Sandwich, U.K. ............ 25 D11  51 16N   1 21 E
Sandy, U.K. ............... 25 B8    52  8N   0 17W
Sandy, U.S.A. ............. 110 B4   40 35N 111 50W
Sandy L., Canada .......... 108 C10  53  2N  93  0W
Sanford, U.S.A. ........... 111 E10  28 48N  81 16W
Sanford, Mt., U.S.A. ...... 108 B5   62 13N 144  8W
Sangihe, Pulau, Indonesia . 83 C4     3 35N 125 30 E
Sangli, India ............. 84 L9    16 55N  74 33 E
Sangre de Cristo Mts., U.S.A.  110 C5  37 30N 105 20W
Sanikiluaq, Canada ........ 109 C12  56 32N  79 14W
Sanirajak, Canada ......... 109 B11  68 46N  81 12W
Sankuru →, Dem. Rep. of
  the Congo ............... 96 E4     4 17S  20 25 E
Sanliurfa, Turkey ......... 73 G6    37 12N  38 50 E
Sanmenxia, China ......... 81 C6    34 47N 111 12 E
Sanquhar, U.K. ........... 21 D8    55 22N   3 54W
Santa Ana, El Salv. ....... 114 E7   14  0N  89 31W
Santa Ana, U.S.A. ......... 110 D3   33 46N 117 52W
Santa Barbara, U.S.A. ..... 110 D3   34 25N 119 42W
Santa Catarina □, Brazil .. 121 E5   27 25S  48 30W
Santa Clara, Cuba ......... 115 C9   22 20N  80  0W
Santa Clarita, U.S.A. ...... 110 D3   34 24N 118 32W
Santa Cruz, Bolivia ....... 120 D3   17 43S  63 10W
Santa Cruz, U.S.A. ........ 110 C2   36 58N 122  1W
Santa Cruz de Tenerife,
  Canary Is. .............. 94 C2    28 28N  16 15W
Santa Cruz Is., Solomon Is.  99 C12  10 30S 166  0 E
Santa Cruz Mts., Jamaica . 114 a    17 58N  77 43W
Santa Fe, Argentina ....... 121 F3   31 35S  60 41W
Santa Fe, U.S.A. .......... 110 C5   35 41N 105 57W
Santa Inés, I., Chile ...... 121 H2   54  0S  73  0W
Santa Isabel, Solomon Is. . 99 B10   8  0S 159  0 E
Santa Maria, Brazil ....... 121 E4   29 40S  53 48W
Santa Maria, U.S.A. ....... 110 D2   34 57N 120 26W
Santa Maria →, Mexico .... 114 A3   31  0N 107 14W
Santa Marta, Colombia .... 120 A2   11 15N  74 13W
Santa Marta, Sierra Nevada de,
  Colombia ............... 116 B3   10 55N  73 50W
Santa Rosa, Argentina ..... 121 F3   36 40S  64 17W
Santa Rosa, U.S.A. ........ 110 C2   38 26N 122 43W
Santai, China ............. 80 C5    31  5N 104 58 E
Santana do Livramento, Brazil  121 F4  30 55S  55 30W
Santander, Spain .......... 69 A4    43 27N   3 51W
Santarém, Brazil .......... 120 C4    2 25S  54 42W
Santarém, Portugal ........ 69 C1    39 12N   8 42W
Santiago, Chile ........... 121 F2   33 24S  70 40W
Santiago de Compostela, Spain  69 A1  42 52N  8 37W
Santiago de Cuba, Cuba ... 115 D9   20  0N  75 49W
Santiago de los Cabelleros,
  Dom. Rep. ............... 115 D10  19 30N  70 40W
Santiago del Estero, Argentina  121 E3  27 50S  64 15W
Santo André, Brazil ....... 122 D1   23 39S  46 29W
Santo Domingo, Dom. Rep.  115 D11  18 30N  69 59W
Santos, Brazil ............ 122 D1   24  0S  46 20W
Santos Dumont, Brazil .... 122 D2   22 55S  43 10W
São Bernardo do Campo, Brazil  122 D1  23 45S  46 34W
São Borja, Brazil .......... 121 E4   28 39S  56  0W
São Carlos, Brazil ......... 122 D1   22  0S  47 50W
São Francisco →, Brazil .. 122 B3   10 30S  36 24W
São Gonçalo, Brazil ....... 122 D2   22 48S  43  5W
São João da Boa Vista, Brazil  122 D1  22  0S  46 52W
São João del Rei, Brazil ... 122 D2   21  8S  44 15W
São João do Piauí, Brazil .. 122 A2    8 21S  42 15W
São José do Rio Prêto, Brazil  122 D1  20 50S  49 20W
São José dos Campos, Brazil  122 D1  23  7S  45 52W
São Lourenço, Brazil ...... 122 D1   22  7S  45  3W
São Luís, Brazil ........... 120 C5    2 39S  44 15W
São Marcos →, Brazil ..... 122 C1   18 15S  47 37W
São Marcos, B. de, Brazil .. 120 C5    2  0S  44  0W
São Mateus, Brazil ........ 122 C3   18 44S  39 50W
São Paulo, Brazil ......... 122 D1   23 32S  46 37W
São Paulo □, Brazil ....... 120 E5   22  0S  49  0W
São Roque, C. de, Brazil .. 120 C6    5 30S  35 16W
São Tomé,
  São Tomé & Príncipe .... 90 F4     0 10N   6 39 E
São Tomé & Príncipe ■, Africa  91 F4  0 12S   6 39 E
Saône →, France ......... 68 D6    45 44N   4 50 E
Sapporo, Japan ........... 82 B7    43  0N 141 21 E
Saqqez, Iran ............. 86 B6    36 15N  46 20 E
Sar-e Pol, Afghan. ........ 87 B11   36  10N  66 0 E
Saraburi, Thailand ........ 83 B2   14 30N 100 55 E
Sarajevo, Bos.-H. ......... 71 C8   43 52N  18 26 E
Saranac Lakes, U.S.A. .... 113 C10  44 20N  74  8W
Saransk, Russia ........... 72 D8   54 10N  45 10 E
Sarapul, Russia ........... 72 C9   56 28N  53 48 E
Sarasota, U.S.A. .......... 111 E10  27 20N  82 32W
Saratoga Springs, U.S.A. .. 113 D11  43 5N  73 47W
Saratov, Russia ........... 73 D8   51 30N  46  2 E
Sarawak □, Malaysia ...... 83 C3    2  0N 113  0 E
Sarda →, India ........... 85 F12   27 21N  81 23 E

Sardinia, Italy ........... 70 D3    40  0N   9  0 E
Sargasso Sea, Atl. Oc. .... 103 D20  27  0N  72  0W
Sargodha, Pakistan ........ 84 C8    32 10N  72 40 E
Sarh, Chad ............... 95 G9     9  5N  18 23 E
Sārī, Iran ................ 87 B8    36 30N  53  4 E
Sark, Iran ................ 27 J9    49 25N   2 22W
Sarlat-la-Canéda, France .. 68 D4   44 54N   1 13 E
Sarmiento, Argentina ...... 121 G3   45 35S  69  5W
Sarnia, Canada ........... 109 D11  42 58N  82 23W
Sarreguemines, France .... 68 B7   49  5N   7  4 E
Sarthe →, France ......... 68 C3   47 33N   0 31W
Sasebo, Japan ............ 82 G1   33 10N 129 43 E
Saskatchewan □, Canada .. 108 C9   54 40N 106  0W
Saskatchewan →, Canada .. 108 C9   53 37N 100 40W
Saskatoon, Canada ........ 108 C9   52 10N 106 38W
Sássari, Italy ............ 70 D3    40 43N   8 34 E
Sassnitz, Germany ........ 66 A7   54 29N  13 39 E
Satara, India ............. 85 G12   24 35N  80 50 E
Satna, India .............. 85 G12  24 35N  80 50 E
Satpura Ra., India ........ 84 J10   21 25N  76 10 E
Satu Mare, Romania ....... 67 E12  47 46N  22 55 E
Saudi Arabia ■, Asia ...... 86 E5    26  0N  44  0 E
Sault Ste. Marie, Canada .. 109 D11  46 30N  84 20W
Sault Ste. Marie, U.S.A. ... 109 D11  46 30N  84 21W
Saumur, France ........... 68 C3    47 15N   0  5W
Saunders C., N.Z. ......... 71 B9   44 50N  20 26 E
Sava →, Serbia & M. ...... 71 B9   44 50N  20 26 E
Savai'i, Samoa ........... 99 C16  13 28S 172 24W
Savanna-la-Mar, Jamaica . 114 a    18 10N  78 10W
Savannah, U.S.A. ......... 111 D10  32  5N  81  6W
Savannah →, U.S.A. ...... 111 D10  32  2N  80 53W
Savannakhet, Laos ........ 83 B2   16 30N 104 49 E
Savoie □, France ......... 68 D7   45 26N   6 25 E
Savona, Italy ............. 68 D8   44 17N   8 30 E
Sawatch Range, U.S.A. ... 110 C5   38 30N 106 30W
Sawbridgeworth, U.K. ..... 25 C9   51 48N   0  9 E
Sawel Mt., U.K. ........... 29 B7   54 50N   7  2W
Sawston, U.K. ............ 25 B9   52  8N   0 10 E
Sawtry, U.K. ............. 23 H8   52 27N   0 17W
Sawu, Indonesia .......... 83 E4   10 35S 121 50 E
Sawu Sea, Indonesia ...... 83 D4    9 30S 121 50 E
Saxilby, U.K. ............. 23 F7   53 16N   0 38W
Saxlingham Nethergate, U.K.  25 A11  52 32N  1 18 E
Saxmundham, U.K. ........ 25 B12  52 13N   1 30 E
Sayan Mts., Russia ........ 74 D13  54  0N  96  0 E
Sayda, Lebanon ........... 86 C3   33 35N  35 25 E
Saynshand, Mongolia ...... 81 B6   44 55N 110 11 E
Sayre, U.S.A. ............ 112 E9   41 59N  76 32W
Sázava →, Czech Rep. .... 66 D8   49 53N  14 24 E
Scafell Pike, U.K. ........ 22 D2   54 27N   3 14W
Scalby, U.K. ............. 22 D8   54 18N   0 26W
Scalloway, U.K. .......... 18 B15  60  9N   1 17W
Scalpay, U.K. ............ 18 H6   57 18N   6  0W
Scamblesby, U.K. ......... 23 F8   53 17N   0  5W
Scandinavia, Europe ...... 56 C8   64  0N  12  0 E
Scapa Flow, U.K. ......... 19 E11  58 53N   3  3W
Scarba, U.K. ............. 20 B4   56 11N   5 43W
Scarborough, U.K. ........ 22 D8   54 17N   0 24W
Scariff I., Ireland ........ 30 E2   51 44N  10 15W
Scarning, U.K. ........... 25 A10  52 41N   0 54 E
Scarp, U.K. .............. 18 F3   58  1N   7  8W
Scebeli, Wabi →, Somali Rep.  88 G3   2  0N  44  0 E
Schaffhausen, Switz. ...... 66 E5   47 42N   8 39 E
Schefferville, Canada ..... 109 C13  54 48N  66 50W
Schelde →, Belgium ...... 65 C4   51 15N   4 16 E
Schenectady, U.S.A. ...... 113 D11  42 49N  73 57W
Schiedam, Neths. ......... 65 C4   51 55N   4 25 E
Schleswig, Germany ....... 66 A5   54 31N   9 34 E
Schleswig-Holstein □, Germany  66 A5  54 30N  9 30 E
Schœlcher, Martinique .... 114 c   14 36N  61  7W
Schreiber, Canada ........ 112 A4   48 45N  87 20W
Schwäbische Alb, Germany  66 D5   48 20N   9 30 E
Schwarzwald, Germany .... 66 D5   48 30N   8 20 E
Schwerin, Germany ....... 66 B6   53 36N  11 22 E
Schwyz, Switz. ........... 66 E5   47  2N   8 39 E
Scilly Is., U.K. ........... 27 H1   49 56N   6 22W
Scioto →, U.S.A. ......... 112 F6   38 44N  83  1W
Scole, U.K. .............. 25 B11  52 22N   1 10 E
Scone, U.K. .............. 21 B9   56 25N   3 24W
Scopwick, U.K. ........... 23 F8   53  8N   0 24W
Scotland □, U.K. ......... 64 C5   57  0N   4  0W
Scott I., Antarctica ....... 55 C11  67  0S 179  0 E
Scottish Borders □, U.K. .. 21 C10  55 35N   2 50W
Scottsbluff, U.S.A. ....... 110 B6   41 52N 103 40W
Scottsburg, U.S.A. ....... 112 F5   38 41N  85 47W
Scranton, U.S.A. ......... 113 E10  41 25N  75 40W
Scremerston, U.K. ........ 22 A5   55 44N   1 59W
Scunthorpe, U.K. ......... 23 E7   53 36N   0 39W
Seaford, U.K. ............ 25 E9   50 47N   0  7 E
Seaford, U.S.A. .......... 113 F10  38 39N  75 37W
Seaforth, L., U.K. ........ 18 G4   57 52N   6 36W
Seaham, U.K. ............ 22 C6   54 50N   1 20W
Seahouses, U.K. .......... 22 A5   55 34N   1 39W
Seal →, Canada .......... 108 C10  59  4N  94 48W
Seamer, U.K. ............ 22 D8   54 15N   0 26W
Seascale, U.K. ........... 22 D2   54 24N   3 29W
Seaton, Cumb., U.K. ...... 22 C1   54 40N   3 31W
Seaton, Devon, U.K. ...... 24 E2   50 42N   3  5W
Seaton Delaval, U.K. ...... 22 B5   55  5N   1 33W
Seattle, U.S.A. ........... 110 A2   47 36N 122 20W
Sebastián Vizcaíno, B., Mexico  114 B2  28 0N  114 30W
Şebinkarahisar, Turkey .... 73 F6   40 22N  38 28 E
Sedalia, U.S.A. .......... 111 C8   38 42N  93 14W
Sedan, France ............ 68 B6   49 43N   4 57 E
Sedbergh, U.K. ........... 22 D3   54 20N   2 31W
Sedgefield, U.K. ......... 22 C6   54 40N   1 26W
Seend, U.K. ............. 24 D4   51 21N   2  4W
Ségou, Mali ............. 94 F4   13 30N   6 16W
Segovia, Spain ........... 69 B3   40 57N   4 10W
Sehore, India ............ 84 H10  23 10N  77  5 E
Seil, U.K. ............... 20 B4   56 18N   5 38W
Seine →, France ......... 68 B4   49 26N   0 26 E
Sekondi-Takoradi, Ghana . 94 H5   4 58N   1 45W
Selborne, U.K. ........... 25 D7   51  6N   0 56W
Selby, U.K. .............. 23 E6   53 47N   1  5W
Selebi-Pikwe, Botswana ... 97 J5   21 58S  27 48 E
Selenge Mörön →, Asia ... 80 A5   52 16N 106 16 E
Selkirk, Canada .......... 108 C10  50 10N  96 55W
Selkirk, U.K. ............ 21 C10  55 33N   2 50W
Selkirk Mts., Canada ..... 108 C8   51 15N 117 40W
Selma, U.S.A. ............ 111 D9   32 25N  87  1W
Selsey, U.K. ............. 25 E7   50 44N   0 47W
Selsey Bill, U.K. .......... 25 E7   50 43N   0 47W
Selvas, Brazil ............ 120 C3    6 30S  67  0W
Selwyn L., Canada ........ 108 B9   60  0N 104 30W
Selwyn Mts., Canada ...... 108 B6   63  0N 130  0W
Semarang, Indonesia ...... 83 D3    7  0S 110 26 E
Semey, Kazakhstan ........ 79 D10   50 30N  80 10 E
Semnān, Iran ............ 87 C8   35 40N  53 23 E
Sena Madureira, Brazil .... 120 C3    9  5S  68 45W
Sendai, Japan ............ 82 D7   38 15N 140 53 E
Seneca L., U.S.A. ......... 112 D9   42 40N  76 54W
Senegal ■, W. Afr. ........ 94 F2   14 30N  14 30W
Senegal →, W. Afr. ........ 94 E2   15 48N  16 32W
Senegambia, Africa ....... 90 E2   12 45N  12 0W
Senhor-do-Bonfim, Brazil .. 122 B2   10 30S  40 10W
Senja, Norway ........... 63 D7   69 25N  17 30 E

Senlis, France ........... 68 B5   49 13N   2 35 E
Sennen, U.K. ............. 27 G2   50  4N   5 42W
Sens, France ............. 68 B5   48 11N   3 15 E
Seoul, S. Korea .......... 81 C7   37 31N 126 58 E
Seph →, U.K. ............ 22 D6   54 17N   1  9W
Sept-Îles, Canada ........ 109 C13  50 13N  66 22W
Seram, Indonesia ......... 83 D4   3 10S 129  0 E
Seram Sea, Indonesia ..... 83 D4   2 30S 128 30 E
Serang, Indonesia ........ 83 D2   6  8S 106 10 E
Serbia □, Serbia & M. ..... 71 C9   43 30N  21  0 E
Serbia & Montenegro ■,
  Europe ................. 71 B9   43 20N  20  0 E
Seremban, Malaysia ....... 83 C2   2 43N 101 53 E
Sergipe □, Brazil ......... 122 B3   10 30S  37 30W
Sergiyev Posad, Russia .... 72 C6   56 20N  38 10 E
Serov, Russia ............ 72 C11  59 29N  60 35 E
Serpukhov, Russia ........ 72 D6   54 55N  37 28 E
Serrinha, Brazil .......... 122 B3   11 39S  39  0W
Sète, France ............. 68 E5   43 25N   3 42 E
Sete Lagôas, Brazil ....... 122 C2   19 27S  44 16W
Sétif, Algeria ............ 94 A7   36  9N   5 26 E
Settat, Morocco .......... 94 B4   33  0N   7 40W
Settle, U.K. .............. 22 D4   54  5N   2 16W
Setúbal, Portugal ......... 69 C1   38 30N   8 58W
Seul, Lac, Canada ........ 108 C10  50 20N  92 30W
Sevan, L., Armenia ....... 73 F8   40 30N  45 20 E
Sevastopol, Ukraine ...... 73 F5   44 35N  33 30 E
Seven →, U.K. ........... 22 D7   54 11N   0 52W
Sevenoaks, U.K. .......... 25 D9   51 16N   0 11 E
Severn →, Canada ........ 109 C11  56  2N  87 36W
Severn →, U.K. ........... 24 C3   51 35N   2 40W
Severn Beach, U.K. ....... 24 C3   51 33N   2 39W
Severn Stoke, U.K. ....... 24 B4   52  5N   2 12W
Severnaya Zemlya, Russia . 79 B11  79  0N 100  0 E
Severodvinsk, Russia ..... 72 B6   64 27N  39 58 E
Severomorsk, Russia ...... 72 A5   69 5N  33 27 E
Sevier →, U.S.A. ......... 110 C4   39  4N 113  6W
Sevier L., U.S.A. ......... 110 C4   38 54N 113  9W
Seville, Spain ............ 69 D2   37 23N   5 58W
Seward, U.S.A. ........... 108 B5   60  7N 149 27W
Seward Peninsula, U.S.A. . 108 B3   65 30N 166  0W
Seychelles ■, Ind. Oc. .... 91 G9   5  0S  56  0 E
Seyðisfjörður, Iceland ..... 63 A3   65 16N  13 57W
Seydişehir, Turkey ........ 73 G5   37 25N  31 51 E
Seymour, U.S.A. .......... 112 F5   38 58N  85 53W
Sfântu Gheorghe, Romania  67 F13  45 52N  25 48 E
Sfax, Tunisia ............ 95 B8   34 49N  10 48 E
Shaanxi □, China ......... 81 C5   35  0N 109  0 E
Shache, China ............ 80 C2   38 20N  77 10 E
Shaftesbury, U.K. ........ 24 D4   51  0N   2 11W
Shahjahanpur, India ...... 84 F11  27 54N  79 57 E
Shakhty, Russia .......... 73 E7   47 40N  40 16 E
Shaki, Nigeria ........... 94 G6   8 41N  3 21 E
Shaldon, U.K. ............ 27 F6   50 32N   3 31W
Shamo, L., Ethiopia ....... 88 F2   5 45N  37 30 E
Shan □, Burma ........... 85 J21   21 30N  98 30 E
Shandong □, China ....... 81 C6   36  0N 118  0 E
Shanghai, China .......... 81 C7   31 15N 121 26 E
Shangqiu, China .......... 81 C6   34 26N 115 36 E
Shangrao, China ......... 81 D6   28 25N 117 59 E
Shangshui, China ......... 81 C6   33 42N 114 35 E
Shanklin, U.K. ........... 24 E6   50 38N   1 11W
Shannon →, Ireland ....... 30 C4   52 35N   9 30W
Shannon, Mouth of the, Ireland  30 D3  52 30N  9 55W
Shannon Airport, Ireland .. 30 C5   52 42N   8 57W
Shantou, China ........... 81 D6   23 18N 116 40 E
Shanxi □, China .......... 81 C6   37  0N 112  0 E
Shaoguan, China ......... 81 D6   24 48N 113 35 E
Shaoxing, China .......... 81 D7   30  0N 120 35 E
Shaoyang, China ......... 81 D6   27 14N 111 25 E
Shap, U.K. .............. 22 C3   54 32N   2 40W
Shapinsay, U.K. .......... 19 D12  59  3N   2 51W
Shaqrā', Yemen .......... 88 E4   13 22N  45 44 E
Sharjah, U.A.E. .......... 87 E8   25 23N  55 26 E
Shark B., Australia ....... 98 F1   25 30S 113 32 E
Sharm el Sheikh, Egypt ... 88 B1   27 53N  34 18 E
Sharon, U.S.A. ........... 112 E7   41 14N  80 31W
Sharpness, U.K. .......... 24 C4   51 43N   2 28W
Sharya, Russia ........... 72 C8   58 22N  45 20 E
Shashi, China ............ 81 C6   30 25N 112 14 E
Shasta, Mt., U.S.A. ....... 110 B2   41 25N 122 12W
Shawano, U.S.A. ......... 112 C3   44 47N  88 36W
Shawbury, U.K. .......... 23 G3   52 48N   2 39W
Shawinigan, Canada ...... 109 D12  46 35N  72 50W
Shawnee, U.S.A. ......... 111 C7   35 20N  96 55W
Shebbear, U.K. .......... 27 F5   50 51N   4 15W
Sheboygan, U.S.A. ....... 112 D4   43 46N  87 45W
Sheelin, L., Ireland ....... 28 D7   53 48N   7 20W
Sheep Haven, Ireland ..... 28 A6   55 11N   7 52W
Sheerness, U.K. .......... 25 D10  51 26N   0 47 E
Sheffield, U.K. ........... 23 F6   53 23N   1 28W
Shefford, U.K. ........... 25 B8   52  2N   0 20W
Shelburne, Canada ....... 113 D15  43 47N  65 20W
Shelby, U.S.A. ........... 110 A4   48 30N 111 51W
Shelbyville, U.S.A. ....... 112 F5   39 31N  85 47W
Shelekhov G., Russia ..... 79 D17  59 30N 157  0 E
Shenandoah, U.S.A. ...... 113 E9   40 49N  76 12W
Shenandoah →, U.S.A. .... 112 F9   39 19N  77 44W
Shenfield, U.K. .......... 25 C9   51 38N   0 22 E
Shenyang, China ......... 81 B7   41 48N 123 27 E
Shepparton, Australia ..... 98 H8   36 23S 145 26 E
Sheppey, I. of, U.K. ...... 25 D10  51 25N   0 48 E
Shepshed, U.K. .......... 23 G6   52 47N   1 18W
Shepton Mallet, U.K. ..... 24 D3   51 11N   2 33W
Sherborne, U.K. .......... 24 E3   50 57N   2 31W
Sherborne St. John, U.K. .. 24 D6   51 17N   1  7W
Sherbrooke, Canada ...... 109 D12  45 28N  71 57W
Sherburn, N. Yorks., U.K. . 22 D7   54 11N   0 32W
Sherburn, N. Yorks., U.K. . 23 E6   53 48N   1 15W
Shere, U.K. .............. 25 D8   51 13N   0 27W
Sherfield English, U.K. .... 24 D5   51  1N   1 34W
Sheridan, U.S.A. ......... 110 B5   44 48N 106 58W
Sheriff Hutton, U.K. ...... 22 D7   54  5N   1  0W
Sheringham, U.K. ......... 25 A11  52 56N   1 13 E
Sherkin I., Ireland ........ 30 F4   51 28N   9 26W
Sherman, U.S.A. .......... 111 D7   33 40N  96 35W
Sherston, U.K. ........... 24 C4   51 34N   2 14W
Sherwood Forest, U.K. .... 23 F6   53  6N   1  7W
Shetland □, U.K. ......... 18 B15  60 30N   1 30W
Sheyenne →, U.S.A. ...... 111 A7   47 2N  96 50W
Shibām, Yemen .......... 88 D4   15 59N  48 36 E
Shickshock Mts., Canada .. 113 A14  48 55N  66  0W
Shiel, L., U.K. ........... 18 J6   56 48N   5 34W
Shifnal, U.K. ............ 23 G4   52 39N   2 23W
Shihezi, China ........... 80 B3   44 15N  86  2 E
Shijiazhuang, China ...... 81 C6   38  2N 114 28 E
Shikarpur, Pakistan ....... 84 F6   27 57N  68 39 E
Shikoku □, Japan ......... 82 G3   33 30N 133 30 E
Shilbottle, U.K. .......... 22 B5   55 23N   1 40W
Shildon, U.K. ............ 22 C5   54 38N   1 38W
Shiliguri, India .......... 85 F16   26 45N  88 25 E
Shillelagh, Ireland ....... 31 C9   52 45N   6 32W
Shillingstone, U.K. ....... 24 E4   50 53N   2 15W
Shillong, India ........... 85 G17  25 35N  91 53 E
Shimoga, India .......... 84 N9   13 57N  75 32 E
Shimonoseki, Japan ....... 82 G2   33 58N 130 55 E

Shin, L., U.K. ............ 19 F8   58  5N   4 30W
Shinyanga, Tanzania ...... 96 E6   3 45S  33 27 E
Shipdham, U.K. .......... 25 A10  52 38N   0 54 E
Shipley, U.K. ............ 23 E5   53 50N   1 47W
Shipston-on-Stour, U.K. ... 24 B5   52  3N   1 37W
Shipton under Wychwood, U.K.  24 C5  51 51N   1 36W
Shīrāz, Iran ............. 87 D8   29 42N  52 30 E
Shire →, Africa .......... 97 H7   17 42S  35 19 E
Shirebrook, U.K. ......... 23 F6   53 12N   1 13W
Shivpuri, India .......... 84 G10  25 26N  77 42 E
Shizuoka, Japan ......... 82 F6   34 57N 138 24 E
Shkodër, Albania ......... 71 C8   42  4N  19 32 E
Shoeburyness, U.K. ....... 25 C10  51 32N   0 49 E
Shoreham by Sea, U.K. .... 25 E8   50 50N   0 16W
Shreveport, U.S.A. ....... 111 D8   32 31N  93 45W
Shrewsbury, U.K. ........ 23 G3   52 43N   2 45W
Shrewton, U.K. .......... 24 D5   51 12N   1 54W
Shrirampur, India ........ 85 H16  22 44N  88 21 E
Shrivenham, U.K. ........ 24 C5   51 36N   1 38W
Shropshire □, U.K. ....... 23 G3   52 36N   2 45W
Shuangyashan, China ..... 81 B8   46 28N 131  5 E
Shule, China ............ 80 C2   39 25N  76  3 E
Shumagin Is., U.S.A. ..... 108 C4   55  7N 160 30W
Shwebo, Burma .......... 85 H19  22 30N  95 45 E
Si Kiang →, China ........ 81 D6   22  5N 113 20 E
Sialkot, Pakistan ......... 84 C9   32 32N  74 30 E
Šiauliai, Lithuania ....... 72 C3   55 56N  23 15 E
Siberia, Russia .......... 79 C11  60  0N 100  0 E
Siberut, Indonesia ........ 83 D1   1 30S  99  0 E
Sibi, Pakistan ........... 84 E5   29 30N  67 54 E
Sibiu, Romania .......... 67 F13  45 45N  24 9 E
Sible Hedingham, U.K. ... 25 C10  51 59N   0 37 E
Sibolga, Indonesia ....... 83 C1   1 42N  98 45 E
Sibsey, U.K. ............ 23 F9   53  2N   0  1 E
Sibu, Malaysia .......... 83 C3   2 18N 111 49 E
Sibuyan Sea, Phil. ....... 83 B4   12 30N 122 20 E
Sichuan □, China ......... 80 C5   30 30N 103  0 E
Sicily, Italy ............. 70 F6   37 30N  14  30 E
Sicuani, Peru ........... 120 D2   14 21S  71 10W
Sidbury, U.K. ........... 24 E2   50 42N   3 14W
Sidi-bel-Abbès, Algeria ... 94 A5   35 13N   0 39W
Sidlaw Hills, U.K. ........ 21 A9   56 32N   3 2W
Sidlesham, U.K. ......... 25 E7   50 47N   0 47W
Sidmouth, U.K. .......... 24 E2   50 40N   3 15W
Sidney, Mont., U.S.A. ..... 110 A6   47 43N 104  9W
Sidney, Nebr., U.S.A. ..... 110 B6   41  8N 102 59W
Sidney, Ohio, U.S.A. ...... 112 E5   40 17N  84  9W
Sidra, G. of, Libya ....... 95 B9   31 40N  18 30 E
Siedlce, Poland .......... 67 B12  52 10N  22 20 E
Siegen, Germany ......... 66 C5   50 51N   8  0 E
Siena, Italy ............. 70 C4   43 19N  11 21 E
Sierra Blanca Peak, U.S.A.  110 D5  33 23N 105 49W
Sierra Leone ■, W. Afr. ... 94 G3   9  0N  12  0W
Sierra Nevada, Spain ..... 69 D4   37  3N   3 15W
Sierra Nevada, U.S.A. ..... 110 C2   39  0N 120 30W
Sierra Vista, U.S.A. ...... 110 D4   31 33N 110 18W
Sighty Crag, U.K. ........ 22 B3   55  7N   2 38W
Sikar, India ............. 84 F9   27 33N  75 10 E
Sikhote Alin Ra., Russia ... 79 E15  45  0N 136  0 E
Sikkim □, India .......... 85 F16  27 50N  88 30 E
Silesia, Poland .......... 66 C9   51  0N  16 30 E
Silifke, Turkey ........... 73 G5   36 22N  33 58 E
Siling Co, China ......... 80 C3   31 50N  89 20 E
Silloth, U.K. ............ 22 C2   54 52N   3 23W
Silsden, U.K. ............ 23 E5   53 55N   1 55W
Silver City, U.S.A. ....... 110 D5   32 46N 108 17W
Silverstone, U.K. ......... 24 B6   52  5N   1  2W
Silverton, U.K. .......... 24 E2   50 49N   3 29W
Simbirsk, Russia ......... 72 D8   54 20N  48 25 E
Simcoe, Canada .......... 112 D7   42 50N  80 20W
Simcoe, L., Canada ....... 112 C8   44 25N  79 20W
Simeulue, Indonesia ...... 83 C1   2 45N  95 45 E
Simferopol, Ukraine ...... 73 F5   44 55N  34  3 E
Simla, India ............ 84 D10  31  2N  77  9 E
Simonsbath, U.K. ........ 24 D1   51  8N   3 46W
Simonside, U.K. ......... 22 B5   55 17N   1 59W
Simplonpass, Switz. ...... 66 E5   46 15N   8  3 E
Simpson Desert, Australia . 98 F6   25  0S 137  0 E
Simpson Pen., Canada .... 109 B11  68 34N  88 45W
Sinai, Egypt ............ 95 C12  29  0N  34  0 E
Sinai, Mt., Egypt ......... 86 D3   28 33N  33 59 E
Sinai Peninsula, Egypt .... 74 G7   29 30N  34  0 E
Sinclair's B., U.K. ........ 19 E11  58 31N   3  5W
Sind □, Pakistan ......... 84 G6   26  0N  69  0 E
Singapore ■, Asia ........ 83 C2   1 17N 103 51 E
Singaraja, Indonesia ...... 83 D3   8  7S 115  6 E
Singkawang, Indonesia .... 83 C2   1  0N 108 57 E
Singleton, U.K. .......... 25 E7   50 55N   0 46W
Sinkiang □, China ........ 80 C3   42  0N  86  0 E
Sinop, Turkey ........... 73 F6   42  1N  35 11 E
Sion, Switz. ............. 66 E4   46 14N   7 20 E
Sion Mills, U.K. ......... 28 B7   54 48N   7 29W
Sioux City, U.S.A. ....... 111 B7   42 30N  96 24W
Sioux Falls, U.S.A. ....... 111 B7   43 33N  96 44W
Sioux Lookout, Canada ... 108 C10  50 10N  91 50W
Siping, China ........... 81 B7   43  8N 124 21 E
Sir James MacBrien, Mt.,
  Canada ................. 108 B7   62  7N 127 41W
Siracusa, Italy .......... 70 F6   37  4N  15 17 E
Sirajganj, Bangla. ........ 85 G16  24 25N  89 47 E
Sīrjān, Iran ............. 87 D8   29 30N  55 45 E
Sirsa, India ............. 84 E9   29 33N  75  4 E
Sistan, Asia ............. 87 D10  30 50N  61  0 E
Sitapur, India ........... 85 F12  27 38N  80 45 E
Sitka, U.S.A. ............ 108 C6   57  3N 135 20W
Sittingbourne, U.K. ...... 25 D10  51 21N   0 45 E
Sittwe, Burma ........... 85 J18   20 18N  92 45 E
Sivas, Turkey ........... 73 G6   39 43N  36 58 E
Sivrihisar, Turkey ........ 73 G5   39 30N  31 35 E
Siwa, Egypt ............. 95 C11  29 11N  25 31 E
Siwan, India ............ 85 F14  26 13N  84 21 E
Six Cross Roads, Barbados  115 g   13 10N  59 28W
Sixmilebridge, Ireland .... 30 C5   52 44N   8 46W
Sizewell, U.K. ........... 25 B12  52 12N   1 37 E
Sjælland, Denmark ....... 63 F6   55 30N  11 30 E
Skagerrak, Denmark ...... 63 F5   57 30N   9  0 E
Skagway, U.S.A. ......... 108 C6   59 28N 135 19W
Skeena →, Canada ....... 108 C6   54  9N 130  5W
Skegness, U.K. .......... 23 F9   53  9N   0 20 E
Skellefte älv →, Sweden .. 63 E8   64 45N  21 10 E
Skellefteå, Sweden ....... 63 E8   64 45N  20 50 E
Skellingthorpe, U.K. ...... 23 F7   53 15N   0 37W
Skelmersdale, U.K. ....... 23 E3   53 33N   2 48W
Skelton, Cleve., U.K. ..... 22 C7   54 33N   0 58W
Skelton, Cumb., U.K. ..... 22 C3   54 43N   2 51W
Skerries, The, U.K. ....... 26 A4   53 25N   4 36W
Skiathos, Greece ......... 71 E10  39 12N  23 30 E
Skibbereen, Ireland ...... 30 E4   51 33N   9 16W
Skiddaw, U.K. ........... 22 C2   54 39N   3  9W
Skien, Norway .......... 63 F6   59 12N   9 35 E
Skikda, Algeria .......... 94 A7   36 50N   6 58 E
Skipsea, U.K. ........... 23 E8   53 58N   0  3W
Skipton, U.K. ........... 23 E4   53 58N   2  3W
Skopje, Macedonia ....... 71 C9   42 1N  21 26 E
Skovorodino, Russia ...... 79 D14  54  0N 124  0 E
Skowhegan, U.S.A. ....... 113 C13  44 46N  69 43W

**Skull** | **Tamil Nadu**

Skull, Ireland ... 30 E3 51 32N 9 34W
Skye, U.K. ... 18 H5 57 15N 6 10W
Slaidburn, U.K. ... 23 E4 53 58N 2 26W
Slaney →, Ireland ... 31 D9 52 26N 6 33W
Slatina, Romania ... 67 F13 44 28N 24 22 E
Slave →, Canada ... 108 B8 61 18N 113 39W
Slave Coast, W. Afr. ... 94 G6 6 0N 2 30 E
Slave Lake, Canada ... 108 C8 55 17N 114 43W
Sleaford, U.K. ... 23 F8 53 0N 0 24W
Sleat, Sd. of, U.K. ... 18 H6 57 5N 5 47W
Sledmere, U.K. ... 22 D7 54 4N 0 35W
Sleeper Is., Canada ... 109 C11 58 30N 81 0W
Sleights, U.K. ... 22 D7 54 27N 0 40W
Slieve Aughty, Ireland ... 30 B5 53 4N 8 30W
Slieve Bloom, Ireland ... 31 B7 53 4N 7 40W
Slieve Donard, Ireland ... 29 C10 54 11N 5 55W
Slieve Gamph, Ireland ... 28 C4 54 6N 9 0W
Slieve Gullion, Ireland ... 29 C9 54 7N 6 26W
Slieve League, Ireland ... 28 B4 54 40N 8 42W
Slieve Mish, Ireland ... 30 D3 52 12N 9 50W
Slievenamon, Ireland ... 31 D7 52 25N 7 34W
Sligo, Ireland ... 28 C5 54 16N 8 28W
Sligo □, Ireland ... 28 C4 54 8N 8 42W
Sligo B., Ireland ... 28 C4 54 18N 8 40W
Sliven, Bulgaria ... 71 C12 42 42N 26 19 E
Slough, U.K. ... 25 C7 51 30N 0 36W
Slovak Rep. ■, Europe ... 67 D10 48 30N 20 0 E
Slovenia ■, Europe ... 66 F8 45 58N 14 30 E
Slovyansk, Ukraine ... 73 E6 48 55N 37 36 E
Slutsk, Belarus ... 72 D4 53 2N 27 31 E
Slyne Hd., Ireland ... 28 E1 53 25N 10 10W
Smallwood Res., Canada ... 109 C13 54 5N 64 30W
Smederevo, Serbia & M. ... 71 B9 44 40N 20 57 E
Smerwick Harbour, Ireland ... 30 D2 52 12N 10 23W
Smethwick, U.K. ... 23 G5 52 30N 1 57W
Smith Sd., N. Amer. ... 54 B4 78 25N 74 0W
Smithfield, U.K. ... 22 C3 54 59N 2 51W
Smiths Falls, Canada ... 113 C9 44 55N 76 0W
Smoky →, Canada ... 108 C8 56 10N 117 21W
Smoky Hill →, U.S.A. ... 111 C7 39 4N 96 48W
Smolensk, Russia ... 72 D5 54 45N 32 5 E
Snaefell, U.K. ... 29 C13 54 16N 4 27W
Snainton, U.K. ... 22 D7 54 14N 0 35W
Snaith, U.K. ... 23 E5 53 42N 1 1W
Snake →, U.S.A. ... 110 A3 46 12N 119 2W
Snape, U.K. ... 25 B12 52 10N 1 30 E
Snettisham, U.K. ... 25 A10 52 53N 0 31 E
Snizort, L., U.K. ... 18 G5 57 33N 6 28W
Snøhetta, Norway ... 63 E5 62 19N 9 16 E
Snow Hill, U.S.A. ... 113 F10 38 11N 75 24W
Snowdon, U.K. ... 26 A5 53 4N 4 5W
Snowy Mts., Australia ... 98 H8 36 30S 148 20 E
Sobradinho, Reprêsa de, Brazil ... 122 A2 9 30S 42 0W
Sobral, Brazil ... 120 C5 3 50S 40 20W
Soc Trang, Vietnam ... 83 C2 9 37N 105 50 E
Sochi, Russia ... 73 F6 43 35N 39 40 E
Société, Is. de la, Pac. Oc. ... 103 J12 17 0S 151 0W
Socorro, U.S.A. ... 110 D5 34 4N 106 54W
Socotra, Yemen ... 88 E5 12 30N 54 0 E
Söderhamn, Sweden ... 63 E7 61 18N 17 10 E
Sofia, Bulgaria ... 71 C10 42 45N 23 20 E
Sognefjorden, Norway ... 63 E5 61 10N 5 50 E
Sohâg, Egypt ... 95 C12 26 33N 31 43 E
Soham, U.K. ... 25 B9 52 21N 0 21 E
Soissons, France ... 68 B5 49 25N 3 19 E
Sokhumi, Georgia ... 73 F7 43 0N 41 0 E
Sokodé, Togo ... 94 G6 9 0N 1 11 E
Sokoto, Nigeria ... 94 F7 13 2N 5 16 E
Solapur, India ... 84 L9 17 43N 75 56 E
Soldotna, U.S.A. ... 108 B4 60 29N 151 3W
Solent, The, U.K. ... 24 E6 50 45N 1 25W
Solihull, U.K. ... 23 H5 52 26N 1 47W
Solikamsk, Russia ... 72 C10 59 38N 56 50 E
Solingen, Germany ... 66 C4 51 10N 7 5 E
Solomon Is. ■, Pac. Oc. ... 99 B10 6 0S 155 0 E
Solomon Sea, Papua N. G. ... 98 B9 7 0S 150 0 E
Solon, China ... 81 B7 46 32N 121 10 E
Solothurn, Switz. ... 66 E4 47 13N 7 32 E
Solway Firth, U.K. ... 22 C1 54 49N 3 35W
Somali Pen., Africa ... 90 F8 7 0N 46 0 E
Somali Rep. ■, Africa ... 88 F4 7 0N 47 0 E
Sombrerete, Mexico ... 114 C4 23 40N 103 40W
Somerby, U.K. ... 23 G7 52 42N 0 50W
Somerset, U.S.A. ... 112 G5 37 5N 84 36W
Somerset □, U.K. ... 24 D2 51 9N 3 0W
Somerset I., Canada ... 108 A10 73 30N 93 0W
Somersham, U.K. ... 23 H8 52 24N 0 1W
Somerton, U.K. ... 24 D3 51 2N 2 43W
Somme →, France ... 68 A4 50 11N 1 38 E
Songhua Jiang →, China ... 81 B8 47 45N 132 30 E
Songkhla, Thailand ... 83 C2 7 13N 100 37 E
Songpan, China ... 80 C5 32 40N 103 30 E
Sonning, U.K. ... 25 D7 51 28N 0 54W
Sonora →, Mexico ... 114 B2 28 50N 111 33W
Sonoran Desert, U.S.A. ... 110 D4 33 40N 114 15W
Sonoyta, Mexico ... 114 A2 31 51N 112 50W
Sonsonate, El Salv. ... 114 E7 13 43N 89 44W
Sopot, Poland ... 67 A10 54 27N 18 31 E
Sorel-Tracy, Canada ... 113 C11 46 0N 73 10W
Soria, Spain ... 69 B4 41 43N 2 32W
Sorocaba, Brazil ... 122 D1 23 31S 47 27W
Sørøya, Norway ... 63 C8 70 40N 22 30 E
Sosnowiec, Poland ... 67 C10 50 20N 19 10 E
Soufrière, Guadeloupe ... 114 b 16 5N 61 40W
Soufrière, St. Lucia ... 115 f 13 51N 61 3W
Soufrière Bay, St. Lucia ... 115 f 13 51N 61 4W
Sound, The, U.K. ... 27 G5 50 20N 4 10W
Souris →, Canada ... 108 D9 49 40N 99 34W
Sousse, Tunisia ... 95 A8 35 50N 10 38 E
South Africa ■, Africa ... 97 L4 32 0S 23 0 E
South America ... 116 E5 10 0S 60 0W
South Australia □, Australia ... 98 G6 32 0S 139 0 E
South Bend, U.S.A. ... 112 E4 41 41N 86 15W
South Benfleet, U.K. ... 25 C10 51 33N 0 36 E
South Brent, U.K. ... 27 G6 50 25N 3 51W
South Carolina □, U.S.A. ... 111 D10 34 0N 81 0W
South Cave, U.K. ... 23 E7 53 47N 0 37W
South Charleston, U.S.A. ... 112 F7 38 22N 81 44W
South China Sea, Asia ... 83 C3 10 0N 113 0 E
South Dakota □, U.S.A. ... 110 B7 44 15N 100 0W
South Dorset Downs, U.K. ... 24 E4 50 40N 2 26W
South Downs, U.K. ... 25 E7 50 52N 0 25W
South East C., Australia ... 98 J8 43 40S 146 50 E
South Elkington, U.K. ... 23 F8 53 23N 0 5W
South Esk →, U.K. ... 19 J12 56 43N 2 31W
South Foreland, U.K. ... 25 D11 51 8N 1 24 E
South Georgia, Antarctica ... 55 B1 54 30S 37 0W
South Hayling, U.K. ... 25 E7 50 47N 0 58W
South Honshu Ridge, Pac. Oc. ... 102 E6 23 0N 143 0 E
South I., N.Z. ... 99 J13 44 0S 170 0 E
South Korea ■, Asia ... 81 C7 36 0N 128 0 E
South Magnetic Pole, Antarctica ... 55 C9 64 8S 138 8 E
South Molton, U.K. ... 24 D1 51 1N 3 51W
South Nahanni →, Canada ... 108 B7 61 3N 123 21W
South Negril Pt., Jamaica ... 114 a 18 14N 78 30W
South Orkney Is., Antarctica ... 55 C18 63 0S 45 0W

South Ossetia □, Georgia ... 73 F7 42 21N 44 2 E
South Petherton, U.K. ... 24 E3 50 57N 2 46W
South Petherwin, U.K. ... 27 F5 50 36N 4 24W
South Platte →, U.S.A. ... 110 B6 41 7N 100 42W
South Pole, Antarctica ... 55 E 90 0S 0 0W
South Pt., Barbados ... 115 g 13 2N 59 32W
South Ronaldsay, U.K. ... 19 E12 58 48N 2 58W
South Sandwich Is., Antarctica ... 55 B1 57 0S 27 0W
South Saskatchewan →, Canada ... 108 C9 53 15N 105 5W
South Shetland Is., Antarctica ... 55 C18 62 0S 59 0W
South Shields, U.K. ... 22 C6 55 0N 1 25W
South Tawton, U.K. ... 27 F6 50 44N 3 55W
South Tyne →, U.K. ... 22 C4 54 59N 2 8W
South Uist, U.K. ... 18 H3 57 20N 7 15W
South Woodham Ferrers, U.K. ... 25 C10 51 39N 0 37 E
South Yorkshire □, U.K. ... 23 F5 53 27N 1 36W
Southam, U.K. ... 23 H6 52 18N 1 23W
Southampton, U.K. ... 24 E6 50 54N 1 23W
Southampton I., Canada ... 109 B11 64 30N 84 0W
Southborough, U.K. ... 25 D9 51 9N 0 16 E
Southend-on-Sea, U.K. ... 25 C10 51 32N 0 44 E
Southern Alps, N.Z. ... 99 J13 43 41S 170 11 E
Southern Indian L., Canada ... 108 C10 57 10N 98 30W
Southern Ocean, Antarctica ... 53 H13 62 0S 60 0 E
Southern Uplands, U.K. ... 21 D8 55 28N 3 52W
Southery, U.K. ... 25 A9 52 31N 0 24 E
Southminster, U.K. ... 25 C10 51 40N 0 51 E
Southport, U.K. ... 23 E2 53 39N 3 0W
Southwell, U.K. ... 23 F7 53 4N 0 57W
Southwold, U.K. ... 25 E8 50 50N 0 13W
Sovetsk, Russia ... 72 C3 55 6N 21 50 E
Sowerby, U.K. ... 22 D6 54 14N 1 21W
Soweto, S. Africa ... 97 K5 26 14S 27 54 E
Spain ■, Europe ... 69 B4 39 0N 4 0W
Spalding, U.K. ... 23 G8 52 48N 0 9W
Spanish, Canada ... 112 B6 46 12N 82 20W
Spanish Town, Br. Virgin Is. ... 115 e 17 43N 64 26W
Spanish Town, Jamaica ... 114 a 18 0N 76 57W
Sparkford, U.K. ... 24 D3 51 2N 2 33W
Sparks, U.S.A. ... 110 C3 39 32N 119 45W
Spartanburg, U.S.A. ... 111 D10 34 56N 81 57W
Spartivento, C., Italy ... 70 F7 37 55N 16 4 E
Speightstown, Barbados ... 115 g 13 15N 59 39W
Speke, U.K. ... 23 F3 53 21N 2 52W
Spencer, U.S.A. ... 111 B7 43 9N 95 9W
Spencer G., Australia ... 98 G6 34 0S 137 20 E
Spennymoor, U.K. ... 22 C5 54 42N 1 36W
Sperrin Mts., U.K. ... 29 B7 54 50N 7 0W
Spey →, U.K. ... 19 G11 57 40N 3 6W
Spilsby, U.K. ... 23 F9 53 10N 0 6 E
Spithead, U.K. ... 24 E6 50 45N 1 10W
Spitzbergen = Svalbard, Arctic ... 55 B8 78 0N 17 0 E
Split, Croatia ... 70 C7 43 31N 16 26 E
Spofforth, U.K. ... 23 E6 53 57N 1 27W
Spokane, U.S.A. ... 110 A3 47 40N 117 24W
Spratly Is., S. China Sea ... 83 C3 8 20N 112 0 E
Spree →, Germany ... 66 B7 52 32N 13 13 E
Spring Hall, Barbados ... 115 g 13 18N 59 36W
Springfield, Ill., U.S.A. ... 111 C9 39 48N 89 39W
Springfield, Mass., U.S.A. ... 113 D11 42 6N 72 35W
Springfield, Mo., U.S.A. ... 111 C8 37 13N 93 17W
Springfield, Ohio, U.S.A. ... 112 F6 39 55N 83 49W
Springfield, Oreg., U.S.A. ... 110 B2 44 3N 123 1W
Springhill, Canada ... 113 C15 45 40N 64 4W
Springs, S. Africa ... 97 K5 26 13S 28 25 E
Sproatley, U.K. ... 23 E8 53 47N 0 11W
Spurn Hd., U.K. ... 23 E9 53 35N 0 8 E
Srebrenica, Bos.-H. ... 71 B8 44 6N 19 18 E
Sredinny Ra., Russia ... 79 D18 57 0N 160 0 E
Sri Lanka ■, Asia ... 84 R12 7 30N 80 50 E
Srikakulam, India ... 85 K13 18 14N 83 58 E
Srinagar, India ... 84 B9 34 5N 74 50 E
Staffa, U.K. ... 20 B3 56 27N 6 21W
Stafford, U.K. ... 23 G4 52 49N 2 7W
Staffordshire □, U.K. ... 23 G4 52 53N 2 10W
Staindrop, U.K. ... 22 C5 54 36N 1 47W
Staines, U.K. ... 25 D8 51 26N 0 29W
Stainforth, U.K. ... 23 E7 53 37N 1 0W
Stainmore Forest, U.K. ... 22 D4 54 29N 2 5W
Stainton, U.K. ... 23 F8 53 18N 0 24W
Staithes, U.K. ... 22 C7 54 34N 0 46W
Stakhanov, Ukraine ... 73 E6 48 35N 38 40 E
Stalbridge, U.K. ... 24 E4 50 57N 2 23W
Stalham, U.K. ... 25 A12 52 47N 1 31 E
Stallingborough, U.K. ... 23 E8 53 36N 0 12W
Stalybridge, U.K. ... 23 F4 53 28N 2 3W
Stamford, U.K. ... 23 G8 52 39N 0 29W
Stamford, U.S.A. ... 113 E11 41 3N 73 32W
Stamford Bridge, U.K. ... 23 E7 54 0N 0 54W
Stamfordham, U.K. ... 22 B5 55 3N 1 53W
Standish, U.K. ... 23 E3 53 35N 2 41W
Standish, U.S.A. ... 112 D6 43 59N 83 57W
Stanford on Teme, U.K. ... 23 H4 52 17N 2 26W
Stanhope, U.K. ... 22 C5 54 45N 2 5W
Stanley, Falk. Is. ... 121 H4 51 40S 59 51W
Stanley, U.K. ... 22 C5 54 53N 1 41W
Stannington, U.K. ... 22 B5 55 7N 1 40W
Stanovoy Ra., Russia ... 79 D14 55 0N 130 0 E
Stansted Mountfitchet, U.K. ... 25 C9 51 52N 0 11 E
Stanwix, U.K. ... 22 C3 54 55N 2 56W
Stapleford, U.K. ... 23 G6 52 57N 1 16W
Staplehurst, U.K. ... 25 D10 51 9N 0 34 E
Stara Zagora, Bulgaria ... 71 C11 42 26N 25 39 E
Staraya Russa, Russia ... 72 C5 57 58N 31 23 E
Starbuck I., Kiribati ... 103 H12 5 37S 155 55W
Starcross, U.K. ... 27 G6 50 15N 3 39W
Start Pt., U.K. ... 27 G6 50 13N 3 39W
Staryy Oskol, Russia ... 73 D6 51 19N 37 55 E
State College, U.S.A. ... 112 E9 40 48N 77 52W
Staten, I., Argentina ... 121 H3 54 40S 64 30W
Staunton, U.K. ... 24 C4 51 57N 2 17W
Staunton, U.S.A. ... 112 F8 38 9N 79 4W
Stavanger, Norway ... 63 F5 58 57N 5 40 E
Staveley, Cumb., U.K. ... 22 D3 54 23N 2 48W
Staveley, Derby, U.K. ... 23 F6 53 16N 1 21W
Stavropol, Russia ... 73 E7 45 5N 42 0 E
Steinkjer, Austria ... 66 E8 47 26N 15 0 E
Steinkjer, Norway ... 63 E6 64 1N 11 31 E
Stellarton, Canada ... 109 D14 45 32N 62 30W
Stephenville, Canada ... 109 D14 48 31N 58 35W
Steppe, Asia ... 74 D9 50 0N 50 0 E
Sterling, U.S.A. ... 110 B6 40 37N 103 13W
Sterlitamak, Russia ... 72 D10 53 40N 56 0 E
Steubenville, U.S.A. ... 112 E7 40 22N 80 37W
Stevenage, U.K. ... 25 C8 51 55N 0 13W
Stevens Point, U.S.A. ... 111 B9 44 31N 89 34W
Stewart, Canada ... 108 C6 55 56N 129 57W
Stewart →, Canada ... 108 B6 63 19N 139 26W
Stewart I., N.Z. ... 99 K12 46 58S 167 54 E
Steyning, U.K. ... 25 E8 50 53N 0 18W
Steyr, Austria ... 66 D8 48 3N 14 25 E
Stikine →, Canada ... 108 C6 56 40N 132 30W

Stillington, U.K. ... 22 D6 54 6N 1 6W
Stillwater, Minn., U.S.A. ... 111 A8 45 3N 92 49W
Stillwater, Okla., U.S.A. ... 111 C7 36 7N 97 4W
Stiperstones, U.K. ... 23 G3 52 36N 2 55W
Stirling, U.K. ... 21 B8 56 8N 3 57W
Stockbridge, U.K. ... 24 D6 51 7N 1 29W
Stockport, U.K. ... 23 F4 53 25N 2 9W
Stocksbridge, U.K. ... 23 F5 53 29N 1 35W
Stockton, U.S.A. ... 110 C2 37 58N 121 17W
Stockton-on-Tees, U.K. ... 22 C6 54 35N 1 19W
Stoer, Pt. of, U.K. ... 18 F7 58 16N 5 23W
Stoke, U.K. ... 25 D10 51 26N 0 41 E
Stoke Ferry, U.K. ... 25 A10 52 34N 0 31 E
Stoke Fleming, U.K. ... 27 G6 50 19N 3 37W
Stoke Mandeville, U.K. ... 25 C7 51 47N 0 47W
Stoke-on-Trent, U.K. ... 23 F4 53 1N 2 11W
Stoke Prior, U.K. ... 23 H4 52 19N 2 4W
Stokesley, U.K. ... 22 D6 54 28N 1 12W
Stone, Bucks., U.K. ... 25 C7 51 48N 0 52W
Stone, Staffs., U.K. ... 23 G4 52 55N 2 9W
Stonehaven, U.K. ... 19 J13 56 59N 2 12W
Stonehouse, U.K. ... 24 C4 51 45N 2 16W
Stonham Aspal, U.K. ... 25 B11 52 12N 1 8 E
Stony Stratford, U.K. ... 25 B7 52 3N 0 50W
Stora Lulevatten, Sweden ... 63 D7 67 10N 19 30 E
Storavan, Sweden ... 63 D7 65 45N 18 10 E
Store Bælt, Denmark ... 63 F6 55 20N 11 0 E
Stornoway, U.K. ... 18 F5 58 13N 6 23W
Storsjön, Sweden ... 63 E6 63 9N 14 30 E
Stort →, U.K. ... 25 C9 51 46N 0 2 E
Storuman, Sweden ... 63 D7 65 5N 17 10 E
Stotfold, U.K. ... 25 B8 52 1N 0 13W
Stour →, Dorset, U.K. ... 24 E5 50 43N 1 47W
Stour →, Kent, U.K. ... 25 D11 51 18N 1 22 E
Stour →, Suffolk, U.K. ... 25 C11 51 57N 1 4 E
Stour →, Worcs., U.K. ... 23 H4 52 21N 2 17W
Stourbridge, U.K. ... 23 H4 52 28N 2 8W
Stourport-on-Severn, U.K. ... 23 H4 52 21N 2 17W
Stow, U.K. ... 22 A3 55 42N 2 50W
Stow Bardolph, U.K. ... 25 A9 52 38N 0 24 E
Stow-on-the-Wold, U.K. ... 24 C5 51 56N 1 42W
Stowmarket, U.K. ... 25 B10 52 12N 1 0 E
Strabane, U.K. ... 28 B7 54 50N 7 27W
Stradbroke, U.K. ... 25 B11 52 19N 1 16 E
Stralsund, Germany ... 66 A7 54 18N 13 4 E
Strangford L., U.K. ... 29 C10 54 30N 5 37W
Stranraer, U.K. ... 20 E5 54 54N 5 1W
Strasbourg, France ... 68 B7 48 35N 7 42 E
Stratford, Canada ... 112 D7 43 23N 81 0W
Stratford St. Mary, U.K. ... 25 C10 51 58N 1 0 E
Stratford-upon-Avon, U.K. ... 23 H5 52 12N 1 42W
Strath Spey, U.K. ... 19 H10 57 9N 3 49W
Strathaven, U.K. ... 20 C7 55 40N 4 5W
Strathmore, U.K. ... 19 J11 56 37N 3 7W
Strathpeffer, U.K. ... 19 G8 57 35N 4 32W
Strathroy, Canada ... 112 D7 42 58N 81 38W
Strathy Pt., U.K. ... 19 E9 58 36N 4 1W
Stratton, U.K. ... 27 F4 50 49N 4 32W
Stratton St. Margaret, U.K. ... 24 C5 51 35N 1 44W
Streatley, U.K. ... 24 C6 51 31N 1 8W
Street, U.K. ... 24 D3 51 8N 2 44W
Strensall, U.K. ... 22 D6 54 3N 1 4W
Stretford, U.K. ... 23 F4 53 28N 2 17W
Stroma, U.K. ... 19 E11 58 41N 3 7W
Strómboli, Italy ... 70 E6 38 47N 15 13 E
Stromeferry, U.K. ... 18 H6 57 21N 5 33W
Stromness, U.K. ... 19 E11 58 58N 3 17W
Stronsay, U.K. ... 19 D12 59 7N 2 35W
Stroud, U.K. ... 24 C4 51 45N 2 13W
Stuart L., Canada ... 108 C7 54 30N 124 30W
Studland, U.K. ... 24 E5 50 39N 1 58W
Studley, U.K. ... 23 H5 52 16N 1 52W
Sturgeon Bay, U.S.A. ... 112 C4 44 50N 87 23W
Sturgeon Falls, Canada ... 112 B8 46 25N 79 57W
Sturminster Marshall, U.K. ... 24 E4 50 47N 2 5W
Sturminster Newton, U.K. ... 24 E4 50 55N 2 18W
Sturton, U.K. ... 23 F7 53 19N 0 39W
Stuttgart, Germany ... 66 D5 48 48N 9 11 E
Stuttgart, U.S.A. ... 111 D8 34 30N 91 33W
Suakin, Sudan ... 95 E13 19 8N 37 20 E
Subotica, Serbia & M. ... 71 A8 46 6N 19 39 E
Suceava, Romania ... 67 E14 47 38N 26 16 E
Suck →, Ireland ... 28 E5 53 17N 8 3W
Sucre, Bolivia ... 120 D3 19 0S 65 15W
Sudan ■, Africa ... 95 E11 15 0N 30 0 E
Sudbury, Canada ... 109 D11 46 30N 81 0W
Sudbury, Derby, U.K. ... 23 G5 52 54N 1 45W
Sudbury, Suffolk, U.K. ... 25 B10 52 2N 0 45 E
Sûdd, Sudan ... 95 G12 8 20N 30 0 E
Sudeten, Europe ... 67 C9 50 20N 16 45 E
Suez, Egypt ... 95 C12 29 58N 32 31 E
Suez, G. of, Egypt ... 95 C12 28 40N 33 0 E
Suez Canal, Egypt ... 95 B12 31 0N 32 20 E
Suffolk □, U.K. ... 25 B11 52 16N 1 0 E
Suglok, Canada ... 109 B12 62 14N 75 38W
Şuhār, Oman ... 87 E9 24 20N 56 40 E
Suihua, China ... 81 B7 46 32N 126 55 E
Suir →, Ireland ... 31 D8 52 16N 7 9W
Sukabumi, Indonesia ... 83 D2 6 56S 106 50 E
Sukhona →, Russia ... 72 C6 61 15N 46 39 E
Sukkur, Pakistan ... 84 F6 27 42N 68 54 E
Sulaiman Range, Pakistan ... 84 D6 30 30N 69 50 E
Sulawesi □, Indonesia ... 83 D4 2 0S 120 0 E
Sullana, Peru ... 120 C1 4 52S 80 39W
Sullom Voe, U.K. ... 18 B15 60 27N 1 20W
Sulu Arch., Phil. ... 83 C4 6 0N 121 0 E
Sulu Sea, E. Indies ... 83 C4 8 0N 120 0 E
Sumatra, Indonesia ... 83 C2 0 40N 100 20 E
Sumba, Indonesia ... 83 D3 9 45S 119 35 E
Sumbawa, Indonesia ... 83 D3 8 26S 117 30 E
Sumburgh Hd., U.K. ... 18 C15 59 52N 1 17W
Sumenep, Indonesia ... 83 D3 7 1S 113 52 E
Summer L., U.S.A. ... 110 B2 42 50N 120 45W
Summerside, Canada ... 109 D13 46 24N 63 47W
Sumqayıt, Azerbaijan ... 73 F8 40 34N 49 38 E
Sumter, U.S.A. ... 111 D10 33 55N 80 21W
Sumy, Ukraine ... 73 D5 50 57N 34 50 E
Sun Valley, U.S.A. ... 110 B4 43 42N 114 21W
Sunart, L., U.K. ... 18 J6 56 42N 5 43W
Sunbury, U.S.A. ... 112 E9 40 52N 76 48W
Sunda, Selat, Indonesia ... 83 D2 6 20S 105 30 E
Sunda Is., Indonesia ... 102 H2 5 0S 105 0 E
Sundarbans, Asia ... 85 J16 22 0N 89 0 E
Sunderland, U.K. ... 22 C6 54 55N 1 23W
Sundsvall, Sweden ... 63 E7 62 23N 17 17 E
Sungaipenuh, Indonesia ... 83 D2 2 1S 101 20 E
Sunk Island, U.K. ... 23 E8 53 38N 0 7W
Sunninghill, U.K. ... 25 D7 51 24N 0 39W
Superior, U.S.A. ... 111 A8 46 44N 92 6W
Superior, L., N. Amer. ... 109 D11 47 0N 87 0W
Sür, Lebanon ... 86 C3 33 19N 35 16 E
Sura →, Russia ... 72 C8 56 6N 46 0 E
Surabaya, Indonesia ... 83 D3 7 17S 112 45 E

Surakarta, Indonesia ... 83 D3 7 35S 110 48 E
Surat, India ... 84 J8 21 12N 72 55 E
Surgut, Russia ... 79 C9 61 14N 73 20 E
Surigao, Phil. ... 83 C4 9 47N 125 29 E
Suriname ■, S. Amer. ... 120 B4 4 0N 56 0W
Surrey □, U.K. ... 25 D7 51 15N 0 31W
Surt, Libya ... 95 B9 31 11N 16 39 E
Susquehanna →, U.S.A. ... 112 F9 39 33N 76 5W
Sussex, Canada ... 113 C15 45 45N 65 37W
Sutherland, U.K. ... 19 F8 58 12N 4 50W
Sutlej →, Pakistan ... 84 E7 29 23N 71 3 E
Sutterton, U.K. ... 23 G8 52 55N 0 6W
Sutton □, U.K. ... 25 D8 51 21N 0 11W
Sutton Bridge, U.K. ... 23 G9 52 47N 0 10 E
Sutton Coldfield, U.K. ... 23 G5 52 35N 1 49W
Sutton Courtenay, U.K. ... 24 C6 51 39N 1 16W
Sutton in Ashfield, U.K. ... 23 F6 53 8N 1 16W
Sutton-on-Sea, U.K. ... 23 F9 53 18N 0 16 E
Sutton Scotney, U.K. ... 24 D6 51 9N 1 20W
Suva, Fiji ... 99 D14 18 6S 178 30 E
Suvorov Is., Cook Is. ... 103 J11 15 0S 163 0W
Suwałki, Poland ... 67 A12 54 8N 22 59 E
Suzhou, China ... 81 C7 31 19N 120 38 E
Svalbard, Arctic ... 55 B8 78 0N 17 0 E
Svealand □, Sweden ... 63 E7 60 20N 15 0 E
Sverdrup Is., Canada ... 54 B3 79 0N 97 0W
Svir →, Russia ... 72 B5 60 30N 32 48 E
Swadlincote, U.K. ... 23 G5 52 47N 1 33W
Swaffham, U.K. ... 25 A10 52 39N 0 42 E
Swakopmund, Namibia ... 97 J2 22 37S 14 30 E
Swale →, U.K. ... 25 D11 54 5N 1 20W
Swan Hill, Australia ... 98 H7 35 20S 143 33 E
Swan River, Canada ... 108 C9 52 10N 101 16W
Swanage, U.K. ... 24 E5 50 36N 1 58W
Swansea, U.K. ... 27 D6 51 37N 3 57W
Swartberge, S. Africa ... 90 K6 33 20S 22 0 E
Swaziland ■, Africa ... 97 K6 26 30S 31 30 E
Sweden ■, Europe ... 63 F7 57 0N 15 0 E
Sweetwater, U.S.A. ... 110 D6 32 28N 100 25W
Swellendam, S. Africa ... 97 L4 34 1S 20 26 E
Swift Current, Canada ... 108 C9 50 20N 107 45W
Swilly, L., Ireland ... 28 A6 55 12N 7 33W
Swindon, U.K. ... 24 C5 51 34N 1 46W
Swineshead, U.K. ... 23 G8 52 57N 0 10W
Swinford, Ireland ... 28 D4 53 57N 8 58W
Swinton, Borders, U.K. ... 22 A4 55 43N 2 15W
Swinton, Gt. Man., U.K. ... 23 E4 53 31N 2 20W
Swinton, S. Yorks., U.K. ... 23 F6 53 29N 1 19W
Switzerland ■, Europe ... 66 E5 46 30N 8 0 E
Swords, Ireland ... 29 E9 53 28N 6 13W
Sydney, Australia ... 98 G9 33 53S 151 10 E
Sydney, Canada ... 109 D14 46 7N 60 7W
Syktyvkar, Russia ... 72 B9 61 45N 50 40 E
Sylhet, Bangla. ... 85 G17 24 54N 91 52 E
Sylhet □, Bangla. ... 85 G17 24 50N 91 50 E
Symington, U.K. ... 21 D8 55 35N 3 36W
Symonds Yat, U.K. ... 24 C3 51 51N 2 38W
Syracuse, U.S.A. ... 113 D9 43 3N 76 9W
Syrdarya →, Kazakhstan ... 79 E8 46 3N 61 0 E
Syria ■, Asia ... 86 C4 35 0N 38 0 E
Syrian Desert, Asia ... 86 C4 32 0N 40 0 E
Syston, U.K. ... 23 G6 52 42N 1 3W
Syzran, Russia ... 72 D8 53 12N 48 30 E
Szczecin, Poland ... 66 B8 53 27N 14 27 E
Szechwan = Sichuan □, China ... 80 C5 30 30N 103 0 E
Szeged, Hungary ... 67 E11 46 16N 20 10 E
Székesfehérvár, Hungary ... 67 E10 47 15N 18 25 E
Szekszárd, Hungary ... 67 E10 46 22N 18 42 E
Szolnok, Hungary ... 67 E11 47 10N 20 15 E
Szombathely, Hungary ... 67 E9 47 14N 16 38 E

**T**

Tabas, Iran ... 87 C9 33 35N 56 55 E
Tablas I., Phil. ... 83 B4 12 25N 122 2 E
Table B., S. Africa ... 97 L3 33 35S 18 25 E
Table Mt., S. Africa ... 97 L3 34 0S 18 22 E
Tabora, Tanzania ... 96 F6 5 2S 32 50 E
Tabriz, Iran ... 86 B6 38 7N 46 20 E
Tabuaeran, Kiribati ... 103 G12 3 51N 159 22W
Tacheng, China ... 80 B3 46 40N 82 58 E
Tacloban, Phil. ... 83 B4 11 15N 124 58 E
Tacna, Peru ... 120 D2 18 0S 70 20W
Tacoma, U.S.A. ... 110 A2 47 14N 122 26W
Tacuarembó, Uruguay ... 121 F4 31 45S 56 0W
Tadcaster, U.K. ... 23 E6 53 53N 1 16W
Tadley, U.K. ... 24 D6 51 21N 1 7W
Taegu, S. Korea ... 81 C7 35 50N 128 37 E
Taejŏn, S. Korea ... 81 C7 36 20N 127 28 E
Taganrog, Russia ... 73 E6 47 12N 38 50 E
Taguatinga, Brazil ... 122 B2 12 16S 42 26W
Tagus →, Europe ... 69 C1 38 40N 9 24W
Tahiti, Pac. Oc. ... 103 J13 17 37S 149 27W
Tahoe, L., U.S.A. ... 110 C2 39 6N 120 2W
Tahoua, Niger ... 94 F7 14 57N 5 16 E
T'aichung, Taiwan ... 81 D7 24 9N 120 37 E
Taimyr Peninsula, Russia ... 79 B11 75 0N 100 0 E
Tain, U.K. ... 19 G9 57 49N 4 4W
T'ainan, Taiwan ... 81 D7 23 0N 120 10 E
Taipei, Taiwan ... 81 D7 25 2N 121 30 E
Taiping, Malaysia ... 83 C2 4 51N 100 44 E
Taitao, Pen. de, Chile ... 121 G2 46 30S 75 0W
T'aitung, Taiwan ... 81 D7 22 43N 121 4 E
Taiwan ■, Asia ... 81 D7 23 30N 121 0 E
Taiyuan, China ... 81 C6 37 52N 112 33 E
Ta'izz, Yemen ... 88 E3 13 35N 44 2 E
Tajikistan ■, Asia ... 79 F8 38 30N 70 0 E
Tak, Thailand ... 83 B1 16 52N 99 8 E
Takamatsu, Japan ... 82 F4 34 20N 134 5 E
Takasaki, Japan ... 82 E6 36 20N 139 0 E
Takhâr □, Afghan. ... 87 B12 36 40N 70 0 E
Takla Makan, China ... 80 C3 38 0N 83 0 E
Talara, Peru ... 120 C1 4 38S 81 18W
Talaud, Kepulauan, Indonesia ... 83 C4 4 30N 126 50 E
Talca, Chile ... 121 F2 35 28S 71 40W
Talcahuano, Chile ... 121 F2 36 40S 73 10W
Taldyqorghan, Kazakhstan ... 79 E9 45 10N 78 45 E
Talgarth, U.K. ... 24 C2 52 0N 3 14W
Taliabu, Indonesia ... 83 D4 1 50S 125 0 E
Tallahassee, U.S.A. ... 111 D10 30 27N 84 17W
Tallinn, Estonia ... 72 C3 59 22N 24 48 E
Taloyoak, Canada ... 108 B10 69 32N 93 32W
Taltal, Chile ... 121 E2 25 23S 70 33W
Tamale, Ghana ... 94 G5 9 22N 0 50W
Tamana, Kiribati ... 99 A13 2 30S 175 59 E
Tamanrasset, Algeria ... 94 D7 22 50N 5 30 E
Tamar →, U.K. ... 27 G5 50 27N 4 15W
Tambov, Russia ... 72 D7 52 45N 41 28 E
Tame →, U.K. ... 23 G5 52 44N 1 42W
Tamerton Foliot, U.K. ... 27 G5 50 25N 4 11W
Tamil Nadu □, India ... 84 P10 11 0N 77 0 E

**Tampa**                                                                                 **Two Rivers**

| Name | Ref | Lat | Long |
|---|---|---|---|
| Tampa, U.S.A. | 111 E10 | 27 57N | 82 27W |
| Tampa B., U.S.A. | 111 E10 | 27 50N | 82 30W |
| Tampere, Finland | 63 E8 | 61 30N | 23 50 E |
| Tampico, Mexico | 114 C5 | 22 20N | 97 50W |
| Tamworth, Australia | 98 G9 | 31 7S | 150 58 E |
| Tamworth, U.K. | 23 G5 | 52 39N | 1 41W |
| Tana →, Kenya | 96 E8 | 2 32S | 40 31 E |
| Tana →, Norway | 63 C9 | 70 30N | 28 14 E |
| Tana, L., Ethiopia | 88 E2 | 13 5N | 37 30 E |
| Tanami Desert, Australia | 98 D5 | 18 50S | 132 0 E |
| Tanana →, U.S.A. | 108 B4 | 65 10N | 151 58W |
| Tandil, Argentina | 121 F4 | 37 15S | 59 6W |
| Tandragee, U.K. | 29 C9 | 54 21N | 6 24W |
| Tanga, Tanzania | 96 F7 | 5 5S | 39 2 E |
| Tanganyika, L., Africa | 96 F6 | 6 40S | 30 0 E |
| Tanggula Shan, China | 80 C4 | 32 40N | 92 10 E |
| Tangier, Morocco | 94 A4 | 35 50N | 5 49W |
| Tangshan, China | 81 C6 | 39 38N | 118 10 E |
| Tanimbar, Kepulauan, Indonesia | 83 D5 | 7 30S | 131 30 E |
| Tanjungbalai, Indonesia | 83 C1 | 2 55N | 99 44 E |
| Tanjungkarang Telukbetung, Indonesia | 83 D2 | 5 20S | 105 10 E |
| Tanjungpandan, Indonesia | 83 D2 | 2 43S | 107 38 E |
| Tanjungredeb, Indonesia | 83 C3 | 2 9N | 117 29 E |
| Tanna, Vanuatu | 99 D12 | 19 30S | 169 20 E |
| Tanta, Egypt | 95 B12 | 30 45N | 30 57 E |
| Tanworth, U.K. | 23 H5 | 52 20N | 1 50W |
| Tanzania ■, Africa | 96 F6 | 6 0S | 34 0 E |
| Taolanaro, Madag. | 97 K9 | 25 2S | 47 0 E |
| Taos, U.S.A. | 110 C5 | 36 24N | 105 35W |
| Tapachula, Mexico | 114 E6 | 14 54N | 92 17W |
| Tapajós →, Brazil | 120 C4 | 2 24S | 54 41W |
| Tapi →, India | 84 J8 | 21 8N | 72 41 E |
| Tarakan, Indonesia | 83 C3 | 3 20N | 117 35 E |
| Taransay, U.K. | 18 G3 | 57 54N | 7 0W |
| Táranto, Italy | 70 D7 | 40 28N | 17 14 E |
| Táranto, G. di, Italy | 70 D7 | 40 8N | 17 20 E |
| Tarawa, Kiribati | 102 G9 | 1 30N | 173 0 E |
| Taraz, Kazakhstan | 79 E9 | 42 54N | 71 22 E |
| Tarbagatai Ra., Kazakhstan | 79 E10 | 48 0N | 83 0 E |
| Tarbat Ness, U.K. | 19 G10 | 57 52N | 3 47W |
| Tarbert, Arg. & Bute, U.K. | 20 C5 | 55 52N | 5 25W |
| Tarbert, W. Isles, U.K. | 18 G4 | 57 54N | 6 49W |
| Tarbes, France | 68 E4 | 43 15N | 0 3 E |
| Tarcoola, Australia | 98 G5 | 30 44S | 134 36 E |
| Taree, Australia | 98 G9 | 31 50S | 152 30 E |
| Tarfaya, Morocco | 94 C3 | 27 55N | 12 55W |
| Târgoviste, Romania | 67 F13 | 44 55N | 25 27 E |
| Târgu-Jiu, Romania | 67 F12 | 45 5N | 23 19 E |
| Târgu Mures, Romania | 67 E13 | 46 31N | 24 38 E |
| Tarija, Bolivia | 120 E3 | 21 30S | 64 40W |
| Tarim Basin, China | 80 B3 | 40 0N | 84 0 E |
| Tarim He →, China | 80 C3 | 39 30N | 88 30 E |
| Tarleton, U.K. | 23 E3 | 53 41N | 2 50W |
| Tarn →, France | 68 E4 | 44 5N | 1 6 E |
| Tarnów, Poland | 67 C11 | 50 3N | 21 0 E |
| Taroudannt, Morocco | 94 B4 | 30 30N | 8 52W |
| Tarporley, U.K. | 23 F3 | 53 10N | 2 40W |
| Tarragona, Spain | 69 B6 | 41 5N | 1 17 E |
| Tarsus, Turkey | 73 G5 | 36 58N | 34 55 E |
| Tartu, Estonia | 72 C4 | 58 20N | 26 44 E |
| Tashkent, Uzbekistan | 79 E8 | 41 20N | 69 10 E |
| Tasikmalaya, Indonesia | 83 D2 | 7 18S | 108 12 E |
| Tasman Sea, Pac. Oc. | 99 H10 | 36 0S | 160 0 E |
| Tasmania □, Australia | 98 J8 | 42 0S | 146 30 E |
| Tassili n'Ajjer, Algeria | 94 C7 | 25 47N | 8 1 E |
| Tatarstan □, Russia | 72 C9 | 55 30N | 51 30 E |
| Tatnam, C., Canada | 109 C10 | 57 16N | 91 0W |
| Tatra, Slovak Rep. | 67 D11 | 49 20N | 20 0 E |
| Tatta, Pakistan | 84 G5 | 24 42N | 67 55 E |
| Tattenhall, U.K. | 23 F3 | 53 7N | 2 46W |
| Tatvan, Turkey | 73 G7 | 38 31N | 42 15 E |
| Taubaté, Brazil | 122 D1 | 23 0S | 45 36W |
| Tauern, Austria | 66 E7 | 47 15N | 12 40 E |
| Taunton, U.K. | 24 D2 | 51 1N | 3 5W |
| Taunton, U.S.A. | 113 E12 | 41 54N | 71 6W |
| Taunus, Germany | 66 C5 | 50 13N | 8 34 E |
| Taurus Mts., Turkey | 73 G5 | 37 0N | 32 30 E |
| Tavistock, U.K. | 27 F5 | 50 33N | 4 9W |
| Taw →, U.K. | 27 E5 | 51 4N | 4 4W |
| Tawas City, U.S.A. | 112 C6 | 44 16N | 83 31W |
| Tawau, Malaysia | 83 C3 | 4 20N | 117 55 E |
| Tay →, U.K. | 19 J10 | 56 37N | 3 38W |
| Tay, Firth of, U.K. | 21 B9 | 56 25N | 3 8W |
| Tay, L., U.K. | 20 A7 | 56 32N | 4 8W |
| Taylor, Mt., U.S.A. | 110 C5 | 35 14N | 107 37W |
| Tayport, U.K. | 21 B10 | 56 27N | 2 52W |
| Taza, Morocco | 94 B5 | 34 16N | 4 6W |
| Tbilisi, Georgia | 73 F7 | 41 43N | 44 50 E |
| Tebay, U.K. | 22 D3 | 54 26N | 2 35W |
| Tébessa, Algeria | 94 A7 | 35 22N | 8 8 E |
| Tees →, U.K. | 22 C6 | 54 37N | 1 10W |
| Teesdale, U.K. | 22 C4 | 54 37N | 2 10W |
| Teesside, U.K. | 22 C6 | 54 36N | 1 15W |
| Tegal, Indonesia | 83 D2 | 6 52S | 109 8 E |
| Tegucigalpa, Honduras | 114 E7 | 14 5N | 87 14W |
| Tehrān, Iran | 87 C7 | 35 44N | 51 30 E |
| Tehuantepec, Mexico | 114 D5 | 16 21N | 95 13W |
| Tehuantepec, G. de, Mexico | 114 D5 | 15 50N | 95 12W |
| Tehuantepec, Istmo de, Mexico | 114 D6 | 17 0N | 94 30W |
| Teifi →, U.K. | 26 C4 | 52 5N | 4 41W |
| Teign →, U.K. | 27 F6 | 50 32N | 3 32W |
| Teignmouth, U.K. | 27 F6 | 50 33N | 3 31W |
| Tejen, Turkmenistan | 87 B10 | 37 23N | 60 31 E |
| Tekirdağ, Turkey | 73 F4 | 40 58N | 27 30 E |
| Tel Aviv-Jaffa, Israel | 86 C3 | 32 4N | 34 48 E |
| Tela, Honduras | 114 D7 | 15 40N | 87 28W |
| Telegraph Creek, Canada | 108 C6 | 58 0N | 131 10W |
| Teles Pires →, Brazil | 120 C4 | 7 21S | 58 3W |
| Telford, U.K. | 23 G4 | 52 40N | 2 27W |
| Tell City, U.S.A. | 112 G4 | 37 57N | 86 46W |
| Tellicherry, India | 84 P9 | 11 45N | 75 30 E |
| Telpos Iz, Russia | 72 B10 | 63 16N | 59 13 E |
| Teluk Intan, Malaysia | 83 C2 | 4 3N | 101 0 E |
| Tema, Ghana | 94 G5 | 5 41N | 0 0W |
| Teme →, U.K. | 24 B4 | 52 11N | 2 13W |
| Temiscaming, Canada | 112 B8 | 46 44N | 79 5W |
| Temple, U.S.A. | 111 D7 | 31 6N | 97 21W |
| Temple Combe, U.K. | 24 D4 | 51 0N | 2 24W |
| Temple Ewell, U.K. | 25 D11 | 51 8N | 1 17 E |
| Temple Sowerby, U.K. | 22 C3 | 54 38N | 2 36W |
| Templemore, Ireland | 30 C7 | 52 47N | 7 51W |
| Temuco, Chile | 121 F2 | 38 45S | 72 40W |
| Tenbury Wells, U.K. | 23 H3 | 52 19N | 2 35W |
| Tenby, U.K. | 26 D4 | 51 40N | 4 42W |
| Tenerife, Canary Is. | 94 C2 | 28 15N | 16 35W |
| Tengchong, China | 80 D4 | 25 0N | 98 28 E |
| Tennant Creek, Australia | 98 D5 | 19 30S | 134 15 E |
| Tennessee □, U.S.A. | 111 C9 | 36 0N | 86 30W |
| Tennessee →, U.S.A. | 111 C9 | 37 4N | 88 34W |
| Tenterden, U.K. | 25 D10 | 51 4N | 0 42 E |
| Teófilo Otoni, Brazil | 122 C2 | 17 50S | 41 30W |
| Tepic, Mexico | 114 C4 | 21 30N | 104 54W |
| Teraina, Kiribati | 103 G11 | 4 43N | 160 25W |
| Téramo, Italy | 70 C5 | 42 39N | 13 42 E |
| Teresina, Brazil | 120 C5 | 5 9S | 42 45W |
| Ternate, Indonesia | 83 C4 | 0 45N | 127 25 E |
| Terni, Italy | 70 C5 | 42 34N | 12 37 E |
| Ternopil, Ukraine | 67 D13 | 49 30N | 25 40 E |
| Terrace, Canada | 108 C7 | 54 30N | 128 35W |
| Terrassa, Spain | 69 B7 | 41 34N | 2 1 E |
| Terre Haute, U.S.A. | 112 F4 | 39 28N | 87 25W |
| Teruel, Spain | 69 B5 | 40 22N | 1 8W |
| Tesiyn Gol →, Mongolia | 80 A4 | 50 40N | 93 20 E |
| Teslin, Canada | 108 B6 | 60 10N | 132 43W |
| Test →, U.K. | 24 E6 | 50 56N | 1 29W |
| Tetbury, U.K. | 24 C4 | 51 38N | 2 10W |
| Tete, Mozam. | 97 H6 | 16 13S | 33 33 E |
| Tetney, U.K. | 23 F8 | 53 29N | 0 1W |
| Teton →, U.S.A. | 110 A4 | 47 56N | 110 31W |
| Tétouan, Morocco | 94 A4 | 35 35N | 5 21W |
| Tetovo, Macedonia | 71 C9 | 42 1N | 20 59 E |
| Teuco →, Argentina | 121 E3 | 25 35S | 60 11W |
| Teutoburger Wald, Germany | 66 B5 | 52 5N | 8 22 E |
| Teviot →, U.K. | 21 D10 | 55 29N | 2 38W |
| Teviotdale, U.K. | 22 B3 | 55 25N | 2 50W |
| Teviothead, U.K. | 24 C4 | 55 20N | 2 56W |
| Tewkesbury, U.K. | 24 C4 | 51 59N | 2 9W |
| Texarkana, U.S.A. | 111 D8 | 33 26N | 94 3W |
| Texas □, U.S.A. | 110 D7 | 31 40N | 98 30W |
| Texel, Neths. | 65 A4 | 53 5N | 4 50 E |
| Teynham, U.K. | 25 D10 | 51 20N | 0 50 E |
| Tezpur, India | 85 F18 | 26 40N | 92 45 E |
| Thabana Ntlenyana, Lesotho | 97 K5 | 29 30S | 29 16 E |
| Thabazimbi, S. Africa | 97 J5 | 24 40S | 27 21 E |
| Thailand ■, Asia | 83 B2 | 16 0N | 102 0 E |
| Thailand, G. of, Asia | 83 B2 | 11 30N | 101 0 E |
| Thal Desert, Pakistan | 84 D7 | 31 10N | 71 30 E |
| Thame, U.K. | 25 C7 | 51 45N | 0 58W |
| Thame →, U.K. | 24 C6 | 51 39N | 1 9W |
| Thames →, Canada | 112 D6 | 42 20N | 82 25W |
| Thames →, U.K. | 25 D10 | 51 29N | 0 34 E |
| Thane, India | 84 K8 | 19 12N | 72 59 E |
| Thanet, I. of, U.K. | 25 D11 | 51 21N | 1 20 E |
| Thanh Hoa, Vietnam | 83 B2 | 19 48N | 105 46 E |
| Thanjavur, India | 84 P11 | 10 48N | 79 12 E |
| Thar Desert, India | 84 F8 | 28 0N | 72 0 E |
| Thargomindah, Australia | 98 F7 | 27 58S | 143 46 E |
| Thatcham, U.K. | 24 D6 | 51 24N | 1 15W |
| Thaxted, U.K. | 25 C9 | 51 57N | 0 22 E |
| The Crane, Barbados | 115 g | 13 6N | 59 27W |
| The Dalles, U.S.A. | 110 A2 | 45 36N | 121 10W |
| The Pas, Canada | 108 C9 | 53 45N | 101 15W |
| The Settlement, Br. Virgin Is. | 115 e | 18 43N | 64 22W |
| Theale, U.K. | 24 D6 | 51 26N | 1 5W |
| Thebes, Egypt | 95 C12 | 25 40N | 32 35 E |
| Thelon →, Canada | 108 B9 | 64 16N | 96 4W |
| Thermopolis, U.S.A. | 110 B5 | 43 39N | 108 13W |
| Thessalon, Canada | 112 B6 | 46 20N | 83 30W |
| Thessaloníki, Greece | 71 D10 | 40 38N | 22 58 E |
| Thetford, U.K. | 25 B10 | 52 25N | 0 45 E |
| Thetford Mines, Canada | 109 D12 | 46 8N | 71 18W |
| Thiers, France | 68 D5 | 45 52N | 3 33 E |
| Thiès, Senegal | 94 F2 | 14 50N | 16 51W |
| Thika, Kenya | 96 E7 | 1 1S | 37 5 E |
| Thimphu, Bhutan | 85 F16 | 27 31N | 89 45 E |
| Thionville, France | 68 B7 | 49 20N | 6 10 E |
| Thíra, Greece | 71 F11 | 36 23N | 25 27 E |
| Thirlmere, U.K. | 22 C2 | 54 32N | 3 4W |
| Thirsk, U.K. | 22 C5 | 54 14N | 1 19W |
| Thlewiaza →, Canada | 108 C9 | 60 29N | 94 40W |
| Thomasville, U.S.A. | 111 D10 | 30 50N | 83 59W |
| Thompson, Canada | 108 C10 | 55 45N | 97 52W |
| Thornaby on Tees, U.K. | 22 C6 | 54 33N | 1 18W |
| Thornbury, U.K. | 24 C3 | 51 36N | 2 31W |
| Thorndon, U.K. | 25 B11 | 52 17N | 1 9 E |
| Thorne, U.K. | 23 E7 | 53 37N | 0 57W |
| Thorney, U.K. | 23 G8 | 52 37N | 0 6W |
| Thornham, U.K. | 25 A10 | 52 58N | 0 35 E |
| Thornthwaite, U.K. | 22 C2 | 54 37N | 3 13W |
| Thornton, U.K. | 23 E3 | 53 52N | 2 59W |
| Thornton Dale, U.K. | 22 D7 | 54 15N | 0 42W |
| Thorpe, U.K. | 25 A11 | 52 38N | 1 22 E |
| Thorpe le Soken, U.K. | 25 C11 | 51 51N | 1 11 E |
| Thrapston, U.K. | 23 H7 | 52 24N | 0 32W |
| Threlkeld, U.K. | 22 C2 | 54 37N | 3 3W |
| Threshfield, U.K. | 22 D4 | 54 4N | 2 1W |
| Thunder B., U.S.A. | 112 C6 | 45 0N | 83 20W |
| Thunder Bay, Canada | 109 D11 | 48 20N | 89 15W |
| Thüringer Wald, Germany | 66 C6 | 50 35N | 11 0 E |
| Thurlby, U.K. | 23 G8 | 52 45N | 0 22W |
| Thurles, Ireland | 30 C7 | 52 41N | 7 49W |
| Thurmaston, U.K. | 23 G6 | 52 40N | 1 5W |
| Thursby, U.K. | 22 C2 | 54 51N | 3 2W |
| Thurso, Canada | 112 C8 | 45 36N | 75 15W |
| Thurso, U.K. | 19 E10 | 58 36N | 3 32W |
| Thurso →, U.K. | 19 E10 | 58 36N | 3 32W |
| Tian Shan, Asia | 80 B3 | 40 30N | 76 0 E |
| Tianjin, China | 81 C6 | 39 8N | 117 10 E |
| Tianshui, China | 80 C5 | 34 32N | 105 40 E |
| Tiaret, Algeria | 94 A6 | 35 20N | 1 21 E |
| Tiber →, Italy | 70 D5 | 41 44N | 12 14 E |
| Tiberias, L. = Galilee, Sea of, Israel | 86 C3 | 32 45N | 35 35 E |
| Tibesti, Chad | 95 D9 | 21 0N | 17 30 E |
| Tibet □, China | 80 C3 | 32 0N | 88 0 E |
| Tibet, Plateau of, Asia | 74 F12 | 32 0N | 86 0 E |
| Tiburón, I., Mexico | 114 B2 | 29 0N | 112 30W |
| Ticehurst, U.K. | 25 D9 | 51 3N | 0 25 E |
| Ticino →, Italy | 68 D8 | 45 9N | 9 14 E |
| Tickhill, U.K. | 23 E6 | 53 26N | 1 6W |
| Ticonderoga, U.S.A. | 113 D11 | 43 51N | 73 26W |
| Tideswell, U.K. | 23 F5 | 53 17N | 1 47W |
| Tierra del Fuego, I. Gr. de, Argentina | 121 H3 | 54 0S | 69 0W |
| Tiffin, U.S.A. | 112 E6 | 41 7N | 83 11W |
| Tighina, Moldova | 73 E4 | 46 50N | 29 30 E |
| Tignish, Canada | 113 B15 | 46 58N | 64 2W |
| Tigris →, Asia | 86 D6 | 31 0N | 47 25 E |
| Tijuana, Mexico | 114 A1 | 32 30N | 117 10W |
| Tikhoretsk, Russia | 73 E7 | 45 56N | 40 5 E |
| Tikhvin, Russia | 72 C5 | 59 35N | 33 30 E |
| Tikrīt, Iraq | 86 C5 | 34 35N | 43 37 E |
| Tiksi, Russia | 79 B14 | 71 40N | 128 45 E |
| Tilburg, Neths. | 65 C5 | 51 31N | 5 6 E |
| Tilbury, U.K. | 25 D9 | 51 27N | 0 22 E |
| Till →, U.K. | 22 A4 | 55 41N | 2 13W |
| Tillmanstone, U.K. | 25 D11 | 51 12N | 1 18 E |
| Tilt →, U.K. | 19 J10 | 56 46N | 3 51W |
| Timaru, N.Z. | 99 J13 | 44 23S | 171 14 E |
| Timișoara, Romania | 67 F11 | 45 43N | 21 15 E |
| Timmins, Canada | 109 D11 | 48 28N | 81 25W |
| Timor, Indonesia | 83 D4 | 9 0S | 125 0 E |
| Timor Leste = East Timor ■, Asia | 83 D4 | 8 50S | 126 0 E |
| Timor Sea, Ind. Oc. | 83 E4 | 12 0S | 127 0 E |
| Tingewick, U.K. | 24 C6 | 51 59N | 1 2W |
| Tinogasta, Argentina | 121 E3 | 28 5S | 67 32W |
| Tintagel, U.K. | 27 F4 | 50 39N | 4 46W |
| Tintagel Hd., U.K. | 27 F4 | 50 40N | 4 47W |
| Tipperary, Ireland | 30 D6 | 52 28N | 8 10W |
| Tipperary □, Ireland | 30 C7 | 52 37N | 7 55W |
| Tipton, U.K. | 23 G4 | 52 32N | 2 4W |
| Tiptree, U.K. | 25 C10 | 51 48N | 0 46 E |
| Tirana, Albania | 71 D8 | 41 18N | 19 49 E |
| Tiraspol, Moldova | 67 E15 | 46 55N | 29 35 E |
| Tirebolu, Turkey | 73 F6 | 40 58N | 38 45 E |
| Tiree, U.K. | 20 A3 | 56 31N | 6 55W |
| Tiree, Passage of, U.K. | 20 B2 | 56 30N | 6 30W |
| Tirich Mir, Pakistan | 84 A7 | 36 15N | 71 55 E |
| Tirol □, Austria | 66 E6 | 47 3N | 10 43 E |
| Tiruchchirappalli, India | 84 P11 | 10 45N | 78 45 E |
| Tirunelveli, India | 84 Q10 | 8 45N | 77 45 E |
| Tiruppur, India | 84 P10 | 11 5N | 77 22 E |
| Tisa →, Serbia & M. | 71 B9 | 45 15N | 20 17 E |
| Tisbury, U.K. | 24 D4 | 51 4N | 2 5W |
| Tisdale, Canada | 108 C9 | 52 50N | 104 0W |
| Titchfield, U.K. | 24 E6 | 50 50N | 1 15W |
| Titicaca, L., S. Amer. | 120 D3 | 15 30S | 69 30W |
| Titusville, U.S.A. | 112 E8 | 41 38N | 79 41W |
| Tiverton, U.K. | 24 E2 | 50 54N | 3 29W |
| Tizi-Ouzou, Algeria | 94 A6 | 36 42N | 4 3 E |
| Tlaxiaco, Mexico | 114 D5 | 17 18N | 97 40W |
| Tlemcen, Algeria | 94 B5 | 34 52N | 1 21W |
| Toamasina, Madag. | 97 H9 | 18 10S | 49 25 E |
| Toba, Danau, Indonesia | 83 C1 | 2 30N | 97 30 E |
| Tobago, Trin. & Tob. | 120 A3 | 11 10N | 60 30W |
| Tobermory, Canada | 112 C7 | 45 12N | 81 40W |
| Tobermory, U.K. | 18 J5 | 56 38N | 6 5W |
| Tocantins →, Brazil | 120 C5 | 1 45S | 49 10W |
| Toddington, U.K. | 25 C7 | 51 57N | 0 32W |
| Todmorden, U.K. | 23 E4 | 53 43N | 2 6W |
| Todos os Santos, B. de, Brazil | 122 B3 | 12 48S | 38 38W |
| Toe Hd., U.K. | 18 G3 | 57 50N | 7 8W |
| Togliatti, Russia | 72 D8 | 53 32N | 49 24 E |
| Togo ■, W. Afr. | 94 G6 | 8 30N | 1 35 E |
| Tok, U.S.A. | 108 B5 | 63 20N | 142 59W |
| Tokat, Turkey | 73 F6 | 40 22N | 36 35 E |
| Tokelau Is., Pac. Oc. | 99 B16 | 9 0S | 171 45W |
| Tokushima, Japan | 82 F4 | 34 4N | 134 34 E |
| Tokuyama, Japan | 82 F2 | 34 3N | 131 50 E |
| Tōkyō, Japan | 82 F6 | 35 45N | 139 45 E |
| Toledo, Spain | 69 C3 | 39 50N | 4 2W |
| Toledo, U.S.A. | 112 E6 | 41 39N | 83 33W |
| Toliara, Madag. | 97 J8 | 23 21S | 43 40 E |
| Tolima, Colombia | 120 B2 | 4 40N | 75 19W |
| Tollesbury, U.K. | 25 C10 | 51 45N | 0 51 E |
| Toluca, Mexico | 114 D5 | 19 20N | 99 40W |
| Tomakomai, Japan | 82 B7 | 42 38N | 141 36 E |
| Tomaszów Mazowiecki, Poland | 67 C10 | 51 30N | 20 2 E |
| Tombador, Serra do, Brazil | 120 D4 | 12 0S | 58 0W |
| Tombigbee →, U.S.A. | 111 D9 | 31 8N | 87 57W |
| Tombouctou, Mali | 94 E5 | 16 50N | 3 0W |
| Tomintoul, U.K. | 19 H11 | 57 15N | 3 23W |
| Tomsk, Russia | 79 D10 | 56 30N | 85 5 E |
| Tonbridge, U.K. | 25 D9 | 51 11N | 0 17 E |
| Tone →, U.K. | 24 E2 | 50 58N | 3 20W |
| Tong, U.K. | 23 G4 | 52 40N | 2 18W |
| Tonga ■, Pac. Oc. | 99 D16 | 19 50S | 174 30W |
| Tonga Trench, Pac. Oc. | 99 D16 | 18 0S | 173 0W |
| Tongareva, Cook Is. | 103 H12 | 9 0S | 158 0W |
| Tongatapu Group, Tonga | 99 E16 | 21 0S | 175 0W |
| Tongchuan, China | 81 C5 | 35 6N | 109 3 E |
| Tonghua, China | 81 B7 | 41 42N | 125 58 E |
| Tongue, U.K. | 19 F9 | 58 29N | 4 25W |
| Tongue →, U.S.A. | 110 A5 | 46 25N | 105 52W |
| Tonk, India | 84 F9 | 26 6N | 75 54 E |
| Tonkin, G. of, Asia | 81 D5 | 20 0N | 108 0 E |
| Tonle Sap, Cambodia | 83 B2 | 13 0N | 104 0 E |
| Tonopah, U.S.A. | 110 C3 | 38 4N | 117 14W |
| Toowoomba, Australia | 98 F9 | 27 32S | 151 56 E |
| Topeka, U.S.A. | 111 C7 | 39 3N | 95 40W |
| Topolobampo, Mexico | 114 B3 | 25 40N | 109 4W |
| Topsham, U.K. | 24 E2 | 50 41N | 3 28W |
| Tor B., U.K. | 27 G6 | 50 25N | 3 33W |
| Torbay □, U.K. | 27 G6 | 50 26N | 3 31W |
| Torne →, Sweden | 63 D8 | 65 50N | 24 12 E |
| Torneträsk, Sweden | 63 D7 | 68 24N | 19 15 E |
| Tornio, Finland | 63 D8 | 65 50N | 24 12 E |
| Toro, Cerro del, Chile | 121 E3 | 29 10S | 69 50W |
| Toronto, Canada | 109 D12 | 43 39N | 79 20W |
| Torpoint, U.K. | 27 G5 | 50 23N | 4 13W |
| Torquay, U.K. | 27 G6 | 50 27N | 3 32W |
| Torre del Greco, Italy | 70 D6 | 40 47N | 14 22 E |
| Torrens, L., Australia | 98 G6 | 31 0S | 137 50 E |
| Torreón, Mexico | 114 B4 | 25 33N | 103 26W |
| Torres Strait, Australia | 98 C7 | 9 50S | 142 20 E |
| Torridge →, U.K. | 27 E5 | 51 0N | 4 13W |
| Torridon, L., U.K. | 18 G6 | 57 35N | 5 50W |
| Torthorwald, U.K. | 22 B1 | 55 6N | 3 32W |
| Tortola, Br. Virgin Is. | 115 e | 18 19N | 64 45W |
| Tortosa, Spain | 69 B6 | 40 49N | 0 31 E |
| Toruń, Poland | 67 B10 | 53 2N | 18 39 E |
| Torver, U.K. | 22 D2 | 54 20N | 3 6W |
| Tory I., Ireland | 28 A5 | 55 16N | 8 14W |
| Totland, U.K. | 24 E5 | 50 41N | 1 32W |
| Totley, U.K. | 23 F5 | 53 20N | 1 32W |
| Totnes, U.K. | 27 G6 | 50 26N | 3 42W |
| Totton, U.K. | 24 E6 | 50 55N | 1 29W |
| Tottori, Japan | 82 F4 | 35 30N | 134 15 E |
| Toubkal, Djebel, Morocco | 94 B4 | 31 0N | 8 0W |
| Touggourt, Algeria | 94 B7 | 33 6N | 6 4 E |
| Toul, France | 68 B6 | 48 40N | 5 53 E |
| Toulon, France | 68 E6 | 43 10N | 5 55 E |
| Toulouse, France | 68 E4 | 43 37N | 1 27 E |
| Touraine, France | 68 C4 | 47 20N | 0 30 E |
| Tournai, Belgium | 65 D3 | 50 35N | 3 25 E |
| Tournon-sur-Rhône, France | 68 D6 | 45 4N | 4 50 E |
| Tours, France | 68 C4 | 47 22N | 0 40 E |
| Towanda, U.S.A. | 112 E9 | 41 46N | 76 27W |
| Towcester, U.K. | 25 B7 | 52 8N | 0 59W |
| Town Yetholm, U.K. | 22 A4 | 55 33N | 2 17W |
| Townsville, Australia | 98 D8 | 19 15S | 146 45 E |
| Towraghondi, Afghan. | 84 B3 | 35 13N | 62 16 E |
| Towson, U.S.A. | 112 F9 | 39 24N | 76 36W |
| Toyama, Japan | 82 E5 | 36 40N | 137 15 E |
| Toyohashi, Japan | 82 F5 | 34 45N | 137 25 E |
| Toyota, Japan | 82 F5 | 35 3N | 137 7 E |
| Trabzon, Turkey | 73 F6 | 41 0N | 39 45 E |
| Trafalgar, C., Spain | 69 D2 | 36 10N | 6 2W |
| Trail, Canada | 108 D8 | 49 5N | 117 40W |
| Tralee, Ireland | 30 D3 | 52 16N | 9 42W |
| Tralee B., Ireland | 30 D3 | 52 17N | 9 55W |
| Tramore, Ireland | 31 D8 | 52 10N | 7 10W |
| Tramore B., Ireland | 31 D8 | 52 9N | 7 10W |
| Trang, Thailand | 83 C1 | 7 33N | 99 38 E |
| Transantarctic Mts., Antarctica | 55 E12 | 85 0S | 170 0W |
| Transylvania, Romania | 67 E12 | 46 30N | 24 0 E |
| Transylvanian Alps, Romania | 67 F13 | 45 30N | 25 0 E |
| Trápani, Italy | 70 E5 | 38 1N | 12 29 E |
| Traverse City, U.S.A. | 112 C5 | 44 46N | 85 38W |
| Trawsfynydd, U.K. | 26 B6 | 52 54N | 3 55W |
| Tredegar, U.K. | 24 C2 | 51 47N | 3 14W |
| Tregaron, U.K. | 24 B1 | 52 14N | 3 56W |
| Treinta y Tres, Uruguay | 121 F4 | 33 16S | 54 17W |
| Trelew, Argentina | 121 G3 | 43 10S | 65 20W |
| Trent →, U.K. | 23 E7 | 53 41N | 0 42W |
| Trentham, U.K. | 23 G4 | 52 58N | 2 11W |
| Trento, Italy | 70 A4 | 46 4N | 11 8 E |
| Trenton, U.S.A. | 113 E10 | 40 14N | 74 46W |
| Tres Arroyos, Argentina | 121 F3 | 38 26S | 60 20W |
| Três Corações, Brazil | 122 D1 | 21 44S | 45 15W |
| Três Lagoas, Brazil | 120 E4 | 20 50S | 51 43W |
| Três Pontas, Brazil | 122 D1 | 21 23S | 45 29W |
| Tres Puntas, C., Argentina | 121 G3 | 47 0S | 66 0W |
| Três Rios, Brazil | 122 D2 | 22 6S | 43 15W |
| Tresco, U.K. | 27 H1 | 49 57N | 6 20W |
| Trevose Hd., U.K. | 27 F3 | 50 32N | 5 3W |
| Tribal Areas □, Pakistan | 84 C7 | 33 0N | 70 0 E |
| Trichur, India | 84 P10 | 10 30N | 76 18 E |
| Trier, Germany | 66 D4 | 49 45N | 6 38 E |
| Trieste, Italy | 70 B5 | 45 40N | 13 46 E |
| Trim, Ireland | 29 D8 | 53 33N | 6 48W |
| Trimdon, U.K. | 22 C6 | 54 42N | 1 24W |
| Trimley, U.K. | 25 C11 | 51 59N | 1 20 E |
| Trincomalee, Sri Lanka | 84 Q12 | 8 38N | 81 15 E |
| Trindade, I., Atl. Oc. | 52 F8 | 20 20S | 29 50W |
| Trinidad, Bolivia | 120 D3 | 14 46S | 64 50W |
| Trinidad, Cuba | 115 C9 | 21 48N | 80 0W |
| Trinidad, Trin. & Tob. | 115 E12 | 10 30N | 61 15W |
| Trinidad, U.S.A. | 110 C6 | 37 10N | 104 31W |
| Trinidad & Tobago ■, W. Indies | 115 E12 | 10 30N | 61 20W |
| Trinity →, U.S.A. | 111 E8 | 29 45N | 94 43W |
| Trinity B., Canada | 109 D14 | 48 20N | 53 10W |
| Trinity Is., U.S.A. | 108 C4 | 56 33N | 154 25W |
| Tripoli, Lebanon | 86 C3 | 34 31N | 35 50 E |
| Tripoli, Libya | 95 B8 | 32 49N | 13 7 E |
| Tripolitania, N. Afr. | 95 B8 | 31 0N | 13 0 E |
| Tripura □, India | 85 H18 | 24 0N | 92 0 E |
| Tristan da Cunha, Atl. Oc. | 52 F9 | 37 6S | 12 20W |
| Trivandrum, India | 84 Q10 | 8 41N | 77 0 E |
| Trnava, Slovak Rep. | 67 D9 | 48 23N | 17 35 E |
| Trois-Rivières, Canada | 109 D12 | 46 25N | 72 34W |
| Trois-Rivières, Guadeloupe | 114 b | 15 57N | 61 40W |
| Trollhättan, Sweden | 63 F6 | 58 17N | 12 20 E |
| Trombetas →, Brazil | 120 C4 | 1 55S | 55 35W |
| Tromsø, Norway | 63 D7 | 69 40N | 18 56 E |
| Tronador, Mte., Argentina | 121 G2 | 41 10S | 71 50W |
| Trondheim, Norway | 63 E6 | 63 36N | 10 25 E |
| Trondheimsfjorden, Norway | 63 E6 | 63 35N | 10 30 E |
| Troon, U.K. | 20 C6 | 55 33N | 4 39W |
| Trostan, U.K. | 29 A9 | 55 3N | 6 10W |
| Trou Gras Pt., St. Lucia | 115 f | 13 54N | 60 53W |
| Trout L., N.W.T., Canada | 108 B7 | 60 40N | 121 14W |
| Trout L., Ont., Canada | 108 C10 | 51 20N | 93 15W |
| Trowbridge, U.K. | 24 D4 | 51 18N | 2 12W |
| Troy, Turkey | 73 G4 | 39 57N | 26 12 E |
| Troy, Ala., U.S.A. | 111 D9 | 31 48N | 85 58W |
| Troy, N.Y., U.S.A. | 113 D11 | 42 44N | 73 41W |
| Troy, Ohio, U.S.A. | 112 E5 | 40 2N | 84 12W |
| Troyes, France | 68 B6 | 48 19N | 4 3 E |
| Trujillo, Honduras | 114 D7 | 16 0N | 86 0W |
| Trujillo, Peru | 120 C2 | 8 6S | 79 0W |
| Trujillo, Venezuela | 120 B2 | 9 22N | 70 38W |
| Truk, Micronesia | 102 G7 | 7 25N | 151 46 E |
| Trull, U.K. | 24 E2 | 51 0N | 3 6W |
| Trumpington, U.K. | 25 B9 | 52 10N | 0 6 E |
| Truro, Canada | 109 D13 | 45 21N | 63 14W |
| Truro, U.K. | 27 G3 | 50 16N | 5 4W |
| Tsetserleg, Mongolia | 80 B5 | 47 36N | 101 32 E |
| Tsiigehtchic, Canada | 108 B6 | 67 15N | 134 0W |
| Tsimlyansk Res., Russia | 73 E7 | 48 0N | 43 0 E |
| Tskhinvali, Georgia | 73 F7 | 42 14N | 44 1 E |
| Tsugaru Str., Japan | 82 C7 | 41 35N | 141 0 E |
| Tsumeb, Namibia | 97 H3 | 19 9S | 17 44 E |
| Tsuruoka, Japan | 82 D6 | 38 44N | 139 50 E |
| Tsushima, Japan | 82 F1 | 34 20N | 129 20 E |
| Tuam, Ireland | 28 D4 | 53 31N | 8 51W |
| Tuamotu Arch., Pac. Oc. | 103 J13 | 17 0S | 144 0W |
| Tuamotu Ridge, Pac. Oc. | 103 K14 | 20 0S | 138 0W |
| Tuapse, Russia | 73 F6 | 44 5N | 39 10 E |
| Tubarão, Brazil | 121 E5 | 28 30S | 49 0W |
| Tubruq, Libya | 95 B10 | 32 7N | 23 55 E |
| Tubuai Is., Pac. Oc. | 103 K13 | 25 0S | 150 0W |
| Tucson, U.S.A. | 110 D4 | 32 13N | 110 58W |
| Tucumcari, U.S.A. | 110 C6 | 35 10N | 103 44W |
| Tucupita, Venezuela | 120 B3 | 9 2N | 62 3W |
| Tucuruí, Brazil | 120 C5 | 3 42S | 49 44W |
| Tuktoyaktuk, Canada | 108 B6 | 69 27N | 133 2W |
| Tula, Russia | 72 D6 | 54 13N | 37 38 E |
| Tulancingo, Mexico | 114 C5 | 20 5N | 98 22W |
| Tulare, U.S.A. | 110 C3 | 36 13N | 119 21W |
| Tulcán, Ecuador | 120 B2 | 0 48N | 77 43W |
| Tulcea, Romania | 67 F15 | 45 13N | 28 46 E |
| Tulita, Canada | 108 B7 | 64 57N | 125 30W |
| Tulla, Ireland | 30 C5 | 52 53N | 8 46W |
| Tullamore, Ireland | 31 B7 | 53 16N | 7 31W |
| Tulle, France | 68 D4 | 45 16N | 1 46 E |
| Tullow, Ireland | 31 C9 | 52 49N | 6 45W |
| Tulsa, U.S.A. | 111 C7 | 36 10N | 95 55W |
| Tumaco, Colombia | 120 B2 | 1 50N | 78 45W |
| Tumbes, Peru | 120 C1 | 3 37S | 80 27W |
| Tumucumaque, Serra, Brazil | 120 B4 | 2 0N | 55 0W |
| Tunis, Tunisia | 94 A7 | 36 50N | 10 11 E |
| Tunisia ■, Africa | 94 B6 | 33 30N | 9 10 E |
| Tunja, Colombia | 120 B2 | 5 33N | 73 25W |
| Tunstall, U.K. | 25 B11 | 52 9N | 1 27 E |
| Tupelo, U.S.A. | 111 D9 | 34 16N | 88 43W |
| Tupiza, Bolivia | 120 E3 | 21 30S | 65 40W |
| Turfan Depression, China | 74 E12 | 42 40N | 89 25 E |
| Turgutlu, Turkey | 73 G4 | 38 30N | 27 43 E |
| Turin, Italy | 68 D7 | 45 3N | 7 40 E |
| Turkana, L., Africa | 96 D7 | 3 30N | 36 5 E |
| Turkey ■, Eurasia | 73 G6 | 39 0N | 36 0 E |
| Türkmenbashi, Turkmenistan | 73 G9 | 40 5N | 53 5 E |
| Turkmenistan ■, Asia | 79 F7 | 39 0N | 59 0 E |
| Turks & Caicos Is. □, W. Indies | 115 C10 | 21 20N | 71 20W |
| Turku, Finland | 63 E8 | 60 30N | 22 19 E |
| Turnberry, U.K. | 20 D6 | 55 18N | 4 49W |
| Turneffe Is., Belize | 114 D7 | 17 20N | 87 50W |
| Turpan, China | 80 B3 | 43 58N | 89 10 E |
| Turriff, U.K. | 19 G13 | 57 32N | 2 27W |
| Tuscaloosa, U.S.A. | 111 D9 | 33 12N | 87 34W |
| Tuscany = Toscana □, Italy | 70 C4 | 43 25N | 11 0 E |
| Tutbury, U.K. | 23 G5 | 52 51N | 1 41W |
| Tuticorin, India | 84 Q11 | 8 50N | 78 12 E |
| Tutuila, Amer. Samoa | 99 C16 | 14 19S | 170 50W |
| Tutume, Botswana | 97 J5 | 20 30S | 27 5 E |
| Tuvalu ■, Pac. Oc. | 99 B14 | 8 0S | 178 0 E |
| Tuxford, U.K. | 23 F7 | 53 14N | 0 54W |
| Tuxpan, Mexico | 114 C5 | 20 58N | 97 23W |
| Tuxtla Gutiérrez, Mexico | 114 D6 | 16 50N | 93 10W |
| Tuz Gölü, Turkey | 73 G5 | 38 42N | 33 18 E |
| Tuzla, Bos.-H. | 71 B8 | 44 34N | 18 41 E |
| Tver, Russia | 72 C6 | 56 55N | 35 55 E |
| Tweed →, U.K. | 21 C11 | 55 45N | 2 0W |
| Tweedmouth, U.K. | 22 A5 | 55 45N | 2 0W |
| Tweedshaws, U.K. | 22 B2 | 55 26N | 3 29W |
| Twenty, U.K. | 23 G8 | 52 47N | 0 17W |
| Twin Falls, U.S.A. | 110 B4 | 42 34N | 114 28W |
| Two Harbors, U.S.A. | 111 A8 | 47 2N | 91 40W |
| Two Rivers, U.S.A. | 112 C4 | 44 9N | 87 34W |

**Twyford**

Twyford, Hants., U.K. ... 24 D6 51 1N 1 19W
Twyford, Wokingham, U.K. ... 25 D7 51 28N 0 51W
Tychy, Poland ... 67 C10 50 9N 18 59 E
Tydd St. Mary, U.K. ... 23 G9 52 45N 0 7 E
Tyler, U.S.A. ... 111 D7 32 21N 95 18W
Tyne →, U.K. ... 22 C5 54 59N 1 32W
Tyne & Wear □, U.K. ... 22 B6 55 6N 1 17W
Tynemouth, U.K. ... 22 B6 55 1N 1 26W
Tyrol = Tirol □, Austria ... 66 E6 47 3N 10 43 E
Tyrone □, U.K. ... 29 B7 54 38N 7 11W
Tyrrhenian Sea, Medit. S. ... 70 E5 40 0N 12 30 E
Tyumen, Russia ... 79 D8 57 11N 65 29 E
Tywardreath, U.K. ... 27 G4 50 21N 4 42W
Tywi →, U.K. ... 26 D5 51 48N 4 21W
Tywyn, U.K. ... 26 B5 52 35N 4 5W
Tzaneen, S. Africa ... 97 J6 23 47S 30 9 E

# U

U.S.A. = United States of America ■, N. Amer. ... 110 C7 37 0N 96 0W
U.S. Virgin Is. ☑, W. Indies ... 115 e 18 20N 65 0W
Uaupés →, Brazil ... 120 B3 0 8N 67 16W
Ubá, Brazil ... 122 D2 21 8S 43 0W
Ubaitaba, Brazil ... 122 B3 14 18S 39 20W
Ube, Japan ... 82 G2 33 56N 131 15 E
Uberaba, Brazil ... 122 C1 19 50S 47 55W
Uberlândia, Brazil ... 122 C1 19 0S 48 20W
Ubon Ratchathani, Thailand ... 83 B2 15 15N 104 50 E
Ucayali →, Peru ... 120 C2 4 30S 73 30W
Uckfield, U.K. ... 25 E9 50 58N 0 7 E
Udagamandalam, India ... 84 P10 11 30N 76 44 E
Udaipur, India ... 84 G8 24 36N 73 44 E
Udine, Italy ... 70 A5 46 3N 13 14 E
Udmurtia □, Russia ... 72 C9 57 30N 52 30 E
Udon Thani, Thailand ... 83 B2 17 29N 102 46 E
Udupi, India ... 84 N9 13 25N 74 42 E
Uele →, Dem. Rep. of the Congo ... 96 D4 3 45N 24 45 E
Ufa, Russia ... 72 D10 54 45N 55 55 E
Uffculme, U.K. ... 24 E2 50 54N 3 20W
Ufford, U.K. ... 25 B11 52 8N 1 23 E
Uganda ■, Africa ... 96 D6 2 0N 32 0 E
Ugborough, U.K. ... 27 G6 50 22N 3 53W
Uig, U.K. ... 18 G5 57 35N 6 21W
Uinta Mts., U.S.A. ... 110 B4 40 45N 110 30W
Uitenhage, S. Africa ... 97 L5 33 40S 25 28 E
Ujjain, India ... 84 H9 23 9N 75 43 E
Ujung Pandang, Indonesia ... 83 D3 5 10S 119 20 E
Ukhta, Russia ... 72 B9 63 34N 53 41 E
Ukiah, U.S.A. ... 110 C2 39 9N 123 13W
Ukraine ■, Europe ... 73 E5 49 0N 32 0 E
Ulaangom, Mongolia ... 80 A4 50 5N 92 10 E
Ulaanjirem, Mongolia ... 80 B5 45 5N 105 30 E
Ulan Bator, Mongolia ... 80 B5 47 55N 106 53 E
Ulan Ude, Russia ... 79 D12 51 45N 107 40 E
Ulceby Cross, U.K. ... 23 F9 53 15N 0 7 E
Ulhasnagar, India ... 84 K8 19 15N 73 10 E
Ullapool, U.K. ... 18 G7 57 54N 5 9W
Ullswater, U.K. ... 22 C3 54 34N 2 52W
Ulm, Germany ... 66 D5 48 23N 9 58 E
Ulster □, U.K. ... 29 B7 54 35N 6 30W
Ulungur He →, China ... 80 B3 47 1N 87 24 E
Ulva, U.K. ... 20 B3 56 29N 6 13W
Ulverston, U.K. ... 22 D2 54 13N 3 5W
Ulyasutay, Mongolia ... 80 B4 47 56N 97 28 E
Uman, Ukraine ... 73 E5 48 40N 30 12 E
Ume älv →, Sweden ... 63 E8 63 45N 20 20 E
Umeå, Sweden ... 63 E8 63 45N 20 20 E
Umlazi, S. Africa ... 97 L6 29 59S 30 54 E
Umnak I., U.S.A. ... 108 C3 53 15N 168 20W
Umtata, S. Africa ... 97 L5 31 36S 28 49 E
Umuarama, Brazil ... 121 E4 23 45S 53 20W
Unalakleet, U.S.A. ... 108 B3 63 52N 160 47W
Unalaska, U.S.A. ... 108 C3 53 53N 166 32W
Unalaska I., U.S.A. ... 108 C3 53 35N 166 50W
Uncía, Bolivia ... 120 D3 18 25S 66 40W
Ungava, Pén. d', Canada ... 109 C12 60 0N 74 0W
Ungava B., Canada ... 109 C13 59 30N 67 30W
Unimak I., U.S.A. ... 108 C3 54 45N 164 0W
Uniontown, U.S.A. ... 112 F8 39 54N 79 44W
United Arab Emirates ■, Asia ... 87 F8 23 50N 54 0 E
United Kingdom ■, Europe ... 64 E6 53 0N 2 0W
United States of America ■, N. Amer. ... 110 C7 37 0N 96 0W
Unst, U.K. ... 18 A16 60 44N 0 53W
Upavon, U.K. ... 24 D5 51 18N 1 48W
Upington, S. Africa ... 97 K4 28 25S 21 15 E
'Upolu, Samoa ... 99 C16 13 58S 172 0W
Upper Heyford, U.K. ... 24 C6 51 56N 1 15W
Upper Klamath L., U.S.A. ... 110 B2 42 25N 121 55W
Upper Red L., U.S.A. ... 111 A8 48 8N 94 45W
Uppingham, U.K. ... 23 G7 52 36N 0 43W
Uppsala, Sweden ... 63 F7 59 53N 17 38 E
Upton, U.K. ... 23 F3 53 13N 2 53W
Upton-upon-Severn, U.K. ... 24 B4 52 3N 2 12W
Upwey, U.K. ... 24 E4 50 39N 2 29W
Ur, Iraq ... 86 D6 30 55N 46 25 E
Ural →, Kazakhstan ... 73 E9 47 0N 51 48 E
Ural Mts., Eurasia ... 72 C10 60 0N 59 0 E
Uranium City, Canada ... 108 C9 59 34N 108 37W
Uraricoera →, Brazil ... 120 B3 3 2N 60 30W
Urbana, Ill., U.S.A. ... 112 E3 40 7N 88 12W
Urbana, Ohio, U.S.A. ... 112 E6 40 7N 83 45W
Ure →, U.K. ... 22 D5 54 5N 1 20W
Urganch, Uzbekistan ... 87 A10 41 40N 60 41 E
Urmia, Iran ... 86 B6 37 40N 45 0 E
Urmia, L., Iran ... 86 B6 37 50N 45 30 E
Urmston, U.K. ... 23 F4 53 27N 2 21W
Uroyan, Mts. de, Puerto Rico ... 115 d 18 12N 67 0W
Uruaçu, Brazil ... 122 D1 14 30S 49 10W
Uruapan, Mexico ... 114 D4 19 30N 102 0W
Urubamba →, Peru ... 120 D2 10 43S 73 48W
Uruguai →, Brazil ... 121 E4 26 0S 53 30W
Uruguaiana, Brazil ... 121 E4 29 50S 57 0W
Uruguay ■, S. Amer. ... 121 F4 32 30S 56 30W
Uruguay →, S. Amer. ... 116 G5 34 12S 58 18W
Ürümqi, China ... 80 B3 43 45N 87 45 E
Usa →, U.K. ... 72 A10 66 16N 59 49 E
Uşak, Turkey ... 73 G4 38 43N 29 28 E
Usakos, Namibia ... 97 J3 21 54S 15 31 E
Ushant, France ... 68 B1 48 28N 5 6W
Ushuaia, Argentina ... 121 H3 54 50S 68 23W
Usk →, U.K. ... 24 C3 51 33N 2 58W
Üsküdar, Turkey ... 86 A2 41 0N 29 5 E
Uspallata, P. de, Argentina ... 121 F3 32 37S 69 22W
Usselby, U.K. ... 23 F8 53 26N 0 21W
Ussuriysk, Russia ... 82 B2 43 48N 131 59 E
Ust-Ilimsk, Russia ... 79 D12 58 3N 102 39 E
Ústí nad Labem, Czech Rep. ... 66 C8 50 41N 14 3 E
Ustyurt Plateau, Asia ... 79 E7 44 0N 55 0 E
Usu, China ... 80 B3 44 27N 84 40 E
Usumacinta →, Mexico ... 114 D6 17 0N 91 0W
Utah □, U.S.A. ... 110 C4 39 20N 111 30W
Utah L., U.S.A. ... 110 B4 40 10N 111 58W
Utica, U.S.A. ... 113 D10 43 6N 75 14W
Utrecht, Neths. ... 65 B5 52 5N 5 8 E
Utsunomiya, Japan ... 82 E6 36 30N 139 50 E
Uttar Pradesh □, India ... 84 F12 27 0N 80 0 E
Uttaradit, Thailand ... 83 B2 17 36N 100 5 E
Uttaranchal □, India ... 84 D11 30 0N 79 30 E
Uttoxeter, U.K. ... 23 G5 52 54N 1 52W
Utuado, Puerto Rico ... 115 d 18 16N 66 42W
Uusikaupunki, Finland ... 63 E8 60 47N 21 25 E
Uvalde, U.S.A. ... 110 E7 29 13N 99 47W
Uvs Nuur, Mongolia ... 80 A4 50 20N 92 30 E
Uyuni, Bolivia ... 120 E3 20 28S 66 47W
Uzbekistan ■, Asia ... 79 E8 41 30N 65 0 E
Uzhhorod, Ukraine ... 67 D12 48 36N 22 18 E

# V

Vaal →, S. Africa ... 97 K4 29 4S 23 38 E
Vaasa, Finland ... 63 E8 63 6N 21 38 E
Vadodara, India ... 84 H8 22 20N 73 10 E
Vadsø, Norway ... 63 C9 70 3N 29 50 E
Vaduz, Liech. ... 66 E5 47 8N 9 31 E
Vail, U.S.A. ... 110 C5 39 40N 106 20W
Val-d'Or, Canada ... 109 D12 48 7N 77 47W
Valahia, Romania ... 67 F13 44 35N 25 0 E
Valdai Hills, Russia ... 72 C5 57 0N 33 30 E
Valdés, Pen., Argentina ... 121 G3 42 30S 63 45W
Valdez, U.S.A. ... 108 B5 61 7N 146 16W
Valdivia, Chile ... 121 F2 39 50S 73 14W
Valdosta, U.S.A. ... 111 D10 30 50N 83 17W
Valença, Brazil ... 122 B3 13 20S 39 5W
Valence, France ... 68 D6 44 57N 4 54 E
Valencia, Spain ... 69 C5 39 27N 0 23W
Valencia, Venezuela ... 120 A3 10 11N 68 0W
Valencia I., Ireland ... 30 E2 51 54N 10 22W
Valenciennes, France ... 68 A5 50 20N 3 34 E
Valera, Venezuela ... 120 B2 9 19N 70 37W
Valladolid, Mexico ... 114 C7 20 40N 88 11W
Valladolid, Spain ... 69 B3 41 38N 4 43W
Vallejo, U.S.A. ... 110 C2 38 7N 122 14W
Vallenar, Chile ... 121 E2 28 30S 70 50W
Valletta, Malta ... 70 a 35 54N 14 31 E
Valley, U.K. ... 26 A4 53 16N 4 34W
Valley City, U.S.A. ... 110 A7 46 55N 98 0W
Valparaíso, Chile ... 121 F2 33 2S 71 40W
Van, Turkey ... 73 G7 38 30N 43 20 E
Van, L., Turkey ... 73 G7 38 30N 43 0 E
Van Buren, U.S.A. ... 113 B13 47 10N 67 58W
Van Wert, U.S.A. ... 112 E5 40 52N 84 35W
Vancouver, Canada ... 108 D7 49 15N 123 10W
Vancouver, U.S.A. ... 110 A2 45 38N 122 40W
Vancouver I., Canada ... 108 D7 49 50N 126 0W
Vanderhoof, Canada ... 108 C7 54 0N 124 0W
Vänern, Sweden ... 63 F6 58 47N 13 30 E
Vanino, Russia ... 79 E16 48 50N 140 5 E
Vännäs, Sweden ... 63 E7 63 58N 19 48 E
Vannes, France ... 68 C2 47 40N 2 47W
Vanrhynsdorp, S. Africa ... 97 L3 31 36S 18 44 E
Vanua Levu, Fiji ... 99 D14 16 33S 179 15 E
Vanuatu ■, Pac. Oc. ... 99 D12 15 0S 168 0 E
Varanasi, India ... 85 G13 25 22N 83 0 E
Varangerfjorden, Norway ... 63 C9 70 3N 29 25 E
Varberg, Sweden ... 63 F6 57 6N 12 20 E
Vardak □, Afghan. ... 87 C12 34 0N 68 0 E
Varginha, Brazil ... 122 D1 21 33S 45 25W
Varna, Bulgaria ... 71 C12 43 13N 27 56 E
Vasa Barris →, Brazil ... 122 B3 11 10S 37 10W
Västerås, Sweden ... 63 F7 59 37N 16 38 E
Västervik, Sweden ... 63 F7 57 43N 16 33 E
Vaté, Vanuatu ... 99 D12 17 40S 168 25 E
Vatersay, U.K. ... 18 J2 56 55N 7 32W
Vatican City ■, Europe ... 70 D5 41 54N 12 27 E
Vättern, Sweden ... 63 F6 58 25N 14 30 E
Vaughn, U.S.A. ... 110 D5 34 36N 105 13W
Vava'u Group, Tonga ... 99 D16 18 40S 174 0W
Vega, Norway ... 63 D6 65 40N 11 55 E
Vega Baja, Puerto Rico ... 115 d 18 27N 66 23W
Vegreville, Canada ... 108 C8 53 30N 112 5W
Velhas →, Brazil ... 122 C2 17 13S 44 49W
Velikiye Luki, Russia ... 72 C5 56 25N 30 32 E
Vellore, India ... 84 N11 12 57N 79 10 E
Velsk, Russia ... 72 B7 61 10N 42 5 E
Vendée □, France ... 68 C3 46 50N 1 35W
Vendôme, France ... 68 C4 47 47N 1 3 E
Venezuela ■, S. Amer. ... 120 B3 8 0N 66 0W
Venezuela, G. de, Venezuela ... 120 A2 11 30N 71 0W
Vengurla, India ... 84 M8 15 53N 73 45 E
Venice, Italy ... 70 B5 45 27N 12 21 E
Venlo, Neths. ... 65 C6 51 22N 6 11 E
Ventnor, U.K. ... 24 E6 50 36N 1 12W
Ventoux, Mt., France ... 68 D6 44 10N 5 17 E
Ventspils, Latvia ... 72 C3 57 25N 21 32 E
Veracruz, Mexico ... 114 D5 19 10N 96 10W
Veraval, India ... 84 J7 20 53N 70 27 E
Vercelli, Italy ... 68 D8 45 19N 8 25 E
Verde →, U.S.A. ... 110 D4 33 33N 111 40W
Verdun, France ... 68 B6 49 9N 5 24 E
Vereeniging, S. Africa ... 97 K5 26 38S 27 57 E
Verkhoyansk, Russia ... 79 C15 67 35N 133 25 E
Verkhoyansk Ra., Russia ... 79 C14 66 0N 129 0 E
Vermont □, U.S.A. ... 113 D11 44 0N 73 0W
Vernal, U.S.A. ... 110 B5 40 27N 109 32W
Vernon, Canada ... 108 C8 50 20N 119 15W
Vernon, U.S.A. ... 110 D7 34 9N 99 17W
Verona, Italy ... 70 B4 45 27N 10 59 E
Versailles, France ... 68 B5 48 48N 2 8 E
Vert, C., Senegal ... 94 F2 14 45N 17 30W
Verviers, Belgium ... 65 D5 50 37N 5 52 E
Verwood, U.K. ... 24 E5 50 53N 1 52W
Veryan, U.K. ... 27 G4 50 13N 4 56W
Veryan B., U.K. ... 27 G4 50 13N 4 51W
Vesoul, France ... 68 C7 47 40N 6 11 E
Vesterålen, Norway ... 63 D7 68 45N 15 0 E
Vestfjorden, Norway ... 63 D6 67 55N 14 0 E
Vesuvio, Italy ... 70 D6 40 49N 14 26 E
Veszprém, Hungary ... 67 E9 47 8N 17 57 E
Vianópolis, Brazil ... 122 C1 16 40S 48 35W
Vicenza, Italy ... 70 B4 45 33N 11 33 E
Vichada →, Colombia ... 120 B3 4 55N 67 50W
Vichy, France ... 68 C5 46 9N 3 26 E
Vickerstown, U.K. ... 22 D2 54 6N 3 15W
Vicksburg, U.S.A. ... 111 D8 32 21N 90 53W
Victoria, Canada ... 108 D7 48 30N 123 25W
Victoria, Chile ... 121 F2 38 13S 72 20W
Victoria □, Australia ... 98 H7 37 0S 144 0 E
Victoria, L., Africa ... 96 E6 1 0S 33 0 E
Victoria de las Tunas, Cuba ... 115 C9 20 58N 76 59W
Victoria Falls, Zimbabwe ... 97 H5 17 58S 25 52 E
Victoria I., Canada ... 108 A8 71 0N 111 0W
Victoria Ld., Antarctica ... 55 D11 75 0S 160 0 E
Victoria Str., Canada ... 108 B9 69 31N 100 30W
Victoriaville, Canada ... 113 B12 46 4N 71 56W
Viedma, L., Argentina ... 121 G2 49 30S 72 30W
Vienna, Austria ... 66 D9 48 12N 16 22 E
Vienne, France ... 68 D6 45 31N 4 53 E
Vienne →, France ... 68 C4 47 13N 0 5 E
Vientiane, Laos ... 83 B2 17 58N 102 36 E
Vieques, Isla de, Puerto Rico ... 115 d 18 8N 65 25W
Vierge Pt., St. Lucia ... 115 f 13 49N 60 53W
Vierzon, France ... 68 C5 47 13N 2 5 E
Vietnam ■, Asia ... 83 B2 19 0N 106 0 E
Vieux Fort, St. Lucia ... 115 f 13 46N 60 58W
Vigo, Spain ... 69 A1 42 12N 8 41W
Vijayawada, India ... 85 L12 16 31N 80 39 E
Vikna, Norway ... 63 E6 64 55N 10 58 E
Vila Velha, Brazil ... 122 D2 20 20S 40 17W
Vilaine →, France ... 68 C2 47 30N 2 27W
Vilhelmina, Sweden ... 63 E7 64 35N 16 39 E
Villa Bella, Bolivia ... 120 D3 10 25S 65 22W
Villa María, Argentina ... 121 F3 32 20S 63 10W
Villach, Austria ... 66 E7 46 37N 13 51 E
Villahermosa, Mexico ... 114 D6 17 59N 92 55W
Villarrica, Paraguay ... 121 E4 25 40S 56 30W
Villavicencio, Colombia ... 120 B2 4 9N 73 37W
Ville-Marie, Canada ... 112 B8 47 20N 79 30W
Villeneuve-sur-Lot, France ... 68 D4 44 24N 0 42 E
Vilnius, Lithuania ... 72 D4 54 38N 25 19 E
Viluy →, Russia ... 79 C14 64 24N 126 26 E
Vilyuysk, Russia ... 79 C14 63 40N 121 35 E
Viña del Mar, Chile ... 121 F2 33 0S 71 30W
Vincennes, U.S.A. ... 112 F4 38 41N 87 32W
Vindhya Ra., India ... 84 H10 22 50N 77 0 E
Vineland, U.S.A. ... 113 F10 39 29N 75 2W
Vinnytsya, Ukraine ... 67 D15 49 15N 28 30 E
Virden, Canada ... 108 D9 49 50N 100 56W
Vire, France ... 68 B3 48 50N 0 53W
Virgenes, C., Argentina ... 121 H3 52 19S 68 21W
Virgin →, U.S.A. ... 110 C4 36 28N 114 21W
Virgin Gorda, Br. Virgin Is. ... 115 e 18 30N 64 26W
Virgin Is. (British) ☑, W. Indies ... 115 e 18 30N 64 30W
Virgin Is. (U.S.) ☑, W. Indies ... 115 e 18 20N 65 0W
Virginia, U.S.A. ... 111 A8 47 31N 92 32W
Virginia □, U.S.A. ... 112 G8 37 30N 78 45W
Visalia, U.S.A. ... 110 C3 36 20N 119 18W
Visby, Sweden ... 63 F7 57 37N 18 18 E
Vishakhapatnam, India ... 85 L13 17 45N 83 20 E
Vistula →, Poland ... 67 A10 54 22N 18 55 E
Vitebsk, Belarus ... 72 C5 55 10N 30 15 E
Viterbo, Italy ... 70 C5 42 25N 12 6 E
Viti Levu, Fiji ... 99 D14 17 30S 177 30 E
Vitória, Brazil ... 122 D2 20 20S 40 22W
Vitória da Conquista, Brazil ... 122 B2 14 51S 40 51W
Vitoria-Gasteiz, Spain ... 69 A4 42 50N 2 41W
Vizianagaram, India ... 85 K13 18 6N 83 30 E
Vlaardingen, Neths. ... 65 C4 51 55N 4 21 E
Vladikavkaz, Russia ... 73 F7 43 0N 44 35 E
Vladimir, Russia ... 72 C7 56 15N 40 30 E
Vladivostok, Russia ... 79 E15 43 10N 131 53 E
Vlissingen, Neths. ... 65 C3 51 26N 3 34 E
Vlorë, Albania ... 71 D8 40 32N 19 28 E
Vltava →, Czech Rep. ... 66 D8 50 21N 14 30 E
Voe, U.K. ... 18 B15 60 21N 1 16W
Vogelkop, Indonesia ... 83 D5 1 25S 133 0 E
Vogelsberg, Germany ... 66 C5 50 31N 9 12 E
Vohimena, Tanjon' i, Madag. ... 97 K9 25 36S 45 8 E
Voi, Kenya ... 96 E7 3 25S 38 32 E
Vojvodina □, Serbia & M. ... 71 B9 45 20N 20 0 E
Volga →, Russia ... 73 E8 46 0N 48 30 E
Volga Hts., Russia ... 73 D8 51 0N 46 0 E
Volgodonsk, Russia ... 73 E7 47 33N 42 5 E
Volgograd, Russia ... 73 E7 48 40N 44 25 E
Vologda, Russia ... 72 C6 59 10N 39 45 E
Vólos, Greece ... 71 E10 39 24N 22 59 E
Volsk, Russia ... 72 D8 52 5N 47 22 E
Volta →, Ghana ... 94 G6 5 46N 0 41 E
Volta, L., Ghana ... 94 G6 7 30N 0 0W
Volta Redonda, Brazil ... 122 D2 22 31S 44 5W
Volzhskiy, Russia ... 73 E7 48 56N 44 46 E
Vorkuta, Russia ... 72 A11 67 48N 64 20 E
Voronezh, Russia ... 73 D6 51 40N 39 10 E
Vosges, France ... 68 B7 48 20N 7 10 E
Vostok I., Kiribati ... 103 J12 10 5S 152 23W
Votkinsk, Russia ... 72 C9 57 0N 53 55 E
Vryburg, S. Africa ... 97 K4 26 55S 24 45 E
Vryheid, S. Africa ... 97 K6 27 45S 30 47 E
Vung Tau, Vietnam ... 83 B2 10 21N 107 4 E
Vyazma, Russia ... 72 C5 55 10N 34 15 E
Vyborg, Russia ... 72 B4 60 43N 28 47 E
Vychegda →, Russia ... 72 B8 61 18N 46 36 E
Vyrnwy, L., U.K. ... 24 A1 52 48N 3 31W
Vyshniy Volochek, Russia ... 72 C5 57 30N 34 30 E

# W

Waal →, Neths. ... 65 C5 51 37N 5 0 E
Wabasca →, Canada ... 108 C8 58 22N 115 20W
Wabash, U.S.A. ... 112 E5 40 48N 85 49W
Wabash →, U.S.A. ... 112 G3 37 48N 88 2W
Waco, U.S.A. ... 111 D7 31 33N 97 9W
Wad Medani, Sudan ... 95 F12 14 28N 33 30 E
Waddenzee, Neths. ... 65 A5 53 6N 5 10 E
Waddesdon, U.K. ... 25 C7 51 51N 0 55W
Waddingham, U.K. ... 23 F7 53 27N 0 32W
Waddington, U.K. ... 23 F7 53 10N 0 31W
Waddington, Mt., Canada ... 108 C7 51 23N 125 15W
Wadebridge, U.K. ... 27 F4 50 31N 4 51W
Wadhurst, U.K. ... 25 D9 51 3N 0 20 E
Wadi Halfa, Sudan ... 95 D12 21 53N 31 19 E
Wager B., Canada ... 109 B11 65 26N 88 40W
Wagga Wagga, Australia ... 98 H8 35 7S 147 24 E
Wah, Pakistan ... 84 C8 33 45N 72 40 E
Wahiawa, U.S.A. ... 110 H15 21 30N 158 2W
Waigeo, Indonesia ... 83 D5 0 20S 130 40 E
Wailuku, U.S.A. ... 110 H16 20 53N 156 30W
Wainfleet All Saints, U.K. ... 23 F9 53 7N 0 15 E
Wake I., Pac. Oc. ... 102 F8 19 18N 166 36 E
Wakefield, Jamaica ... 114 a 18 26N 77 42W
Wakefield, U.K. ... 23 E6 53 41N 1 29W
Wakkanai, Japan ... 82 A7 45 28N 141 35 E
Walberswick, U.K. ... 25 B12 52 19N 1 40 E
Walbrzych, Poland ... 66 C9 50 45N 16 18 E
Walbury Hill, U.K. ... 24 D6 51 21N 1 28W
Walcheren, Neths. ... 65 C3 51 30N 3 35 E
Waldron, U.K. ... 25 E9 50 56N 0 13 E
Wales □, U.K. ... 26 C4 52 19N 4 43W
Walgett, Australia ... 98 G8 30 0S 148 5 E
Walker L., U.S.A. ... 110 C3 38 42N 118 43W
Walla Walla, U.S.A. ... 110 A3 46 4N 118 20W
Wallaceburg, Canada ... 112 D6 42 34N 82 23W
Wallachia = Valahia, Romania ... 67 F13 44 35N 25 0 E
Wallasey, U.K. ... 23 F2 53 25N 3 2W
Wallingford, U.K. ... 24 C6 51 35N 1 8W
Wallis & Futuna, Is., Pac. Oc. ... 99 C15 13 18S 176 10W
Walls, U.K. ... 18 B14 60 14N 1 33W
Wallsend, U.K. ... 22 C5 54 59N 1 31W
Walmer, U.K. ... 25 D11 51 11N 1 25 E
Walney, I. of, U.K. ... 22 D2 54 6N 3 15W
Walpole, U.K. ... 23 G9 52 45N 0 13 E
Walsall, U.K. ... 23 G5 52 35N 1 58W
Walsenburg, U.S.A. ... 110 C6 37 38N 104 47W
Walsham, U.K. ... 23 G9 52 41N 0 11 E
Waltham, U.S.A. ... 23 E8 53 3N 0 7W
Waltham Abbey, U.K. ... 25 C9 51 41N 0 1 E
Waltham Forest □, U.K. ... 25 C9 51 35N 0 0 E
Waltham on the Wolds, U.K. ... 23 G7 52 50N 0 48W
Walton-on-the-Naze, U.K. ... 25 C11 51 51N 1 17 E
Walvis Bay, Namibia ... 97 J2 23 0S 14 28 E
Wanborough, U.K. ... 24 C5 51 33N 1 42W
Wandsworth □, U.K. ... 25 D8 51 27N 0 11W
Wanganui, N.Z. ... 99 H14 39 56S 175 3 E
Wansbeck →, U.K. ... 22 B5 55 10N 1 32W
Wantage, U.K. ... 24 C6 51 35N 1 25W
Wapakoneta, U.S.A. ... 112 E5 40 34N 84 12W
Warangal, India ... 84 L11 17 58N 79 35 E
Warboys, U.K. ... 23 H8 52 24N 0 4W
Wardha, India ... 84 J11 20 45N 78 39 E
Wardington, U.K. ... 24 B6 52 7N 1 17W
Wardle, U.K. ... 23 F3 53 7N 2 35W
Ward's Stone, U.K. ... 23 D3 54 1N 2 36W
Ware, U.K. ... 25 C8 51 49N 0 0W
Wareham, U.K. ... 24 E4 50 42N 2 7W
Wark, U.K. ... 22 B4 55 6N 2 14W
Warkworth, U.K. ... 22 B5 55 21N 1 37W
Warley, U.K. ... 23 H5 52 30N 1 59W
Warminster, U.K. ... 24 D4 51 12N 2 10W
Warrego →, Australia ... 98 G8 30 24S 145 21 E
Warren, Mich., U.S.A. ... 112 D6 42 30N 83 0W
Warren, Ohio, U.S.A. ... 112 E7 41 14N 80 49W
Warren, Pa., U.S.A. ... 112 E8 41 51N 79 9W
Warrenpoint, U.K. ... 29 C9 54 6N 6 15W
Warrington, U.K. ... 23 F3 53 24N 2 35W
Warrnambool, Australia ... 98 H7 38 25S 142 30 E
Warsaw, Poland ... 67 B11 52 13N 21 0 E
Warsaw, U.S.A. ... 112 E5 41 14N 85 51W
Warsop, U.K. ... 23 F6 53 12N 1 9W
Warta →, Poland ... 66 B8 52 35N 14 39 E
Warwick, U.K. ... 23 H5 52 18N 1 35W
Warwick, U.S.A. ... 113 E12 41 42N 71 28W
Warwickshire □, U.K. ... 23 H5 52 14N 1 38W
Wasatch Ra., U.S.A. ... 110 B4 40 30N 111 15W
Wash, The, U.K. ... 23 G9 52 58N 0 20 E
Washburn, U.K. ... 24 D2 51 9N 3 21W
Washington, U.K. ... 22 C6 54 55N 1 30W
Washington, D.C., U.S.A. ... 112 F9 38 54N 77 2W
Washington, Ind., U.S.A. ... 112 F4 38 40N 87 10W
Washington, Pa., U.S.A. ... 112 E7 40 10N 80 15W
Washington □, U.S.A. ... 110 A2 47 30N 120 30W
Washington, Mt., U.S.A. ... 113 C12 44 16N 71 18W
Washington I., U.S.A. ... 112 C4 45 23N 86 54W
Wasilla, U.S.A. ... 108 B5 61 35N 149 26W
Waskaganish, Canada ... 109 C12 51 30N 78 40W
Wast Water, U.K. ... 22 D2 54 26N 3 18W
Watampone, Indonesia ... 83 D4 4 29S 120 25 E
Watchet, U.K. ... 24 D2 51 10N 3 19W
Waterbeach, U.K. ... 25 B9 52 16N 0 12 E
Waterbury, U.S.A. ... 113 E11 41 33N 73 3W
Waterford, Ireland ... 31 D8 52 15N 7 8W
Waterford □, Ireland ... 31 D7 52 10N 7 40W
Watergate B., U.K. ... 27 G3 50 26N 5 4W
Waterloo, Canada ... 112 D7 43 30N 80 32W
Waterloo, U.S.A. ... 111 B8 42 30N 92 21W
Watertown, N.Y., U.S.A. ... 113 D10 43 59N 75 55W
Watertown, S. Dak., U.S.A. ... 111 B7 44 54N 97 7W
Waterville, U.S.A. ... 113 C13 44 33N 69 38W
Watford, U.K. ... 25 C8 51 40N 0 24W
Watlington, Norfolk, U.K. ... 23 G9 52 40N 0 24 E
Watlington, Oxon., U.K. ... 24 C6 51 38N 1 0W
Watrous, Canada ... 108 C9 51 40N 105 25W
Watseka, U.S.A. ... 112 E4 40 47N 87 44W
Watson Lake, Canada ... 108 B7 60 6N 128 49W
Watton, U.K. ... 25 A10 52 34N 0 51 E
Waukegan, U.S.A. ... 112 D4 42 22N 87 50W
Waukesha, U.S.A. ... 112 D3 43 1N 88 14W
Wausau, U.S.A. ... 111 B9 44 58N 89 38W
Wauwatosa, U.S.A. ... 112 D4 43 3N 88 0W
Waveney →, U.K. ... 25 A12 52 35N 1 39 E
Waver →, U.K. ... 22 C2 54 50N 3 15W
Wâw, Sudan ... 95 G11 7 45N 28 1 E
Wawa, Canada ... 112 B5 47 59N 84 47W
Waycross, U.S.A. ... 111 D10 31 13N 82 21W
Wayne, U.S.A. ... 112 F6 38 13N 82 27W
Waynesboro, U.S.A. ... 112 F8 38 4N 78 53W
Waynesburg, U.S.A. ... 112 F7 39 54N 80 11W
Wazirabad, Pakistan ... 84 C9 32 30N 74 8 E
Weald, The, U.K. ... 25 D9 51 4N 0 20 E
Wear →, U.K. ... 22 C6 54 55N 1 23W
Weardale, U.K. ... 22 C4 54 44N 2 5W
Wearhead, U.K. ... 22 C4 54 45N 2 13W
Weatherford, U.S.A. ... 110 D7 32 46N 97 48W
Weaver →, U.K. ... 23 F3 53 17N 2 35W
Weaverham, U.K. ... 23 F3 53 16N 2 35W
Webster Springs, U.S.A. ... 112 F7 38 29N 80 25W
Weddell Sea, Antarctica ... 55 D1 72 30S 40 0W
Wedmore, U.K. ... 24 D3 51 13N 2 48W
Wednesbury, U.K. ... 23 G4 52 34N 2 1W
Wednesfield, U.K. ... 23 G4 52 37N 2 2W
Weedon Bec, U.K. ... 23 H6 52 15N 1 5W
Weifang, China ... 81 C6 36 44N 119 7 E
Weipa, Australia ... 98 C7 12 40S 141 50 E
Weiser, U.S.A. ... 110 B3 44 10N 117 0W
Welch, U.S.A. ... 112 G7 37 26N 81 35W
Weldon, U.S.A. ... 22 B5 55 17N 1 46W
Welford, Northants., U.K. ... 23 H6 52 25N 1 3W
Welford, West Berkshire, U.K. ... 24 D6 51 27N 1 24W
Welkom, S. Africa ... 97 K5 28 0S 26 46 E
Welland, Canada ... 112 D8 43 0N 79 15W
Welland →, U.K. ... 23 G8 52 51N 0 5W
Wellesley Is., Australia ... 98 B6 16 42S 139 30 E
Wellingborough, U.K. ... 23 H7 52 19N 0 41W
Wellington, N.Z. ... 99 J13 41 19S 174 46 E
Wellington, Somst., U.K. ... 24 E2 50 58N 3 13W
Wellington, Telford & Wrekin, U.K. ... 23 G3 52 42N 2 30W
Wellington, I., Chile ... 121 G2 49 30S 75 0W
Wells, U.K. ... 24 D3 51 13N 2 39W
Wells-next-the-Sea, U.K. ... 25 A10 52 57N 0 51 E
Wellsboro, U.S.A. ... 112 E9 41 45N 77 18W
Wellsville, U.S.A. ... 112 D9 42 7N 77 57W
Welney, U.K. ... 25 A9 52 31N 0 15 E
Wels, Austria ... 66 D8 48 9N 14 1 E
Welshpool, U.K. ... 23 G2 52 39N 3 8W
Welton, U.K. ... 23 F8 53 18N 0 29W
Welwyn Garden City, U.K. ... 25 C8 51 48N 0 12W
Wem, U.K. ... 23 G3 52 52N 2 44W

**Wem**

**Wembury**                                                                    **Zwickau**

| Place | Ref | Lat | Long |
|---|---|---|---|
| Wembury, *U.K.* | 27 G5 | 50 19N | 4 6W |
| Wemindji, *Canada* | 109 C12 | 53 0N | 78 49W |
| Wenatchee, *U.S.A.* | 110 A2 | 47 25N | 120 19W |
| Wendover, *U.K.* | 25 C7 | 51 45N | 0 44W |
| Wenlock Edge, *U.K.* | 23 H3 | 52 30N | 2 43W |
| Wensu, *China* | 80 B3 | 41 15N | 80 10 E |
| Wensleydale, *U.K.* | 22 D4 | 54 17N | 2 0W |
| Wensum →, *U.K.* | 25 A11 | 52 40N | 1 15 E |
| Wenzhou, *China* | 81 D7 | 28 0N | 120 38 E |
| Weobley, *U.K.* | 24 B3 | 52 11N | 2 50W |
| Werrington, *U.K.* | 27 F5 | 50 39N | 4 23W |
| Weser →, *Germany* | 66 B5 | 53 36N | 8 28 E |
| West Auckland, *U.K.* | 22 C5 | 54 38N | 1 43W |
| West Bank ☑, *Asia* | 86 C3 | 32 6N | 35 13 E |
| West Bend, *U.S.A.* | 112 D3 | 43 25N | 88 11W |
| West Bengal □, *India* | 85 H16 | 23 0N | 88 0 E |
| West Berkshire □, *U.K.* | 24 D6 | 51 25N | 1 17W |
| West Beskids, *Europe* | 67 D10 | 49 30N | 19 0 E |
| West Bridgford, *U.K.* | 23 G6 | 52 55N | 1 8W |
| West Bromwich, *U.K.* | 23 G5 | 52 32N | 1 59W |
| West Burra, *U.K.* | 18 B15 | 60 5N | 1 21W |
| West Calder, *U.K.* | 22 A1 | 55 51N | 3 33W |
| West Coker, *U.K.* | 24 E3 | 50 55N | 2 40W |
| West Falkland, *Falk. Is.* | 121 H3 | 51 40S | 60 0W |
| West Fen, *U.K.* | 23 F8 | 53 5N | 0 5W |
| West Frankfort, *U.S.A.* | 111 C9 | 37 54N | 88 55W |
| West Grinstead, *U.K.* | 25 E8 | 50 58N | 0 19W |
| West Haddon, *U.K.* | 23 H6 | 52 20N | 1 3W |
| West Kirby, *U.K.* | 23 F2 | 53 23N | 3 11W |
| West Linton, *U.K.* | 22 A2 | 55 46N | 3 21W |
| West Lulworth, *U.K.* | 24 E4 | 50 37N | 2 14W |
| West Malling, *U.K.* | 25 D9 | 51 17N | 0 26 E |
| West Meon, *U.K.* | 24 D6 | 51 1N | 1 5W |
| West Mersea, *U.K.* | 25 C10 | 51 46N | 0 56 E |
| West Midlands □, *U.K.* | 23 H5 | 52 26N | 2 0W |
| West Moors, *U.K.* | 24 E5 | 50 49N | 1 53W |
| West Palm Beach, *U.S.A.* | 111 E10 | 26 43N | 80 3W |
| West Point, *U.S.A.* | 112 G9 | 37 32N | 76 48W |
| West Pt., *Canada* | 113 A15 | 49 52N | 64 40W |
| West Rasen, *U.K.* | 23 F8 | 53 23N | 0 24W |
| West Seneca, *U.S.A.* | 112 D8 | 42 51N | 78 48W |
| West Siberian Plain, *Russia* | 74 C11 | 62 0N | 75 0 E |
| West Sussex □, *U.K.* | 25 E8 | 50 55N | 0 30W |
| West Virginia □, *U.S.A.* | 112 F7 | 38 45N | 80 30W |
| West Yorkshire □, *U.K.* | 23 E5 | 53 45N | 1 40W |
| Westbourne, *U.K.* | 25 E7 | 50 52N | 0 55W |
| Westbrook, *U.S.A.* | 113 D12 | 43 41N | 70 22W |
| Westbury, *Shrops., U.K.* | 23 G3 | 52 41N | 2 55W |
| Westbury, *Wilts., U.K.* | 24 D4 | 51 15N | 2 11W |
| Westbury-on-Severn, *U.K.* | 24 C4 | 51 50N | 2 25W |
| Westerham, *U.K.* | 25 D9 | 51 16N | 0 5 E |
| Western Australia □, *Australia* | 98 F2 | 25 0S | 118 0 E |
| Western Dvina →, *Latvia* | 72 C3 | 57 4N | 24 3 E |
| Western Ghats, *India* | 84 N9 | 14 0N | 75 0 E |
| Western Isles □, *U.K.* | 18 G3 | 57 30N | 7 10W |
| Western Sahara ■, *Africa* | 94 D3 | 25 0N | 13 0W |
| Westerschelde →, *Neths.* | 65 C3 | 51 25N | 3 25 E |
| Westerwald, *Germany* | 64 C4 | 50 38N | 7 56 E |
| Westfield, *U.S.A.* | 25 E10 | 50 55N | 0 35 E |
| Westhill, *U.K.* | 19 H13 | 57 9N | 2 19W |
| Westhoughton, *U.K.* | 23 E3 | 53 33N | 2 31W |
| Westmeath □, *Ireland* | 28 D6 | 53 33N | 7 34W |
| Westminster, *U.K.* | 25 D8 | 51 30N | 0 9W |
| Westmoreland, *Barbados* | 115 g | 13 13N | 59 37W |
| Weston, *U.K.* | 23 G4 | 52 51N | 2 1W |
| Weston, *U.S.A.* | 112 F7 | 39 2N | 80 28W |
| Weston-super-Mare, *U.K.* | 24 D3 | 51 21N | 2 58W |
| Westport, *Ireland* | 28 D2 | 53 48N | 9 31W |
| Westray, *U.K.* | 19 D11 | 59 18N | 3 0W |
| Westruther, *U.K.* | 22 A3 | 55 45N | 2 35W |
| Westward Ho!, *U.K.* | 27 E5 | 51 2N | 4 15W |
| Wetar, *Indonesia* | 83 D4 | 7 48S | 126 30 E |
| Wetaskiwin, *Canada* | 108 C8 | 52 55N | 113 24W |
| Wetherby, *U.K.* | 23 E6 | 53 56N | 1 23W |
| Wetwang, *U.K.* | 23 D7 | 54 1N | 0 35W |
| Wewak, *Papua N. G.* | 98 A7 | 3 38S | 143 41 E |
| Wexford, *Ireland* | 31 D10 | 52 20N | 6 28W |
| Wexford □, *Ireland* | 31 D10 | 52 20N | 6 25W |
| Wexford Harbour, *Ireland* | 31 D10 | 52 20N | 6 25W |
| Wey →, *U.K.* | 25 D8 | 51 22N | 0 27W |
| Weybourne, *U.K.* | 25 A11 | 52 57N | 1 9 E |
| Weybridge, *U.K.* | 25 D8 | 51 22N | 0 27W |
| Weyburn, *Canada* | 108 D9 | 49 40N | 103 50W |
| Weymouth, *U.K.* | 24 E4 | 50 37N | 2 28W |
| Wha Ti, *Canada* | 108 B8 | 63 8N | 117 16W |
| Whale →, *Canada* | 109 C13 | 58 15N | 67 40W |
| Whale Cove, *Canada* | 108 B10 | 62 10N | 92 34W |
| Whales, B. of, *Antarctica* | 55 D12 | 78 0S | 165 0W |
| Whaley Bridge, *U.K.* | 23 F5 | 53 20N | 1 59W |
| Whalley, *U.K.* | 23 E4 | 53 49N | 2 24W |
| Whalsay, *U.K.* | 18 B16 | 60 22N | 0 59W |
| Whalton, *U.K.* | 22 B5 | 55 8N | 1 46W |
| Whangarei, *N.Z.* | 99 H13 | 35 43S | 174 21 E |
| Whaplode, *U.K.* | 23 G8 | 52 42N | 0 3W |
| Wharfe →, *U.K.* | 23 E6 | 53 51N | 1 9W |
| Wharfedale, *U.K.* | 23 E5 | 54 6N | 2 1W |
| Wheatley Hill, *U.K.* | 22 C6 | 54 45N | 1 23W |
| Wheeler Pk., *U.S.A.* | 110 C4 | 38 57N | 114 15W |
| Wheeling, *U.S.A.* | 112 E7 | 40 4N | 80 43W |
| Whernside, *U.K.* | 22 D2 | 54 14N | 2 24W |
| Whicham, *U.K.* | 22 D2 | 54 15N | 3 21W |
| Whimple, *U.K.* | 24 E2 | 50 46N | 3 20W |
| Whipsnade, *U.K.* | 25 C7 | 51 51N | 0 32W |
| Whissendine, *U.K.* | 23 G7 | 52 43N | 0 46W |
| Whitby, *U.K.* | 22 D7 | 54 29N | 0 37W |
| Whitchurch, *Devon, U.K.* | 27 F5 | 50 32N | 4 9W |
| Whitchurch, *Hants., U.K.* | 24 D6 | 51 14N | 1 20W |
| Whitchurch, *Hereford, U.K.* | 24 C3 | 51 51N | 2 39W |
| Whitchurch, *Shrops., U.K.* | 23 G3 | 52 59N | 2 40W |
| White →, *Ark., U.S.A.* | 111 D8 | 33 57N | 91 5W |
| White →, *Ind., U.S.A.* | 112 F4 | 38 25N | 87 45W |
| White →, *Utah, U.S.A.* | 110 B5 | 40 4N | 109 41W |
| White Esk →, *U.K.* | 22 B2 | 55 13N | 3 11W |
| White Horse, Vale of, *U.K.* | 24 C5 | 51 37N | 1 30W |
| White Horse Hill, *U.K.* | 24 C5 | 51 34N | 1 33W |
| White Mts., *Calif., U.S.A.* | 110 C3 | 37 30N | 118 15W |
| White Mts., *N.H., U.S.A.* | 111 B12 | 44 15N | 71 15W |
| White Nile →, *Sudan* | 95 E12 | 15 38N | 32 31 E |
| White Sea, *Russia* | 72 A6 | 66 30N | 38 0 E |
| Whiteadder Water →, *U.K.* | 22 A4 | 55 51N | 2 25W |
| Whitecourt, *Canada* | 108 C8 | 54 10N | 115 45W |
| Whitefish Point, *U.S.A.* | 112 B5 | 46 45N | 84 59W |
| Whitehaven, *U.K.* | 22 C2 | 54 33N | 3 35W |
| Whitehorse, *Canada* | 108 B6 | 60 43N | 135 3W |
| Whitesand B., *U.K.* | 27 G5 | 50 21N | 4 18W |
| Whitewater, *U.S.A.* | 112 D3 | 42 50N | 88 44W |
| Whithorn, *U.K.* | 20 E7 | 54 44N | 4 26W |
| Whitley Bay, *U.K.* | 22 B6 | 55 3N | 1 27W |
| Whitney, Mt., *U.S.A.* | 110 C3 | 36 35N | 118 18W |
| Whitstable, *U.K.* | 25 D11 | 51 21N | 1 3 E |
| Whittington, *Derby, U.K.* | 23 F6 | 53 16N | 1 26W |
| Whittington, *Shrops., U.K.* | 23 G3 | 52 52N | 3 0W |
| Whittlesey, *U.K.* | 23 G8 | 52 33N | 0 8W |
| Whittlesford, *U.K.* | 25 B9 | 52 7N | 0 9 E |
| Whitwell, *Derby, U.K.* | 23 F6 | 53 17N | 1 12W |
| Whitwell, *I. of W., U.K.* | 24 E6 | 50 36N | 1 15W |
| Whitwick, *U.K.* | 23 G6 | 52 45N | 1 22W |
| Whitworth, *U.K.* | 23 E4 | 53 39N | 2 11W |
| Wholdaia L., *Canada* | 108 B9 | 60 43N | 104 20W |
| Whyalla, *Australia* | 98 G6 | 33 2S | 137 30 E |
| Wiarton, *Canada* | 112 C7 | 44 40N | 81 10W |
| Wiay, *U.K.* | 18 H3 | 57 24N | 7 13W |
| Wichita, *U.S.A.* | 111 C7 | 37 42N | 97 20W |
| Wichita Falls, *U.S.A.* | 110 D7 | 33 54N | 98 30W |
| Wick, *U.K.* | 19 F11 | 58 26N | 3 5W |
| Wickford, *U.K.* | 25 C10 | 51 36N | 0 33 E |
| Wickham, *U.K.* | 24 E6 | 50 54N | 1 11W |
| Wickham Market, *U.K.* | 25 B11 | 52 9N | 1 23 E |
| Wicklow, *Ireland* | 31 C10 | 52 59N | 6 3W |
| Wicklow □, *Ireland* | 31 C10 | 52 57N | 6 25W |
| Wicklow Hd., *Ireland* | 31 C11 | 52 58N | 6 0W |
| Wicklow Mts., *Ireland* | 31 C10 | 52 58N | 6 26W |
| Wickwar, *U.K.* | 24 C4 | 51 36N | 2 23W |
| Widdrington, *U.K.* | 22 B5 | 55 15N | 1 35W |
| Widecombe, *U.K.* | 27 F6 | 50 34N | 3 49W |
| Widemouth, *U.K.* | 27 F4 | 50 47N | 4 34W |
| Widnes, *U.K.* | 23 F3 | 53 23N | 2 45W |
| Wiener Neustadt, *Austria* | 66 E9 | 47 49N | 16 16 E |
| Wiesbaden, *Germany* | 66 C5 | 50 4N | 8 14 E |
| Wigan, *U.K.* | 23 E3 | 53 33N | 2 38W |
| Wight, Isle of □, *U.K.* | 24 E6 | 50 41N | 1 17W |
| Wigmore, *U.K.* | 23 H3 | 52 19N | 2 51W |
| Wigston, *U.K.* | 23 G6 | 52 35N | 1 6W |
| Wigton, *U.K.* | 22 C2 | 54 50N | 3 10W |
| Wigtown, *U.K.* | 20 E7 | 54 53N | 4 27W |
| Wigtown B., *U.K.* | 20 E7 | 54 46N | 4 15W |
| Wilhelm, Mt., *Papua N. G.* | 98 B8 | 5 50S | 145 1 E |
| Wilhelmshaven, *Germany* | 66 B5 | 53 31N | 8 7 E |
| Wilkes-Barre, *U.S.A.* | 113 E10 | 41 15N | 75 53W |
| Willemstad, *Neth. Ant.* | 115 E11 | 12 5N | 69 0W |
| Willenhall, *U.K.* | 23 G4 | 52 36N | 2 2W |
| Willesborough, *U.K.* | 25 D10 | 51 8N | 0 56 E |
| Williams Lake, *Canada* | 108 C7 | 52 10N | 122 10W |
| Williamsburg, *U.S.A.* | 112 G9 | 37 17N | 76 44W |
| Williamson, *U.S.A.* | 112 G6 | 37 41N | 82 17W |
| Williamsport, *U.S.A.* | 112 E9 | 41 15N | 77 0W |
| Willingdon, *U.K.* | 25 E9 | 50 47N | 0 17 E |
| Williston, *U.S.A.* | 110 A6 | 48 9N | 103 37W |
| Williston L., *Canada* | 108 C7 | 56 0N | 124 0W |
| Williton, *U.K.* | 24 D2 | 51 9N | 3 19W |
| Willmar, *U.S.A.* | 111 A7 | 45 7N | 95 3W |
| Willoughby, *U.K.* | 23 F9 | 53 13N | 0 12 E |
| Wilmington, *U.K.* | 24 E2 | 50 47N | 3 7W |
| Wilmington, *Del., U.S.A.* | 113 F10 | 39 45N | 75 33W |
| Wilmington, *N.C., U.S.A.* | 111 D11 | 34 14N | 77 55W |
| Wilmslow, *U.K.* | 23 F4 | 53 19N | 2 13W |
| Wilnecote, *U.K.* | 23 G5 | 52 36N | 1 39W |
| Wilton, *U.K.* | 24 D5 | 51 5N | 1 51W |
| Wiltshire □, *U.K.* | 24 D5 | 51 18N | 1 53W |
| Wimblington, *U.K.* | 23 G9 | 52 31N | 0 4 E |
| Wimborne Minster, *U.K.* | 24 E5 | 50 48N | 1 59W |
| Wincanton, *U.K.* | 24 D4 | 51 3N | 2 24W |
| Winchelsea, *U.K.* | 25 E10 | 50 55N | 0 43 E |
| Winchester, *U.K.* | 24 D6 | 51 4N | 1 18W |
| Winchester, *Ky., U.S.A.* | 112 G6 | 38 0N | 84 11W |
| Winchester, *Va., U.S.A.* | 112 F8 | 39 11N | 78 10W |
| Wind →, *U.S.A.* | 110 B5 | 43 12N | 108 12W |
| Wind River Range, *U.S.A.* | 110 B5 | 43 0N | 109 30W |
| Windermere, *U.K.* | 22 D3 | 54 23N | 2 55W |
| Windhoek, *Namibia* | 97 J3 | 22 35S | 17 4 E |
| Windrush →, *U.K.* | 24 C6 | 51 43N | 1 24W |
| Windsor, *Canada* | 109 D11 | 42 18N | 83 0W |
| Windsor, *U.K.* | 25 D7 | 51 29N | 0 36W |
| Windward Is., *W. Indies* | 115 E12 | 13 0N | 61 0W |
| Windward Passage, *Caribbean* | 115 D10 | 20 0N | 74 0W |
| Wing, *U.K.* | 25 C7 | 51 53N | 0 43W |
| Wingham, *U.K.* | 25 D11 | 51 16N | 1 13 E |
| Winisk →, *Canada* | 109 C11 | 55 17N | 85 5W |
| Winkleigh, *U.K.* | 27 F6 | 50 50N | 3 58W |
| Winkler, *Canada* | 108 D10 | 49 10N | 97 56W |
| Winnebago, L., *U.S.A.* | 112 D3 | 44 0N | 88 26W |
| Winnemucca, *U.S.A.* | 110 B3 | 40 58N | 117 44W |
| Winnipeg, *Canada* | 108 D10 | 49 54N | 97 9W |
| Winnipeg, L., *Canada* | 108 C10 | 52 30N | 97 0W |
| Winnipegosis L., *Canada* | 108 C9 | 52 30N | 100 0W |
| Winona, *U.S.A.* | 111 B8 | 44 3N | 91 39W |
| Winooski, *U.S.A.* | 113 C11 | 44 29N | 73 11W |
| Winsford, *U.K.* | 23 F3 | 53 12N | 2 31W |
| Winslow, *U.K.* | 25 C7 | 51 57N | 0 52W |
| Winslow, *U.S.A.* | 110 C4 | 35 2N | 110 42W |
| Winster, *U.K.* | 23 F5 | 53 9N | 1 39W |
| Winston-Salem, *U.S.A.* | 111 C10 | 36 6N | 80 15W |
| Winterborne Abbas, *U.K.* | 24 E3 | 50 42N | 2 33W |
| Winterhur, *Switz.* | 66 E5 | 47 30N | 8 44 E |
| Winterton, *N. Lincs., U.K.* | 23 E7 | 53 39N | 0 37W |
| Winterton, *Norfolk, U.K.* | 25 A12 | 52 43N | 1 41 E |
| Winton, *Australia* | 98 E7 | 22 24S | 143 3 E |
| Wirksworth, *U.K.* | 23 F5 | 53 6N | 1 35W |
| Wirral, *U.K.* | 23 F2 | 53 25N | 3 0W |
| Wisbech, *U.K.* | 23 G9 | 52 41N | 0 9 E |
| Wisborough Green, *U.K.* | 25 D7 | 51 2N | 0 30W |
| Wisconsin □, *U.S.A.* | 111 B9 | 44 45N | 89 30W |
| Wishaw, *U.K.* | 22 C8 | 55 46N | 3 54W |
| Wiske →, *U.K.* | 22 D6 | 54 19N | 1 27W |
| Witbank, *S. Africa* | 97 K5 | 25 51S | 29 14 E |
| Witham, *U.K.* | 25 C10 | 51 48N | 0 40 E |
| Witham →, *U.K.* | 23 G8 | 52 59N | 0 2W |
| Withern, *U.K.* | 23 F9 | 53 18N | 0 8 E |
| Withernsea, *U.K.* | 23 E8 | 53 44N | 0 1 E |
| Witley, *U.K.* | 25 D7 | 51 9N | 0 39W |
| Witney, *U.K.* | 24 C6 | 51 48N | 1 28W |
| Wittersham, *U.K.* | 25 D10 | 51 0N | 0 43 E |
| Wiveliscombe, *U.K.* | 24 D2 | 51 2N | 3 19W |
| Wivenhoe, *U.K.* | 25 C10 | 51 51N | 0 59 E |
| Wkra →, *Poland* | 67 B11 | 52 27N | 20 44 E |
| Włocławek, *Poland* | 67 B10 | 52 40N | 19 3 E |
| Woburn, *U.K.* | 25 C7 | 51 59N | 0 36W |
| Woburn Sands, *U.K.* | 25 B7 | 52 1N | 0 39W |
| Woking, *U.K.* | 25 D7 | 51 19N | 0 34W |
| Wokingham, *U.K.* | 25 D7 | 51 24N | 0 49W |
| Wolf Rock, *U.K.* | 27 H2 | 49 57N | 5 49W |
| Wolfsburg, *Germany* | 66 B6 | 52 25N | 10 48 E |
| Wollaston Is., *Canada* | 108 C9 | 58 7N | 103 10W |
| Wollaston Pen., *Canada* | 108 B8 | 69 30N | 115 0W |
| Wollongong, *Australia* | 98 G9 | 34 25S | 150 54 E |
| Wolsingham, *U.K.* | 22 C5 | 54 44N | 1 52W |
| Wolverhampton, *U.K.* | 23 G4 | 52 35N | 2 7W |
| Wolverton, *U.K.* | 25 B7 | 52 3N | 0 47W |
| Wolviston, *U.K.* | 22 C6 | 54 38N | 1 18W |
| Wombwell, *U.K.* | 23 E6 | 53 32N | 1 24W |
| Wŏnsan, *N. Korea* | 81 C7 | 39 11N | 127 27 E |
| Wonston, *U.K.* | 24 D6 | 51 8N | 1 18W |
| Woodbridge, *U.K.* | 25 B11 | 52 6N | 1 20 E |
| Woodbury, *U.K.* | 24 E2 | 50 41N | 3 24W |
| Woodhall Spa, *U.K.* | 23 F8 | 53 10N | 0 12W |
| Woodhouse, *U.K.* | 23 F6 | 53 22N | 1 21W |
| Woodley, *U.K.* | 25 D7 | 51 27N | 0 53W |
| Woodroffe, Mt., *Australia* | 98 F5 | 26 20S | 131 45 E |
| Woods, L. of the, *Canada* | 108 D10 | 49 15N | 94 45W |
| Woodstock, *N.B., Canada* | 113 C13 | 46 11N | 67 37W |
| Woodstock, *Ont., Canada* | 112 D7 | 43 10N | 80 45W |
| Wookey, *U.K.* | 24 D3 | 51 13N | 2 41W |
| Wookey Hole, *U.K.* | 24 D3 | 51 14N | 2 40W |
| Wool, *U.K.* | 24 E4 | 50 40N | 2 12W |
| Woolacombe, *U.K.* | 27 E5 | 51 10N | 4 13W |
| Wooler, *U.K.* | 22 A4 | 55 33N | 2 1W |
| Woonsocket, *U.S.A.* | 113 E11 | 42 0N | 71 31W |
| Wootton Bassett, *U.K.* | 24 C5 | 51 32N | 1 54W |
| Wootton Wawen, *U.K.* | 23 H5 | 52 16N | 1 47W |
| Worcester, *S. Africa* | 97 L3 | 33 39S | 19 27 E |
| Worcester, *U.K.* | 24 B4 | 52 11N | 2 12W |
| Worcester, *U.S.A.* | 113 D12 | 42 16N | 71 48W |
| Worfield, *U.K.* | 23 G4 | 52 34N | 2 21W |
| Workington, *U.K.* | 22 C1 | 54 39N | 3 33W |
| Worksop, *U.K.* | 23 F6 | 53 18N | 1 7W |
| Worms, *Germany* | 66 D5 | 49 37N | 8 21 E |
| Wortham, *U.K.* | 25 B11 | 52 21N | 1 3 E |
| Worthing, *Barbados* | 115 g | 13 5N | 59 35W |
| Worthing, *U.K.* | 25 E8 | 50 49N | 0 21W |
| Worthington, *U.S.A.* | 111 B7 | 43 37N | 95 36W |
| Wotton under Edge, *U.K.* | 24 C4 | 51 37N | 2 20W |
| Wragby, *U.K.* | 23 F8 | 53 18N | 0 17W |
| Wrangel I., *Russia* | 79 B19 | 71 0N | 180 0 E |
| Wrangell, *U.S.A.* | 108 C6 | 56 28N | 132 23W |
| Wrangell Mts., *U.S.A.* | 108 B5 | 61 30N | 142 0W |
| Wrangle, *U.K.* | 23 F9 | 53 3N | 0 7 E |
| Wrath, C., *U.K.* | 18 E7 | 58 38N | 5 1W |
| Wrekin, The, *U.K.* | 23 G3 | 52 41N | 2 32W |
| Wrentham, *U.K.* | 25 B12 | 52 23N | 1 40 E |
| Wrexham, *U.K.* | 23 F3 | 53 3N | 3 0W |
| Wrigley, *Canada* | 108 B7 | 63 16N | 123 37W |
| Writtle, *U.K.* | 25 C9 | 51 44N | 0 27 E |
| Wrocław, *Poland* | 67 C9 | 51 5N | 17 5 E |
| Wroughton, *U.K.* | 24 C5 | 51 31N | 1 47W |
| Wroxham, *U.K.* | 25 A11 | 52 42N | 1 24 E |
| Wu Jiang →, *China* | 80 D5 | 29 40N | 107 20 E |
| Wuhan, *China* | 81 C6 | 30 31N | 114 18 E |
| Wuhu, *China* | 81 C6 | 31 22N | 118 21 E |
| Wuppertal, *Germany* | 66 C4 | 51 16N | 7 12 E |
| Würzburg, *Germany* | 66 D5 | 49 46N | 9 55 E |
| Wutongqiao, *China* | 80 D5 | 29 22N | 103 50 E |
| Wuwei, *China* | 80 C5 | 37 57N | 102 34 E |
| Wuxi, *China* | 81 C7 | 31 33N | 120 18 E |
| Wuyi Shan, *China* | 81 D6 | 27 0N | 117 0 E |
| Wuzhong, *China* | 80 C5 | 38 2N | 106 12 E |
| Wuzhou, *China* | 81 D6 | 23 30N | 111 18 E |
| Wye →, *U.K.* | 25 D10 | 51 10N | 0 57 E |
| Wye, *U.K.* | 24 C3 | 51 38N | 2 40W |
| Wylye →, *U.K.* | 24 D5 | 51 5N | 1 51W |
| Wymondham, *Leics., U.K.* | 23 G7 | 52 45N | 0 43W |
| Wymondham, *Norfolk, U.K.* | 25 A11 | 52 35N | 1 7 E |
| Wyndham, *Australia* | 98 D4 | 15 33S | 128 3 E |
| Wyoming □, *U.S.A.* | 110 B5 | 43 0N | 107 30W |
| Wyre →, *U.K.* | 23 E3 | 53 52N | 2 57W |
| Wyre Forest, *U.K.* | 23 H4 | 52 24N | 2 24W |

# SATELLITE IMAGE OF THE SEVERN ESTUARY

This Landsat false-colour composite image was captured in October. The cities of Bristol and Cardiff are clearly visible, as are the Black Mountains and the Brecon Beacons in Wales. Images such as this are used for recording and monitoring land use. *(EROS)*